The Pied Piper

The Pied Piper

ALLARD K. LOWENSTEIN AND THE LIBERAL DREAM

By Richard Cummings

GROVE PRESS, Inc./New York

First Hardcover Edition published in 1985

Library of Congress Cataloging in Publication Data

Cummings, Richard

    The pied piper.

    1. Lowenstein, Allard K. 2. Legislators—United States—Biography. 3. United States. Congress. House—Biography. 4. Liberalism—United States—History—20th century. 5. United States—Politics and government—1945–xxxx. I. Title.
E840.8.L68C85 1984   328.73′092′4   [B] 83-49377
ISBN 0-394-53848-X

Manufactured in the United States of America

GROVE PRESS, INC., 196 West Houston Street, New York, N.Y. 10014

10 9 8 7 6 5 4 3 2 1

To my family

Contents

AUTHOR'S NOTE

I wish to express my deepest thanks to Barney and Lisa Rosset of Grove Press for their patience and confidence in me as I proceeded with this project. As my editor at Grove, Fred Jordan provided me with invaluable insights and direction, while my wife Mary supplied meticulous editorial skills in helping me shape the text. I cannot thank them enough.

Without the generous assistance of the Albert and Bessie Warner Fund and the Authors League Fund, I would not have been able to complete this book. Their assistance was more than financial; they gave me the courage to continue.

The Southern Historical Collection of the Wilson Library at the University of North Carolina, Chapel Hill, gave me critical assistance in researching Allard Lowenstein's papers. Frances Weaver and Dr. Richard Shrader made this task possible and I thank them from the bottom of my heart. The Urban Archives Center of Temple University was kind enough to provide me with access to certain of its files which enabled me to get a better grasp of the anti-Communist activities of the union movement.

Research assistance of an extremely valuable nature was provided by Sandra Sherman, whose constructive criticism of the original manuscript led to significant revisions. I am indebted as well to Marc A. Feigen for providing me with his senior thesis, *The March To Washington: Allard K. Lowenstein in the United States House of Representatives 1968–70*, Department of History of the University of Pennsylvania, April 15, 1983. In writing the chapters on Lowenstein's career in Congress, I made considerable use of this work. Amy Bach did important research for me and helped me organize the documents related to the Rooney campaign. Irene Schneider put it all in order at the computer, a monumental task. Preparation of the manuscript would have been impossible without her. I would also like to thank my agent, Timothy Seldes of Russell & Volkening, for his advice and help. Lastly, I would like to mention my sons, Benjamin and Orson, who were so patient while I worked so long on this book.

*   *   *

"Alone I did it."

William Shakespeare
Coriolanus, Act V, Scene VI

Introduction

Allard K. Lowenstein, student leader, civil rights organizer, antiwar activist, one-term congressman, and United Nations ambassador, blazed across the American political scene at a period of continuing crisis. Often characterized as a figure of the sixties, Lowenstein came of age in the forties, part of a generation that believed in America with almost absolute certainty.

The path of his life led from optimism to disillusionment as he committed himself to the liberal ideals of Franklin Roosevelt, John Kennedy, and the Democratic party, only to be cast aside in his effort to win election himself. Although he was a virtually forgotten figure by 1980, his tragic assassination by Dennis Sweeney, a deranged former protégé from the civil rights movement, brought Lowenstein back into the public's consciousness.

Students followed Lowenstein in his quest for a just and peaceful world. But they did not know that his deep sense of patriotism and intense anti-Communism led him to work for the CIA in Africa and Spain and to inform on suspected Communists in the civil rights movement.

In doing this, Lowenstein was a child of his times. In the fifties, McCarthyism had created a paranoia about Communist infiltration, and unless liberals proved their anti-Communism, they risked intense Red-baiting from the right. Lowenstein also remembered a time when liberal democracy was threatened by Stalin and Hitler. The values instilled in him by Algernon Black at the Ethical Culture School in New York City led him to detest both Communism and Fascism. He devoted his life to fighting both. By working for the CIA, he thought he was doing the right thing, but he came to understand that totalitarian currents had been unleashed by the very forces he had served in the interest of saving democracy and halting tyranny.

Because Lowenstein led many lives at the same time, it is difficult to tell his story chronologically. For this reason, I have elected to divide this book into segments, sometimes continuing one aspect of Lowenstein's career to its particular conclusion and then returning to an earlier date to resume another aspect.

Lowenstein's call was to ideals, not to self-interest. There is no indication that he wanted to make a great deal of money. He did want place in history and a major role on the world stage, which he achieved.

Yet Lowenstein remains unknown to the great majority of the public, despite the enormous influence he had on his times, the course of history in southern Africa, American race relations, American foreign policy, the presidential process, and the way the Congress is run. He brought countless people into the system and changed a great many lives. Worshipped by some and condemned by others, Allard Lowenstein lived a remarkable life of passionate intensity. It was marked by controversy, significant accomplishment, and failure.

The span of his life, 1929 to 1980, is a distinct epoch of American history. It saw conservatism and isolationism discredited following the stock market crash and Hitler's aggression, then witnessed the rise of liberalism through the genius of Roosevelt, and ultimately America's disenchantment with that too, as the country adopted neoconservative values and elected Ronald Reagan.

I undertook this project believing Lowenstein to be one man, only to discover he was many men. He was not what he appeared to be, even to those closest to him. His idealism concealed a strong desire for personal recognition; his open criticism of the established order had at its base the objective of preserving it.

The opportunity to examine Lowenstein's papers at the Southern Historical Collection of the Wilson Library at the University of North Carolina, Chapel Hill, including his diary, which he laid out like the front page of *The New York Times*, obliged me to rewrite totally a manuscript of substantial length. Having already conducted numerous interviews, I discovered other people with more of the missing pieces, some as far afield as Johannesburg, South Africa.

Starting with the belief that I had shared many of Lowenstein's experiences and viewpoints, I discovered things about myself that had been hidden as well. Digging deep for the truth is a painful, sometimes tedious, but ultimately exhilarating process. The breaking down of denial is conceivably the most anger-provoking activity possible to engage in. I am aware that much of what I have to say about Lowenstein and people close to him will produce an outcry and charges that I have been unfair. But while I found myself growing to dislike certain aspects of Allard Lowenstein's personality and concluding that deceit was inherent in his career, I came away with a deep respect for his genius and his positions on public policy. The central issue he grappled with—how to achieve change without violent revolution—remains a significant one.

I was also deeply moved by what I consider remarkable similarities between those who have made a cult of Lowenstein and are struggling to revive his memory, and the early Christians. The book of writings by and about Lowenstein edited by his nephew Douglas Lowenstein with Gregory Stone, a self-proclaimed "authoritative record" that makes not a single reference to the heretical works of either Teresa Carpenter or David Harris, has the ring of the Gospels to it. The film *Citizen*, which presents taped interviews of his friends and clips of Lowenstein himself, comes as close as possible to an attempt to resurrect him.

Was Lowenstein the model citizen this film portrays, or was he Saul Bellow's "Dangling Man," who for want of any other talent tried to make of citizenship an art form? Lowenstein was no ordinary person doing his duty as a citizen. He had other gifts. He was an athlete, a talented actor, a musician, a teacher, a writer, and a spellbinding orator. He was born into a wealthy and talented family and received a superb education. Lowenstein had resources other people did not have and access to the rich and powerful.

Lowenstein was called the "conscience" of the liberals for his role in the famous "Dump Johnson" movement that deposed the most powerful president in America's history. Curtis Gans, Lowenstein's associate in that movement, says, "Allard taught me the meaning of ambivalence." Americans have, in their naïveté, always wanted to see things in neat, clean images: all good or all bad. Some will say the disclosures about Lowenstein confirm their high or low opinion of him. They do neither. They confirm that nothing is as it appears to be, a lesson that goes far beyond politics.

Richard Cummings
Bridgehampton, New York
March, 1984

Starting

I

1.

When Allard Lowenstein was born on January 16, 1929, in Newark, New Jersey, his family was so busy that there was no time to give him a name. "Boy Baby Lowenstein" was hastily scrawled on the birth certificate. His father, Gabriel, a Jewish immigrant from Lithuania, was anxious to get back to his flourishing restaurant business, and his mother, Augusta, was restless to return to her other children, Bert and Larry, and her family responsibilities.

They finally called the baby Allard Augustus Lowenstein, the Augustus for his mother, Augusta Goldberg. Before he was even a year old, she died of breast cancer and Gabriel remarried. His new wife was Florence Goldstein, an elementary school teacher with whom he had worked teaching English to immigrants at the ERON school, which he had founded. She stopped teaching as soon as she was married and devoted her life to the family. While technically a stepmother, she was regarded as the real mother. The memory of Augusta faded. "She was a very bright woman. I hardly knew her because I was seven years old when she died," Larry Lowenstein, the second son, recalls. "My mother's name was Augusta Goldberg, and then Florence Goldstein. My father remarried because he felt we needed a mother."

It wasn't as if their mother had died. It was rather as if she had simply changed her name. Struggling to reach the top in America, the Lowensteins apparently had little time to dwell on the past or on personal problems. The feeling that Florence was the real mother became so intense that a decision was made not to tell Allard Lowenstein that another woman had given birth to him. Undertaken in the child's own interests, the concealment was not regarded by the family as a betrayal. They wanted him to grow up believing that Florence Goldstein was his mother, and no one was allowed to tell him otherwise.

Yet his father kept in touch with the Goldberg family, Augusta's parents (Grandpa and Grandma Goldberg, as the young Allard was told to call them), as well as her brother and sister. As a child, he was taken to see Aunt Ruthy and Uncle Victor in Queens. He loved these people and felt close to them, and the bond established with old people was something that Allard Lowenstein kept all his life. Friends spoke of his "need for grandparents."

When he was twelve, Allard approached Florence and said to her, "Mother, I know you're not my real mother, but I love you very much."

Unable to conceal the truth any longer, his stepmother told him what had happened. Lowenstein apparently accepted the explanation calmly, having learned something about life at an early age: even the most important things might be deliberately hidden by the people you trust and love the most, by the authority with power over your life.

From this authority, in this case his father, he also learned to avoid digging too deeply into personal problems, an activity that can distract from the accomplishment of higher goals. He learned that if, in the struggle to accomplish those goals, he felt dejected, demoralized, or defeated, he would have to pick himself up and fight on. He learned he would have to deploy people, including himself.

It had been an odd conspiracy, and Lowenstein had uncovered it. In later life, he seemed to feel that the initial ambiguity concerning his identity entitled him to a certain self-indulgence in creating his own persona. In high school, he started calling himself Allard Kenneth Lowenstein, dropping Augustus, the last trace of his real mother. He didn't like the name Allard and hoped his friends would call him "Ken." They didn't. He would finally settle on "Al" Lowenstein. In a sense, he named himself.

2.

Gabriel Lowenstein was a young Jew in Lithuania on the run. No one knows for certain what actually happened. Sitting in the elegantly Old World apartment of her half brother Larry on Central Park West, Dorothy DiCintio talked about their father.

"The story was that he was active in anti-Czarist activities and was jailed. Through some prearranged set of circumstances, he escaped from jail, went home, got his toothbrush, and went to America. He traveled with the clothes on his back. It was through Germany, I believe. And two minutes after he left, the police came after him again. So he really escaped."

Gabriel Lowenstein landed in New York, knowing no English, and got a job in a shirt factory, a sweatshop laborer in the garment industry working with other cheap labor from Eastern Europe.

Arriving without material possessions, Gabriel Lowenstein had brought with him ample resources of intellectual energy and the ideology that motivated him—Socialism.

At the shirt factory he began to organize for the union and was soon regarded as a leading Socialist in his community. He also worked with and for his people, the Jews. He set up the ERON school to teach English to the Yiddish-speaking immigrants and recruited teachers from the public school system to teach at night. He threw himself into the activities of the Madison Settlement House, helping Jewish immigrants assimilate, and he also found time to manage the impassioned mayoral campaign of Socialist Morris Hillquit, with its packed rallies at Madison Square Garden.

Gabriel Lowenstein was also a passionate Zionist. He founded the United Palestine Appeal, which later became the United Jewish Appeal, and with Abraham Wechsler he organized the very first program to be called "Night of the Stars." Cleverly blending business with politics, Gabriel Lowenstein brought together some of the biggest names in the entertainment business to raise money for the United Palestine Appeal, a technique his younger son would one day successfully imitate. The event raised what was then a considerable sum by filling Madison Square Garden, which had a seating capacity of about 17,000.

While zealously committing himself to his causes, Gabriel Lowenstein also achieved amazing things for himself in his new country. Working all the time, he managed to finish high school and gain admission to Columbia University. He received his B.S. in 1912, his M.A. in 1914, and his Ph.D. in biochemistry in 1915, and was hired to teach at Columbia University College of Physicians and Surgeons. A professor at one of the best universities in the world, a teacher of doctors, a maker of physicians, Gabriel Lowenstein began to make plans for his children. Though he was said to have had little respect for the medical profession—complaining that doctors knew nothing about nutrition and never read a medical book once they had graduated—he decided that his children should be doctors and change the profession. But for this to happen there would have to be more money than he was making at Columbia.

His brother Willie had followed Gabriel Lowenstein to the United States. Seemingly out of nowhere, from nothing, a small restaurant was opened. Larry Lowenstein describes it: "I use the word 'restaurant' carefully because it was a coffee shop—what we used to call in the old days a 'coffee pot,' a place where you had a counter and a few tables and served coffee, donuts, and hamburgers, mostly. And he was making a lot of money—at least it was a lot for those days." By this time, Gabriel Lowenstein, known as "Doc" or "Gabe," had Augusta, Bert, and Larry to support, and his brother Willie convinced him that he could make a lot more money running a coffee shop than he could teaching.

When Gabriel Lowenstein finally agreed to work part-time to supplement his income, he told his children, "I'm going to take a year off and make a lot of money and I'll come back and teach again." Then, according to the account he gave them, he went to the legendary president of Columbia, Nicholas Murray Butler, and said, "I want a leave of absence. I want to take a year off and make a lot of money." And Butler replied, "Doc, I'll give you a leave of absence, but mark my words, if you take it, you'll never come back."

He never did. He was sorry the rest of his life, because his first love was science and teaching. But he did make the money to give his children the things he never had. And he did keep up his medical knowledge, reading scientific periodicals. He was also an avid sports fan and loved music.

One coffee shop became two. A third brother, Lazar, joined them. It was the twenties, the America of Warren G. Harding, Calvin Coolidge, business, and optimism. A chain of cafeterias called WILLOW emerged. These flourished from the late twenties into the thirties, well into the Depression. They were sold at a profit, and a new cafeteria, Stuart's, appeared. It became a landmark known for its low prices and the quality of its food.

As these cafeterias went out of fashion, other restaurants opened that catered to the more affluent. The Lowensteins also had a concession on the Staten Island ferry, a lucrative enterprise. Jimmy Wallace, a friend of Allard Lowenstein's from his Chapel Hill days, remembers that the family lived well.

Gabriel Lowenstein seemed to expect the same kind of performance from his family that he extracted from himself. He knew how to withhold love, how to suspend approval pending perfection. Dorothy DiCintio, Allard Lowenstein's half sister, remembers her father as a difficult person. He wanted his children to be successful, and whenever one of them failed to follow his plan, he became frustrated.

People close to the family remember Gabriel Lowenstein as aloof and reserved, even a "cold" person. He had a distinguished manner and never became excited.

Dorothy DiCintio believes that her father's influence was "tremendous." "If anything was worth doing," she paraphrases him, "it should be done the best. A 95 was not good enough. If a child received a 98 on a test or in a subject, Gabriel would ask why it wasn't 100. If you knew everything and did everything you would succeed." To make sure of this, he spent large sums providing his children with all kinds of lessons.

His oldest son, Bert, was, as Dorothy describes him, "the apple of his father's eye." But Allard wanted the same measure of affection, a yearning that seemed to remain with him throughout his life. Dorothy DiCintio maintains that her father loved his children but did not understand Allard's interests. And because Allard Lowenstein loved and admired his father, he did not want to challenge him in open rebellion, preferring to develop strategies that would allow him to lead his own life without alienating his father. Lowenstein's step-mother, Florence Goldstein, was described by a cousin as very close to her stepson but also very anxious for him to be conventional. From his early years, Lowenstein chafed against this conventionality even as he craved the love and comfort of his mother and father.

Moreover, the bourgeois conventionality that the Lowensteins sought for their children also held contradictions. In fact, Gabriel considered himself something of an eccentric genius and wanted his sons to follow his lead. Yet, according to Bronia Kupsick, whose husband handled the advertising for the restaurants, Gabriel Lowenstein was not affectionate, did not touch the boys, and his youngest son partic-ularly resented the distant and formal tone his father used when he called him "Allard."

In fact, Gabriel Lowenstein's gruffness was often a facade; when he was caught in a kindness, he was embarrassed. He gave jobs in the restaurant business to countless relatives, aware that most of them criticized him behind his back. On the other hand, he could be a ruthless competitor. Several restaurant deals left partners burned but Lowenstein flourishing.

Though Allard Lowenstein was small and wore glasses, he was not a bookworm or a typical intellectual prodigy. He was as interested in baseball as he was in current events, and while the rest of the family rooted for the New York Giants, he was an avid Brooklyn Dodgers and Cleveland Indians fan.

He loved cars, flashy ones, fast ones. Glamour dazzled him. Movie stars fascinated him. Katharine Hepburn, whom he worshipped, would always be his favorite.

When American institutions like baseball, Hollywood, and cars captivate a youth, then it is safe to assume that the mythology of America has taken hold of him in a very fundamental way. He is a believer. Things may be wrong, very wrong, but in appreciating those wrongs, he does not feel alienated from his country. He loves it, wants to embrace it, be part of it. Little Allard Lowenstein may have looked like a typical, bright Jewish New York kid, but he surely felt more like Stover at Yale or maybe Frank Merriwell; he was the guy who got the home run in the last of the ninth inning or scored the winning touch-down with seconds left in the game.

Lowenstein did, in fact, possess gifts and interests that set him apart from his New York playmates as well as his brothers and sister. Bronia Kupsick's daughter, Rita Kupsick Katz, remembers Allard at six, poring over *The New York Times* like an adult. His brother Larry and his sister, Dorothy, recall that he memorized the World Almanac. This reinforced his image as the "professor," as his father called him, "the genius," the "quiz kid." But when a member of the family would ask him for some esoteric fact, he would shoot back: "Don't ask me that."

Lowenstein was combative from the beginning with his brothers and sister and with his friends. His cousin Alice Levien remembers him as full of fight, never letting himself be put down by someone older or bigger than he was. Indeed, by the time he was seven or eight, Lowenstein had already made a conscious decision to change his "genius" image, and he started the process by campaigning to get rid of the little collars and ties his parents dressed him in.

Because his oldest son, Bert, who was graduated from Harvard at fifteen, was deeply interested in science, "Doc" Lowenstein had a special affinity for him. His Phi Beta Kappa key seemed to confirm to his father that Bert would be a physician who would break new ground in the profession. But although Bert went on to Columbia College of Physicians and Surgeons, became a brilliant internist, and wrote an important work on diabetes, he did not achieve the great fame his father had envisioned for him. Perhaps Bert sensed his father's disappointment. As an adult, he would suffer from serious emotional problems and was briefly hospitalized.

Larry Lowenstein, the second son, never considered becoming a doctor. Following in his father's footsteps, he entered Columbia, then quickly switched to Cornell. He found the restaurant business exciting and made it his vocation. Although it had been a second choice for Gabriel Lowenstein, he had been elected president of the National Restaurant Association and was considered "almost a genius in the field," according to his friend Abraham Wechsler. To his son Larry, the decision to enter the family business seemed natural.

Allard was immensely proud of his brother Larry's record as a paratrooper in the Second World War. It was important to him that a member of his family had fought against Hitler. It confirmed to him that there were instances when armed might was justifiable. William F. Buckley, Jr., observes that Lowenstein never regarded himself as an enemy of the military establishment, even at the peak of his opposition to the American intervention in Vietnam.

3.

The Allard Lowenstein of the thirties was a boy deeply involved with his moral sense. This preoccupation was further developed by the school to which his parents sent him, Ethical Culture. Gabriel Lowenstein would not send his children to a public school because they were to have the best. Ironically, after years of stressing egalitarianism, Allard Lowenstein would come around to his father's thinking, advocating tuition tax credits because he considered the public school system a failure. This kind of ambiguity would forever infuriate Lowenstein watchers.

But Ethical Culture was unique. Although it was private, it was not elitist. It was regarded as the most liberal school in New York. The Society for Ethical Culture was founded in 1876 by Felix Adler, an educational reformer who in 1878 established The Free Kindergarden, the first school of its kind in the city of New York. The school was later known as the Workingman's School of the United Relief Works for the Society for Ethical Culture, and finally, in 1895, as the Ethical Culture School.

Adler, who became Professor of Social and Political Ethics at Columbia in 1902, was a colleague of John Dewey. In his Ethical Culture school, he stressed Dewey's "learning by doing," believing the task of education to be one of "penetration, revelation, turning potentialities into potencies." Adler's ultimate goal was "to train reformers."

The school was innovative in other ways: it was coeducational, and its curriculum included ethics as a subject for very young children. Adler's philosophy rejected total individualism as well as various forms of Socialism, favoring instead a pluralistic view of what he called "organized democracy." In a sermon to his father's congregation entitled "Judaism of the Future," which offended the trustees of Temple Emanuel, Adler had asserted that "Judaism ever claimed to be a religion not of the creed but of the deed, and its destiny is to embrace in one great moral state the whole family of man." His opposition to the self-segregation of ethnic groups and his support of a brand of Judaism that responded to the desire of educated Jews in New York to assimilate, while still retaining their identity, attracted some of the brightest students in the city.

Economic diversity, also a factor in Adler's philosophy, was apparently a matter of necessity as well as idealism. Originally, his pupils were only the children of the poor. The school was tuition-free, and no child whose family could afford to pay was admitted. But expenses increased as the school became bigger and better, and in 1890, to help defray the costs, a decision was made to admit some tuition-paying students. "A class school, whether for the poor or the rich, is a mistake," Adler proclaimed, and encouraged people from all income brackets to send their children to his school. Eventually, however, the number of poor children diminished and Ethical Culture became a haven for the privileged. Adler's ethics were perpetuated, though, by Algernon Black, an Ethical Culture alumnus from a poor Jewish family, who returned to the school after graduating magna cum laude from

Harvard in 1923 and became its most prominent faculty member. A disciple of both Adler and Roger Baldwin, under whom he had worked for the American Civil Liberties Union (ACLU), Algernon Black would, like them, reject the right and the left. Though he did not go as far as Baldwin, who expelled all Communists from the board of the ACLU, Black was impassioned in his battle against any form of authoritarianism. When Lowenstein entered the school, Black was chairman of the ethics department. He would remain an influence on him throughout his life.

4.

Bronia Kupsick recalls, "I had a daughter in the same kindergarten class and was immediately impressed about this little boy who seemed to lead the whole class. I said to the teacher 'Isn't that amazing, the way he leads these children around?' She said, 'He not only leads them around. I want you to know that he's two years younger than all the other children in the class.'"

Yet Bronia Kupsick and her daughter, Rita, were surprised when Lowenstein chose politics as a career. In spite of his leadership qualities, Rita admits, "We thought Allard was a little strange."

The image of Allard Lowenstein, with his horn-rimmed glasses, was that of a potential intellectual. People like Bronia Kupsick thought he would be a scientist. He was not "social" enough for the other children but spoke instead of "trying to save the world."

Lowenstein was very affected by Algernon Black. As head of the Ethical Culture Society and of the school's ethics department, Black gave weekly lectures which held everyone mesmerized. He told the children that good would triumph over evil. He stressed honesty and their responsibility to the starving people in the world.

Some former students remember Black as almost too moralistic and unyielding, placing too heavy a moral burden on very young children. Others recall that Black was considered extremely left-wing. Though his ideology never went beyond advocating a mixed economy and strong support for New Deal and reform politics, his passionate intensity gave the impression of radicalism.

Judge Richard Wallach, who attended Ethical Culture with Lowenstein, remembers that Lowenstein listened to Black in a way that the other students did not. "He was head and shoulders above his classmates," Wallach recalls, very much under the influence of Algernon Black. Black stood for "ethics and goodness," Wallach stresses, and could speak with "final authority."

"Al Lowenstein didn't emerge full grown from nowhere," Wallach insists. "Right from the beginning, he showed the traits that would characterize him all his life: concern with injustice, world events, the need to act."

The first objects of his concern with injustice were the teachers at Ethical Culture themselves. Strict New Englanders of the old mold, they tolerated no nonsense during class. Miss Paine, who was best known for her campaign against what she described as the fifth graders' "animal instinct," and Miss Puritan were the most feared.

Richard Wallach, who was "sometimes on the wrong side of the law," as he puts it, remembers that whenever one of the teachers was harsh with him, Allard Lowenstein would rush to his defense. In fact, Lowenstein not only defended Wallach and others, he organized a delegation to protest what he considered minor classroom tyranny imposed by the severe, uncompromising teachers. And while most of the classmates he organized were not as deeply concerned as Lowenstein was, teachers were obliged to take seriously the small, unathletic child with thick glasses who had been audacious enough to challenge their authority in the name of justice.

In confronting what he perceived as injustice, Lowenstein drew on skills developed by the kinds of games he preferred—games that involved either intellect or dexterity or both. Because he was not well coordinated, he did not participate in competitive sports but excelled instead in bridge and jacks. He even used a Culbertson machine to improve his bridge. He used game skills to accomplish his ends with people who were older and had power.

To Lowenstein it seemed that if an institution stood for something, those who were part of it had an obligation to act according to its principles. And those in a position of authority should be held to the highest standards, which, in the case of the Ethical Culture School, were clearly set forth by Algernon Black.

Lowenstein was not in rebellion against the school. He merely expected people and the institutions they created to live up to their ideals. To get them to do so, he learned to deploy individuals, to get the other children to act and the teachers to listen.

While not a religious institution, Ethical Culture taught values that were of the nature of theology, the highest of which was a form of nonideological democracy. To one of the faith, the highest calling was not a right; it was a privilege. Lowenstein, who believed that the way of life he was being taught was absolutely right, was ripe for that calling. To choose it was a way of being special, of succeeding in a dimension beyond the ordinary and of having an impact on life. Most of all, it was a way of being loved.

His father, the legitimate authority figure in Allard Lowenstein's life, tried to prove that there was no contradiction between wealth and a sense of social justice. While he had thrown his lot in with the moneymakers, Gabriel Lowenstein still spoke in the language of the social conscience of his early years as a labor organizer and Socialist. Only now he was a liberal Democrat. This created an ambivalence in Allard Lowenstein, who was as impressed by his father's sense of social justice as he was by Algernon Black's lectures, but who saw a contradiction in his father's professed values and the way the family lived.

While Lowenstein's stepmother indulged him, it was his father for whom he had the deepest love. His cousin Alice describes how Allard loved to call his father "papa," a very conscious term of affection. He loved the color green because it was his father's favorite color.

Because his father was successful and he wanted his father's love, Lowenstein would not condemn this aspect of Gabriel's existence. He himself would not want to be rich, but he would not challenge the wealth of others. His father had made his money for his children and given up what he believed in so that he could give them what he had been denied. Thus, as a "citizen," Lowenstein's calling would not lead him to attack those with more, but rather to help those who had less. He would be the realization of his father's lost ideals, that part of him which sought truth and justice rather than profit.

Unfortunately, Gabriel Lowenstein did not comprehend this effort to win his affection. It was one thing to show concern for the disadvantaged, another to devote your whole life to them. Despite that lack of understanding, his father was a tremendous force in Lowenstein's life, the source of his fervent belief that you could make things better without destroying the order in which you lived.

What Lowenstein developed, ironically, was a certain sense of patrician obligation, though he would always be somewhat embarrassed by the trappings of material well-being, be they good clothes, furniture, or other conveniences. He would make a point of denying himself material things even when he could afford them.

Another source of Allard Lowenstein's ambivalence was the school itself. Originally for the poor, it had become predominantly for the affluent, putting Algernon Black in no position to advocate the dissolution of private wealth to the children of parents who were paying tuition.

Because most of the Ethical Culture parents were Jewish, many of whom had experienced institutional anti-Semitism in Europe, there was a great emphasis at the school on the evils of prejudice. The enemy was the Klan, the *Bund*, the Nazis. Bronia Kupsick deliberately chose Ethical Culture for her daughter because it was the only school she knew of where there were black children.

If Fascism was the enemy on the right because it was anti-Semitic, Communism was a threat on the left because it would take away the wealth accumulated in the New World through suffering and sacrifice.

The correct position was in the middle: poised against the bigotry of the right and the collectivism of the left. And this was the main thrust of an essay the young Lowenstein wrote on Socialism when he was only thirteen years old.

This would be Allard Lowenstein's creed, and he would act on it. Bob Wechsler, his classmate at Ethical, remembers being recruited by Lowenstein to stand on street corners distributing literature for Franklin Delano Roosevelt. He also remembers standing on the steps of the austere red brick school building on Central Park West raising money for the Spanish loyalists. They were eight years old at the time.

Lowenstein's total involvement in the Spanish Civil War mystified his family, and friends like Richard Wallach and Bob Wechsler were amazed that he knew so much about what was going on in the world. On an adult level politically, Lowenstein was keenly aware of the rise of Hitler. From Algernon Black he got his understanding of the importance of what was going on in Spain and his enthusiasm for Roosevelt.

During the 1936 Roosevelt-Landon campaign, Lowenstein put up Roosevelt posters at day camp, and organized the other campers to help. When Franco won in Spain and Madrid fell, Lowenstein cried for two days, refusing to come out of his room. He was then just ten.

Injustice clearly affected him deeply, but Lowenstein also understood that politics, was, in fact, a game, and that playing it was absorbing. At the house in Hartsdale, Westchester, where the family summered, Lowenstein and his friend Samuel Heyman used to play at arranging a newspaper front page. "The Game of Politics," a board game, was another favorite: players competed for the electoral votes in each state by rolling the dice. So involved was Lowenstein with America and its political structure that he was always able to draw a freehand map of the United States, with all the states and their capitals. He knew their electoral votes by heart. Later, during the Second World War, when his brother Larry was in the paratroopers, Lowenstein played a war game on the roof with his sister involving fictional countries. Not surprisingly, he always won.

Lowenstein's competitiveness, which his Little Lord Fauntleroy suits could not entirely camouflage, manifested itself at Ethical Culture in a rivalry between school newspapers. One paper was put out by Richard Wallach, who acknowledges that his publication, produced by the hectograph method, was inferior to Lowenstein's, which he managed to have mimeographed. Wallach had access to the office machinery of his coeditor's father, a vice-president of RCA. But both Wallach and Harold Kingsburg published primarily to get the attention of their classmates, while Lowenstein's paper tended, in Wallach's words, "to be on a much more adult level. And he was, even then, interested in politics and current events, the rise of Hitler in Germany, things that left some of his classmates a little wide-eyed." Lowenstein was also clearly interested in journalism and saw this as the most likely career for satisfying his passion for politics.

Wallach thinks of Lowenstein during the years of 1937, '38, and '39 as "extremely articulate, bright, fun," and always ready to mount a protest. His seriousness could give way to playfulness when he was organizing a protest against the strict teachers or rushing around with his newspaper. The solution for him, as a child somewhat apart, neither particularly social nor athletic, was to merge his moral concerns with his vocation as a leader, publicist, and organizer.

Once when the Lowenstein family was visiting with the Kupsicks, Bronia Kupsick remembers recounting a conversation she had had with a young revolutionary at the railway station in Lukow, Poland. As she ended her story, on a somewhat ambiguous note, she remembers that Allard Lowenstein implored her not to stop, saying, "Go on. What happened?"

The idea of the revolution—the possibility that everything could be changed—had intrigued him. But the Lowenstein family was hardly one to approve the concept. Passionately for Franklin Roosevelt and the New Deal, the family aligned itself with a brand of liberals who never questioned their right to live well, even in the depths of the Depression. They were upwardly mobile, and the Democratic Party, which they supported, with its reformist legacy of Woodrow Wilson and Al Smith, would take care of the poor and the unemployed. Socialism had become alien to them, a relic of the immigrant experience.

When Allard Lowenstein was born in Newark, New Jersey, it was a middle-class white ethnic community. Soon the Lowensteins moved into a comfortable Manhattan apartment and rented a series of large houses in Westchester and Long Island for the summer. Allard was aware that the money that enabled them to do this had been generated largely by his Uncle Willie, whose rough-and-ready business style had inspired one friend to describe him as "Runyonesque."

After he was graduated from Ethical Culture, Lowenstein transferred into the seventh grade of the Horace Mann School in Riverdale. He was pleased because he thought the school, which ranks among the foremost private schools in America, having produced graduates such as William Carlos Williams, Rockwell Kent, James Schlesinger, and Anthony Lewis, would be more challenging academically. But its elitism and wealth were in conflict with the values he had been taught at Ethical Culture.

At the same time, his father purchased a very imposing house in the wealthy community of Harrison, New York. An apartment was kept in Manhattan for the winter months, when the drive into the city was particularly hazardous. Employing a full staff, the Lowensteins lived up to the standards of that community. Because Gabriel didn't drive and his wife was considered a menace on the roads, there was a black chauffeur, Rex. There was also a gardener, a full-time maid, and a cook—a Spanish woman whose English was poor.

Lowenstein had a great affinity for this woman, and took pains to include her in the family. He recognized in her, and in Rex, people who had to struggle to be included. It was how he considered himself.

Something of a "grande dame," Mrs. Lowenstein kept a kosher home, although her husband had no use for religion. On passover, Dr. Lowenstein had a separate refrigerator brought in to save the trouble of moving the food as required by religious law. This was perhaps not a major event, but to the man moving the refrigerator in the middle of the Depression it might have seemed an extravagance, particularly as it was done in the name of religion, during a celebration of the liberation of a people from bondage. And Allard Lowenstein wondered about the significance of this religion and about the bondage of others in the America in which he lived.

Meanwhile, in Europe, there had been the anschluss, the Munich Pact, the Hitler-Stalin Pact, and in 1939, the Nazi invasion of Poland. Spain had fallen to the Franco forces. There was open persecution of Jews and a threat to civilization unequaled in the history of the human race. While to almost everyone else in Lowenstein's school life these events were remote, they hovered like a dark cloud over him. Still, he himself was not immune to the culture that surrounded him.

Lowenstein read about world problems and became fascinated with the politics of New York, but he also had political interests in school. He was constantly running for class office at Horace Mann, where he began a practice he would continue throughout his life: keeping a book of his constituents with their names, addresses, and phone numbers.

Lowenstein was elected vice-president of his junior class, although some students thought of him as manipulative, even "Machiavellian," says his close friend Sandy Friedman. "The idea of Al as the pure reformer is ridiculous," he asserts. "He was a skillful politician and could make deals, even in high school."

Lowenstein's campaign for school president was a prolonged struggle, which he waged with what Friedman describes as a "Teddy Roosevelt impulse and drive." While other candidates were less knowledgeable, many students supported them over Lowenstein, who was not elected, because they were perceived as more straightforward. Yet Lowenstein was a formidable competitor whose best weapons were information and a band of intensely loyal supporters, whom he cultivated with care.

Lowenstein relied on *The New York Times* as his main source of information. His cousin Alice would help him file vast piles of old editions in his own special *New York Times* room in the big house in Harrison.

Though he was passionately interested in politics, Lowenstein was not single-minded. He was determined to be a wrestler, and finally made the Horace Mann team. Edging out Roy Cohn, who had also sought the position, Lowenstein became editor of *The Record*, the school newspaper that Anthony Lewis had edited before him.

On his own, Al Lowenstein put out another publication, one that was at odds with his image as a brilliant student with a moral mission. It was called *The Progressive*, a misleading title because it had absolutely nothing to do with politics. It was concerned exclusively with pop culture. He wrote articles about movie stars and popular songs, picked the records which he thought would reach the top of the Hit Parade, and printed the ratings of popular songs as they stood on the charts. He took a school poll on the question of whether Katharine Hepburn or Bette Davis was the bigger box office draw.

This was what Sandy Friedman calls the theatrical side of Allard Lowenstein, the show-biz aspect of his personality that was always there. In high school, he was an actor and a member of the Drama Club, which Friedman headed. With Friedman, he coauthored a play that was never finished, but in which he was deeply interested. During the summer, he attended a farm camp in Vermont, where he and Friedman put on plays in which he was the chief performer. If he sometimes spoke of becoming a rabbi, he more often mentioned the possibility of a theatrical career.

"It was all there," Friedman concludes—"the love of pop, movies, plays, songs. He adored pop. He wanted to be an actor."

Friedman nevertheless was aware that Lowenstein had other, more profound, concerns that enabled him to make use of his theatricality. He recognized that Lowenstein's ability as an actor, combined with his intellect and vast knowledge, made him "the most remarkable public speaker I have ever heard."

His public speaking and debating skills were enhanced by participation in the Debating Club; his brilliance was recognized by election to the Archon Society, an honor society. An outstanding student, Lowenstein could occasionally be seen writing copy for *The Progressive* while simultaneously absorbing difficult classwork.

Even with all these gifts and interests, Lowenstein wanted desperately to be elected to class office. Friedman suggests that Al was very insecure, the sufferer of what was then called an "inferiority complex." Lowenstein, he affirms, was "the most complicated person I have ever met. It was crucially important that he have that affirmation of approval and popularity that being elected president meant."

As he sought approval from his peers, Lowenstein continued to grapple with his family. According to Friedman, Allard wanted the approval of his father—who was often described as "authoritarian" in an Old World sense—more than anything else. Yet he desperately needed to rebel against a suffocating, rigid, Jewish family code.

There was also the complication of the stepmother. Friedman recalls that when he and Al were about twelve, Lowenstein's stepmother became quite ill. At this time, largely because of her illness, Friedman says, "I doubt that there was much warmth coming from Florence." In addition, there was a severity in Gabriel, a coldness that left Allard feeling more alone than ever. Having lost one wife, Gabriel was fearful of another tragedy and he reacted by withdrawing further from his son. Allard felt the need to be loved more than ever.

Florence recovered and again became warm and affectionate. She considered herself close to Allard and always kept a room for him in the apartment where he and his friends could stay. She ran his errands, picked up the laundry he dumped on the floor. But she never wanted him to "make waves," and he made some effort to accommodate her. Because she was religious, Al became involved in a Sephardic temple, even suggesting to her that he might become a rabbi. His cousin Alice does not believe that Lowenstein was ever seriously religious, though he maintained throughout his life that he believed in God and called himself a theist. Later on he did attend temple, and when his children were born, he thought of them as Jewish, even though it is the mother's faith that determines if a child is a Jew, according to Jewish religious law, and his wife, Jenny, was not Jewish.

Mostly, though, he rebelled. His mother, who prided herself on setting a beautiful table, was distressed by Allard's habit of smearing his food with ketchup and mustard. She was furious when he would turn up with a motley crew of friends, some of them black, at the Fenway Golf Club in Scarsdale.

Gabriel, on the other hand, took a bemused attitude toward his youngest son's eccentricity. Though Dr. Lowenstein was a nutritionist, with a syndicated column in some thirty papers, he was indulgent when Allard ate watermelon and ravioli together. And the father's manner of dress influenced the son. According to Alice Levien, Gabriel, who was usually disheveled, with his tie askew, took pride in such displays of reverse snobbery. In fact, it was said of Gabriel before it was said of Allard that he marched to a different drummer. He never cared about the condition of the house or car. What he did care about was knowledge and performance, especially in his children.

Sandy Friedman saw Allard's slovenliness and notorious tardiness as rebelliousness, but also as an emulation of his father's idiosyncrasies. Dorothy was amazed at the way her brother was able to handle this demanding and eccentric father. Yet she felt that Gabriel Lowenstein did not understand many of his son's later achievements, since they were often performed out of the public eye and he got no credit for them.

Gabriel Lowenstein apparently believed that if you did something worthwhile, people should know about it and you should get credit. Dorothy called it "the old syndrome of the immigrant. 'I want you to get the credit and be wealthy, successful, and whatever it is ˙that makes you happy.'"

The Lowenstein children were often reminded by their father that he had to walk ten miles to school except in the winter, when he crossed a frozen lake, shortening the walk by five miles. "So if you complained because you were out in the cold too long," Dorothy recalls, "he would say, 'When I was your age . . .' And if you were trying to lift something, he would say, 'When I was your age, I could lift this piano.'"

Larry Lowenstein, who, like his sister, remembers Gabriel as a difficult but loving father, saw a change in Allard's attitude toward his father. "As the years went on, Al could wind him around his little finger, but then again, he could wind anybody around his little finger. Whatever he would say to Al, Al would put him down in a way that he couldn't argue with." According to Larry, Gabriel once said to Al, "When I was your age, I was running twenty-two restaurants," to which his son replied, "But, Papa, when Lincoln was your age, he was president of the United States."

While Gabriel was the intellectual, Uncle Willie was the tycoon, a tough and adventurous businessman who was responsible for building the restaurant empire. Gabriel's youngest son knew early on that he wasn't on that track. While he liked to bring his crowd of unconventional friends into the restaurants, he did not consider himself part of them.

At thirteen or fourteen, Lowenstein was, in Sandy Friedman's words, "the stereotype of a liberal." The ultraliberal afternoon newspaper *p.m.* was a source of tremendous excitement to him. "This is the kind of paper I would publish if I were an editor," Lowenstein said. The good guys were the underdogs and those who fought for them. And the way you fought for them was in politics.

5.

His passion for politics increased. After every election, he pored over the vote, district by district, state by state. As he grew older, every minute fluctuation was studied and saved. No one knew why he did it. The newspapers piled up as his own cache of political information reached encyclopedic proportions. But the idea of actually entering politics didn't occur to him. This was something they didn't teach at Ethical Culture or Horace Mann, and in any case, according to Friedman, Lowenstein was not then thinking in career terms. His identification with the underdog came, Friedman believes, from a feeling of being a "wallflower"; he suffered from some "hidden handicap" that plagued him and made him feel apart.

"Al wanted power much more than he was aware of," Friedman maintains. "It was one of his central drives. I'm not sure Allard didn't perceive power until much later as something not negative. As a result, until he understood that power was something necessary, he had to find an altruistic motive for all of his actions. Once he was in Congress, he understood that power was not pejorative. He saw it as something necessary. But early on, he didn't like this motive in himself." He preferred to believe that people in public life were selfless and did not want power.

Lawrence Rossbach from Horace Mann remembers Lowenstein from the farm camp, Camp MacArthur, in Waitsville, Vermont. It was 1943, the middle of the war, and the campers worked from 9:00 to 5:00 on local farms to help the war effort. The boys, most of them Jewish, planted 300 tomato plants and picked 30 tons of beans.

Recreation after work was swimming and theatrics under the direction of Charlotte Baruth, a former silent film star who cofounded the camp with her husband Alfred, an English teacher from Horace Mann. Her production of *George Washington Slept Here* with Al Lowenstein as the leading man was so successful that it moved to the Oddfellows Hall in Waitsfield. The cast, strongly influenced by Lowenstein, voted to donate the proceeds to the town. Its success there prompted the company to perform at many area town halls. Before the summer was over, a thousand people had come to see Camp MacArthur's first real theatrical endeavor, and to Rossbach it seemed that Lowenstein had found an activity that gave him the recognition he craved. But Rossbach also felt that Lowenstein was not in the social swim; he appeared to be unhappy except when he was performing.

Though he may not have been entirely happy there, the summer at work camp helped to improve Lowenstein's self-image. The farmwork developed him physically and he saw the possibilities for changing his body into a powerful, athletic one. He also became aware of his ability to perform in public, to hold the attention of large audiences and make them believe what he was saying.

Lowenstein's patriotism, which had always been strong, grew stronger. He took pride in his brother Larry's record as a paratrooper during World War II, fighting against democracy's enemies. According to their sister, the three brothers were "very, very different," and had never been very close. After the war, however, Larry Lowenstein began to get to know and understand his younger brother. Unlike his father and mother, he perceived that Allard would have a unique calling in this new postwar world.

The Lowenstein family was now living in Scarsdale. Low prices at Stuart's had given way to elegance at the Sherbrook and Monte's on the Park, new Lowenstein restaurants. Bert was a doctor, having completed his medical studies, and Larry would go into the family business. Dorothy was at Fieldston, another exclusive secondary school.

For Allard Lowenstein, the question now was college. His father and mother assumed it would be a major Ivy League school, probably Harvard. With his outstanding record and his IQ of 143 he could have been admitted anywhere. But again he chose to be different. In search of America, he wanted to learn something new about his country. He was interested in state schools, where he would find ordinary Americans who were athletes and not bookworms. He had heard of Frank Porter Graham, a great liberal educator and social reformer who was president of the University of North Carolina at Chapel Hill. Lowenstein decided to go south to Chapel Hill and seek him out.

II

South

6.

Chapel Hill was a beautiful and optimistic place, full of the hope of
the forties. Both it and Frank Graham would become established in
Lowenstein's mind as ideals by which institutions and leaders should
be measured. But when he entered, Lowenstein was an obscure
freshman looking to make friends.

It was June 30, 1945, the beginning of the summer term, according
to the semester system then in use, and the stately old campus of the
University of North Carolina was alive with the activity of students on
a sultry night.

If a Hollywood director were looking for the perfect campus of an
American university, one that would be quintessentially beautiful and
convey instantly all the longings and aspirations of the halcyon undergraduate experience, he would find it at Chapel Hill. Although the
particular beauty of its campus and the grace which characterized human relationships there still gave it a distinct southern flavor, by 1945
Chapel Hill was no longer just a fine southern university; it was an
American institution attracting people from many different regions.
And along with the southern gentlemen and the scions of the landed
gentry came new kinds of people—advocates of change, serious intellectuals, liberals, radicals, even some Communists.

It was, however, still a white institution in a segregated society,
where blacks were prohibited by law from attending white schools.
And while its president, Frank Graham, was able to capture a good
portion of Columbia's statistics department, a black still couldn't get a
hamburger at a lunch counter. Jewish students were assigned, for the
most part quite routinely, to the same dormitory because the administrator in charge of room assignments assumed that Jews "preferred
it that way."

Fraternities were housed in magnificent antebellum mansions
staffed by black servants, but no one in them sipped any bourbon;

North Carolina was completely dry. Traditionally all-male, there was the beginning of a break with sexual segregation; women were now allowed to do their first two years at the all-female campus at Greensboro and then finish at Chapel Hill.

James Wallace, who would one day become mayor of Chapel Hill and a professor at North Carolina State, remembers his first encounter with Lowenstein in 1945. He was then the dorm advisor at Steele, the building to which Lowenstein had been assigned, and he had left the door to his ground-floor room at No. 4 Steele open to catch any faint breeze that might have been stirring on a hot North Carolina evening. With him was Douglas Hunt, also from North Carolina, and the two were deep in discussion of "the grand affairs of campus politics," as Wallace puts it.

At the time Wallace had already received his bachelor's degree in physics and was enrolled in the law school. Hunt, a senior, was what is generally called a "big man on campus," very involved in student government, while Wallace was known as the "campus radical." Wallace recalls that while they were engaged in what had become a habitual late-night conversation, someone shuffled down the stairs toward the water fountain. He had a clock in one hand and poked his head in the door to ask the time.

He added, "I'm Allard Lowenstein. From New York."

Wallace, somewhat curious, invited him in. Having accepted the invitation, Lowenstein stayed until three in the morning, talking. Lowenstein's head was still full of New York politics, but the two southerners tired of that and turned the conversation to other topics. Among them was what they called "the Race Problem" in the South, something to which Lowenstein had given little thought up until then.

What Wallace did not know that night was that Allard Lowenstein was only sixteen years old. Lowenstein confided this to him two months later when he and Wallace had become friends, but made him swear that he wouldn't reveal it to anybody.

Douglas Hunt recalls that Lowenstein sounded very often "as if he had the wisdom of the ages at his beck and call—extremely articulate, very quick of mind, nimble of tongue, and with a kind of wisdom in dealing with human beings, a kind of kindly view of them, a willingness to be outgoing, much beyond the years of a person only sixteen years old."

That long conversation put Lowenstein on a course from which he would never diverge. Wallace represented the radical populist tradition of the American south, an indigenous, grassroots, antiauthoritarian, antiracist mentality. Hunt was more the southern liberal, and what Lowenstein saw in him was a different kind of person, a man capable of showing warmth and friendship to another man, in a manner totally southern.

Looking back, Wallace recalled the impression Lowenstein left with him: "So here comes this person down from New York, a strange and foreign land. . . . And here we were, two southerners, suddenly confronted with this person who had come down for whatever reason—I think that it was the liberalism and the view that at UNC that was the thing." And what he said afterward to Hunt was, "You know, he's a very smart person, with a remarkable acuity and understanding of a tremendous number of things." He remembers that Hunt concurred.

In the South, campus politics traditionally provided a training ground for future leaders, and it was not unusual for high-ranking state politicians to retain their interest in student affairs and to recruit talent from the ranks of politically active undergraduates. In North Carolina a student leader might become governor or a United States senator by virtue of his undergraduate political connections at Chapel Hill. And the excitement of the undergraduate political experience was something to which Lowenstein was particularly susceptible.

The absence of blacks and his own minority status as a Jew at Chapel Hill provoked a culture shock in Lowenstein that the segregation of Jewish students into one dormitory did nothing to lessen. It was the exclusion of blacks, however, the total segregation of the South, that was most shocking to him.

Among those who openly opposed racial segregation were leaders of the North Carolina Jewish community, through whom Lowenstein was introduced to the unusual role of southern Jews. After frequent visits to the home of E. J. Evans, who served as the mayor of Durham, North Carolina, from 1951 to 1963, Lowenstein, although originally convinced that a Jewish state amounted to a form of self-segregation, became a confirmed Zionist and supporter of Israel. He joined the Hillel at Chapel Hill, but he also joined Rev. Charles Jones's Community Church and found himself allied with Christians who shared his political beliefs. The president of the university was himself a devout Christian with a deep respect for Jews and a hatred for any kind of prejudice. Frank Graham set the tone for the university.

Just as at Ethical Culture he had challenged the teachers for behaving in a manner inconsistent with their expressed beliefs, Lowenstein was impelled to take action at Chapel Hill. He could have joined a Jewish fraternity, but recoiled against moving into a Jewish ghetto. And he resented the dormitory arrangements which segregated Jews.

Lowenstein went to Douglas Hunt with evidence that Jews were being assigned to a single dormitory. In fact, there had been some anti-Semitic incidents involving baseball bats and threats. Hunt took the evidence to Graham and was told that according to university policy student requests for a particular room or roommate were to be met to the extent possible. In the absence of specific requests, "we just start with the dorms in South Building and go out in ever-widening circles until we fill all of the dorms as the applications come in and that is our unvarying policy."

Informed by Hunt that it was not happening that way, Graham asked for evidence. At Lowenstein's request, the Jewish students then copied names off the dorm doors and Hunt returned to Graham with the list, telling him that Allard Lowenstein had been responsible for compiling it. When Claude Teague, the administrator under whose jurisdiction room assignments fell, denied that students were assigned by "race" but confirmed that they were placed with the understanding "that certain people would prefer to be together," Graham ordered the practice stopped.

Hunt had made it clear to Graham that it was Lowenstein who gathered the evidence, and Graham was intrigued. For his part, Lowenstein recognized in Graham a legitimate authority figure who had done the right thing.

The highest honor a student can achieve at Chapel Hill is not a Phi Beta Kappa key or a varsity football or basketball letter. It is to be tapped by the Order of the Golden Fleece. Frank Graham, a true democrat in politics and education, was tapped not once but three times, and it did not seem a contradiction to him to oppose fraternities, racism, and a class system while awarding high prestige to the Golden Fleece and those whom it honored.

Lowenstein, who was tapped, was attracted to this secret society because of the camaraderie and sense of belonging which its members enjoyed. It was an elite of men close to each other in almost a classic sense who shared the view that nothing in life could equal the friendship of excellent minds in athletic bodies. Born with the mind, Lowenstein transformed his body at Chapel Hill by a sheer act of will into that of a powerful athlete. He neither smoked nor drank and worked out so much that friends considered him fanatical. A compact 5 feet 11 inches, 175 pounds, he was always looking for a good match, a good debate, mind and body now both ready for competition. In fact he became so involved in extracurricular activities that the academic Lowenstein briefly declined and he actually flunked a math course, an experience he would wear like a badge of honor.

Lowenstein decided to major in history, and the debates he had with his professors sometimes caused a campus stir. His career plans at the time were for some kind of newspaper work, probably in management, so he worked on the *Tar Heel*, the student paper.

Jimmy Wallace describes Lowenstein's rise on the campus as "meteoric," while fellow undergraduate Richard Murphy describes him as "controversial." Murphy, who describes himself at Chapel Hill as "a flunky of Lowenstein," says "People were violently for Al or violently against him. , , , You were either a follower or a nonfollower. . . . He was a . . . lightning rod, around which people were either on one side or the other."

Lowenstein was attracted to the movement to abolish fraternities because he was self-conscious about his own privilege. Douglas Hunt remembers that Lowenstein would deliberately run the heels down on his saddle shoes. Yet he did keep a car on campus, a Nash Rambler. He would wear a T-shirt under an open plaid shirt, khakis, and a sailor hat, with his thick glasses always on his nose.

North Carolina was more of a home to Lowenstein than his own, and his friends were a new family in which he was freer to be himself than he had ever been. He was loosening his ties with the narrow world he had left in New York, becoming assimilated into a wider America. Clearly, evil existed in it, but the good far outweighed the bad and things could be made better.

At Chapel Hill Lowenstein wanted to abolish fraternities that excluded Jews. He wanted to rid the campus of racial segregation. What he felt was needed was a framework of government on the campus through which he and his friends could attack the fraternities.

Lowenstein was a member of the Dialectic Senate or the "Di," the leading literary and debating society, which along with Phi, the other major society, ran the honor code. Membership in the Di had helped to prepare such major political figures as James Polk for political careers in the past, a fact which was not lost on Lowenstein, who, Jimmy Wallace asserts, "had aspirations to be president" of the United States. "He was extremely ambitious," he concludes. Meanwhile, his dynamic role in the Di projected him as a major leader on the campus.

Lowenstein backed a resolution in the Di to abolish fraternities that discriminated against Jews, but Hunt, who headed the student government, helped to change it to one that would abolish any organization on campus that discriminated on the basis of religion. This encompassed the Jewish fraternities that excluded Gentiles. After a heated debate, in which Lowenstein displayed the oratory that would give him a national reputation, the resolution carried. But the Di had no power to implement it.

Frank Graham introduced Lowenstein, Wallace, and Hunt to another issue which eventually led to an organized movement for comprehensive change at Chapel Hill. The issue was one that would become paramount during the sixties: free speech. Through Graham, the students learned about Homer Price Raney, who had been fired from the University of Texas because he had refused to remove *U.S.A.* by John Dos Passos from the shelves of the library. Graham encouraged them to attend meetings on the campus supporting Raney and intellectual liberty, and the discussions sparked by this issue eventu-

ally led them to conclude that there should be a new student constitution that would prohibit discrimination and promote freedom of
speech.

At the beginning of this movement, there were two major parties
on campus, the University party, which was a prime supporter of fraternities, and the Campus party. The small band of liberal student
constitutionalists formed a coalition of supporters in the major parties
and created a new entity, the United Carolina party, the UCP. Lowenstein played a significant role in its creation.

This "strange coalition," as Wallace calls it, lasted for only one semester, but it did make the constitution possible. The constitution,
however, did not get rid of fraternities. The deep conservatism of the
majority of the students was resistant to such fundamental change and
those favoring fraternities continued to gravitate toward the University party, while those against—Hunt, Wallace, Lowenstein, and the
rest—joined the new Student party. At eighteen, seeing himself as a
kind of undergraduate Willkie, free from the ties to any political machine and drafted by his supporters, Lowenstein strove to effect fundamental change at Chapel Hill within the new constitutional framework.

Elections were held on the campus every six months, and Lowenstein, with his extraordinary energy level, organized and participated
in most of the campaigns. He invariably lost his own races by narrow
margins, with the one exception of his election as vice-president of
the student legislature. Through his participation in the passionate
student politics of the state of North Carolina, he also drew closer to
Frank Graham.

The race question in higher education simmered as an issue and
then burst open. The statewide student legislature still excluded representatives from black colleges and Lowenstein found himself em-
broiled in the fight to admit them. He was preparing to represent
Chapel Hill in Raleigh, where the student legislature was meeting in
the state legislative chamber, when he began to worry about the consequences of his position pressing for the admission of blacks.

Rev. Charles Jones remembers: "I got a phone call about eleven
o'clock one night, and it was Al, and he said, 'Preacher, we're thinking
about introducing a resolution to open the state student legislature to
students of any higher educational institution in the state.' And he
says, 'What do you think of it?' Well, he knew what I thought of it."
Lowenstein then disclosed his concern, telling Jones, "We don't want
to destroy Dr. Frank's budget."

Declining to make a judgment on the question thus framed, Jones
arranged for the delegation to meet with Graham, who was to return
to Raleigh on War-Labor Board business the next day, so that they

could speak to him directly about their problem. Graham had only about ten minutes to spare after a scheduled speech and before boarding a train, but he told Jones, "If you bring them down and ride me across, I can talk to them." Jones recalls that they explained their dilemma, telling Graham, "We don't want to hurt the university, but we think that it ought to be done." And he remembers Graham's reply: "Well, you let me take care of the University and you follow your conscience."

Graham was risking his career. He was not only president of Chapel Hill, he was also head of the Consolidated Universities, the statewide system of higher education, and segregation was the policy of the state. Lowenstein was deeply impressed, and Jones believes that from the moment Graham gave his support to the students, there was a bond between them.

Students from all over the state congregated in the state capital. Many of them were former GIs returning to school with a broad perspective on social questions. The debate raged in a packed chamber, with Wake Forest moving to table the resolution to admit blacks. The white students who were proposing integration of the body were regarded as extreme radicals, even Communists. They were told that it was too soon to take this kind of action and that the question was too serious for a student forum. Jimmy Wallace, a member of the Chapel Hill delegation of which Lowenstein was chairman, protested, asking, "How long will we wait before they will be seated in these hallowed seats? The least we can do at this time, as young people, as people who see an injustice having been done, is to say, 'The time is now!'"

Someone suggested that if the motion to admit the blacks carried, if the students from the University of North Carolina did not "shut up and back off," if in fact any state-supported institution did not back off on the motion, then the appropriations would be cut. To that Wallace boldly replied: "If it comes to a question of whether the students of this University of North Carolina can speak in public their own minds regarding politics, or whether the university appropriations shall be curtailed, then I say, to hell with the appropriations."

To wild cheers, the resolution was carried. But the press picked up the quote and calls poured into Frank Graham's office demanding Wallace's expulsion.

Graham's response was to assure Wallace, "Before any of the students are thrown out of the university, they will have to dispose of me as president."

In their jubilation, Lowenstein's friends were puzzled by an incident that revealed a side to him that had not previously been evident.

During the debate at the state capital, Lowenstein had grown increasingly anxious about a paper he had to submit for a required course. His friends Jimmy Wallace, Doug Hunt, and Mary Elizabeth Bolick were planning to return to Chapel Hill by bus, but when they arrived at the station with Lowenstein they discovered that the bus was going to be late.

Lowenstein, who was becoming desperate, insisted that he had to get back to work on the paper. He wanted his friends to share a taxi with him from Raleigh to Chapel Hill. Because they considered the fare for all of them entirely too steep, and Lowenstein didn't have the money himself, his friends lent him the money and he went alone.

According to Douglas Hunt, Lowenstein felt that his friends had failed a personal loyalty test. He was hurt when they didn't come with him in the taxi after the tumultuous victory.

Douglas Hunt describes Lowenstein's need for reassurance: "There was a quality of that in Al, not terribly egocentric, but a quality of sort of testing his friends early on for loyalty if he felt that he wanted to be close to them, before he got *too* close. And we talked about it that evening and I said, 'Well, Al, if I had seen it in those terms at all, I would have given up a week's pay, because I think that much of you.' But I didn't see it in those terms. It was to me a simple question of whether to take a taxi or a bus to get a paper written, and it seemed to me that he had ample time to do it, and I guess, from my point of view, the amount that the taxi would have cost us would have been what I could earn for my education for the next week."

Yet in many ways Lowenstein was extremely lighthearted. Still interested in sports he wrestled intramurally as a middleweight after an injury kept him off the varsity team. Pop music, about which he talked endlessly, continued to be a passion, and he was dating a beautiful girl, the daughter of Charles W. Tillet, who had been Frank Graham's roommate at college, and Gladys Child Tillet, national vice-chairman of the Democratic party under both Roosevelt and Truman.

His courtship of Sarah Tillet was characteristically eccentric. On the evening of a formal dance, Lowenstein, who had lent his respectable dinner jacket to a friend, appeared in chocolate-brown pants and the jacket from a blue suit. At the predance party, he and Sarah, who wore an elegant black evening dress, danced in a little back room at a coffee house called Danziger's. Lowenstein, the undergraduate from New York, who had arrived knowing nobody, now had the world of Chapel Hill in the palm of his hand. For the first time in his life, he was not only part of things but at the center of them.

Late one night he was out on the street in front of Frieda Altschul's Viennese coffee shop. Frieda and Otto Altschul were "Old World" Viennese Jews whose place was a hangout for the students because Frieda had a special feeling for them.

"You shouldn't be out without a coat," she shouted at him. "Go home to sleep."

Lowenstein laughed and called her "grandma," but he was back the next day, asking her about Vienna and staying all morning. She and her husband became surrogate grandparents with whom Lowenstein would keep in touch, visiting them when he returned to Chapel Hill, and later in Berkeley when they moved.

If the Altschuls were his surrogate grandparents, Frank Graham was now his father figure. Graham was fifty-nine when Lowenstein came to Chapel Hill. He came from a large family himself, but he and his wife Marian had no children of their own and in many ways Lowenstein, who shared his values, became the son Graham always wanted.

Though puritan in his habits—Graham neither smoked nor drank—and religious in outlook—he often spoke of life as "this pilgrimage toward the kingdom of God"—Graham was also a brilliant politician who possessed a keen sense of justice and the courage to act on it, qualities which inevitably drew Lowenstein to him. Jimmy Wallace observes that Lowenstein too was a politician, but Wallace believes that in some ways Lowenstein must have been afraid to succeed; Wallace recalls the elections Lowenstein repeatedly lost by one or two votes. Unlike his real father, Graham made Lowenstein comfortable with himself. There was no need to rationalize his concerns or his mode of life. In Graham's eyes, Lowenstein was living the way one should, devoted to the cause of justice, humanity, and freedom, and Wallace believes that Graham was the mentor Lowenstein needed to bolster his confidence.

Graham had defied the establishment in North Carolina during the twenties, supporting the right of the Communists to express their views during the period when the labor movement was growing. But his experience with the Communists left him with considerable doubt about their motives, something he would impart to Lowenstein.

Graham had been active in the Southern Conference for Human Welfare, a force for social progress in the South based in Atlanta. Southern academics and intellectuals were involved as well as activists from the entire South.

According to Douglas Hunt, the Communists "infiltrated" the conference and tried to take it over. Graham did not try to get rid of them. As a civil libertarian, he insisted that they were entitled to their opinion. But he resented their methods and believed it to be dangerous for them to hide in an organization without stating their real affiliation. He believed that their loyalty to Russia was paramount, above the interests of those he was trying to help. Later, very conscious that in poor regions such as the South the Communists could be an effective organizing force, he warned his young disciples against falling in with them.

Graham's view of the Communists arose from his conviction that any totalitarian view of life was wrong, whether on the right or left. Like Algernon Black, he was passionately committed to the progressive center.

Catching Graham's fervor, Lowenstein developed a sense of mission; he felt he must work to prevent a swing to totalitarianism. Sounding like Graham, he spoke of a "mystical" quality in his own life and believed he could see the consequences of things and understand what had to be done to prevent the worst from happening. Like Graham, he tried to be detached and said he had a sense of "seeing with the Third Eye," a reference to the Indian mystics who had the capacity to be involved with detachment. Like Graham, he feared that after World War II there might be a period of disillusionment and cynicism resembling the twenties. He wanted to proceed, as did Graham, with Roosevelt's agenda. And like Graham, he believed that with energy and vigorous engagement there could be a democratic politics capable of effecting change without violent revolution.

The essence of the politics Lowenstein was formulating lay in action, deeds, and speech; passivity and ideological rigidity, he concluded, led to dictatorship. But while he knew that action aimed at breaking down the barriers between people was more important than developing a private career or aquiring personal wealth, personal power remained an ambiguity. Lowenstein liked getting his way, being admired. But from Graham, as from Algernon Black, he had learned that wanting this power was somehow unworthy.

In fact, Lowenstein was more different from Graham than he may have imagined. When the legislature tried to oust Graham from his position as president of the Consolidated Universities, Graham survived, but precariously. Attacked throughout his life from the right and the left, Graham remained outwardly serene. But serenity was not Lowenstein's nature. He took any attack on Graham as a personal one, and would view attacks on himself the same way. He was deeply hurt by the wounds of political combat.

Jimmy Wallace says Lowenstein was "compelled, driven. He never had a relaxed moment." His friends remember he spoke often of getting exhausted and they were aware of how important to him it was to get rest, sunshine, and physical exercise. But he did have brief interludes of quiet or recreation. After lunch, he and his friends, including Sarah Tillet, would often sit in the sun, doze in the yard of the Presbyterian church, or linger over a coke and dessert. They played twenty questions, at which Lowenstein was ingenious, using abstruse American historical facts and figures. He would play the piano and sing popular songs in a voice somewhat nasal and forced at the top. And when he wasn't singing himself he loved to listen to Jimmy Wallace sing Irish songs, sometimes with a group Wallace had formed with a number of friends, known as "Mr. Wallace and his Cohorts."

7.

Lowenstein returned to Chapel Hill for his senior year, still undecided what he would do after graduation in 1949. At his father's urging he applied and was admitted to Yale Law School. Lowenstein was also given the John J. Parker Award for distinguished student leadership at Chapel Hill. Then the governor of North Carolina, W. Kerr Scott, announced that he was going to name Frank Porter Graham to fill a vacancy in the Senate.

When Graham went to Washington he asked Lowenstein to come with him as a staff member, and Lowenstein convinced Yale Law School to postpone his entrance. He was, quite suddenly, in a position close to the center of power in America. President Truman appointed Graham to his Civil Rights Commission and Lowenstein worked as his advisor. All this, as Jimmy Wallace says, "back when it was not chic— not only was it not chic, it was terribly heretical, unbelievably bad, that anyone could evenhandedly view civil rights problems in relation to blacks and whites."

It was neither surprising nor unusual for Lowenstein to be outspoken as a Graham staff member. Having moved beyond the "doctor-student" relationship (Graham was called Dr. Frank although he never completed his Ph.D.), in which they had functioned more or less as equals anyway, both Graham and Lowenstein considered their development of policy on issues as a joint venture. In Washington, Graham now relied increasingly on Lowenstein's advice, particularly concerning the race question. Yet as an advisor to Graham, Lowenstein found himself, at one point, in conflict with his own idealism.

Debate raged in the Senate in 1950 on key civil rights legislation, the Fair Employment Practices Act, and a vote was to be taken on cloture. If Graham voted to cut off debate and force a vote he would be seen as breaking longstanding southern tradition, which dictated that senators be allowed to speak as long as they liked. Worse, he would be called a supporter of the blacks. On the other hand, his position against racism was already well known in his home state; his political opponents had been calling him a Communist for years, and yet he had never been forced to yield the university. Moreover, even local people who disagreed with his views were proud of the prestige that he had brought to North Carolina, giving it one of the best universities in the country.

When the question of cloture came up, Graham had only a short time before him as an appointed senator. The campaign for a full term was just months away. If he voted to cut off debate, his chances of avoiding a serious contest would be greatly reduced.

While Frank Graham wrestled with his conscience, Lowenstein

sought out Jimmy Wallace at Nags Head, North Carolina, to talk with him about the ramifications of Graham's vote. They both knew that Graham did not believe in forcing things on people. And they knew too that, in the past, this had led him to a contradictory position, opposing discrimination, while at the same time refusing to support civil rights legislation. In 1936, as a participant in a forty-member commission on civil rights, Graham had, according to Jones, "voted all the way down the line until the final thing; it called for legislation and he voted against that."

Wallace remembers little of what they said at Nags Head, only the agony. They sat in the dark on the grass a hundred feet from the memorial to the Wright brothers. "The issue," recalls Wallace, "was whether Graham could do more good for the civil rights movement by voting *against* cloture—retaining influence among other white southerners for future advantage—or by voting *for* cloture, sealing off all future possibilities."

Lowenstein apparently concluded that the future advantage should not be sacrificed, and fearing that Graham had already decided otherwise, he attempted to change his mind. Rev. Charles Jones remembers Lowenstein confiding in him that "Dr. Graham was going to vote the wrong way." According to Jones, Lowenstein and some of the other young members of Graham's staff "went over and saw Senator Richard Russell to see if he would talk Dr. Frank into voting against cloture." But Russell's response was an angry admonition not to "tamper with Frank Graham's conscience."

Jones himself was astonished by Lowenstein's action: "I was surprised when he told me that he and the boys had gone over to see Russell, it surprised me greatly." He suggests that Lowenstein must have decided that it was "so important that Dr. Frank be there in the Senate, where he was, that after all, well, the outlook was not going to be changed by his vote, and I can see him reasoning that way; on the other hand, I should think, if Dr. Frank had started to vote against anything against Dr. Frank's principles, Al would have argued the other way."

In the end, Lowenstein and a number of other staff members formulated a compromise and enlisted liberal senators to communicate with Graham, urging him to go along with it.

Graham had been ill and was in North Carolina. According to the plan, he was simply to authorize Senator Clyde Hoey, the other senator from North Carolina, to say, as he voted against cloture, "And if my colleague Senator Graham were here, he, likewise, would vote 'nay.'" By doing this, Hoey maintained, Graham would pick up another 50,000 votes in the election and eliminate the need for a runoff. Hoey, a staunch segregationist, respected his liberal colleague even though he disagreed totally with his philosophy. Frank Graham's biographer, Warren Ashby, recounts:

> Graham was in anguish. He felt he was betraying all his friends who were clamoring for him to perform what they saw as a simple, uncomplicated act. He too saw it as a simple, uncomplicated act, but from the other side; lying on a sickbed in Raleigh, he could not know what his judgment might lead him to do if he were on the Senate floor. . . . Perhaps he also felt that such an act would be self-serving and that he would later find it hard to justify to himself. . . . He turned, in the dimness of the hotel room, to Lowenstein. "What would you do if you were in my place?"
>
> "That's not fair to ask," said Lowenstein. "I'm not the Senator. You're the Senator."

Graham could not bring himself to ask Hoey to speak for him, and because of his participation on Truman's Civil Rights Commission, which issued a report supporting a compulsory Fair Employment Practices Commission, his silence was interpreted as a vote for cloture. In fact, Graham had written a dissenting opinion in the report, outlining his position against any compulsory fair-employment legislation, but mud-slinging clouded the facts. Graham was labeled a Communist, antisouthern, and pro-Negro by his enemies.

Lowenstein had been prepared to do what was necessary to get Graham elected. But Graham, though he recognized the risk, had hoped that his prestige was so great that even the loss of the die-hard vote could not be his undoing. A win, after voting his conscience, would have signaled that the South had finally changed forever. And if he won in North Carolina with his views, it was more than likely that he could win elsewhere. Though, like Lowenstein, Graham thought it somehow unworthy to aspire to leadership and power, he knew that a Frank Graham who did not vote against cloture and who won a seat in the Senate would be more formidable nationally than Hubert Humphrey—or any other Democrat.

North Carolina in 1950 was virtually a Democratic monopoly. All shades of political opinion were contained in the monolithic structure of the Democratic party, from the racist reactionaries to the integrationist liberals. As a folk hero in the state, Graham had been able to appeal across the boards to a wide constituency. Convinced that this was the most important thing they could do, the liberal students from Chapel Hill, Jimmy Wallace, Douglas Hunt, Richard Murphy, and John Sanders, president of the student body in 1950, joined with Lowenstein to work in Graham's Senate campaign. Graham stood for all their ideals: racial equality, economic justice, the United Nations, and world peace. Most of all, he stood for a new South, no longer insular and hostile to the forces of change.

There were two other candidates, a minor North Carolina politician named Robert R. Reynolds and Willis Smith, a former president of the American Bar Association. To avoid a run-off Graham needed fifty percent of the vote. While his enormous popularity did not seem to have been seriously eroded by the cloture issue, Graham's opponents had neither popularity nor organization.

At the end of the first balloting, Graham fell just short of the required fifty percent, and *The New York Times* wrote that his 49.5 percent indicated that "a resurgent tide of race prejudice" appeared to have been turned back. Robert R. Reynolds withdrew. Willis Smith, who had finished second, had ten days to call for a run-off.

With weak support, Smith was on the verge of announcing his withdrawal when the Supreme Court issued its first desegregation order, unanimously striking down segregation practices at the Universities of Texas and Oklahoma and on the railroads, stating that equal facilities were required in higher education as well as in public transportation in interstate commerce. A small group of segregationists persuaded Smith to stay in the race and demand a run-off. Among those supporting the Smith campaign was political commentator Jesse Helms, then involved in radio and television and later a "New Right" leader, elected to the Senate in the seventies.

A media blitz depicted Graham as a Communist sympathizer who advocated racial mixing at all levels. Composite photographs showing Graham with blacks were distributed. His membership on Truman's civil rights commission became a red flag.

The campaign was worst in the eastern part of the state, where Lowenstein watched as Graham was vilified and spat on by angry whites when he tried to address them. He heard even people who were sympathetic to Graham snipe at what they considered self-righteousness. They said that Graham was a good man, and that he would go to heaven, but when he got there, he would "discover that he was not God Almighty."

Graham's supporters waited in the Sir Walter Raleigh Hotel in Raleigh for the returns of the second primary. They sat up through the night until the bad news was confirmed. By 20,000 votes Graham lost to Smith, who, as Jimmy Wallace tersely put it, "had the nerve to die six months after the election."

Frank Graham's defeat taught Lowenstein something about the strength of the right and the power of the forces of hate and reaction. It also led him to conclude that political manipulation for a good end could be justified. He was convinced that Graham should have let Hoey speak for him on cloture in order to win the election.

Lowenstein's friend from Chapel Hill, Richard Murphy, remembers what it was like during the vigil at the Sir Walter Raleigh Hotel: "I remember the morning of Dr. Graham's defeat was when the North Koreans invaded South Korea. I remember hearing that on the radio. That morning we got to bed, we woke up, and it was horrendous. We, of course, had the defeat of Dr. Graham that evening, and when we woke up the next morning I remember turning on the radio and hearing that the North Koreans had invaded South Korea. And, of course, that was terrible news to receive also. We did not know at that time that we were going to be involved in the Korean War, but of course we felt that there was a good likelihood that might happen. And President Truman later that day took action."

The Cold War had become hot.

III

The National Student Association

8.

During Allard Lowenstein's years as an undergraduate at the University of North Carolina at Chapel Hill, from 1945 to 1949, he became deeply involved in the postwar student movement, both in the United States and internationally. As a committed liberal, he was attracted to those emerging organizations that embodied the values he supported.

After the Americans for Democratic Action (ADA) held its first meeting in January of 1947, Lowenstein became involved. An assemblage of the leading lights of American liberalism, faithful to the legacy of Franklin Delano Roosevelt, it organized to offer an alternative to Marxism on the left and anti-New Deal conservatism on the right. Present at the first meeting were Eleanor Roosevelt, Thomas Finletter, Averell Harriman, Helen Gahagan Douglas, and labor lawyer Joseph Rauh. This was the vanguard of the non-Communist left and it was natural that Lowenstein would be attracted to it. When Students for Democratic Action (SDA), the campus offshoot of the ADA, was formed and headed at Chapel Hill by his friend Richard Murphy, Lowenstein signed on.

After the Second World War the liberal Democrats were still in power but in retreat. The group that formed the ADA, while strongly anti-Communist, was attacked from the right as being sympathetic to the Communists, soft on Communism, or Communist "dupes." The entire left in America was faced with a crisis caused by the anti-Communist politics of the postwar era.

Lowenstein saw himself as a fighter against both the reactionary right and the Communists. Most of his activities in student government at the University of North Carolina had revolved around the question of racial and religious intolerance. Now, because of the rising tide of McCarthyism and the need on the part of liberals to distance themselves from anything tainted by Communism, as well as his own conviction that Communism was evil, Lowenstein's involvement in student politics in the wider national and international arenas took on an increasingly anti-Communist and anti-Soviet quality. He reflected the general direction of liberalism at this time and participated with vigor to promote its objectives.

The American liberals undertook to fight the Communists for control of the growing student movement. In so doing, they believed they would insulate themselves from attacks from the right, which was itself trying to mobilize student support at Catholic schools and gain a constituency of college students who would take the leadership in the future. But it was in Europe, where Marxist ideology was a powerful force among young people, that the democratic values Lowenstein believed in faced their first serious challenge from Communist-backed student groups.

In 1945, a World Student Youth Congress was organized by the Paris-based World Federation of Democratic Youth (WFDY) to form the International Union of Students. Predominantly Marxist, the WFDY received support from European Communist parties and ultimately fell under the control of the Soviet Union. The preliminary meeting was held in 1945, to prepare for the 1946 congress in Prague.

After the first American youth organization, the American Federation of Youth, was founded in 1925, it was dissolved after a battle between liberals and Communists. When the liberal National Student Federation of America (NSFA), also founded in 1925, merged in 1934 with the American Youth Congress, in which Eleanor Roosevelt and Joseph Lash were active, the Communists once again moved to take control. When World War II broke out, the American student movement came to an end.

After the war, while the Europeans were rebuilding their student movement, there was no similar organizational activity in the United States. The liberals feared that if the Communists infiltrated any new student organization, it would be the object of attacks from the right. Worse, it would become a vehicle for Soviet propaganda.

Just at the time when the WFDY was organizing the Prague congress, the United Nations conference in San Francisco was also being planned. State Department officials came to the Chapel Hill campus and told students that it would be attended by "grassroots" people from all over the country. The officials invited the students to form their own group and send representatives, and Frank Graham encouraged them to do so. Created "at the behest of the State Department observers," according to Douglas Hunt, to send student delegates to the United Nations conference in San Francisco, the new organization was called the Conference of Southern Students.

When the Conference of Southern Students convened in Chapel Hill the weekend that Franklin Roosevelt died, Douglas Hunt, a delegate, was approached by State Department observers and invited to attend the World Student Youth Congress in Prague. Hunt declined because he thought it was "more important for us to get the Conference of Southern Students going." What the State Department apparently had in mind was the formation of regional student organizations to lead eventually to the creation of a national student organization, liberal but not Communist, which would represent America at international student meetings. It was the students themselves, however, who raised the money to bring the delegates to the campus for the first meeting, according to Hunt.

In April of 1945, in violation of the state's segregation laws, black and white students met in Graham Memorial on the Sunday morning after President Roosevelt's death. President Graham, in defiance of those state laws, came to greet them. "And then we sent a black and a white to San Francisco and elected a black as president of our conference," says Hunt.

Although Lowenstein was not in Chapel Hill for the first meeting of the Conference of Southern Students, he became involved in planning for the next one, and when the organization reconvened, Lowenstein was a leading figure. The gathering was held in the Chapel of the Cross where Lowenstein was scheduled to speak. The atmosphere was tense; the audience was racially mixed, and a group of white students was objecting to the presence of blacks. This was Lowenstein's first address before a large audience and it was, according to Douglas Hunt, "a real stem-winder."

When, in the middle of it, someone in the group opposed to the presence of blacks shouted, "We don't want niggers here," Lowenstein charged from the speaker's podium, grabbed Junius Scales, the agitator who he believed had made the remark, and put a hammerlock on him. The two men had to be separated, but Lowenstein finished his speech. After that, whenever Lowenstein mentioned Scales, it was as the personification of everything he despised. Though not many schools were represented, Lowenstein's address received considerable recognition and his reputation began to spread.

An American Preparation Committee was formed for the 1946 international youth congress to be held in Prague to establish the International Union of Students. The committee's role was to determine which American institutions would send delegates to the Prague conference. While a strong leftist bent among many of the European students came as no surprise, the Americans who were organizing to participate in the International Union of Students congress were ideologically mixed. Battle lines were being drawn between the Marxists and the liberals with the understanding among the liberals and their supporters in the State Department that any Marxist-dominated American student organization was bound to be pro-Soviet.

Chapel Hill was selected to be one of ten campuses to send delegates. Nonacademic organizations selected to send delegates included the YMCA, the YWCA, the American Association of Interns and Medical Students, the Methodist Youth Fellowship, the National Federation of Catholic Students, and the American Youth for Democracy, the youth affiliate of the Communist Party. Harvard picked Douglass Cater, who would be an advisor to Lyndon Johnson, as its delegate.

At Chapel Hill, a battle was fought over who should represent the university at the Prague congress. A screening committee was set up, its eighteen members representing the various factions on campus. The committee members themselves all pledged to put up money to send the delegate. "You see," Wallace recalls, "anybody who made a contribution" could become a member of the committee. They were traveling by boat and would be in Europe for about three or four weeks.

In the end, there were three candidates: Herbert Bodman, who later taught in the Arab Studies Department of UNC; Lowenstein's nemesis, Junius Scales, a well-known local student, the scion of a former governor of North Carolina, blond, blue-eyed, handsome, and soft-spoken, "the natural choice," as Wallace puts it, "of the fraternity block"; and James Wallace, "campus radical."

What nobody knew then, but which later became public knowledge, following his 1947 announcement, was that Junius Scales had during the entire time been the secretary of the Communist party for North and South Carolina. He was ultimately sent to prison under the Smith Act.

When the field was narrowed to Scales and Wallace, Wallace found himself one vote short for a tie. Allard Lowenstein, who had been summoned as a proxy for Robert Morrison, a committee member whose duties as editor of the *Tar Heel* kept him from being present, arrived quite late. He finally walked in and said, *"Wallace,"* producing a tie, which was promptly broken by Walter Stewart, the chairman, in favor of Wallace. Lowenstein would always mistakenly believe that his vote had decided it for his friend.

9.

A new institution created by legislation enacted in 1947, the Central Intelligence Agency, began to play an increasingly important role in the effort to contain Communism. A creation of the Truman administration, it would be cloaked in complete secrecy by legislation enacted in 1949, which authorized the CIA director to spend funds secretly and to conceal information from the public as well as from Congress. The CIA attracted to its fold such liberal student leaders as Cord

Meyer, who as a young World Federalist had grown frustrated with the constant attempts by the Communists to take over student organizations in America and use them for their own ends. An idealistic writer and antiwar activist, he became a CIA agent. Meyer claims that no sooner was the international student movement launched than the Communists began trying to take it over. Thus he argues that it was legitimate for the CIA to become involved. In fact, the CIA and the NSA came into existence at about the same time for many of the same reasons. And they would be inexorably drawn to each other.

Jimmy Wallace, Douglas Hunt, and Allard Lowenstein had been encouraged by people from the State Department before there was a CIA. But these State Department observers were from the American intelligence establishment, and what ultimately became the CIA did, in fact, form the National Student Association. It had created the Conference of Southern Students; it had encouraged the conference to join in the formation of a delegation to Prague.

Jimmy Wallace, Charles Proctor, the black who had been elected president of the Conference of Southern Students, and the other delegates went to Prague. The International Union of Students (IUS) was formed and, according to Wallace, was Communist dominated. Wallace also noted that American delegates from the Catholic Youth were traveling on diplomatic passports, kept a close watch on leftist groups, and were known to have made reports to the State Department. Moreover, Wallace was disturbed because of all the countries represented at the conference, only the United States lacked a national student organization.

The Americans traveled together through Europe. It was the autumn of 1946. They traveled down from Paris to Rouen and boarded a Liberty ship that was coming home for the last time to be mothballed. "All the way across the ocean in this old ship, this old tub called the *George Washington*," Wallace recalls, "we were sitting out there on deck getting sunburned, plotting the formation of what came to be known as the National Student Assocation."

Their ship was diverted to Mobile Bay and the students disembarked at Mobile. "And the first thing," Wallace says, "in September, after all those people, all these races and everybody else, we had to take two taxis in Mobile because Charles Proctor was black and rode in one and we rode in the other, and I knew I was back in the United States, the Southern United States, and it was 1946."

At an organizational meeting that winter in Chicago, the delegates who had been to Prague scheduled their first actual National Student Association meeting for the summer on the campus of the University of Wisconsin at Madison. The fledgling organization survived an attack from the right by conservative Catholics and grew. (Upon hearing of the plans to create a National Student Association in America, John

Courtney Murray, editor of *America*, instructed the Catholic Youth to "take it over or bust it up.")

Wallace immediately involved Allard Lowenstein in the new organization. Richard Murphy, a successor to Lowenstein as president of the NSA, gives the orthodox explanation of how the NSA came into existence, noting that it was formed just after World War II by a "group of veterans" who had returned from the Prague Congress unhappy that the United States was unique in lacking a national student union. They decided to found one that would have "an interest in international affairs," an interest "in doing something about the racial situation in America,"and that would involve itself "in issues of academic freedom." For students from southern colleges, he adds, it was also to provide "contact with the rest of the world."

Lowenstein threw himself into NSA work, organizing in the South and fighting to keep the Catholic colleges in the fold. Notre Dame remained a member, although Jimmy Wallace insists it did so just to obtain information. Yet it became the campus at which Lowenstein would be most popular, one which provided countless volunteers for his congressional campaigns, bestowing on him its highest medal for outstanding service to the country.

While Lowenstein was still at Chapel Hill, the university became an affiliate member of the NSA, giving him a base. He moved up to chairman of the Virginia-Carolinas region, attending the NSA regional meetings, the only integrated meetings held in the South. The national organization grew until there were about 300 member institutions nationwide, a network of young liberals prepared to work within the system for change in America. With his newfound charisma, boundless energy, and grasp of the issues, it was highly probable that Allard Lowenstein would become their leader. But he had yet to be discovered on a national level.

It was Alice Brandeis Popkin, the granddaughter of Justice Louis Brandeis, who helped give Lowenstein his first national exposure. She and Lowenstein had first met at dancing classes while she was a student at the Horace Mann School for Girls. Later, at Radcliffe, she became active in the NSA.

Not having seen each other for many years, she and Lowenstein met at the 1948 NSA convention, which was again held at the University of Wisconsin at Madison. Lowenstein, a delegate from Chapel Hill, aspired to prominence. "Where else was there to be but marching?" Alice Popkin asks, looking back on the idealism of the period. Popkin nominated Lowenstein for vice-president of the NSA.

Upon being nominated, Lowenstein made a stirring speech from the floor on racism in America which took the delegates by surprise. They wondered who this persuasive, powerful speaker was who talked to them about something that until then had been outside their expe-

rience. Although he was not elected, Lowenstein made an overwhelming impression. That a southern school should have sent the
delegate that brought this question to the consciousness of the young
activists from all over the country was startling.

Popkin believes that Lowenstein knew he would lose that election,
but saw it as an opportunity to make contacts and to build both issues
and organizations for a future effort. The nomination gave him a
chance to perform, and his performance established him as a likely
leader of the NSA, somebody to be reckoned with.

10.

In the summer of 1948, Lowenstein participated in two very different
kinds of youth gatherings.

The first gathering was the Encampment for Citizenship, headed
by Algernon Black, his former ethics teacher at Ethical Culture.
Black, head of the Ethical Culture Society, had founded the encampment after the war because he believed that in a democracy which
had been threatened from the right during the Great Depression by
Nazi and Fascist movements, and from the left by Stalinist Communism, a special training ground for future leaders was needed.

In the thirties, Black had helped to found "work camps" for young
farmers and union organizers to promote the ideology of the New
Deal. Now Black was shifting his focus away from the farmer-labor
commitments of the thirties to the new elite of American students.
His goal was to "educate young people in the field of social and community organization and civic responsibility to enable them to understand and participate in democratic society." To accomplish this, he set
up an education program in a "camp setting," with formal classes, lectures by a full-time faculty and visiting lecturers, discussion groups,
workshops, forums, field trips, and other educational experiences.

Black got grants from the Schwarzhaupt Foundation for Citizenship and the Ford Foundation, which also sponsored a review of the
encampment by the Social Research Bureau at Columbia, and opened
the first encampment on the campus of the Fieldston School in Riverdale in 1946. From bottom-up grassroots democracy, Black had now
shifted to top-down patricianism.

The first encampment attracted 128 students, and the number increased each year. With further help from the Schwarzhaupt Foundation, a Berkeley, California, encampment was opened. Eleanor Roosevelt, who became a major force in the encampment experiment,
gave the opening reception. Other encampments opened in Denver,
Great Falls, Montana, San Antonio, Louisville, and in 1961, Puerto

Rico, attracting students not only from all over the United States, but from Latin America, Europe, Africa, and Asia.

Lowenstein's application to the second encampment lists his experience as a "farm laborer," a reference to his work at summer camp in Vermont, where, in fact, he spent much of his time performing in theatrical productions. He also lists his father Gabriel's occupation as "scientist," although he had not taught at Columbia for years and was running a hugely successful restaurant business. Among the community groups of which he listed himself a member were the United World Federalists, the Presbyterian Student Group, the Hillel Foundation, the ADA and "the National Conference of Students (NSA)."

To the question on the application "Is there any issue in the local, national, or international situation about which you feel very strongly? Explain," he replied: "Spain. I think the Civil War was my greatest emotional jolt—one from which I've never quite recovered. The Republican Government must be restored!"

Discussing the reasons that he wished to participate in the encampment, he wrote:

> I would like to meet, and have an opportunity to know and work with, people I should otherwise only read about, from places I may never get to and from backgrounds now strange to mine. It would be fun to learn and to play and work with a group, which by its very nature demonstrates the "practicality" of the American, Judeo-Christian ideal. In North Carolina a summer spent thus will horrify some and make no dent on others, but to many it will symbolize much that they want to know can happen, though not yet in their own villages and towns. Properly interpreted, the experience of this interlude would have a sobering effect on the racially wayward and a most encouraging effect on the Timid Souls, who don't quite believe "it" possible "now" . . . I would be so glad to have the opportunity to practice what I preach. . . .

Lowenstein, who saw himself at the vanguard of race relations while still a junior at college, suggested that the leadership he could exercise on this issue might be his most valuable contribution to the encampment:

> Perhaps all this adds up to a feeling I have that I might be able to contribute a process of thought and feeling on racial matters which has undergone all the changes necessary for an honest-with-himself Northern person of "broad" outlook who has moved South, and which outlook has emerged basically the same. I have learned to distrust and disapprove of "self-segregation" as wholeheartedly as segregation. The world is not composed of "People"

and "Other People" and that which tends to build up this fiction is dangerous.

The experience of the encampment had a profound effect on Lowenstein. Black's ethics were reasserted there, confirming Lowenstein in his faith that change could be achieved within existing democratic institutions. And for the first time, he met Eleanor Roosevelt who, one day each summer during the encampment, would invite its participants to her retreat at Val Kill. It was the beginning of what was to be a special relationship between Allard Lowenstein and Eleanor Roosevelt.

But if the encampment was the embodiment of Allard Lowenstein's faith, the other youth gathering he attended that summer was the opposite. As a representative of the National Student Assocation, Lowenstein was to attend an international youth conference sponsored by the International Union of Students in Geneva. Sidney Cohn, the labor attorney who represented the workers in the Lowenstein restaurants, recalls Lowenstein confiding that the "State Department" had requested him to write a report for them on the meeting. Once in Geneva, Lowenstein was disturbed to find that the only people there who supported his positions were from the British and West German delegations. In his view, the British were colonialists and the Germans still symbolized the destruction of the Spanish Republic, the Holocaust, Hitler. Students from other countries repeatedly asked Lowenstein why the United States wanted to start another war.

Deeply shaken, Lowenstein went to Cohn for guidance about his "assignment." Cohn told him that he should write the truth, which, according to Cohn, he did, indicating to what extent the National Student Association was at odds with the majority of the other student organizations. Asked whether there was any CIA connection with Lowenstein, Cohn replied that you have only to look at who Lowenstein's idols were—Frank Graham and Eleanor Roosevelt—to reject that conclusion.

But even if the State Department officials who requested the report were not CIA undercover, the report most probably fell into the hands of the new intelligence agency. In any event, the government did feel it had the right to ask a young undergraduate to report back to it on a student meeting.

Ironically, just as the CIA and the State Department began to conceive of the NSA as a vehicle for intelligence gathering and combatting the influence of the Communists, the FBI began to look upon the NSA with suspicion. Since the FBI and the CIA did not communicate with each other, each jealous of the other's prerogatives, both proceeded without knowledge of the other's activities. Massive files were accumulated by the FBI, dossiers collected on individuals whose anti-Communism was so evident to the CIA that it made every effort to use them for CIA purposes. One of those spied upon by the FBI was Allard Lowenstein, whose dossier, obtained under the Freedom of Information Act by his lawyer and friend Gary Bellow in the 1970s, comes to over 1,300 pages, a lifetime of surveillance.

But when Lowenstein became president of the NSA, his reputation was that of a strong anti-Communist liberal. Frank Graham had been defeated for the senate in North Carolina, and the conservative tide was rising in America. FBI informers swarmed all over the NSA conventions, while Gus Hall's Communists distributed literature denouncing Truman and NSA plans for withdrawal from the Communist-dominated IUS.

11.

In August of 1950, Allard Lowenstein attended the NSA congress at the University of Michigan at Ann Arbor, where the Korean War was the main topic of concern. Americans were being drafted and sent to fight with the United Nations peace-keeping force as the result of President Truman's decision, one which, according to Richard Murphy, a delegate from Chapel Hill, was being "heavily challenged" by some students. Leading the opposition, recalls Murphy, was the American Association of Interns and Medical Students under Halsted Holman, whom he believes had strong pro-Communist sympathies.

In fact, Lowenstein was uncertain about his own future. Frank Graham, who had taken him with him to Washington as his Senate aide, had been defeated in the run-off primary and Lowenstein was now scheduled to go to Yale Law School in September if he were not taken by the military.

The California delegation introduced a special resolution calling on the NSA to back the United States' and the United Nations' move in Korea, but its supporters were temporarily thwarted. It was later learned that the resolution had been blocked by the international vice-president, Erskine Childres of Stanford, who felt that its adoption might put NSA students who had not yet returned from an IUS meeting in Prague, in jeopardy. He apparently feared that approval of a resolution hostile to the Communist position at that time "might have direct consequences on the lives of those students in Prague, if they were, in fact, still there."

Thwarted several times by its opponents, the resolution was repeatedly reintroduced. Finally, Allard Lowenstein, addressing the convention from the floor, delivered a spontaneous, spellbinding speech supporting the resolution. The great majority of the students burst into applause, approved the resolution, and then, as a demand for his leadership grew, elected him president of the NSA.

Lowenstein telephoned Jimmy Wallace in North Carolina. Should he accept? he asked Wallace. The answer was yes. Allard Lowenstein, the man who would gain international acclaim in the anti-Vietnam War and "Dump Johnson" movements in the sixties, had won the presidency of the National Student Association by vigorously supporting armed intervention in Korea.

Later in 1950, Lowenstein, as president of the NSA, went to Helsinki for the International Union of Students World Youth Festival sponsored by the World Federation of Democratic Youth and found that the Communist countries were winning the support of Third World students. "He was incensed by the Communist manipulation," says William Dentzer, Lowenstein's successor as president of NSA. "Lowenstein took the position that it was a waste of time debating with the Communists at Communist-run youth festivals," he adds. Lowenstein concluded that a separate, non-Communist international student movement was necessary.

Joining him in pressing for such an organization, a Coordinating Secretariat of the National Unions of Students, or COSEC, was Olof Palme of the Swedish National Union of Students. But the NSA, together with the British National Union of Students, took the lead in founding COSEC, which Richard Murphy, NSA president after Dentzer, describes as the organization "of those national unions of students that did not choose to be affiliated with the IUS because the IUS was a complete propaganda organization that was run out of Prague . . . paid for by the Czechoslovakian government."

Following Helsinki, Lowenstein went to Stockholm in January of 1951 "by invitation of Olof Palme," William Dentzer recounts, to participate in an "ad hoc" conference of international student groups that had been called by Palme's Swedish National Union of Students "to establish COSEC as the non-Communists had agreed to in Helsinki." According to Barbara Boggs Sigmund, daughter of Louisiana Congressman Hale Boggs, an active NSA supporter and Lowenstein's fiancée in the early sixties, the Stockholm conference was "CIA-sponsored."

In a major address, Lowenstein attacked the influence of the Soviet Union in the international student movement, issuing as William Dentzer tells it, "a clarion call for a non-Communist organization." Like Palme, Dentzer felt that Lowenstein was too blatant. In overdoing his anti-Communist rhetoric, he says, "Al was his own worst enemy." Although some criticism did come from the far left, most came from the more subtle anti-Communists.

Reporting on Lowenstein's trip to Stockholm, the *Journal Ameri-*

can wrote on January 2, 1951: "The Communist-controlled International Union of Students (IUS) was accused of using unscrupulous deceit, distortion of facts and confusion in carrying on a propaganda campaign against democratic nations. The charge was made by Allard K. Lowenstein, 21, Scarsdale, New York, President of the United States National Student Association (NSA), which has steadfastly refused to join the IUS."

When Lowenstein's term as president ended in August of 1951, William Dentzer was elected to succeed him, defeating Kenneth Kurtz from Swarthmore, though he had difficulty winning, he maintains, because of his friend Lowenstein's support. Identified with Lowenstein, Dentzer became the target of criticism from the less strident anti-Communists, such as Kurtz, who disapproved of a strategy based on blatant attacks on the Soviet Union, as well as from left-wing students who wanted the NSA to join the International Union of Students.

At the same NSA congress, Avrea Ingram, a Harvard graduate student, was elected an NSA vice-president, defeating a Lowenstein-supported candidate. Ingram, whose election had been opposed by Dentzer, who was identified with Lowenstein and his entire slate of candidates, was from the anti-Lowenstein faction which disagreed not with Lowenstein's anti-Communism but with his style. Ingram's opponent had delivered a Lowenstein-like anti-Communist address, while Ingram had chosen to soft-pedal the issue.

In Dentzer's opinion, Lowenstein regarded "all opposition to him as immoral." After news stories revealing CIA support of the NSA broke in 1967, Lowenstein would point to Ingram's defeat of his candidate in 1951 and say to his wife, Jenny, "My God, that explains the convention I couldn't figure out."

Nevertheless, Dentzer insists that Lowenstein's goal of combatting the Communists was basically accepted. "This position was generally supported by the NSA," he states, "but there was a disagreement over tactics."

In 1952, the non-Communist students who had previously met in Stockholm met again. In January, William Dentzer, now president of NSA, went to Edinburgh as head of the American delegation, and with other anti-Communist student groups, elected a committee to form COSEC. The National Union of Students of Holland donated a small headquarters in Leyden, and that October, Dentzer joined its secretarial staff. His task there was to help found the International Student Conference, the ISC, which, he explains, "was the conference part of COSEC, to compete with the Communist-run youth festivals." He was joined in Leyden by Avrea Ingram.

The CIA told Dentzer, when he joined the COSEC in Leyden, that it had channeled money to NSA for several years without anyone knowing, "on an ad hoc basis and rarely," up until 1952. "The CIA provided funding and let the students decide their own policy," he asserts. "The CIA funding of NSA international activities had been ad hoc up until this point. When the anti-Communist Americans were set up in Leyden by the Dutch, the CIA began funding on a regular basis."

Both Dentzer and Ingram knew of CIA funds channeled through the Foundation for Youth and Student affairs in New York to COSEC. Ingram eventually went to work for the foundation itself. On February 5, 1957, he was found dead in a hotel room, naked with a belt tied around his neck and attached to a dresser. His death was considered to be a suicide unrelated to politics. The presence of homosexual literature found in the room suggests that Ingram's concern over his sexual preference was a motivating factor in taking his life. If he was in the CIA, he certainly knew that homosexuals were barred from employment in the agency. At the funeral, Dentzer told Ingram's parents, conservative southerners, that they had every reason to feel comforted. "I told them that their son had participated in some very important anti-Communist work."

Dentzer, who was Ingram's best friend and close enough to Lowenstein for Lowenstein to be an usher at his wedding, went on to hold important positions in the State Department and the Agency for International Development (AID). As for the CIA funding of the NSA, he quips: "Oh, someone must have called up Allen Dulles and said, 'Give these people a few bucks.'" To him, COSEC seemed the logical extension of the ideology of the students themselves and not the product of CIA manipulation.

Certainly, Lowenstein's intense anti-Communism at that time was well known and reached back to his undergraduate days at Chapel Hill, where, as Richard Murphy describes him, "he would be very liberal and very anti-Communist. When I first met Al, Al was a Willkie Republican." Murphy, as head of the Students for Democratic Action, the student branch of the ADA, was supporting the reelection of Harry Truman, but he recalls that Lowenstein "was very much opposed to Truman in every way, shape and form." He adds, "He never approved of any president of the United States within his lifetime, that I can recall."

Lowenstein's ire in 1948 had been particularly directed at Henry Wallace. His admiration for Norman Thomas, whom he supported for president that year, stemmed not from any Socialist sympathies, but from Thomas's strong anti-Communism. Says Murphy, "He regarded Henry Wallace as being much too soft with regard to Communists. He regarded Wallace's foreign policy as misleading."

Yet Lowenstein strongly opposed Joseph McCarthy, the House Un-American Activities Committee, and the Smith Act. And when the

NSA came out against the HUAC in 1961, Lowenstein was generally credited with having led it to this position, even though he had left the organization's formal leadership years before. He didn't believe in putting Communists in jail because they were Communists. He wanted them exposed and opposed.

Aware of Lowenstein's ideology, those close to him during his NSA presidency, such as Dentzer and Murphy, maintain that he acted on his own, without any knowledge of CIA funding or direction. Jimmy Wallace, who exonerates Lowenstein, insists that "when Richard Murphy took over, the CIA funding started," describing Murphy as an idealist-turned-opportunist. "He quit graduate school," Wallace snaps. "He was too busy with the NSA. He survived the Eisenhower years, deep in Democratic politics. He got close to JFK and became assistant postmaster general under Johnson. He is part of the Democratic establishment in Washington and a lobbyist for Sperry-Univac. He is close to Charles Manatt, reorganizing the Democratic National Committee." Wallace concludes: "His association with the CIA is transparent."

Murphy would become head of Youth for Kennedy in 1960 and a member of the Kennedy and Johnson administrations, rising to a subcabinet level under Johnson. He and Lowenstein drifted apart and did not see each other until the revelations about the CIA-NSA connection, when Lowenstein went to Murphy's office to ask him what he knew.

Murphy strongly denies any personal knowledge of the CIA funding. He explains that the CIA probably became involved around 1951, but that he became aware of it only when his "duties in the government" as assistant postmaster general put him in a position to inform himself about some of what had happened. Though he prefers not to elaborate on how he learned what he did, Murphy explains that the grants from the Foundation for Youth and Student Affairs, of which the CIA was subsequently revealed as the source, were to be used solely for the international affairs activities of the NSA.

Murphy, who succeeded Dentzer as NSA president in August of 1952, argues that the organization was overwhelmingly financed out of membership dues and that there was a bitter disagreement with some of the officers during his term as president over the use of funds that were allocated strictly for the International Commission of NSA. That money, he asserts, could not be commingled with the funds allocated for anything domestic. By the time he became president, the Foundation for Youth and Student Affairs had already been contributing funds for the NSA's international programs. "So I made my request to it as a matter of course," he recounts, "together with other foundations to which I also applied and received money. They weren't the only foundation we got money from. But they were evidently the conduit through which CIA funds were applied, and I say 'evidently' because I cannot speak first-hand about it."

Murphy further insists that no one ever gave anyone instructions, not to Lowenstein when he went to Helsinki and Stockholm, not to Murphy when he went to Copenhagen for the ISC. "I don't know what my attitude would have been during that time had I been knowledgeable about it," Murphy continues. "I think I probably would have approved of it, which is one of the reasons that, as I pointed out to Al, I felt fairly decent about the relationship. It had not compromised the NSA, because he and I made our decisions completely without the knowledge of any kind of financing or complication." And William Dentzer adds, referring to the founding by Lowenstein of COSEC in Helsinki, "I am certain that any action he took there was completely an action of his own, that he had nothing to do with any kind of funding or information from the CIA or connection with the CIA."

Such writers as David Halberstam and Milton Viorst have declared Lowenstein the last NSA president to have been untainted by the CIA connection. But when that connection was revealed in 1967, critics to Lowenstein's left contended—though they have never been able to substantiate their claim—that he had taken the NSA out of the IUS on behalf of the CIA.

But Lowenstein's work was considered sufficiently important for him to avoid serving in the Korean War. A basic tenet of the Lowenstein myth was that he had to force his way into the army because he kept getting rejected on account of his bad eyes. *Newsday* reporter Ed Hershey wrote in a 1970 interview with Lowenstein, "When his poor eyesight exempted him from military service in 1954, Lowenstein kept on trying until he found an Army doctor who would declare him fit. He served from 1954 to 1956."

Apart from the dates of service, these assertions are untrue. Lowenstein did serve as a private in the army from 1954 to 1956 and was stationed in Germany. His records indicate that on June 24, 1955, he earned the designation of "marksman" in his rifle training program. But the reason for the delay in Lowenstein's service was not the one given by journalists or by Lowenstein himself. Though requiring thick glasses, his eyesight was adequate for the draft.

Lowenstein had been elected president of the National Student Association after his "spellbinding" speech in support of America's military support for South Korea. But although Lowenstein was an enthusiastic supporter of this military intervention, he avoided participating in it. His classification questionnaire was mailed to him on September 11, 1950. On December 15, 1950, he was classified 1-A and was called for his physical on January 5, 1951. The result of his Armed Forces Physical Examination was "Accepted," meaning he was pronounced fit to serve. After a hiatus, during which time Lowenstein was not drafted, he received his formal classification on September 20, 1951: 2A-S. 2-A stood for "Registrant deferred because of civilian occupation." Lowenstein's "civilian occupation" was president of the NSA. 2-S stood for "Registrant deferred because of activity in study." Lowenstein was entering Yale Law School, having deferred this in order to serve as NSA president for a year. On February 21, 1952, and again on March 6, 1952, Lowenstein was reclassified 1-A, showing that his physical had disclosed no reason for him not to serve in the military. Lowenstein was ordered on April 25, 1952, to report for induction on May 8, 1952. But while a law student, Lowenstein applied for and received a further deferment, the army writing him on April 25, 1952, that he was classified 1-S, as a full-time student. On May 2, 1952, he received a 1-Sc classification (student deferred by statute-college) and finally a 2-S classification on July 9, 1953 (student deferment). Only when the Korean War was over and he had been graduated from Yale Law School did Lowenstein get himself reclassified and volunteer for induction. According to William Dentzer, Lowenstein was "drafted." Ellison Capers Wynn, Lowenstein's friend and commanding officer in Germany, states that "Al wanted to be in the military because he knew it would help his political career."

Lowenstein confided in his attorney Gary Bellow that he had an NSA deferment and then a law school deferment. Throughout the NSA's relationship with the CIA, it was standard practice for NSA officers who cooperated with the CIA to be given draft deferments on the basis of their "occupation vital to the national interest." It remained in force as long as that person was an NSA officer, at which time he could be admitted to graduate school and receive a student deferment.

Letters of recommendation addressed to the local draft board on behalf of the NSA official asserted that the staff member was needed for activities that affected the national interest. The letter stated: "NSA is largely responsible for the creation and maintenance of the International Student Conference, which was established in 1950 to combat the Communist-controlled International Union of Students."

During the Vietnam War, when Lyndon Johnson began his escalations in 1965 and '66, NSA officers were reclassified 1-A, precipitating panic among NSA staff members. Phil Sherburne, then president of NSA, responded by appealing to both General Hershey and the Selective Service Presidential Review Board. No NSA staff members were drafted.

The documents on which the extract of Lowenstein's classification record is based have been destroyed by the Selective Service System. But the NSA and its international wing were major propaganda tools for the United States during a period when the Cold War reached critical proportions and as Czechoslovakia fell to the Communists.

Lowenstein provided trustworthy leadership at the time of the Korean crisis and the widespread activity of the International Union of Students. Best of all, he was not just anti-Communist and anti-Soviet. He was a liberal.

Lowenstein chose to conceal his true draft status and the CIA had every reason to get him a deferment. In a major speech before the 1951 NSA congress, Lowenstein, as president, urged American students to reach "out to students all over the world in a national emergency," in order to preserve western-style democracy. "It seems a great tragedy," he declared, "that the NSA has been forced into international affairs because the Communists got there first." He went on to condemn the International Union of Students as "the arm of the Cominform—Soviet dominated," to point out the need for money to sustain the NSA's desperately needed international programs and to exhort his listeners to support the NSA and its cause, concluding that "that cause is freedom."

An important figure in a government-supported movement with a critical, if hidden, agenda to which he subscribed, Lowenstein was playing a role which was bound to be extremely attractive to him, as the Rev. Charles Jones relates:

> The National Student Association, I think, was one of the most interesting phases of his life. . . . He became president of it and they received a big grant from the government during the war years and this enabled them to put up big offices, and have a very extensive program. He said to me, "Now, look, I want to get some student leaders from major Southern state universities and I want to have a Catholic priest, and I want you to be advisors, because they have no notion about what being a liberal means in the South. We've got the money and I don't expect you to make programs for them, but these are going to be carefully picked and they're going to be leaders." And so we took it, about two years of that, and they did have a lot of money. Years later, it turned out that the CIA had made a big grant to the National Student Association, and that was during the period that Al was there. Now, I say that is interesting because it's a fact kind of contrary to his nature, if he knew it, and I never felt like I should ask him because I never felt it was my business.

12.

While Lowenstein was the president of NSA, its headquarters were in Madison, Wisconsin. He was paid a stipend and his traveling expenses. When Richard Murphy took over in 1952, headquarters were in Philadelphia, where he met Ruth Hagy, the associate editor of the *Philadelphia Evening Bulletin*, who ran the Philadelphia Bulletin Forum, an annual three-day conference on current affairs.

Told that Hagy "would raise millions for the NSA," Murphy arrived for the meeting to find an ebullient woman who reached out her hand to him, saying, "You must be Dickie. I'm Ruthie. I will raise one million dollars." According to Murphy, it was she who raised the money for the NSA to establish itself in Philadelphia and for its domestic programs for the next five years, although he does not specify how she accomplished this. A mover and shaker in wealthy political communications circles, she was apparently devoted to the cause of the NSA and would become, in time, just as devoted to the cause of Allard Lowenstein.

Close to Joseph Clark, then the mayor of Philadelphia, Hagy was also on good terms with the influential district attorney Richardson Dilworth, Bernard Gimble, and Walter Annenberg, all of whom responded when she appealed to them on behalf of the NSA. With Annenberg's help, she launched the College Press Conference on WFIL, an Annenberg station and ABC affiliate, and asked the NSA to supply student body presidents and news editors to appear on it.

This was now a politically moderate NSA. Radical, leftist organizations had been excluded by the regulations requiring that delegates be elected exclusively from student councils or student bodies and could not come from independent student organizations. On the right, the presence of what Murphy calls the "little Catholic girl schools," with figures like Mother O'Burn from Sacred Heart on the NSA board, helped them to deflect the assaults of Joseph McCarthy and the right-wing Students for America.

Among the 300 to 350 members under Murphy's presidency were big state universities, Ivy League schools (with the notable exception of Princeton, which disdained any political involvement), the small Catholic girls schools, and other private liberal arts institutions.

Lowenstein was pleased by the makeup of the NSA conventions in the fifties and the general absence of the left and the right. He told Milton Viorst, author of *Fire in the Streets*:

> The value of NSA was that it reached a broad stream of American students. It was a mass movement, and at the convention every year were fraternity jocks and Midwestern pom-pom girls, kids from little Catholic colleges and student body presidents who were not particularly interested in partisan politics. It was not narrowly based, like the SDS conventions, where the students were mostly intellectuals, and some of them fanatic. I think if you took a vote in the NSA congresses on the Eisenhower-Stevenson

races in 1952 and 1956, Eisenhower would have won. Yet I think NSA contributed to liberalizing a wide range of student opinion.

And, according to Richard Murphy, "The people of Al's time remained in politics and government during the last thirty years. Everyone would say that the NSA was the most valuable experience they had. Democrats, Republicans, and Independents. They were and are all very political. Lowenstein had been a tremendous influence on their lives, even if they disagreed with him."

What Lowenstein and his friends had in common, even those who disagreed with him, was a strong distaste for what they regarded as the political extremes. Lowenstein was not only anti-Communist. He feared backlash if the NSA moved too far to the left. And he saw himself as a force for the gradual liberalization of mainstream American students. Later on, his legacy would be contested by those who believed that Lowenstein had kept certain political views out of mainstream politics, an exclusion which, they would contend, caused the liberalism he supported to lose its dynamism. They would say that he had been aided in excluding those views by the CIA when it became involved in NSA affairs.

According to Paul Sigmund, later a professor of politics at Princeton, "The NSA was ignored by the establishment. There was a change in this when actual movements were generated. The government did have sophisticated relationships with some of these people through the CIA connection."

His wife, Lowenstein's one-time fiancée Barbara Boggs, who was herself active in the NSA, observes pessimistically that "there was no way for young people to become part of the political system. No one will let an ideological movement among students exist in America. Al gave them a channel to the system that no one else did."

What Lowenstein and his friend Ruth Hagy shared was a vision of liberalism in which the NSA would be a huge Encampment for Citizenship, with young people carrying the banner of liberal democracy into the future. But the hopes of the forties were dimming. The right was on the rise. After twenty years of Democratic rule, the country was ready to go Republican. "I Like Ike" buttons appeared across the nation. Weary of the Korean War, which the people blamed on Truman and the Democrats, they wanted peace and quiet. The Rosenbergs were executed in the electric chair and "The Fifties" came over the land. The only rebels were those without a cause.

13.

Lowenstein entered Yale Law School in 1951, where as a first year student, he argued as an alternate in the Yale Moot Court of Appeals

Prize Argument. The participants were selected on the basis of outstanding arguments made in the spring term. Lowenstein had enormous talent as a debater, and it was said of him that he could argue
from any side of any issue.

At Yale, Lowenstein stepped up his political activities. Calvin Trillin of *The New Yorker* describes the level of those activities as "awesome" and relates that when people telephoned New Haven information to get his number, they got an instantaneous reply, "as if they had
asked for the number of the New York, New Haven Hartford Railroad."

Eleanor Roosevelt recruited him as head of Students for Stevenson, a position that enabled him to travel widely, rallying campus
youth to the Democratic standardbearer. Lowenstein was also asked
to write speeches and develop issues. Stevenson grew to rely on him
and used much of Lowenstein's material. For a first year law student,
it was a heady experience.

But Lowenstein also spent hours rehearsing Gilbert and Sullivan
productions in which he often starred, and he took a personal interest
in the well-being of the fourteen women law students in his class.
Anne Feldman, one of the fourteen (his friend Alice Brandeis was
another) and later an organizer of Lowenstein's 1972 campaign for
Congress in Brooklyn, remains bemused at Lowenstein's efforts to see
that they had dates. She recalls a sweet side of her friend which enabled him to empathize with the women, who were regarded as un-
suitable companions by most of the male law students because they
were in competition with them.

Lowenstein also served as a college counselor to undergraduates.
He befriended a troubled student named Gary Bellow, who was upset
about a process at Yale called "healing," which required that an undergraduate interested in a particular student activity be subjected to a
rigorous form of hazing before he could participate. Bellow wandered
out of his room very late at night to find Lowenstein's light on and the
window open. He went inside to speak to Lowenstein, who responded
by suggesting they go somewhere and talk about it.

At an all-night luncheonette they talked until early morning,
agreeing on the injustice of the procedure. Bellow would feel better,
Lowenstein told him, if he could analyze the problem and then do
something about it. Bellow responded by launching a small movement
to change the "healing" system. Although it wasn't much, Bellow felt
the fact that he understood how he could act made the situation better
for him.

Throughout his years at Yale, Lowenstein continued to attend the
NSA conventions. His continued presence prompted observer
George Kaufmann to remark in the early fifties that "the student
leader of today is the student leader of tomorrow." Lowenstein retorted that the student movement was essential to American democ-

racy and that those who were active in it would indeed be the leaders of the country.

In 1956, Lowenstein was graduated from Yale Law School with fair grades, having relied to a considerable extent on Alice Brandeis's notes. He did outstandingly well in Psychiatry and Law and excelled in Labor Law. He did not bother to take the bar exam.

His tour of duty with the army was a period of relative relaxation. Lowenstein turned down the chance for a Judge Advocate General (JAG) appointment as a lawyer. "He would not take a high office," the Rev. Charles Jones explains, "he didn't want to be anything but low-down, because he wanted to be where he could defend people. He would defend privates who didn't know how to defend themselves and tell them what to do."

When he was at boot camp at Fort Jackson, Lowenstein would often turn up at Jones's church with a group of young men. Jones recalls one incident when he arrived with a black Catholic from Pennsylvania, a white Baptist from Mississippi, and an Episcopalian. After church, Lowenstein introduced his friends to Jones and asked, "Can we have dinner with you?" Lowenstein told Jones that the Baptist was in his platoon and that he had met the Episcopalian somewhere else. "How did you meet this black fellow?" Jones asked him. "I was driving down from Washington," Lowenstein replied, "and this fellow was thumbing and I just picked him up on the road."

In Mannheim, Germany, where Lowenstein was stationed with the CCA 2nd Armored Division as company clerk, his commanding officer was Ellison Capers Wynn. The first black soldier to be a headquarters commandant of a combat division of an armored division, Wynn remembers that Lowenstein crashed Grace Kelly's wedding to Prince Rainier in Monte Carlo.

"Have you got an invitation?" Wynn remembers asking when he learned of Lowenstein's plans to attend.

Lowenstein had replied, "No, but I'll get in."

Driving the Volkswagen he had bought with money from his father, and wearing a rented tuxedo, Lowenstein and a friend, Tom Jones, went off to the wedding where Lowenstein descended periodically to give reporters, clustered downstairs, a running account of the events upstairs. Later, back in New York after his discharge, Lowenstein was at the theater with his brother Larry, when he caught sight of the actress Rita Gam walking up the aisle. "Rita," he shouted, "I haven't seen you since the wedding."

Wynn remembers Lowenstein as enormously good-humored and not an abstainer at this time, drinking a little beer or wine on special occasions. He spoke to Wynn about his friendship with Eleanor Roosevelt, but the officer was incredulous until one day when the phone rang and Lowenstein told him that she was on the other end of the line. Wynn recalls that he did not believe it until he put the phone to his ear and heard the familiar voice say to him, "This is Eleanor Roosevelt. Can Al Lowenstein come to Paris?"

Wynn agreed and Lowenstein went off to see his mentor.

Having completed an army course in tax law and represented GIs with their tax problems, Lowenstein had seen enough of the practice of law to know it did not interest him. Ruth Hagy Brod, his friend from Philadelphia who had founded the College Press Conference and who was now married to New York financier Al Brod, contacted Lowenstein to recruit him to work for her program. A condition of the job was that he be enrolled as a graduate student in an American university.

Extensive correspondence ensued between Lowenstein and his parents. He wanted them to talk to the dean of the graduate school of Yale about enrollment. At the same time, he gained admission to the University of North Carolina at Chapel Hill in the history department. "I can always register at George Washington or Georgetown for a course or two and be around Washington, I imagine," he wrote his parents.

Brod then insisted that he report to her in Chicago on August 7, 1956, to help get Adlai Stevenson on her program just before the Democratic convention, a task, he wrote to his parents, which left him "sour." Persuading Stevenson to be on a broadcast "the day before the fate of his political ambitions is to be settled is not my idea of an attractive chore," he added. Having learned from Brod that she wanted him around Washington "to be a general factotum," he decided it would be best to register at one of the District of Columbia universities (he selected Georgetown) and then transfer to either Yale or Chapel Hill.

Lowenstein petitioned for early separation from active duty, asking to be released on August 4, 1956, after serving twenty-one months. In support of his application, Ruth Hagy Brod filed a certificate alleging that she wanted him to report to her Washington office to start work on August 12 and to be in Chicago on August 13, the day the Democratic National Convention started, to cover it.

Having managed to satisfy Ruth Hagy Brod's criteria, with the help of his parents, and believing that all the legal requirements had been met for early discharge from the army, Lowenstein was incensed when the army proved recalcitrant, rejecting his request. He had been counting on attending the NSA congress as well as both the Republican and Democratic conventions. Lowenstein pressed his father to help with the army, which he was evidently able to do. He was out of the service on August 4, in time for everything.

Lowenstein wanted to enroll in a graduate school that would not demand too much of his time since he would have to be in Washington several days a week. He finally decided that the program at Chapel Hill was the most flexible. He involved himself in the 1956 Stevenson campaign and resumed his attendance at the NSA conventions.

Previously, Lowenstein had taken very liberal positions at the NSA conventions on a wide range of issues. In 1953 he had been instrumental in getting the NSA to pass a resolution condemning apartheid in South Africa as it affected higher education, and he pressed hard for the adoption of a strong academic freedom statement. His speeches before the NSA congresses were generally punchy and to the point. But he was very much out of character in 1956.

At the Democratic convention, which had nominated Stevenson, a debate had taken place over a civil rights plank in the platform. Roy Wilkins, chairman of the Leadership Conference on Civil Rights, had joined with Walter Reuther of the United Auto Workers (UAW) in leading the fight for a strong plank. Their strategy had been to wait for the Platform Committee to submit its weak plank, then to demand a roll call vote and introduce a resolution substituting the strong minority report. Reuther had promised that labor would support the minority report. When the time came, however, no call for a roll call vote was issued. Irate blacks, like James Forman of Roosevelt University, watched as the "ayes" carried the weak plank.

Forman then went to the NSA convention and urged that organization to adopt the five points contained in the minority report drafted at the Democratic convention: the establishment of a Civil Rights Commission, of a civil rights section in the Justice Department, of a national conference on civil rights, implementation of the 1954 Supreme Court decision, and the repeal of Senate Rule 22, which required a two-thirds vote to end debate (and which was traditionally used by segregationists to sustain filibusters against civil rights legislation). Forman felt that the NSA would be more liberal than the Democrats. He says that he was told, however, that adoption of the platform would be difficult because Allard Lowenstein, "who had enormous influence in the NSA," was opposed.

In fact, the resolution on the five points passed easily, but someone moved that the vote on the repeal of Rule 22 be reconsidered on the grounds that the NSA should not be telling the United States Congress how to conduct its affairs. Forman recalls Lowenstein encouraging a black student, the chairman of the delegation from City College, to speak against the Roosevelt University position: "There are some faces and expressions that one does not forget. And to this day I remember the expression on the face of Allard Lowenstein as he pushed that black cat down the aisle. This was the young white who would later build a big liberal image by organizing students to work in the south and by his trips to Africa."

Forman, who, as head of the Student Nonviolent Coordinating

Committee (SNCC) in the sixties, would be one of Lowenstein's chief enemies in the civil rights movement, observes further: "The 1956 NSA convention was the first and last one I attended. I knew almost nothing about the organization before this experience. Afterwards I felt NSA was irrelevant to the struggle of black people, since it was an extremely conservative organization, dominated by a body of students and former officers who saw themselves moving in governmental circles. But I underestimated the influence of NSA's International Affairs Commission. Since the 1967 disclosure about its involvement with the CIA, its relationship to African students has caused some of us great concern."

But if Forman was disillusioned with the NSA and with Lowenstein, the great majority present in 1956 were moved by a strange, almost Victorian address Lowenstein gave on August 29, known as the "antiseptic generation speech." In it, Lowenstein appealed to the idealism of his contemporaries.

"We are the privileged and antiseptic generation," he told them. "We move in the backwater of great events, well clothed, well housed and well fed. Struggle is not our hallmark and greatness is not our necessity. We are become lazy on the victorious sacrifices of our older brothers and on the nonfulfillment of gloomy prophesies. . . .

"A few warners and mourners prattle about Asians and atoms from their convertibles," he conceded. "But their timing is out of joint; and most of them come to relax too, because the prettier wives who are, with less effort, producing healthier children and more nutritious meals, marry unaware of our undaunted epic premonitions. . . . If destiny wishes to rendezvous with this generation she will first have to find us."

Speaking to them of the "folly of playing hide-and-seek with the fates," he warned of the grim consequences "if one generation's evasions are to be its children's doom," and exhorted them to action: "It is time long since that helpfulness galvanized and kindness liberated became symbols of our unparalleled and unearned great national luck; that energies more than ever were turned to the intangibles provided by our abundance; that generous impulses and high instinct were nourished by a society arrived at unimaginable technological achievement."

Concluding on a religious note, Lowenstein asserted that "the Lord in His goodness has given us the material to win, if we but grasp the stakes and rouse the will. In our wealth we have the wherewithal to be more nearly generous; in our content we have the incentive to awake in ourselves our finest; in our democratic concept we have the vehicle best suited to carry men's chiefest hopes. It is almost as if we are dared to selfishness in our well-being so we may know finally that all the vast material gifts cannot by themselves preserve themselves or their masters. Survival of man may ever be in balance and survival of freedom will long be in doubt, but we cannot but have the faith of men who know the love of the Lord for His creatures that if we seek to do right contagiously He will help us to see realized the gentler, crisper world men could be heir to."

The speech gave outer form to Lowenstein's inner ponderings, which he often typed up for his own reference. (Convinced that he would have a substantial role in the coming struggle, Lowenstein once wrote: "I detest false modesty." On another occasion, he noted, "If you are a bystander, you are not innocent.")

George Cohen, the president of the student body of Northwestern, who later traveled to the Soviet Union with Lowenstein, repeated the speech virtually word for word when he was back on his own campus. As a precursor of John Kennedy's call to greatness and sacrifice, the speech had put into words a longing which would find full expression in the sixties.

After his stint as an assistant to Ruth Hagy Brod for the College News Conference, Lowenstein got a job, through the efforts of Eleanor Roosevelt, as educational consultant to the Association for the United Nations, an organization she had helped launch to develop support for the U.N. at a time when it was being attacked by isolationists. His assignment there was to work with the Collegiate Council for the United Nations lecturing on the U.N. at college campuses and helping to build a base for international community by increasing interest in and support for the U.N. To the liberals, the United Nations was the center of American foreign policy. It had been the vehicle for halting the Communists in Korea, and Mrs. Roosevelt now perceived it as the best instrument for developing close ties between the United States and the emerging countries of Africa.

Lowenstein enrolled as a graduate student at Chapel Hill, ostensibly to get an M.A. He was also named as an assistant to the Dean of Students, Fred Weaver, and as dorm counselor in the Cobb dormitory, engaging in an experimental counseling program for football players. He also tried to pick up where he had left off with the NSA when he was at law school. He had been the driving force behind much of the movement of the NSA then and had developed considerable influence within what Paul Sigmund describes as the "Old Boy, NSA network." Lowenstein had cultivated his own "acolytes" at each NSA campus and would notify them that he was coming; they were part of his personal army.

The tenth NSA congress in 1957 was a long, drawn-out celebration of a decade of student activities, with past presidents delivering tedious speeches. The delegates were completely bored as William Dentzer delivered his earnest address. Then Lowenstein took the podium as the final speaker. He cracked a few slightly off-color jokes and captured everyone's attention in seconds. Using apt, funny, and original stories, he soon had the whole congress in uproarious laughter. When the roar died down, Lowenstein gave a brief, inspiring speech which brought him a standing ovation. He was in the spotlight again before the students. But his friends had all gone on to careers, while he found himself immersed in undergraduate politics at Chapel Hill.

At the time Lowenstein was enrolled as a graduate student there, a flu epidemic was predicted, and the *Tar Heel*, under the editorship of Neal Bass, denounced the infirmary doctor, Dr. Hedgepath, for not preparing adequately. According to Jimmy Wallace, Lowenstein became inflamed because Hedgepath's position had not been presented. Irate over what he perceived to be a substantial injustice, Lowenstein led the movement to "Dump Bass."

Wallace remembers, "To denounce an adversary, Al had to get him in a morally indefensible position. This was the first *Tar Heel* editor to be recalled. He came in with *Tar Heel* clippings, showing unfairness to Dr. Hedgepath. He got geared up, to a point where a vindictiveness welled up in him."

The fight over Bass brought Lowenstein into contact with Curtis Gans, a third-year undergraduate who wrote a column and did some editing for the *Tar Heel*. While Gans was critical of Bass, he opposed the recall movement. In the fall of 1957, however, Bass was ousted from his position on the paper and Lowenstein moved on to the issue of fraternities, the first concern of his undergraduate days, and the reform of the honor code. Lowenstein no longer sought to abolish the Greek letter societies, but wanted instead to defer the "rushing," or selection process, by either a semester or a year. According to Gans, Lowenstein made a series of tactical judgments which led to a loss of these issues. "He wove a complex web and it all fell apart," he asserts.

As to why Lowenstein felt it necessary to become involved in these matters, Gans concludes: "Allard could not congenitally resist being at the center of controversy, wherever he was. It was in that set of battles that I learned something about Al, which was that there were times when he had the capacity to outsmart himself. He was single-handedly responsible for the 'demise' of that editor of the *Tar Heel*. You could say that Al instinctively moved, when he saw something that bothered him, to do something about it. But why take on an issue that is peripheral, as this was? My sense is that there was an ego need always to be at the center of controversy. If he was going to be in Chapel Hill, he was going to be in the center of controversy in Chapel Hill."

Gans believes that Lowenstein was not unlike Huey Long in the way he could both rouse people and damage them, and Jimmy Wallace observes that he had a touch of the prosecutor in his personality. Wallace compares this trait with the character of Joseph McCarthy.

That he resorted to demagoguery when he believed it necessary was not lost on his friends; neither was the fact that people could be hurt by his tactics. If he felt himself to be in the right, he could hound an opponent relentlessly.

Gans ran for the editorship of the *Tar Heel* in the spring of 1958, and Lowenstein became his campaign manager. They had much in common. Gans was also a New Yorker (from Brooklyn) who had gone to an exclusive private school in the Bronx, and had come to Chapel Hill because he admired Frank Graham. Though Graham was no longer there, Gans identified with the kinds of politics that the university stood for. Lowenstein imbibed endless amounts of Coke; Gans, Pepsi.

Gans drafted a lengthy platform on how to improve the paper, while Lowenstein instructed him on how to win the election. There were "nightly seances," with the graduate student explaining to the undergraduate what moves were necessary for victory. Gans was elected. The political chemistry between Gans and Lowenstein would be of considerable significance in the sixties, but more immediately, the two had begun a working relationship that led to Gans's involvement in the NSA, enabling him to be useful to Lowenstein.

As the *Tar Heel* editor, Gans attended the NSA congress in 1958 on the campus of Ohio Wesleyan University. There he ran into Lowenstein, who had driven Eleanor Roosevelt to the convention where he had arranged for her to speak. Gans was disturbed because he felt his friend was behaving sycophantically toward Mrs. Roosevelt. It occurred to Gans at the time that Lowenstein had a peculiar pecking order of senior people: Eleanor Roosevelt first, then Frank Graham, Norman Thomas, and Adlai Stevenson. Later, he would add Robert Kennedy to the list. Gans felt that Lowenstein had set himself up as a "fawning protégé" of these people and he didn't approve. A new political consciousness was rising among American students. Less respectful of authority figures, it would manifest itself in the SDS, which Gans joined briefly in its early period.

There were some peculiar events at the 1958 congress, involving the election of the new NSA president. Emory Bundy, a delegate from the University of Washington in Seattle was being encouraged by many people to run for the position, though he says he had no desire at the time to be an NSA officer. The heir apparent to the incumbent was an NSA vice-president from Notre Dame, a man named Robert Kiley, who, according to Bundy, "later became a CIA operative." Delegates with negative feelings about Kiley approached Bundy, but while he was making up his mind, the incumbent president pressured him not to seek the presidency and was "unkind," as Bundy puts it. Then the president of the University of Washington student body publicly denounced Bundy, charging that he wasn't a legitimate delegate.

Bundy, earlier elected president of the University of Washington student body himself, insists that the charge was false. Outraged, he moved closer to becoming a candidate. He discussed the decision with Lowenstein, whom he had heard speak at the NSA congress in 1957, but received no encouragement. "He could have gotten me to run," Bundy states, "but he didn't exert pressure for me."

Bundy did not run and Kiley was elected. In 1967, when "the CIA thing came out," Bundy relates, Lowenstein explained to him that Kiley had been "witty," a CIA code word indicating that he was knowledgeable about the connection between the CIA and the NSA, including the extensive funding. Because Bundy was an "outsider," Lowenstein said he believed pressure had been put on him not to run. Had he been elected, Bundy might have discovered the clandestine relationship with the CIA and gone to Lowenstein with the information. "They did what was necessary to keep you from being an officer," Lowenstein told him.

In 1959, Curtis Gans was elected national affairs vice-president of NSA. Lowenstein attended too, this time without Mrs. Roosevelt, who was elderly by then, curtailing her activities, and apparently confident that the organization was in good hands.

At the congress, held at the University of Illinois in Urbana, Lowenstein spoke about his mission to South West Africa earlier that summer. At his urging, and with NSA Vice-President Curtis Gans's help, $750 was raised so that Hans Beukes, a South West African student whom Lowenstein had smuggled out of South Africa, could fly to New York and testify at the United Nations.

During the summer of 1959, the Communist-backed World Youth Festival was held in Vienna. This presented a serious problem to Lowenstein, by now a foreign policy aide to Senator Hubert Humphrey. Largely through Lowenstein's own efforts, the NSA had refused to join the IUS. Now the Soviet bloc was threatening to one-up the West by holding a world youth conference in a neutral, but essentially pro-Western democracy, Austria. Nonparticipation in the Communist-backed festivals was NSA policy; but nonparticipation in this case would be an insult to the Austrians and a coup for the Communists.

To solve the problem, Lowenstein wrote a letter for Humphrey's signature, which was mailed to the editors of the student newspapers on all NSA campuses. It opened with this passage:

> You may be aware that this summer in Vienna the leading Communist international student and youth organizations will stage their seventh biennial World Youth Festival. For some time I have followed with great concern the vigorous efforts of the Communists to gain the sympathy and, whenever possible, the support of young people in general, and of the intellectual leadership

of the great emerging areas of the world in particular. The vast significance of the impending Youth Festival in this Communist effort becomes clearer every day, and the importance of an informed and vigorous reaction to it by American students can hardly be overemphasized.

The letter went on to commend the National Student Association for its "invaluable contributions to the creation and support of the Coordinating Secretariat of the International Student Conference," an organization which it stated "has become a most effective forum through which the non-Communist international student community can discuss ideas, arrange personnel exchanges, and extend assistance to oppressed or needy students wherever they may be."

Noting that the chief representatives of American students and youth organizations "have wisely decided not to participate officially in the Vienna gathering," the letter went on to assert that "mere nonparticipation is clearly an inadequate response to the opportunity and challenge that will be presented in Vienna," and to assert that well-informed, well-briefed, enthusiastic American students should "be encouraged to attend the events in Vienna in their individual capacities."

For such briefing purposes, the text of remarks on the festival made by Humphrey in the Senate were included with the letter which recommended that any students interested in participating as individuals contact the Independent Service for Information on the Vienna Youth Festival, located in Cambridge, Massachusetts. It concluded by urging the editors to "inform as many as possible of the qualified students on your campus about the pitfalls and challenges which will abound at the Festival."

Lowenstein received this letter back from another Humphrey aide who had reviewed it for Humphrey. Accompanying it was a handwritten note dated May 14, 1959, stating simply, "Al, as requested, Cyril." Lowenstein then sent the materials referred to and the Humphrey letter to Gloria Steinem and Leonard Bebchick on May 20, along with a short note, saying he thought she "might like to have a copy of this" for her "files." He looked forward to seeing her "in Vienna if not before." Lowenstein also sent the material to his uncle Lazar, a partner in the family restaurant empire, who, like Lowenstein's father, had come to America from Lithuania. Lazar Lowenstein was on a first name basis with Hubert Humphrey and presumably endorsed his anti-Communist positions.

The Independent Service for Information on the Vienna Youth Festival, which was technically founded by Gloria Steinem and Paul Sigmund, and which came to be known as the Independent Research Service, was funded by the Independence Foundation, one of the conduits of CIA funds into the NSA. In 1965, it was the Independence Foundation which leased its posh offices in Washington to the NSA, signing a fifteen-year, rent-free agreement.

The Independent Service diligently recruited hundreds of American students to attend the 1959 Vienna festival and later the 1962 Communist-backed Helsinki festival, to oppose the Communists as vigorously as possible. According to Eugene Theroux, who served as chairman of the Metropolitan New York region chapter of NSA in 1958, the Americans went "to cause trouble."

Dennis Shaul, who was the director of the Independent Research Service at the time of the Helsinki Youth Festival, was elected president of the NSA directly afterward, then received an Independence Foundation "scholarship" in 1964. Not only were travel expenses for all the delegates paid, but the Independent Service picked up the bill for a jazz group, an exhibition of famous American painters, and the cost of printing a daily newspaper published in five languages. Gloria Steinem attended the Helsinki festival as part of the independent American delegation.

Lowenstein attended the Vienna Youth Festival with Emory Bundy on the way back from their trip to South West Africa. They met with the "antifestival" Americans and were issued forged passes and documents enabling them to get into the events. "I'm sure this had something to do with the CIA," says Bundy.

With the CIA-supplied documents, Lowenstein and Bundy entered the grounds where the delegates were staying. Moments later, Bundy says Lowenstein was already engaged in conversation with members of the American delegation. "One guy was a convinced Communist and Al got into an argument with him," Bundy recalls. As the argument grew hotter, a crowd gathered. "Al was his usual very persuasive self," says Bundy. As the two men argued, they began to insult each other and Bundy feared that it would soon become physical. "Al dared him to take a poke at him," he remembers.

According to Bundy, Lowenstein was "much the master of the argument," but decided to leave in a hurry because he grew apprehensive that they would be found out and get into trouble. When they were a good distance from the scene of the confrontation, Lowenstein asked Bundy what he thought of his argument. Bundy told him that he was brilliant but that there was no chance of Lowenstein's persuading the Communist. Lowenstein laughed and explained to him that he was really speaking to the crowd that had gathered.

Lowenstein then went with Bundy to a huge celebration of Soviet culture held in a giant indoor stadium which the USSR had rented. It was in sharp contrast to the Americans' small group of folksingers with guitars. "It was intimidating. They had the Bolshoi ballet, gymnasts, and Chinese dancers with flags," Bundy remembers. A special hidden sound system had been placed in the stadium, and at the end, the singing of the *Internationale* broke out. The voices were clear and strong, and Lowenstein and Bundy found themselves surrounded by a ringing musical affirmation of Soviet ideology. "It was almost unreal," Bundy concludes. "There were over 30,000 people. You felt you were surrounded by perfection, that history was on their side, there was so much power and momentum." Lowenstein and Bundy walked a mile before either of them said a word. Eugene Theroux would hear Lowenstein deliver an impassioned speech at a banquet for past NSA presidents on what it was like to attend one of those massive Communist youth festivals at which the United States was constantly denounced. "Today, it would be considered a right-wing speech," Theroux notes.

It is evident from the Humphrey letter, which Lowenstein wrote while he was not only on his staff but working under the direction of Ernest Lefever (a top Humphrey liaison to the Foreign Relations Committee, a vehement anti-Communist, and ultimately Ronald Reagan's choice to head the Office of Human Rights in the State Department), that Lowenstein was a driving force behind the CIA-funded United States effort to disrupt the Communist youth festival in Vienna. The Helsinki effort was simply a duplication of what had taken place before.

By 1960, the assault on the NSA at home was coming not from the left but from the right. The Young Americans for Freedom, under Howard Phillips, the president of the Harvard student body, was seeking to take over the American student movement. Founded by William F. Buckley, Jr., and Fulton Lewis III, the YAF sought to replace Eleanor Roosevelt's liberalism with a tough brand of right-wing conservatism as the dominant ideology of American youth.

Lowenstein, who might have been expected to be involved in the struggle with the YAF, reduced his activities in the NSA. He was becoming preoccupied with his courtship of Barbara Boggs, whom he met at the 1960 NSA convention at the University of Minnesota. Seen there walking with his arm around her, Lowenstein was clearly more interested in her than in the growing threat of the right. The 1961 congress, which Curtis Gans notes was the one at which the critical challenge of the YAF was met, Lowenstein missed altogether. There, against right-wing objections, NSA came out against the House Un-American Activities Committee. This had long been Lowenstein's position, but he was not there for the victory.

While the international activities of the NSA remained tightly in the grip of the CIA, its domestic posture after 1961 became increasingly liberal. But Lowenstein's activities in NSA were noncontroversial from 1962 through 1964. As a dean and professor at Stanford, and then as a professor at North Carolina State, he was called on as a resource person. In this capacity, in 1964, he tried to establish a relationship with the NSA and the Peace Corps, as he extended his own activities in African affairs. But by 1965, the war in Vietnam had become a cause of concern, with radical students in the SDS seizing on the issue. The NSA was once again torn ideologically.

Lowenstein would find himself debating the radicals and the conservatives in 1966 at the NSA congress in Urbana, Illinois, on the draft and the Vietnam War. And in 1967, he would make his historic address at the NSA congress at College Park, Maryland, officially launching the Dump Johnson movement.

But by 1967, a cloud of suspicion hung over the NSA. Unlike their American counterparts, Third World students had always assumed that both Western and Soviet bloc student movements were supported by their respective governments. They had benefited with free rides from the Americans through COSEC and from the Russians through the IUS. It was common knowledge that both groups used "ringers" for the international conferences, "perennial students," much older than the others and unlikely to be taken in by the party lines of the opposition in the Cold War.

Yet the Americans refused to believe that their government would secretly fund and direct the activities of what was supposed to be an independent student organization.

Lowenstein was invited to a meeting of officers and staff members of the NSA in November of 1966 and was told that there was a crisis; the CIA had been funding the international activities of the NSA since the fifties and through the sixties. Since the story would now likely come out, they had to find a way to present what had happened without destroying the organization.

Lowenstein, who was serving as chairman of the National Supervisory Board of NSA, told them that he had suspected this was the case, but that he had had no direct knowledge. He later told the press that the students had confided in him because he was "one of the few past officers who was not involved in or in favor of the CIA connection." On a piece of paper, he scrawled a list of names, among them, Dentzer and Ingram. Lowenstein's advice was to push as hard as possible to cut the CIA connection, even at the risk of hurting programs.

In January of 1967, Ed Schwartz, an NSA vice-president, was told that a story would be run in *Ramparts* in March that would reveal the CIA connection. When that issue of the radical San Francisco publication appeared, it was revealed that, in addition to the Foundation for Youth and Student Affairs, the other foundations through which CIA funds had been channeled to the NSA were the Independence Foundation, the San Jacinto Foundation, the Sidney and Esther Rabb Foundation, and the J. Frederick Brown Foundation. Michael Wood, the NSA director of development, or fund raising, was in a position to know, and had decided to tell all, betraying the confidence of the then-president of NSA, Phil Sherburne.

The CIA, in its almost exclusive interest in the NSA's international programs, had developed its own method of communication with NSA staffers, used whenever they discussed their operation in public. The CIA was the "firm," and agency bureaucrats were the "fellas," or the "boys." Those in NSA who knew of the CIA relationship were "witty." NSA staffers had code names. The Covert Action Division No. 5 conducted the face-to-face encounters, and by the sixties, on the estimate of a former international vice president, all the CIA agents the students dealt with were former NSA people themselves.

The NSA became a major recruiting ground for agents, with over 70 percent of its officers taking positions in "intelligence." And money kept pouring into the NSA from the foundations, most of it CIA funds, until by 1964 $370,000 of the NSA's budget of $400,000 was CIA funding. In 1965, it was $440,000 of $760,000. The 1966 budget was $735,000, of which $355,000 came from the Agency.

An international staff member of NSA would consult with a CIA agent and then international policies would be formulated concerning overseas programs. Reports on foreign student leaders would also be passed by the cooperating NSA official to one of the CIA agents. This was exactly the kind of report that the State Department had asked Lowenstein to write in 1948.

In this way, NSA delegates to international youth conferences often functioned in much the same way as the delegates to the NSA congresses who reported back to the FBI. But the FBI considered left liberals unreliable, while the CIA sought out such people as representatives of the American non-Communist left. Michael Wood, however, had been considered unreliable even by the CIA because of his radical politics, and he had never been told about the CIA relationship until Sherburne explained it to him.

When Lowenstein learned that the NSA article was to be published in *Ramparts*, he went to see his old friend Richard Murphy, then an assistant postmaster general. Discussing the problem at length, "we both came to find out," Murphy states, "that neither of us had knowledge of this situation during the time that we were NSA presidents." According to Murphy, both he and Lowenstein agreed that the CIA funding had not affected the decisions they had made. They talked about specific people who had been knowledgeable and had been involved, "who were well known to him and me," Murphy recalls. "I don't want to go into a long list of names," he then adds, "but I simply say that the statement that came from the government in 1967 was that most of the presidents from 1953 on knew about the arrangement and most of the international vice-presidents and a few others at that time knew about it."

Lowenstein later argued that the CIA had been wrong to put "direct pressure" on the students and to maintain the "secrecy of the relationship with NSA." It was his position that the CIA, had it wanted to, could have given "financial support" and "used its influence to channel money to the students . . . without involving the students in direct relations with CIA agents." Lowenstein said he told the students at the November meeting that "I was the one they kept it all secret from." And he stated in 1967 that while he was president of NSA, he "was not involved in any relationship with the CIA." He had, he insisted, "neither sought nor accepted any funds" from the CIA or from "any foundations" and had no knowledge of the connection until he was told about it by the students before the *Ramparts* article appeared. But he did say that before he went to the Stockholm youth congress, he had received a "suspicious offer" of funds to pay for the trip. He rejected it, he said, and paid his own way. "It might have been from the Communist party," he speculated. In Lowenstein's view, the truth had been kept from him because he was independent and not reliable from the CIA's point of view. "Curiously enough," Lowenstein observes (referring to his successor as president of NSA, William Dentzer), "Dentzer never confided in me after his election."

Lowenstein did write a statement for the NSA which justified the relationship and which enraged some incumbent NSA officers. The past presidents of NSA, including William Dentzer, who believed the relationship with the CIA was justified, issued their own statement, which Lowenstein did not sign, while Eugene Groves, the NSA president, Richard Stearns, the international vice-president, and Edward Schwartz, the national affairs vice-president, issued their own, deploring the CIA support. The National Supervisory Board announced that its policy in future would be to terminate the relationship and to prohibit the use of CIA funds for any NSA program.

In Curtis Gans's opinion, there was considerable hostility toward Lowenstein from the NSA people with CIA connections. While he speculates that this may have been because Lowenstein was regarded as a traitor in what amounted to a family fight, it is also possible that it was simply the result of Lowenstein's opposition to Johnson and the war. He continues to wonder about the trips and the huge credit-card phone bills, the mobility that Gans describes as being "beyond us mere mortals." And responsible antiwar activists, such as Mary Lou Oates, later of the *Los Angeles Times*, split with Lowenstein because they were convinced that he knew of the CIA connection. Emory Bundy states: "The CIA issue was something unresolved about Al in my mind. Al always maintained he was unaware of it. But I believe that someone that bright and aware must have had knowledge of it."

Jenny, Lowenstein's wife, remembers in the early seventies, being taken to dinner at the Fifth Avenue apartment of Helen Jean Rogers Secondari, an old NSA friend whom Lowenstein had not seen for some time. In the middle of dinner, Lowenstein asked her, "What about the CIA-NSA connection?" According to Jenny, Secondari pretended she hadn't heard him and changed the subject. Al raised it again and again, and each time Secondari acted as though she had not heard him and changed the subject. Lowenstein dropped it, but afterward, when they left, he appeared shaken. "He was profoundly disappointed that he was suspect," Jenny recalls. He also told Alice Brandeis Popkin how hurt he had been by the disclosures.

Jenny also tells the story of her trip to California to join Lowenstein when he was working for Jerry Brown in the summer of 1975. Driving with her were her three children, Frankie, Tommy, and Kate, and a friend, Nancy Pierce. They stopped in Wichita Falls, Texas, to stay with an old friend of Lowenstein's from the NSA who had become a Texas state legislator. The first evening, the friend told Jenny "how deeply and appallingly sorry he was that he knew of the NSA-CIA connection but couldn't tell Al." The friend went on to relate how he had met with "nameless" CIA people who had made a "not terribly oblique reference" to what might happen to him if he told.

But in light of all the other evidence, it is difficult to accept Jenny's version as final. The problem is that no one was really free to tell everything. As Sam Brown, who is a former head of the National Student Association Advisory Policy Board and who became a leader of the antiwar movement and a key operative in the Eugene McCarthy campaign, told authors David Wise and Thomas B. Ross, the CIA would select one or two association officers as its contacts. The officers were told that "they should be aware of certain secrets and were asked to sign an oath pledging silence. Then," Brown said, "they were told, 'You are employed by the CIA.' At that point they were trapped, having signed a statement not to divulge anything. . . . This is the part of the thing that I found to be most disgusting and horrible. People were duped into this relationship with the CIA, a relationship from which there was no way out."

One of the NSA students who went on to become executive assistant to CIA Director Richard Helms posed as an official of the Agency for International Development to "entrap unsuspecting NSA officers, revealing his 'cover' only after extracting pledges of secrecy and even NSA commitments to cooperate with specific CIA programs."

When news of the CIA-NSA connection was made public, President Johnson appointed a special committee to study the problem, including Under Secretary of State Nicholas Katzenbach as chairman, Richard Helms, CIA director, and John Gardner, secretary of HEW. On May 29, 1967, the committee recommended and Johnson accepted as "national policy" that "no federal agency shall provide any covert financial assistance or support, direct or indirect, to any of the nation's educational or private voluntary organizations." The report indicated that exceptions could be made in case of "overriding national security interests" but that none of the organizations currently being used, such as the NSA, fit that description.

Presumably, this policy invalidated Cord Meyer's argument that since the Soviet Union had infiltrated the international student movement after the Second World War, the United States was correct in taking countermeasures as a matter of national security. Writing in *Mademoiselle* in August 1967, Rick Stearns, who had served as international vice-president of the NSA and presumably knew of the CIA-NSA link, argued that although it was possible to be "historically compassionate" about the situation, given the existence of the Cold War and the paranoia of McCarthyism, "at no time, even granted the conditions—and there certainly were mitigating conditions in 1952—was the relationship justified." Stearns later served as a chief organizer for the campaign of George McGovern in 1972.

CIA agents bristled, and pointed out that in Britain, information about the use of private organizations by British intelligence is voluntarily suppressed out of patriotism and that such activities were legitimate and essential. Richard Bissell, former chief of Clandestine Services so told the Council on Foreign Relations in 1968:

> If the agency is to be effective, it will have to make use of private institutions on an expanding scale, though those relations which have been "blown" cannot be resurrected. We need to operate under deeper cover, with increased attention to the use of "cut-outs" (i.e., intermediaries). CIA's interface with the rest of the world needs to be better protected. If various groups hadn't been aware of the source of their funding, the damage subsequent to disclosure might have been far less than occurred. The CIA interface with various private groups, including business and student groups, must be remedied.

Dennis Shaul, president of NSA from 1962–63, who supported the CIA funding, put it bluntly: "The National Student Association was organized partially to serve as a bulwark against Communist organizations that were active both here and abroad shortly after World War II." Shaul is correct in this assessment. Lowenstein himself was not modest in describing his own contribution to the anti-Communist effort of the NSA. In a letter dated September 29, 1959, to Nathan Straus, former New Deal official and the powerful head of WMCA Radio, he wrote: "While I was with the NSA, we launched the representative non-Communist international student organization, to whose first conference in Stockholm I was the American delegate. This organization, known as the International Student Conference, has done wonderful and insufficiently appreciated work since its formation in combatting the efforts of the Communist International Union of Students."

Others point out that this justification does not take into account the risk that a totally secret CIA might involve itself in an ever-increasing sphere of activities in the name of anti-Communism, eventually threatening the democracy it was created to protect. Indeed, there has been an ongoing disclosure of CIA funding of numerous organizations and activities—*Encounter* magazine, the Asia Foundation, the American Council for the International Commission of Jurists, to name a few. The United Auto Workers was used as a conduit of funds for various political purposes that the CIA wished to promote. It has also been revealed that numerous books were published with CIA assistance.

In 1967, Sam Brown, acting on the policy set by the National Board, cut the remaining CIA ties with the NSA. The College Park congress, at which Lowenstein rallied the students to oppose Johnson, brought vast numbers of young people, including Brown, into the democratic process to end the war in Vietnam. But this was not only the final chapter of Lowenstein's influence on the NSA. It was really the end of the organization itself. In debt and cut from government support, it waned.

The students themselves now lacked the motivation to be involved. Lowenstein observed at the 1968 NSA congress at the University of Kansas that the young people had changed. "They're turning inward," he remarked. "When things are going well, they tell you about the political stuff they're working on. Now it's all personal. They feel so damn ineffectual. They feel activism is meaningless. They're all too tired and too beaten out. . . . All they can see is the collapse. They can't see what they've accomplished."

Lowenstein would give his last speech to the NSA at this 1968 congress in Kansas after Eugene McCarthy had been defeated and Robert Kennedy was dead. He would try to make the young people feel they had won a victory, that they had forced Johnson from office. He acknowledged that liberalism had failed in many ways, but said there was still hope.

Two years before Allard Lowenstein's death in 1980, the NSA merged with the National Student Lobby to create the United States Student Association. It claims a membership of two million and lobbies on such bread-and-butter issues as tuition increases and student loans. It is currently in court, continuing the suit filed by the NSA in 1977 under the Freedom of Information Act, to force the CIA to release files on the agency's covert relationship with the student group from 1947 through 1967: 1947, not 1952. But the CIA does not respond.

Iberia and Africa
Part One

14.

As a graduate student at Chapel Hill, Allard Lowenstein had begun his own courtship of Hubert Humphrey, an affable and responsive man always on the lookout for new talent for the political movement that he believed would one day bring him to the presidency. Lowenstein saw in Humphrey a way out of the seemingly dead-end situation he found himself in as 1958 began. When Ruth Hagy had hired Lowenstein to work for the College Press Conference in 1956 and requested his early separation from the army so he could assume his duties covering the Chicago Democratic convention on August 13, she had insisted that he actually be a student. To satisfy this requirement, he had dutifully enrolled in the graduate school at the University of North Carolina at Chapel Hill to do a master's in history. He had his degree from Yale Law School, but since he had never taken the bar exam, only becoming a member of the New York bar when the state passed a law exempting veterans who were law school graduates from the requirement of taking it, the job offer was a godsend at the time. But at Chapel Hill he ended up involved in campus politics, as if he were an undergraduate once again, and far removed from the great issues of the world.

Lowenstein knew Humphrey from the NSA congresses, in which the activist senator had taken a serious interest. They had both given major addresses at the 1957 congress at the University of Wisconsin at Madison and had been received enthusiastically. When he visited Chapel Hill during a speaking engagement in North Carolina, Humphrey found himself assisted by an enthusiastic Lowenstein. And when a favorable editorial about Humphrey appeared in the *Durham Morning Herald*, Lowenstein quickly sent it to him on February 17, 1958, with a letter. Lowenstein also contacted Ruth Hagy, who belonged to a community of wealthy and dedicated anti-Communists in

Philadelphia and was close to Humphrey, and suggested to her that he might be of use to Humphrey.

Humphrey wrote back to Lowenstein on February 27, 1958, thanking him for his letter and for his "helpfulness" during his visit to Chapel Hill. "I have seen Ruth Geri Hagy," Humphrey wrote, "and we have had a good talk about you. She should be seeing you shortly, or at least you should hear from her." Humphrey had conveyed Lowenstein's good wishes to Muriel, his wife, who remembered Lowenstein well and who asked Humphrey "to say that she is looking forward to seeing you on one of your trips to Washington." Humphrey concluded by thanking Lowenstein for sending him the editorial. "Not bad!" he exclaimed. The Senator finished up with a quip about the weather in North Carolina, which had been inclement. "Sorry to have bothered you with that Minnesota weather. It was unintentional."

Lowenstein stayed in close touch with Humphrey. He also worked on a United States-Soviet exchange program which brought six Soviet editors of youth publications to America under the auspices of the National Student Association, while a counterpart group of American editors toured the USSR at the same time. Lowenstein met with the editors in New York and in Chapel Hill-Raleigh-Durham. In Manhattan, he took them to dine at one of the Lowenstein family restaurants, and in North Carolina set up their visits at universities and with local politicians. He also helped to arrange their interviews with Adlai Stevenson, Eleanor Roosevelt, William O. Douglas, and other American leaders.

Walter C. Clemens, a professor of political science at Boston University who was then a graduate student at Columbia and who served as an escort, guide, and interpreter for the delegation, recalls that Lowenstein was extremely effective with the Soviet editors: "What Al had to say to them was just as meaty as what Douglas, for example, said in his interview. But Al was closer to them in age and had better rapport. He could be more informal—more blunt, more humorous, and more aggressive—but they seemed to like and respect him for these qualities. For these reasons, he made probably the deepest impression on them of any U.S. citizen encountered in the month-long tour."

Lowenstein took one editor, Vladen Troshkin, for a tour of the Chapel Hill-Raleigh-Durham area in his convertible, giving Troshkin an opportunity to take motion pictures. But the Russians believed that people like Lowenstein were fighting a losing battle, and carried away with them a negative image of the country.

The exchange program between the USSR and the United States was financed by the Foundation for Youth and Student Affairs, a conduit for money from the CIA. And that summer, during July and August, Lowenstein traveled to the Soviet Union as part of a group to meet an official Soviet youth group. With him were George Cohen, the president of the student body of Northwestern, and Perris Henderson, the captain of the Chapel Hill wrestling team. Cohen and Henderson paid their own way, and Cohen believes that Lowenstein probably did as well, although he acknowledges that he did not know this for a fact. "Al might have had some official connection of some kind," he adds, "because he brought letters from Hubert Humphrey and Eleanor Roosevelt."

On the way to the Soviet Union, they toured Germany, visited Lowenstein's old army base, and met with survivors of a concentration camp. In Russia, they visited Young Pioneer camps where Lowenstein suggested that wrestling matches be staged between himself, Henderson, and some Russians. But Cohen had to participate in the toasting afterward because Lowenstein would not drink vodka. Later at a track meet, a Russian soldier came over to Cohen to say, "I wrestled with Al Lowenstein."

While in Europe, Lowenstein met a Princeton undergraduate named Bill Boyd, whom he asked to come along on a trip to South Africa later that summer. The genesis of this expedition was a conversation he had during the Christmas holidays with another Princeton undergraduate, his friend Adlai Hardin. Adlai Stevenson's cousin and a member of the prestigious and exclusive Ivy Club, Hardin was the kind of undergraduate Lowenstein sought to cultivate as a friend and traveling companion. Lowenstein was "excited and enthusiastic about the idea," Hardin recalls. "He said he wanted to go to Africa also and we planned to meet that summer in Cape Town." Hardin gave Lowenstein his African itinerary and Lowenstein, in turn, gave him contacts in some of the countries he was planning to visit on the way to South Africa. The list was impressive. "He gave me introductions to Tom Mboya in Kenya and Julius Nyerere in Tanganyika," relates Hardin, who has the distinct impression that Lowenstein must have already visited Africa because of his knowledge and associations.

Hardin went down the east coast of Africa until he reached South Africa in August. Lowenstein traveled to Israel and Egypt, and then appeared with Boyd to meet Hardin, as they had planned. As to why Lowenstein had gone to South Africa, Hardin was puzzled. "I can't say he didn't mention Hubert Humphrey," he speculates. "I was mystified as to why he was going to Africa. Al certainly had definite purposes."

Emory Bundy, who would later journey with Lowenstein to South West Africa, says that this African trip was made as a "foreign policy advisor to Hubert Humphrey," a contention that others support. Humphrey was collecting information on Soviet influence in Africa and African students in the Soviet-bloc countries for his own reports, and Lowenstein's findings would have been useful. But Lowenstein did not actually work in Humphrey's office until 1959. His situation at the time of the trip is consequently unclear. Humphrey had a history of letting people serve as staff members on a voluntary basis for which they received no pay, a role that would have suited Lowenstein at that time.

In Cape Town, Hardin and Boyd did some sightseeing on their own while Lowenstein took care of his own business. Then they picked up a Volkswagen that somebody wanted driven to Johannesburg, and with Hardin at the wheel most of the time, they took a dangerous drive late into the night to Fort Hare University College, then the only institution of higher education for blacks in South Africa. There Lowenstein had an appointment to meet with student leaders.

The three Americans went into a room where the African student leaders were waiting for them. At first, Lowenstein, Hardin, and Boyd spoke with them in small clusters, then Lowenstein addressed the whole group. According to Hardin, Lowenstein was "spellbinding," as the students listened. "Al was charismatic in the way he spoke," Hardin asserts. "It was like a preacher. Al was preaching the political process. But he was not preaching revolution. His message was not in any way incendiary. His basic message was 'I'm here as a friend.'"

Hardin, who leaves no doubt that he believes Lowenstein was in the CIA, was overwhelmed by Lowenstein's performance. "This experience, which was quite extraordinary," he maintains, "was one of the things that led me to believe that some smart s.o.b. in Washington thought it would be a good thing if a guy like Al Lowenstein talked to the students at Fort Hare. I was impressed that this was an extraordinary person I was listening to and that it had to have a profound impact on the people listening to him."

Lowenstein spoke for about forty minutes in general terms about racial politics and legal and economic issues, comparing the United States and South Africa. Afterward, there was dialogue, with Lowenstein answering questions from the students. There was considerable student hostility toward American racial attitudes and United States policies, particularly what the students perceived as America's support for the regime in South Africa. Lowenstein argued that most Americans really knew nothing about apartheid in South Africa and that if they did, they would disapprove of it. He assured them that many powerful Americans who were "right-thinking" did not support apartheid or the Nationalist regime in South Africa, and were working through the political process to change South African racial policies.

According to Lowenstein, this proved to be his first encounter with Jariretundu Fanuel Kozonguizi, who was then, or appeared to be, an angry student from South West Africa, the territory over which South Africa ruled. Kozonguizi reproached him: "You say your people don't see that they were responsible for the things that are done to the black man in South Africa. Well, I come from a place for which your country and the United Nations are directly responsible, and there things are so much worse that I must come here to get a breath of fresh air."

After Kozonguizi's criticism of America and its indifference to the problems of South Africa and his country, Lowenstein asked him if he could spend a "little time" talking with him about South West Africa. They conversed until dawn.

Kozonguizi, who would be one of Lowenstein's advisors before he embarked on his trip to South West Africa, went on to have an extraordinary career. His meeting with Lowenstein at this point on Lowenstein's trip, whether entirely fortuitous or not, became one strand in a web that would entangle Lowenstein in the intricacies of South West African politics, with its rival organizations struggling to position themselves for power on the eventual day of independence. It also projected Lowenstein into a major role in the American effort to shape the outcome of that political struggle for control of an area which was to assume enormous importance for the West twenty-five years later. Kozonguizi, a Herero, was to play a significant part in this political struggle, as the leader of a party that split the independence movement, as an associate of CIA-funded organizations in Britain and the U.S., and eventually as a paid employee of the Republic of South Africa.

Lowenstein, Hardin, and Boyd were in Fort Hare for over an hour and it was well past midnight when they finally departed. From Fort Hare they drove through the night until they reached Durban, where Lowenstein had an appointment to see Alan Paton, the white South African author of *Cry the Beloved Country* who was also chairman of the Liberal party of South Africa. After lunch with Paton, they continued their drive to Johannesburg, where Lowenstein met with white student leaders at the universities. In Pretoria he met and spent time with the son of then Prime Minister Vorwoerd, a student leader at Stellenbosch University. Then Hardin went to Ghana, while Lowenstein continued on with Boyd.

When Lowenstein returned from his trip to South Africa in 1958 he went to the National Student Association congress at Ohio Wesleyan University. He escorted Eleanor Roosevelt to the congress, where he had arranged for her to speak and for himself to deliver an address on South Africa and South West Africa. While he was there, he ran into Emory Bundy from the University of Washington, with whom he had become friendly in Seattle during the spring of 1957.

Lowenstein had gone to Seattle to speak at the University of Washington at the same time Bundy was elected president of the student body of the university. A distant relation of McGeorge Bundy, Kennedy's national security advisor, Bundy came from a poor family in Seattle with good connections. He was introduced to Lowenstein, who joined him at the banquet at which Bundy's election was celebrated. In typical Lowenstein fashion, they then adjourned to Bundy's home, where they talked late into the night and where Lowenstein slept. That summer, Bundy went to an NSA congress for the first time and met Lowenstein at the University of Wisconsin at Madison. He heard Lowenstein deliver a brilliant address, fell totally under his spell, and joined him on a tour of the Southeast. Traveling with him, Bundy learned all about the NSA and became enthralled with Lowenstein, whom he found to be "the smartest person I ever met," and the most charismatic.

After the 1958 NSA congress, Bundy joined Lowenstein again, this time for a trip by car to New York. Bundy recalls that they knocked around the city and visited the U.N., where Bundy became acquainted with Mburumba Kerina, who had left South West Africa in 1952 and was the first nonwhite South West African to make it to New York. Lowenstein noticed that Father Michael Scott would be speaking at the Trusteeship Committee. Scott, an Anglican priest who headed Africa Bureau in London (an organization later identified by *Ramparts* as a conduit for CIA funds that served as the model for the American Committee on Africa headed by George Houser), had been appearing since 1949 at the United Nations on behalf of the Herero people to represent the tribal interests of South West Africa because the tribal leaders were not allowed out of the country to plead their own case.

Lowenstein wanted to meet Scott and approached his former mentor, Frank Graham, who, after the loss of his seat in the United States Senate, had gone to work at the United Nations. Graham obliged him. He arranged to have Michael Scott meet both Lowenstein and Bundy, and Lowenstein, in turn, invited Scott to join Bundy and him for dinner at the Hyde Park, a Lowenstein family restaurant.

Scott had first gone to South West Africa in 1947, at the time of the formation of the international mining consortiums which sought to exploit the territory's vast mineral wealth. His explanation was that he had been invited by some tribal chiefs who had asked him to come and observe conditions there. After his appearance at the United Nations and his open criticism of the government of South Africa, he had been prevented from returning.

Lowenstein later wrote that he had not come to hear Scott as an admirer because he was rumored to have "Communist connections" and some people called him a "crackpot." He added: "Nothing I had heard about Father Scott had prepared me for the remarkable impact of the man. There was a great strength and simplicity to what he said that evoked the deference of diplomats and touched that which makes men want to cheer and weep at once. He was somehow both blunt and gentle, a lean pacifist lion full of a restraining patience of a man certain that time would bring victory, an impatience that men do not prod time as much as they could."

Lowenstein concluded that "if this man was a crackpot, so were all men who take the burdens of other men as their own," and described Scott as he was surrounded by a crowd of people: "Always there is the great patience-impatience, always the people pushing and pulling and seeking this and that; but never is there a show of pique or of self-importance on his part."

As Emory Bundy related, Lowenstein "got more closely acquainted with Scott." Scott was frustrated with the United Nations. He feared that a lack of interest in the problems of South West Africa would cause it to be dropped from the agenda. If this happened, peaceful independence under U.N. supervision would never be achieved, and the repressive policies of South Africa would lead inevitably to violent revolution. Although two native South West Africans, Kozonguizi and Kerina, had appeared before the U.N., there was still no action. Scott himself had not been able to visit South West Africa since 1948. He conceived the plan to have an outsider go and document what was going on, talk to the chiefs and other non-Europeans, observe, and then report the findings. In this way world opinion might be mobilized and pressure put on South Africa to change its racial policies in South West Africa or to give up the territory itself. Scott envisioned this impartial observer coming before the United Nations with tape-recorded statements by tribal chiefs and other African leaders, photographs of living conditions and personal impressions. He implanted in Lowenstein the idea that he would be this person.

While he pondered the possibility of going to South West Africa for Michael Scott, Lowenstein took up his position as a foreign policy advisor to Hubert Humphrey. A friend observed: "Al never was too good on Hubert's staff. He was always saying yes to every request, putting Hubert's name on everything, when his job really was to keep Hubert's name *off* everything." But Lowenstein and Humphrey shared a common political philosophy and some specific political goals. One of them concerned the draft.

Humphrey had managed to avoid doing military service during the Second World War. But he would single out "draft dodgers" as the target of his wrath. Lowenstein had avoided military service during the Korean War by getting an occupational deferment as president of the National Student Association. Later he volunteered for induction in the peacetime army. But he too would be fiercely critical of draft evaders at the time of Vietnam.

Lowenstein set out to get the young aides in the Senate to persuade their bosses that the draft was not functioning equitably and that the system should be changed to a lottery so the rich and influential could not get out of it. Among those he approached was the former tennis star and Rhodes scholar Hamilton Richardson of Louisiana, executive secretary and legislative assistant to Senator Russell Long. Lowenstein then arranged to meet with Armed Services Committee chairman, Senator Richard Russell of Georgia, with Richardson accompanying him to support his efforts. But Russell balked. "Boys, don't open this up," he instructed them. "If we do, everyone opposed to the draft would testify against it, those people who are totally for peace, and we'll end up passing it as it is. Leave it alone."

Lowenstein became close to Richardson, who introduced him to the powerful people in Washington from Louisiana. Among them were Congressman Hale Boggs and his wife, to whose daughter, Barbara, Lowenstein would later become engaged. Richardson and Lowenstein would often be seen having lunch together in the Senate cafeteria, where Lowenstein would expound on politics.

Africa continued to be an important focus of his activities. Humphrey, too, was deeply involved in the power struggle under way between the United States and the Soviet Union to fill the vacuum left in Africa by departing European colonial powers. In 1960, a press agency, International Features Service, was established, and it began disseminating the thoughts of Hubert Humphrey to the people of the Third World including Africa. International Features became the not-for-profit Peace with Freedom when it was reorganized under Murray Barton, the vice-chairman of the New York Liberal party and was liberally supported with CIA funds through the International Development Foundation, a conduit, and the dummy Price Fund. Barton involved both the NAACP's Roy Wilkins and the UAW's Walter Reuther in the operation and continued to promote Humphrey's message in twenty-two languages.

Lowenstein saw to it that Humphrey got help from George Houser's American Committee on Africa, a bastion of American liberalism. Houser, a theologian who had done a year in prison in 1940 with Howard E. Spragg for refusing induction into the army because of his religious convictions about nonviolence, and who had cofounded CORE, a civil rights organization that endorsed nonviolence, with James Farmer in Chicago in 1944, resigned from his position as national secretary of CORE to support the "Defiance" campaign, becoming executive secretary of Americans for South African Resistance. He had studied at both Union and Chicago Theological Seminaries, promoted a trip to Africa in 1954, and returned to found the American Committee on Africa to oppose the racial policies of South Africa and its rule in South West Africa, where apartheid had also been instituted. Houser familiarized himself with all of the movements against South Africa in South West Africa and began to give them assistance.

Chairman of the American Committee on Africa's executive board was Unitarian minister Donald Harrington, who later served as chairman of the New York Liberal party. And on the national committee were such luminaries as Eleanor Roosevelt, Norman Thomas, A. Philip Randolph, Martin Luther King, Jr., Senator Eugene McCarthy, Arthur Schlesinger, Jr., Angier Biddle Duke, and Hubert Humphrey himself. Included on the executive board were Edward F. Gray of the United Auto Workers, who worked with Lowenstein on Spain, Bayard Rustin, who worked with him on civil rights and Africa, and public relations executive· Gilbert Jonas. The general counsel was Robert Delson, of the firm of Delson & Gordon, which would employ Lowenstein in the late seventies. Lowenstein came to have close ties to the American Committee on Africa, an organization of influential liberal anti-Communists who feared the spread of Communism in Africa.

Early in 1959, Lowenstein went to work with Houser to make arrangements for "Africa Freedom Day" on April 15, an annual event planned by the Accra Conference of Independent African States to focus world attention on Africa's struggle for independence. A public meeting was to be held in Carnegie Hall, with Eleanor Roosevelt as the first honorary chairman of the affair. The other honorary chairmen were contralto Marian Anderson and former Secretary of the Air Force Thomas Finletter. Cochairmen were the head of the AFL-CIO George Meany and baseball great Jackie Robinson. The list of sponsors included Mrs. John Dewey and Adam Clayton Powell as well as Allard Lowenstein's elementary school ethics teacher, Algernon Black of the Ethical Culture Society.

Lowenstein's and Houser's choice of a speaker for the event fell on Tom Mboya, chairman of the All-Africa Peoples' Conference, who had emerged as a leading spokesman of those proindependence Africans who supported the West, and those Westerners who believed African independence was in their interests. Only twenty-eight years old at the time, Mboya was a conservative anti-Communist on Kenya's legislative counsel who also served as head of the CIA-supported Kenya Federation of Labor. He had become a superstar of a kind and traveled extensively on funds provided by Africa Bureau (funded by the CIA) and the International Confederation of Free Trade Unions (IFCTU), which was supported by the AFL-CIO and which was later identified by *Ramparts* as a conduit for CIA money to stop the spread of Marxism in Africa. Mboya wrote articles for the International Student Conference of the Coordinating Secretariat of the National Unions of Students, which Lowenstein had helped set up as president of the NSA. On a world tour to promote his "Africa Freedom Fund," Mboya made a six-week lecture tour of America under the auspices of the American Committee on Africa.

Mboya was a natural choice to speak at Carnegie Hall for a variety of reasons. He opposed Kwame Nkrumah's militant pan-Africanism that would have forged the emerging African states into a mammoth, leftist African federation instead of the separate moderate-to-conservative African nations that America hoped to be able to lead at the U.N. The AFL-CIO maintained that the pan-African movement was manipulated by the Communists and had formed close links with the IFCTU to take on the radical All African Trade Union Federation (AATUF), which embraced Nkrumah's position. Mboya was being groomed by America's anti-Communist trade union movement, and Humphrey and Lowenstein had especially close ties to it.

From his Humphrey staff office, Lowenstein spoke on the phone with George Houser, and Houser agreed to get Mboya's Africa Freedom Day speech written. Houser then wrote to Lowenstein on February 19, 1959:

This is just to follow up on our telephone conversation. We will have some kind of draft of the speech sent to you in another week. Will you let me know as soon as you have a date set for coming to New York so that we can get together for discussion of this in more detail? I also would like to have at least one other person who has been working on it meet with us. If my schedule should shape up so that I come to Washington before you get to New York I will let you know. I don't know what the form of a resolution to be presented to the Senate on the observance of African Freedom Day should be. But this is a detail that I am sure you will know the answer to.

Houser went on to ask Lowenstein whether the thirteenth or fourteenth of April were "good" for having Mboya in Washington. "I would like to know as soon as possible so that we can begin to tie down some aspects of his schedule," Houser concluded.

On March 9, 1959, Houser wrote to Lowenstein again to tell him that Peter Weiss, an executive board member of the American Committee on Africa, and husband of heiress and peace activist Cora Weiss, had prepared the speech: "I am enclosing a first draft. There is still a lot more that we could do with it here but it seemed better to send something along so that you and others there can take a look at it and see what ideas you have. You will notice that in a few spots there are some blank spaces for some statistics. We have the general facts but we wanted to be certain of the accurate statistics before filling in those blanks. . . ."

Mboya appeared onstage at Carnegie Hall in colorful African garb while the crowd shouted "Uhuru!" the Swahili word for *freedom,* even before he started speaking. He called for an "internationalism of democracy" dedicated to freedom, independence, and the elimination of disease, poverty, and ignorance all over the world. The course he charted, Mboya asserted, would "match the internationalism of Communism" and deliver "a death blow to the root causes of most of the 'isms' that currently bedevil the world." Addressing himself further to the fear of Communism, Mboya stated: "Too often we have heard of those who insist that African freedom is a risk towards Communism. To them, all I want to say is that if they spent all their efforts in practicing the democracy that they preach they would have nothing to fear from Communism."

On May 8, 1959, Mboya conferred with Vice-President Nixon. Then, on May 9, both Humphrey and Mboya addressed the Americans for Democratic Action in Washington. In a speech reflecting the thoughts and language of Lowenstein (this should not be surprising since Lowenstein wrote many of Humphrey's speeches), Humphrey urged America to meet the "growing Soviet challenge with a grand design for peace—a seven-year plan of our own." This included keeping defenses at "the peak of efficiency," the wiping out of "the last vestiges of discrimination of color under law" so all Americans would realize the dream of dignity and well-being, and a $2 billion a year technical and economic assistance program to "free people everywhere."

Mboya, meanwhile, asked for more support for African freedom and suggested a program for America in its relations with Africa, including more aid and an attempt "to mitigate and change the inhuman South African policy of apartheid." Mboya would repeat these words a week later to the International Ladies Garment Workers Union in Miami. He was received enthusiastically all over America. But on June 9, when Mboya returned to Nairobi, the police seized documents after searching his luggage. Pro-West as he was, there was still resistance by the colonizers to the inevitable.

Mboya's economic plan for Africa was to create an urban middle class through the establishment of a new government bureaucracy to run the country after independence. This middle class would, in turn, through its demand for consumer goods, stimulate the development of industry. In the meanwhile, their middle-class life-style was to be supported by vast amounts of economic aid from America, which he presumed would keep coming because of the fear of Communism.

American liberals responded to this approach because it was anti-

Communist and nonconfrontational. But the new African countries became increasingly dependent on the foreign aid program, while the aid bureaucracy sought to perpetuate the state of dependency to assure its own survival.

15.

At approximately the same time that Lowenstein was working on Africa Freedom Day, his attention was directed to Spain. Another Humphrey staff member sent a memo on March 6, 1959, to the senator, with a copy to Humphrey aide Ernest Lefever. The memo informed Humphrey that Norman Thomas wanted to arrange a meeting between Juan Manuel Kindelan, a "boy" who was a refugee from Spain and a leader of a student group based in Peru, and some of the senators and congressmen of the Foreign Relations and Foreign Affairs Committees. Thomas wanted it to be an off-the-record discussion of the problem of "anti-Americanism in Spain," and he wanted it to take place by March 13.

Kindelan's uncle, the memo stated, was a former Franco general turned anti-Franco. Thomas and the magazine *Iberica* had sponsored Kindelan in America to publicize his message, which was that the American ambassador in Spain was considered to be "Franco's Charlie McCarthy," and that the situation was much like that in Cuba "until recently." The memo noted that there had been an excellent press conference in New York and that *Iberica* was willing to pay all expenses to bring Kindelan to Washington. The magazine also wanted to hold another press conference in Washington, to be handled by an *Iberica* aide.

Attached was a *New York Times* article dated March 6, 1959, which identified Kindelan as the twenty-six-year-old leader of a student union opposed to Franco. His father was Gen. Alfredo Kindelan, chief of General Franco's air forces during the Spanish Civil War. The younger Kindelan, who lived in Paris, was returning from Lima, where he had attended an international conference. A Socialist, he criticized the Voice of America for being so close to the Franco regime that its broadcasts were integrated with daily Spanish radio propaganda. Because of this, he argued, the United States was identified with the policies of the Spanish government in the mind of the Spanish public. Kindelan stated that the effect was "damaging to the United States irrespective of the broadcast's content." He said that in the six months before he left Spain, he had heard Voice of America three-minute broadcasts "on the regularly scheduled Spanish Government afternoon program of domestic and foreign news." The interview with Kindelan, the *Times* pointed out, was held at the offices of *Iberica*, "a publishing concern at 112 East 19th Street."

The United States Information Service explained that tapes were routinely sent to Spanish radio stations to be used at their discretion and that they did not know how or when the material went on the air. But the matter was considered of sufficient importance to have it called to Humphrey's attention. He scrawled on the memo, "Ernest L—What do you think we should do?—H.H."

On March 10, Ernest Lefever responded to Humphrey:

Since the Foreign Relations Committee rarely takes testimony from a non-American, and since the concerns of this refugee student are under constant consideration by Senator Sparkman, Chairman of the European Affairs Subcommittee, it would seem appropriate to tell Norman Thomas to have this student prepare a carefully documented memorandum for the use of Senator Sparkman's Committee, assuring him that it would be [sic] careful consideration.

If you, as a member of the European Affairs Subcommittee, wish to see this student personally, I will be glad to arrange it. I will also be happy to see him in your place if you so desire.

I believe in the principle which Harlan Cleveland has enunciated, namely, that our government must find ways and means of keeping in contact with the opposition in a country as well as with the government in power. And it may be that we are not accomplishing this purpose sufficiently at the present time in Spain. Many people are aware of this problem, but it is difficult to figure out how to accomplish this important function within the traditional diplomatic structure.

Because of the lateness of time, I suggest that you or I call Norman Thomas rather than write him a letter.

Lefever then sent all the memos and the article along to Lowenstein with a note: "Al—This matter is in your hands. Senator agrees with my memo—Ernie."

The solution to the problem turned out to be Allard Lowenstein. He met with Juan Manuel Kindelan and started a relationship with the non-Communist Spanish underground that lasted until Franco's death. Lowenstein would spend so much time with these groups that for a period there would be demands that he register as a foreign agent. After Franco finally died, Lowenstein wrote in 1976:

By this time I had been attending "meetings" in Spain on and off for some 17 years, ever since the son of the chief of Franco's air force made his way to Hubert Humphrey's office, where I was working at the time, to plead that someone come to see the evils of the government that his father had helped to put in power. That was the beginning of my association with some of Franco's new enemies. It had never occurred to me that the risky politics of opposing a dictatorship would attract the pride and heirs of the realm; wealthy, tough, bright young men who were to display a gallantry that would have been notable at the Round Table. Men like these—Juan Kindelan, Carlos de Zayas, and the others— scions of grandees and dukes and Nationalist generals, with lives of almost guaranteed success ahead of them, impelled by no discernible force but conscience, chose to throw away the most privileged positions in a land of protected privileges to languish at times in jails of peculiar inhumanity. Their sacrifices, whispered across a moribund countryside, reminded a drained people of hope and, in the process, wrenched at families whose loyalties to God and Spain were not prepared for a clash with loyalty to Family itself.

And they provided a remarkable introduction to the continuing involvement that led me back to Madrid all these years later.

Lowenstein's specialty, his profession really, became the untraditional development and maintenance of ties with opposition groups outside of regular diplomacy. It is what he did both in Spain and in Africa, with varying degrees of success. And the seeming chaos of his method would have a structure that only he and a few others would know. But the purpose would always be the same: to cultivate the non-Communist alternative to an existing structure that was bound to fall. And while Lowenstein spoke frequently of the need for change and for justice, it was also his burning anti-Communism that motivated him to act.

The problem in Spain stemmed from the 1953 treaty of cooperation the United States had signed with Franco. After that, anti-Americanism was rampant among the Spanish left. Since it was feared that Franco was creating a power vacuum that the Communists would eventually fill, the United States needed to cultivate an opposition to Franco within Spain that, if it came to power, would not damage European defenses against the Soviet Union and which also appealed to popular Spanish sentiment. As romantic as Lowenstein makes it seem, Juan Kindelan's visit had not been spontaneous. It had been arranged by Norman Thomas, who was concerned with the threat of a Communist takeover in Spain after Franco's death. The Communist party in Spain had been the only political organization to stay fully intact after the civil war. It had gone underground, waiting for its chance to reemerge and take over the country. In a sense, Juan Kindelan was Lowenstein's Michael Scott in Spain. They were both attractive, aristocratic figures and sophisticated anti-Communists. And Norman Thomas, with whom Lowenstein would work closely on numerous issues, was not some figure of America's political fringe, but a distinguished member of the American establishment, one with considerable influence who was treated with respect and even deference by Hubert Humphrey and his staff. He became, along with Eleanor Roosevelt, Frank Graham, and Adlai Stevenson, one of Lowenstein's great heroes in his hierarchy of venerated figures, to which only Robert Kennedy would be added eventually. Hubert Humphrey, in fact, was not included.

On March 26, 1959, Lowenstein's working relationship with Humphrey was changed significantly. Instead of working directly for Humphrey, Lowenstein was to be responsible for a subcommittee on disarmament. Humphrey's memo read:

> You will be assigned to the Subcommittee on Disarmament as of April 1. Your salary will be $6,500. I have spoken to Miss Goetz, who is the Subcommittee staff director and she knows of these arrangements.
>
> Your first responsibility will be to Miss Goetz and the work of the Subcommittee. I am hopeful you will be able to help us with general foreign policy matters. After all, the Subcommittee is part of the Foreign Relations Committee. There will be plenty of work to do, but I want you to follow the general direction of Miss Goetz. She is responsible and I hold her strictly accountable for work performance. So you are on the job with a specific assignment and I know you will find it very interesting.
>
> The work of the Subcommittee is becoming much more important every day, so you have an opportunity to do yeoman service for the cause of peace.
>
> Just in case you are interested as to the relationship between Miss Goetz and Ernest LeFever. Betty is on the Foreign Relations payroll. Ernest LeFever works for me personally. However there is a good cooperative friendly relationship and Betty works with Ernest and there will be no problem at all as long as you recognize that your first responsibility is to Betty, who in turn takes her orders from me.
>
> Secondly, if you have any work with Ernest you can clear it with Betty. She will be cooperative and will have her general line of instructions from me.

The shifting nature of Lowenstein's responsibilities for Humphrey has caused former Governor of North Carolina Terry Sanford to question whether Lowenstein was ever actually on Humphrey's staff. Lowenstein's file at North Carolina State, where he taught in the sixties, lists 1959 as the only year during which he was employed by Humphrey; he did, however, indicate elsewhere that his employment began in 1958. As in other instances, Lowenstein's formal appointment simply provided pay for what he was already doing, a circumstance which was largely explained by the arcane and often incongruous world of anti-Communism, where Humphrey's constituencies mixed their ideological concerns with their special interests.

Humphrey was invited to a dinner in Washington on April 8 given by the Council against Communist Aggression, a political arm of the Upholsterers International Union, whose director of Civic, Education and Governmental Affairs was a verbose ideologue named Arthur McDowell. McDowell also headed the Council against Communist Aggression.

One of the purposes of this particular dinner was to win over important black African countries. A contingent of West African diplomats attended, spending most of the evening with Lowenstein, who also ran into his friend Philip Willkie, an Indiana state legislator and son of the late Wendell Willkie, the Republican candidate for president against Roosevelt in 1940. Also in attendance was James Roosevelt, son of the late Democratic president. Lowenstein wrote to Willkie on April 23, 1959: "Dear Philip: It was an unexpected treat to see you at the Dinner Versus Communist Aggression. I am sorry you missed out on the West Africans, who turned out to include in their midst the new Ambassador from Guinea, a most delightful fellow."

McDowell had pressed his pet project at the dinner, "the Orlando Plan," to establish a Freedom Commission and a Free World Academy to teach the dangers of "the Communist conspiracy, ruthlessly and inflexibly set upon organizing the whole world on a slave basis."

At the United States Information Agency, however, Conger Reynolds pointed out that ideological training programs were already under way at numerous American universities such as Columbia, Georgetown, Johns Hopkins, Syracuse, and others. He was correct. A large-scale, subtle anti-Communist effort was in process, involving not only universities but other private institutions. What McDowell wanted done on a giant public scale was the formalization of what was already happening. In Africa, for example, to combat the growing influence of the Communists (the South African Communist party was an old and established institution with an increasing appeal to blacks), the United States was supporting a variety of anti-Communist organizations through private groups. The AFL-CIO was backing the ICFTU (the International Confederation of Free Trade Unions) and such unions as the Kenya Federation of Labor, headed by Tom Mboya, which rejected Marxist-Leninism. Missionaries involved included Methodists who were actually training Africans to resist "Communist brainwashing." And Lowenstein had functioned as a kind of one-man anti-Communist crash course during his visit with the African students at Fort Hare in South Africa.

Meanwhile, Tom Mboya had explained to the American union leaders that South Africa was a major stumbling block to American interests in Africa. It became an established dogma of the anti-Communist left that apartheid had to be overturned rapidly, or else the Soviet Union would capitalize on the issue and win over the newly independent African countries, such as those represented at McDowell's dinner. A strategy for South Africa had to be developed that forced the whites to give up their policy of racial segregation and the exclusion of blacks from political power.

The emergence of the Pan-Africanist Congress in South Africa coincided with all of these political and economic objectives. A new organization of blacks, it was more militant that the old African National Congress, from which it splintered away. It was challenging the restrictive "passbook" laws imposed on South African blacks, a source of humiliation that the South African Communist party was using as a major issue and which both it and the African National Congress had jointly challenged in the past. And the Pan-Africanist Congress was also planning a drive to form new unions for black workers in South Africa to improve working conditions and to appeal to the rising nationalist spirit among all black people in a country that denied them the rights of citizenship.

The issue of South West Africa was no less significant. It was a relic of the kind of colonialism Mboya counseled America to oppose if it was to gain the support of independent black Africa. By this time, Lowenstein had decided to make the trip to South West Africa, for which Humphrey granted him a leave of absence. Lowenstein quotes Michael Scott as saying to him: "But we would never want anyone to go whose integrity and objective judgment were the least in doubt. How would such a trip help? It's the facts we're after, you know."

After a recruitment process that Emory Bundy describes as "largely fiction," Lowenstein persuaded Bundy, who was married and had a child, to leave his job in Seattle and join the expedition to South West Africa. Lowenstein also convinced Sherman Bull, a Yale graduate and a medical student at Columbia P & S to join them. Bundy and Bull each had to put up $2,500, while Lowenstein raised the balance of the funds to finance the trip.

Africa was not a subject of great interest in the United States in the fifties. Only a handful of universities offered courses on it, and apart from Gwendolyn Carter, who did research on Africa under the auspices of the Rockefeller Foundation, academic interest was minimal. This would change dramatically and swiftly as America, the Soviet Union, and China intensified their competition for the minds of the African leaders and the power to control the vast continent's wealth.

But in 1959, in spite of its importance, South West Africa was particularly obscure. There was virtually no knowledge about it and the problems of those who lived there who wanted freedom from South African rule.

Theo-Ben Gurirab, the chief representative of the SWAPO (South West Africa Peoples' Organization) Permanent Observer Mission to the United Nations, says that Lowenstein's name became familiar "in the ranks of the Namibian freedom fighters" because "he was among the first people to write a book about Namibia, cast in a modern context, about the struggle of the Namibian people for freedom."

According to the Rev. Donald Harrington, the chairman of the executive board of the American Committee on Africa, Lowenstein sought the help of the committee to get to South West Africa, and spent a considerable amount of time at its offices. George Houser acknowledges that he did advise Lowenstein on people he should contact in London on the way, but says that no financial assistance was provided by ACOA. The committee, however, did important coordinating work for Lowenstein, and its interest in the expedition was considerable.

Michael Scott was no longer available for consultations, having gone off on a mission to the Sahara. But available was Jariretundu Fanuel Kozonguizi, the angry Herero student from South West Africa Lowenstein had met on his trip to South Africa the year before and with whom he had debated long into the night at Fort Hare. Kozonguizi now based himself in London with Africa Bureau, having founded with other Herero intellectuals and students the South West African Union (SWANO) as a rival to SWAPO's forerunner, the Ovamboland People's Organization (OPO).

Lowenstein, Bundy, and Bull gathered as much information as they could through consultations with Kozonguizi and Mburumba Kerina, whose wife, Jane, was American. The most valuable person Lowenstein could talk to, they told him, was Hosea Kutako, the paramount chief of the Herero people. Almost ninety years old, he had long opposed the policies of South Africa in the territory. But he remained a conservative tribal leader. Lowenstein wrote: "The Kerinas are a remarkable couple who for a number of years had borne the brunt of the year-round effort to keep the issue of South West Africa before the world."

Kerina, like Kozonguizi, turned out to be an enigmatic figure. A cofounder of SWAPO and Lincoln University graduate, he had at one time been accused of being a "police informer," became chairman of SWAPO, later was expelled from it, worked for the Liberian Mission to the U.N., and then for the Peace Corps in Bechuanaland (later called Botswana after independence), and became involved in organizing a series of political parties in South West Africa. In 1976 a special SWAPO commission was to identify him (and Kozonguizi) as a participant in a conspiracy with the South African government and several Western powers to undermine SWAPO's armed struggle and to help support the South African-backed Turnhalle Conference, which Theo-Ben Gurirab of SWAPO says was established so South Africa could run Namibia "like a puppet."

Whether Allard Lowenstein was aware of it or not, the three people most significant in mobilizing him for his trip to South West Africa, Michael Scott, Kerina, and Kozonguizi, all had connections of a dubious nature. Scott's Africa Bureau was a conduit for CIA funds, Kozonguizi turned out to be in the employ of the South African government, and Kerina was working for the Americans. What all of them had in common was a desire to defeat the radical elements of what was to become SWAPO. Scott was religious and idealistic, but his CIA-supported Africa Bureau was seeking to promote non-Communist alternatives in South West Africa, an objective with which the CIA and he agreed. Hated and banned by the white racist South African government and with restrictions placed on his U.S. visa, Scott had considerable credibility with African liberation movements. Kozonguizi may well have been authentic when he started out, but the likelihood is that when Lowenstein met him at Fort Hare, he was a plant. And Kerina, from the beginning, was a dubious opportunist playing all sides for his own personal gain.

Emory Bundy relates that "during the course of the trip, Al was concerned about Communism and talked about it. We had conversations with the liberal, democratic opposition in South Africa and this was an element of the discussions." Lowenstein stressed to Bundy that he had a "deep philosophical abhorrence of the regime in South Africa" but that the Americans did little to help the opposition, while the Communists, whom he also abhorred, were giving assistance. Bundy insists that Lowenstein was tolerant of those struggling against the regime no matter where they sought help, even if they looked to the Soviet Union when the West would not act. "His preference," Bundy argues, "was for the peaceful solution. He admired Oliver Tambo. And we saw Luthuli on the trip." Tambo was the deputy president of the African National Congress, and Albert Luthuli, a chief who won the Nobel Peace Prize and served as president of the African National Congress, was made honorary president of the National Union of South African Students.

In contact with black South Africans who advocated nonviolence, Lowenstein was also in touch with white South African liberals, many of whom were Jewish. In Cape Town, he, Bundy, and Bull stayed with Neville Rubin, president of the National Union of South African Students. In Johannesburg, they stayed with Helen Suzman. Both are part of what Bundy terms the "nonviolent democratic opposition."

"A nonracial movement seemed less and less practical," Bundy concludes. "Al was trying to keep the groups which opposed the regime, but had divergent interests, in touch with each other." He describes Lowenstein's work as a "two-front set of discussions": "How do you keep this on a democratic course and cope with the Communists, and also deal with opposing the regime?" While Lowenstein allegedly had made the trip to promote the issue of South West Africa before the United Nations, his participation in the racial politics of South Africa, with his strong anti-Communist predilections, diverged from this original intent. But he did gain credibility among the white liberals who assisted him.

Lowenstein also spoke to Afrikaner Nationalists. At one university where he spoke, he told them:

You are quite right that I had been misled about what I would find in South Africa. I came expecting to find a group of Nazis pursuing such mad racial policies that they were going to be pushed into the sea, and I expected to be glad that they were going to be pushed into the sea. Instead, I have found some of the most generous and wonderful people I have ever met. I have felt more at home with you than at any other place outside my own country; this has become, in some magic way, my country too. These are very different things from what I had expected— this deep affection, this feeling of somehow being part of your country. And feeling these things, I cannot be glad that you are pursuing such mad racial policies that you are going to be pushed into the sea, and that no one will help you then because you will have brought it all on yourselves.

Lowenstein had been invited to give a greeting to the annual congress in Johannesburg of the National Union of South African Students (NUSAS), the federation of college students of the English-speaking universities open to students of all races. He went alone because he had dispatched Bundy and Bull to obtain a Volkswagen for the excursion into South West Africa. Unable to afford a Land Rover, Lowenstein's first choice, he settled for this alternative.

The congress of some 300 delegates elected to represent 16,000 black, white, and colored (mixed race) was tumultuous. Lowenstein spoke. "There may be moments when you feel alone and isolated, but it is your tormentors, not yourselves, who are alone and isolated. Your cause is the cause of men of good will everywhere, and your behavior is their inspiration."

Throughout the congress, students repeatedly expressed their outrage over government harassment of NUSAS members. Passports had been withdrawn or denied, offices raided, mail opened, and documents confiscated by the police because the government regarded the nonracialism of the organization as subversive. This differed only in degree from what the FBI had done to the National Student Assoca-tion when it monitored its activities and placed informers at its con-gresses. There was even a report of a statement by the minister of education that the government had planted spies at the universities in England, where many South African students were enrolled. This, combined with the knowledge that such spies existed among the stu-dents in South Africa itself, created an environment of paranoia and anger.

The *cause célèbre* of the NUSAS congress was Hans Beukes, a "Cape colored" student from Rehoboth, South West Africa, who had received a scholarship to study in Norway and had been given a pass-port which was subsequently revoked "in the best interests of the state." South Africa's reversal was attributed to their desire to intimi-date NUSAS. Another reason for it, Lowenstein wrote, was that Beukes had been found with a book by Adlai Stevenson, which the government considered "Communist." Had he been permitted to leave, Beukes would have been only the second nonwhite (Kerina being the other) from South West Africa to get out of the country to study abroad.

Because of the Beukes affair, students who had been critical of the NUSAS, having been influenced by charges made against it by the government, were now supporting it. Parliament was picketed and a "Hans Beukes Fund" was established, receiving a steady flow of con-tributions. And according to Emory Bundy, "Al wanted to look up Beukes when he was denied a passport. Under the original mandate, South Africa was to contribute to the education of all South West Af-ricans. This was an example of South Africa's not carrying out its man-date."

Lowenstein wanted Beukes to register a protest, as an individual, to the United Nations by sending a cable. But he wrote that he found the tall, unhappy man unresponsive. "He had a wonderful opportu-nity to study in Norway," Bundy explains, "and he was cut off." Bundy insists that "Hans Beukes was conservative. It had been impressed on him by his family. His opportunity for higher education required him to be entirely free from politics. He had not occupied himself with any politics because it was risky for him if he wanted to continue his edu-cation." Beukes had not been enthusiastic about the idea of sending the cable because he believed it would jeopardize whatever chances he had not only of getting to Norway, but of any further education.

But then Beukes addressed NUSAS himself, electrifying the audi-ence with his simplicity as he spoke about his life in South West Af-rica. Beukes then approached Lowenstein and told him he wanted Lowenstein's help in getting out of the country. Lowenstein later wrote that Beukes explained to him that it would be better if he appeared before the U.N. to testify about conditions in his country than if he sent a cable, but Emory Bundy contradicts this. "Al didn't know why they should do this," he states. "Hans had no well-defined politics or objective. This was only for his personal pursuit." But he adds: "Al found Hans had a well-formulated knowledge about South West Africa and Hans impressed him with his tenacity. Al became impressed with him."

Sources report that while Lowenstein was in Johannesburg he was contacted by the CIA and asked to perform a mission which must have been highly appealing to his romantic side, while at the same time allowing him to strike what he felt was a telling blow against the apartheid government of South Africa. The mission was to smuggle Hans Beukes out of the country.

Just who it was who recruited Lowenstein for this assignment remains a matter of conjecture, although it is known that Frank Carlucci, later deputy director of the CIA, ambassador to Portugal during the Portuguese revolution, and eventually a close friend of Lowenstein's, was stationed in the American consulate in Johannesburg as a Foreign Service officer at the time of Lowenstein's visits in 1958 and 1959. He would become a legend for his daring exploits in Africa. Carlucci himself has denied having been a CIA agent, although he concedes that he and Lowenstein might have met in Johannesburg in 1959. In any event, for Lowenstein the assignment, which he readily accepted, turned into a smuggling caper that was not without its humorous overtones.

Lowenstein was clearly on his own, along with Bundy and Bull, when it came to getting Beukes out of South Africa. They would have to smuggle this large person out of South Africa in a tiny Volkswagen. A detour was planned, through difficult terrain, to get Beukes to the British Protectorate of Bechuanaland, the vast, sandy territory between South Africa and South West Africa. From there, he would be free to leave.

The Beukes story had filled the papers for days, making the escape all the more dangerous. Money had to be raised abroad for the trip to New York and there was no guarantee that Beukes would be able to make it out of Bechuanaland even if they got him there. Lowenstein insisted that Beukes's visa problem was solved when he came up with the news that, by treaty, access was assured to New York for those with official business at the United Nations. How Lowenstein acquired his knowledge of this obscure point of international law is speculation; the information might have been provided by the CIA, or he might have picked it up from a course in international law at Yale, on one of those rare occasions when Lowenstein was in New Haven. But Lowenstein was dramatizing. The visa was in hand, but still they had no knowledge of how the British would react to Beukes and what he intended to do.

As they drove in the Volkswagen with the very recognizable Beukes, his large frame was bent over in the small car, clearly visible through the window. Along the route, several policemen spun their heads around at the sight of the vehicle containing three white men and a nonwhite. But their car was not stopped. The youthful travelers, with their confidence carrying them into the countryside, pressed on over the bumpy African terrain.

Waiting at the border while Bull struggled to repair the car, which had broken down, they decided as soon as they saw some headlights coming at them that Beukes would have to be less visible. He would have to be jammed into the tiny space between the rear seat and the rear window. They quickly removed a laundry bag full of documents and assorted objects, and in its place, stuffed the six-foot Beukes. As the headlights came closer and closer, Bull finally diagnosed the problem as a snapped accelerator cable. He fixed it in a few moments and they sped across the border, just as the other vehicle, its lights bearing down, pulled to a halt on the other side of the road.

Once inside Bechuanaland, they proceeded to the home of Lowenstein's friend, Oxford-educated Seretse Khama, who was serving at the time as a cabinet member of the government of what would become Botswana. There they discussed Hans Beukes's status and how he would get to New York. Letters were sent off to various people in New York and London, explaining Beukes's requirements. Lowenstein wrote that they were afraid to use the telephone or telegraph because they were run by a white South African.

Why did the CIA want Beukes out of the country and in Norway? Or, for that matter, testifying before the United Nations? The sources that reveal Beukes was smuggled out for the CIA describe Beukes as being "opposed to SWAPO." While at the time Beukes's antigovernment credentials may have appeared impeccable, later events have cast doubt on his real commitment to the cause of freeing South West Africa from apartheid domination. Some of his former associates point out that Beukes, who settled in Norway after marrying a Norwegian woman, was expelled from SWAPO in 1976 and charge that he was later involved in a conspiracy inspired by the South African government "to undermine SWAPO's armed struggle and leadership." Lowenstein himself would laugh sarcastically when referring to Beukes in the seventies as a "freedom fighter." The picture of Beukes that emerges in retrospect is of a conservative "Cape colored" from a poor but prominent family in Rehoboth where his grandfather was on the Rehoboth Council, who pursued his personal ambition to study in Norway and consequently clashed with the South African government's restrictive policies. It never turned him into a political firebrand. Having such a person testify at the United Nations along with an American who smuggled him out would be a tremendous plus for America in the international community, demonstrating that, contrary to Communist claims, Americans *did* care and that South West Africa's opposition to South Africa was not revolutionary. It was, in a nutshell, Lowenstein's own view of how the antiapartheid position could best be served without recourse to violence and with "democratic" means.

It is difficult to discern how much of what Lowenstein later wrote in *Brutal Mandate* was fact or fiction, concerning the degree of danger they were actually in. Although Bundy insists that the South African police were a constant threat and that their personal belongings were taken, there is considerable exaggeration. Hilarious passages describe how Beukes was concealed in a hotel room with Sherman Bull, while Lowenstein protested as his own room was searched. "You'll get a hell of a lot of Americans to stay here when we're through telling about this," he shouted. He also recounts how they drove a bit in the morning and deposited Hans Beukes alone on the road, leaving him on his own to make contact with the British authorities. But Beukes himself states that he remained the guest of Seretse Khama while Lowenstein was back in New York, "parading my need of aid to get out of Botswana." With the assistance of Lowenstein's friend, Curtis Gans, who was a vice-president of the National Student Association, $750 was collected at the annual NSA congress that summer for Beukes's trip to New York. Beukes also observes that the NSA's "foreign secretary at the time expressed her suspicions that he was parading my need of aid to get out of Botswana as a stalking-horse to recoup his own outlays. He was fairly broke, I had the feeling."

Whether Beukes was left in the home of Khama or on the road, the three Americans did proceed with the original objective of the trip: the gathering of testimony in South West Africa to present at the United Nations on the abuses of South Africa in the exercise of its mandate. They drove back to Johannesburg to collect their belongings, load and repair the car, make a few contacts and set off for South West Africa.

A series of mishaps discouraged them. Their car was broken into and all their clothes stolen, and so were carbon copies of letters asking for financial assistance. The Americans concluded that their phone had been tapped and that it all had been the work of the Special Branch, the political arm of the South African police. But Sherman Bull insisted, "Let's get on with it!" and Lowenstein, Bundy, and Bull trekked into South West Africa to record the facts that they would report to the United Nations.

They visited tribal chiefs, taped the conversations, and took extensive notes. They went to churches and slept in the homes of people who could have been punished severely for testifying to them. The conditions were arduous. Bull's diary reads at one point: "Desolate drive—thick dust—we are covered, almost buried, coughing and blowing—we go into drifts. Few signs of life."

Most of the meetings with Africans were held at night, when there were fewer police around. And everywhere they went, they heard the same story: oppression, poverty, little or no education, tyrannical rule by the white man. There were statements by chiefs, clergymen, and unknown farmers. One said, "The dogs of white men live ten times better than I do."

The last person to be interviewed was Chief Hosea Kutako of the Herero tribe. Lowenstein wrote of him:

> It is Chief Kutako who has set much of the tone of the African opposition since World War II. He is a devout Christian, a disciple of nonviolence who once studied for the ministry; and he has insisted that change must come through action by the United Nations. If Hosea Kutako's efforts do not produce results, it is unlikely that his successors will wish, much less be able to restrain Africans indefinitely from less gentle tactics in the seeking of freedom.

But Lowenstein's advocacy of nonviolence was not an indication of total passivity on his part. Emory Bundy recalls that Lowenstein had strong opinions about what measures should be adopted to force South Africa's hand. "In 1959, I was completely naive about African affairs," he relates, "and didn't have the kind of sophistication Al had. He believed American interests should boycott South Africa. American companies with mining interests in South Africa were, in his opinion, aiding and abetting apartheid. He rejected the argument that the investments helped the blacks. He was searching for the way to minimize violence and have a multiracial society. He advocated as total a boycott as possible—if not governmental, then private."

The government's attitude to him was one of total hostility. He, Bundy, and Bull were in serious danger when they were followed by a police car from Kutako's. They jumped from the truck and fell to the ground until the searchers, speaking in Afrikaans, were gone. Picked up and transported to Windhoek, they stayed at the home of a sympathetic white and spirited most of their notes, tapes, and photographs out of the country.

Lowenstein flew alone to Johannesburg. Of the South African city, he wrote:

> There are no other cities like Johannesburg; there should be no others. One such place is too many. Yet what magic there is in this strange, teeming, undigested mixture of El Dorado and the

Black Hole, of Wall Street in the '20s and Berlin in the '30s, this bush village exploded by gold and diamonds in less years than a man's life into bottomless slums and endless suburbs and all the pulsating racket of the metropolis between; exploded until it has become, without design or conscious choice, Mecca to black men seeking work and Westchester County to white women seeking play, and how much more to how many others; and to me, as no foreign place before or since, home.

On the day of the flight, Lowenstein was joined by Bundy, who had just come in from Windhoek. When the BOAC hostess called their flight, three uniformed men surrounded Bundy, and Lowenstein was escorted by several others. The police began rummaging through their baggage piece by piece, even though they had been passed through customs. Fearing that they were being delayed by the police so they would miss the plane, Lowenstein called the hostess. When the police suddenly disappeared, they rushed to the aircraft and boarded. But Bull had not yet arrived. He was waiting for his contact person for his ticket. The plane was to leave at 12:45 and it was already 12:17. "I'm sunk," he wrote in his diary. Then he stuffed notes and film into his shoes and rolled-up pairs of socks, crumpled his diary into his flashlight and went through customs. "I stride up terrified but look enthusiastic," he wrote later in his diary, "like a touring white hunter. They say I'm late for the plane and never ask a question. Now all I need is a ticket!" Twelve minutes before departure, the contact with the ticket arrived. Bull dashed through the gate to the ramp where he was greeted by a "pack of cops." But Bull, "fully expecting to be pinched," flew past them onto the plane and collapsed into an empty seat.

Bull left them to climb Mt. Kilimanjaro, and Lowenstein and Bundy stayed in Nairobi to visit Tom Mboya and then flew to Addis Ababa, where Lowenstein had some appointments the nature of which was not disclosed. "Al must have seen someone important because they held the flight for us for over an hour," Bundy recalls. From Addis Ababa, they flew to Vienna to attend the Communist-backed Vienna Youth Festival, which they entered with the forged documents Bundy believed had been provided by the CIA. It was here that Lowenstein debated with the American Communist who was part of the United States delegation and attended the vast Soviet cultural display. Soviet-backed world revolution seemed to him inevitable.

A confidential priority memorandum from the American embassy in Madrid to the State Department dated August 17, 1962, discloses that Lowenstein turned up in Spain in the summer of 1959 after the African trip. He went to the embassy accompanied by anti-Communist oppositionist Carlos Zayas, described in the memorandum as an

"opposition figure of some prominence who was at that time a Socialist, but who subsequently joined the more radical Frente de Libera-
cion Popular (FLP)." In 1962, when Lowenstein returned to Spain,
and again turned up at the embassy, he explained to embassy personnel that he had been working for Senator Humphrey in the summer
of 1959, "in which capacity he had gone to Africa and then to Spain."

On his return to the U.S., Lowenstein was busily engaged in pub-
licizing the findings of his trip to South Africa and South West Africa.
George Houser, Michael Scott, and Dr. Homer Jack, the new associate executive director of the American Committee on Africa, helped
organize a press conference on September 8 at the committee's new
offices at 801 Second Avenue in New York.

Developments at the United Nations following the press conference indicated a significant and dramatic shift in American policy with
regard to Africa. And the smuggling out of Hans Beukes contributed
to the effectiveness of this United States diplomacy in the world body.
With the money raised by the National Student Association to pay for
his plane ticket, Beukes arrived in time to testify before the Fourth
Committee of the General Assembly on Trusteeships on the plight of
the "colored" people in South West Africa. To have the American students put up the money on the spot for him was a tremendous propaganda coup because it was spontaneous, sincere, and independent.

The events at the Fourth Committee of the General Assembly on
Trusteeships, before which Lowenstein, Bundy, Bull, and Beukes testified, revealed the new policy. Donald Grant, a staff correspondent
of the *St. Louis Post-Dispatch* (whom Hans Beukes describes as "a
Republican who had closely followed the African scene up to then and
was posted at the U.N."), reporting from the United Nations on October 28, 1959, wrote that "United States policy on Africa is moving
to a perceptible degree away from a cautious desire to please the
Union of South Africa and the colonial powers who are our European
allies. It is moving toward positive support for the emerging peoples
of the African continent."

Grant was enthusiastic about the United States attempt to get an
International Court of Justice, or World Court, decision on the case of
South West Africa. The 1950 decision that South West Africa had international status which South Africa could not alter, and that the old
League of Nations mandate was still in force, had been advisory. Now
America was backing an effort in the General Assembly in 1959 to
adopt a resolution calling the attention of the members of the United
Nations to the compulsory jurisdiction of the World Court, under Ar-
ticle 37 of its charter, in any dispute with South Africa concerning its
interpretation of its mandate over South West Africa. This was because, as Lowenstein later wrote, under Article 7 of the Mandate
Treaty, any country that was a member of the League of Nations could

require a state that had a mandate over a territory to "defend its stewardship before the court." It was believed that South Africa was in
contempt of the 1950 ruling prohibiting any change in South West
Africa's international status because it was illegally applying its apartheid policies to the territory over which it held a League of Nations
mandate. The General Assembly resolution was a procedural requirement, which had to be fulfilled before an appropriate nation or group
of nations could bring the action before the World Court to hold South
Africa in contempt. It was Michael Scott who had first raised the possibility of using this approach, and Lowenstein followed up by making
such a resolution a primary objective of the appearances before the
Fourth Committee.

Before Lowenstein presented his "evidence" to the Fourth Committee, Boston patrician Mason Sears, the chief American delegate to
the Trusteeship Committee, had made a speech against racial oppression, but without specifics concerning American policy. He had been
arguing for years within the State Department that America needed
to take a far more positive position on Africa. And just as Lowenstein
and his associates were preparing to make their appearances, American delegates began working closely with African diplomats at the
United Nations on the South West African question, particularly with
those representing Ghana, Liberia, and Tunisia. Ambassador Angie
Brooks of Liberia, a graduate of Shaw University, a black institution in
Raleigh, North Carolina, took the most important role in pressing for
the resolution. This brought her close to Lowenstein, and the two
became excellent friends. Later, while he was teaching at North Carolina State in Raleigh in 1963, Lowenstein joined with her in "integrating" several restaurants in Raleigh.

The strategy was to pass the resolution after all the evidence gathered on the mission to South West Africa had been submitted and the
Americans and Beukes had testified. Then, some African countries
friendly to the United States (they turned out to be Liberia and Ethiopia, the only black African countries to be members of the old League
of Nations) would go to the World Court for the ruling. Armed with
such a ruling, they planned to return to the United Nations General
Assembly and demand that South West Africa be transferred from the
Union of South Africa and placed directly under the rule of the United
Nations in preparation for eventual independence. And no evidence
proved to be more important in this process than the testimony of
Chief Hosea Kutako.

It was the most intelligent way of bypassing the radical elements
in what became SWAPO, whose rush to independence threatened to
follow an agenda that included policy elements sympathetic to the
Soviet Union. With the vast mineral wealth of the territory at stake,
and the threat of armed struggle imminent, this approach represented

the enlightened self-interest of the United States. Britain, still hoping to keep the Union of South Africa in the Commonwealth, took a placatory attitude toward South Africa's intransigent position on South West Africa. The British hopes were ultimately dashed, though, when the Union of South Africa pulled out of the Commonwealth and became the Republic of South Africa.

Britain marshaled all of its resources in the United Nations to try to defeat the American initiative. Surprisingly, Krishna Menon, the Indian defense minister, worked behind the scenes to aid Britain in this effort, although taking a public position against "white domination." The explanation offered was that India feared Chinese aggression and wanted to be assured of the backing of the entire British Commonwealth, of which it was a member along with South Africa. But there were also wealthy Indians functioning in South Africa in spite of its racial policies, and Menon was unquestionably taking this into consideration.

The Soviet position was strangely ambiguous, most probably because it wanted China's designs on India contained. Donald Grant wrote: "Finally, American support of African aspirations in the South West Africa case seems doubly attractive to United States diplomacy here because the Soviet Russian position is ambiguous to say the least. Though often talking loudly in behalf of African rights, Russia opposes use of the World Court. In the present case, the Soviet Union is at least tacitly on the side of British 'imperialism' in Africa."

But there was more to it than that. If the jurisdiction of the World Court could be successfully invoked against South Africa with regard to South West Africa, it could be invoked against the Soviet Union too, with regard to Latvia, Lithuania, and Estonia, which it had gobbled up without legal justification. In 1959, public international law was on the side of the United States, even if the American right failed to perceive it.

When the South African Foreign Minister Eric Louw denounced the Americans who had prepared the evidence for making false statements on their visa applications, saying they were "discredited" people in their own country and part of a sinister international network of "spies and subversives," an American congressman then serving as a temporary ambassador to the Fourth Committee told Lowenstein that the United States would have to abstain when the vote on whether to permit them to testify came up. The abstention was necessary, he said, in order not to jeopardize Americans who needed visas to travel to South Africa. But Lowenstein read aloud statements from Eleanor Roosevelt, Adlai Stevenson, Hubert Humphrey, and Frank Graham expressing respect for his integrity and pride in his enterprise on behalf of an oppressed people. Hans Beukes remembers: "The African, Asian, and Latin American delegates, on their part, responded with much enthusiasm—and in the face of all this it seemed clear to us that the U.S. delegation didn't have much choice but to vote for the application."

With Ambassador Sears and Senator Wayne Morse supporting them in the Fourth Committee, Lowenstein, Bundy, Bull, Hans Beukes, and Kozonguizi, the five new petitioners, were all permitted to appear, as well as Michael Scott and Mburumba Kerina. Six additional petitioners who had been approved were unable to appear in person, prevented by their inability to pay for the trip to New York. Beukes received particularly enthusiastic support from Mason Sears, as Beukes explains:

I had personal occasion to find out that the U.S. representative in the Fourth Committee, Mason Sears, was in fact something of a maverick, as far as the U.S. policies on Africa and on Southern Africa in particular were concerned. My visa had run out and the South Africans were using this fact to put pressure on the Americans to have my movements in the U.S. curtailed. Al suggested that I go to Washington, to the offices of Senator John Kennedy and Vice-President Nixon to speak to friends he had there. It was Senator Kennedy's man who helped me most, calling various offices in the labyrinth with the magic phrase, "Senator Kennedy is interested in this." I had an indefinite extension to my visa in a day. The thought occurred to me to pay a visit to Ambassador Sears, to whom I had in fact taken a liking, to ask him who I should see in Washington. "Oh, it's a good thing you're going there," he burst out when I entered his office. "You give them hell, tell them what it is like to live under the South Africans. Just this morning, I had to make forty calls down to Washington to get support for the vote I cast last night."

Sears was referring to his support for the resolution on the compulsory jurisdiction of the World Court over the South African mandate in South West Africa. And prior to that vote, Beukes had what he calls "a several weeks' object lesson in lobbying, under the direction of Al," during which Lowenstein became furious with Beukes when he failed to speak to two black congressmen whom he had been told to get in touch with. Lowenstein himself spoke at numerous student forums, sometimes with Beukes present. Ruth Hagy Brod, Lowenstein's friend from the College Press Conference, arranged to have them both appear together on *Face the Nation*, a Sunday noontime nationwide TV show. They also addressed the Overseas Press Club in New York, and on October 30, they appeared at a reception honoring "the Rev. Michael Scott and several petitioners from South West Africa to the United Nations," which was jointly sponsored by the American Committee on Africa and the International League for the Rights of Man, and which was held at the home of Mr. and Mrs. Walter Frank (Adelaide Schulkind).

On October 13, the chairman of the Fourth Committee, the Honorable N. Pilar of Indonesia, invited the petitioners to take seats at tables in the center of the great hall where the Fourth Committee met. Lowenstein observed, "All at once History was not somewhere else."

Kerina listed South Africa's violations of legal obligations, and Kozonguizi presented a detailed statement about the daily life of the nonwhites, while Hans Beukes stressed his personal story as an example of the position of the colored population of South West Africa. Eric Louw had gone to great lengths to vilify him, quoting what were purported to be accurate statements in newspaper articles by Beukes's friends and family repudiating him. Beukes rebutted the charges eloquently by reading letters from the same people who were supposed to have been quoted.

Emory Bundy and Sherman Bull made short, moving appeals, setting out what they found in South West Africa. Bull, speaking as a medical student, pointed out that hospital wards for nonwhites were filthy and overcrowded while the facilities for whites were "resplendent." Lowenstein was the last of the three to testify. After denouncing South Africa at great length, he argued that it was unfit to

> continue as the Trustee for the conscience of civilization. . . . It is an ironic challenge and opportunity that the one government in the world based on racial discrimination should also be the one government in defiance of the United Nations, and of opinions of the International Court, about its responsibilities in an international territory. . . . We urge that steps be taken this year to carry the problem of the status of South West Africa to the International Court of Justice for determination under its compulsory jurisdiction. . . . In the troubled scales of the human travail, few situations have required less action to produce hope for results.

In support of their own testimony, Lowenstein, Bundy, and Bull then introduced the tape recordings they had made of African chiefs, Christian ministers, and others. The one that received the most publicity was the recording of Hosea Kutako, who told how the Germans first came to the territory and "plundered everything." His country, he stressed, had been under the rule of African people for a long time before the Germans had conquered it. Kutako reminded the U.N. that the African tribes had not accepted the German conquest, "but rose and fought; even without guns or anything, and we want to impress upon the world that we did not just give this land as a present to the Germans." In actuality, it had been even worse. Africans starved to death and resembled the Jews in the concentration camps after World War II.

Donald Grant wrote for the *St. Louis Post-Dispatch* on October 30: "The United States has chosen the South West Africa issue as the basis for a major change in its Africa policy. American diplomats, quietly but firmly, are supporting measures proposed in the Trusteeship Committee on the South West Africa issue by the independent African nations. So great is the influence of the United States that what might seem a small change in policy on a minor issue has resulted in a profound shift in the alignment of powers and people."

In his first policy address, Mason Sears, head of the American delegation, had called for a revival in some form of the League of Nations Mandate for South Africa. This would have meant keeping South African control over the territory, but with some mode of international supervision.

India introduced the Commonwealth resolution calling for further negotiations between South Africa and the United Nations. Then the African-backed resolution to use the World Court was offered, guided by Liberian Ambassador Angie Brooks. "At a critical moment in the debate," Donald Grant wrote, "Sears consulted two Africans who recently escaped from South West Africa, and aligned American policy to their wishes and judgment. It was this action perhaps more than any other that convinced African opinion, as represented here, of American sincerity and goodwill. . . . The two Africans—Fanuel Kozonguizi and Hans Beukes—were consulted at that point. Neither had any faith in a change of South African policy, and consequently did not believe the people of South West Africa could be benefited by an attempt to revive the League Mandate. Both wanted emphasis on World Court action—which might lead to taking the Territory from South African control altogether." When the vote on the African-supported resolution was postponed, America joined the Africans in protest.

The debate lasted three weeks, with Sears working closely with Angie Brooks of Liberia, Quaison Sackey of Ghana, Caba Sory of Guinea, and Tesfaye Gebre-Egzy of Ethiopia. To see the Soviets allied with the British, whose representative, Sir Andrew Cohen, the former British governor of Uganda, was pushing what Grant called "a modified 'empire' line—hoping to keep the Union in the Commonwealth"—was a reminder to the Africans that America had been the first antiimperialist country which had thrown the British out by force. America appeared to be acting on principle while the Soviet Union was playing power politics. Grant gleefully identified Cohen, Krishna Menon, and the Soviet Union as an anti-African lobby. Pulling out all the stops, he described how Sears was relying on the advice of two young Africans, Beukes and Kozonguizi. Finally at Sears's urging, the resolution calling for the compulsory jurisdiction of the World Court passed, with the Soviet Union supporting the American initiative. Lowenstein wrote: "It was nice that the United States ultimately voted for the South West African resolution in the Fourteenth Session."

The United States moved further on its new policy. The old ambassador to South Africa, Henry Byroade, who had excluded Africans from contacts with the embassy and concentrated on keeping good relations with the white racist government in Pretoria, was replaced. South Africa replaced the fanatic foreign secretary E. H. Louw in the United Nations with a polite and soft-spoken diplomat named B. G. Fourie, and rumors spread that it was considering a change in its racial policies.

But far more important was the position into which the United States had forced the Soviet Union as a supporter of an American policy. The headlines of the *St. Louis Post-Dispatch* proclaimed the American coup: "U.S. Scores Victory in U.N. by Identifying Itself With South West Africans' Hopes. Mason Sears Takes Initiative and Russia Is Forced to Support His Position—Native Leaders Convinced of Washington's Sincerity."

The story was told again by Donald Grant, whose coverage had taken on a euphoric and partisan ring so pronounced as to create the impression that he was working not for a newspaper but for a propaganda agency. The United States had "won the first round—in the only sense in which victory is possible in the U.N."—in the new series of debates in the United Nations on Africa. "Mason Sears," he continued, "the American representative on the U.N. Trusteeship Council and head of the American delegation in the U.N. Assembly Trusteeship Committee, has managed to identify the United States with African aspirations in the issue of South West Africa. The extent and significance of this accomplishment is difficult to exaggerate."

In an effort to keep the momentum going, Lowenstein worked diligently to organize student involvement. On October 16, he participated in a meeting at the Student Council office of Columbia University called by Michael Horowitz, the acting coordinator of the Student Appeal for South Africa. In attendance besides Lowenstein and Horowitz were Ann Morrissett of the American Committee on Africa, college representatives from about six colleges in the New York area, and officials from the National Student Association.

The NSA officers expressed interest in an "educational campaign" in which funds raised on American campuses would be channeled to South Africa through the World University Service, later revealed to be a CIA conduit. Lowenstein, who had been on a speaking tour of campuses with Hans Beukes, offered to coordinate use of the funds for "general educational, defense, and welfare purposes" in South Africa with two of his contacts there, Neville Rubin, head of the National Union of South African Students, and Bishop Ambrose Reeves, the Anglican bishop of Johannesburg, who would certify the expenditures in South Africa. Ann Morrissett agreed that the banking facilities of the American Committee on Africa could be used to receive the funds raised by Lowenstein and Beukes and the Student Appeal for South Africa. In this way, a "voluntary" fund-raising effort was used to bolster the CIA-financed programs in South Africa of the International Commission of the National Student Association.

A few weeks later, Ethiopia and Liberia, one a conservative monarchy and the other descendants of American slaves, announced their intention to bring an action in the International Court of Justice in The Hague for a compulsory ruling. Lowenstein observed: "The concept of world law would soon have its best opportunity to challenge injustice and lawlessness successfully." But he also wrote, "Neither is it likely that the creaking apparatus of international law will affect events anywhere if it cannot affect them in an international territory, or if it can be flouted by the most isolated and friendless governments."

Lowenstein had now established himself as an "expert" in the new and expanding field of African affairs. On August 4, 1960, Catherine Raymond, a staff associate of the American Committee on Africa, would write to him requesting that he permit the committee to list him in a brochure being prepared by its speakers' bureau service as part of their South Africa Emergency Campaign. Any group inviting him would be responsible for his transportation costs and other expenses, such as overnight accommodations. Catherine Raymond told him, "We are hoping to be able to announce in our brochure that all honoraria will be contributed by the speakers to our South Africa Emergency Campaign and our Africa Defense and Aid Fund, and we would also like to have your reaction to this proposal." Lowenstein was expected to perform for nothing, which would irk him more and more.

Lowenstein finished 1959 by helping the American Committee on Africa raise funds to help the Rev. Markus Cooper, a black clergyman in South West Africa whom he had taped for the U.N. Cooper had been living in a reserve area which had been the traditional land of his people but was forcibly removed by South Africa because that land had been decreed "for whites only." The committee, in a letter signed by Donald Harrington, used Cooper's own words, which Lowenstein had taped and played at the United Nations: "The police stabbed some people including women on their stomachs with bayonets. . . . Two policemen grabbed me and threw me in a . . . lorry originally built to carry animals. The same treatment was meted out to my crippled wife, my daughter of fifteen years, my four sons, and all my valuable property."

As the African activity increased in the United States, gradually the issue began to enter the American consciousness. Lowenstein's last communication of 1959 came from the Coordinating Secretariat of National Unions of Students in Leyden, Holland, in a letter dated December 31, requesting him to write an article of about 1,500 words on his personal experiences during his trip to South West Africa. It was ironic that the COSEC, which Lowenstein had formed in Helsinki in 1951 when he was still president of the National Student Association, should be the one to approach him for an article. The organization was an anti-Communist invention to combat the powerful Soviet-backed International Union of Students and World Federation of Democratic Youth, the sponsor of the huge International Youth Festival in Vienna, which he had attended with Bundy. And it was bothersome that he was still being asked to write as a "student," about student life. He was now, after all, thirty years old. But the suggestion became the basis for his book, *Brutal Mandate*.

16.

Because Lowenstein was not ready to support Humphrey for president in 1960, he did not remain on the senator's staff, but stayed on excellent terms with Humphrey. On January 30, 1960, Humphrey wrote him: "Dear Al: Forgive me for not thanking you long ago for that wonderful cooked ham. It was simply delicious and was enjoyed by all the Humphreys. You are a wonderful and dear friend. Our best wishes to you. Sincerely yours, Hubert."

But Lowenstein did not have a job. He set himself up as a lawyer, practicing out of his parents' apartment. As he told the embassy personnel in Spain during one of his trips, he "had practiced law for a while in New York" but found it a "hideous exploitation." An FBI report on Lowenstein at this time suggests he was, in fact, serving as legal counsel to the Hyde Park Restaurant, which was owned and operated by his father and brother Larry.

For Lowenstein, making a living was a serious concern, although his friends took for granted that he didn't mind living on a shoestring. In spite of their ostensible wealth, the Lowensteins had known financial disaster. In the early fifties, Lowenstein's father, Gabriel, who had been enormously successful in the restaurant business after leaving academic life, went bankrupt. The elder Lowenstein brother, Willie, who had founded the business and was, according to Allard's sister,

Dorothy DiCintio, "totally uneducated," built what she describes as "fancy restaurants"—the bigger the better. A cycle of successes had propelled Gabriel Lowenstein to build the Sherbrook on Park Avenue and 54th Street. But "Doc" Lowenstein's forte was in buying unsuccessful restaurants and turning them around, and the Sherbrook, his shot at a big-time, class operation, was his undoing.

At about the same time the Sherbrook was draining Gabriel Lowenstein's resources, his son Bert was having what Dorothy DiCintio calls "serious emotional problems." A childhood genius who was graduated from Harvard when he was fifteen and became a physician, he had married and set himself up in a medical practice that cost, in his sister's words, "hundreds of thousands of dollars." When Bert had to be hospitalized, Gabriel Lowenstein took on the responsibility of paying for Bert's practice. "This all caused the bankruptcy," DiCintio concludes. Gabriel Lowenstein, who had worked himself up from a Yiddish-speaking garment worker, getting a Ph.D. from Columbia, joining the faculty of Columbia P & S, then making a fortune after serving in the army in World War I, experienced the humiliation of losing everything he owned, including his house in Westchester and his 1949 Oldsmobile. As they took it away, he resolved to get it all back—which he did—but he realized that it could all be lost again. Furthermore, the business was divided among the three brothers, with other relatives in charge of running some of the restaurants.

In all, Gabriel Lowenstein had ten restaurants, which supported numerous families. The most lucrative was the Post & Coach in the Port Authority bus terminal. But Uncle Willie's nephews-in-law ran it, and according to DiCintio, it supported five families and the extravagant life-style of Gabriel's brother Willie, who lived at the Sherry Netherland.

Another highly successful venture was the food concession on the Staten Island ferries. But Gabriel gave his brother Lazar a job with this business. "Lazar never takes anything that isn't his," the family would say, according to DiCintio. "The problem is that he thinks everything is his." And when her mother (Al's stepmother) was dying in the hospital in 1967, and Lowenstein had just returned from Africa, DiCintio explained to him how the Riese brothers were taking over the concession. Standing by her mother's bedside, she told Lowenstein, "The ferries are being taken from us. Can't you use your influence with Mayor Lindsay and his commissioners?"

But Lowenstein refused. Disdaining commerce and what he considered money grubbing, he didn't want anything to do with the business. Moreover, his father was not going to be able to sustain his energetic involvement with the restaurants. Gabriel Lowenstein would soon develop a serious heart problem, and his wife was waging a protracted struggle with cancer.

What Lowenstein wanted was some form of high service to the country that would also enable him to support himself. He wanted a career in politics based in New York, and he wanted to be able to write about his foreign exploits and to sell his articles to major publications. But both of these fields were difficult to break into, as Lowenstein discovered. In 1958, he had tried to sell an article that he had written after a trip to Russia with George Cohen, president of the student body of Northwestern, and Perris Henderson, captain of the Chapel Hill wrestling team. James A. Skardon, senior editor of *Coronet*, wrote him on November 20, 1958: "I found your article on Russia thoughtful and well written. . . . However, I am sorry to say that the recent picture story we did on Russia precludes our using your story." With this rejection in mind, he had resolved to get photographs for his writing on South West Africa, but as Bundy explained, his efforts were a failure. According to Bundy, Lowenstein had "hoped to mobilize a lot of concern about South West Africa." But his vision of the *Life* Magazine piece on the trip faded. "Apart from John McCann Phillips at *The New York Times*, there was no interest," Bundy concludes.

Lowenstein wanted to establish himself in New York and become known. And he believed that in the liberal circles he needed to cultivate, the dramatic issues of South Africa and South West Africa would provide the material.

Eleanor Roosevelt did devote most of her "My Day" column on November 27, 1959, to the South West Africa trip, but begins it not with Lowenstein but by relating the pleasure she had of "meeting two young men from South West Africa." She praised Mburumba Kerina, saying he had "forged his way out" of South West Africa, because he wanted to study in America and "now would like to go back to his own country as soon as it is safe for him to do so, for he wants to work for his people. In the meanwhile, he is trying to become a lawyer, as he feels that will fit him better than anything else for usefulness."

Mrs. Roosevelt describes Hans Beukes as "the other young African" who was "smuggled out with the help of some young Americans who had got themselves into South West Africa posing as tourists." She then wrote, "They were deeply interested in the situation as it existed in that country and came home to appear before the committee of the General Assembly of the U.N. on trusteeships. The three young Americans who made this trip were Al Lowenstein, Emory Bundy, and Sherman Bull." In typical Eleanor Roosevelt fashion, she refused to single out her friend Allard Lowenstein and instead lumped him together with Bundy, Bull, Beukes, and Kerina. "All five showed great courage," she concluded.

Even Mrs. Roosevelt's column, though, was the work of a friend with a political ax to grind, not the news coverage Lowenstein had hoped for, and he decided to write a book himself. *"Brutal Mandate* arose out of the lack of media coverage," Emory Bundy explains, "although the events at the U.N. much exceeded what we fairly expected to happen." Bundy was convinced that although Lowenstein believed the issues to be important, his ego was a factor, that he wanted recognition for what he had done. But "Al found it hard to write the book," Bundy recalls. Later, Lowenstein also persuaded Lou Shaw to do a screenplay of *Brutal Mandate* and even went to Hollywood to meet with Marlon Brando and Paul Newman with the hope of getting them involved in a media project. None of this came to fruition. Lowenstein had to promote the book himself when it finally came out in 1962. As Bundy remembers, "Al tried to get *Brutal Mandate* to be a best-seller. He had a million friends and he felt the publisher was not promoting the book. He badgered people to buy or give away the book."

Lowenstein might not have had time to write *Brutal Mandate* had he succeeded in getting a nomination to run for office, his primary objective after leaving Humphrey's staff. Mrs. Roosevelt had suggested that on his return from Africa he talk to James Wechsler, the liberal columnist for the *New York Post* about his trip and U.N. appearance, and he became enthralled with the idea of immersing himself in New York liberal politics.

It was logical that the vehicle Lowenstein should choose for entry into elective politics was the New York reform movement. The lament of liberals within the Democratic party was that its basic organization was corrupt and closed to the issue-oriented citizens to whom the idea of subservience to a political boss was repugnant. Eleanor Roosevelt, one of the leading critics of the Democratic machine, joined with Senator Herbert Lehman, the former governor of New York, former Secretary of the Air Force Thomas Finletter, and the Ethical Culture Society's Algernon Black, who had founded the Encampment for Citizenship, to create this new force within the Democratic party. Lowenstein's old friends who were prominent in Ethical Culture, Alice "Nanny" Pollitzer and her sister Lucille Kohn, and other leading patrician Democratic reformers also participated.

The major centers of this reform liberalism in New York were the Upper West Side and Greenwich Village. Liberal, intellectual, predominantly Jewish, these communities featured left-wing politics and comfortable life-styles. Former Socialists and even one-time Communists from the thirties, all now respectable, part of what became known as the "Old Left," filtered into the Democratic party because it was the established and legitimate organ for participation in the system. Artists, writers, entertainers, and rich patrons of the arts flocked to the liberal reform banner. They were for peace, disarmament, racial integration, and good government. Often with powerful connections (Alice Pollitzer was, for example, the mother-in-law of Louis Weiss, a founder of the prestigious Paul, Weiss, Rifkind, Wharton & Garrison law firm), they still saw themselves as ultraliberal, and even radical. They lived in spacious apartments in lovely old buildings with doormen on Central Park West and Riverside Drive, housing made affordable by rent control. And because Allard Lowenstein's family was from the Upper West Side and had the kind of Old World credentials this group identified with, it was inevitable that Lowenstein himself would be drawn to their orbit, and to such organizations as the National Committee for a Sane Nuclear Policy (NCSNP, or SANE) and the American Civil Liberties Union.

SANE was typical of the organizations in which Lowenstein was involved. A struggle to prevent its takeover by the Communist party was being waged, and an FBI source advised on May 14, 1958, that the National Committee of the Communist Party, USA, was "very anxious to direct and control the activities of the NCSNP; however the CP at the present time lacks the necessary leadership and large number of persons necessary to bring this about." Lowenstein's FBI file notes that Trevor Thomas, the executive secretary of the national committee, advised that the group would "object to any attempts by the Communist Party to take over the NCSANE or any of its local groups," and would "fight any organized effort by the CP to take over any of its local groups." The Upper West Side had one of the most active SANE groups. It also had people with sympathies for the Communist party, whom Lowenstein would passionately oppose. So identified would Lowenstein become with West Side liberal Democratic politics that the FBI would forward memos to the White House when Lyndon Johnson was president "regarding the West Side Liberal Democrats and Allard Kenneth Lowenstein."

His intense anti-Communism notwithstanding, Lowenstein was constantly caught in a crossfire between the right and the left. The FBI took note that "Allard Lowenstein was among a large number of Americans who attended the Seventh World Youth Festival in Vienna, Austria, in 1959. (The House Committee on Un-American Activities has described the Seventh World Youth Festival as 'communist-arranged.')" They did not have any idea that he went there to help disrupt it, as part of an organized effort financed by the CIA. And because he continued his antiapartheid activities, he was written up favorably by *The Daily Worker*, the Communist newspaper. The FBI took note of this as well.

The reform movement was exploding. During 1959, Lowenstein made his bid for the Democratic nomination for Congress in the 20th C.D. on the Upper West Side, the district of which he was a resident. He recruited his friend from Chapel Hill and the National Student Association, Brooklynite Curtis Gans, to help him, and he began speaking on street corners. His father, who had spoken on soapboxes as a young Socialist on the Lower East Side, came to listen. Gabriel Lowenstein would become stern when someone in the crowd was not paying attention to his son. In his Lithuanian accent, he would order the bystander: "Listen!"

It was a field of three: Lowenstein, William Fitz Ryan, and James Scheuer. Intense pressure was put on Lowenstein to withdraw because the leading reformers were supporting Scheuer. There was also an apparent reluctance on the part of Lowenstein's friends to support him for elective office. He had been away from New York for some time, and others had become better known and had stronger ties to the movers and shakers of New York politics. Since his discharge from the army, he had been living in North Carolina and Washington, keeping his Raleigh, North Carolina, residence until nearly the end of the fifties. Among those who were the most forceful in pressuring him out of the race were Eleanor Roosevelt and West Side reformer Ethel Grossman, an older woman who served as bookkeeper for Gabriel Lowenstein's restaurants and became Lowenstein's chief secretarial assistant. Grossman told him that it "wasn't necessary" to run for Congress "in order to make a contribution to the Reform movement." Her suggestion was that there was an "enormous amount of good to be accomplished upstate," and that "this could be done conveniently using Albany as a base." The implication was that he should seek state office, probably the state senate.

At an evening reform meeting, Lowenstein announced his decision to withdraw, stating that he had been guided in his decision by "Ethel and Mrs. R." Those who wanted him out of the congressional race turned and smiled at Grossman while the others glared at her. Later that night, hedging on her suggestion that he run for state office, Grossman approached him to say that Lowenstein's own supporters were telling her that "it wasn't necessary for you to go to Albany at all in order to make this contribution to the reform movement—everything that needed to be done upstate could be done from New York City by making periodic field trips, and you would be wasted unless your base of operations was New York City."

Ethel Grossman had in turn been put under tremendous pressure by Herbert Lehman. Thanking Lowenstein for his decision, Grossman wrote: "You said that you would call Scheuer sometime today to announce your decision, and also that you would tell your own supporters. I would also suggest that you tell Mrs. R., and I would like your permission to tell the Senator myself of your decision, and as quickly as possible. . . . If you don't think I should be the one to tell him, you might like to ask Mrs. R. to do so, but please let me know. After all, we want his backing and blessing for your senatorial candidacy, don't we? I could not tell you of the Senator's own attitude before now, or the pressure to which he had been subjected, because this would have been an indirect method of putting pressure on you, which I have sworn never to do."

Ethel Grossman proceeded to discourage Lowenstein from ever seeking elective office. "I am on your personal bandwagon, not your political one," she wrote him. "I think that you have a great and important mission in life, although at this moment you may not know what that mission is, or perhaps only a little of it has been revealed to you. I also believe that you have had, and will continue to have, divine guidance to assist you in your mission, and that this is true even though you may be an atheist (I have no idea of your religious inclinations, if any). For want of a better description, when I think of you and of your mission in life, I think of it as 'helping people.'" Politics, she told him, was a "dirty business," and she said she would be "especially sorry" if he went into it because he was "so nice, so fine, so honest, decent, and upstanding" that he "would be sure to be hurt in the process."

As for election to the State Senate, which Lowenstein announced he planned to seek, she said: "It does not matter very much if you run for state senate or assembly or governor or dogcatcher. Neither does it matter very much if you should win or if you should lose. No matter what you *decide* to do, or if you do nothing, you will still be called upon to fulfill the same destiny. It is not your nature to run away from destiny; in any case, it would seek you out. You have already proved this. You have accomplished more in your short span of years than most people dream of accomplishing in an entire lifetime. . . .

"You were born to lead, but not necessarily from the front ranks. One may lead merely by setting the right example to the right people at the right time."

Once again, Lowenstein was thwarted by Eleanor Roosevelt in his plans to seek elective office. Catherine Hemenway, wife of Russell Hemenway, who became head of the National Committee for an Effective Congress, promised to support him for the State Senate in the 25th Senatorial District, also on the Upper West Side. Both Hemenways were early and active reformers, with Catherine winning election as the district leader of the FDR-Woodrow Wilson Club on 96th Street, below the Riverside Club, William Fitz Ryan's base. But according to Lowenstein's old Ethical Culture friend Bob Wechsler, Al "got screwed out of that" when Catherine Hemenway threw her support to Manfred Ohrenstein, who was deadlocked with him. That race was so close and there was so little time that full procedures were abandoned. The clubs called in the Committee for Democratic Voters, headed by Thomas Finletter, to decide.

At a late-night meeting at the Hemenways, Lowenstein fought for the nomination, pulling out what he thought was his ace; Eleanor Roosevelt would have "great difficulty" supporting the reform ticket without him, he insisted. Contacted by phone, however, Eleanor Roosevelt said that Lowenstein was great, but even without him, she would support the reform ticket. Her position was that because she was so close to Lowenstein, she should remain impartial. Accepting her as human, he would point to a small bust of her on his desk, joking that Eleanor Roosevelt's bust was on his desk.

The final result of the reform battles was that William Fitz Ryan and not James Scheuer was nominated for Congress and Ohrenstein was designated for the state senate. Ryan would become one of the great liberals in Congress, Ohrenstein the minority leader of the upper New York State chamber. And as a consolation prize, Lowenstein was made the chairman of the Ryan-Ohrenstein Campaign Committee, heading a *Who's Who* in the reform movement listed on the stationery as honorary vice-chairmen and members of the advisory board. Included were such luminaries as Helen Gahagan Douglas, Susan Brandeis, Robert Lekachman, Richard Neustadt, Alice Kohn Pollitzer, Lucille Kohn, Paul O'Dwyer, Ted Weiss, Rita Aid, Albert Blumenthal, Robert Wechsler, and James Scheuer, among others. And Lehman endorsed the ticket, even though Scheuer wasn't on it, saying, "I very much hope that the Democratic voters of the 20th Congressional district will vote overwhelmingly for Bill Ryan and Fred Ohrenstein. . . ."

Lowenstein's final effort that year in elective politics was to seek election as a delegate for Adlai Stevenson, Eleanor Roosevelt's candidate, at the Democratic convention in Los Angeles. Both he and his old friend from Ethical Culture Bob Wechsler, who had also failed to win support for a congressional race of his own, presented themselves as prospective Stevenson delegates to the reformers but found that William Ryan, whom Lowenstein was aiding in his campaign, was backing R. Peter Straus and Stanley Lowell. Straus and Lowell were the winners, with Lowenstein and Wechsler elected as alternates. Lowell supported Stevenson, but Straus, in going for Kennedy, indicated the mood which prevailed in the New York delegation.

At a caucus of New York delegates in Albany, Wechsler and Lowenstein, as alternates, had to take seats in the back. The hard-core groups of Stevenson supporters were swamped by State Chairman Mike Prendergast and Tammany Hall boss Carmine DeSapio, who supported Kennedy. When Lowenstein was refused the right to speak for Stevenson, he charged to the front of the room and struggled to get to the microphone but was dragged off bodily by the sergeant at arms. Wechsler wanted to leave but Lowenstein insisted on staying so he could apologize. They waited for two hours before Lowenstein was able to get to Prendergast.

At Los Angeles, Lowenstein introduced Eleanor Roosevelt to John Kennedy, but she refused to switch. She didn't like the fact that Kennedy had been close to Joseph McCarthy. And the antagonism between Stevenson supporters and the Kennedy organization mounted. Stevenson was short on committed delegates, but David Garth, who was working for him, decided that they should get as many Stevenson backers as possible on the convention floor, with the hope that a demonstration there might turn the tide. As alternates, Lowenstein and Wechsler did not have floor passes, but Garth had some of his people dress as state troopers to get Stevenson supporters in.

Suddenly, Stevenson appeared on the floor of the convention, breaking with a longstanding tradition that candidates for the presidency remain out of sight. There was electricity in the air when he got up to speak. But with the crowd in the palm of his hand, in a situation to turn things around, he indulged in self-deprecation. He finished with a wry remark that got a laugh and walked off, in an anticlimax.

Several delegations still wanted the demonstration. Herbert Lehman picked up the New York State standard in order to participate, but to Lehman's shock, Mitch Bloom, an old-line regular district leader who was for Kennedy, threw a body block at him and grabbed the banner. Suddenly, Lowenstein appeared. He waded into the hostile crowd and attacked Bloom, grabbing him and wrestling him to the ground. Lowenstein shouted at him, "You stupid jerk! This is Lehman!"

Eugene McCarthy made a brilliant nominating speech for Stevenson, and Eleanor Roosevelt seconded, warning that this was no time to turn away from experienced leadership. And Joe Rauh joined with Bobby Kennedy in warning everybody against Lyndon Johnson as the vice-presidential candidate. But when the smoke cleared it was Kennedy and Johnson. On August 2, 1960, Frank Graham wrote to Lowenstein: "McCarthy's nominating speech was the best in either convention and for a great cause. Now all hands for J.F.K. and L.B.J.!!"

Lowenstein could not share Graham's enthusiasm because there seemed no place for him in all the great Democratic action. He spoke to his good friend Lucille Kohn, who set up an appointment for him with her influential sister, Alice Kohn Pollitzer. In a sympathetic letter to him on November 16, 1960, she wrote:

I've just written Ruth Hagy and now I want to send you a little note which has been wanting to be written for several weeks. You just don't sound yourself over the telephone, so I have been worried about you. I wish you wouldn't take such a dim view of A.K.L. for he is one of the most remarkable people I know. I realize you can't make a living by taking care of all humanity, but that God of yours should pay you a big salary for taking care of his unfinished business. The world desperately needs people like you even though they have no tags or titles and small emoluments. I hope the book comes through as earnest of a rush of good things in the future.

17.

Lowenstein scrawled on a piece of Ryan-Ohrenstein Campaign Committee stationery: "The great fact is that everywhere this generation is the vanguard of the push forward—a generation stirred to action by goals beyond its own comforts, its energies and training turned to providing leadership for a justice unmarred by prejudices and for freedom unfettered by exceptions. What a banner our contemporaries hold high: 'I exist,' in the words of Francis Lieber, 'as a human being, and I have a right to exist as a human being.'"

Demands for the right to exist as a human being were being made by black people in 1960 in both the south of the United States and in South Africa, compelling Lowenstein to become deeply involved in both movements.

In 1955, Rosa Parks had refused to move to the rear of the bus in Montgomery, Alabama, triggering the bus boycott that made Martin Luther King, Jr., a national figure. Then, catching everyone by surprise, on February 1, 1960, four young students from North Carolina Agricultural and Technical College, a black school in Greensboro, North Carolina, sat down at the lunch counter of the local Woolworth's and asked to be served.

Curtis Gans, as the vice-president for internal affairs of the National Student Association, went down to Greensboro on February 3 to work as a tactical advisor to what was beginning to resemble the "Defiance Campaign" in South Africa eight years before. Gans was given a $25,000 grant from the Taconic Foundation after a five-minute talk with Steven Currier, to publicize the sit-ins in order to increase their impact. And at the NSA congress in 1960, the major issue was whether expanded NSA support should be given, with the southern students strongly in opposition. The great majority of the delegates voted approval, causing the NSA to move in a sharply liberal direction.

According to Gans, the sit-ins had been "peripheral" to Lowenstein, who was more concerned with South Africa. Gans asked Lowenstein to be a trouble-shooter in Alabama, to help Bernard Lee, a black activist who was president of the student body of a black school in Alabama and who later served as an aide to Martin Luther King, Jr. Lee had been expelled by a conservative black administration fearful of repercussions because of Lee's civil rights activities, and Lowenstein was sent down by the NSA, on its funds, to resolve the problem.

And from this first effort, Lowenstein became a central figure in the South. "That's initially how Al made certain connections in the civil rights movement," Gans explains. "Al always became involved in the same way. He wanted to help the cause and he wanted to be in the center of the cause."

Lowenstein participated in a colloquium at Yale on March 11, 12, and 13, 1960, called "Challenge" which was organized by Yale undergraduates. In attendance were 2,000 college students from every college on the northeast coast. On Friday evening, March 11, at 11:00 P.M., Lowenstein conducted one of the sessions in Dwight Hall. He explained the issues and urged the students to return to their college communities and organize demonstrations in support of southern Negro college students. On May 6 and 7 of 1960, at the New England Student Conference on Civil Rights convened at Wesleyan University in Connecticut, Lowenstein also exhorted students to join the civil rights movement.

An article in *The New York Times* on the Yale colloquium appeared on March 20, the day before a date of monumental significance, as it turned out, in South Africa. There, events similar to those taking place in the American South produced catastrophic consequences.

On March 21, in what has come to be known as the Sharpeville Massacre, police fired into a crowd of unarmed demonstrators, killing 70 people and wounding 200. In the aftermath of the killings, more than 21,000 activists and opponents of apartheid were arrested, the Pan-Africanist Congress and the African National Congress were banned, a state of emergency giving police dictatorial powers was declared, and Dr. Hendrick Verwoerd, the South African prime minister, took South Africa out of the Commonwealth.

Lowenstein was shaken and horrified by Sharpeville, comparing it to the killing of Hungarian freedom fighters by the Soviet army. He wrote in a statement intended for the press: "The 'incident' of the Sharpeville Massacre prompted one observer to write of the 'shame of South Africa.' What an understatement! The Union of South Africa is the shame of the West. . . . If there is one thing the rulers of South Africa wish to make absolutely clear, it is that there will be no slow march forward for South Africa—there is to be only the pell-mell impossibility of an accelerated mad race back to the 10th century."

Lowenstein wanted a prohibition of the South African team from the 1960 Olympics and a trade boycott, which the International Confederation of Free Trade Unions, the AFL-CIO, and the American Committee on Africa all called for. America had advocated nonviolent action, and Lowenstein had given his services to this cause endorsed by liberals in the U.S. as well as in South Africa itself. Instead of change, nonviolence had lead to violence and repression.

The ferment in South Africa had been building for years. Liberals, including Humphrey and Lowenstein, feared that Communists would exploit the unrest, and this led to American support of the antiapartheid struggle. The Communist party had supported the African National Congress; but younger, more activist members broke away from the ANC in 1959 to form the militantly anti-Communist Pan-Africanist Congress. At Orlando, Johannesburg, in December of that year, the PAC called on black South Africans to destroy and to refuse to carry their passbooks. The passbook was the instrument used by the South African government to restrict the movements of Africans and was the symbol of third-class citizenship. Past protests, including the "Defiance" campaign had been directed in measure against the pass. Because of all the regulations attached to it, in 1956 alone, 1,700,000 Africans out of an African population of some 10,000,000 were arrested for passbook violations even though, at the time, only males over 16 were required to carry passbooks. Only later were females forced to do so.

Lowenstein had written about the pass in *Brutal Mandate*:

Most important, neither Coloureds nor Indians are required to carry the passbooks that are the most hated symbol and instrument of the oppression of the Africans by the whites. A few 'exemptions' have been granted, and a pass is solemnly issued to certify that the bearer is exempted from carrying a passbook; but he had better have this strangest of all, the pass that says he need not have a pass, on his person at all times.

And Susan Mariaki Monanoe of the Pan-Africanist Congress, stated:

On 19th December 1959, my organization, the Pan-Africanist Congress, at its annual National Conference held at Orlando, Johannesburg, resolved to embark upon a campaign directed against the Pass Laws, which subject the African people to the humiliation of constant arrests. We, as an organization concerned with the rights and freedom of our people, felt we could no longer tolerate the persecution of these arrests and gaol confinement, and therefore set a date upon which we would call upon the people to support us when we surrendered ourselves for arrest in protest and in an attempt to have the Pass Laws repealed. I might mention, too, that the other aims and objects of our Pan-Africanist Organization are: the inculcation of Nationalism in our people and the pursuance of a struggle to achieve complete freedom from the foreign domination and the oppression and exploitation which go together with rule by foreigners; the creation of African Trade

Unions and their right to recognition; a minimum wage for all Africans of thirty-five pounds per month.

The South African Communist party accused the PAC of being supported by the CIA as well as the AFL-CIO. There is ample reason to believe the Communist assessment, which also charged that the CIA had infiltrated labor organizations throughout Africa. Certainly, the American labor movement had become increasingly involved in Africa, backing Mboya and looking to halt Soviet influence. The CIA's collaboration with American unions in Africa is well documented before 1959, emerging into public view in 1965 with the formation of the African-American Labor Center, a joint AFL-CIO–CIA project which backed anti-Communist unions in Africa and became a base for CIA operations in forty African countries. Its goal was to push the African union movement on a "reformist" path and away from Communist influence.

Although Lowenstein must have felt a dreadful remorse about what happened at Sharpeville, he never called for violent retaliation or revolution; all he advocated was more pressure on the government of South Africa. He had shown that he was not irresponsible and that he could be trusted. He had proved his mettle by not losing his head in the worst possible crisis: a miscalculation in which he had shared had resulted in a massacre.

As George Houser tells it, his own contacts with Lowenstein in working on Africa were "spasmodic. He was not an easy guy to work with," and they "did not have a close working relationship." Houser describes Lowenstein as "running his own show. He was a free-lance kind of guy, a political animal. But the objectives he had for Africa and civil rights were the same as my own. He was a non-Communist, maybe an anti-Communist. That was not a problem because our organization was never in anybody's hip pocket. We acted independently. Ours was the only organization in the field a person like Al could have been associated with." But other facts indicate that Lowenstein and the American Committee on Africa were deeply involved with each other.

On April 13, 1960, a little over two weeks after Sharpeville, Lowenstein received a telegram: "Invite you to attend meeting called by American Committee on Africa to discuss mobilization of American resources to meet deepening crisis in South Africa Thursday April 21 at 3:00 P.M. 477 Madison Avenue 20 floor.—Donald Harrington and A. Philip Randolph."

Harrington was well known to Lowenstein as the chairman of the executive board of the American Committee on Africa, the pastor of the famous Community Church, and the titular head of the Liberal party. Randolph was the top black union leader of the country (he was the founder of the Brotherhood of Sleeping Car Porters), who had earlier advocated a march on Washington by blacks. An advisor on civil rights matters to presidents since FDR, he was a Socialist of the persuasion of Norman Thomas, which meant that he too was firmly against the Communists.

The outcome of their meeting with Lowenstein is suggested by subsequent events. Various African countries called for a complete quarantine of South African "terror." The sworn statements of eighteen Africans who had been wounded in the Sharpeville Massacre reached Lowenstein in New York, where he presented the evidence to the eighty-two delegates of the member countries of the United Nations. This evidence, Lowenstein insisted, showed "definitely" that the South African police opened fire without provocation and that the Africans who were demonstrating peaceably were shot in the back as they fled for their lives. Lowenstein explained that the documents reached him by a "roundabout route" from Bishop Ambrose Reeves, the Anglican bishop of Johannesburg, who was obliged to flee to Switzerland. In an article in the Communist newspaper the *Daily Worker* covering the story, Lowenstein was described as "a New York lawyer . . . who represents other victims of South Africa's racial policy, the populations of South West Africa, before the United Nations Trusteeship Committee."

Lowenstein and Beukes had raised funds on American campuses, and their expenditure in South Africa had been certified by Bishop Reeves and Neville Rubin, president of the National Union of South African Students. Collected for the Student Appeal for South Africa, the money had been put into the bank account of the American Committee on Africa. In a memorandum written on October 22, 1959, Ann Morrissett wrote that the funds were to "be treated as the rest of our special funds, with some part of them used for administrative and promotional expenses." And it was Neville Rubin who had directed Lowenstein in Johannesburg to the Hans Beukes matter at the meeting of the National Union of South African students. Beukes, in turn, had been used with dexterity at the United Nations by Mason Sears.

George Houser was close to virtually all of the African liberation movements and was a proponent of Ghandi-like passive resistance, which Martin Luther King, Jr., a member of the national committee of the ACOA, was advocating in the American civil rights movement. Whether the American Committee on Africa gave the Pan-Africanist Congress direct advice is not altogether clear. But there is sufficient evidence of American involvement in the activities of the Pan-Africanist Congress—which was both antiapartheid and anti-Communist—to suggest that the money in the Committee's special fund found its way to those movements in South Africa that were advocating passive resistance against apartheid. From Morrissett's memorandum it can also be inferred that the National Student Association's CIA-supported International Commission provided help as well.

There is other evidence that the American Committee on Africa was deeply involved in providing monetary and other forms of assistance to African national liberation groups, such as the Pan-Africanist Congress, against the wishes of some of its board members. On March 1, 1960, Ben Wechsler, a member of the executive board of the ACOA, wrote to Executive Board Chairman Donald Harrington:

> With feelings of mixed relief and regret, I submit my resignation from the Executive Board of the American Committee on Africa.
>
> As you know, I have been considering this resignation for many months, in fact since the Board was 'purged' of those people whom I considered to be its most responsible members. . . . As I am sure you are aware, this is a most unpleasant letter to write, but I am so deeply concerned with the growing trend of irresponsibility in the American Committee on Africa that I feel I must formally report some of the reasons why my resignation appears to be an absolute necessity.
>
> From the moment I first participated in the decisions of the Executive Board, I was astounded by the lack of democracy, as well as the chaotic and unparliamentary procedures characteristic of all Board meetings. Time and time again persons holding a minority position were told that debates were not in order in the Executive Committee; that questions and arguments should be taken up at subcommittees, but attendance at subcommittee meetings was strongly discouraged. Meetings were held without notification; other techniques were utilized to throttle debate. A perusal of Executive Board minutes will show a number of occasions on which illegal procedures had to be corrected at subsequent meetings.
>
> I am even more concerned with the use to which publicly subscribed funds have been put, and evidently will continue to be put in the future. Letters which gave every indication of being solicitations for the South Africa Defense Fund were interpreted, unjustifiably, I believe, as requests for general funds for the ACOA. I have tried repeatedly to get the exact breakdown of income and expenditure to which I, as a Board member, am legally entitled. When I volunteered to work out the figures myself, George Houser refused even to allow me to check the files.
>
> It is my view that much more of the general funds belongs properly to the South African Defense Fund. This behavior is a symptom of the staff and some Board members' preoccupation with competition for funds that cover salary and overhead. As a result the South African Defense Fund has been pursued timidly,

and the sharp increase in the funds spent for salaries and overhead has produced an unjustifiable ratio. . . .

Your entire list of national committee members and several of your officers exercise no influence whatsoever in the ACOA's activities. In fact, they are generally unaware as to your activities and their implications. At this time, this has constituted an abuse, or misuse, of these prominent figures.

You are immorally pressing your request for tax exemption while broadly extending your political activities. Staff and various Board members are choosing sides and are offering support among the many African nationalist groups throughout the continent. I cannot be associated with an attempt to secure tax exemption for this kind of procedure.

If you feel there are answers to any of the questions this letter may have raised, I can only point out that honest efforts on my part to obtain them have been frustrated in the past.

This letter will be distributed among the many persons and organizations who have asked me to justify my membership on your Board.

Houser's explanation for the letter is that the executive board entered into a contract in 1958 with the public relations firm of Harold Oram for fund raising and to build up the mailing list. H. L. Oram, Inc., would later figure significantly in Lowenstein's work on Spain with the American Committee for Iberian Freedom. According to Houser, some members of the board disagreed with Oram's strategy, and Wechsler, who was part of the "Oram organization," tried to replace Donald Harrington as chairman. Others in the Oram faction, Houser states, were Oram public relations executive Gilbert Jonas, and Elliot Newcomb. Houser insists that the Oram clique was trying to push the American Committee on Africa to the right and away from its very liberal image, which, it maintained, was hurting fund-raising efforts. "Oram put pressure on us to get A. J. Muste off the board because he was too far left," Houser relates. But while Houser defends the presence of Muste, the pacifist antiwar leader and fellow member of the Fellowship of Reconciliation, on his board, the leftist stance of the American Committee on Africa was itself something of a pose. It persisted in one of its main objectives: the preempting of the Communists in Africa. The full story of the American Committee on Africa is in the archives of the Amistad Research Center in New Orleans, which purchased the organization files while George Houser still served as its executive director. Houser retired in 1981 and was then hired by the Amistad Research Center as an archivist to catalog the documents. At the writing of this book, Houser keeps a busy schedule in Africa, working out of the United Church Board for Homeland Ministries in New York. Howard Spragg, the man who went to jail with Houser in 1940 rather than go into the army, has offices in the same building, where he works on Christian education projects.

Paradoxically, the clandestine manipulation aimed at producing change in South Africa had brought the results that the liberals wanted to avoid. Not only had they misjudged the Afrikaners, who became more recalcitrant, now there was no way to protest by nonviolent means because the black organizations had been banned and there were severe penalties for passive resistance. The disenfranchised blacks, four-fifths of the population of South Africa, were without any voice. Oliver Tambo of the African National Congress began a reappraisal of his tactics, and the hand of the revolutionaries, who argued that only violence and armed struggle could change the situation, had been strengthened. In their fear of Communism, the liberals had given the far right a rationale for total repression and the far left a justification for its program of total revolution. A survey of middle-class Africans by the South African Institute of Race Relations found a majority prepared to accept violence as a method of political action, and almost half believed that the use of force was inevitable. On December 16, 1961, Nelson Mandela, Oliver Tambo's law partner and a key figure in the African National Congress, formed Umkhonto We Sizwe, Zulu for "Spear of the Nation." Thought to be the military arm of the ANC, it began a campaign of sabotage against "the symbols of apartheid," staging rocket attacks against police stations. Not to be outdone, the remnants of the Pan-Africanist Congress established Poqo, a mass movement modeled on the Mau Mau in Kenya. It claimed a membership of 150,000 and engaged in acts of terrorism. The situation had gotten out of hand, and the government retaliated, not only against the black groups but against the sympathetic whites.

On June 21, 1960, the Liberal party of South Africa, which was very close to Lowenstein, appealed to him for help. On stationery with its insignia of a black hand shaking a white hand, Marion V. Friedman, the acting honorary secretary, wrote to him that under the South Africa Emergency Regulations, 2,000 people were being held "without any charge having been brought against them." In detention for three months, many had lost their livelihoods and had their families broken up. They were, according to Friedman, "almost destitute."

In addition to the Africans who were being held, the national chairman and nine members of the Liberal party also had been detained without any charges brought against them. According to Friedman, the Liberal party had appealed to the government to end the State of Emergency because it was "intimidating South Africans of all races to the point where they are fearful of legitimate opposition to the Government." Also requested was a lifting of the ban against the African political organizations.

Lowenstein was asked to add his voice to the Liberal party's by sending a cable during the first two weeks of July. "Can you get others—persons and organizations—1,000 or more if possible—to do the same?" Friedman requested, signing off with regards from Lowenstein's friend Theodore. Clearly, Lowenstein had a serious working relationship with this organization. Just prior to this formal call for help, he had joined with the Kerinas, following Sharpeville and the State of Emergency, in launching Action for South Africa, an organization of Africans and Americans that called on "Americans to join in the fight against racial tyranny in the Union of South Africa and South West Africa." Pledged to keep this cause "constantly before the American public," it supported a boycott of all South African goods "in response to the appeal from the National Congresses in South Africa." It also urged sanctions by the United Nations and an end of the "de facto annexation" by South Africa of South West Africa and the placing of the territory under United Nations trusteeship "as a first step toward responsible self-government and independence." And it prepared to send aid to those who had been detained by the South African government during the State of Emergency. Lowenstein drafted the constitution for the group, which sponsored fund-raisers—parties, and social gatherings in Harlem with African music—United Nations demonstrations, and picketing in front of the South African Consulate. On an invitation to an Action for South Africa meeting scheduled for August 18, Jane Kerina, Mburumba Kerina's white American wife, wrote a message to Lowenstein, saying that it was important to meet with him "before we take final decisions." Sharpeville was going to be used as the basis for mobilizing public opinion in America.

On November 3, 1960, Lowenstein attended another New York meeting of Action for South Africa. Held in the Harlem apartment of Mary Delaney as a "closed meeting," it was attended by Oliver Tambo, still deputy president of the African National Congress, as well as the London Representative for the South African United Front. Also present was Mvusi (Vus L.) Make, the national executive of the Pan-Africanist Congress and Cairo representative of the Front. Though they were competitors, the two African congresses still felt it was necessary to have some kind of working agreement in this period of crisis.

Then, in late December of 1960, Lowenstein met with a public relations account executive from the Harold L. Oram firm, Gilbert Jonas, who was also a member of the Executive Board of the American Committee on Africa. The Pan-Africanist Congress's Vus L. Make, who was taking an increasingly important role in the South African United Front, was also at the meeting. Jonas and Make also met alone. On December 30, Jonas wrote to Make at the South African United Front in London setting forth their agreement.

Jonas was to organize a public relations fund-raising campaign on behalf of the South African United Front from which the organization could anticipate "a gross income of $175,000" during the first year of Jonas's efforts. Jonas stated three conditions for his work to be successful: there would have to be "high level" leadership, including South African and world figures; a "basic and dramatic manifesto" of about 1,000 words that set out the charges against the South African government and the program of the South African United Front; $5,000 to pay for a full-page advertisement in *The New York Times* "announcing the Front, its manifesto, and the world leaders supporting the cause."

The leaders Jonas wanted from South Africa were "the heads of the major organizations associated with the Front, Alan Paton, Z. K. Matthews, the archbishop of Cape Town, Roman Catholic archbishop of Durban, the chief rabbi, Ellen Hellman, and many others of equal stature." The African leaders he thought necessary were Nkrumah, Toure, Mboya, Nyerere, Banda, Bourguiba, Senghor, Dia, Houphouët-Boigny, the king or prime minister of Morocco, Telewa, and Olympio. "In addition, we can use a representative assortment of world figures," Jonas wrote, "(leaving the question of which Americans to ask until you return) such as: Nehru, U Nu, Tengku Abdul Rahman, Ngo Dinh Diem, John Chang, Ayub Kahn, Sukarno, Carlos Garcia, and any other governmental leaders of similar stature in Europe, the Middle East, or Latin America. (The Declaration of Conscience brochure I gave you can serve as a guide.) As for England, the logical names include Bishop Reeves and Revs. Huddleston and Scott. And of course, any names such as the Huxleys, Toynbees, Bertrand Russell, Olivier etc. The association of these eminent persons can be in the form of an international board of sponsors or honorary patrons."

Jonas was prepared to draft the manifesto and get the support of the prominent names he listed. He explained that this was "not essentially a fund-raising operation," but a "promotional and public relations drive" to mobilize American and world support for the cause of freedom in South Africa "as embodied by the Front," and to provide financial assistance "to victims of the apartheid policy" in South Africa and to people who fled South Africa. Jonas also explained that the Front would have to pay nothing because Oram's fee would come out of the funds the firm raised. So as a package deal, which would bring Jonas's firm $36,000 (half for PR, half for fund-raising), the South Africa United Front got a list of world leaders, Nobel Prize winners, South Africans, prominent Americans, and assurances of sufficient income to launch the campaign necessary to pressure the government of South Africa to change its ways before it was too late. But the money that came in first would have to go to the printer, Make was told. Make was also advised to keep costs at the Front's New York office down. "If the costs of the office are minimal (less than $1,000 per month)," Jonas wrote, "we could place that in second priority, but I believe Lowenstein's suggestion that a minimum budget for your office be provided by London is the wisest course until we have four or five months of experience under our belts. . . . Meanwhile, if we raise funds according to plan, we will have enough to expand the work of your office later on."

Jonas then hedged on the question of his fee. If insufficient funds were raised, the deal was off and the campaign would end. But he did not envision such an event. "As I have noted," he added, "I believe we can run this campaign successfully in both major regards: propaganda impact and amount of funds raised. We have been involved in virtually every other campaign of a like nature in this country relating to Africa and any other liberal or internationalist cause. Among our clients have been the NAACP Legal Defense Fund (since 1943), the American Committee on Africa, Africa South etc. There is no other firm of similar background in the United States and, however immodest it sounds, none of similar philosophic views and professional ability either. Though nothing is certain in life, we feel this has a reasonably good chance of success. Otherwise, it would be difficult for us to undertake it so speculatively."

Jonas reiterated that "we will have to register and report on our activities with the U.S. Justice Department as agents of a foreign political group in order to stay within the law. This in no way inhibits us and it should not bother you." In closing, he states: "Finally, I will repeat my offer to provide you with temporary office space for your Front activities when you return, assuming we are going to have some kind of relationship. . . . Please convey to your colleagues (and, if you see him, Bishop Reeves) my sincerest good wishes for a fruitful and rewarding New Year."

Harold Oram and Gilbert Jonas profited from conservative as well as liberal anti-Communism. The Oram firm did public relations for South Vietnam Premier Ngo Dinh Diem and the American Friends of Vietnam, with Jonas serving as "campaign director" of the Vietnam account. Both Oram and Jonas were registered foreign agents acting for the Republic of Vietnam. Jonas, who would handle the PR for Lowenstein's book, *Brutal Mandate*, was a presidential campaign advisor for John Kennedy, whose name was listed on the American Friends of Vietnam stationery along with Arthur Schlesinger, Jr., and Norman Thomas. One of the cochairmen was General "Wild Bill" Donovan, founder during World War II of the OSS, the precursor organization of the CIA. Oram also did PR for the International Rescue Committee, which aided refugees from Communist countries, and the Committee of One Million Against the Admission of Communist China to the U.N. Ex-Communist Marvin Liebman, who worked for H. L. Oram, served as an advisor to William F. Buckley, Jr.'s, Young Americans for Freedom and collaborated with Buckley in setting up the Committee for Freedom of All Peoples, which staged a giant protest against Krushchev's visit to the United States.

Jonas had explained to Vus Make that liberalism was a business like any other and that his firm produced the goods for a fee. The New York office of the South Africa United Front was to be run from the headquarters of a hot-shot PR company. But Lowenstein was still working *pro bono*. He had concluded that Action for South Africa, as it was run by the Kerinas, had not mobilized sufficient support because they were spending too much time in Harlem. Something much bigger was needed, something that would galvanize white public opinion in the United States: hence, the South Africa United Front.

The Liberal party of South Africa continued to press Lowenstein for support. And Ethel Grossman, having derailed Lowenstein from his political career in New York, did everything in her power to keep him involved with the concerns of the South African Liberals, while he involved her in his African activities. She corresponded extensively with leaders of the Liberal party, conveying to them Lowenstein's thoughts as he discussed them with her. And they responded, cleverly articulating their basic position that liberalism was the only hope in South Africa against all forms of totalitarianism, including Communism, and that the United States was the only country that could save South Africa by forcing its government to change.

In the Spring of 1961, Grossman wrote to Ernest Wentzel, the chairman of the Transvaal Provincial Division of the Liberal Party of South Africa in Johannesburg and former president of the National Union of South African Students, with whom Lowenstein stayed on his 1959 trip, telling him that Lowenstein was completing a book on his trip to South West Africa and that he wanted to know what Americans could do to help the South African Liberals.

On June 28, 1961, Wentzel wrote back: "I am very pleased that Al is finishing his book, and that his book will give us some opportunity to make propaganda for the right of the South African Liberal Party. I do hope—the Government willing—to visit London in August. More about this later when I hope that Al and I will be able to arrange to meet."

The situation for the Liberals was becoming increasingly difficult. Peter Brown, their chairman, was jailed in 1960, with Alan Paton resuming his chairmanship. A leading Liberal, John Lang, had his house searched in the early hours of the morning, after which the intruders moved on to the offices of the party itself, searching there for the rest of the day. Discouraged, Lang left the country. As for the black Africans, Wentzel related how both the African National Congress and the Pan-Africanist Congress had been declared unlawful. Then he asked rhetorically: "Would it not be true to say that the world is divided into the supporters of authoritarianism and democracy? Those who reject democracy are found in all countries of the world and give themselves many names but they all, whether they be communist, fascist or Afrikaner nationalist, destroy the individuality and human dignity of men."

Wentzel explained that the Liberal party was unique in South Africa in that it was entirely nonracial and supported the Universal Declaration of Human Rights. Summing up basic strategy, his letter continued:

There seems no possibility that white South Africa will make many concessions to the growing non-white demand for fundamental human rights unless powerful pressure is brought to bear on Dr. Verwoerd's government. It is here that Americans can help. The United States has a long history of opposition to colonialism. In its recent actions in the United Nations, by voting for resolutions censuring apartheid, it has been true to this history. We Liberals are deeply encouraged by this and we believe that Americans should continue to oppose South Africa at the United Nations with all the power at its command. Your government in America is able to bring powerful direct pressure to bear on the South African government.

The most specific form of help that could be provided, he declared, was financial. And the reasons for providing this support had to do with the self-interest of the United States:

There is an ideological battle in Africa between Communism, black nationalism, and liberalism. If liberalism is to prevail we must be able to compete powerfully with our adversaries. If we can put many more organizers into the field, if we can provide them with adequate transport, if we can open more offices and staff them properly, if we can print more and better literature, there is hope that we will have the victory. Even now, with small resources, we are growing daily. Branches are being formed in the towns and in the rural areas, and the prestige of the party is ever increasing. With your help we believe that nothing can stop us.

In her letter to Wentzel, Ethel Grossman had written that Lowenstein also wanted to know what his personal experiences had To this Wentzel replied that he had been jailed for three months during the Emergency of 1960 and that Walter and Adelain Hain, Maritz van den Berg and Colyn van Reenen had been arrested one night in Lady Shelborne, Pretoria, while handing out Liberal party literature. The pretext for the arrests was that the four constituted a "gathering"; all gatherings had been banned for the month of May. Like many others, the four were held without bail and then released without any charges being brought.

Grossman also wrote to Adrian Leftwhich, the new president of the National Union of South African Students, saying that her communication was on behalf of Lowenstein. He replied to her on stationery bearing the NUSAS insignia—a jackboot crushing the pillar of academic freedom—and expressed sentiments which echoed those of the South African Liberal party.

The National Union of South African Students, Leftwhich told her, had passed resolutions "condemning outright the government's policy of apartheid in all its manifestations, and consequent upon this, adopted a resolution outlining a campaign against educational apartheid."

Leftwhich told Grossman that he was pleased to hear from Lowenstein through her since communications addressed to Lowenstein in Hollywood, where he was promoting the screenplay of *Brutal Mandate* with Marlon Brando and Paul Newman, had not reached him. NUSAS, like the Liberal party of South Africa, was in desperate need of funds. Its goal was to expose the "sham of educational apartheid and the tribal colleges in particular" by bringing out a critical publication for wide-scale distribution and by sponsoring speaking tours by ex-students from the tribal colleges. "All this means that we need financial assistance more than ever," Leftwhich wrote.

He outlined a program of seminars and conferences to be held on a regional basis in South Africa to "cultivate a continuous growth of a strong cadre of student leadership which is militant in its opposition to apartheid and prepared to take active steps to implement its beliefs." Leftwhich added: "Once again we are completely hamstrung through lack of finances, and if you and Al are at all able to assist us, we would be deeply appreciative."

The program of the National Union of South African Students bore a striking resemblance to that of the National Student Association while Lowenstein was its president in 1951. At that time, Lowenstein had explained to the Rev. Charles Jones of Chapel Hill that the NSA was going to get a big grant to develop liberal leaders in the South who would fight segregation. Lowenstein was, like the leaders of the National Union of South African Students, strongly anti-Communist and saw social change in race relations as essential to prevent the appeal of the Communist Party.

The closeness of Lowenstein to the South Africans who were promoting the programs of the National Union of South African Students and the new liberal publications explains the influence he was able to exert in shaping these programs. He was using the model of his own experiences with the NSA and grafting them onto the South African situation. And because of his wide range of connections, he was able to muster support for the liberal South Africans the way he had been able to get various forms of support for the NSA.

18.

People like Ethel Grossman, who were involved in shaping Lowenstein's career, kept pressuring him to get married. Grossman wrote to him: "You should marry as soon as you find the right partner, and the right partner is one who will understand you and who will be proud to share you with the world. For you and for your future happiness, this understanding is much more important than beauty, wealth, and physical appeal."

Lowenstein had an undeniably magnetic quality that attracted women as well as men. Barbara Boggs, his new girlfriend, felt that attraction. A student at Manhattanville College at Purchase, New York, she was the daughter of the powerful Louisiana Congressman Hale Boggs, the Democratic whip. As a participant in the NSA convention in 1960 at the University of Minnesota in Minneapolis, Barbara Boggs was confronted by a man whose attraction came not only from his personal vitality but his reputation. What made Lowenstein attractive to her and to so many other women was, in her words, "his articulate idealism combined with wit and a totally consuming and flattering expression of interest in you as a person. He was an attractive man to women. He was attracted to women."

He was immensely attracted to Barbara Boggs; she was beautiful and she was from the center of political power in America by virtue of her birth. He pursued her. Following her return to Manhattanville after the 1960 NSA congress, Boggs began dating Lowenstein in New York where he took her to West Side reform club meetings and to political events organized for the Ryan-for-Congress campaign and Ted Weiss's city council race.

On December 3, 1960, Boggs wrote Lowenstein that a friend of theirs from South Africa, Sean Bond, had seen her safely to 14th Street on the subway. "We had a few good belly laughs picturing Cardinal Spellman in Bishop Reeve's britches and the like; we discussed the future of the world, South Africa and Sean Bond, and bid each other a fond farewell."

Boggs jokingly expressed concern about Lowenstein traveling to New Orleans, particularly since her father was there. "My New Orleans musings provide me with nightmare material. I can just picture the front page of the *Times-Picayune*, as its ever-vigilant cameramen have caught you in an immortal pose with fist raised in righteous indignation as you spew forth your wrath upon the mobbing mothers of the Crescent City. If it *must* happen, please wear your new glasses— I'm sure they will photograph *much* better than the old ones!"

Two days later, she wrote again to tell him that she had "gone out with an NCB (local shorthand for Nice Catholic Boy) and decided that he was not among the 'dozens' with whom I once so blithely declared I could live happily ever after." She had also taken a test in American foreign policy and noted ironically that in all her reading, "the only thing that I can remember is that someone called NATO a 'bold and imaginative' plan (What a snare and a delusion!)." Then she added: "I know that I shouldn't say this and all, but I miss you terribly and am praying that your trip is a happy and successful one. Please remember that I'll always think that you are—well, you know—just darlin'. My love always, Barbara."

They continued to see each other, and by the end of the summer of 1961, they were engaged, although no public announcement was made.

Lowenstein and Barbara Boggs shared more than their mutual personal attraction. Their politics were virtually the same; NSA anti-Communist liberalism. They shared an interest in the independence movements to which the Cold War was shifting. Boggs believed that "if the liberal Democrats did not become involved in Third World liberation movements, they would be left to the Communists." She shared Lowenstein's intense dislike of the Communists. "Al was very much a patriotic American, there is no doubt about it," she reflects. "He was violently anti-Communist."

Lowenstein was also involved in changing careers, or at least in starting one. He had toyed with the idea of an academic life: it was the way Frank Graham had proceeded. And he had other friends in high academic positions, such as William Craig, who were urging him to teach and go into university administration.

Lowenstein had met Craig in 1951. As president of the NSA, Lowenstein was then visiting Washington State University, where he helped to organize a new chapter. At the time, Craig was dean of students, the youngest dean in the United States. He was a rising star of American academic life, as well as a member of the National Advisory Committee of the NSA. By 1960, Craig was the dean of men at Stanford University and he wanted Lowenstein to join his staff. He contacted Lowenstein in New York at the time Lowenstein was actively pursuing the nomination for Congress, and urged him to come to Stanford as assistant dean of men and as a lecturer in political science.

Craig himself arrived in New York in the early summer of 1960 to press Lowenstein for a decision. And before Craig left, Lowenstein had decided to go to Stanford as his assistant and as the director of the Stern Dormitories, where he was to live and where he would have a staff of graduate students assisting him. His teaching assignments included a course on the politics of South West Africa called "The Politics of Sub-Saharan Africa," which he gave in the fall term, and constitutional law in the spring.

Lowenstein then devoted his energies to the completion of his book on his mission to South West Africa. He left New York early in 1961 and went down to Hollywood, Florida, where he labored on the manuscript. Writing was a painful process to Lowenstein. He needed help, and in addition to getting help from his editor at Macmillan, Peter Ritner, Lowenstein enlisted the assistance of Curtis Gans, then working in Miami as a journalist.

He gave Gans several chapters to read and rewrite, using research done by Brooke Aronson, a Smith College graduate and friend now working at the American Society of African Culture, later exposed by *Ramparts* magazine as a CIA front. Peter Ritner encouraged him: "So far as I knew, when you signed your contract, you might not have been able to write a word. Lots of men who are fluent speakers can't. But it turns out that you *can* write. In fact, I think you'll have no trouble soaring way over your word-limit on the first draft. Then will come the next phase, of integrating the 'chunks' together, modeling the contours of the book as a whole, setting a sustained tone for it, bringing the high points and characters into bold relief, etc. You won't have any real trouble with this, I think, but you'll have to work like a dog."

Besides helping him with the book, Curtis Gans shared with Lowenstein his experiences before coming to Miami. After graduating from Chapel Hill, Gans in the winter of 1961 had gone to Berkeley where he did graduate work in European intellectual history. Berkeley then was at the vanguard of the new student protest movement against authoritarianism in university administration and Gans himself became involved briefly as a member of the new Students for a Democratic Society. When he left Berkeley and came back East, hooking up with Lowenstein, Gans brought with him a sense of the new dynamic in the student movement, a radicalism that was pulling from the left and the right. The "progressive center" that had been so carefully cultivated by Lowenstein in the NSA was being torn apart. There had been widespread rage on the left. And when the radicals rioted against HUAC (the House Un-American Activities Committee), the right responded in kind. William Buckley, Jr., who had joined with Howard Phillips and Fulton Lewis III in founding the Young Americans for Freedom, rushed to denounce the demonstrators and to support the committee.

Lowenstein had enormous contempt for the House Un-American Activities Committee. He regarded it as crude and primitive, an unbecoming vestige of the obsolete far right which gave America a bad name.

Sensing the rising student antipathy to rigid authority and the need to fill the vacuum left by the fifties, during which there had been no serious dissent, Lowenstein became a leading liberal spokesman against the HUAC, stressing the need for a more subtle brand of anti-

Communism that did not overtly challenge the civil liberties guaranteed by the Constitution. In 1961, he went to Exeter Academy in New Hampshire to debate William Buckley, Jr., on the subject of the HUAC. Greg Craig, William Craig's son, was by then a student at Exeter, and he recalls the episode in which Lowenstein, the champion of the non-Communist left, took on Buckley, the dragon of the New Right.

"I have no memory of what Al looked like from those early days. As I said, he was more of a presence than a real person to me then. I was really too young, perhaps, to be conscious of the way people dressed or looked. I think I really 'saw' Al while I was a student at Phillips Exeter Academy in New Hampshire, aged sixteen. I remember spotting the notice on the bulletin board announcing that William F. Buckley, Jr., would debate Allard K. Lowenstein, 'a lawyer from New York City' about the House Un-American Activities Committee (HUAC) and 'Operation Abolition,' a film about the student demonstration against HUAC in San Francisco. (Al Lowenstein was to 'lawyer from New York City' as Clark Kent is to 'mild-mannered reporter.') Again, I faced the problem of telling my friends that I knew and, in fact, was friends with this man named Allard K. Lowenstein. We had discussions in the dining hall about the upcoming debate. Everyone had heard of William F. Buckley, Jr., but who was this New York lawyer, Allard K. Lowenstein, and why was he, of all people, the one who would be debating Buckley? I couldn't answer those questions to my own satisfaction. I didn't think I could possibly explain who Al Lowenstein was, so I kept my silence, hoping that Al, in the course of his appearance, would strip away the mystery once and for all.

"I arrived very early to get a front row seat in the chapel in the Academy Building. I came by myself. The room was filled to overflowing. There were many townspeople there as well as students, because the event was being cosponsored by some local organizations and, I think, the local Catholic church.

"I remember seeing Al on the stage and being disappointed in what he looked like. It was, in fact, the first time in my life that I focused on Al's looks, and I was genuinely surprised at how unprepossessing he appeared. I began to tremble for him as I watched him hunched in his armchair on the stage. Buckley would make mincemeat of him. Al would be humiliated. He would probably be too ashamed to stay around to say hello to his friends after the debate, and I prepared to make a rapid and invisible exit at the end of the program, to slink off into the night and return quietly to my dormitory.

"First, the film was shown. It was a black-and-white documentary largely assembled from news film, a brutal, violent, carefully edited and slanted (by the right) portrayal of the student demonstrations against HUAC in San Francisco. The theme of the movie was that the demonstrations were inspired, organized, and carried out by the Communists, and although there were surely some well-meaning non-Communists who participated in the demonstrations, they were, at best, dupes. (I recall that the phrase 'Communist dupe' was particularly popular in those days.)

"After the film, the house lights remained down, and the rostrum was lit with bright spotlights. Buckley walked to the podium, red rose in lapel, bathed in warm, welcoming applause. It is my recollection that the people in the audience did not share Buckley's politics but were really there to observe the performance of a master debater, much the way Spaniards would crowd in the bull ring to watch El Cordobés dispatch the bull. Not so many people had heard of Buckley then [1961] but his reputation among those that knew him was not very different from what it is today. Then, however, he was younger, more aggressive, and still a phenomenon. But this audience—me included—had never seen Buckley perform before, and the Buckley style cut through the room like a rapier. He was arrogant, condescending, outrageous, witty, brilliant, biting, literary, arch, caustic, all of these and more. He curved his back and swept up onto his tiptoes, hands gripping the sides of the podium, nose and chin lifted high, patronizing, supremely confident. On his toes, he swayed slowly from side to side like a cobra, hypnotizing the audience, choosing his time to stroke, to pierce, to paralyze. He was, in short, absolutely terrifying.

"Al followed. He padded up to the microphone in a baggy suit, a complete and utter unknown to all of the people in the audience. He leaned on the rostrum, took off those heavy glasses and rubbed the bridge of his nose. The audience was deathly still. I was embarrassed for him. He was not the most elegant or dashing champion in the world. He was so homely, he was so rumpled, he seemed so terribly unorganized, he was the last person in the world one would actually choose to do battle with the Buckley dragon. He began to speak, and I held my breath. Maybe it was going to be all right. In fact, it was going to be terrific.

"The ugly duckling took flight and began to soar like an eagle. He started slowly, circling upward almost lazily, gaining altitude, bringing up the speed and starting to cover ground. His speech developed a rhythm, gaining power and volume and force slowly, moving faster and faster, building, building, building, and then crashing through to irrefutable conclusions. Then a pause, a joke, a quip, and he would start over again.

"Al's speech was always the essence of argument—one point connected to the next, leading to a third, moving always toward a conclusion. He stitched the case together right before your eyes. There was no hocus-pocus. He was never mean-spirited, never shrill, never angry, never insulting, always reasoning, always logical. His words swept over the audience like an avalanche. They came so fast, you had little time to savor them. His speech was studded with historical and political references—to Eleanor Roosevelt, to Adlai Stevenson, to Frank Porter Graham—as if everyone in the room agreed with Al that, of course, these were America's greatest living public figures.

"He met Buckley's satire with his own. His wit was just as quick. But Al was never arrogant, never pompous. He was, however, hilariously funny. Al was everything you ever wanted a speaker to be without once losing his dignity or his composure or his control. And when people finally stood and applauded for him (and for Buckley), I could scarcely restrain the tears."

IV
Iberia and Africa
Part Two

19.

At Stanford, Lowenstein was an extremely popular lecturer, attracting the bright and the curious to his course on South West Africa. He was instrumental in bringing Stanford back into the NSA. On a conservative campus, he was perceived as someone who empathized with the students. According to a political science professor at Stanford who was a friend of John Tyler Caldwell, the chancellor of North Carolina State, Lowenstein was "a regular Pied Piper. If he started to say anything to students, they just followed him, just like the old Pied Piper." But Lowenstein was by no means a radical, although many students were confused by his passionate rhetoric and took him to be one. "At the time, I didn't understand this," says Kris Kleinbauer, an undergraduate from Los Angeles who took Lowenstein's course and was greatly impressed by him. "Al was an anti-Communist. He was the best of these people; he was an honest force."

And undeterred by distance, Lowenstein kept up his relationship with Barbara Boggs, who was now working in the White House for President Kennedy. Sometimes Lowenstein would fly to Washington to see her, sometimes she would jet out to California to be with him. Having previously worked for the Extension Volunteers, a Roman Catholic organization charged with recruiting students for assignments in poor rural areas where they helped church programs and worked on basic social problems, Boggs had returned to Washington when her parents persuaded her to take a position with the president. As a liaison to citizen groups, she worked in the White House drafting messages from Kennedy to the various groups who wanted action on any number of issues.

In the "heady preassassination days," as Barbara Boggs refers to them, Lowenstein would descend on Washington with twenty friends and arrive at the White House to see her. It was a hectic engagement, more of a "group courtship" in which she felt as if she were engaged not to Allard Lowenstein but to many groups, his South African group, his civil rights group. And most of his camp followers were what she describes as Lowenstein's "blond, WASP-y acolytes," the talented and attractive elite who found in him a focal point for their concerns about society and the world. She was unconcerned about his obvious attraction to these young men, with the inevitable wrestling matches and the overt demonstrations of affection. Coming from New Orleans, she accepted this as natural; men there frequently walked with their arms around each other. In Lowenstein's case, she also recognized "the eternal feeling" on his part of wanting to appropriate the characteristics of the young men he was close to. He was attracted, she concludes, to both the "physical and manor-born characteristics that more easily fit the American ideal."

In December of 1961, Allard Lowenstein and Barbara Boggs became engaged. The wedding was set for December 8, 1962 and it would have been a major liberal-establishment event.

Lowenstein joked with Hale Boggs that he would agree not to campaign for him in Louisiana in order to improve his chances of reelection. But while Boggs appreciated Lowenstein's sense of humor, he objected to Lowenstein as a husband for his daughter. Boggs thought Lowenstein didn't have the ability to stick to a vocation, and also felt his Jewishness was a problem.

Barbara Boggs thinks of Lowenstein as a person who was, most of all, fun to be with. But in spite of her feelings for him, their relationship began to be strained. While her mother Lindy looked forward to the wedding enthusiastically, ordering expensive towels and other household items for them, Allard and Barbara began to drift apart. Lindy Boggs admired Lowenstein for his rebel spirit and his outrageous sense of humor. Since she too was a rebel at heart, the idea of the marriage appealed to her enormously. But some of the very qualities that she found so appealing made her daughter think twice. "He never figured out his restlessness," she reflects. "He never got beyond the crisis of justification for leaving what he was doing at the moment to do something else." Also citing "religious differences" as a cause for their breakup, she said she came to the conclusion that Lowenstein had a "Messiah complex," which would ultimately make marriage to him impossible. And he, in turn, understood that the religious issue was a major obstacle. When Barbara's sister later married a Jewish man, Lowenstein joked that a Jew had finally made it into the Boggs family.

Boggs also insists that while her Catholic upbringing had socialized her for a life as a wife, accomplishing good in the world through serving her husband, she was rebelling against this: "For reasons I don't understand yet, I found this wasn't so. You couldn't live your life through someone else. Although I enjoyed dinner with twenty people at once, I might get a little tired of having them in various combinations around together while he would be in South Africa or Mississippi, where it was exciting, and I would be home with his followers and the children."

Late in the summer of 1962, she broke off the engagement.

20.

Both politically and personally, 1962 was a watershed year for Allard Lowenstein. Events in Africa were taking a disturbing direction. Nelson Mandela was arrested when the South African police discovered the underground headquarters of the African National Congress in Rivonia, a suburb of Johannesburg. If convicted of the charges against him, he faced death by hanging. In a secret interview with Patrick O'Donovan on May 30, 1961, the notes of which were given to Lowenstein by his friend in London, Mary Benson, Mandela had said that "the question is whether we can continue talking peace and nonviolence, whether in future campaigns we can hope to muster support from the African people if we talk nonviolence. I think increasing numbers of Africans are coming to consider it futile and consider it useless to use nonviolence in view of government reaction to those methods." Mandela was thinking along the lines of massive strikes in South African industry and agriculture and added, "The basis on which we have conducted our struggle so far will have to be seriously reconsidered where the government's reaction is to crush by naked force."

Mandela discounted the Pan-Africanist Congress because, he asserted, "there is no doubt in my mind that they preached an extreme form of racialism." And he pointed to the failure of their attempt to organize a demonstration in Cape Town as evidence of their lack of support. Mandela's liberal sympathizer, Mary Benson, inserted in the notes of the interview that his comments on the possibility of violence should not be credited to him publicly, but Mandela concluded strongly: "No leader is going out to say we want peaceful discussions because the government is making that kind of talk senseless. Instead of getting a favorable response, the government is more arrogant. The African reaction can only be a show of force."

In line with this resolve, Oliver Tambo fled the country in 1962 to rebuild the African National Congress abroad, establishing his headquarters in Zambia. Acts of sabotage, which Lowenstein documented in a series of memoranda, began to occur in South Africa with increasing frequency.

On May 31, 1962, the Accra Freedom Fighters Conference called by Kwame Nkrumah met in Ghana to promote the cause of those Africans who were fighting for independence. Jacob Kuhangua, the National Secretary of SWAPO, attended the conference with other SWAPO leaders and met with the organizers of SWANU to attempt the establishment of a united front against South Africa to win independence for South West Africa. From Accra, he proceeded to Dar es Salaam, Tanganyika, where Sam Nujoma had set up SWAPO's headquarters in exile. From Dar, Nujoma organized for the liberation of South West Africa by armed struggle. This happened just as the South African Communist Party was calling for armed struggle on the grounds that peaceful means had been exhausted. The specter of the Soviet Union's influence in Africa was becoming more menacing, while the American position was eroding, weakened by U.S. ties to South Africa, continued racial segregation at home, and a lack of trained personnel capable of establishing personal contacts with the new African leadership. It was a situation ripe for Lowenstein's participation.

Meanwhile, Lowenstein had become a controversial figure on the Stanford campus. Lawrence de Bivort, a student at Stanford at the time, recalls that Lowenstein was "free-wheeling" and very supportive of the undergraduates on a campus that was generally "staid." "Ultimately," according to de Bivort, "Al was too eclectic for any organization."

Barbara Boggs describes Stanford as "in crisis" during the time Lowenstein worked there. The students were critical of the limitations placed by the administration on their access to political and religious speakers. They were, according to William Craig, also agitating for reasonable rules on drinking. Dean Craig's office, in which Lowenstein worked, stood on the side of increased freedom for the students. Faced with President Wallace Sterling's intransigence, both Craig and Lowenstein decided to leave.

Boggs insists that Lowenstein "left Stanford because there was a crisis at Stanford which created a noble self-justification for leaving." In reality, Craig resigned before Lowenstein, whose relations with the administration were more cordial than Lowenstein's friends acknowledge. The vice-president for financial affairs, Kenneth Cuthbertson, was a close friend, and President Sterling continued to seek Lowenstein's advice on student affairs. In 1965, Sterling would arrange for Stanford to pay Lowenstein's air fare to California in order for them to continue their discussions. Lowenstein relished the role of the *enfant terrible*. It gave him ever-increasing credibility with students who were becoming more restless as they embraced the spirit of the sixties. But it also made his life unsettled and deprived him of the continuity which is essential for anyone who is advancing an academic career.

This was Lowenstein's situation in 1962 when, according to sources with background in intelligence work, he was formally recruited by the Central Intelligence Agency. Although the author's attempts to obtain Lowenstein's CIA file under the Freedom of Information-Privacy Act from the CIA and from his lawyer Gary Bellow proved unavailing, other evidence overwhelmingly supports these sources. One of these sources states that Lowenstein was brought in initially to work on South West Africa. Having traveled to South West Africa, then written a book and taught a course on the subject at Stanford, Lowenstein had as much expertise and practical experience as any American in South West Africa affairs. And the critical issue of South West Africa, or Namibia, as it came to be called, continued to require the attention of the United States as it formulated its Africa policy in the tumultuous years of the independence movements.

As Victor Marchetti, who worked for the CIA and coauthored *The CIA and the Cult of Intelligence* with John D. Marks, pointed out to me, there are many ways a person can be associated with the CIA. Marchetti does not know if Lowenstein was employed by the CIA but says that "there are so many ways he could have been connected." Marchetti observes that the CIA tried to make use of "so many people." They might be professors, authorities on particular areas, who were briefed and debriefed, without any financial compensation. Or such people might be "contract agents," on a career, long-term, or job-by-job basis. According to a document obtained by the Africa Research Group, the career agent is defined as someone with a "status midway between that of classical agent used in a single compartmented operation, perhaps for a limited period of time, and that of a staff member involved through his career in many operations and well-informed of the agency's capabilities." The most difficult thing, Marchetti explains, is to pin down "if the person is receiving money." He notes that "there is a big difference between signing a piece of paper and receiving money, and cooperating with each other." Even if, in the latter case, funds are provided for specific projects, the distinction remains, "particularly in the mind of the recipient." And, as Marchetti asserts, "This often gets lost in the eyes of the agency people."

The CIA has many people it regards as "allies," "contacts," "friends," and the like, both foreign nationals and Americans, who have varying relationships with the agency, involving money, assignments, and degrees of trust. When Victor Marchetti did a study for the director of the CIA on the people associated with the agency, he encountered problems in deciding exactly who should be included. "It's difficult to pin down," he says. "Is he a contact or a contract agent?" Such people would be assigned a code name, a cryptograph, to cover them from exposure, even within the agency itself.

Particularly confusing is the fact that different CIA administrators might come to differing conclusions about an individual. Marchetti speaks hypothetically about the head of the African Desk, who might say, "We have five guys we're using at X universities." Another officer might say that the agency didn't have anybody at those universities. Then too, Marchetti explains, there were some people who thought they were working for the CIA but were not so regarded by the agency itself.

Lowenstein's exact relationship with the CIA is vague, as it no doubt was meant to be, and as it was with many of their people. It is not possible to pinpoint what, if any, his compensation was, although his ability to travel abroad extensively and stay at excellent hotels when he was, for example, on leave of absence from his job as a professor and received no salary, reinforces the conclusion that the sources are correct. As Marchetti advises, "Stick with the circumstantial evidence. What matters is the close association and cooperation." This is what reveals a person's role with the CIA.

The CIA could recruit a person while letting him believe he was still independent. But at what point does he stop being a professor and his job become a cover? When the hotel is paid for? When they give him money for a political cause he supports in Spain or Africa? When they tell him to keep the money because he could have been making it doing something else instead of cooperating with them? When a consultantship is arranged, or a book contract? Or when he finally signs a piece of paper and swears never to reveal that he has been working for them?

Lowenstein's relationship with the CIA was, in fact, much like his sexuality: ambivalent. It was not permissible to be overtly homosexual and work for the CIA. Yet Lowenstein was physically close to young, attractive men. At what point does an encounter between men become a sexual encounter? When they wrestle? When they embrace? When one of them takes off his clothes and goes to bed with the other, as Lowenstein did? Lowenstein denied he was gay even as he made advances to a man, and he denied he was working for the CIA, even as he collected information and acted to influence the internal affairs of other countries.

The CIA divides its covert operations into two categories for some purposes: intelligence collection, which is espionage or the obtaining of intelligence by covert means; and covert action, attempts to influence the internal affairs of other nations—sometimes called "intervention"—by covert means. Lowenstein was involved in both of these activities.

He clipped and analyzed newspaper reports on African affairs extensively. He saved thousands of newspaper and magazine articles, which he outlined carefully. He subscribed to numerous magazines on

Africa, and to others likely to carry information of relevance. He relied heavily on *Africa Report*, the publication of the American Committee on Africa that became the vehicle of the CIA-backed African-American Institute. In detailing the incidents of violence in South Africa and the government's response, starting in 1962, Lowenstein transcribed portions of articles from papers such as the *Sun Johannesburg*, which contained information on how much the Nationalist government was spending on military and police equipment.

Lowenstein wrote numerous reports on his trips to Spain and Africa, which he could rationalize as support work for the political groups he championed at home and abroad that the CIA also happened to be encouraging. Likewise, he could look at the personal relationships he had cultivated with key players in the politics of the countries in which he was involved as having the purpose of advancing his cause. His offering of financial support to his contacts furthered this end as well. But his relationships with these people allowed him to gather needed information and to influence their actions. Lowenstein was trusted and he often served as the carrier of information which one group or another wanted brought to the attention of the government in Washington. He invariably offered financial support, and was regarded by members of such groups as a friend and supporter, unless, of course, they themselves fell into the hazy orbit of CIA contact-contracts, doing the bidding of Washington.

Lowenstein became involved in the politics of Spain and in Africa in ways that constituted "covert action." As Richard Bissell explained, the "operational types" would be risk-takers, which Lowenstein was. Bissell, who was chief of Clandestine Services of the CIA under President Kennedy until he was forced to resign after the Bay of Pigs, classified the various forms of covert action: "(1) political advice and counsel; (2) subsidies to an individual; (3) financial support and 'technical assistance' to political parties; (4) support of private organizations, including labor unions, business firms, cooperatives, etc.; (5) covert propaganda; (6) 'private' training of individuals and exchange of persons; (7) economic operations; and (8) paramilitary or political action operations designed to overthrow a regime (like the Bay of Pigs and the programs in Laos). These operations can be classified in various ways: by the degree and type of secrecy required, by their legality, and, perhaps, by their benign or hostile character." Lowenstein's actions can be seen to fall into most, if not all, of these categories.

Lowenstein's handwritten notes on key African leaders are illuminating. There is a considerable amount of information, giving a concise background, political affiliation, and ideology. Next to the mini-dossier of one political leader, there is a sum of money.

Sekou Toure, trade-union, (CGT) Muslim parentage, "We prefer poverty in liberty to riches in slavery." (Nouveau franc 1,136,000

- 57,000); Kwame N. Nkrumah, Lincoln Univ, in Econ. Soc; Lecturer in Poli Sci at same, Garvey supporter, jailed, Jan. '50 P.M. Mar. '57, . . . Julius Nyerere, . . . TANU, "Uhuru Na Kazi" (freedom & work)—Socialist and Pan Africanist; Albert Lithuli . . . Jomo Kenyatta roomed in London with Robeson & Abrahams . . . English wife, 1 son . . . Tom Mboya . . . Luo Sanitary Inspector, Trade Unions in lieu of political support-KANU-ICFTU cost him Pan African support; Haile Selassie . . . at 14 Gov. of region, 16 of province; William Vacanarat Shadrach Tubman . . . True Whig.

After the information on the leaders, Lowenstein jotted down three issues: Economic Investment, Communist Penetration, Regional Groupings. He asked, "Does independence help or impede economic development? 2. Are tribal and other traditional forces adjusting? 3. What is the significance of the cold war on African thinking?" Then, he scribbled: "re Chicuarra (Mozambique) we have Pedro CHIKUEKA (Angola) at Lincoln. re Nhambiu (Mozambique) no record re Paul Muonjani (Basutoland)—no record (no students from High Commission Territories at Lincoln)." He was gathering information, analyzing issues, and developing contacts.

Starting in 1957, the CIA had worked with Israel in gathering intelligence on the independent African countries. The Church Committee wrote:

> In the early 1960's the decolonization of Africa sparked an increase in the scale of CIA clandestine activities on that continent. CIA actions paralleled growing interest on the part of the State Department and the Kennedy Administration in the "third world countries." . . . Prior to 1960, Africa had been included in the European or Middle Eastern Division. In that year it became a separate division. Stations sprang up all over the continent. Between 1959 and 1963 the number of CIA stations in Africa increased by 55.5%.

In the Congo, where Lowenstein's friend Frank Carlucci was sent after his tour of duty in Johannesburg, the CIA engaged in a struggle with leftist Congolese influenced by the Soviet Union, and plotted the assassination of Patrice Lumumba. Cash was given to various pro-West politicians and arms were supplied to the supporters of Joseph Mobutu and Cyrille Adula. Carlucci got so close to Adula that when the Congolese premier attended a state luncheon at the White House in 1962, he asked, "Where is Carlucci?" Embarrassed, President Kennedy whispered, "Who the hell is Carlucci?" After a search, the young Foreign Service officer, then on the State Department's Congo desk, was found having lunch across the street with lower-level State Department officers. He was rushed to the White House.

In 1960, in Angola, the CIA recruited Holden Roberto, the leader of an anti-Soviet faction in the war that was raging for control of the Portuguese colony; the Soviet Union was supporting the MPLA, or Popular Movement for the Liberation of Angola. And in South Africa, the CIA worked closely with the South African secret police.

Lowenstein's work in the CIA involved southern Africa, and because Franco supported Portugal and South Africa, it also involved Spain, where Lowenstein worked with the anti-Communist left opposed to Franco. The CIA wanted as much pressure put on South Africa as possible to get it to give up the mandated territory of South West Africa, and on Portugal to force it to relinquish its colonies of Angola and Mozambique, thus eliminating a source of friction between the United States and black Africa. Lowenstein also worked to cultivate the leaders of the African liberation movements who were potential allies of America, to make sure the colonies became friendly independent countries, while continuing to promote the cause of the antiapartheid, anti-Communist liberals in South Africa.

Harris Wofford, a friend of Lowenstein's who served as President Kennedy's special assistant for civil rights from 1961 to 1962, then as special representative to Africa from 1962 to 1964, and finally, associate director of the Peace Corps from 1964 to 1966, observes: "There is the possibility, of course, that Al was tied to the CIA. I don't know that he was. I never thought he was until recent times have made me think conceivably in the mid-fifties, when NSA was getting involved . . . the people promoting the NSA tie were people that were saying, 'We're supporting liberal-left people around the world, we're supporting Democratic Socialists in Latin America and India,' and that Al could have cooperated. I know a CIA fellow that it turns out later was involved in all that stuff, and I didn't know about the stuff at the time, but his thesis to me was, 'If you only knew what we're really doing, the liberals and leftists, the democratic leftists, what we're supporting around the world, you'd see that we represent the good wing in the CIA.' I could see that someone representing the 'good wing' got some kind of collaboration with Al. I could imagine it. It would not surprise me if for a while he saw this as a good thing."

While Wofford denies any express knowledge of Lowenstein's CIA connection, he asserts that the matter is worth pursuing. "I think you need to," he told me. "It's an interesting question. The thing your book can do is, through the complexity of Al's life, convey some of the complex plot of our time. There was a 'good wing' that had the theory that America's interests called for supporting the democratic left in Latin America, India, and elsewhere. I picked up its trail in India. It wanted to support the non-Communist Socialists in India and in the end, it hurt them because they got several of the Indian Socialist leaders involved in the Congress for Cultural Freedom and some other things and they got money to them, and it all got exposed. And suddenly some of these militant Socialists in India had on record in the United States that they had been getting money from CIA fronts."

Wofford is certain that this approach was used in Africa as well. And Lowenstein was the ideal person to have operating as a member of the so-called "good wing" of the CIA, which needed people with credibility who could gain the trust of the Third World leaders the CIA wanted in the fold.

Lowenstein was a leading figure in this effort. Before he was recruited by the CIA, he was already involved, doing work that the CIA wanted him to continue. He was the contact person for the anti-Communist resistance in Spain, for the liberals in South Africa, and for the black African liberation organizations in South Africa and South West Africa—all groups that America needed to cultivate in case they did come to power. And since he was their messenger to the American power structure, they all wanted Lowenstein in the government in some capacity as their spokesman. Indeed, had he continued to work for them, he would have had to register as a foreign agent.

Lowenstein shared, as his good friend, the antiwar leader Rev. William Sloane Coffin observes, the view held by the CIA at the time: the way to defeat Communism was with a different form of the left, not from the right. Coffin, himself a CIA operative for three years during which time he worked on Soviet affairs, says that he was recruited for the CIA while at Yale because he was "too liberal for the State Department" and points out that Joseph McCarthy denounced the CIA for being a "nestbed for liberals and radicals."

Lowenstein was the outstanding student leader of his generation, the way Cord Meyer had been of his. And like Cord Meyer, who joined the CIA, Lowenstein came to believe that his greatest enemies were to his left. Lowenstein was, before anything else, an anti-Communist, to whom liberalism was the most effective strategy for defeating Communism. He was, according to Buckley, a "meliorist," someone who believed in incremental change to make things modestly better. That William F. Buckley, Jr., whom he debated and who also served in the CIA, became one of his closest friends, is not as incongruous as some might believe. They came together as dedicated anti-Communists who differed on strategy. Buckley, the archconservative, feared that any change would simply let down the floodgates; Lowenstein, the archliberal, believed change was the way to let the steam out of the pressure cooker and thus prevent revolution. Martin Peretz, who backed the candidacy of Eugene McCarthy with his family's fortune and became the publisher of *The New Republic*, once commented to Wendell Willkie II that the difference between himself and

Lowenstein was that he was a non-Communist but Lowenstein was an anti-Communist. His passionate advocacy of moderate change was Lowenstein's greatest incongruity and led the right to regard him as a dangerous radical. Sophisticated conservatives like Buckley were the exception; they saw Lowenstein as a valid force in American politics. But it was also a tenet of Lowenstein's liberalism that excessive conservatism, in stifling the process of change, aided the Communists, giving them issues they would otherwise be denied.

Lowenstein's politics disallowed anything to his left within the United States and anything that was Communist abroad. Those to his right in America, he sought to educate and convert.

In the spring of 1962, Lowenstein was contacted by both the American Committee on Africa and the CIA-supported American Society of African Culture, which were joining forces for a demonstration and protest march on behalf of Nelson Mandela, Walter Sisulu, and the seven others who had been arrested by the South African police when the African National Congress underground headquarters was discovered. The arrested leaders were on trial and faced the possibility of the death penalty, which in South Africa was administered by hanging.

The rally literature featured a quotation from John F. Kennedy: "Freedom is indivisible and when one man is enslaved, who are free?" On June 4, 1962, the public was invited to join in protesting "bannings, jailings, torturing, and trials of thousands of opponents of apartheid," and to march in "solidarity" with Mandela and his associates. The South African Consulate on Madison Avenue was to be picketed, followed by a march to the United Nations where a rally was scheduled with speeches by union leader Leon Davis, popular black actors Ossie Davis and Ruby Dee, the National Director of CORE James Farmer, Morley Nkosi, a representative of the Pan-Africanist Congress, "and others." The event was sponsored by the American Committee on Africa, the American Society of African Culture, the Association of Artists for Freedom, Campus Americans for Democratic Action, CORE, Local 1199, RWDSU, the NAACP, the Student Action Committee of Union Seminary, SDS, SNCC, the United Auto Workers, and the U.S. National Student Association.

Mandela was a cult figure of the left who had enormous appeal. Until his capture, his ability to elude the police had made him a folk hero. What is significant about the demonstration was that all of the sponsors were anti-Communist, thus preempting the Communist party's gathering its front groups in a major protest. The American Society of African Culture was CIA-supported and the Association of Artists for Freedom was one of those "cultural" groups with distinct Cold War overtones. And as late as 1962, the fledgling SDS and SNCC were still establishment-supported organizations, receiving funds from the union-backed League for Industrial Democracy and Martin Luther King, Jr.'s, SCLC. The Kennedy quotation put the world on notice that America opposed apartheid, just as the mounting civil rights movement demonstrated that there was determined opposition to segregation within the United States. And because of this organized pressure, Mandela and Sisulu were not executed but sentenced to life in prison, with Mandela remaining, even behind bars, the preeminent figure in the African National Congress.

In July of 1962, *Brutal Mandate* was published by Macmillan, with an introduction by Eleanor Roosevelt. She wrote:

I have known Mr. Lowenstein for many years. He is a person of unusual ability and complete integrity. I think he will always fight crusades because injustice fills him with a sense of rebellion. He wants to be of help in some way, and it must have been a great satisfaction to him and his companions when the recordings they had succeeded in smuggling out of South West Africa were finally played for members of the Fourth Committee of the United Nations. Their own testimony made a deep impression, so deep that they awakened much new interest in South West Africa and gained new respect for their own country.

And Lowenstein, in turn, wrote of her in his acknowledgement: "There is Mrs. Franklin D. Roosevelt, the greatest of human beings, if greatness can be measured by numbers of people helped and quantities of energy guided to useful purposes."

Lowenstein was also preparing to leave Stanford for a new teaching position at North Carolina State in Raleigh. As an assistant professor in the department of social studies, his salary was to be $7,000 a year. He stepped up his African activities and his involvement in Spain, moving along at a breathless pace.

21.

Lowenstein sat in his office at North Carolina State devouring a plate of spaghetti and washing it down with two glasses of chocolate milk while he spoke with reporter Lawrence Maddry. He told Maddry that he had toured Spain in 1958 as an aide to Hubert Humphrey and made a report on the Franco regime for the Foreign Relations Committee. Later, he was asked by Fred Zinnemann, the producer of *High Noon*, to serve as technical advisor for *Behold the Pale Horse*, a Columbia Pictures film starring Gregory Peck and Anthony Quinn. "Roughly, the movie is a story of Spanish opposition fighters exiled in

France, but anxious to return to Spain," Lowenstein explained. "It all started when I picked up a phone in my office and a voice asked if I knew Fred Zinnemann. . . . I said I'd heard of him," Lowenstein added modestly. The film, most of which was shot in France, angered the Franco regime, which charged that Columbia Pictures had not treated the Spanish government fairly.

Part of Lowenstein's work involved being as hard as possible on the Franco administration, something which he was eager to do since he despised the Spanish dictator. But Lowenstein had to demonstrate greater anti-Franco sentiments than the Communists, who were pushing to position themselves as the only true opponents of Spanish Fascism.

In 1961, the Committee for a Democratic Spain was established in New York. Violently anti-Franco, it was suspected of having Communist ties. Its statement of purpose, which was widely distributed, read:

> The time has come for a new effort to persuade our government to withdraw its moral and economic support from the Fascist Franco regime put into power in Spain by Hitler and Mussolini. For this purpose, and to give such aid as is possible to the forces inside and outside Spain seeking freedom from the Franco dictatorship, the Committee for a Democratic Spain has been formed.
>
> The Committee will issue a newsletter that will report the significant developments in the struggle for a free Spain. Through public meetings, such as this initial one, the committee intends to inform and arouse the American people about the true character of the Franco regime and the real prospects for liberation in Spain.
>
> Special efforts will be made to influence the Kennedy administration and the Congress to act in accordance with our American traditions of democracy and in the interest of our true national security by breaking the bonds of aid to Franco and encouraging the democratic impulses inside Spain.

The New York Committee for a Democratic Spain was ostensibly a "Liberal-Socialist" organization founded by Spanish exiles Alvarez Del Vayo and Mario De Salegui, but FBI sources described both Del Vayo and De Salegui as "pro-Communist." Lowenstein quickly joined the effort, supported by the CIA and the United Auto Workers, to displace this organization.

The anti-Communist Spanish opposition began to organize late in 1961. A secretariat was formed called the Unión de Fuerzas Democráticas uniting the Izquierda Demócrata Christiana (IDC) and the Partido Socialisto Oberero Español (PSOE). Radical Carlos Zayas of the Frente de Liberación Popular (FLP) described it in a letter to Lowenstein dated December 10, 1961: "as you know, the centre-left opposition." Zayas told Lowenstein that America needed a new policy in Spain. "This would consist in having ready a body of non-compromised politicians and army officers whom you can trust, able to seize power at the crumbling of the dictatorship. . . . But above all it will be necessary to be able to give to the recently liberated masses a clear justification of your former attitude to the dictatorship." He concluded with the "hope that Bowles' change is not equivalent to a swing to the right in the State Department." Chester Bowles, a liberal and a proponent of working with the anti-Communist left abroad, had been Dean Rusk's under secretary of state but was forced out of that position following a visit Rusk paid to Franco after a NATO meeting. His appointment as under secretary by Kennedy had given Spanish oppositionists like Zayas hope that America would withdraw its support from the Falangists in Spain and back instead the opposition that was still pro-American. The anti-Communist, anti-Franco Americans also had that hope.

On July 5, 1962, Curtis Gate, the European editor of *The Atlantic Monthly*, who was based in Paris, wrote a memorandum on the growing crisis in Spain which was distributed to key members of the American liberal community, including Allard Lowenstein. It was Gate's thesis that a political vacuum was developing in Spain and that the powerful Spanish Communist party would fill it unless something were done quickly. While the Soviet Union was aiding its allies in Spain, America and the other Western democracies were allowing the situation to deteriorate. Gate announced the formation of a new group to reverse this inaction. He wrote, in part:

This silence or passivity on the part of the western democracies gives Moscow and the Spanish Communist Party a free field for exploiting all forms of internal unrest. It allows them to assume unwarranted credit for all upheavals that may take place. Above all, it establishes a dangerous situation whereby the Spanish Communist Party is the only organized opposition force in the country which can influence and orient an explosive situation by being able to issue broadcast directives to its agents, sympathizers and the disoriented masses in the industrial and urban centers of the country.

The exact means for breaking the Communist monopoly have yet to be determined. What is imperative is that this abnormal and potentially disastrous situation should be brought to the attention of the United States and other Western governments. To this end, a "Liberal Spanish Opposition Aid Committee" is being formed.

Because the Communists were already using the name "Committee for a Democratic Spain," it was decided that the new group should be given a name as similar as possible and filled with anti-Communists. Choosing a name everyone could agree on proved surprisingly difficult but the objective was clear: to give support to the anti-Communist liberals and leftists in Spain, so that when Franco died or his regime collapsed, an alternative to the Communists would be in a position to take over the country. Working with the Americans were such leading Spanish anti-Communist oppositionists as Dionisio Ridruejo, a poet who had been propaganda chief of Franco's Falange (Fascist) party in Spain until 1942, and was the leader of the Social Party for Democratic Action as well as the organizer of the Union of Democratic Forces in Spain; Jesus Prados Arrarte, professor of economics at Madrid University; Julian Gorkin, secretary of the Congress for Cultural Freedom (Congres pour la liberté de la Culture), a CIA-supported organization based in Paris, and the editor of its monthly magazine, *Cuadernos*; and Lowenstein's good personal friend, Amadeo Cuito, also based in Paris, who served as Lowenstein's contact with the other Spaniards.

Lowenstein traveled abroad that summer to assess the Spanish problem and to mobilize support for the new committee. It was the period of the Asturian strikes in Spain and the Munich Conference of Spanish exile groups in Europe. In Geneva, Lowenstein spent time with Gil Robles, a leading oppositionist figure. In Paris, he saw Ridruejo, Prados Arrarte, Dr. Rodolfo Llopis, the Socialist leader of the Spanish exiles in France who had resigned as head of the Spanish government in exile in 1947 after a break with the Communists, and Curtis Gate, the *Atlantic Monthly* representative whose memo had warned of the Communist danger in Spain. In Italy, he met with Spanish oppositionist groups and encountered resistance within their exile committees to his insistence on excluding all Communists and their sympathizers. To them, Dolores Ibarruri, La Pasionaria, a Communist, was the single greatest symbol of resistance to Franco. Moreover, while Stalin had sent aid to the embattled Spanish republic during the civil war, Roosevelt had declined to intervene.

The purpose of the meetings that took place all over Europe was to study "ways and means" of channeling funds, once they had reached Spain, so that the money would contribute in the greatest measure possible to the overthrow of the Franco regime. Later, when Lowenstein called on the American embassy in Madrid, he indicated that there was no shortage of funds available for this purpose, "both from interested persons in the United States and a variety of other non-Spanish sources."

To avoid trouble with the police Lowenstein entered Spain by car over obscure motor roads, staying at small pensions, or with contacts.

He immediately contacted opposition groups in Barcelona and attended and actually participated in many of their "secret meetings," before coming to Madrid, the last leg of what Lowenstein referred to as his "assignment." Lowenstein did not believe the police would "touch him" because of his nationality and his prominent backers, but acted discreetly so as not to endanger his Spanish "fellow-workers."

Lowenstein called on the American embassy in August and expressed his chagrin that Adlai Stevenson, Kennedy's ambassador to the United Nations, had ended his recent visit to Spain without meeting with opposition groups, though he *had* met with Franco. A confidential priority State Department memorandum dated August 17, 1962, states:

> An energetic young American writer and teacher, Allard K. Lowenstein, called at the Embassy on August 8 and 9 to express his personal dissatisfaction and that of "a very wide range of Spanish opposition personalities" with whom he claims (with apparent justification) to be in close touch, regarding the visit of Ambassador Stevenson to Spain. Lowenstein is obviously violently opposed to the Franco regime on ideological grounds and seemed to be extremely disappointed when informed that there would be no chance for an "opposition delegation" (he stated that he came to the Embassy on their behalf) to call on Mr. Stevenson, as the latter had already left Spain.

Lowenstein engaged in conversations with the embassy's minister-counselor and with an embassy officer. The memorandum reports:

> He made it clear from the outset that he was diametrically opposed to U.S. policies in and toward Spain and that he found it difficult to even talk with Embassy personnel as he was so deeply engaged in activities directly contrary to U.S. policies; namely, in personally trying to overthrow the Franco regime as soon as possible. He added that it would probably be possible to achieve success in this effort within the next six to eight month.

Lowenstein was convinced that Spain could "take care of itself once Franco is out of the way" and was impervious to embassy suggestions that a new regime would not necessarily be an improvement. He did not agree that there would be post-Franco problems. Lowenstein said he had talked with Spanish Communists and was certain that they would not constitute any danger to a successor government. He did not, he added, consider the maintenance of U.S. bases in Spain important.

Explaining who he was, Lowenstein told of his past work for Hubert Humphrey and his recent position at Stanford. After finishing his present "assignment," he said he planned to return to North Carolina State to teach but expected "to return to Spain periodically" in view of his interest in developments there. Lowenstein then produced a copy of *Brutal Mandate*, with its highly laudatory foreword by Eleanor Roosevelt. Although he did not mention it at the time, Lowenstein was hoping that a Spanish edition of the book would be published to influence anti-Franco groups to oppose apartheid in South Africa and support independence for Namibia.

Lowenstein expressed his support for his friend, the prominent oppositionist Carlos Zayas, who had been imprisoned along with a number of FLP associates, all of whom were charged with a series of minor bombings. He called Zayas "a person of sterling character" and said he had watched him "upholding the non-Communist point of view" at various opposition meetings. Lowenstein expressed his disappointment with the embassy for its failure to challenge the authorities over the arrest of his friend. He believed that an effort to at least save Zayas from "probable" torture at the hands of the police should have been made.

Upon his arrival in Madrid, Lowenstein had told the embassy personnel of his close and constant contacts with "all the active opposition leaders," particularly those of the left, but including some "conservative oppositionists." He refused, though, to name them, muttering that one Inigo Caveiro had been sent to the Canary Islands shortly after talking to an embassy officer. He said he was currently talking with "lower level" oppositionists at meetings largely devoted to efforts to advise them of what was being done for them abroad, particularly in the United States, and to weld the various opposition groups together. He wanted to be certain that the opposition did not fly apart, as it had in the past. Because of the arrangements he had made for funding opposition activities, and the distribution channels that had been established, he did not see this as a problem any longer. Before returning to the United States, Lowenstein said he planned to meet with oppositionists in Vitoria and Bilbao. He indicated that he would see Antonio Amat in Vitoria, but would give no other names. He also informed the embassy that he planned to tape record the statements of oppositionists for use in the United States, and added that, in fact, he had already taped the remarks of one woman from Ovieb who claimed that her husband had been tortured by the police. "She was either a very good actress or else telling the truth," Lowenstein said, adding that he thought there were many more instances of police brutality than had been publicly aired.

Lowenstein commented that many oppositionists he had seen were "disgusted" with the embassy, which "hadn't done anything concrete for them," merely "maintaining contact." But Lowenstein added that he personally felt the embassy was probably doing all it could because "after all, the president of the United States is himself very pro-Franco." Because they were confident that, in the months ahead, they would succeed in their struggle against what he called "Fascist tyranny," Lowenstein concluded that it was possible the oppositionists felt that they did not any longer "need the U.S. Embassy or indeed the U.S." and therefore felt justified in taking "an independent attitude" toward the maintenance of embassy relations. New strategies and tactics were going to be very effective, he believed, as the success of recent strikes proved.

The embassy was puzzled by Lowenstein, as the memo indicates. "He refused to be drawn out as to who was financing his present trip (he was staying at the Hilton in Madrid and obviously had ample funds), but by constant references to Mrs. Roosevelt, Norman Thomas and Walter Reuther, he conveyed the impression that the first two personages highly endorsed his activities and that the latter might be helping to finance it."

Lowenstein finally brought up the matter of the Spanish committee. The memorandum describes what took place:

Lowenstein mentioned briefly that he is one of several who are trying to replace the present New York "Committee for a Free Spain" with a new group, the "Committee for Democratic Spain." He seemed somewhat uncertain, however, as to whether he had mixed the names of these two groups. He initially remarked that the reason for the proposed change was due to the fact that the older group was "Communist infiltrated," but subsequently seemed to regret having made this statement. He seemed, however, quite enthusiastic about the proposed new committee saying it would include Mrs. Roosevelt and Norman Thomas. Somewhat surprisingly, he added that the backers of this group would find a few "well-known Protestants" to give the group "respectability." These persons would, he said, be willing to join due to their dislike of Catholic Church activities in Spain.

Totally confused, the embassy concluded:

It will be obvious from the foregoing that Mr. Lowenstein's activities do not appear to conform to U.S. objectives in Spain and there are also indications that his activities are tending to drive a wedge between the Embassy and certain opposition factions. Any information available to the Department with regard to him would consequently be appreciated. His address is A. Lowenstein, 25 West 81 Street, New York City. [Signed for the Ambassador, Robert H. McBride, Minister-Couselor.]

The naïveté of the embassy is puzzling. Anyone serious about overthrowing Franco would not walk into the American embassy in 1962 and announce his plans. It was important for Lowenstein to have credibility with the opposition groups that were now disappointed with the Kennedy administration for being pro-Franco. The illusion of radicalism was necessary to prevent the opposition from going over to the Communists. The United States was trying to have it both ways: to maintain good relations with Franco, who supplied America with needed air bases, and at the same time, to develop credible ties with the oppositionists by offering them the hope that some Americans who were not Communists were prepared to support drastic action against Franco.

Lowenstein was traveling first class, something he avoided in America, where he preferred to give the impression that he had barely enough funds to survive. From Spain, he went on to Africa.

In Africa, Lowenstein went to Dar es Salaam where he had extensive talks with SWAPO President Sam Nujoma at SWAPO headquarters. He also met SWAPO aide Theo-Ben Gurirab there, the first of many meetings. Lowenstein's purpose in undertaking this South West Africa mission was to convince the Spanish opposition groups to oppose retention by the Portuguese of its colonies in Africa. On this point, he had been resisted by some oppositionists who did not want to become involved in Portugal's colonial wars. Some had even suggested that after Franco, Spain should keep the Sahara. But independence for Mozambique and Angola was crucial to America's African policy; as long as Portugal kept them, colonialism would remain an issue which Moscow could use against America. Instead, America wanted these colonies to become friendly independent countries. As new "front line" states, they would then add to the pressure on South Africa to give up its domination of South West Africa, granting it the independence that America had fostered elsewhere on the continent. Lowenstein had two big items on his personal agenda: the end of South African rule in South West Africa and the eventual defeat of Franco. As far as he was concerned, the CIA was on the right side of these issues. They were letting him do what he was doing.

Lowenstein's performance at the embassy in Madrid had been a *tour de force*. It was so effective that the FBI pursued its investigation of him to determine whether he should be required to register under the Foreign Agents Registration Act as a foreign agent working for the Spanish groups. He had successfully cultivated a reputation for romantic radicalism as the leading anti-Franco activist among the Americans.

Edward F. Gray, the New Jersey education and political action director of the United Auto Workers, called a meeting of the Working Committee for a Free Spain on August 21, 1962. He wrote: "Dr. Al Lowenstein has just returned with much up-to-date information about the current situation inside Spain. We will meet to hear his report at the UAW office, 855 Sixth Avenue (at 30th Street)."

Following the meeting, Victor Reuther, administrative assistant to his brother, Walter Reuther, the president of the UAW, wrote Lowenstein in care of Norman Thomas at 112 East 19th Street, New York (also the address of Iberica, the publishing company that had sponsored young anti-Franco oppositionist Juan Kindelan's U.S. visit while Lowenstein was still working for Humphrey). Reuther wrote that he was very eager to hear from Lowenstein as to whether or not arrangements had been made for a meeting with Stevenson since he was very anxious to participate. Then he continued: "My second reason for writing is that I would very much appreciate receiving as quickly as possible any summary report which you do on your meetings and discussions within Spain. I want to assure you that the contents of such a report would be treated with the greatest confidence so that you will feel free to report frankly and in detail."

Plans for the committee moved along. At a luncheon meeting called by Gray on September 10, and attended by Lowenstein, Irwin Suall, and Dan Shulder, Shulder agreed to go to work immediately for what Gray called, in a letter addressed to Victor Reuther that same day, "our Spanish Committee." Lowenstein drafted an appeal letter which read in part:

Accurate reports from men with Spanish soil still on their shoes indicate that the long night of the Spanish tyranny may be nearly over—*if* the democratic leaders in the West read the time with their hearts and their devotion to freedom. With help, a new democratic alliance in Spain will bring about the rebirth of a free and democratic Spain. . . .

Yet, at this moment when the dedication to freedom of the Spanish people is about to be transformed into a heroic impulse that could electrify the cause of democracy in the world, they hear only two voices in their land—the suave accent of the Communists from Prague, and the Spanish Fascist broadcasts. Franco and the Communists, each for their own purposes, pretend that the only alternative to Fascism in Spain is Communism. . . .

In response to these new pressures, a new opposition coalition has been formed which includes the right-wing Christian Democrats, the Basque Nationalist Party, Socialist Party, and the trade unions, but excludes the totalitarian communists and fascists. . . .

It ended with a plea:

For these purposes we are constituting a Committee of Americans to Support Freedom in Spain. Will you help? Will you give us your permission to use your name in company with us for this cause which has the most profound implications, both for our country and our conscience?

It was vintage Lowenstein, using the Communist threat to spur liberal action against the far-right and excluding Communists from any alliance. It was very difficult to suggest this in Spain since the Communists had fought and died in the civil war and were regarded as genuine "Loyalists" by the non-Communists. Lowenstein knew how to play to American public opinion, though; exclusion of the Communists was essential to get support.

Ed Gray sent several copies of Lowenstein's letter to Victor Reuther enclosed with his own letter, which summarized the conclusions of the luncheon meeting. They were to secure additional signatures for the appeal letter, to be added to those of Walter Reuther, Norman Thomas, and Eleanor Roosevelt, who had already agreed to sign. The appeal would then go out to some 200 prominent citizens in an effort to build up a much larger committee of sponsors. A press conference would then be called at which the material collected by Lowenstein—the names of some 200 prisoners and taped testimonials of torture by Franco's henchmen—would be made public.

In concluding, Gray noted that "our Spanish committee is still very much in the formative stage." Having alternated as chairman with Joel Jacobson, executive vice-president of the New Jersey State AFL-CIO, Gray said he expected to function as the treasurer in the future, while Jacobson would "continue temporarily as chairman until we have persuaded someone, such as George Schuster, to become chairman." At the committee's suggestion, he requested a grant of $2,000 to support its work during the initial period. He asked that the check be made payable to the National Committee for a Free Spain and sent to him at his office, noting that "the name of the committee is not necessarily final."

Lowenstein's relationship with the UAW was deep and strong, and the union's relationship with the CIA was well-established. Tom Braden, who was head of the CIA's International Organizations Division from 1950 to 1954 had once gone to Detroit, at Victor Reuther's request, and given Walter Reuther $50,000 in $50 bills. "Victor spent the money, mostly in West Germany, to bolster labor unions there," Braden explained. And David Halberstam relates that President Kennedy planned to replace John McCone as CIA director with Jack Conway, Walter Reuther's chief political lobbyist. The CIA could seduce liberals and labor into believing that it shared their goals. And the anti-Communist left thought it could use the CIA to defeat their Communist enemies and keep alive the Liberal-Socialist alliance.

While Vincente Sirban, a key oppositionist, was reporting that the "setting up of the committee is well advanced," Victor and Walter Reuther met in Oslo with potential supporters and offered their assistance. These were not radical Spaniards whom they were cultivating. Some were not even liberals. So it was necessary to have the appearance of dynamic activism to give the impression of movement. Lowenstein's key contact, Amadeo Cuito, to this end, promised that "this fall we will try very hard to stir things up."

The Communists in Spain were the most important political force in the unions, which had taken the lead in opposing Franco. An important CIA motive in having the American unions become active was to counter Communist influence and foster an international anti-Communist union movement. Spain was very much on the agenda in this respect. The difficulty was that the American unions were obliged to work with Spaniards who were really more to the right than anyone wanted to admit, straining the working relationship. Even getting the Spaniards to agree on a name for the committee continued to be a problem, and the Spaniards still expressed anger over Adlai Stevenson's failure to meet with them, in their eyes a sign of bad faith. Though Lowenstein knew that Kennedy was pro-Franco, he had to sustain the confidence of the oppositionists in the president and persuade them that, if they organized, pressure could be successfully brought to bear on the Kennedy administration so that it would change its policies.

After intense infighting, the oppositionist factions finally agreed on a program to be submitted to the American committee and on the three names to be used in connection with it: Dionisio Ridruejo, Joseph Pallach, and Julian Gorkin. Amadeo Cuito cabled Lowenstein: "Confirm agreement on names Ridruejo Pallach Gorkin. Letter follows. Cuito." The CIA, using its front, the Congress for Cultural Freedom, then "invited" Gorkin (he ran the Spanish section and was regarded as the top official in the entire operation, which was financed by the CIA) and Ridruejo to the United States. Cuito, in a letter to Lowenstein dated September 19, 1962, indicated that he knew where the money was coming from, and what Gorkin's role was. "They have been invited by the Congres pour la liberté de la culture which Gorkin heads in Paris (at least the Spanish section) and which I believe is financed with American money."

Cuito then gave Lowenstein his instructions with regard to Ridruejo and Gorkin: "They will no doubt get in touch with you and you could take them to see Mrs. Roosevelt, Walter Reuther, etc. . . ."

Cuito planned to leave for Spain the following week to bring back two letters from general committees in Barcelona and Madrid approving the three names. He wanted to know from Lowenstein the outcome of the Oslo meeting and the extent of the support he could expect from the UAW, and he warned Lowenstein that Ridruejo was resisting the idea of pushing for independence for the Portuguese colonies in Africa. He informed Lowenstein:

> I have seen Ridruejo yesterday. I think you proposed to him the idea to get in touch with the Angolan nationalists etc. and to take a strong anti-colonialist stand. Ridruejo is very much opposed to that idea and thinks it is silly since it would give an opportunity to Franco to accuse the democratic opposition of being responsible for the loss of the colonies. I think it is Ridruejo who is silly especially when you think how easy it was for Franco to lose Spanish Morocco, and how important is Africa for the American opinion today. Anyway I am telling you that, so when you see Ridruejo, you are careful in pushing forward this idea. He thinks it is your idea but not the Reuthers' or Mrs. Roosevelt's idea. I don't think this is too important in this first stage but I wanted to advise you he believes that this is a naive idea. I hope Ridruejo and Gorkin visit will help you in getting things set.

But it was vitally important to Lowenstein that the Spanish committee take a strong position on the question of the Portuguese colonies. It was the reason he was involved in setting it up. As far as CIA policy was concerned, it was imperative that two new "front-line" states be created in Angola and Mozambique to add to the pressure on South Africa to give up South West Africa and change its apartheid policies. Lowenstein's job was to work with the nationalist groups in the Portuguese colonies to keep them anti-Soviet, and to manipulate the Spanish committee to this end.

When Ridruejo continued to resist the idea, Lowenstein's enthusiasm for the project dampened. He wanted a Spanish committee to help get rid of Franco so Spanish assistance to Portugal and South Africa would be eliminated, not strengthened. That was the covert American policy Lowenstein was expected to implement. The CIA, defined as the "covert arm of the presidency" by former CIA agent Ralph McGehee, had established that as the primary objective, and the conflict prompted Lowenstein to follow a pattern typical of his involvement with critical movements. He would launch them to accomplish his hidden agenda and then diffuse them when they moved in opposite directions, until they came around to his way of thinking, or were dispersed in confusion. And while this was partly a function of his personality and ideology, it was primarily a direct result of his affiliation with the CIA.

Lowenstein met with Walter Reuther and Eleanor Roosevelt at her home in late September and gave them a firsthand report on the Spanish situation. The three were, as Cuito understood, in agreement on the Portuguese colonies and the position of the Spanish committee.

Lowenstein sent a copy of *Brutal Mandate* to Walter Reuther. Reuther wrote to thank him for the book, "which I look forward to reading at the first opportunity." He had also been pleased to get Lowenstein's Spanish report. "I have been doing some quiet work on the matter of creating a committee and the UAW has appropriated $2,000 as seed money for the purpose," he wrote. "I hope to be able to talk to George Meany about this matter in the coming week."

By the end of September, Gorkin and Ridruejo were in the United States, visiting Washington, New York, and other cities where Spanish oppositionists were centered. Mysteriously, they failed to appear at an important meeting called by Ed Gray at UAW headquarters in New York. Among the participants were UAW operative Lew Carliner and Frank Arricola, a full-time employee on the Spanish project. Arricola's first assignment was to call on Father Hesburgh, president of Notre Dame University, to ask him to serve on the committee. One of Hesburgh's functions was to endow liberal committees with an ecumenical flavor by allowing his name to appear on their letterheads.

On October 10, Gray wrote to Lowenstein, who was by then back at North Carolina State, informing him that Gorkin and Ridruejo had not shown for the meeting and suggesting that one of the AFL-CIO officials working on the Spanish project may have objected to their participation and suggested other courses of action. "If so, this alters the approach we planned concerning the press conference next week," Gray wrote. "We will attempt to track them down and find out why they failed to appear as scheduled. I will write you again as soon as I know more of the details." Gray also told Lowenstein that he was sending a "filtered tape" that Carliner had brought along to the meeting, without indicating the contents, and promised to write again by the end of the week.

The elusive Gorkin and Ridreujo were located at the Alamac Hotel in Manhattan, but Lowenstein made no attempt to get in touch with them or to involve himself deeply with the oppositionists in New York at this time. Gorkin and Ridruejo were the featured speakers at a rally organized for them by the Sociedades Hispanas Confederades at the Casa Galicia, a Spanish restaurant on West 41st Street. Lowenstein received two tickets for the rally from J. Gonzales Malo, but "sources" close to the Spanish oppositionists reported to the FBI that he was not present among the 250 people who attended. These "sources" also reported that the Spanish opposition groups in New York were not being reorganized and that Lowenstein's name had not come to their attention as proposing a reorganization of any of the Spanish opposition groups in New York. He had apparently decided to cool it since Ridruejo was stonewalling him on the question of the Portuguese colonies.

Things began falling apart. George Meany and Walter Reuther not only disagreed on policy but disliked each other personally. And the Portuguese colonies stood as an obstacle to further action. On October 19, 1962, Joel Jacobson and Ed Gray called an emergency meeting of the Committee on Free Spain for October 25. It was to be a "very short, but extremely important meeting." Hiding the crisis, Gray wrote: "Recent developments which are of crucial significance, and definitive progress which seems to assure the initial success of our work, must be discussed and analyzed. The Committee's desires, advice and directives are needed to continue the good that has been accomplished." In fact, everything was going wrong.

On November 7, Eleanor Roosevelt, who had been an important figure in the Spanish equation and who had been Lowenstein's most important mentor, died after a period of declining health. "News is devastating," Lowenstein wrote in the strange diary which he assembled in the style of the front page of *The New York Times*. He dropped everything and raced to Val Kill for the funeral. "God weeps as Mrs. R. is Laid to Rest in Hyde Park," he recorded. "Last Visit to Val Kill a Trying One." Lowenstein arrived at the grave site just ten minutes before she was laid to rest, and mourned the loss of his greatest idol.

Turning his attention back to Spain and southern Africa, Lowenstein found pressure mounting at the United Nations, where the African states were supporting sanctions against South Africa, while the Kennedy administration, including Adlai Stevenson, Kennedy's ambassador to the U.N., opposed them. Kennedy was also moving away from the position that linked the Spanish situation with Angola and Mozambique. Lowenstein recorded his understanding of events in his newspaper diary: "Effort to Link African Fight Iberian Fails; Indication Mounts of U.S. Swing Towards Portugal. Domestic Foe's Views Held to Preclude Alliance." And early in December, he made this entry: "Meany Reuther Bitterness Blamed for Non-Formation of Anti-Franco Committee."

The position of the CIA liberals was being undermined by domestic reactionaries and Cold War hard-liners, whom Kennedy—who had always operated according to the motto "No Enemies on the Right"— felt he could not buck. Kennedy's preoccupation with the right and with a "tough" posture internationally became the dominant concern of his administration and Lowenstein was now a dissenter within the CIA. His was a liberal voice in the hardening atmosphere in which State Department moderates like Chester Bowles were being pushed aside.

William Dentzer, Lowenstein's good friend from the National Student Association, who had become a top AID official, scoffed at Bowles, suggesting that his point of view represented a "wrong drift." But the Bay of Pigs disaster in the spring of 1961 had offered some hope that the "dovish" thrust of the moderates might regain its momentum. Richard Bissell, the CIA's chief of Clandestine Services, who had, at one point, favored using covert agency operations in support of the anti-Communist left and the "progressive political forces" promoted by Bowles during his brief tenure as under secretary of state, nevertheless went down with the hard-line Bay of Pigs operation; he was fired by Kennedy. Bowles stayed in the Kennedy administration as special representative and advisor for Asian, African and Latin American affairs. He was offered his old job back as ambassador to India and was trying to find a way to bring Lowenstein along with him. But notwithstanding Bissell's collapse, Kennedy stuck to his hawkish instincts. Though Bissell had not made it to the top of the CIA, his point of view prevailed in defeat; he was replaced by Richard Helms. John McCone, who had succeeded Allan Dulles as head of the CIA in 1961, was also a hard-liner. The "good wing" of the CIA that Harris Wofford describes found itself in an ambiguous situation.

Nevertheless, early in 1963, the Reuthers, who were allies of Chester Bowles, and Lew Carliner began to push their Spanish committee again. In March, when Lowenstein's friend Zayas and several others from the FLP were given two-year sentences for the bombings, officials in the AFL-CIO urged the formation of the committee. They argued that if Franco continued to crush the anti-Communist opposition to his regime, there would be no one left after his death but the Communist party to take over. By now, the focus of opposition to Franco had shifted from the exiles to the Socialists inside Spain. It was important that they be reached before widespread anti-Americanism could turn the Spanish into a dangerously hostile force.

Also in 1963, President Kennedy appointed Tom Hughes director of intelligence and research at the State Department, and Hughes asked Lowenstein for information on Spain. Lowenstein wrote in his diary during the winter of 1963, "Tom Hughes Asks Spanish Data; 'Salazar' Aid Plan Makes Little Progress." Hughes, who would head the Carnegie Endowment for International Peace after leaving the government, observes: "It could have happened. He came to the State Department in the 1960s. He dropped into everybody's office. He had lots of friends in the State Department." As to whether Lowenstein had a working relationship with the government, Hughes asserts: "He could have. But I didn't know it." Hughes's bureau was the State Department's liaison with the rest of the intelligence community and had access to what John D. Marks, who worked for it, calls "the whole network of American spying."

Hughes had been an aide to Chester Bowles in Congress and again when Bowles became under secretary of state. Like Lowenstein, at one point in his career he had worked for Hubert Humphrey and, like Lowenstein, was close to the Reuthers. He was part of the Bowles clique in the State Department and the CIA. By supplying the kind of information Hughes needed, Lowenstein in his Spanish engagement was functioning in two capacities, as it became normal for him to do. He was both activist and provider of information. And as often as not, his agitations were designed as much to produce information as to provoke change. He could even tolerate violence, as he did in the case of the Spanish bombings in which Zayas had been involved, as long as it furthered his ends.

In February of 1963, a new Spain effort was launched with Norman Thomas and Amadeo Cuito "as keys," as Lowenstein put it. In July 1963 Lowenstein began a seven-month leave of absence without pay from North Carolina State. The leave had been granted so that he could work for the Peace Corps. He did not take a position with the Peace Corps, but instead pursued other interests. He was involved in civil rights work in Mississippi, traveled to London to get information about South African liberation groups from exiles, and went to Spain in November. He telephoned the embassy on November 23 and was visited the next day at the Madrid Hilton by Livingston D. Watrous, embassy counselor for political affairs. Although he was receiving no salary from NC State (his reported income for the year was $3,500, plus $400 from other sources), Lowenstein still managed to travel abroad extensively and stay at the best hotels.

Lowenstein told Watrous that since his last visit to Spain, opposition to Franco had increased in size and bitterness. But he admitted that the various opposition groups were more divided than ever. Lowenstein said that as a "friend and advisor" of the opposition, he constantly hammered on the theme of unity and tried to convey to them the urgency of harnessing their energies toward fighting the regime rather than each other. After several weeks of traveling all over the country, except in the south, he found that only the Catalan opposition parties were cooperating with each other to some degree but that discord between the various factions was rampant everywhere else.

Of particular concern to Lowenstein was the increasing bitterness against the United States. Spanish people generally disliked Americans, he told Watrous, and the opposition, which sensed this feeling, considered it advantageous to adopt an anti-American stance. Watrous countered by telling him that thousands of Spaniards had come to the embassy to express their sorrow over the assassination of President Kennedy, but Lowenstein insisted that it was precisely the most liberal opposition leaders who were the most grieved over the president's death. The opposition leaders felt, he said, that it was U.S. policy to shore up the Franco regime and resented the fact that they never received any assistance or spiritual help from the embassy. They were prepared, he insisted, to take power when Franco fell without being identified with the U.S. embassy.

Although Adlai Stevenson did return to Spain in 1963 and talked with some intellectuals commonly identified as being in opposition to the regime, Lowenstein remained adamant that Stevenson's failure to meet with oppositionists in August, 1962, when he had held extensive talks with Franco, had been a blow from which the oppositionists had never recovered. But Watrous had the distinct impression that what was bothering Lowenstein was the memory of his own failure to produce Stevenson for a meeting with an "opposition delegation" at that time. "His inability to produce Stevenson for the opposition still rankles and seems to have poisoned Lowenstein's mind," Watrous reported. "From some of his remarks and his apparent obsession with Embassy-opposition relations, or the lack thereof, it appears quite possible that he *is* influencing opposition groups and warning them of the danger of maintaining contact with the Embassy," Watrous concluded.

Lowenstein indicated to Watrous that he wanted to give the embassy an understanding of the "mood" of the opposition in order to be of help. He told him that the "interior" Socialists definitely had the upper hand and that the number of Socialists following the orders of the French exile group under Llopis had decreased sharply. And while he was no longer in contact with any Spanish Communists, Lowenstein said he had heard that the "Chinese" faction was giving the Moscow-oriented leadership of the Communist party a "hard struggle."

Watrous pressed Lowenstein on the subject of who was paying for his trip and what its purpose was, but Lowenstein studiously avoided giving any reasons for being in Spain other than "sympathy" with the opposition. He would not say what group, if any, was paying for him to be in Spain or who provided funds he might have passed on to the opposition. But he did say he expected to return to Spain in June of 1964 for a "more extended stay."

The new Spanish effort was critically hampered, at a time when Franco was believed to be faltering, by the divisions among the anti-Communist opposition groups and by the shift away from the exiles in France to the "interior" Socialists in Spain. Gorkin and Ridruejo were reporting an agreement in the army that a junta should replace Franco in three to four years, while the Pallach group was insisting that the committee had been deliberately "sabotaged." And there were bitter splits among the Socialists in Spain as well. Also, after Stevenson's coyness and Kennedy's death, there was a reluctance on the part of the Spanish opposition to get too close to the Americans. So Lowenstein distanced himself from his old idol Stevenson. He retained his credibility and waited for another opportunity to put together a Spanish committee to aid the anti-Communist opposition. In 1965, the student riots in Madrid seemed to offer an opening, but things did not get rolling again until the autumn of 1966. By this time, Lowenstein was getting more public recognition, and when he arrived at the embassy in late October, he was received with much more respect than in the past.

On October 29, Lowenstein was received there by a counselor and then Ambassador Angier Biddle Duke. He told them he had been in Madrid for four or five days and had made contact, on his own initiative, with members of the Spanish opposition whom he knew from previous trips. He insisted he was there on his own, having refused financial assistance from the Reuther brothers and Norman Thomas so that he would not have to see people they wanted him to see and look into matters that interested them. He preferred, he said, to pay his own way so that he would have complete freedom to do what he wanted and see whom he wanted. He said he regretted limiting this voyage to Madrid, and not being able to go to Barcelona and Bilbao.

In actuality, his trip to Spain was the last leg of an extensive trip to Africa where Lowenstein had conferred in Dar es Salaam, Tanzania, with the African National Congress's Oliver Tambo and with Lowenstein's friend Eduardo Mondlane, the American-educated head of Frelimo, the Mozambique liberation group. He cut his trip short in Spain to return for his wedding, which was to take place in Boston, but said he hoped to return in the spring, if he could "save the money for the trip." In fact, that spring Lowenstein traveled again in Africa, staying at the best hotels and conferring with African leaders and American ambassadors. Shortly after that, his travels would take him to Vietnam, from which he would return to help launch the movement to "dump" Lyndon Johnson as president of the United States.

Although Lowenstein's contacts in 1966 still centered on the left-wing of Spain's opposition, he startled the ambassador by making a strong pitch in favor of U.S. support for Don Juan, the father of Juan Carlos, whom Franco was grooming for the throne. It was the first time that Lowenstein had expressed any interest in the monarchy. He indicated that he had also met with some moderates and had made suggestions about who would make a good prime minister. He explained that the opposition was now looking to the future much more than previously. All elements of the opposition, he said, were now focusing on what role they would assume in the post-Franco period, and none of them were intent on overthrowing the Franco regime by force, as they had been at the time of his earlier visits. Lowenstein expressed his concern about the Alianza Sindical Obrera (ASO), suggesting that it was not an authentic opposition labor group but was in actuality being used by forces in the Franco regime for their own purposes. He cited a study of the Spanish labor scene conducted by a German sent to Madrid under the auspices of the Social Democratic Party which confirmed that view. Lowenstein said he expected to meet with Tierno Galvan, the Spanish Socialist, in Princeton. He had contacted Raul Morodo, Tierno's political deputy in Madrid, before visiting the embassy, but did not see Dionisio Ridruejo, meeting instead with various university student elements. Ridruejo was regarded as obsolete and the new Spanish effort was putting its money elsewhere.

Lowenstein met with four students from Madrid University in a group, then approached one of them for further conversation, saying that he had found him more "wide awake" and aware of what was going on than the others. Lowenstein then offered financial assistance from unspecified groups which he said he represented in the United States. It would be provided to help them carry on their work of "liberalizing" conditions in Spanish universities, but he said he would need a written description of the students' project, which should be sent to him in New York. The student reported Lowenstein's overture to his colleagues, who made inquiries about Lowenstein at the embassy. They were told that Lowenstein usually came to the embassy when he visited Spain, but he had no connection officially or otherwise with the U.S. government, and that he was acting completely on his own initiative. While the embassy would not officially encourage or discourage the students' dealing directly with him along the lines he suggested, the embassy officer pointed out the "dangers" inherent in soliciting help from outside Spain in a "manner which might become known to the Spanish authorities."

The embassy did not expect the students to send any documentation to Lowenstein on the basis of this one meeting in Madrid. In a memo on Lowenstein's 1966 visit, an embassy official (presumably Ambassador Duke) summed up:

> Mr. Lowenstein is an intense activist and a genuine political enthusiast. His free-wheeling approach to the opposition and his Lanny Budd-like interest in dealing behind the scenes on a personal basis must cause a great deal of confusion among them as to who he is and what he stands for, especially since he frequently mentions in his conversation the names of prominent people in the U.S. with whom he is in close contact and presumably whom he can commit to his programs and ideas.

Lowenstein's role, whether concealed from the embassy or known to it at certain levels and not at others, was to keep the opposition believing that there was still hope that the United States would come around. This he had done with consummate skill until the oppositionists had grown weary of waiting for Franco to fall and were ready to cooperate in a gradual transformation of the country along the lines of constitutional democracy. He had helped the anti-Communists to buy time so the pro-Western parties could become forces capable of winning elections and governing.

As for the idiosyncratic behavior that the embassy in Madrid took note of, it was not unlike that of other great liberals such as Stevenson and Mrs. Roosevelt, or of CIA types like Kermit Roosevelt, who had overthrown Mossadegh in Iran and returned the Shah to power in the fifties. Flaky on the surface, few took them seriously. But their behavior was an affectation, designed to make them seem naive and simplistic. In fact, they were tough, clever, hard-nosed people.

During the Nixon administration, Henry Kissinger complained that Frank Carlucci was soft because he would not act against the left in Portugal. Lowenstein was of the same mold and it made him extremely effective, though it worked against him later when, as a candidate for office, his constituency was too unsophisticated to understand his subtlety. But he was a whiz in intelligence matters. He knew every Spanish opposition group and its leadership inside and out, and he knew what had to be done to get them moving in a particular direction. Lowenstein knew the language and the culture of Spain and was trusted in a country where Americans were suspect. And he brought the same sophistication to Africa.

The FBI, which found that Lowenstein did not represent any particular Spanish group and was consequently not required to register under the Foreign Agents Registration Act, had anticipated reaching that conclusion in a 1962 report where it was written that "the expected results . . . would not justify the embarrassment which would possibly result because of subject's sensitive position. . . ." The report suggests that the FBI was considering Lowenstein for employment in some capacity but gave up the idea. (The report reads: "In view of subject's employment by Stanford University and his residence on the campus of the university, it is not considered desirable to employ . . ." What follows is blacked out.) Lowenstein's ability to function in a way recognized as valuable to such organizations attested to deep divisions within him. Whether it was his work that caused these divisions or his personality that made him perfectly suited for it is uncertain. What is clear is that he shifted roles with ease and rarely stood still to analyze the implications of what he was doing. There was mental illness in his family; his brother Bert had been hospitalized for a nervous breakdown. Lowenstein appeared to have at least two selves which could be reconciled only by constant action. According to his close friend, Jimmy Wallace, "Al was as schizophrenic as a person could be." He had to stay in motion to survive. He was an "action freak," and like an addict, he had to follow the action, to be not only part of it but at the center of it. When the action shifted from Spain to Vietnam, Lowenstein shifted with it. As the Spanish Civil War had been the central event for the "Old Left," Vietnam would be the watershed experience

for the "New Left." Lowenstein had cultivated the old and it was slow-
ing down. He needed the new, and the intoxication of involvement.

Spain, more than any other place, had symbolized the romantic
yearnings characteristic of the liberal CIA mentality. In the service of
those who opposed revolution, Americans of that mold sought excitement abroad, where they could be with the rebels for the sake of
fighting Communism. If Lowenstein chose to work out the contradictions in his personality with anti-Franco anti-Communism, it was
really quite natural. And before Vietnam took all of his attention, he
returned to the Spanish issue and his "Old Left" anti-Communist compatriots, the clique of people who made careers out of their disillusionment with the Soviet Union. Franco was the unfinished business
of this group. They saw Spain as their personal cause that was sometimes complicated by the presence of the Spanish.

Lowenstein's old National Student Assocation now got into the act.
Richard Stearns, the international affairs vice-president, later a top
coordinator of George McGovern's 1972 presidential campaign, was at
the time in charge of the NSA's International Commission (which
would shortly be exposed as a long-time recipient of CIA funding). In
December, 1966, he wrote to Lewis Carliner, the assistant to the director of the UAW who had been one of the original contingent working with Lowenstein in 1962 to launch the Spanish committee.
Stearns enclosed a lengthy memorandum written by NSA's Frederick
E. Berger, which reviewed "contemporary Spanish student politics"
and which set out a suggested "program of aid conducted by American
labor and students, for students in Spain working for the restoration
of democratic government." Stearns was optimistic. "We feel that the
time is propitious for such assistance. The promulgation of reforms
recently by Franco is a reminder of the shortening life of his regime,"
Stearns wrote.

The "joint international program of such important consequences"
that Stearns was proposing to Carliner would have involved CIA funds
coming through the NSA; that is where the International Commission's money came from. The UAW might also be expected to get CIA
money for such a project. Berger's memorandum reviewed developments in the new Spanish student movement, which had been
launched in 1962, the year Lowenstein started working for the CIA,
and which was organizing along the lines of the U.S. National Student
Assocation. Following demonstrations in the early sixties, the anti-
Communist, anti-Franco students had forced the government-backed
Sindicato Español Universitario to liberalize itself, and the new democratic procedures allowed many students to join and participate.
Clandestine student groups battled each other for control of the Spanish student movement, and by 1965 the elected officers of the SEU
were operating openly against the government. "Free Assemblies"

had been organized, with thousands attending in cities all over Spain. The attempt by the police to disperse them had led to serious confrontations in Barcelona, Valencia, and Madrid.

At the time of the Madrid riots, Lowenstein had believed it might be necessary for him to go to Spain. In fact, had Frederick E. Berger's name not appeared on the detailed report to Carliner, setting out the history and nature of all the student organizations, it would have been reasonable to assume that the memorandum had been written by Allard Lowenstein, particularly since the main purpose of his trip to Madrid in 1966, at a time when he was deeply involved in NSA affairs, had been to gather information on the student movement. A copy of the report was in his personal papers.

By 1966, the students were frustrated by government "reforms" that led to the abolition of the SEU and the creation of the Asociaciones Profesionales de Estudiantes (APE), an organization that had democratic procedures but no function. It was largely boycotted by the students, though in some cities it was taken over and used to promote anti-Franco activity.

Once again, the problem was the Communist party. The NSA report to Carliner explained that the Communists were backing the powerful Confederación Universitaria Demorática de España (CUDE), a clandestine student organization that included, besides the Communists, various left-wing Socialist groups and certain radical Catholic elements. Affiliated were other powerful student groups based in Madrid, Barcelona, Valencia, Bilbao, and Granada. What it added up to was a well-organized Communist-led student movement.

In opposition to this grouping were the Unión de Estudiantes Demócraticos (UED), which was Christian-Democratic, and the Frente Nacional de Estudiantes Catalanes (FNEC), separatist and conservative. If the students were the wave of the future in Spain, that wave was Red and the NSA memo justified its program stating that it would create "a non-Communist opposition to Franco." The memo indicated that relations with the Christian Democrats, "a more homogeneous and reliable group," should be pursued, but it would also be necessary to establish contacts with certain elements in the radical student organizations "in order to erode the communist strength in these groups." Among the activities suggested were leadership training programs, funding and publicity for the anti-Communist student activities, scholarship programs, a Spanish Solidarity Meeting in the United States, and a Committee on Solidarity with the Students of Spain, using the NSA and the UAW. All of this, the report concluded, would require a basic administrative staff, one full-time person "experienced and knowledgeable in Spanish student affairs," and a secretary. The NSA volunteered its offices in Washington, and the memo suggested that the program could benefit from NSA's "wide experience in international student relations." The staff would engage in research and travel in Spain to establish and pursue contacts. Overall administrative costs for such a program would be between ten and fifteen thousand dollars. If funds were not available for a full-time staff, "it would be entirely feasible for USNSA to accept specific assignments from the Committee for the implementation of particular aspects of its programs," stated the memo.

In essence, the NSA was offering to spy on the Spanish student movement for the purpose of eroding support among the Communists, the left Socialists, and the radical Catholics and to build up the anti-Communists of the center-right. And the man they approached for help was Lew Carliner of the UAW, Lowenstein's coworker on the old Spanish committee.

Meanwhile, the UAW had approached Spanish Refugee Aid, Inc., in New York to help revive the old idea of an American committee for a free Spain. Spanish Refugee Aid, of which Lowenstein was a member and "sponsor," was headed by Nancy Macdonald, a veteran of the Spanish scene who had once been married to the literary critic Dwight Macdonald. The list of sponsors and board members was a *Who's Who* of liberalism, and included Victor Reuther of the UAW, Roger Baldwin of the ACLU, Algernon Black of Ethical Culture, the Rev. Donald Harrington, Lillian Hellman, Lewis Mumford, Mrs. George Orwell, Mme. Albert Camus, A. Philip Randolph, Norman Thomas, Arthur Schlesinger, Jr., painter Esteban Vicente, journalist Barbara Probst Solomon, and a host of others.

On February 21, 1967, a special meeting of Spanish Refugee Aid was held at Hannah Arendt's Manhattan apartment to discuss the UAW proposal. "They want the cooperation of SRA, our know-how and aura. We must discuss," Nancy Macdonald wrote to Lowenstein on February 15. Lowenstein was abroad and unable to attend but Macdonald sent him the notes on the meeting.

At the meeting, she had read a telegram from Victor Reuther of the UAW inviting SRA to join "like-minded groups" in forming a committee supporting a free Spain, a proposal that Hannah Arendt found "vague."

Arendt asked if funds were to be provided by the UAW or whether SRA was expected to raise the money by itself, and was informed by Nancy Macdonald that the UAW intended to pay start-up expenses, with the hope that the committee could raise its own money eventually. Just why the UAW wanted a Spanish committee at this point remained a point of confusion at the meeting and no one mentioned that the real purpose of the Spanish committee was the derailment of the Communists inside Spain.

Nancy Macdonald did comment that she "would not like to see the new group fall into the hands of the exiled Spanish Socialists," while

Frances O'Brien added that Carliner seemed to have in mind "not an exile group but one staffed and controlled by Americans." Asked whether Carliner had approached other groups besides SRA, O'Brien replied that "it appeared that some student groups may have been talked to," referring to the role of the National Student Association. In its report on the Spanish situation, the NSA had warned of the Socialist-Communist alliance, making it clear that the Spanish Socialist exiles were not to be trusted, and that only Americans could be relied on. In the end, those attending the SRA meeting agreed to give their help and support "only on condition that the new committee work for a free Spain *as understood by Spaniards in Spain*." Presumably the UAW and the National Student Association's CIA-supported International Commission would make the determination as to which Spaniards.

On March 1, Nancy Macdonald sent the notes of the meeting to Lowenstein. She told him that the "committee of six" would meet again the following week, that she was planning a meeting with the "UAW people" which she hoped he would attend, and she solicited his suggestions for other participants. On October 17, 1967, SRA held its annual membership meeting and a meeting of the board of directors. But Lowenstein was now totally immersed in Vietnam, and the Spanish committee was once again suspended. Without Lowenstein's full attention, nothing was going to happen.

According to sources, Lowenstein was separated from the CIA sometime in 1967 (the sources say Lowenstein "was in the agency from 1962 to 1967"), a year when he neglected to pay his dues to both Spanish Refugee Aid and the American Committee on Africa. There was no further movement on the Spanish committee until 1976, after the election of Jimmy Carter, in whose administration Lowenstein served as U.S. representative to the Human Rights Commission in Geneva and then as an ambassador to the United Nations under Andrew Young. By then, Franco was dead and constitutional monarchy was established in Spain under Juan Carlos. The Communist party remained a powerful force in Spain in the elections and in the unions.

During 1975, Lowenstein became deeply involved in the politics of Portugal because of his relationship with Portugese Socialist Mario Soares, who was foreign minister at a period when the Portugese revolution was pushing increasingly leftward. Involving Lowenstein was his friend Frank Carlucci, who served as U.S. ambassador to Portugal from 1975 to 1978 and then as Jimmy Carter's deputy director of the CIA. On March 14, 1975, Carlucci wrote Lowenstein that the coup attempt in Portugal, which he described as "unbelievably ill-conceived, poorly organized and badly led," was suspected of being organized by the powerful Communist party. Carlucci disagreed with this assessment, but added: "I think it is a serious question about whether your friend Mario Soares will remain as Foreign Minister. With the parties to the center coming under attack and almost certain to be banned, the whole spectrum shifts to the left and the Socialists in turn must be considered a center or center-right party! This is hard to conceive of through our eyes but that is what is indeed happening, particularly since there are a number of small splinter groups to the left of the Communists." Carlucci was looking for a way to restore the equilibrium but acknowledged that "certainly life will become more difficult." Asking Lowenstein to "please keep the above in confidence," he concluded, "I will not hesitate to call on you if I think you can be useful."

Lowenstein made trips to Portugal several times while he was an ambassador to the U.N. in the Carter administration. He visited Carlucci and his wife, Marsha, in Lisbon on various occasions and stayed with them at the ambassador's residence. Ronald Brownstein and Nina Easton, writers for Ralph Nader, have reported accusations against Carlucci that he was a CIA agent, stating: "But if Carlucci, as he maintains, was never involved in any of the CIA's covert intrigues during the 1960s, he at least seemed regularly to pop up in the vicinity of some of the agency's sleazier operations." The controversial *Dirty Work 2: the CIA in Africa* devotes a whole chapter to Carlucci, and while Carter's appointment of him as deputy director of the CIA does not in itself confirm the allegations, it lends credence to the argument that Carlucci had previous experience, making him a logical candidate for the position.

Lowenstein was extremely useful to Carlucci. According to Carlucci, Lowenstein "had a relationship with Mario, I think through the Socialist Internationale. And he knew him and Soares liked him and he would call on him when he came to Lisbon."

Lowenstein admired Carlucci. He had a well-formulated knitting needle approach to Communist revolution; to work it from the inside out, opening the knot with subtlety with the fine instrument of a Mario Soares. Carlucci's bland exterior concealed a tough core. Lowenstein was helpful to Carlucci when he was having what Carlucci refers to as a "difference of opinion" with Henry Kissinger over policy toward Portugal. He had a "range of contacts from right to left," as Carlucci describes them, and used those contacts to help Carlucci. Lowenstein spoke with Senator James Buckley, William Buckley, Jr.'s brother (Lowenstein was close to William Buckley, Jr., who, like Lowenstein, had served in the CIA) and asked him to persuade Kissinger to be more supportive of Carlucci's approach. The Carlucci strategy was to ride the situation out until the pro-American moderate left, which Soares represented, could be put into power. According to Brownstein and Easton, Carlucci was ambassador "at a time when the CIA was shoring up conservative elements there with money and manpower to prevent the Communist Party from taking power. During that period Carlucci led a minority of policy makers who argued—against Secretary Henry Kissinger—in favor of supporting Portugal's leftist military government in 1975 'as long as appearances of democracy remained extant,' as one official said. Carlucci's position eventually gained the White House's support."

It was alleged that Kissinger complained during a meeting, "Whoever sold me Carlucci as a tough guy?" and although the State Department denied the report of Kissinger's complaint, Carlucci did have to work feverishly to prevent Kissinger from imposing an arms embargo on the independent Socialist government, firing off cables to counter those opposing Carlucci's U.S. military assistance plan for Portugal. Carlucci reported that the most satisfying aspect of his experience as the ambassador to Portugal "was watching the Portugese people move from the brink of communism to equilibrium."

The Portugese Communist party then published a 167-page book called *Dossier Carlucci CIA* accusing him of working to "subvert the revolutionary process initiated in Portugal." After he became deputy director of the CIA, they charged: "What should one think of the president of one country whose representative to the president of another country afterwards becomes director of the spying service?" But Carlucci was doing what the CIA did often, and continues to do, and which has never been appreciated by the right or the left in America. With Allard Lowenstein's assistance, he was defeating the Communists with another form of the left; the pro-American, anti-Communist Socialists. According to Carlucci, Lowenstein's "contacts with the Socialists were very close"; Lowenstein knew Soares through the German Socialists who "were very close to Mario Soares. He was also close to the British Socialists and the Socialists were all very chummy." Carlucci describes Soares, who eventually became Prime Minister of Portugal, as "a very pro-American, pro-NATO Socialist who's now trying to turn back some of the government-owned banks to the private sector."

Carlucci has expressed his gratitude to Lowenstein for his assistance in stopping the Communists in Portugal. "He was very supportive. He was definitely helpful," Carlucci concludes. "The U.S. government was of two minds," Carlucci explains. "One was the fatalistic frame of mind that said Portugal was lost and that the best thing to do was to insulate them from the rest of NATO, and in effect, ostracize them. I was arguing that Portugal was not lost, that it had too many ties to NATO, to the West, and that while most of the country was in the hands of the Communists our only logical course of action was to work with the moderate non-Communist elements, and that included at that time in particular the Socialists, who were the strongest non-Communist political force."

How close were Carlucci and Lowenstein? According to Carlucci, their friendship went back to the late sixties when Lowenstein was elected to Congress and he was with the Office of Economic Opportunity in the Nixon administration. But Carlucci had also been heavily involved in Africa as a Foreign Service officer and was in Johannesburg in 1959 at the same time Lowenstein was asked by the CIA to smuggle Hans Beukes out of the country. Carlucci became a legend because of his daring exploits in Africa. Was he the man who gave Lowenstein the request? Carlucci says, "It's entirely possible that we met at the time but didn't remember it. I was in South Africa in the late fifties, but I was a very minor functionary." Carlucci also insists that he never heard of the Hans Beukes affair although he was vice-consul at the consulate in Johannesburg in 1959, and by both Lowenstein's and Emory Bundy's accounts, it was a major story in the South African press. Carlucci maintains that Lowenstein "had no association with the CIA other than knowing me or knowing people in the CIA, as anybody does who travels around the world." But he adds that "those of us who have been associated with the CIA neither confirm nor deny any kind of association with it," and says "even if he had been in the CIA, there's nothing wrong with it." When the story of how Lowenstein smuggled out Beukes is related to Carlucci, he just smiles, revealing the slightest hint of amusement. In Carlucci's office at the headquarters of Sears World Trade in Washington, where he works as its head, having resigned as deputy secretary of defense in the Reagan administration, there is a color photograph of him and his attractive wife, Marsha, beaming in front of a partially visible big Central Intelligence Agency insignia. They are being honored.

Franco died in 1975. In 1976, Spanish Refugee Aid was infused with new life under the leadership of Nancy Macdonald who also joined with Lowenstein to form the American Committee for Iberian Freedom (Spain and Portugal). Heading the new organization was Lowenstein's friend James I. Loeb, the former U.S. ambassador to Peru and Guinea. Loeb worked for H. L. Oram, Inc., the firm which had handled public relations for Diem, the American Friends of Vietnam, the American Committee on Africa, and which, at Lowenstein's urging, had allowed its offices to be used by the South African United Front for which Gil Jonas had served as fund-raiser. Jonas had also handled the PR for Lowenstein's book, having gone into business for himself. Now Oram was making its offices available as the headquarters of the American Committee for Iberian Freedom, and Loeb was volunteering his full-time services to direct it.

Loeb met with Lowenstein and others to set up the Committee and prepare the statement of purpose, as well as a letter to prospective supporters to be signed by Lowenstein and Nancy Macdonald. On February 11, 1976, Loeb sent drafts to Lowenstein with a note thanking him for his participation and enthusiasm, which he said was of "enormous importance." The letter, entitled "To Organize the American Committee for Iberian Freedom" assured prospective participants that the committee's aims would be accomplished "with the minimum of cost." This they could do because Loeb was donating his services and an office had been made available without cost.

The letter also stressed the committee's intention "to avoid any involvement in the specific political arrangements of Spain and Portugal." Its purpose was only "to encourage the rebirth of freedom in these two nations which have suffered so much and so long."

Those who received the statement of purpose for the American Committee for Iberian Freedom were asked to consider the state of the Iberian world—Portugal was threatened now, after ousting its 48-year-old dictatorship with "a dictatorship from the left," thwarted thus far only by the "courageous leadership of such men as Mario Soares"; and Spain was the victim of a bloody civil war, followed by a 40-year dictatorship, its official democratic republic having been "betrayed by the world's democracies, and most especially by the United States which, on the other hand, supported the dictatorship for 40 years with vast financial aid, much of it in payment for military bases of increasingly dubious value."

Now, with Franco dead, the statement continued, his successor, King Juan Carlos I, "has given some indications of seeking to build a new Spain in which conciliation will replace tyranny. But 60,000 railroad workers striking on behalf of their grievances have only recently been conscripted, labor lawyers have been arrested, and scheduled free elections have been postponed for a year and a half." Moreover, since recently announced plans for "spurious reforms" had provoked additional grievances, the probable results, they predicted, "will once more be tyranny—either from the extreme right or the extreme and equally undemocratic left."

Americans were called on to fulfill their "solemn obligation" to see to it that the actions of the U.S. government would encourage "a new birth of freedom within the Iberian peoples." Specifically they were urged to insist that aid to Spain "be predicated on Spain's commitment to the democratic process." And they called for a general amnesty to be declared by the Spanish government, not only to free those imprisoned in Spain, but to allow "some 40,000 Spanish patriots living in France, many since 1939," to return home.

A press release was prepared announcing the formation of the American Committee for Iberian Freedom and listing prominent people who had agreed to support it. Among the names were those of sociologist Daniel Bell; historian James MacGregor Burns; critic Malcolm Cowley; Frances B. Grant, director of the Inter-American Association for Freedom and Democracy; Jack Greenberg, the director of the NAACP Legal Defense Fund; philosopher Sidney Hook of NYU; Irving Howe, the editor of *Dissent*; Joseph Rauh; and Arthur Schlesinger, Jr. There were many others and it was not a bad list, but it was not the catalog of leading personalities that the American Committee on Africa had succeeded in enlisting in the sixties. They were distinguished names but the Spanish question had lingered so long, and they had been used so often, they were getting stale.

In 1976, Lowenstein himself mused on its long duration:

If we had helped when so many Spaniards bought time for Western democracy at such dreadful cost to themselves, might Prague have been spared, or Paris or London or Bataan or Guadalcanal? Was Munich inevitable, and Dachau, and the Hitler-Stalin pact, and so on to Hiroshima and the Berlin Wall and the bridge at Andau and the Bay of Pigs and Vietnam? Could Communist misbehavior in Spain and Poland have been avoided or tempered if ours toward Spain and Czechoslovakia had been, and so perhaps some kind of understanding if not cooperation preserved that would have minimized the post-war ordeal of Eastern Europe and the polarizing of the post-Hitler planet? If it is foolish to underestimate the chasm that separated Western and Soviet attitudes so fatefully in the Thirties and Forties, it is also simplistic not to wonder whether the paranoid viciousness of emergent communism might have been modified had the Western democracies resisted sooner the calculated viciousness of emergent fascism. But even if nothing anyone could have done in or about Spain could have averted World War II or the Cold War, what if democratic countries had helped the republic during the Civil War instead of driving it to dependence on the Soviet Union? Is it inconceivable that democracy triumphant in Spain could have headed off extremes of anti-clerical misconduct and thus diffused the antagonism over Franco that poisoned relations between American Catholics and liberals at a time that was so critical? What a difference it might have made if McCarthy and Nixon had not been helped in their rise by the extravagant emotions about Spain that led so many Catholics to suspect liberals of being soft on communism, and so many liberals to suspect Catholics of being soft on fascism: isn't it just possible that a different Spanish experience, perhaps even a concern shared as it is now about Portugal, could have spared America the unhappy period of the exploited neurosis that led first to such destructive mistrust at home and then to such devastating consequences in Indochina?. . . I still wonder at times whatever got into otherwise thoughtful people like Adlai Stevenson where Spain was concerned. Political considerations can explain many things, and there was certainly a price to pay in the United States in the Fifties and Sixties for outspoken opposition to Franco; the few who were prepared to pay the price were people like Herbert Lehman and Eleanor Roosevelt, people who were extraordinary in any event. But Adlai Stevenson twice chose to go to Spain and pose with high officials after his elective career was over, both visits coming at moments of special difficulty for the opposition; and the second visit was even less understandable than the first, because it took place after Walter Reuther, Norman Thomas and I had sent him a petition signed by Socialist and Christian Democratic leaders whom he had refused to meet on his first visit, pleading that he not "damage" Spanish democrats in the same way again. The "damage" referred to was two-sided: it helped the Spanish government at a rough moment; and it helped the Spanish Communist Party, perhaps even more than it helped the government. These were the concerns of the people who sent the petition; they were of course concerns of mine, too, but I had another: the drain on what Wendell Willkie had called the "reservoir of good will" for America around the world.

22.

In February of 1963, Norman Thomas urged Lowenstein to leave North Carolina and run for the House of Representatives in the 19th Congressional District in New York. Lowenstein informed the chairman of his department at NC State, George Gullette, that he was considering leaving in order to make the race. But Lowenstein did not run for Congress; he made other plans instead.

William Craig, who had once before recruited Lowenstein as his assistant dean at Stanford, was now the director of training in Puerto Rico for the Peace Corps and looking for a way to get Lowenstein to work with him again. Craig ran the training center at the University of Puerto Rico where Peace Corps volunteers were prepared for foreign assignments. It was one of several outposts designed for this purpose.

"There were certain aspects of it that were not working," Craig related. "I was very much interested, of course, in getting him involved in the Peace Corps, and he came down, and looked it over, and I was hopeful that we could get him involved in the training program."

Lowenstein delivered several lectures to the volunteers; and when Craig was named director of training for the entire Peace Corps in Washington under Sargent Shriver, he asked Lowenstein to replace him in Puerto Rico. The salary offered was $14,500—twice what Lowenstein was being paid by NC State. Lowenstein discussed the offer with George Gullette, who offered him a semester's leave of absence and a pay raise on his return. Lowenstein could try out the job to see if he liked it, with the assurance that his teaching spot at NC State would remain available to him. He was, in the words of Chancellor John Tyler Caldwell, "an extraordinary teacher." One of three professors chosen by students at NC State while Lowenstein taught there for the "Blue Key Award," symbolizing extraordinary service to the school, he taught contemporary issues and the history and sociology of science, both extremely popular courses. Lowenstein knew almost nothing about science, though, and went over to Durham on the eve of each lecture to be prepared by Jimmy Wallace, who taught history of science at Duke. Lowenstein was winging it at NC State, but Lowenstein winging it was apparently better than most people with their nose to the grindstone.

In May, Gullette sent a note explaining the situation to Dean Fred Cahill, and effective July 1, 1963, Lowenstein was granted a seven-month leave so that he could "accept a temporary assignment with the Peace Corps."

The first director of training in Puerto Rico had been an "Outward Bound" person from England, with a military background. Also at the outset, Peace Corps Director Shriver had convinced the Rev. William Coffin to come down. Coffin had stayed about six months, then left. "I never knew why he didn't continue," former Associate Director of the Peace Corps Harris Wofford comments, "but it very well could be that Coffin was in the CIA and Shriver, very early in the beginning of the Peace Corps, took this absolute position that no one ever associated with the CIA could have any relationship with the Peace Corps. He carried it very far and he was very serious about it. Now later, I know that Coffin had either been with the CIA or its predecessor organization. So that could have come to light and could have been the reason Coffin didn't continue there. My recollection is that Coffin launched it, so that he could well have recommended Al."

The Puerto Rico training center was, in Wofford's words, "a big operation" which combined Outward Bound adventures with intensive courses in the various countries in which volunteers would be stationed. Although Lowenstein was well suited for a position at the training center, he was not named to one. William Craig recalls that "he was interested but nothing ever came of it. We just didn't put it together."

Craig maintains that his discussions with Lowenstein concerning a position with the Peace Corps had "nothing to do with his taking a leave of absence from North Carolina State." He insists that Lowenstein "didn't take the leave at North Carolina State with the expectation of coming in the Peace Corps. That was one of the options he was talking about. And I was trying to get him to come in, but we just couldn't get it set up right for him."

Nevertheless, Lowenstein's file at NC State explicitly states that he was granted leave to join the Peace Corps, and that is confirmed by John Tyler Caldwell, who was chancellor at the time.

Wofford finds it "fascinating" that Lowenstein did not join the Peace Corps and insists that he "never heard about it." "I mean I don't remember it," he adds. "I find I often don't remember things." Wofford, who describes himself as an "anti-Communist," concedes that one possible explanation is that Lowenstein was "tied" to the CIA. In his book, *Of Kennedys and Kings*, Wofford has noted that "the FBI and Civil Service Commission were asked to inform Sargent Shriver if the background investigations of Peace Corps applicants, either volunteers or staff, uncovered any previous connection with intelligence work. Not only would no one with CIA ties be selected, but the ban extended to volunteers' later careers and beyond the CIA to the whole so-called intelligence community." The issue is not whether the FBI found something "left-wing" about Lowenstein; he was a known anti-Communist. It was whether it found any CIA association. And since Lowenstein was not able to work for the Peace Corps, Wofford's speculation on Lowenstein's association with the CIA is tantamount to a confirmation of it.

A man who has had an impressive career in the liberal establishment, a veteran of the Kennedy administration, a former law professor at Notre Dame, and at one time president of Bryn Mawr College, Wofford is currently a partner in Schrader, Harrison, Segal & Lewis, a major Philadelphia law firm. He is also a leading figure in the United States-South Africa Leader Exchange Program (USSALEP), which is supported by leading South African and American corporations, including Anglo-American, and expresses his disapproval of Oliver Tambo and the African National Congress. It was Wofford who advised John Kennedy to phone Martin Luther King, Jr., a personal friend of Wofford's, offering to help when King was imprisoned in Montgomery, Alabama, an act that is credited with winning for Kennedy the approval of millions of black Americans. He was called in to advise the embattled pro-American president of Kenya, Daniel Arap Moi, and headed the Alan Cranston for President campaign. Suave and urbane, he is the quintessential liberal insider. In *Of Kennedys and Kings*, he suggests that both John and Robert Kennedy knew about and approved the attempts on Fidel Castro's life. Yet he remains a Kennedy loyalist, believing the best strategy is to admit the sins and stress the good points.

Gullette told associates that Lowenstein came to him at North Carolina State "very embarrassed" and told him that the assignment had "fallen through." His file there notes that "he expressed a desire to work on a novel," and he was allowed to take leave anyway "as a replacement had already been found."

Eventually it came out that Lowenstein had used part of his leave to work in the civil rights movement in Mississippi at the time of the critical "Freedom Vote." But Lowenstein's extensive travels to Spain to promote the cause of the anti-Communist opposition groups and to London to meet with South African exiles and gather information about their plans, remained unknown to all but those with whom he was working.

Before he left on his leave of absence, Lowenstein had worked to create African Freedom Day Action against Apartheid (AFDAAA), which was based in Oberlin, Ohio. Joining him in the effort were George Houser and Donald Harrington of the American Committee on Africa, Norman Thomas, A. Philip Randolph, Roy Wilkins, and a host of prominent liberals, activists, and academics. Also working with Lowenstein and listed as a sponsor was Dennis Shaul, the international affairs vice-president of the U.S. Youth Council, who as the international vice-president of the NSA had channeled CIA funds to NSA's various international programs. The purpose of African Freedom Day Action against Apartheid was to increase the pressure on South Africa to change its policies, by promoting a trade embargo and discouraging private American investment, among other things. A national conference on the weekend of April 10–11, 1963, including a demonstration, was planned at Georgetown University to coincide with African Freedom Day on April 14.

Lowenstein also participated in the American Society of African Culture's Fourth International Conference at Howard University before his departure. From April 11 to April 13, the conference focused on "Southern Africa in Transition," and featured the major leaders of most of the southern African independence movements: Oliver Tambo, acting president of the African National Congress of South Africa; Eduardo Mondlane, leader of the Mozambique Liberation Front; Kozonguizi of SWANU; Kerina of SWAPO; as well as leaders from the various political factions in Angola, Zimbabwe (Rhodesia), and Zambia.

The American Society of African Culture, which had convened the conference and which was composed of leading black American scholars, writers, and professional people, had been formed allegedly to promote African culture and to build bonds between American blacks and black Africans who had their struggle for freedom in common. Brooke Aronson (Trent), who worked for AMSAC and did research for Lowenstein on *Brutal Mandate*, said it was created "as a link between the American black community and the new African leadership" because "the only people who knew anything about Africa were American blacks."

When AMSAC was first launched, it shared the office of the Council on Race and Caste in World Affairs, a "paper" organization established by the CIA that specialized in collecting and analyzing data on racial problems worldwide and assessing their impact on international relations—in essence examining the extent to which the Communists were capitalizing on racial conflicts globally. The council and AMSAC merged in 1957, and the council served as a conduit to channel funds to the new organization, which was not officially incorporated until February 1960. *Ramparts* reported contributions to AMSAC from Pappas Charitable Trust ($65,000), Marshall Foundation ($25,000), Benjamin Rosenthal Foundation ($26,000), J. Frederick Brown Foundation ($103,000), Colt Foundation ($47,000), C. H. Dodge Foundation ($28,000), Rabb Foundation ($40,000), and the Ronthelym Foundation ($20,000), all CIA conduits. Serving as the group's assistant director until 1961 was Lowenstein's friend and predecessor at the NSA, DAR Medal winner James T. ("Ted") Harris. A black expert in international affairs and a linguist, Harris has been accused of participation in CIA covert operations and is currently in prison in Tanzania.

The statement of purpose of the American Society of African Culture declares an intention "to study the effects of African culture on American life, examine the cultural contributions of African peoples to their societies; to appraise the conditions affecting the development of ethnic national and universal culture; to cooperate with international organizations with a view to . . . exchange of information on African culture. . . ." The Howard conference was stretching this purpose to include a study of revolution in southern Africa. It was strictly hard politics, not a conga drum to be heard anywhere.

Observers of the 1963 conference, the fourth sponsored by AMSAC in four years, thought it resembled a "revolutionary round table in Havana." *Ramparts* wrote: "The Howard University meeting provided an ideal opportunity for the CIA to look over the top African revolutionaries while providing an illusion of U.S. concern for their cause."

Lowenstein observed as Kerina presented a paper on *South West Africa—Past, Present and Future*, then joined with John Marcum, a University of Pennsylvania professor, in giving a scholarly paper entitled, *Force: Its Thrust and Prognosis*. A sweeping analysis of all of the revolutionary movements in southern Africa, it was subsequently published in 1966 by Praeger, the publishing company whose CIA affiliation was later documented by *Ramparts*, in a book entitled *Southern Africa in Transition*, a collection of the papers given at the conference. The main premise of this paper was that southern Africans were being thwarted in their efforts to obtain peaceful change and were consequently turning to violence. Marcum and Lowenstein set forth their basic thesis:

> In the absence of internal collapse in Portugal and of external intervention in South Africa and Southern Rhodesia, the period of violent upheaval may be prolonged. Neither collapse nor intervention now appears likely, and the legacy of European settlement in southern Africa may consequently be hatred and destruction of catastrophic proportions. This prospect will not dissuade Africans from force. It will be recalled that Americans fought an extended War for Independence that was prompted by grievances that look paltry compared to those now present in southern Africa.

In its account of the origins of the Angolan war for independence, the paper—an extremely sophisticated document—awards Holden Roberto and his U.S.-backed National Front for the Liberation of Angola (FNLA) the main role. The Soviet-backed MPLA (Popular Movement for the Liberation of Angola), headed by poet-physician Dr. Agostino Neto, who became Angola's first president, is characterized as "peripheral."

Holden Roberto had been recruited by the CIA in 1960. After the MPLA took control, the CIA began a prolonged effort to overthrow the MPLA and install a pro-American faction, spending many millions of dollars on ammunition, air support, and mercenaries. Their most notable ally in this effort was UNITA's Jonas Savimbi, whom Lowenstein visited on his swings through Lusaka, Zambia.

Marcum and Lowenstein detailed Dr. Eduardo Mondlane's efforts to achieve independence for Mozambique through diplomatic channels and his creation of the Mozambique Liberation Front (Frelimo). A good friend of Lowenstein's and of the United States, Mondlane was later assassinated in Dar es Salaam, where Frelimo was based.

The main body of the Marcum-Lowenstein effort was devoted to South Africa. Since Sharpeville, they argued, the drift among all but one of the opposition groups was toward violence. (Chief Albert Luthuli maintained that he would not engage in violence under any circumstances.) There were two basic approaches: one, that of the African National Congress's military arm, Nelson Mandela's Spear of the Nation and its ally, the National Liberation Committee, advocated sabotage and hit-and-run tactics against communications and industrial installations; the other, advocated by Poqo ("We Are Alone"), the Pan-Africanist Congress organization for mass violence, put the emphasis on dramatic and brutal action.

Lowenstein's own warnings, already expressed in *Brutal Mandate*, of the potential for a cycle of violence in Africa until all the European liberals have fled, were also set forth. If that were allowed to happen, he observed, it would lead to the rise of bloodthirsty black leaders, "Communists, black racists, gangsters, religious fanatics, and political opportunists, and countless individuals angling for power or glory," and all vying for control of an increasingly "ugly and chaotic situation."

The paper includes a brief analysis of South West Africa, where violence was said not to be imminent but where the credibility of the United Nations was at stake, and Southern Rhodesia, where it was imminent, and of the soon-to-be independent High Commission Territories of Basutoland, Bechuanaland, and Swaziland, to which opponents of apartheid were fleeing, causing a situation of increasing tension. The authors then examined the relationship between Portugal, Spain, and South Africa. "Portugal and South Africa can count on active support only from each other and from Spain," Marcum and Lowenstein wrote. "Their fear of effective international intervention, however, is not overwhelming as long as the Western powers do not support such an intervention."

There was a growing competition, the writers argued, between Pan-Africanism and Communism. They concluded with these sobering words:

> Meanwhile, in southern Africa bitterness proliferates, lines harden, and an explosion approaches. If the explosion is violent, it will be because the world outside, and especially the United States, permitted non-violence to fail. If it is anti-West, it will be because the present white governments have sustained themselves by courtesy of the West. If it is anti-white, it will be because white men failed for so many years to oppose convincingly that which is anti-black. As things are going now, it is likely to be all three. And nothing within southern Africa can change the somber prognosis.

Following the conference, Kozonguizi blasted Lowenstein, calling him a "white tool," explaining that he had "waited four years" to "expose him." The SWANU organizer was motivated either by fear of his own exposure or a need to separate himself from his American contact, or both.

In London, in November of 1963, Lowenstein found that exiles from South Africa agreed on very little. Patrick Duncan, a Liberal who supported the anti-Communist Pan-Africanist Congress and believed that only an anti-Communist revolution could save South Africa from a Communist revolution, and Nelson Mahomo, a member of the PAC executive bureau, met with Lowenstein. They assured him that the PAC was strong in South Africa. But while they insisted that an uprising was "imminent," other sources told Lowenstein otherwise. Some reported that the PAC was "finished," while the African National Congress-National Liberation Committee alliance was "blossoming"; and there were still others who told Lowenstein that only Spear of the Nation had any underground capacity, though they added that no one really expected much in the way of organized upheavals or effective United Nations sanctions.

Fearing that the "neutrality" of the other Africans might destroy the Pan-Africanist Congress, which he looked to as a clear alternative to the Communists, Lowenstein suggested that an attempt be made to get aid for the PAC from the United States, although he conceded that he was pessimistic about the outcome. To stop revolution, the CIA was willing to play with revolution, at least on Lowenstein's level. Yet at the same time, Lowenstein was urging on Oliver Tambo of the ANC a strategy according to which African heads of state would make a "quiet approach" to President Kennedy. Lowenstein was pressing the notion of an African "Démarche" with the ANC leaders while he was talking revolution with the anti-Communist PAC.

There was, however, no time to talk to Kennedy. On November 22, he was assassinated.

23.

While African groups like the All-African People's Conference and the Pan African Freedom Movement for East, Central, and Southern Africa (PAFMECSA) called for sanctions against South Africa, for a boycott of Portugal unless it agreed to independence for its African colonies, and publicized their eagerness to assist in the fight against apartheid and colonialism, Lowenstein noted with frustration that there was considerable hypocrisy. He and Marcum had written: "In fact, many African states still enjoy profitable trade relations with Angola or South Africa, or both."

One African leader made no attempt to hide his beneficial relationship with South Africa; Dr. Hastings Kamuzu Banda, the eccentric, dictatorial head of state in the newly independent nation of Malawi, which until 1964 had been the British colony of Nyasaland. In 1958, after forty years away from his country, Banda returned. A physician, he had lived in America, Scotland, and South Africa, and was practicing medicine in Ghana when the young people called him back to lead the movement that would break up the Rhodesian Federation, which linked Nyasaland to Southern and Northern Rhodesia. The British detained Banda for a year in 1959 for his activism, but by late 1963 the colony was well on its way toward independence, with the blessing of the United States. Peace Corps volunteers were already being sent to Malawi, supplementing an aid program designed to assure that the newly independent black African nation would play the role American had in mind for it.

It was United States policy to use the new "front-line" states, the independent countries that shared a border with South Africa, to pressure South Africa to change its racial policies and relinquish control of South West Africa.

But "Banda was always a disaster," says Kris Kleinbauer, Lowenstein's former student at Stanford who later joined the Peace Corps in Malawi. As soon as the British flag was lowered and the flag of Malawi went up on July 6, 1964, Banda became president with no opponents permitted. His political party was the only party allowed by law. He railed against the Russians and the Chinese, denouncing Communism so vehemently that his speeches might have been written in Pretoria. Banda quickly became an embarrassment to the United States, an easy target for Communist ridicule. A cultural as well as a political reactionary, Banda further antagonized the United States by criticizing what he called its lack of morals.

Worst of all, from the beginning Banda had insisted that his country would accept assistance from whoever he chose. "I would take help from the devil if that would benefit Malawi," he was reported as saying, and indeed, Banda received assistance openly from South Africa, eventually entering into diplomatic relations with the South Africans, the only black African country to do so. The ideal of a black African country working for nonviolent change in South Africa was tainted by Banda. He was clearly in the way.

At the same time, the young people in Malawi who had originally looked to Banda as a leader, "started a ferment against him," as Kris Kleinbauer recalls. And it wasn't long before the temptation to encourage this ferment became irresistible to the Americans, who saw an opportunity to topple Banda without overtly opposing him.

There had been rumors of other attempts to overthrow ultraconservative leaders in Africa. Some said that the coup attempt against Haile Selassie by young officers in 1960 had been assisted by the United States. The rationale there was apparently that if young anti-Communist progressives did not take over, the Emperor would hang on until only the Communists remained to take over when he finally collapsed, a prediction that eventually proved true, in a sense.

Peace Corps volunteers Kris Kleinbauer and novelist-to-be Paul Theroux both became involved in the movement to overthrow Dr. Banda. In the end it failed, but their involvement in the effort, along with the complicity of Allard Lowenstein, with his ties to the CIA, undermines the notion of a CIA-free Peace Corps.

The Peace Corps was attractive to people who wanted to serve their country by helping others, to adventure seekers, and to some who were not able to follow through on other plans. It attracted Kris Kleinbauer and Paul Theroux.

Kris Kleinbauer had been inspired to join the Peace Corps by Allard Lowenstein, who was her professor in a course on southern African politics. At Stanford, she recalls, Lowenstein was regarded as "radical" because "introducing the National Student Association seemed a very radical thing to do." Kleinbauer and Lowenstein became close. She was attractive and he was a legendary figure whose adventures gave him a special aura. "We had a romance," she remembers, "but it was always in the airport. He was always on the phone." But Kleinbauer also recalls that it was difficult to get too close to him. "Al was not one for deep personal relationships. He was closer to the guys than to women."

Kleinbauer was among the second group of volunteers to go to Malawi in late 1963 while it was still a British colony. In addition to the Americans, Banda had the South Africans there as well. Kleinbauer worked as a teacher in Zomba, the capital, and lived in a Catholic convent. She recalls that there were Europeans and Americans everywhere, many of them giving encouragement to the students who were opposing Banda. "When things came to a head with Banda, many of them went underground," Kleinbauer recalls. "They brought us into the American ambassador's office and told us that these people were on the run. We shouldn't alienate them, but we should keep our distance."

The government began arresting people. Shortly after independence, they arrested some of her students and she went with a friend to the police station to vouch for them. The two of them were the only whites at the station, where the atmosphere was "festive," as Kleinbauer describes it. "You couldn't tell who was for or against the government."

In 1964, Paul Theroux was "terminated" as a volunteer and sent home from Malawi for "getting involved in anti-regime politics in that country," according to Wofford's account. Wofford explains that Theroux smuggled a revolutionary out of Malawi with a message for the anti-Banda forces, then smuggled guns back in.

Kris Kleinbauer was also expelled from Malawi in 1964. Greg Craig, Lowenstein's close friend whose father was then director of training for the Peace Corps, says that Kleinbauer was forced out because she hid an anti-Banda revolutionary. Kleinbauer herself says she was sent home before the government could deport her.

During the period of the anti-Banda activity, Kleinbauer had been in touch with Lowenstein, who, having left North Carolina State, was dividing his time between Mississippi, New York, Europe, and during the Democratic convention, Atlantic City. But as her situation became more precarious, he began to grow apprehensive about her safety and dubious about the success of any action against Banda. Lowenstein clearly knew what Kleinbauer and Theroux were doing, and he contemplated flying over to Malawi to be closer to the situation.

Starting in mid-October of 1964, Lowenstein began recording "headlines" in his newspaperlike diary that seemed to mix romance with international intrigue.

"Q IS PUT BY WIRE, CHANCES 'NOT TOO BRIGHT'; TIMING LEFT OPEN, NEXT FALL PREFERRED."

"Theroux a Problem; Trip Over Possible."

"HOPES FADING IN CONTINUING SILENCE; 'IMMEDIATE ACTION' NOW OUT, OLD PLANS RESTORED."

"Concern for safety rises, but 'odds' favor an 'awkward negative'."

"SAYS ABSENCE OF WORD BEGINS TO SEEM PECULIAR; 'CHECK UP' IS WEIGHED."

"K SILENCE CONTINUES; E.B. TO ASK IF FAMILY HAS HEARD 'ANYTHING.'"

And on Election Day, 1964: "K EXPELLED FROM MALAWI BY P.C., DUE IN TOMORROW; CABLE ASKS 'HELP,' IS SILENT ON LARGER QUESTIONS; HOPES REVIVE FOR 'A NEW ARRANGEMENT' NEXT AUTUMN. D.C. RENDEZ VOUS SET."

Right after the election, which Lyndon Johnson won by a landslide over Barry Goldwater, Lowenstein wrote: "K AFFIRMATIVE BOTH AGREE 'THERE'S NO RUSH' AND SET RENDEZ-VOUS IN AFRICA IN AUGUST; FINAL DECISIONS ARE DEFERRED UNTIL THEN. (DAR TRIP VIA ASIA LIKELY) VIEWS VERY SIMILAR. P.C. FIGHT TAKES TURN FOR BETTER, BUT TRANSFER STILL SEEMS UNLIKELY."

Kris Kleinbauer was a trusted Peace Corps volunteer close to Lowenstein, a CIA operative, and shared his antipathy to Dr. Banda. Lowenstein's entries in his diary, his direct interest in Theroux's activities as well as Kleinbauer's, indicate a supervisory role on his part in their activities against Banda. But when Banda's own intelligence found out (he had the best in the business, South Africa's secret police), the Peace Corps had no choice but to act, refusing to give Kleinbauer money due her. Theroux says that he met Lowenstein only once.

Kleinbauer was "crazy about Al," Emory Bundy (the E.B. in one of the "headlines") relates. And Lowenstein was notorious for using people. His penetration of the Peace Corps may have been the only such incident, but there is no escaping the fact that Kleinbauer and Theroux were involved in what the CIA would define as a covert paramilitary operation, whether they realized it or not.

Lowenstein was able to get Kleinbauer her Peace Corps money, and then suggested to her an assignment working with Eduardo Mondlane of Frelimo, who was based in Dar es Salaam. Mondlane was a Lowenstein contact who received U.S. support for his liberation war against the Portuguese in Mozambique. Lowenstein gave the development this headline: "K in L.A., Likes Idea of Job With Mondlane." Kleinbauer made plans to go to Dar ostensibly with a teaching job in a Catholic school.

In 1965, Kleinbauer was with Lowenstein again, recruiting in Berkeley for the Encampment for Citizenship. Lowenstein was also helping his friend Martin Meyerson, the president of Berkeley under Chancellor Clark Kerr, to weather the stormy free-speech movement. He arranged for Kleinbauer to meet William Craig and then drive cross-country. A 1965 entry in his diary records that at one point she drove him to Los Angeles. "K. Drives A. to L.A. Mustang Safely There; Digs Outlook Hopeful." The Mustang was Al's, which he cherished. "Warmth of K. Reunion Suggests 'Reappraisal' Before African Trip," he inscribed.

Kleinbauer insists that all she did in Dar was teach school. "People thought I was a CIA agent," she admits. "In Dar, they thought you were either a CIA agent or a missionary." Kleinbauer says that many of her friends were in exile in Tanzania, and since she had no money for graduate school, this seemed the best alternative. She stayed in Dar, meeting such black Americans as SNCC leader James Forman and expatriate Bill Sutherland, who, she adds, "works with the liberation movements."

In 1968, Kris Kleinbauer returned to America to work for Lowenstein's congressional campaign. Although she worked hard for Al, she says they were very far apart politically. "I wasn't a Democrat," she explains, stressing her left-wing views. "I wasn't too keen on all that." Taking her radical politics with her back to Los Angeles, she started a career as a private investigator, a career for which her African work undoubtedly helped to prepare her.

Harris Wofford insists that he never heard of Kris Kleinbauer, whose expulsion from Malawi had caused a sensation within the Peace Corps. Since Wofford negotiated the Malawi Peace Corps deal, this is odd. He certainly was very aware of Paul Theroux, and very interested in the "newspaper" diary entries which Lowenstein recorded under Malawi headlines. Wofford asked for copies of them as well as of several of the letters written by Peace Corps volunteers, which invariably opened with the salutation, "Dear Family."

The "Dear Family" letters were definitely another dimension to the Peace Corps. They were not letters home to mom and dad. There was nothing personal in them. They were intelligence reports to the "family" of trusted Americans within or at the periphery of that amorphous mass known as the "intelligence community." They were invariably marked "for private circulation only" or "not for publication." Who to include in "the family" was a matter to be decided by those who used the term. According to Victor Marchetti, people in the CIA used "a lot of terms invented by different minds, by little groups and individuals, out of boredom." So when Lowenstein writes in his diary that Emory Bundy is to see if the "Family has heard anything" about Kris Kleinbauer, he is not referring to Kleinbauer's parents, although they were probably asked; he is referring to that group of people Lowenstein himself designated as "the family," a term derived from the opening used by Peace Corps volunteers and others in the numbered and duplicated intelligence reports Lowenstein was receiving. He was a member of this "family," and so was Emory Bundy.

Lowenstein was on the mailing list of many authors of these "Dear Family" letters, keeping in touch with innumerable people who had gone to live in Africa. Among them was Carol Hardin Kimball, sister of Adlai Hardin, who had traveled in South Africa with Lowenstein in 1958, and wife of a young Mobil executive in Nigeria Geoff Kimball. Another was Peace Corps Volunteer Steve Bingham, who had worked with Lowenstein in Mississippi and was the nephew of Lowenstein's friend, liberal Congressman Jonathan Bingham. Writing from Njama via Tabe, Sierra Leone, in 1966, Bingham apologized for his failure to keep the letters coming: "My daily entries for May and June are all very small and so I am going to try within a week or so to get off another letter to you bringing us up to June. That can all make one mimeo letter. I am sorry I've fallen far behind again."

After making the trip to South West Africa with Lowenstein in 1959, Bundy had taught at Millbrook, then gone to work for the State Council of Churches in Seattle. Later, at UCLA he had studied under James S. Coleman, then director of what Bundy calls the "best African studies program in the country." Kris Kleinbauer and Bundy had Lowenstein in common and their paths crossed in Los Angeles before Kleinbauer left for Malawi. In 1965, Bundy was hired by the Rockefeller Foundation for their field staff in Uganda where he worked as assistant to his former professor James S. Coleman. When Bundy returned to America, he joined the faculty of Oberlin College and encountered Kris Kleinbauer again when they both worked for Lowenstein's 1968 congressional campaign. Bundy then went to Washington with Lowenstein as his chief of staff. He would leave this position with some bitterness and return to Seattle for a career in television, leaving African affairs and politics.

Another Communist-backed youth festival was planned by the IUS for the summer of 1965 in Algiers, and Lowenstein made preparations to go there in order to disrupt it. Planning to join him this time was Paul Theroux's brother Eugene, who, as an NSA leader in 1958, had met Lowenstein and been inspired by him to work on behalf of South West Africa and black students in the South. Eugene Theroux had been recruited in 1965 by Gloria Steinem to work for the CIA front Independent Research Service. They were to be part of a delegation to "cause trouble" as Theroux puts it, or to "engage people in debate," as he corrects himself. But the youth festival never took place. As Theroux recalls it, Ben Bella was overthrown in Algeria and the festival was rescheduled for Accra in 1967. But "Nkrumah ran into trouble," Theroux says, and was overthrown as well, with the CIA deeply implicated in the effort.

24.

Late in 1965, a groundswell of support among American whites developed for Ian Smith, the white Rhodesian who had taken control of the country and declared it independent from Britain. Rhodesia, once multiracial, was now heading toward its own brand of apartheid. Black Africans, who became aware of this attitude toward Smith, seethed. Clearly, all the post-Sharpeville activity had produced nothing permanent and some public action was needed to show that the U.S. was not abandoning black Africa.

Lowenstein, who was then living in New York, was called upon to draft a statement for the American Committee on Africa to stress collective action by the United Nations against Rhodesia. In a document dated December 20, 1965 (his handwriting identifies Lowenstein's authorship), he said for the ACOA: "We believe the only effective way of doing this is under Chapter VII of the U.N. Charter which involves naming the Rhodesia crisis a 'threat to the peace.' It is such a threat because the economies of Zambia and Malawi are jeopardized by events in Rhodesia."

Lowenstein's work with the American Committee on Africa in 1965 and 1966 was especially helpful to the committee, which was having budget problems at the time. Lowenstein did not have to be paid. Such volunteer work could supply CIA support to organizations deemed worthy without having it known.

Lowenstein was drafted once again to press the New Jersey Region of the National Conference of Christians and Jews against proceeding with its plan to give a "brotherhood" award to Charles W. Engelhard, a business partner of Harry Oppenheimer, the South African multimillionaire. He wrote a letter of protest, signed by Donald Harrington and A. Philip Randolph, which called Engelhard "the symbol of United States financial support for the pernicious system of apartheid in South Africa," and expressing outrage at an act of "public recognition to one who is so closely tied in with the system of racial exploitation in South Africa." (A first draft, in a passage ultimately cut from the final letter, noted that Engelhard had "the dubious reputation of having served as the model on which Ian Fleming based his character

Goldfinger" and that he claimed to have a stewardess aboard his $1 million personal Convair 404 named Pussy Galore.)

By this time, the executive board of the ACOA had some new names, including writer James Baldwin; James Farmer of CORE; Stanley Levison, Martin Luther King, Jr.'s, lawyer; Joseph Jablow; Bayard Rustin; Mason Sears, the U.S. representative to the Trusteeship Council who had heard Hans Beukes's testimony; and Victor Reuther of the United Auto Workers. These were Lowenstein's people, and he was writing the ACOA's material.

In March 1966, while Lowenstein was trying to get reform backing for his candidacy for Congress in Manhattan, he published an article on South West Africa in *The Record*. The World Court would soon hand down its decision on the case brought by Liberia and Ethiopia determining what the United Nations could do about South West Africa. If the court failed to side with two black African countries against South Africa, Lowenstein warned that there would be dire consequences: "If the United Nations cannot protect its own ward—when and where can world law be taken seriously?" Lowenstein then summed up his position eloquently, noting:

"It is high time we tried to understand the bitterness of people held in bondage in what we call the 'Free World' because of the 'practical considerations' of the Cold War. Democracy's strength is that to her, decency is universal and concerned with the freedom of *all*. But even ignoring ethical considerations, we should realize that to support tyrants is to court the hatred of the oppressed. We have spawned too many Batistas not to realize that Batistas inevitably spawn Castros."

He went on to take his country to task for "the lingering double standard that has made our record on race relations so shoddy at home, and encourages the suspicion that we are less concerned about the suffering of non-whites than whites." The long-awaited World Court ruling, he said, "may provide the last opportunity for the civilized world to act peacefully against the most barbarous racism since Hitler."

By 1966 Robert Kennedy, having resigned his position as attorney general and having won election to the Senate in New York, was increasingly regarded by liberals like Lowenstein as the government in exile. He was seen as entirely problack, an image he cultivated at a time when there was enormous support for the civil rights cause. In the fall of 1965, the National Union of South African Students, an organization with whom Lowenstein had close ties, invited Robert Kennedy to address its annual Day of Affirmation in Cape Town to be held in June 1966. NUSAS saw the visit as "providing an opportunity for the democratic opposition in South Africa to show that it has the support of a prominent member and policymaker of a Western democracy. In particular, we are interested that the appeal of the Kennedy family to youth should be felt in South Africa."

Robert Kennedy and his staff thought the perfect person to help them accomplish this was Allard Lowenstein. Lowenstein had the South African experience they needed; he had connections with NU-SAS, he appealed to the young, and he was potentially a useful political ally. Having managed Congressman William Ryan's unsuccessful mayoral campaign in New York in 1965, and having lost only narrowly himself when he made a bid for reform endorsement in a congressional race, Lowenstein's reform credentials were interesting to Kennedy, who had backed organization candidate Abe Beame for mayor of New York and now felt it necessary to forge links with the growing movement of which Lowenstein was a part. And since Lowenstein had written extensively on South Africa, he would know what buttons to press in a major speech such as the one Kennedy was to give to students in Cape Town during Day of Affirmation ceremonies. It was the first time Lowenstein and Kennedy ever worked together and evidently they each found the collaboration inspiring. Lowenstein wrote the most moving part of the speech, not knowing at the time that his words would be inscribed on the monument near Robert Kennedy's grave.

"Some believe there is nothing one man or woman can do against the enormous array of the world's ills," Kennedy told the overflow crowd. "Yet many of the world's great movements of thought and action have flowed from the work of a single man.

"A young monk began the Protestant Revolution. A young general extended an empire from Macedonia to the borders of the earth. A young woman reclaimed the territory of France, and it was a young Italian explorer who discovered the New World, and the thirty-two-year-old Thomas Jefferson who explained that all men are created equal."

And he told them, "Each time a man stands for an ideal, or acts to improve the lot of others, or strikes out against injustice, he sends forth a tiny ripple of hope. And crossing each other from a million different centers of energy and daring, those ripples build a current that can sweep down the mightiest walls of oppression and resistance. . . ."

No sooner had Kennedy returned than Lowenstein prepared for his own trip to Africa in the summer of 1966. Lowenstein wrote in his diary that the assassination of South African white supremacist Prime Minister Verwoerd might "muddle" the trip, but he proceeded on schedule. The assassination was not politically motivated but the act of a deranged white. He conferred in Washington with Helen Suzman, who was there to see Robert Kennedy. He also spoke with

George Houser at the American Committee on Africa who wrote letters to several African liberation movement leaders to arrange meetings for Lowenstein.

To Oliver R. Tambo, head of the African National Congress,
Houser wrote that Lowenstein was expected to be in Africa "towards
July or August," when he would be "most anxious" to meet with Tambo
in Dar es Salaam. Eduardo Mondlane, head of Frelimo, also received
a brief note from Houser advising him of Lowenstein's plans for an
African trip and requesting a meeting in Dar.

Shortly before the trip, Lowenstein was invited by A. Philip Randolph to be a sponsor of the Committee of Conscience against Apartheid, just formed by the American Committee on Africa. As he wrote
Lowenstein on July 22, Randolph himself had already agreed to chair
the new group, which planned to "carry on a campaign for the next six
months, appealing to both individuals and organizations to withdraw
their accounts from the First National City and Chase Manhattan
Banks" because they were "symbolic of the international financial support that has helped to make South Africa so prosperous and powerful." Randolph pointed to the success of a demonstration on April 20
when 300 people marched "in dignified fashion" to the First National
City Bank branch at 111th Street and Broadway. The demonstrators
who held accounts with the bank withdrew them and those who did
not deposited a letter of protest with the bank management. Organized by students and faculty from Jewish Theological Seminary, Columbia, and Barnard, it was, according to Randolph, "in a sense, a
pilot project." It was a sign that pressure was once again being put on
South Africa, just as Lowenstein was making plans to meet with liberation leaders to find out their plans and urge them to be patient.

Lowenstein was also involved with his personal plans. He was
planning to marry Jenny Lyman, a young Barnard graduate from a
wealthy old Boston family who had spent some time in Nigeria and
had worked briefly for the American Committee on Africa. Lowenstein had started courting Jenny while she was working in his reform
campaign for Congress in Manhattan that winter. Jenny's sister Muffie
was a friend of Geoff Kimball, the Mobil executive working in Nigeria.
His wife was Lowenstein's friend Carol Hardin, author of some of the
"Dear Family" letters from Africa and the sister of Adlai Hardin, who
had traveled to South Africa with Lowenstein in 1958. It was, in a
way, all in the "family."

Lowenstein told Jenny Lyman that he was going on a "fact-finding
trip" to confer with his friends in the resistance in Spain and with
South African exiles in London before going down to Africa to visit a
number of countries where he had friends in national liberation organizations. She was amused by the official-sounding title he gave his
expeditions and refers to them instead as "fact-finding adventures."

She was, she insists, not certain where the funds for them came from. "He must have had money," she concludes.

Lowenstein's father had died in March of 1965 and there were a number of insurance policies, but the estate was tied up in legal tangles and family disagreements. Moreoever, Lowenstein had a reputation among even his friends for being a tightwad, rarely paying for anything that somebody else might pay for. As for the purpose of the trip, Jenny explains that "there was never a cause he considered finished. He had more back burners and front burners. Intellectually, causes were the most interesting thing to him. He loved history and politics and was very moved by unusual people who were courageously fighting for a particular cause. Those around him were 'source material' for his own politics and inspiration."

James Forman of SNCC, who had clashed with Lowenstein in Mississippi, differed with this interpretation of Lowenstein's motives. In 1966, while traveling in Africa with Howard Moore, a political associate, Forman ran into Lowenstein. Forman would later write:

Allard Lowenstein popped up while we were in Dar es Salaam, like a sudden nightmare. We assumed that he was there on behalf of the State Department or the CIA. We knew that he did not have the Tanzanian Government's interest at heart, and saw his presence in the framework of the liberal-labor syndrome's efforts to maintain control even in faraway Africa. The influence of that treacherous element in Africa has been great, especially in some of the trade unions. Lowenstein turned up again on the plane with us as we headed for Zambia and the Seminar on Apartheid, Racism and Colonialism in Southern Africa.

When Lowenstein got back to the United States, he received a letter from Kris Kleinbauer in Dar es Salaam dated August 10:

Forman and Howard Moore have returned—I happened to wind up in a big group with them the other night. Forman is a lot less articulate and less obnoxious than I expected. Bill Sutherland came round to our house the following night to take us out with them. I wouldn't go as we had guests, but Bill insisted we all must get together since "there is something interesting going on between Lowenstein and Forman." To say the least! If this meeting ever takes place, I'll let you know. Things get more interesting here all the time but I am thinking vaguely of coming home at the end of the year. Just a thought at the moment but I'm beginning to feel it's time for a change. Also the "Great Society" seems to be ready to fall apart—maybe a reason for staying away, but it draws me back somehow!

More than the "Great Society" was falling apart. On July 18, 1966, the World Court had shocked the international law community by deciding that Ethiopia and Liberia did not have standing to bring the South West African case on the question of the South African mandate because they could not show how they were harmed by it. The timing couldn't have been worse for Lowenstein, who was trying to persuade the Africans to eschew violence and rely on the United Nations. Robert Kennedy's message had raised hopes that could not be fulfilled in Africa. Bitterness and cynicism took hold as international law went out the window. While the United States was spending fortunes establishing law schools all over Africa (the biggest in Ethiopia), the World Court had handed down a decision that made the whole enterprise look like a farce as far as the Africans were concerned.

After the World Court decision, Lowenstein wrote in his diary in August, "Court Decision Means Violence. Sanctions Out. Anti-S.A. Groups Agree; SWAPO asks A to organize. Jolt is 'Devastating.'"

Sensing the disillusionment and seeing their opportunity, the Maoist Chinese rushed in with large amounts of money for the liberation groups based in Dar es Salaam. China handed the money over to the government of Tanzania to be distributed to the various liberation organizations to which it was host in order to keep the assistance relatively covert. So much money was there that in some cases ethics were strained to the breaking point. One story which made the rounds in Dar es Salaam told of Julius Nyerere's minister charged with dispensing the money, who packed a suitcase with over a million dollars and bought a ticket to London. When customs officials at Nairobi Airport opened the fleeing minister's suitcase, bills flew in every direction. But instead of arresting the culprit, the officers ran after the money while the minister shut his bag, grabbed it, and ran to the plane that carried him to luxurious retirement in London.

At the headquarters of the liberation movements in Dar es Salaam, however, the big pictures of Mao Zedong were going up, as guerrilla garb replaced suits and dashikis. They were instant Maoists, living by the slogan of Mao: "Power grows from the barrel of a gun." The once nonviolent African National Congress was now committed to violence, as was SWAPO, whose militant uniforms and graphically stylish posters began to look as though they had been designed by a Marxist Gucci. The gun was in.

Even so, Americans continued to come and go in Africa as if nothing were happening. They acted as though they were still in charge, still running things. They poured fortunes into Ethiopia, the only country in Africa with an emperor. They sent professors, dancers, doctors, and judges. (Some of them wrote "Dear Family" letters. And if the Peace Corps volunteers went on the cheap, others did not.)

In 1967 Lowenstein performed the last of the series of African missions begun in 1962. Having cultivated the African liberationists as well as the influential white Americans with an interest in Africa during those years, Lowenstein found himself in an ambiguous position: he had one foot in the past and another in the future. His present was a frenzy of activity to reconcile going in both directions.

When revelations about CIA-funding of numerous organizations were published in the March 1967 issue of *Ramparts*, the American Committee on Africa, in a fund-raising letter signed by Donald Harrington, expressed its shock. Harrington wrote that he had been "amazed at the recent revelations about CIA support to private organizations operating in the field of foreign affairs." He said that the disclosures "highlighted the need for truly independent organizations, free from all governmental pressures and inducements, free to criticize and bring influence to bear on American policies toward other areas of the world," and affirmed that the ACOA had always maintained "a completely independent policy," supported entirely by its "members and contributors." He mentioned that, programatically, the most important new element in the ACOA's work was the addition of two people to its staff in Washington, an expensive, but indispensable measure, he said, "if a growing number of Congressmen are to be provided with facts to do their part in setting the direction of U.S. policy towards Africa."

It would take two full-time staff people in Washington to replace Al Lowenstein, who was moving on to other things. He had been a one-man lobbying organization of enormous power, a gatherer of information covering a whole continent, and a mover and shaker of liberation movements, directing them in the interests of the United States. But the Vietnam War was becoming a preoccupation with him, and his position was becoming increasingly untenable.

There had been an attempt to woo him back into the fold. Tom Hughes, director of intelligence and research at the State Department, had sent him a memo on December 9, 1966, with a copy of an off-the-record speech Hughes had delivered at Stanford Law School. In it, Hughes had attempted to justify America's role in the Vietnam War on legalistic grounds. "You may find a few stalks of general application rising from this underbrush of legalisms," Hughes wrote to Lowenstein. But Lowenstein was moving away from them. Increasingly, he came under criticism from CIA people who had previously been friendly to him. But Lowenstein was becoming more independent as he moved to center stage in the antiwar movement, and he was not concerned over the criticism. He had his own inheritance, his wife's trust, which provided a modest income, and most important, a growing conviction that in some sense his time was finally coming. He had his issue and he was running with it. With his wife three months pregnant, Lowenstein would take off for Africa once more, this time to wind up his southern African work for the CIA.

Lowenstein's situation at the time was a precarious one. Still engaged in African intelligence work, he was publicly opposing American policy in Vietnam. Shortly before his departure for Africa, in the spring of 1967, Lowenstein arrived at Chapel Hill to debate a State Department official in an event, sponsored by the Political Speakers Society that had been organized by undergraduate Robin West. Hal Minus, another undergraduate, whose father was head of the chemistry department at Chapel Hill, and who was majoring in Africa studies, wanted to meet Lowenstein. West told him that a few people were going to have dinner with Lowenstein before the lecture and that he could come if he wanted.

Lowenstein arrived at a predebate dinner in his usual tumultuous state. He needed a particular *New York Times* article and Hal Minus volunteered to help Lowenstein find it.

The two became friends during the week Lowenstein spent at Chapel Hill, where, according to Minus, Lowenstein "wiped out the State Department person" at the debate. Having arranged to stay a few more days to lecture on Vietnam, Lowenstein was "tireless and articulate," Minus recalls. "I never had the feeling of a power-hungry person. He put on no airs. The issues were more important." But Lowenstein did astonish Minus with his diet. The undergraduate looked on in bewilderment as Lowenstein wolfed down junk-food, milkshakes, and ice cream, as well as fresh fruit and juice. "I have to get exercise," Lowenstein would say. "If I get tired, I must work out." Minus would wrestle with him as part of the routine. "He was very strong, really powerful. His arms were gigantic," Minus remembers.

In May, when another recruit who was to have accompanied him on his African trip dropped out, Lowenstein invited Minus to join him. He insisted that he was going on his own and needed Minus to assist him. He said that his objective was to "bring change in southern Africa" and that he was in a position to help by drawing publicity to the problem.

Minus met Lowenstein in New York and was given a variety of assignments. He obtained visas and studied assigned "background information," including reports prepared by the African-American Institute, an organization later revealed by the Africa Research Group to be CIA-supported, and which had become the publisher of *Africa Report* after the American Committee on Africa stopped publishing it. Through them, he familiarized himself with the African independence movements, particularly those in Rhodesia and Mozambique, and with developments in the "front-line" states. "We were going to renew contacts," Minus explains. "We would meet in his brother's restaurant and he would be carrying on four conversations at the same time. He wanted to assist the independence movements. His involvements with the early independence movements were profound. His contacts were good."

The trip was to take three weeks. Lowenstein went through Europe and hooked up with Minus two weeks later in Nairobi. At the Norfolk Hotel, a "horrendously expensive" old establishment that catered to the old British colonial crowd, Lowenstein's attempt to bargain down the rates was unsuccessful, and Minus felt obliged to choose another hotel. On their first full day in Nairobi, they looked up Lowenstein's friend Jack Block, the white owner of the posh New Stanley Hotel in Nairobi, as well as a big farm near Lake Nawasha. Block, a man with powerful contacts, was born in Kenya, married to a white South African and entertained Lowenstein whenever he passed through Nairobi.

Lowenstein himself had run into a little cash-flow problem before Minus joined him. On July 3, his wife Jenny wrote him from Maine, where she was vacationing with her sister and Tim Hogen, a friend and political confidant of Lowenstein's: "I've been here for a week now and plan to leave on Sunday. As a result you won't get any mail until Dar (if not Israel). . . . FDR, the bearded IIIrd, just phoned to say you were in financial straits. Oh Lord. I guess you must have cabled me and I wasn't there to send you money—you poor thing—I hope nothing bad went wrong. You perhaps did nothing more unusual than have your plane ticket stolen? Anyway, Franklin is dispatching the money immediately and I'll reimburse him as soon as I get home."

Jenny's sister, Muffie Huntington, scribbled a facetious note on the same letter: "During a secret caucus of Democratic political leaders from New York City, the candidacy of Allard Lowenstein for Congressman from the 19th C.D. was a heated subject of discussion. The candidacy was proposed by Jenny Lowenstein and seconded by T. L. Hogen, a close political associate of Mr. Lowenstein. Muffie Huntington expressed some reservations to the proposal on the basis that the candidacy had not been submitted to a family caucus. Steve Smith promised his support. Neither Robert Kennedy nor Mr. Lowenstein could be reached for comment. P.S. News of county leadership fight will follow Monday." (Steve Smith was Kennedy's brother-in-law and a power in New York politics.)

In a short note, Hogen added: "Hope I'll catch a glimpse of you before your trip to V.N." Lowenstein was planning to fly to Vietnam after returning from Africa via Israel, a country he visited often. Deeply involved in covert operations in Africa, Israel had a superb intelligence operation there that worked closely with the CIA.

In Dar es Salaam, capital of the liberation movements, Lowenstein met with Oliver Tambo of the African National Congress, Sam Nujoma of SWAPO, and the leaders of the Zimbabwe liberation groups. At the airport he also met briefly with Mozambique liberation leader Eduardo Mondlane, who was himself returning from a trip and had only a short time to spend with Lowenstein. No one was permitted to go with Lowenstein to these meetings, which Minus gathered were of a sensitive nature. But Minus knew that Lowenstein enjoyed "good personal relations" with Mondlane and that he had also been in contact that June with Mondlane's American wife, director of the Mozambique Institute, concerning their efforts to "improve Mozambique education."

Lowenstein told Minus that he had hoped to get into Mozambique to get an exclusive story on Frelimo. When he found he could not, he decided to stay in Dar to talk to a group of African National Congress "freedom fighters." Lowenstein took Minus with him to this encounter at ANC, headquarters where a picture of Mao Zedong was prominently displayed. When Lowenstein asked them how he could be of help, the black South Africans told him that what they needed was money for arms. They were engaged in armed struggle and wanted weapons, not the limited support Lowenstein had provided in the past, and which China had eclipsed.

Lowenstein was now disillusioned with the ANC and it had little further use for him. Just as the gap between Lowenstein and the radical wing of the civil rights movement in the United States had widened before, so now the gap separating Lowenstein from the African National Congress, and SWAPO as well, was widening. Because it wanted an end to Portuguese colonialism, and there was no compromise with this issue, the United States considered armed struggle justifiable in Mozambique. But in South Africa, Rhodesia, and South West Africa, the goal was multiracialism, and pro-West capitalist regimes. For their parts, Sam Nujoma of SWAPO, Robert Mugabe and Joshua Nkomo of ZAPU and ZANU in Rhodesia, and Tambo and Mandela in South Africa had all abandoned these goals. America had failed to get the white southern Africans to move, and as Lowenstein had predicted, the blacks turned to uncompromising violence. They had also turned from the West to the Communist bloc.

Lowenstein and Minus left Tanzania for Zambia, where they visited camps of refugees from South West Africa, Mozambique, and Rhodesia, and where Lowenstein was to see President Kaunda. Before the appointment, Minus dropped Lowenstein at the home of the American ambassador in Lusaka where he had been invited to have lunch. Minus arrived late to pick up Lowenstein for their meeting with Kaunda, and Lowenstein snapped: "Next time I say pick me up, don't let me spend too much time at the ambassador's house." By the time Lowenstein and Minus arrived where Kaunda and his entourage had been waiting, it was too late for a meeting. Instead, Kaunda inscribed copies of a book he had written and gave them to the Americans.

Minus then completed his own swing through West Africa before returning to America with a certain sense of failure. "I felt I let Al down," he laments. "I felt I was too young to do what I should have to help. But Al presented opportunities to me and left me with the choice of being involved." After graduating from Chapel Hill, Minus joined the Peace Corps, then earned a degree in planning, then took a job at the Research Triangle Institute in North Carolina, a nonprofit corporation which, among other things, conducts research on African development for the AID.

Meanwhile, Lowenstein spent a day with Emory Bundy and his wife in Kampala, Uganda, painting a somber picture of events in the United States. Bundy wrote Lowenstein on July 23: "It was *great* to see you Al—so good to learn something about the contemporary USA (even if it sounds pretty grim)."

When Lowenstein returned to New York, more than political events were somber. His mother was dying. After the funeral, he would undertake the nationwide speaking tour on the Vietnam War, and the challenge to Lyndon Johnson that would make him a national figure, a symbol of resistance within the system. When he would speak in August at the famous College Park, Maryland, NSA Congress, the first to be free of CIA ties for years, and formally announce "Dump Johnson," SDS protestors would call him a CIA agent. They would hound him with this charge which he would not or could not answer. He planned to run for Congress and his supporters expected a denial that *he* at least was unaware of the NSA's CIA funding.

From a friend who had attended a dinner honoring Bayard Rustin that spring with him, Lowenstein received a postcard expressing the hope "that the hysteria surrounding the CIA mess (which touches most of us somewhere—probably the reason for the reaction and emotion) has tapered off, and that you can get back to business single-mindedly."

Lowenstein was convinced that what Johnson was doing in Vietnam, a country that Lowenstein felt was of little strategic importance, would hand the colonialism argument back to the Soviet Union in Africa and elsewhere, in countries where the United States had a much greater stake and where it might have to intervene later. He did not advocate surrender in Vietnam. He believed that negotiations were the price that had to be paid to keep a generation of young Americans from joining a revolution at home. He had kept his options open as long as possible; now he needed to be free to act. But could he be free, given his involvements?

Whether Lowenstein was on loan to the peace movement or whether he joined it and the effort to relieve the nation of the excesses of Lyndon Johnson in the purity of democratic conviction may never be known. What matters is his impact on events, which was considerable.

25.

Directly after Lowenstein was sworn into Congress in January of 1969, he made a sensitive and dangerous trip to Biafra in the midst of the bloody civil war that was tearing Nigeria apart. The area the Biafrans claimed as the territory of their secessionist state had much of the oil Nigeria was counting on to make it rich. The French were actively backing Biafra against Nigeria, which was supported by the British, who were seeking to exploit the Nigerian oil. France, if they succeeded in gaining independence for Biafra, counted on replacing the British in what would then be the Biafran oil fields. It was much the same game the Belgians had played in the Congo in 1960 when they backed the attempted secession of mineral-rich Katanga under Moise Tshombe.

The United States' position was difficult. In sympathy with the British, with whom the Americans worked closely in Africa, the U.S. nevertheless could not ignore the growing public sentiment in favor of Biafra, a sentiment Nigeria had helped to engender by its failure to expedite efforts to ease widespread famine in the rebel-controlled areas. What the United States wanted was a negotiated solution that would preserve Western interests. The basic goal was to keep Nigeria intact, to prevent secession. For any such disruption in a pro-Western African country, it was feared, would only present opportunities for the Soviets to increase their influence. Moreover, America was closer to Britain than to France in that the American oil companies were closer to British Petroleum (BP) than they were to Total, France's state-controlled oil monopoly.

Lowenstein's trip was not a congressional one. According to Emory Bundy, who had left a teaching job in Oberlin to become Lowenstein's chief of staff in Washington, "The trip to Biafra really started *before* Al took office. None of that planning went through the office."

According to Greg Craig, who accompanied Lowenstein on the Nigerian trip, a foundation, the name of which he knows but chooses not to reveal, paid for the expedition. Craig says that Lowenstein appeared before a large committee at the offices of the foundation, explained the nature of the trip, and obtained funding. "Al went to Nigeria on Ted Kennedy's behalf," Craig insists. "Al was sympathetic to Biafra, and Kennedy was their leading spokesman. Al was pro-Biafra."

But by the time the trip was over, Lowenstein would be responsible for undermining Biafra's position.

In January 1969, Greg Craig, then a student at Yale Law School, accepted an invitation to go to Biafra with Lowenstein. They had come to know each other through William Craig, Greg's father, and in 1964 Lowenstein had recruited Greg to work with him in Mississippi when the younger Craig had just graduated from Exeter and was about to enter Harvard.

The two flew first to London for meetings with the American mission and with representatives of the Wilson government, which was backing the federal government of Nigeria. The British wanted to defuse the starvation issue. Because neither the Biafrans nor the federal government would let foreign planes land, it was impossible to get food to the Biafrans who were isolated and starving. And as photographs appeared in the newspapers of Biafran children near death, sympathy grew for the cause of secession. To counter this, the British under secretary for foreign affairs told Lowenstein when he met with him, "If you can get an agreement from both sides that planes can land with food, we'll have them here."

The Biafrans depended on outside supplies for the guns and ammunition they needed to keep up the war. To keep the military supplies out, Nigeria imposed a quarantine, which had the effect of cutting off food as well. Aggravating the situation was the Biafran troops' refusal to eat any food that had been previously inspected by federal troops. Lowenstein's solution was to propose that planes should land with food in the Biafran-controlled areas. If the Biafrans turned this down, then they would be suspect. But it would be difficult for them to accept the proposal because the planes might be air support for Nigerian troops or they might be filled with paratroopers. Lowenstein was proposing a "no-win" situation for Biafra.

Lowenstein and Craig went on to Lagos to meet with the American ambassador. American politicians like liberal Republican Senator Charles Goodell were also flying in as the scene became a circus of sixties media hype. The romantic vision of independent African countries was losing its gloss, and the show was on the nightly TV news. The message was that the Biafrans were an industrious but oppressed people, struggling to free themselves from a corrupt and backward country.

Lowenstein met with Major Gowan, the Nigerian head of state, and with all the major Nigerian officials, obtaining what Craig calls a "firm commitment" to permit planes to land on Obilago air strip. He was able to achieve this with the help of President Kenneth Kaunda of Zambia. After consultations with Kaunda, Lowenstein concluded that the Organization of African Unity was key to a settlement. Since the OAU had its headquarters in Addis Ababa, Ethiopia, and Emperor Haile Selassie was still a highly influential African leader, Low-enstein planned to enlist the emperor as a mediator.

A Swedish count who was a noted adventurer in Africa personally flew Lowenstein from Lagos to Addis Ababa, from where he traveled to Haile Selassie's summer palace for his audience with the emperor. He would later regale Craig with stories of how the emperor inter-rupted their discussions to caress his tiny pet dog. While Haile Selas-sie was preoccupied with his chihuahua, Lowenstein explained that it would be best to convene a strategic conference on food in the Biafran crisis. He reasoned that once the parties were assembled to discuss the food question, it would then be possible to negotiate a cease-fire and a political solution, and the war would end. This had been Kaun-da's advice to Lowenstein, and he was relaying it to Haile Selassie.

Lowenstein was also prepared to show that Colonel Ojukwu, the Biafran secessionist leader, was exploiting the food issue. As soon as the federal government of Nigeria agreed to the plan for an OAU-sponsored mediation on the food question, it would be up to Biafra to take the next step. If they cooperated, the war could be brought to an end. If they did not, as it could be readily assumed they wouldn't, Lowenstein could point to this as a sign of bad faith. The Biafran lead-ership could be blamed for the starvation of millions, world opinion would turn against them, and they could be forced to give up the critical oil industry.

Lowenstein was heavily assisted by the State Department. He stayed at the ambassador's residence in Lagos and used the embassy offices. Lowenstein also stayed at the home of the American ambas-sador to what was then called Dahomey (now Benin), the country from which he and Craig flew into Biafra.

Showing a flair for the dramatic, Lowenstein left a note with the American ambassador in Lagos, not to be opened unless they failed to return. It read: "In trying to get Biafran agreement to the shipment of food, we will use the argument that Biafra will suffer in the eyes of world opinion if the only opposition to the plan was the Biafran gov-ernment. If something should happen to us, Biafran interests should not be beyond suspicion."

Lowenstein sealed the message and gave it to the ambassador be-fore setting out for Biafra via Dahomey. The night flight had no seats and was filled with fish for the starving Biafrans. Both Lowenstein and Craig were aware that the Nigerian government had expressed its clear intention of shooting down all unauthorized flights into the coun-try. The old DC–3 flew through the night, down along the coast past Lagos and then into Biafra, approaching the darkened airstrip with extreme caution. The lights went on briefly and they hit the runway. Immediately, it was totally dark again. Lowenstein looked with amaze-ment at the pilot who was using a flashlight to wheel in his aircraft.

They drove all night to see Ojukwu, meeting first with the chief of staff of the Biafran troops, who had no objection to the food plan. Then they went in to talk with Ojukwu.

No sooner had they entered his office than there was a bombing raid. Lowenstein, his arm in a sling following an accident suffered in Washington, hit the floor. All of them huddled together, Lowenstein, Craig, and Ojukwu, waiting for the all-clear. When it came, Lowenstein asked Craig to leave the room.

Afterward, Lowenstein told Craig that Ojukwu had temporized, claiming that he didn't make all the decisions. He said he couldn't give Lowenstein a commitment on the food negotiations without consulting first with the ruling council. According to Craig's secondhand account, a stern Lowenstein informed Ojukwu that he had already spoken to the chief justice and to all the top military leaders of the council and they had agreed to his plan. When Ojukwu continued to insist on convening the council, Lowenstein responded, according to what he told Craig: "It is vital to give a positive response because it would be too bad if I had to report to the world that the only obstacle was the Biafran government. Senator Kennedy would be greatly distressed."

Lowenstein and Craig traveled to a remote feeding station in Biafra and then left without an answer. Lowenstein intended to report that the Biafran government had decided that the only hope for them and for Biafra was to starve the Biafran people. Craig asserts that he and Lowenstein felt they were "morally bound" to report their findings. "As such," he stresses, "we were a threat to the Biafrans."

Fearing for their lives, Lowenstein and Craig were caught in a firefight during the frightening drive out to the airstrip. A car pulled over and troops with guns got out. Craig was terrified. "Stay in the car," Lowenstein told him as he got out to talk to the soldiers. He returned quickly and they continued on their way, rushing onto the plane while the airstrip was being bombed. "Al was in pain," Craig relates. "His shoulder was killing him. We were both exhausted and everyone on the plane was frightened. Al became Eleanor Roosevelt. He went around talking to the crew. He was so saintly, I was pissed off."

They got back to Dahomey and stayed again with the U.S. ambassador, waiting for a reply from Ojukwu that never came. They returned to the United States, where Craig wrote Lowenstein's speech on the Biafran question and Lowenstein filed his full report "to Ted Kennedy," says Craig.

26.

After a hiatus, Lowenstein's African activities were resumed in the midseventies. By then the exploitation of uranium in South West Africa had made South Africa's role there a major international issue again, as the large block of nonwhite Third World countries pressed for its independence. In April 1975 Lowenstein was invited by the Johnson Foundation (funded by the Johnson & Johnson pharmaceutical company) to a key symposium on South Africa that explored ways to prevent the worst from happening from the point of view of the American companies that had invested heavily there. South Africa was described as "the Saudi Arabia of minerals," and South West Africa had once again become vitally important to the West because of Britain's dependence upon it for uranium. Rio Tito Zinc, a multinational mining company based in Britain, was exploiting that uranium at the Rossing mine, the world's largest single source of uranium.

Lowenstein's analysis at the Wingspread symposium was classic "good-wing" CIA. The Soviet Union and the People's Republic of China were supporting liberation movements throughout the world, including Africa. They were giving "particular encouragement" to the freedom fighters of Namibia, Angola, Mozambique, and Rhodesia. "Once independent," Lowenstein warned, "those countries can become anti-United States on the assumption that we have not aided them but have sympathized with their colonial oppressors." Lowenstein asked, "Will we identify with the oppressed people, including those of South Africa?" Because Africans were finding that the only way to produce change was through violence, this was playing "into the hand of the Soviet Union and China," who were providing money and training which were, in fact, producing results.

Lowenstein asked the rhetorical question "Can we influence Africans to accommodate their demands to less violent ways?" His answer was that of those who, since Magna Carta have understood the best way to avoid violent revolution: "Only if we pressure for the necessary reforms at an acceptable pace." With respect to the specific question of South Africa, with which the conference was concerned, Lowenstein postulated: "This means finding ways to get South Africa out of Namibia and Rhodesia, to permit Black regimes to develop in both states. Instead of 'buffer states' there might emerge on the border of South Africa the appearance of priviliged sanctuaries so that the pressure for change within South Africa would be stepped up. As the international dimensions proceed, they are the priority; the domestic ones should follow.

"Eventually, changes within South Africa will have to occur. If they do not come non-violently and in a rapid, evolutionary way, they will be forced with sabotage, violence, and warfare."

Lowenstein believed the change in American policy would not come until after a new election in 1976, but beyond 1977 he saw no rigid or fixed policies. The election of an enlightened Democrat meant to Lowenstein that "we have a chance to suggest priorities that will be realistic and humane." Loosely translated, this meant finding ways to retain the important American interests while making those concessions that were essential to stave off Communism. Implicit in the implementation of this approach is the understanding that governments established in Third World countries should be controllable, not reactionary.

In 1976 Jimmy Carter won the presidency. As a white southerner with a conservative image, Carter had needed help in holding the traditionally Democratic black vote. He got it from a fellow Georgian, the black Congressman from Atlanta, Andrew Young. A former aide to Martin Luther King, Jr., and a good friend of Allard Lowenstein's from the civil rights movement, Young was named Carter's permanent representative to the United Nations, a position to which some of Lowenstein's friends had hoped he would be named. Lowenstein himself had hoped to be appointed ambassador to South Africa. Instead, in the winter of 1977 he was offered and accepted the job of U.S. representative to the Human Rights Commission in Geneva, and then, ambassador to the United Nations for special political affairs, both positions obtained on the recommendation of Andrew Young. The ambassadorship, a high-ranking position which paid $52,000, made him one of the five ambassadors in the U.S. delegation and put him under Young, whose job had cabinet status.

Lowenstein's deputy in Geneva was Brady Tyson who had worked with missionaries in Brazil when Frank Carlucci was serving there, having arrived in Rio de Janeiro just a few months after a CIA-backed military coup had ousted the elected Goulart regime. At the time, the CIA was funneling money to the ruling junta, but it was never the intention of the United States to have indefinite military rule. As in so many similar cases, however, the United States, in seeking an alternative to a pro-Communist administration, had allowed things to get out of hand.

Brady Tyson was, as Carlucci explains, expelled from Brazil during this period for "political activities." Carlucci confirms that "Tyson was helping left-wing groups" and adds that Lowenstein was "involved in Brazil" as well. He does not elaborate on the nature of this involvement.

One of Lowenstein's aides in Geneva was Tom Flynn. Having worked with Lowenstein as a student intern in California during the summer of 1975 while Lowenstein was working for Governor Jerry Brown, Flynn was dispatched to London with the names of 120 South African exiles who were living there. Flynn's assignment was to inform them that Lowenstein was now in the State Department and to "get as much information from them as possible."

When the session in Geneva was over, Lowenstein assumed his duties at the United States Mission to the United Nations, involving himself deeply in the affairs of southern Africa: in Rhodesia, the violent civil war and struggle for majority rule; the struggle for Namibian independence; and the effort to effect policy changes, both internal and external, in South Africa. Lowenstein was routinely briefed by CIA people in New York. He received the documents he wanted and had access to top intelligence and policymaking people. Tom Flynn notes that Lowenstein dealt with the CIA and State Department as though they were interchangeable and observes that, in fact, very often they were the same people. He adds that there are "lots of CIA people at the United Nations."

The Nationalist government was firmly in power in South Africa. The Liberal party had disbanded rather than obey the Prohibition of Political Interference Act of 1968, which prohibited multiracial political parties. Lowenstein's friend Helen Suzman, elected to parliament from a Johannesburg suburb, was a member of the Progressive Federal party, a tiny group with little popular support. The old United party of Jan Smuts had also disappeared and the black nationalist groups were banned. The periodic acts of sabotage by supporters of the African National Congress were disturbing, but no danger to the state. The unsettling events in Rhodesia, Mozambique, and Angola, however, were causing a new perspective to take hold among the Afrikaners. The *verlicht* or "open-minded" Afrikaners (as opposed to the *verkrampt* or "constipated" Afrikaners) began to move glacially toward an understanding that some change, however minimal, was necessary in South Africa if the country were not to be totally isolated in the world.

Ambassador Donald Bell Sole, the South African ambassador, took a liking to Lowenstein. He believed that the points Lowenstein was making about South Africa could be helpful to the government in Pretoria. *Brutal Mandate*, which had caused Lowenstein to be "banned" from entering South Africa, became something of a textbook in the Nationalist government.

While he was at the United Nations, Lowenstein was approached by a young South African in the Foreign Office attached to the embassy in Washington. Sean Cleary, an elegant and aristocratic young man, spoke of his desire to continue living in South Africa but also acknowledged that the situation there was "untenable," and that change was necessary. Cleary asked Lowenstein to come to South Africa to initiate a dialogue in which all the different groups in the South African equation would participate: the Afrikaners, the English-speaking population, the black nationalists, the front-line states. The Nationalist government was convinced that Lowenstein was the only person who could act as a liaison at a time when communication had become virtually impossible. He had impeccable credentials among the black African leaders; he knew Kaunda and Nyerere. Tambo and

Mandela. And because in recent days he had expressed his sympathy for the white minority, he was trusted by the whites.

As a spokesman for human rights in the Carter administration, Lowenstein, while an ambassador to the U.N. in 1977, made four major trips to different parts of the world: Eastern Europe, Latin America, including Nicaragua, where he aided opponents of the dictatorial Somoza regime, the black African countries, and Western Europe and South Africa. The arrangements for all of them were handled by the ICA or International Communications Agency, or USIA (at one time, also known as the USIS, United States Information Service). Invariably, Lowenstein passed through Spain and Portugal. The expeditions, each of about three weeks in duration, involved appearances, a press conference, a speech, and side meetings with dissidents. The invitation from Cleary enabled Lowenstein to add South Africa to his already planned Western European human rights voyage.

In South Africa, Lowenstein made a live speech on radio. (He had told the South Africans that this had been allowed in Eastern Europe and informed them that Americans would be distressed if it were not permitted in South Africa.) In the speech, Lowenstein called on South Africa to release Nelson Mandela and other black nationalists from prison. His message was that the South Africans had to change, or change would come without their being part of it. Lowenstein was tough with the whites but he impressed them with his concern for them. "Lowenstein was concerned with everyone's welfare, not just the blacks," the radio announcer interpreted.

After the broadcast, Lowenstein met with Afrikaner officials at the Foreign Office headquarters. They held copies of *Brutal Mandate* and asked him, "How can we show the world we are sincere?" They wanted to know what they had to do to end their isolation from the West. Lowenstein replied that they had to negotiate directly with black nationalist leaders like Mandela, who were in prison and who should be released. Lowenstein also told them to accept the Western plan for South West African elections. The Afrikaners responded favorably, expressing their willingness to hold secret negotiations with the United States on these suggestions. Lowenstein's participation and his personal assistance as a government official were considered of vital importance in this process by the Nationalist government.

By this time, Ken McComiskey, a young friend of Lowenstein's who had recently graduated from Cornell, had started working with Lowenstein on his southern African endeavors. Lowenstein, who was planning another trip to South Africa and distrusted the State Department bureaucracy, asked McComiskey to go to South Africa on his behalf to set up appointments for him. He also asked McComiskey to find out if there had been "tangible change or sentiments for change to a majority government" in Rhodesia, and to inform him if Bishop

Abel Muzorewa, head of the "transitional" government in Rhodesia, was a puppet. Lowenstein planned to meet McComiskey in South Africa, be briefed, and continue on with the trip.

McComiskey set up meetings with a wide range of people, including Helen Suzman, her husband, Dr. Mosie Suzman, Ismail Ayob, a lawyer and apartheid opponent, and the white dissident, Helen Joseph, whom Lowenstein had never met. But when South African troops made a raid into Angola, killing blacks in the SWAPO camps in Kassinga, the trip was canceled. McComiskey relates that he was instructed by Lowenstein to inform the Afrikaner contacts that the cancellation was intended as a punishment for the raid into Angola. But Lowenstein added that, in his opinion, the real reason was that the State Department was "afraid" of his going. "He was too independent," McComiskey asserts. "Southern Africa was Andy Young's baby."

Lowenstein believed that Young had forced the cancellation of the trip and that Secretary of State Cyrus Vance had gone along with Young. To his surprise, Lowenstein was supported by National Security Adviser Zbigniew Brzezinski; he told McComiskey that he had not expected Brzezinski to be so receptive to his plans. But it didn't shock McComiskey. "Al was tough on Russia and the Commies," he states, adding: "Al didn't want to think Young was stopping him, but concluded he had. Al was disillusioned with Young."

William Buckley, Jr., puts Lowenstein's feelings about Young more strongly. "He didn't trust Andy Young," he states. "He didn't believe what Young was telling him." The situation with Young was a major factor in Lowenstein's decision to resign from the United Nations in the spring of 1978; he had wanted to go to South Africa as a member of the government, something the South Africans had wanted as well.

"I had to indicate to Cleary that Lowenstein was getting resistance in the State Department for taking any initiative, while Lowenstein thought it was just from Andy Young," McComiskey recounts. "I couldn't indicate this to Cleary, that it wasn't a unified push. I had to tell him Al was resigning because of the raid into Angola." McComiskey states that Lowenstein "didn't want a dictatorial government, black or white. He saw in nuances. Young said anyone who didn't back SWAPO was a sell-out. Al wasn't for making Sam Nujoma king. He wanted a democratic process."

Lowenstein had now decided to run for Congress in Manhattan, and the decision worried the South Africans, who were afraid he would lose his ability to be of help to them. At the Rand Club, a symbol of the established order in South Africa, McComiskey met with Sean Cleary to reassure him. Reporting back to Lowenstein on the meeting, McComiskey wrote that the two had spent four hours talking. Describing Cleary as "confused" about why the cancellation of Lowenstein's trip had been necessary, McComiskey said he did not think he had adequately dispelled that confusion in taking the agreed-upon stance that Lowenstein's "hands were tied." As for the concern over Lowenstein's resignation from the U.N., which had led to fears that future momentum for change would be lost if Lowenstein no longer held a "credible" and "potent" government position enabling him to sell his agenda effectively, McComiskey felt he had been more successful with his reassurances: "I pretty adequately explained to him that your relationship with Andy would preclude any ill feeling that would jeopardize future working relations with the government people," he wrote. He added that he had also emphasized that "the administration needs you, and that in Congress, you would be a very potent force in government." Concluding his report, McComiskey wrote, "In all, I think everything went very well."

A show of sincerity with regard to elections in South West Africa was attempted but with disastrous consequences. The United States, Britain, France, West Germany, and Canada, the Contact Group of Western countries pressuring South Africa on the Namibian question, were investing heavily in Namibia. Urangesellschaft, a West German company, was prospecting for uranium there and had helped to develop the Rossing mine, which Western Knapp Engineering of the United States designed, engineered, and constructed. The Société Nationale Elf Aquitaine (SNEA) and Pechiney-Ugine Kuhlmann of France, and Falconbridge Nickel Mines of Canada, controlled by the Superior Oil Company of Texas, were developing new deposits of uranium in Namibia. Britain was heavily involved with Rio Tinto Zinc. Meanwhile, Anglo-American also had begun to prospect for uranium, increasing the South African interest in Namibia, where Consolidated Diamond Mines, a subsidiary of DeBeers, remained a mining giant and economic power.

President Carter took the initiative in 1977 to get the Contact Group of nations, all members of the Security Council, to obtain agreements from South Africa to hold free and fair elections under United Nations supervision in Namibia, leading to independence.

The unilateral elections held by South Africa in Namibia on December 4–8, 1978, took place in a climate of widespread intimidation emanating from the South African Defense Force, white employers, and the South African-supported Democratic Turnhalle Alliance (DTA). Voters were forced to register and take out DTA membership cards; others were beaten or threatened with the loss of their jobs. South African troops manned many of the polling places, and the government transport fleet was assigned to the DTA to get out the vote. SWAPO members were arrested or detained, and SWAPO condemned the elections, refusing to participate.

Yet when Lowenstein visited South West Africa/Namibia in 1979, he told Ivor Willkins of the *Sunday Times* that the atmosphere he described 20 years ago in his book *Brutal Mandate* had changed vastly. "The contrast between what I found in SWA/Namibia 20 years ago and the situation now is the most remarkable example of people being able to change more than they think they can," he insisted. "People, who 20 years ago were suspicious, distrustful and hostile, were now sitting down and taking decisions to erase social injustice." The statement could easily be attributed to excessive optimism on Lowenstein's part, but later revelations indicate that, in 1979, he was traveling in southern Africa in a unique capacity that contributed to that optimism. "No 'Brutal Mandate,'" the headline in the *South African Digest* proclaims in reporting Lowenstein's statement. And Lowenstein's old friend from Chapel Hill, Jimmy Wallace, maintains that Lowenstein moved away from his "self-righteous" position in *Brutal Mandate* to a "more realistic" understanding of the problems of South Africa. The suggestion is that his pursuit of nuances had led him away from absolutes. But viewed from another angle his statements on SWAPO look increasingly like those of Sir Mark Turner, chairman of Rio Tinto Zinc, who said in 1977, "Why must we talk, if I may say so, in a slightly trendy way about SWAPO eternally, when as far as I can see we've yet to see what the people of Namibia want?" Clearly, Lowenstein felt the Democratic Turnhalle Alliance was "something to work with," as Emory Bundy puts it.

According to Ken McComiskey, Lowenstein "wasn't a big fan of Nujoma. Al was more interested in process than in groups. He wanted to bring about a democratic process in the area so people could have the opportunity to voice their own preference. He was not in favor of recognizing SWAPO as the sole representative of the Namibian people."

Emory Bundy wrote to Lowenstein in 1978 suggesting to him that he reissue *Brutal Mandate* because it was relevant again. It was. But it was also now an embarrassment.

After Lowenstein lost his last bid for Congress in 1978, he turned his attention increasingly to the problems of Zimbabwe/Rhodesia, working out of his law office at the firm of Delson & Gordon. Headed by prominent international lawyers Max and Robert Delson, who had served as general counsel to the American Committee on Africa, the firm had offices in New York, Washington, DC, and Djakarta. Later he would switch to Layton & Sherman, headed by another prominent international lawyer from his own class at Yale Law School, Robert Layton. Layton & Sherman maintained offices in New York, Tokyo, and London.

The Rhodesia/Zimbabwe situation was not unlike the South West Africa/Namibia situation. A white supremacist regime under Ian Smith was pushed to relinquish power by external pressure. Inside the country, a group of conservative black clergymen led by Bishop Abel Muzorewa, was being included in an "internal settlement" that established a transitional government in which the whites still played a dominant role with biracial elections scheduled for April of 1979. Opposing the settlement were Robert Mugabe and Joshua Nkomo, the leaders of the Patriotic Front who were relying on armed struggle to take power from the whites. Supporting the Front were the black African "front line" states that had a common border with Rhodesia.

There were tensions between Andrew Young and Lowenstein on the whole question of Zimbabwe/Rhodesia. "Young said anyone who found merit in the transition government in Rhodesia was a sell-out," Ken McComiskey asserts. "He said anyone who tried to work with Ian Smith was a sell-out. Al believed there would be lots of whites in Zimbabwe and that they would have to be dealt with. He was an anti-Communist. He knew Stalinism for what it was: oppressive, treacherous, and murderous. He wasn't interested in seeing that imposed anywhere, including South West Africa. The others just wanted the whites out and whatever came afterwards was acceptable."

Lowenstein viewed Mugabe and Nkomo in the same light as he viewed Sam Nujoma of SWAPO. As Wendell Willkie II, to whom Lowenstein spoke after his last Africa trip, puts it, Lowenstein "got distressed over Andy Young's role. He felt that Young was pushing the Carter administration toward supporting the revolutionaries. His feeling was that Bishop Muzorewa was elected and that there were problems with that and that there should be more elections. He was on the conservative side, or to the right, of the Carter administration on Rhodesia. Al perceived Mugabe, who was waging a revolutionary war, as a rigid Leninist and felt Nkomo had a Russian connection. He saw the Carter administration pushing in a direction that was not helpful to democratic values. After Muzorewa, he wanted to do more."

At the heart of Lowenstein's differences with Young was Lowenstein's position on the role of the white liberals in southern Africa. He saw them as central to any solution there. Young differed, going so far as to suggest that Helen Suzman was irrelevant to southern Africa. "Al thought this was the height of stupidity," McComiskey recalls. "She had been fighting for democratic majority-rule government for years."

Lowenstein told his aide at the U.N., Tom Flynn, that he thought Muzorewa and the Rhodesian white liberals could form the center of a biracial coalition. And he told James Symington that Bishop Muzorewa deserved a chance in spite of his white support. It was his opinion that Robert Mugabe and Joshue Nkomo could not form a government because they were guerrillas. Wendell Willkie II speaks of Lowenstein's "frustration" with Andrew Young's approach to foreign policy and says that Lowenstein "believed in the possibility of peaceful

change in southern Africa. He was hostile to violent revolution."
Willkie adds that Martin Luther King, Jr., had greatly influenced
Lowenstein, but did not mention that Young had been King's aide.

Lowenstein's approach was to let the interim government hold
elections. When Muzorewa won, McComiskey recalls that Lowenstein stressed the necessity for another round of elections, though he
proclaimed that the first vote had been a "positive sign." Lowenstein
wanted a constitution drawn up as soon as the first round of elections
was completed, so that it would be in place for the next round, in
which all the parties should participate. "He didn't want to see Nkomo
and Mugabe imposed on the people without elections," McComiskey
adds.

When fifty whites were murdered at a Christian mission at Gutu,
in Rhodesia, "Andy Young automatically took the position that it had
been zealous black scouts under Ian Smith," McComiskey explains.
"He would dismiss the idea that Mugabe's people could do it." Mc-
Comiskey asserts that the killers were Mugabe's people and that this
was evidence, in Lowenstein's opinion, that Mugabe was being imposed by force. The solution, which Gwendolen Carter supported,
was to let Muzorewa's election stand and then go to the "front-line"
states and have them insist on further elections.

Young disagreed with all of this. He believed that Mugabe and
Nkomo had to be included in any interim government and that the
United States should work with them in trying to protect the interests
of the whites in the economy, which he perceived as the major issues,
not the promotion of "democratic values."

The British were closer to Lowenstein's approach than was the
Carter administration. Arthur Schlesinger, Jr., wrote that David Harlech, British ambassador to the United States during the Kennedy
administration and British emissary to the front-line African nations
during the Rhodesian negotiations, and Lowenstein "were in basic
agreement on what ought to be done about Rhodesia," and that Harlech "regularly consulted with Al on his visits to Washington over the
last year on the difficult mission of persuading the Carter administration to accept a sensible solution." Lord Harlech himself wrote in 1980
that he and Lowenstein worked closely on the Rhodesian question. "I
had met him briefly in 1968," Harlech noted, "but saw a great deal of
him last year in connection with Rhodesia. His energy was superhu-
man and the encouragement and support he gave me made a tremendous difference to the success."

Lowenstein had resigned from the U.N. partially because of An-
drew Young and other disagreements with the Carter administration.
But in January of 1979 Carter asked Lowenstein to go to southern
Africa to help "break the diplomatic stalemate."

Once again, the ICA (USIA) arranged the trip. Greg Stone, a former student of Emory Bundy's at Oberlin who became a campaign aide and archivist for Lowenstein, notes that "when Lowenstein joined Delson & Gordon, he still was traveling on behalf of the ICA." A "different shop from the State Department," the ICA, observes Stone, "concentrated on cultural exchanges and good will. They loved to have Al because he made great speeches and got people excited about human rights and they paid his expenses and gave him a *per diem*. This is how he did most of the Rhodesian stuff; the trips were sponsored by the ICA. There wasn't a complete break with Carter foreign policy. Al consulted all the time with Young, the National Security Council, Vance, Jody Powell, and Hamilton Jordan. The lines were still open, but Al felt he could no longer be an ambassador. Southern Africa was a deep emotional commitment to him since *Brutal Mandate*, and he felt he had to try."

Lowenstein met with Ian Smith, Robert Mugabe, Joshua Nkomo and several of the leaders of the "front-line" states. A plan was formulated according to which Smith would resign as prime minister, a liberalized constitution would be drawn up, and international, supervised elections would take place. The plan's benefit to Rhodesia would be that the embargo on its chrome would be lifted by the United States, but the Carter administration did nothing to implement it.

When Smith and the interim government called for elections to be held in April of 1979, Lowenstein returned to Rhodesia with his friend Bayard Rustin under the auspices of Freedom House to observe them. Lowenstein later described it: "It was extremely moving. You saw old people who traveled hundreds of miles for days. . . . The feeling reminded me of Mississippi after the Voting Rights Act. The important thing was that the people were voting less for the government than for the elections to go on." But testifying before a House foreign affairs subcommittee in May 1979, Lowenstein noted bitterly: "Ambassador Young has said since the elections . . . that the elections were stolen a year ago. Now I cite all of that simply to say that if one's position is, in fact, that the elections were stolen a year ago or that it was impossible under the constitution to have fair and free elections, then I am at a loss as to what we are talking about. If that is the fact, then we are not looking to see what occurred; we are saying that what occurred had had no chance of validity."

Lowenstein did recognize that the Patriotic Front had forced the elections, even though they had not participated. "The contributions made . . . by the Patriotic Front have been enormous," he admitted. "Without the effort of those who have been fighting to end white supremacy over the years, there would have been no elections like this. Anyone who tries to put a 'cold war' overlay on this misses the point entirely."

Privately, however, Lowenstein did just that. His position was that without an alliance of liberal whites and moderate blacks, the Communists would be the winners in southern Africa. It was, after all, the position of the white liberals in South Africa with whom he had worked for two decades.

After the elections, which Lowenstein maintained had been relatively fair, Congress pushed to get the sanctions against Rhodesia lifted. Lowenstein, in testifying to Congress, took the position that sanctions should be used in a creative way. The United States, he argued in essence, should make sanctions a carrot for Smith and a stick for the Patriotic Front. If majority rule was not implemented, they would remain in force. But if Mugabe and Nkomo continued to boycott the solution, the threat of lifting the sanctions, thus signaling U.S. approval of what Smith and Muzorewa were doing, might force them to the bargaining table. He told the congressional committee: "I would urge the administration to utilize the leverage it has in the issue of sanctions to encourage further steps in the Zimbabwe situation—internally and externally—without committing what I would do about lifting or not lifting sanctions. The worst mistake I think we have made is in fact to assert that we cannot lift sanctions unless everybody agrees that we should, thus removing the leverage that sanctions provide to utilize our good will and our moral persuasion to produce the goals that you want."

The *Washington Post* described Lowenstein's suggestion as "a promising initiative," and *The New Republic* added that "a middle course solution . . . might enable the Carter Administration to salvage its basic aims in Rhodesia and its prestige both here and in Africa." But others found the suggestion "racist."

On March 15, 1979, the Senate, by a seventy-nine to nineteen margin, voted to end the sanctions. Brooklyn Democrat Stephen Solarz and New Jersey Republican Millicent Fenwick, both allies of Lowenstein's, joined with others to hammer out a resolution giving the president discretion to keep or lift the sanctions depending on developments in Zimbabwe. The resolution was passed unanimously by the House Foreign Affairs Committee, and on June 7, President Carter announced that he was not ending sanctions immediately but would be reviewing them "in light of progress toward majority rule." With Lowenstein lobbying Congress intensely, the resolution passed overwhelmingly and became law. That September, negotiations between Britain, the Muzorewa government, and the Patriotic Front began in London. The government of Prime Minister Margaret Thatcher was represented by Foreign Secretary Lord Carrington, who applied "heavy pressure" on the Rhodesian whites and the Patriotic Front to approve a new liberalized constitution and plans for a new round of democratic elections. In October of 1979, the new constitution was accepted by all sides, and in November a British-administered interim government was approved. The agreement for a formal cease-fire was rounded out in December and both Britain and the United States lifted sanctions as Lord Soames flew to Salisbury to supervise the transition of power and the new elections.

Jack Anderson, in a column in the *Washington Post* on January 20, 1980, related: "Feisty British Prime Minister Margaret Thatcher, stepping in firmly where Carter feared to tread, was able to bring the white-supremacist forces of Ian Smith and the black Rhodesian guerrillas to the conference table and hammer out a negotiated settlement. Though the White House was not reluctant to accept credit for the success of the British-engineered settlement, secret State Department cables make clear that Carter contributed virtually nothing."

Anderson went on to observe that, in fact, the Carter administration had dismissed out of a hand a suggestion proposed by Lowenstein a year earlier for bringing "the Rhodesian imbroglio to a peaceful solution," one that was "roughly the same as the successful one used by the British months later." Anderson elaborated on the Lowenstein plan and its fate at the White House, the State Department, and the National Security Council: "What Lowenstein suggested—and the Carter administration thinkers apparently gagged at—was that the United States use the economic and military sanctions imposed on Rhodesia years before as a means to get both sides to the negotiating table. The black guerrillas would be impressed by a threat to lift the sanctions, which would give the white Rhodesians power to keep control of the country indefinitely. Conversely, the white Rhodesians would be impressed by a threat to continue the sanctions indefinitely."

Anderson went on to support his view that the plan deserved a better reception: "This was no will-o'-the-wisp theory cooked up by a pipe-smoking egghead far removed from the scene. Lowenstein had made an on-the-spot visit to southern Africa last February to sound out leaders on both sides." Moreover, not only had Lowenstein cleared "his 'big stick' sanctions policy with President Kenneth Kaunda of Zambia, but he was told by Ian Smith that Smith had 'no problem' with renegotiation of the whites-only constitution, its submission to the entire nation—blacks and whites—and elections under U.N. supervision in which the black guerrillas would participate."

All that notwithstanding, wrote Anderson, "the U.S. embassy in South Africa denigrated Lowenstein's diplomatic efforts, professing in a cable to Washington that Smith's reasonable attitude 'boggles the mind.' The embassy experts suggested that 'Smith (intentionally) and Lowenstein (unintentionally) were . . . talking past each other.'"

So the administration sat on its hands, the column concluded, and eventually, "the British moved along the lines recommended by Lowenstein and brought the whites and blacks to the conference table. . . ."

Robert Mugabe won the election that was held in February of 1980 and became the prime minister of Zimbabwe, making majority rule a reality, while Ian Smith remained in parliament as an opposition leader. Lowenstein's hopes remained with the white liberals who, he believed, could still form a coalition with anti-Communist blacks and prevent a Communist takeover. With American help, the democratic system had responded in Portugal where he had worked closely with Frank Carlucci. There was reason to believe that a similar joint effort could be arranged in southern Africa.

It was, in fact, Lowenstein's involvement with the white liberals in South Africa and his relationship with Frank Carlucci, appointed deputy director of the CIA by Jimmy Carter, that enabled him to continue his work in southern Africa in the summer of 1979, when he made an extensive trip there with his three children.

Friends of Lowenstein speculated how the trip was financed. Wendell Willkie II is "confident he went on his own." Ken McComiskey says that Lowenstein's expenses were covered but Lowenstein told him he didn't know who paid for them, and suggested that it might have been Oppenheimer money. And Theo-Ben Gurirab relates: "He called me just before he left. I had been in his law office on Park Avenue when he was finalizing his itinerary. He said he called me because he said he was going on a trip to South Africa. Over the years, he had applied for a visa but was turned down. He learned this time that if he wanted to go he would be welcome. He learned from his friends in South Africa that South African leaders had reread *Brutal Mandate* and found some of the points he made which they rejected in 1959 interesting now and wanted to probe him on them. He made reference to the fact that he wasn't paying for his own trip. I didn't think the South African government or the United States government was paying for the trip. It could have been South African or United States friends."

In reality, it was both. On June 12, 1979, Lowenstein's old friend Ernest Wentzel, a former president of the National Union of South African Students (NUSAS) with whom Lowenstein, Bundy, and Bull stayed during their 1959 trip and an official in the defunct South African Liberal party, wrote to Hank Slack, the American director of Anglo-American Industrial Corporation, Ltd., explaining the arrangements for the trip. Wentzel, a Johannesburg barrister, wrote to Slack at 44 Main Street, Johannesburg, the address of Anglo-American's headquarters:

I have finally got hold of Al Lowenstein, who has returned to America. I spoke to him twice yesterday and he has been able to arrange for a postponement of his lecture assignments at Stanford. He would be able to come to South Africa for about six weeks leaving the United States on about the 1st July. He proposes to travel via London and to spend a day with Lord Harlech to discuss matters with him. Al tells me that there was a feature article on Zimbabwe Rhodesia in yesterday's *New York Times* in which his proposals were given prominence and approval although with qualifications. I discussed as much of the detail with Al as I could and it would apparently require the following arrangements.

There followed a seven-point list of Lowenstein's requirements as well as those of his three children and his assistant and godson Mark Childress, for whom Wentzel presumed the necessary air tickets could be arranged through Slack's New York office. Their presence would also require that a "suitable house" be found in Johannesburg, one that would provide "recreational facilities" for them, as well as the proper conditions "for Al to work in and invite for discussions the various people from southern Africa who will be involved." The house would preferably be one with "domestic servants."

Lowenstein would also need a car, secretarial assistance, and compensation for the time away from his law practice and the missed Stanford lectures. In this matter, Wentzel was prepared to accept Lowenstein's own suggestion: "He proposed that $1,000 should be paid to his secretary in the U.S., $1,000 to Childress and $7,000 to him. This seems acceptable." Wentzel indicated that additional expenses would probably not be substantial and offered his wife as escort to take the children to the Kruger Park, "at my expense!"

He closed on an urgent note: "It is very necessary for me to phone Al today or tomorrow to finalize these arrangements if they are acceptable. Do you think you could confirm them immediately? I propose, when you do so, to arrange lectures by Al at Wits, Stellenbosch, UCT, the Institute of Race Relations, International Affairs, etc. to give him some additional reasons for his visit."

H. R. Slack, in addition to his important position at Anglo-American, headed a "personal service" company, R. L. Clare, Inc., with offices in Olympic Towers in Manhattan. When his name was mentioned to the librarian at the South African consulate in New York, she observed: "Mr. Lowenstein must have had something to do with the very top people at Anglo-American." At the very top of Anglo-American was, of course, Harry Oppenheimer.

Oppenheimer was clearly the source of the money that was paid to Lowenstein. Speaking from his chambers on Pritchard Street, Wentzel did not deny that it was Anglo-American that put up the $7,000 for Lowenstein as well as the money for Mark Childress, who accompanied him, and for Lowenstein's secretary who worked on planning the trip. When asked exactly who the source was, he responded "I don't know if I'm very happy to tell you that." To the specific question "Would it have been Anglo-American?" he answered: "What an extraordinary question. You know, I'm not sure I've got the right, he's deceased, to discuss that sort of matter with you. It was kept highly private and personal. Allard and I were friends for a very, very long time, more than twenty years, and that matter was something entirely private between him and me. I raised the money. But I truly don't know that I would feel happy on a telephone just to rattle off what happened in this connection." Wentzel also refused to explain Slack's role, saying, "I really don't think I should have a discussion with you about it. I think it would be quite nutty of me to do that." Nor would Slack himself repond to questions submitted to him.

It may well have been a private matter, but Lowenstein, who was in close contact with the Nationalist government as well as with Harry Oppenheimer, was working hard in the United States to influence American policy decisions affecting southern Africa in the legislative and executive branches of the government as well as at the U.N. He should, in this instance, almost certainly have been required to register under the Foreign Agents Registration Act.

Not only was Lowenstein paid for the trip, which included round-trip fares for himself, Childress, and his children on the Concorde, but he had the assistance of the deputy director of the CIA, Frank Carlucci. According to Carlucci, Lowenstein "would report to me" and "kept the State Department informed" through David Newsome, under secretary of state. "The State Department, the assistant secretary for African affairs, they thought of Al as somebody who kept getting in the way of their negotiations in the State Department," Carlucci asserts. "I, on the other hand, felt that he could make a useful contribution and urged them to listen. Dick Moose was the assistant secretary for African affairs, and they kind of wished Al would stop interfering in their affairs and I said no. He could be useful, because Al did have invitations. He had invitations from South African officials and he had invitations from, of course, the people in Rhodesia. He would come back and tell me what was going on and try to get the State Department to be more, to try and establish some channels between Zimbabwe, South Africa, and the State Department." As for who was paying, Carlucci says, "In fact, I think he was funding the trips himself through his law practice. Certainly the U.S. government wasn't."

Lowenstein thought the problems of South Africa could be "worked out," says Carlucci, who adds, "I don't think Al would have refused the ambassadorship to South Africa" had it been offered to him. A month before Lowenstein was killed, Carlucci had joined him for dinner at a Washington hotel. "It was all very disjointed. People dropped in, dropped out. A delightful evening. He was always inviting people over. There was a South African at the table next to us, the South African ambassador, and he invited him to join us." As for what Lowenstein was doing for a living, Carlucci states that Lowenstein told him he was practicing law, "But I don't know when he had time to do it. For all I know, he paid for the trip himself," he adds, returning to the summer expedition to South Africa. "I don't know it for a fact, I just never questioned it. For all I know, he could have had clients who paid him and he could have coupled that with some legal business."

Carlucci's own financial disclosure statement, issued when he was deputy director of the CIA, lists dividends from family holdings in a handful of companies, one of which was Oppenheimer's DeBeers. While this does not indicate a conflict of interest, it does raise doubts about the kind of role Carlucci had in mind for Lowenstein. Harry Oppenheimer, the man who provided the funds to pay for Lowenstein, was making fortunes using black labor and paying far less than if that labor were white. Anglo-American was the leading corporate presence in Zimbabwe; DeBeers ran the diamond mines of Namibia. Both were controlled by Harry Oppenheimer, who was also financing the political parties backed by the South African government in Zimbabwe and Namibia. Yet Oppenheimer was still regarded as an ally of liberals in South Africa, like Ernest Wentzel.

Like Carlucci, Ernest Wentzel believed that Lowenstein had an important role to play in South Africa and Rhodesia: "I thought that Allard had two very important things that he could do. The first one is that he always had an uncanny ability, in my experience with him, to bring together people of very different opinions and in South Africa, obviously, people of very different racial backgrounds, and get them into the habit of talking the one with the other. And I was pretty anxious that—he had a particular ability to talk to Afrikaners, white Afrikaners in South Africa—and I was very anxious that he should take an increasing interest in southern Africa and, you know, particularly try to show that there are sympathetic people—I was very anxious that he should have some exposure again to South Africa and, more particularly, to Afrikaners, to try to persuade them that the whole world is not entirely hostile and uncaring and unthinking about them, but that they've got to move forward and move in a very perceptible and obvious way. And that was one factor. The other factor was that I wanted at the time for him to take a very much greater interest in Zimbabwe and where the development and future of Zimbabwe at that time was very critically poised. And I wanted him to, in other words, get much more involved in southern Africa than he had been for some time."

But Wentzel denies that there was any particular involvement in South West Africa during this particular trip, although his letter clearly stated that Lowenstein would travel there. Mark Childress, a Yale undergraduate at the time he traveled to Africa as Lowenstein's assistant, and the son of one of Lowenstein's North Carolina friends, gave a lengthy account of Lowenstein's African activities in 1979 in a memo he wrote to Lowenstein's brother Larry:

> In January and February of 1979, and again in July and August, Allard Lowenstein was engaged in discussions with the highest level of the South African government. Mr. Lowenstein, at that time a private citizen, agreed to meet with South African officials on the condition that he have the right to talk to *any* individual within South Africa about any topic. The South Africans' compliance with this demand was a highly unusual concession. Given these assurances, Mr. Lowenstein engaged in intensive discussions on the following topics:
> 1) The peaceful transfer of power to majority rule in Rhodesia, now Zimbabwe;
> 2) A Namibian independence which avoided a disastrous repetition of the 1965 UDI in Rhodesia;
> 3) The dismantling of racial legislation in the Republic itself, within the framework of the eventual goal of a peaceful resolution of the current crisis.
> All parties contacted by Mr. Lowenstein obviously did not support this agenda in full. Nonetheless, compelled by his unusual qualities of persuasion, they undertook negotiations with individuals and groups with which they were in official disagreement—sometimes across battlelines. Mr. Lowenstein's unique mediation abilities were perhaps best demonstrated by a South African Cabinet Minister who remarked incredulously, "That man has done more about Rhodesia in the last two weeks than has been done by the whole bloody diplomatic corps in the last two years." That Minister did not agree with Mr. Lowenstein's assumptions about multiracialism, but he did support his contention that South Africa *must* support the process towards "one-man, one-vote" elections in Rhodesia.
> In Namibia, Mr. Lowenstein met with the Administrator General, the Democratic Turnhalle Alliance, the South West Africa People's Organization and all other major parties. It should not surprise anyone familiar with the complexities of the Namibian situation to learn that "solutions" did not present themselves. However, all groups in the territory agreed on a common concern—political assassinations. Characteristically, Mr. Lowenstein's efforts were central to the creation of an informal anti-assassination agreement. As with any such understanding, there was never a codification of the principles involved. Nevertheless,

members of all groups expressed their gratitude to Mr. Lowenstein during his July visit. It is indeed ironic that a life dedicated
to activities such as this agreement should be ended abruptly by
a gunman's assault.

The efforts within South Africa obviously met more resistance
from South African officials. Mr. Lowenstein was unable to convince the ruling regime that the moral opprobrium associated
with apartheid was deserved. He was, however, able to bring together individuals who had never spoken before. The exchanges
between men and women who occupy the antipodes of South African politics were astonishingly candid. The details can be provided at a later date, but it can be stated now that subsequent
dialogues have taken place. No matter the sub rosa character of
any such encounter, we have the example of Zimbabwe to show
us the most quiet of diplomatic ventures can produce startling
results. Such ventures remain as a testament to Mr. Lowenstein,
despite his tragic death.

A partial list of some of the key figures Lowenstein met with
between January and August of 1979 gives further indication of
the depth and extensiveness of his work: Alan Paton, South African author; Helen Suzman, member of the opposition South African Parliament; Colin Eglin, member of the opposition South
African Parliament; Ntatho Motlana, leader of Soweto Council of
Ten; Harry Oppenheimer, industrialist, chairman of Anglo-American; Samuel DeBeer, member of South African Parliament;
Helen Joseph, "banned" internal dissident; Nelson Mandela,
leading African Nationalist, imprisoned by white regime on Rob-
ben Island; Beyers Naude, South African churchman turned dissident; Gatsha Buthelezi, head of Inkhata, Zulu political organization; Lord Harlech, British Lord, key Rhodesian negotiator;
Kenneth Kaunda, President of Zambia; Julius Nyerere, President
of Tanzania; Paul McCloskey, U.S. Congressman; Millicent Fenwick, U.S. Congresswoman; Doug Walgren, U.S. Congressman;
Cyrus Vance, former Secretary of State; Andrew Young, former
U.N. Ambassador; Ronald Dellums, U.S. Congressman; James
Callaghan, former Prime Minister of Great Britain; Judge Steyn,
former Administrator General, South West Africa/Namibia; Ger-
rit Viljoen, Secretary of Education in South African Cabinet; Pik
Botha, South African Foreign Minister; P. W. Botha, South African Prime Minister; Piet Koornhof, South African Minister for
Cooperation and Development.

Richard Moose, Carter's assistant secretary of state for African affairs, told former CIA analyst Sam Adams that Lowenstein was talking
to "a lot of opposition groups" in southern Africa and that there was

concern about him in the State Department. "State was scared as hell about what Lowenstein was doing in South Africa," Moose told Adams, and he himself had been "worried about the Lowenstein problem," thinking that Lowenstein was "a loose end knocking about Africa." But Moose learned more about Lowenstein's work in Africa and then said he was "surprised that Lowenstein wasn't as doctrinaire a liberal as I thought." In actuality, the strategy Lowenstein pursued in South Africa, Zimbabwe, and Namibia was the same as in Spain: to keep the opposition believing America supported the anti-Communist "left." The power-sharing for the Indians and coloreds that followed, introduced by Prime Minister P. W. Botha, may have been generated by Lowenstein's efforts. And perhaps Mrs. Suzman's visit to Nelson Mandela to inspect prison conditions was the first step toward some kind of negotiations. Lowenstein always believed that some step in the right direction was better than none.

Lowenstein was permitted to appear on South African television and he took the opportunity to broadcast a prophetic warning that South Africa must change. He met with the prime minister, the foreign minister, and Nelson Mandela, who, in a sense, owed his life to Lowenstein, who had helped to organize the pressure groups that stopped the South Africans from hanging him. Lowenstein told Wendell Willkie II that he thought there was "a real possibility for constructive, peaceful movement away from the rigid policy of apartheid." He said he thought there were "people in ruling circles who want to do this but are operating under their own political constraints."

After his return, Lowenstein had lunch with Wendell Willkie II and Joseph Lelyveld, then *The New York Times* correspondent in South Africa. Lowenstein told them that Prime Minister Botha had asked him to see Mandela for him. Lelyveld dismissed this, saying that Botha could see Mandela any time he wanted to, and later commented to Willkie that Lowenstein "is quixotic and is off on a wild goose-chase." Lelyveld said Lowenstein was naive, that there would be bloodshed and violence in South Africa. He thought, Willkie concludes, that Lowenstein was a "noble spirit wasting his energies on a lost cause."

The *New York Times* correspondent in Salisbury, when asked about Lowenstein's efforts in South Africa by the foreign desk of the paper, responded with a memo sent by cable on March 15, 1980, the day after Lowenstein's death:

Al Lowenstein visited South Africa and Rhodesia at least twice in the past year offering himself in an honest broker role. He came with knowledge of Secretary of State Vance and other senior State Department officials but no commission other than encouragement to do whatever he could and to report back if he found openings into which diplomats could move. He was in Rhodesia for "internal" elections in April 1979, and again about three months later. On each occasion he preceded his visit with stops in black capitals . . . involved in the Rhodesia problem and met there—and in Salisbury—with the very top people—Ian Smith, Kenneth Kaunda of Zambia, Julius Nyerere of Tanzania, Bishop Abel Muzorewa, etc. His idea was to develop a peace formula for settling the war between the Patriotic Front and the Salisbury government and step back to allow Britain and the United States . . . to move in and bring things to fruition.

In South Africa, where he spent several weeks trying to bring together parties to the racial dispute—ruling white Afrikaners, white liberals, tribal black leaders, and black nationalists . . .—the effort was hopeless from the beginning (as, to speak bluntly, it was in Rhodesia too, coming as it did from a private American citizen with a strong background in politics . . . but little influence).

Privately, many who dealt with Lowenstein on his trips felt that he was motivated by a desire to promote a new political career for himself at home (New York Senate bid?). Al did not deny this. [To support this, the correspondent quoted] a Rhodesian foreign office official, a white, who was the liaison here when Al came through on his swings: "I think Al saw himself as sort of a king-maker for the future Zimbabwe . . ., a sort of catalyst around which the future Zimbabwe . . . would form, but unfortunately for Al, he was overtaken by events. . . . Al was out on his own, looking for a breakthrough and hoping that if all went well he'd get the kudos. The State Department knew about it and encouraged him, but only on the understanding that if anything went wrong, they could wash their hands of it. He had a sincere concern for the future of the area and was trying to be constructive, but the problems were greater than could have been resolved by anyone."

It depends on whom you speak to if you want to know what Lowenstein accomplished. He himself told the Pretoria Press Club that America's attitude to South Africa should be seen as one of affection, concern, and "brotherly identification." Although America would not prescribe to South Africa how to solve its problems, he said, only decisions supported by all groups in the country would be acceptable. "It is our duty to end white rule and nothing will change that," Lowenstein said, noting that the flexibility and change in Namibia was encouraging and that there was no reason why the same principles could not be applied in South Africa.

Lowenstein remained optimistic and practical. On August 2

he spoke to the South African Institute of International Affairs on "the role of the Administration, of Congress, and of public opinion in the making of American policy." He continued to believe in reason.

For Lowenstein, the trip had undoubtedly held special pleasures because of the presence of his children. They had flown on the Concorde for England on July 3 and then to Johannesburg. He introduced Frankie, Tommy, and Katherine to Helen Joseph and explained her situation to them. Each night, he asked them what they had learned, and talked with them about what he was trying to do.

Mark Childress traveled with Lowenstein on his speaking tour. Then they spent four days at Harry Oppenheimer's game farm just for recreation. There, Frankie, Lowenstein's oldest son, advised his father that, now that he had a good job with a law firm, he should stay at it and get out of politics. "Dad, you've done great but you should stop now," he told him. "I don't like what you're doing in South Africa because it's dangerous."

When they discussed South Africa again, Frankie disagreed with his father. He told him that he thought terrorism was justified if everything else failed. Lowenstein finally agreed that if nothing was done, eventually there would be violence.

From South Africa, they flew to Nairobi and then on to Greece, Geneva, and back to London for several days. They flew to Scotland, where Lowenstein rented a car and they drove to visit Churchill's grave. Then they flew back on the Concorde, he returned his children to their mother on the outskirts of Boston and went home to New York. His African career was over.

V

Civil Rights—
Good-Winging It
In Mississippi

27.

Crossing over from African work to civil rights work and vice versa was not uncommon. Harris Wofford moved easily from one to the other, serving as a chief advisor to President Kennedy on civil rights and then on African affairs, before going to the Peace Corps. And George Houser of the American Committee on Africa had been a founder and director of the Congress of Racial Equality (CORE). Lowenstein's credentials as an opponent of apartheid in South Africa made him a natural for civil rights work, and he himself saw the issues as fundamentally related. Just as change was necessary in South Africa to deprive the Communists of a major issue, so segregation would have to be eliminated in the South and blacks given the right to vote. Moreover, Lowenstein had excellent connections with leading members of the black community in America who shared his ideology. He had met them in such organizations as the American Society of African Culture and the American Committee on Africa. He also had established contacts among union leaders involved in international affairs and civil rights.

Lowenstein himself offered a personal rather than an ideological explanation for his involvement in civil rights. He told author Milton Viorst that because he was small and bookish as a child, and something of an outcast, he "identified with ugly girls at dancing school, with blacks in the back of the bus, with anybody that was in some way hurt or excluded. My political involvement, I think, came from some emotional identification with people like that rather than from some ideology."

Curtis Gans first brought Lowenstein into the civil rights movement by directing his attention to the sit-ins in Greensboro, North

224 • THE PIED PIPER: ALLARD LOWENSTEIN

Carolina, early in 1960. In those early days of the movement, the debate among activists was whether to concentrate on direct action, such as the sit-ins and the freedom rides, or on voter registration. Established black leaders objected to radical tactics (even Martin Luther King, Jr., disassociated himself from the Freedom Rides), and the Kennedy administration, hesitant to upset white southern politicians who had backed Kennedy against Nixon, did what it could to discourage such confrontational tactics. Ella Baker, founder of the Student Nonviolent Coordinating Committee (SNCC), suggested a compromise. Coming down on the side of voter registration, she told direct action proponents that if they opted for voter registration, direct action would be bound to follow.

When SNCC activist Robert Moses started working on voter registration in Mississippi in 1961, his work was supported by the Southern Conference Education Fund, an organization created by leftists Carl and Anne Braden of Louisville, Kentucky, whose activities, as Andrew Kopkind wrote in *The New Republic*, "probably fill volumes in the annals of the House Un-American Activities Committee." SCEF also supported the Southern Student Organizing Committee, a group of white and black students involved in the southern protest movement. According to Kopkind, both the SSOC and SNCC knew that the SCEF money was "tainted" but took it because they were extremely low on funds. SNCC workers subsisted on $10 a week—when they were paid.

In June of 1961, Attorney General Robert Kennedy advised SNCC organizers that funds from private foundations would be available to them if they switched their tactics to voter registration. To sweeten the pot, promises of draft deferments were allegedly offered as well. To follow up, President Kennedy had his friend Harry Belafonte meet with SNCC leaders to discuss the new direction of the civil rights movement. Belafonte apparently gave them to understand that there would be financial support and that the emphasis on voter registration did not necessarily exclude direct action projects.

To assume the leadership of SNCC's voter registration effort in Mississippi, Moses, who had known and admired Ella Baker since he was a small boy, left a New York teaching job. Baker had broken with the NAACP in 1946 because she found it too bureaucratic. Grassroots-oriented, she had helped Martin Luther King, Jr., found the Southern Christian Leadership Conference (SCLC) in 1957 and then, in 1960 at a conference at Shaw University, the black Episcopal school from which she had been graduated, she founded SNCC. Although the money for the conference had been provided by Dr. King's SCLC, Baker wanted SNCC to be completely independent. "SNCC was so innovative and creative," civil rights historian and filmmaker Joanne Grant Rabinowitz asserts, "because Ella was there to make people

listen to the young people and let them make their own decisions."
Southern and unstructured, SNCC became the cutting edge of the
civil rights movement.

In the fall of 1961, a group of SNCC workers was invited by the
Assistant Attorney General for Civil Rights Burke Marshall, and Harris Wofford, to meet with officials from several "liberal" foundations,
including the Field Foundation. One of the workers, Timothy Jenkins,
remembers that what followed in that and subsequent meetings was a
"hard, cold, matter-of-fact political exchange" about how the foundation money could be funneled to the civil rights organizations so as to
benefit President Kennedy and the movement in the South. President
Kennedy's attitude towards civil rights at the time was described by
Arthur Schlesinger, Jr.: "Like most other white politicians, he underestimated the moral passion behind the movement. The protests of
the Freedom Riders on the eve of his departure for the 1961 meeting
with Khruschev irritated him."

Another of the SNCC workers, Lonnie King, observes: "We met
with Bobby Kennedy and a number of other people, but primarily
Bobby Kennedy. The thrust of that meeting was to try and get more
students to move into Mississippi to deal with voting rights, and
Bobby pledged marshals and what-have-you to help us out." Then, in
1962, a year after SCEF, with its "tainted" money, began funding
SNCC's voter registration campaign in Mississippi, the Voter Education Project was launched with grants from the liberal private foundations, as SNCC joined with other more moderate civil rights organizations in Mississippi, in a joint voter registration drive.

Lonnie King, who left SNCC because he thought what the Kennedys were trying to do was "wrong," asserts: "I saw John Kennedy as
being a little bit concerned about how his international image was
being tarnished by all these ragtag black kids wadin'-in and sittin'-in
and kneeling in churches and what-have-you, and really talking about
the conscience of America and how we had a double standard in terms
of democracy. And I felt that what they were trying to do was to kill
the movement, but kill it by rechanneling its energies. . . . I may be
wrong, but I always will feel that the administration had some people
in our group who were keeping them informed on what we were
doing."

28.

As an assistant professor in the School of General Studies at North
Carolina State, a post which he took after leaving Stanford in 1962,
Lowenstein apparently had plenty of time for other things. He had

gotten the job through his college friend, Jimmy Wallace, who was then working as a lecturer in the history of science at Duke but had ties to North Carolina State in Raleigh. Wallace had introduced Lowenstein to George Gullette, chairman of the NC State social studies department. Gullette, who had a vacancy in his department, knew Lowenstein's reputation and hired him "on the spot," as Wallace puts it. In addition to a course on contemporary issues, Lowenstein was also assigned to teach the sociology of science, about which he knew nothing. His appointment, effective July 1, 1962, paid $7,000 a year.

Lowenstein shared an apartment in Raleigh with Joel Fleishman, a former student leader at Chapel Hill, who had gone on to Yale Law School and a job with North Carolina Governor Terry Sanford. Lowenstein's work load was light. Contemporary Issues involved no preparation since Lowenstein was part of the movements he lectured about. To prepare for his lectures on the sociology of science, Lowenstein would drive to the Duke campus to be coached by Jimmy Wallace.

Lowenstein quickly became a popular if controversial figure at NC State. In his second year as a faculty member, he was one of three professors chosen by students for the "Blue Key Award," symbolizing outstanding service to the school. He apparently did not regard his situation as permanent, though. As early as December, 1962, he wrote in his diary "'No' to State for 1963–1964 Now a Virtual Certainty Despite Vague Alternative."

Lowenstein told Gullette that he might leave to run for Congress in Manhattan's 19th Congressional District, at his friend Norman Thomas's urging. Thomas was also working closely with Lowenstein on the anti-Communist Spanish opposition group that would take Lowenstein to Spain that summer. But in March of 1963, Gullette offered Lowenstein a pay raise and a semester's leave of absence as inducements to stay at NC State, and Lowenstein, after a trip to New York to discuss his future, decided to return to NC State. Backers were now urging him to run for Congress in 1966. The leave of absence became effective July 1, 1963, and was to end February 1, 1964.

Though the administration at NC State was apparently unaware that Lowenstein intended to devote part of his time off to civil rights work, by the spring of 1963 he was already deeply involved in the cause in North Carolina, where the atmosphere was becoming tense. Governor Terry Sanford, widely regarded in liberal circles as the heir to the Frank Graham tradition, had established a program to attract distinguished speakers to the state. He was opening up the intellectual life of North Carolina to what he hoped would be the free exchange of ideas. Among those invited to lecture was Angie Brooks, the Liberian assistant secretary of state, who, as her country's delegate to the United Nations, had worked closely with Lowenstein when he had appeared at the U.N. following his trip to South West Africa. Scheduled to speak at her alma mater, Shaw University, one of the black institutions Lowenstein was organizing, Brooks, accompanied by Lowenstein, went first to the Sir Walter Hotel Coffee Shop and the S & W Cafeteria in Raleigh where she was refused service. When Lowenstein insisted that she was the Liberian ambassador and, in effect, the governor's guest in North Carolina, Brooks was finally served at the S & W. Lowenstein noted in his diary, "Caldwell perturbed" [John Tyler Caldwell was the chancellor of NC State] and "S & W to desegregate gradually but not Sir Walter." Early in May, Lowenstein figured prominently in a number of antisegregation demonstrations climaxing with a march of about a thousand people to the governor's mansion.

Sanford says he was aware that there was speculation among "statehouse politicians" at the time "that Lowenstein was there to let Terry Sanford know what was happening," and Sanford's successor, Dan Moore, called Lowenstein an "agitator." Impatient with the demonstrations, the legislature passed a speakers' ban despite opposition from both Lowenstein and Frank Graham. Graham himself telephoned legislators in an unsuccessful effort to have the bill repealed.

Graham's biographer, Warren Ashby describes the sequence of events:

> On the final day of its biennial session in 1963, the North Carolina legislature passed a law forbidding state institutions of higher education to allow any person to speak who was a "known member of the Communist Party," advocated "the overthrow of the Constitution" or had ever pleaded the Fifth Amendment to the United States Constitution. . . . Earlier that spring, some students and faculty members at North Carolina State in Raleigh, including Allard Lowenstein, who at that time was an assistant professor of political science, had joined in a march for racial justice. Five days prior to the introduction of the bill, Lowenstein and others had joined in a demonstration at the Sir Walter Hotel, the residence of many legislators.

In their fury against the Red menace, the segregationists were lumping the liberals with the Communists, and increasingly, in North Carolina, their target was Lowenstein.

But while Lowenstein was making enemies of the North Carolina conservatives and segregationists (a constant critic was senator-to-be Jesse Helms), he was working closely with powerful forces in the labor movement and liberal allies in the Democratic party to give momentum to the civil rights movement. The United Auto Workers, led by his friend and ally on the Spanish issue, Walter Reuther, and the

Americans for Democratic Action, figured prominently in the coalition that was developing to force change in the South. Among Reuther's allies were black union leader A. Phillip Randolph and civil rights activist Bayard Rustin, both associated with Lowenstein at the American Committee on Africa.

Reuther, who had been instrumental in forcing the Communists out of the UAW, was denounced by critics for turning on his old leftist friends, but praised and embraced by those who shared his negative assessment of the Soviet Union and his conviction that the Communist Party U.S.A. was interested only in the well-being of the Soviet Union. Blacks like Randolph and Rustin, who considered themselves socialists in the Norman Thomas tradition, also shared Reuther's hostility to the Soviet Union and Communism, reflecting a point of view that was widespread among blacks active in the unions after the Second World War, who believed that the Communist party did not really care about the problems of American blacks but wanted to use the racial issue to discredit the entire American system. Thus, the "anti-Communist" left, as it called itself, generally barred Communists from membership in its organizations, fearing that Communists would manipulate them for their own ends. The ADA prohibited Communists from membership and the American Civil Liberties Union under Roger Baldwin expelled Communists from its board, insisting on loyalty oaths. The NAACP and its Legal Defense Fund were virulently anti-Communist as well. They all supported Walter Reuther's hard line against any coalition with any organization that did not bar Communists. SNCC was suspect because it had no prohibition against any particular ideology.

Though by the sixties only a few fragments of the Communist party survived and the Democratic party, led by the Kennedys, was the undisputed vehicle for social change, Walter Reuther apparently still considered the Communists his mortal enemy and even believed they were trying to assassinate him for having purged them from the union. Fearful that they could exploit the race issue, and anxious to assure a UAW role in civil rights, Reuther called a meeting sometime in the early sixties which was attended by Martin Luther King, Jr., Whitney Young of the Urban League, James Farmer and Floyd McKissick of CORE, Harry Belafonte, Ralph Abernathy, Andrew Young, Joseph Lowry, and other black leaders, as well as Reuther's lawyer, ADA activist Joseph Rauh. The purpose was to form a coalition of union and church people on civil rights. It was the beginning of the UAW's annual three-day conferences on civil rights, organized by its Fair Employment Council as part of the union's national agenda. The conferences, which took place at leading universities around the country, offered seminars for blacks who had never held union cards before, teaching them grievance procedures. "It involved the blacks in getting some skills on unionism," explains the Rev. Russell K. Williams, an active UAW organizer at the time. "But at the same time it gave the union, the international, a chance to achieve some publicity in what they were doing, not for just black union members, but in the total black community of America."

In the spring of 1963, prior to the March on Washington, the UAW held its three-day Leadership Conference on Civil Rights in Washington, DC. According to Williams, the "prime movers" at the conference, who were pushing for "a coalition group to come to Mississippi to enhance a giant voter registration," were Charles Evers of Mississippi, whose brother, Jackson NAACP leader Medgar Evers, would be assassinated later that spring, and Aaron Henry. Henry, state president of the Mississippi NAACP, was a friend of Lowenstein's, the two having met when Henry was an NSA delegate from Xavier College in Louisiana.

Williams, who had attended civil rights meetings organized by the UAW in New York with Lowenstein, insists that Lowenstein figured prominently at the conference. "He was in these meetings," Williams asserts. "I'd never seen one that he wasn't there. He wasn't always on the program, but he was there. If not in an official capacity, he was there as a spectator. But he was there." Williams remembers attending a civil rights meeting in a Washington office which he maintains was Lowenstein's, though at the time Lowenstein was allegedly still only an assistant professor at North Carolina State in Raleigh.

In June of 1963, Lowenstein went on leave from NC State. An entry in his diary records his intention to write a novel; he also wrote that a planned trip to Spain would be postponed. Then an entry for the week of June 19–23 states: "Early departure for Deep South probable; Higgs says legal help is needed in Jackson."

William Higgs was the white lawyer from Jackson who had filed a law suit earlier that year against Attorney General Robert Kennedy and FBI Director J. Edgar Hoover in behalf of Bob Moses, who was attempting to force prosecution of southern officials "responsible for acts of violence and intimidation against civil rights workers." The suit had failed, the acts of violence were continuing, and Higgs, who also advised Moses on voter registration strategy, was being forced to leave the state. Since he was at the time virtually the only white lawyer there who would take a civil rights case, his inability to carry on had prompted the appeal for help which eventually reached Lowenstein.

The Voter Education Project, meanwhile, which had been launched in 1962 at the urging of Assistant Attorney General Burke Marshall, with funds provided by the Taconic Foundation, Field Foundation, and the Stern Family Fund, was struggling along, coordinated by the "big five" civil rights organizations: the NAACP,

CORE, SCLC, the Urban League, and SNCC. To prevent haggling over the VEP funds and to create a coalition of the major civil rights organizations to coordinate voter registration in Mississippi, the Council of Federated Organizations (COFO) was created, putting the NAACP, CORE, SCLC, and SNCC under one umbrella in Mississippi. Moses became the COFO voter registration director, David Dennis of CORE his assistant. Aaron Henry of the NAACP was elected president.

But serious differences among the groups persisted. Moses was committed to voter registration. But he was becoming increasingly critical of the Kennedy administration for not providing protection from federal marshals for blacks who were trying to register. He also criticized the pending voting rights bill for its requirement of a sixth-grade education. As relations between SNCC, led by outspoken activist James Forman, and the Kennedy administration deteriorated, SNCC workers began to be radicalized by their experiences in Mississippi. While they continued their efforts in behalf of the voter registration project, they developed a sense that voting might not in itself be sufficient. They also questioned whether the tactics endorsed by the old coalition in which the church played such a prominent part, could ever be effective. Irreverently, SNCC workers referred to Martin Luther King, Jr., as "De Lawd," showing their contempt for his rhetoric.

When Assistant Attorney General Robert Doar responded to their demands for federal protection by stating that the government was not in a position to provide protection for each SNCC worker, Bob Moses shot back that it was not a matter of the SNCC workers' safety but one of preventing injury to blacks trying to register at the courthouse. Unless such protection was provided, he argued, the exercise was meaningless and few blacks would be able to register.

Indeed, many SNCC workers began to suspect that this was what the Kennedy administration intended. Eschewing the March on Washington as a waste of time, they were unenthusiastic about such civil rights legislation as public accommodations. Their goals involved far more than the right to be served a hamburger at a lunch counter. They were moving away from liberalism to radicalism.

Unlike the new generation of activists in their overalls, Lowenstein continued to dress "like a college kid of the fifties," in T-shirt, sweat socks, and loafers, according to Greg Craig, son of Lowenstein's friend William Craig. In the Mississippi setting the contrast would be striking.

After Lowenstein went on leave from NC State in June of 1963, he planned his Mississippi itinerary:

  July 4—Tougaloo–Jackson
  July 5—Yazoo City–Clarksdale
  July 6—Greenville–Greenwood

July 7—Lexington–Oxford.
He added mysteriously, "En Route: Arguella, Belzoni, Tchula, Batesville, etc."

On the Mississippi situation, he wrote: "Miss 'No Gains Without Pains' was never more true. Only massive protests seem likely to produce a reappraisal so it will get rougher before there is much progress. White 'liberals' function as in South Africa, but are less numerous and courageous; Racial non-communication almost total."

Lowenstein was in Jackson participating in demonstrations after the assassination of Medgar Evers. In an interview with Stanford historian Clayborne Carson, he said he expected to find Mississippi "only somewhat worse" than North Carolina but found instead that it was "like South Africa, only a little bit better." He wrote in his diary: "Jackson involvement deep, late summer return likely."

White racists were angered by the sight of blacks and whites working together to give blacks the vote. "Biracial groups viewed as treason," Lowenstein noted. "Henry asks to return to Clarksdale now, Brando, Franciosa said to be going," he wrote.

Lowenstein, who was assembling film stars for the march on Washington, had made *Brutal Mandate* into a screenplay and hoped to interest actors Marlon Brando and Anthony Franciosa, both active in civil rights, in it. Later that summer he gave Brando a screen treatment of a novel he had prepared with Hollywood screenwriter Marcia Borie. The novel itself, which was to have been based on his experiences in Mississippi and called "Angus," was still in the planning stages at the time. Still later, describing the novel to journalist Lawrence Maddry, Lowenstein called it "a study of how a town disintegrates under a social crisis with local citizens trying to bridge the chaos." It was not autobiographical, he insisted. "Angus as a person is a local hero. I've never experienced that distinction," he quipped to Maddry. "I think a book of this type was needed. Nobody today is writing about the problems of the white man, caught with his own conscience and feelings of guilt," concluded Lowenstein.

Lowenstein also told Lawrence Maddry his version of how he came to Mississippi in the summer of 1963. "I hadn't planned to go," Lowenstein said, recalling that he had received an appeal from a confederation of civil rights groups in Mississippi. "They said they needed a lawyer. They said the only white lawyer who would take a civil rights case had been run out of the state. So I went." Lowenstein said he had been "shocked" and referred to the situation in Mississippi that summer as "lawless." "People were being dragged out of their homes at night by officers without search warrants."

According to Charles Evers, former head of the Mississippi NAACP, "Al came to Mississippi . . . unannounced and unknown." Evers adds, "The situation was pretty bad then. We had most of our money tied up in the bail bonds, and the police were hounding us.

We couldn't picket or register to vote, or even attract any public attention. Al came in as a lawyer and helped us out in the courts."

Teresa Carpenter, writing in the *Village Voice*, reported that in 1963 "Lowenstein was summoned to Jackson that July by Aaron Henry, head of the Mississippi NAACP. The Movement there was plagued by disputes and Henry appealed to Lowenstein to mediate differences between Charles Evers and Bob Moses, the soulful, softspoken leader of the Student Nonviolent Coordinating Committee. In later years, Lowenstein was to recall that he found the Movement a shambles."

James Forman, who worked closely with Moses in Mississippi, later wrote: "It would take us still longer to understand the full implications of Lowenstein's presence in Mississippi in 1963. We would discover that he represented a whole body of influential forces seeking to prevent SNCC from becoming too radical and to bring it under the control of what I have called the liberal-labor syndrome. The syndrome's first step was just to observe—and I am sure that is why Lowenstein showed up in Mississippi that year."

James Forman relates that Lowenstein, Joe Rauh, Michael Harrington, and Bayard Rustin held several meetings in 1962 and 1963 to decide what to do about the "Stalinists" who had "taken over" SNCC. Labor organizer and writer Paul Jacobs, who was working for the federal government at the time and who attended a key meeting of this group, later related to Forman that a decision was made at the meeting that "Allard Lowenstein should infiltrate SNCC on behalf of the liberal-labor group to check the power of the supposed Stalinists and keep SNCC out of the orbit of the communists." The goal was to keep SNCC in the camp of the social democrats who followed the ideology of Norman Thomas.

Lowenstein had no courtroom experience, and Mississippi gave out-of-state counsel a hard time, facts supporting the conclusion that Lowenstein could have been only minimally effective in a lawyer's role. What Lowenstein was superb at was observing, analyzing, and mobilizing. And by the time he arrived, the voter registration workers were frustrated and fatigued. "When I first got to Mississippi (in July of 1963)," Lowenstein later told Nancy L. Steffen, the editor of the *Stanford Daily*, in an interview "everything was finished. The whites had won. There were a few SNCC kids holding out . . . but the people literally had no hope. . . . They were so scared. What could you do?" He planned to stay a "couple of days—no more." But then, Lowenstein recalled, "it got hard to leave. . . . I was only going to stay for a short time. . . . But people were being beaten and arrested and terrorized and nobody seemed to know or care. . . . So I stayed."

Moses knew he had to find a new strategy. According to Clayborne Carson, "Moses' participation in the Greenwood protests in the spring of 1963 and his use that summer of white workers in the COFO head-quarters in Jackson indicated his awareness of the need for new tactics. He decided that outside intervention alone would make possible a significant breakthrough in voter registration in Mississippi and that this intervention could come about only with greater national publicity regarding Mississippi civil rights activities."

In July of 1963, "while Moses was searching for new alternatives," Lowenstein was searching for him. The itinerary Lowenstein wrote in his diary before he left for Mississippi clearly shows that he knew where he was going. And in spite of protestations that he planned to stay for only a couple of days, the deep involvement he anticipated in his diary quickly became a reality.

Lowenstein conferred on July 4 at Tougaloo College with Ed King. From King, a white chaplain active in the movement, Lowenstein learned of the importance of SNCC to the voter registration drive, and that Bob Moses, director of SNCC's Mississippi project, was central to the effort. King also explained the details of COFO and advised Lowenstein to talk to Moses.

In Clarksdale, where he met with Aaron Henry on July 5, Lowenstein learned more about the tensions in COFO. There were differences between SNCC and CORE. And there was an underlying tension between the SCLC, under the leadership of pacifist Martin Luther King, Jr., and SNCC, with its far more militant inspiration, Ella Baker. The NAACP itself had been critical of the SNCC voter registration project when it first began in 1960 because of the source of its funding. They had even had reservations about the Voter Education Project on the grounds that it was impractical. While Moses suggests these differences arose from a natural struggle for preeminence, there were deep ideological differences. The NAACP, SCLC, and CORE were all distrustful of SNCC.

On July 6, Lowenstein was in Greenwood, headquarters of SNCC's Mississippi project. Not finding Moses in, he set out to locate him. Moses did not know who Lowenstein was and was not aware of what he wanted, but he was told that "somebody was looking for him in Mississippi." Milton Viorst documents their first encounter in McComb, and Moses says it probably was "somewhere in the delta. We moved up to the delta and then opened an office in Jackson."

Lowenstein was evidently very impressed by Moses. Mendy Samstein, a white SNCC volunteer of the period who was close to Moses recalls: "Bob was awesome in terms of his influence on everybody in radical politics, whether it was A. J. Muste, Mario Savio, or Stokely Carmichael. This had to do with his mystique and articulation of the issues. Unlike Allard, he considered any aggrandizement of himself as contrary to the aims of the movement. He was Ghandi-like."

Lowenstein spoke of Moses in the kind of language he reserved for

234 • THE PIED PIPER: ALLARD LOWENSTEIN

Michael Scott or Frank Graham: "Moses had . . . an almost inhuman quality," he observed, "in the sense of angelic. He had such goodness as a person. . . . He reminded me of Frank Graham. . . . He had an extraordinary intellect, capable of grasping people's sensibilities and then becoming them. [He was] a real figure of strength. . . . You always felt when you were with him that you were in the presence of someone better. . . . As a person, Bob Moses was not only indispensable but unparalleled."

"What we had to do," Lowenstein later explained "was to figure out new tactics. . . . It seemed that you couldn't appeal to Washington, because nobody knew or cared. . . . We had to shake people on the outside out of thinking that Mississippi was just another state. . . ."

The "new tactics" Moses and Lowenstein decided on were, in fact, an extension of a device Moses had already used in the delta. According to Moses, there was a history of running candidates in Mississippi to challenge restrictions on voting and to raise the consciousness of blacks. In 1961, at the outset of the registration drive, Bill Higgs, the white Mississippi lawyer, had persuaded a clergyman to run for Congress in the 4th C.D., with Moses as his campaign manager. Higgs, who had a long history of civil rights activity in Mississippi by the time he was run out of the state, had promoted symbolic candidacies, according to Moses. "Ministers ran in the delta," Moses explains, "with no thought of winning. We had no registered voters among the blacks, but we would use whatever tool possible."

Moses was attacked and beaten by whites during that 1961 congressional campaign, but although he learned that this "voting" tactic was extremely dangerous, he also thought it was worth using again. Thus the decision to run Aaron Henry for governor and Ed King, the white chaplain of Tougaloo College in Jackson, for lieutenant governor in 1963, in a separate all black election—what came to be known as the "Freedom Vote"—was nothing more to Moses than an "extension of the voting in 1961 in McComb."

Before Lowenstein's arrival in Mississippi, a Harvard Law School student, then working for COFO, had discovered a provision of Mississippi law that applied to voters who claimed they were being illegally prevented from registering to vote. It gave them the right to go ahead and vote anyway, with their ballots to be counted only when they filed an appeal. Later, when Lowenstein had joined them, he related to Moses and some SNCC workers what had happened on election day in South Africa. He told Milton Viorst:

I remembered that I had been in South Africa on election day. The African National Congress had called a day of mourning so that blacks would demonstrate their discontent. So I thought, in

South Africa, where blacks can't vote, they have a day of mourning but in Mississippi, they are supposed to be able to vote. So why not have a day of voting?

But then the problem arose of how to vote, because if any black in Mississippi tried to vote, he'd be arrested, and the bail would be so great that no one would be able to put it up. That's what led to the idea of the Freedom Vote, which was that you could vote where you would be safe—in black churches, barbershops, community centers, funeral parlors, whatever you could find, as a way of massive protest.

The idea was tried first as a "protest vote" in Greenwood during the primary for governor that August, "but it didn't make any headway," Lowenstein asserted. Nancy L. Steffen, in her article in the *Stanford Daily* based on an interview with Lowenstein, concluded: "Then, Bob Moses translated the 'protest vote' concept into a 'Mock Election' and shifted the context from the primary election to the general state election. Then the 'Aaron Henry for Governor Campaign' with Lowenstein as chairman of the Campaign Advisory Committee began to take shape."

Clayborne Carson insists that Moses was encouraged by the results in the primary election, which led him to formulate the new plan with Lowenstein for a "Freedom Vote" in the general election. As to whose idea it was to actually run Henry and King, Joe Rauh, the civil rights lawyer who later represented the Mississippi Freedom Democratic Party, recalls: "I was aware of the Freedom Vote, and I assumed it was Al's idea. Milton (Viorst) casts some doubt on whether it was Al's idea or someone else's but I have always assumed all my life that the Freedom Vote in 1963 for Aaron Henry was Al's idea."

Charles Evers also attributes the idea to Lowenstein: "He never got credit for it, but running Aaron Henry for governor in a separate all black election, was his idea. That showed black people that their votes could mean something."

SNCC workers who attended the meeting at which Lowenstein mentioned the South African analogy maintain, according to David Harris, that the COFO worker from Harvard Law School had already discovered the Mississippi rule that permitted the vote to take place. Lowenstein's subsequent repetition of his version was seen by some as self-aggrandizement on Lowenstein's part. The Rev. Russell Williams puts it another way. "The various civil rights groups were involved in a battle for control and publicity. There was a lot of animosity. The squabble went further than that. There were people in the movement who wanted white participation limited to money and wanted to go it alone, such as the SNCC. They were adamant about whites being out front. The Jewish groups, such as the American Jewish Congress, gave substantial amounts of money. But there were blacks in the movement who were anti-Semitic. Lowenstein was a victim of this. Lowenstein was a great organizer who could get things going. Certain blacks felt he was trying to take things over."

Lowenstein knew Moses wanted and needed publicity for the Freedom Vote and manpower for COFO, which was wracked by infighting. He seized the opportunity and agreed to recruit students at Stanford and Yale, two campuses where he had close contacts among both faculty and undergraduates. At Yale, where he went in early fall 1963, Lowenstein was assisted by chaplain William Sloane Coffin, a liberal, a former marine and CIA expert on the Soviet Union who was known for his ability to appeal to the idealism of privileged youth. Coffin watched Lowenstein's technique at Yale. He made a brilliant speech, then enlisted volunteers. The editor of the *Yale Daily News*, who had come to cover the speech, stayed and joined up. Lowenstein's Yale organization was then given tasks and instructions as he departed for his next campus. But as Coffin observed, Lowenstein would feel "betrayed" if someone he recruited "passed him" by moving further to the left, revealing not only the ideological limits of his tolerance, but his deep need for personal loyalty.

Lowenstein wrote in his diary: "Yale group passes 50—Coffin the key as Durfee Session ignites massive camp response." He managed to recruit about a hundred students, most of them scheduled to arrive two weeks before the election in November. Some, like Dennis Sweeney of Stanford, arrived late in the summer to begin work. Sweeney was from Oregon, a bright scholarship student who had been close to Lowenstein at Stanford when Lowenstein was assistant dean of men. Apolitical when he first arrived at Stanford, Sweeney had been suspended as a freshman for getting drunk and passing out on the lawn. But when he returned, he earned a reputation as a serious student leader and found a role model in Lowenstein.

In the same way that he made friends of numerous other students who enlisted in his causes, Lowenstein became Sweeney's friend. Sweeney in turn did what many young people did for Lowenstein; he drove him around to his numerous appointments and listened to him expound. Lowenstein, always on the lookout for new talent to be molded into future liberal leaders, talked to him about South Africa and about civil rights and when the opportunity to go to Mississippi arose, Sweeney snapped at it.

When he arrived there, Sweeney was placed by Lowenstein with SNCC's office in Jackson. Lawrence de Bivort, who came with Sweeney from Stanford says he was "gentle and friendly" and remembers that Sweeney "would play his guitar." Things were relatively peaceful at first, according to de Bivort, who says "There was no sense of tension or conflict. We were singing 'We Shall Overcome' in a church."

Occasionally an insensitive remark would, however, lead to an argument, and sometimes Lowenstein himself would become an irritant, with his frenetic style and contacts in high places. "Ella Baker was there doing the Freedom Vote and she was turned off by Al's 'cyclonic' method of operating," Bob Moses observes. "He had lots of ties to important people in the government and the Democratic party like Hubert Humphrey. He was always on the phone with them and Ella Baker had reservations about it. This wasn't the way we were working at the time." But speaking for himself and others who were based in Mississippi, he adds, "We had no problem with Lowenstein." White SNCC organizer Mendy Samstein, then a history professor at Morehouse College in Atlanta, adds: "It didn't bother Bob that Al came and went. He saw him as a valuable resource in opening Mississippi and fended off the criticism."

Moses does acknowledge that there was friction, however, recalling that "students wanted to go into Yazoo where we hadn't been and wouldn't let them." This surprised some of the whites who, in de Bivort's words, "wanted self-asserted heroes while the blacks were savvy about what had to be done." Lowenstein did go to Yazoo with Dennis Sweeney and some other white students, who volunteered to be arrested. Ordered to return, they were picked up by John Lewis, a SNCC worker who had participated in the first sit-ins in Greensboro. As they left Greenwood, Lewis noticed that they were being followed. As the group of whites opened fire on them, Lowenstein covered Lewis with his body so the driver would not be shot and the car forced off the road. "It didn't matter to him if he got killed," de Bivort comments. Such stories were later integrated into Lowenstein's civil rights recruitment speeches.

On October 2, Lowenstein spoke at the Stanford Student Congress meeting, as did Dennis Sweeney. Lowenstein opened his speech by alluding humorously to rumors that were circulating about him: "In Mississippi, I'm just sort of a Communist agitator who comes in and has to be gotten rid of. But here it's always more sophisticated. So far, since I've been back, I've discovered that I'm banned from coast to coast from thirty campuses, at least two of which have offered me jobs, and I thought I'd better phone and tell them that." But he turned serious on the subject of his address, "Mississippi: A Foreign Country in Our Midst?" telling the Stanford students: "I don't think that Mississippi is a foreign country in our midst—and I think one reason it's important to talk about Mississippi is it is very much *ourselves* in our midst. Mississippi is a place where America is at its worst but it is also a place where anyone who is an American can see himself at his worst."

Calling Mississippi "sick," Lowenstein told the students that the federal courts in the state were no better than the state courts, "because one of the two judges that one has to deal with, Judge Cox, was Senator Eastland's law partner and was appointed district court judge because it was necessary at the time—or so the attorney general thought—to appoint somebody that was acceptable to Eastland in order to get other judges in the rest of the country cleared through the Judiciary Committee of which Eastland was chairman."

Lowenstein told of a group of blacks who had been beaten and evicted from the premises when they had tried to register in Rankin County, Mississippi. In the federal court, where the matter was taken "because it is a violation of the federal law to beat people up who are trying to register," the deputy sheriff of Rankin County had denied under oath that he'd been present when the beatings occurred. When "witness after witness" then came forth to testify to the contrary, Judge Cox, having heard all the evidence, "not only dismissed the suit against the sheriff and the deputy sheriff on the grounds that there was no proof that the beatings were connected with their effort to register—although nobody ever adduced any evidence that they were connected to anything else—but also dismissed the perjury of the deputy sheriff on grounds that, after all, the evidence had been improperly received in the courtroom and therefore it was improper to consider whether perjury had been committed in improperly produced evidence."

Lowenstein went on to describe other legal abominations. He also told the students the Kennedys were labeled Communists in Mississippi for supporting civil rights. He concluded by explaining the Aaron Henry campaign and observing that, for the summer of 1964, "we're hoping to be able to get agreement among the Negro civil rights organizations to have a large number of people from outside Mississippi come and help and bring enough people into the state so that there will be an awareness among whites that you can't beat up everybody in the United States, and that every time you beat up one person who is committed to the terribly radical thing of getting people to vote, and this is all that our project is aimed at, ten more will come. . . ."

If Lowenstein's method of operations raised eyebrows, his dedication was not suspect during the Henry campaign. Lowenstein was arrested several times and provoked the police with his offhand disdain. White students were arrested as well. In September, Dennis Sweeney and John Bundy, Emory Bundy's brother, also recruited by Lowenstein, were both arrested. And in late October, Lowenstein and two students from Yale were arrested for breaking the curfew in Clarksdale, a law that the NAACP was challenging. Lowenstein wrote: "A.K., 2 Yalies Jailed in Clarksdale for 'Violating Curfew': Bond Posted, Arrests near 50—NAACP fights curfew—'Intimidation general and growing' Yale reinforcements arriving, car due from Stanford." He then noted: "Stanford sends $5,000. 300 told not come as harassment intensifies. Atmosphere 'Like Cuba' A.K. statement asserts."

To his parents, Lowenstein wrote on October 29, 1963: "We are under a reign of terror and it is not pleasant. . . . We've been in touch with the White House, Justice Dept., Senator Morse, etc., today, and they may help. Norman Thomas, bless his heart, is coming down Thursday. Most astonishing and cheering of all is that Stanford has sent $4,300!—Which is making all the difference in the world. They had 300 people who wanted to come to Miss. (from Stanford). It's an extraordinary response and we are all deeply moved. The Yalies keep coming and are good people. What have you to say for Columbia? (I know, you won a football game.)"

Thirteen Stanford students headed south. On Sunday, October 27, Dennis Sweeney drove with the first contingent of Stanford recruits to Mississippi. Lowenstein's statement was published in the *Stanford Daily* that Monday:

> What is going on in the State of Mississippi in October 1963 is astonishing to an American citizen not experienced in the ways of the state. . . . It could not survive the test of a free election. That is why people will not allow a free election to be held. . . . The atmosphere of this campaign suggests more nearly what a campaign must be like in the Soviet Union or Cuba . . . than in the United States. . . . The courage of the people who are continuing their efforts in the campaign cannot fail to impress and move those of us who have arrived from other parts of the United States.
>
> We shall tell what we have found in Mississippi wherever we go when we leave here and we shall not leave here until we have seen through the rest of this dismal affair. We shall submit evidence of what we have found to . . . the Congress of the United States in the faith that the American people, once they know the facts, will not be willing to allow tyranny to wrap itself in the American flag. . . . It is of course a pity that it should be necessary for people to make such sacrifices in our country at this late date, but it is wonderful to know that there are many prepared to do so long as it may be necessary.

When news of Lowenstein's arrest reached NC State in Raleigh, it caused a furor. The chancellor, John Tyler Caldwell, had been told that Lowenstein was going on leave to train Peace Corps volunteers in Puerto Rico. "That's what he got his leave of absence to do," Caldwell asserts. "I never knew that he wasn't doing that until all of a sudden it turned up that he was in Clarksdale, Mississippi, and put in jail in Clarksdale, Mississippi."

The head of the North Carolina senate criticized NC State for paying Lowenstein $7,500 a year while he was agitating for civil rights, and when reporters called him for a statement, Lowenstein shot back: "Yes, it is disgraceful, $7,500 is far too little." It was not until much later that Caldwell, learned that Lowenstein had also used his leave to go to Europe. "No, this is brand new to me," he asserts, adding that "we never felt any political pressure within the university, at least I never let myself feel any political pressure, and I don't recall any."

In Mississippi, blacks had turned out to vote for Henry and King in sufficient numbers for the drive to be termed a success, and Lowenstein recorded the violent white reaction: "U.S. Marshals 'demanded' as violence and harassment mount; 3 are shot at; 'vote' total at 30,000—may reach 75,000. 4 Yalies assaulted. 'I'm going to kill you, nigger,' cop tells SNCC worker, gun cocked at his head. 'Nightmare Night' in Jackson follows rally." A few days later, he made a further entry: "Henry's race for Gov. 'vote' put at 82,000, Henry asks Congress to investigate 'Pattern of intimidation.' Plan for summer stalled on numbers. Michael Scott to tour Mississippi next week."

Afterward, Moses and Lowenstein discussed plans to bring a thousand white students to Mississippi for the summer of 1964. Moses wanted a monumental confrontation between the Mississippi authorities and the federal government. SNCC's job was to "bring about such a confrontation . . . to change the power structure," according to Moses, who described the SNCC plan as an "annealing process. Only when metal has been brought to white heat, can it be shaped and molded. This is what we intend to do to the South and the country, bring them to white heat and then remold them."

Though militant SNCC blacks and Atlanta separatists were against bringing large numbers of whites into the movement, there was general agreement that the momentum gained by the Henry campaign had to be sustained and a "massive" Mississippi project, as envisioned for the summer of 1964 by Lowenstein and Moses, gained support. Lowenstein wrote: "Decision still far from final but opportunity seems too good to pass up. Moses, Henry, Evers agree; Scott to make 'survey trip.'"

At a COFO meeting on November 14, black SNCC field workers argued against a large white presence, and some complained that the whites were "taking over." Others rejected the argument. "If we're trying to break down this barrier of segregation," insisted Fannie Lou Hamer, "we can't segregate ourselves." Moses agreed. He told the black field workers that whenever white people worked alongside of them, it changed the whole complexion of what they were doing. "So it isn't any longer Negro fighting white, it's a question of rational people against irrational people." As for the role of blacks, Moses added, "I always thought that the one thing we can do for the country that no one else can do is to be above the race issue."

Moses believed that the blacks and whites in the movement shared the same objective and he was impressed by the dedication of the white activists. But while Moses mobilized support for the Summer Project, Lowenstein left to travel to London on a South African assignment and to Spain. According to Lowenstein's diary, Moses made a "plea" to Lowenstein "for 'priority' change." Lowenstein wrote: "Agree Miss. is foremost but 'regretfully' decided to meet commitments."

Lowenstein also had other things on his mind. He wrote in his diary: "Summer 'must have time for writing.' A.K. to insist to 'all'— he balks at remarks by G.G. that teaching will go on till June '65." George Gullette ("G.G."), the chairman of Lowenstein's department, was trying to keep him at NC State, while Lowenstein was looking to get out of Raleigh, to run for Congress in New York, and to succeed as a novelist and screenwriter. But since he also wanted to be a college professor, he remained equivocal about his relationship with NC State, particularly since it provided him with an effective cover. Lowenstein had all of these things going at the same time, but Mississippi increasingly commanded his attention.

In August of 1963, Lowenstein had written in his diary: "A.K. for JFK in '64 almost beyond reconsidering. Endorsement is enthusiastic and linked to Mississippi. 'If every American could spend 2 weeks there we'd have a landslide': But tactics of Kennedys on C.R. [civil rights] and other issues hit, and fear is expressed of reaction to that program and to 'wise' Cold War steps if effort to 'educate' languishes." Lowenstein apparently wanted more subtlety from the Kennedys and expected them to follow the "good-wing" approach to combating Communism. Hence what Lowenstein refers to as "wise" Cold War steps. Unless the Kennedy administration was able to "educate" the American people about the necessity to end all forms of racial segregation in America and support for South Africa abroad, there would be, he feared, a backlash against liberalism, and the hard-liners would take control. America would assume a bellicose position and alienate the rest of the world. But there would be little time for Kennedy to educate America. On November 22, he was assassinated and Lyndon Johnson became president.

Lowenstein had harbored suspicions that SNCC was infiltrated by Communists. Journalist Theodore White shared those suspicions. In the November, 1963, issue of *Life* magazine he wrote that SNCC was the target of "serious penetration by unidentified elements" and charged that SNCC "agents" had attempted "to convert a peaceful march into a violent *Putsch* on government offices" in demonstrations in Jackson and Birmingham. White referred to a SNCC "battle plan" which he alleged had been "rejected by Negro leaders" calling for "nonviolent battle groups . . . to cut Montgomery off from all communication with the outside world—presumably to provoke 'nonviolent' combat between Alabama and the U.S."

But though Lowenstein feared Communist infiltration, he did not oppose radical tactics and did not assume that only Communists would advocate them. Like Moses and other SNCC leaders, he was in favor of forcing confrontation. This set Lowenstein apart from the old-time liberals, who did not have his South African background and did not know that in South Africa, white liberals, fearful of a Communist revolution, had advocated confrontational direct action and support for the Pan-Africanist Congress, the South African equivalent to SNCC. The old-time liberals assumed that radical tactics showed the Communist hand. But Lowenstein viewed the Mississippi Summer Project as an anti-Communist activity, designed to provoke confrontation and force the federal government to take over the state. This was necessary, he believed, to end the abuses that could, in fact, lead to a rise in Communist influence among disenchanted blacks. Consequently, Lowenstein was suspicious of those who opposed the use of whites to cause the confrontation he wanted.

The executive committee of SNCC took up the Summer Project on December 30. Lowenstein recorded the sequence of decisions: "SNCC staff favors 9–1 negro summer ratio. Leaders oppose it and February decision looms. SNCC votes to stress a drive in Miss. Moses phones, due here. A.K. named to head outside buildup, declines—as starts recruiting at once. COFO drops quota, keeps 1,000 as goal. But approval of full project nears as Moses agrees to approach Rustin."

Moses himself observes: "The Freedom Vote gave rise to debate among the organizers in Mississippi. The question was should we have the students down for next summer on a large basis. Al was pushing for it. The staff was deadlocked. I broke the deadlock in favor of the project." Moses, who was named director of the Summer Project, knew this would make manpower available which would pay its own way rather than drain SNCC's already meager resources.

Lowenstein was a dynamic and effective recruiter for the Mississippi project. But, according to Lawrence de Bivort, some of the black SNCC volunteers, whose resources were extremely limited, resented the way Lowenstein's white recruits could "float in and out of their lives, to go back to some prestigious university." When Lowenstein flew Norman Thomas in for "support," the seed of resentment began to blossom into open hostility. James Forman, among others, harbored fears that Lowenstein was taking over, and relates that his suspicions were confirmed as plans for the Summer Project progressed: "Lowenstein was traveling around the college campuses telling students that he had charge of recruitment and people would go to Mississippi under his direction."

Indeed, Lowenstein's preppy recruits did consider him the leader of the movement. They had not been involved before and would not have become involved if not for Lowenstein. He took these conservatives and made them liberals, and they loved his wit, his rumpled appearance and even his Jewishness. From the upper-middle-class WASP culture they came out of, he brought them into the world of social conflict and gave them a cause.

In January, Lowenstein, who was also writing his novel ("135 page 'Angus' nears completion—Novel now 1/4 done"), observed in his diary: "Project to be 'As big as possible' A agrees to Jackson trip tomorrow; JSC [Jackson State College] students riot." As he became more active in recruiting students in the north, hostile whites in North Carolina pressed to have him fired. By February, he was writing: "NC State—Attempts to 'purge' A, Stone says C. R. [civil rights] work makes A 'unfit' to teach at NCS, Demands ouster. Decision to 'Hit Back' likely; Stone, Helms may be target soon." Then he wrote: "Moses says A 'Must' stay on, Appoints him political chief; Pressure to accept mounting."

When Lowenstein made a recruitment appearance at Harvard, Greg Craig, then a freshman, came to hear him speak on voter registration. Craig describes the occasion: "I turned up to say hello, along with approximately six other people who were apparently interested in civil rights. It was in the depths of winter, gloomy and cold and icy outside; the walls of the common room were paneled in dark wood, and the room itself was extremely dark. We were a very small turnout, but we seated ourselves around the room in the overstuffed leather chairs and couches, awaiting Al's arrival."

When he came, Lowenstein was introduced by Barney Frank, then a teaching fellow in the government department. Craig remembers Lowenstein "hunkered on a couch with his legs pulled up underneath him Indian-style," telling the gathering that, after traveling in southern Africa, he had returned to discover that race relations in the American south were every bit as bad as they were in South Africa. "Al said that he had been astonished to discover that in Mississippi, the institutions of the state government—the police, the political parties, and the elected officials—were as thoroughly anti-black as was the South African government. . . . While the repression in South Africa was open and visible and almost acknowledged by the regime, the racism in the South was just as entrenched, just as violent, just as implacable, and the outlook just as grim. The only difference was that the world community was outraged about South Africa but nobody seemed to care about Mississippi."

He told them that Mississippi was the key to the South because if Mississippi could become "unstuck," Alabama and South Carolina and Georgia would follow. The nation's attention needed to be drawn to the "festering sore" and the best way to do that was to demonstrate in some dramatic way that the black people of Mississippi were being denied the most essential and fundamental right of citizenship, the right to vote.

"Al described the campaign that had been conducted in 1963 to elect Aaron Henry governor of Mississippi," recalls Craig, and he told them how the participation of students from Stanford and Yale had given the situation much greater visibility in the North. "Al also described the physical dangers. People had been threatened, followed, arrested, beaten, and jailed. There were no lawyers in Mississippi who would represent civil rights workers or Mississippi blacks who were arrested in connection with their work on Aaron's campaign. The harassment came from the state police, the local police departments (which were generally even more dangerous than the better equipped, trained, and sophisticated state police), and from local white folk who rode around the dusty back roads of Mississippi with gun racks on their pickup trucks."

To illustrate the way traffic violations were used as a pretext to haul civil rights workers into the station house and hold them in a jail cell while the local vigilantes were called, after which they were released in the middle of the night to whatever awaited them outside, Lowenstein told the story of his own arrest. As Craig remembers, "Al told of arriving in McComb at two o'clock in the morning and seeing that, in the city limits, a state police cruiser had pulled in behind him and followed him into town. Al described how carefully he had driven, never going over twenty miles an hour, scrupulously stopping at each intersection, signaling with both blinkers and hand signals, trying to anticipate every possible infraction that he might be accused of having committed." No sooner had he pulled up in front of the hotel, however, than the trooper arrested him for going through a stop sign. He was handcuffed and taken to the police station.

Craig continues the story: "Al realized that none of his friends knew where he was and that no one expected him to arrive anywhere the next day and that the one thing that he had to accomplish for his own safety was somehow to get word to someone where he was and what had happened. When they arrived at the police station, Al insisted that he be given his one telephone call. Somehow he extracted that concession."

While the troopers were standing around him, listening to his side of the conversation, Lowenstein told the operator, "This is a person-to-person collect call to Mr. FRANKLIN DELANO ROOSEVELT THE THIRD." And when his friend answered in Manhattan, Lowen-

stein informed him in a loud voice that he had been arrested by the
Mississippi state police in McComb. "No," he said, "don't call Bobby
yet. No, there's no reason to call anyone at Justice yet. But if you don't
hear from me in the morning, you probably ought to do that. I'll talk
to you again tomorrow and by then I'll know more." The police released Lowenstein twenty minutes later.

Describing the Summer Project to the Harvard students, Lowenstein told them that volunteers would live with black families and
work out of the local black churches, going around door-to-door to
persuade people to appear before the county clerk in the county
courthouse and ask for permission to register to vote. Anyone who
was denied the right to register to vote would then fill out an affidavit
detailing what had happened; that affidavit would then be sent to the
Civil Rights Division of the Department of Justice as evidence of the
systematic exclusion of blacks from the voting rolls in Mississippi. "Al
explained that lawyers from the North were planning to go to Mississippi during the summer to provide legal assistance to the project."

Lowenstein did not specify who these lawyers would be. He told
Greg Craig, who wanted to volunteer for the Summer Project, that
there would probably be violence. Lowenstein said that he couldn't
be certain that Craig wouldn't be hurt and that "if anything happened
to you, I would never be able to face your parents again." Because
Craig was much younger than most of the other volunteers, Lowenstein insisted on speaking first to his parents, who gave their permission. Lowenstein was pleased. "When northern college students got
involved, northern newspapers got interested," he said later.

29.

By March of 1964, a cloud had come over the Summer Project, fueling
suspicions harbored by Lowenstein and other liberals that Communists were infiltrating the civil rights movement. SNCC joined with
SCEF and the Bradens in organizing the Southern Students Organizing Committee (SSOC) to bring more white students from the South
into the movement. A Harvard graduate student who was close to the
organization at the time observed later that "SNCC had become too
radical, too professional, too full-time revolutionary to recruit large
numbers of idealistic college students."

Disdaining the integration of lunch counters, SNCC workers
"shifted from hamburgers to bread," as one worker put it, emphasizing
full-employment and basic economic needs ahead of desegregation.
"The liberals were concerned about blacks getting a tuna fish sand-

wich at a lunch counter, but the SNCC people were talking about jobs and unions," says National Lawyers Guild attorney Sanford Katz. Lowenstein, who stressed politics over integration, was ahead of most of the other liberals. "He felt politics was the key," white SNCC advisor Connie Curry relates. "He always felt that voter registration and political organization was the key to the problem more than desegregation."

But Lowenstein's politics were hostile to radical economics. Stokely Carmichael, then a young SNCC organizer active in the Nonviolent Action Group (NAG), openly advocated such socialistic solutions to the economic problems of poor blacks in the South as nationalization of industry. Another SNCC volunteer was discovered to have participated in a youth festival sponsored by the WFDY, the Communist-backed enemy of COSEC and NSA. Moreover, SNCC refused to take a stand excluding Communists from their ranks or forbidding alliances with Communist-supported groups. Carmichael called on the civil rights movement to "stop taking a defensive stand on communism" because it took "the whole emphasis off the civil rights issue and (put)it on the issue of Americanism vs. anti-Americanism."

All that, plus the high visibility of the writings of Marx and Lenin around SNCC offices and the growing presence of radical lawyers from the National Lawyers Guild there, finally led Lowenstein to describe SNCC as "insufficiently anti-Communist." He also attacked the guild lawyers as "Stalinist" and criticized their "sixties" appearance and their incompetence.

Sanford Friedman, Lowenstein's old friend from Horace Mann, recalls that Lowenstein was upset by what was happening in Mississippi. "During the SNCC period, I had the impression that Al felt there was some very radical faction trying to take over that organization," he maintains. ". . . Al always had facts, names, information he could state. He would say, 'I know this person is trying to do this,' and so forth, and he produced charts as to what was going on, who was with which faction, which he laid out on the table. In his mind, he perceived evidence about this or that. I dimly have the impression that he felt there was not only some Communist source, even Chinese, of revenue, financial backing, influence; that faction, in his mind, was trying to achieve something different from what he was trying to accomplish and was subverting it."

Curtis Gans records the Mississippi period as "the first year that lots of people had mixed feelings about Al. Al had a problem with anyone to his left. He had a tactical analysis that the SDS tactics were self-defeating. But why did he engage in Red-baiting in the summer of 'sixty-four against the Lawyers Guild? Even many of his friends felt this was wrong."

The Lawyers Guild, though it had originally been founded to bolster the fortunes of the New Deal, was by then anathema to anti-Communist liberals. Formed in 1933 as an alternative to the American Bar Association, which had systematically opposed the social legislation of the Roosevelt administration, the Lawyers Guild had also attracted attorneys who were Communist party members and sympathetic to the Soviet Union. By 1940, it was viewed as predominantly leftist with Communist sympathizers, and by the end of the war, as the Cold War began, most of the non-Communist liberals had drifted away.

There were, however, many guild members who were not Communist party members, according to Katz. "It attracted activist lawyers who were dissatisfied with the ABA and who felt that such organizations as the ACLU, which, at Roger Baldwin's urging, had expelled Communists from its board, were not sufficiently dedicated to the principles they claimed to support," he explains. By the sixties, with such radical activist lawyers as Arthur Kinoy, Victor Rabinowitz, and Michael Stander on its rolls, the guild was, Katz asserts, "the cutting edge of legal activism in America and was attracting a new generation of young radical American lawyers."

In 1963, the Lawyers Guild entered the civil rights movement in earnest, setting up civil rights programs and opening an office in Jackson, where George Crockett, a black lawyer from Detroit who had been jailed in the forties under the Smith Act, and Claudia Shropshire, a black woman attorney, became the guild presence. "Through the efforts of guild lawyers Victor Rabinowitz and Michael Stander, they captured the SNCC," according to Katz.

Because, like SNCC—and unlike the ADA, the ACLU, the NAACP, and the UAW—the Lawyers Guild did not prohibit Communists from membership and participation in its programs, its entrance into the civil rights arena upset Lowenstein and other leading ADA liberals. Jack Greenberg, head of the NAACP Legal Defense Fund, was adamant that the guild should be barred from the Summer Project, and he threatened to abort a legal assistance program destined for the project if his group were forced to cooperate with the guild.

Greenberg insists that his objection to the guild was based not on ideology but on the quality of the representation. "Our general feeling was that we thought some arrangement should be made to represent the defendants on some kind of sustained, continuous basis," he argues. "The Lawyers Constitutional Defense Committee and the Lawyers Guild and some other groups . . . would send somebody down for a week, or two or three weeks, but that isn't how a litigation goes, even a minor prosecution. And if lawyers are coming in and out, the representation is basically discontinuous with varying degrees of competence." Greenberg claims that some of the lawyers coming down had no background in civil rights, even if they had the "best of intentions."

During the winter of 1963–64, while Lowenstein was recruiting students, radical lawyer Arthur Kinoy, a professor of law at Rutgers and an active guild member, joined with activist attorney William Kunstler to break down the legal obstacles to civil rights work in the state, what Kinoy called the "large-scale legal persecution" of civil rights workers. Originally, the tactic employed had been to remove the cases to the federal court. Out-of-state lawyers were able to appear in the northern district before Eisenhower-appointee Federal Judge Claude F. Clayton without difficulty. This system broke down, however, when some thirty activists were arrested for disorderly conduct after a voting rights march and demonstration in front of the courthouse in Hattiesburg. William Harold Cox, the known racist and Kennedy appointee whose behavior Lowenstein had so vividly described to his audience at Stanford, was sitting in Hattiesburg, and the federal judge who had once referred to blacks in his court as "chimpanzees" who "ought to be in the movies rather than being registered to vote" refused the removal petitions, announcing a new set of rules: for each person appearing, a $500 bond had to be posted, joint petitions were prohibited, and no petitions could be filed except by a local member of the Mississippi bar. According to George Crockett, who headed the guild project in Mississippi, there were five black lawyers in the state, "but three of them would handle civil rights cases only if they were paid, one wouldn't handle civil rights cases even if you paid him, and the fifth wasn't practicing."

Kinoy tried to have Cox disqualified, and then obtained a writ of mandamus in the Fifth District in New Orleans forcing Cox to hear the removal petitions. "In the argument before the panel," Kinoy writes, "we maintained that the federal remedy of removal enacted back in the 1860's was an essential weapon for the defense of citizens seeking to implement basic rights guaranteed to them by the national Constitution. . . . One point more than any other seemed to move the three judges. The new Mississippi rule, which would throw out any petition for removal that was not signed by a local member of the Mississippi bar, would in reality virtually eliminate the removal remedy for Black citizens fighting for the right to register to vote, since only a tiny handful of lawyers in that state would represent them in this struggle."

Although Kinoy of the Lawyers Guild won the case that allowed outside counsel to function in the Mississippi Summer Project, opposition to the guild continued to mount among many liberal Democrats who were disturbed by its radicalism and fellow-traveling with Communists. On the other hand, among Mississippi blacks, there was a deep distrust of the Democratic party. The other federal judge sitting in Mississippi, Judge Mize, a racist even more venomous than Cox, had been appointed by Roosevelt. The blacks had been kept on hold by the Democrats, while the radical Lawyers Guild was taking on the racist judges the Democrats had appointed. SNCC, looking for help wherever it could get it, saw no reason not to use the services of the Lawyers Guild, and made the decision to accept its aid, disturbing Lowenstein.

Bob Moses was disappointed by Lowenstein's reaction to the presence of the guild, and his subsequent attitude to the Summer Project. "In the early organizing of it, Lowenstein played a big role in it, but broke with it," Moses confides. "He said he wouldn't come down as part of COFO. He was upset about the Lawyers Guild. He saw them as Communists and wanted them banned. We had worked with SCEF and the Bradens were close to Ella Baker. We fought the issue of working with whomever we pleased. There was no giving in on the question of which lawyers would be used. Al tried to persuade Dennis (Sweeney) and the Stanford group not to come, but I flew out and persuaded them to stay with the project. But the Stanford people stayed friends with Al. I didn't see Al that summer. Lowenstein broke with the movement. I was surprised. It was the anti-Communist feeling on the part of certain elements in the Democratic party. But no one else broke with us except Al, although others also disapproved of the guild."

In addition to the Lawyers Guild problem, there was a serious disagreement over the structure and leadership of the project. "The project was very delicate in terms of getting off the ground at all," Moses explains. "Mississippi was the only place where all the civil rights organizations got together. People were skeptical of everybody's motives and who was trying to take over. The key point was who was making decisions about the project. To keep SNCC, it was decided that COFO staff would make the decisions. SNCC believed in decentralized decision-making. Al didn't understand this. He could not accept an organization run this way. In his mind, the staff didn't make the decisions."

According to Moses, Lowenstein wanted William Sloane Coffin to come down as "chairperson of the project." Says Moses, "This was out of the question. It upset Al that this was rejected. He said he had put more time and energy in this project than any in his life, and he felt that it had come to nothing for him. But the only way the project could come off was for people in the center of it to be low key. Otherwise, it could all fall apart. This was built into the nature of it. I don't know if Al understood this."

Coffin himself believes that Lowenstein "wanted a cleaner structure and cleaner political delineation than was possible." He shrugs off Lowenstein's determination to ban all Communists from the movement as a relic of the McCarthy period and a foible in the character of an otherwise brilliant and powerful force for good. He does not recall being asked to be the head of the whole project by Lowenstein.

SNCC workers suspected Lowenstein of working for the CIA, and he suspected them of being Communists. "There were deep ideological differences," Greg Craig asserts, "with each side suspicious of the other's motives. Each faction believed the other had a hidden agenda. To SNCC, Al's agenda was self-aggrandizement and self-promoting, to deliver a major constituency to the Democratic party and to reap the rewards. Al perceived SNCC as having a hidden agenda that had nothing to do with reform but using unrest and social injustice to transform and revolutionize the political system. Al was devoted to our system, the 'product of genius operating over 200 years,' as he described it. And he didn't believe the Democratic party was a corrupt institution hostile to change. He thought it was the most viable instrument for change."

Craig explains that "the central ideological suspicions" which Lowenstein and SNCC members harbored of each other "broke down into intense disputes over narrow issues." The "Freedom Schools" to be set up in Mississippi as part of the Summer Project were at the center of one of them. "Al wanted to address the Freedom Summer to American opinion makers; he wanted a national constituency and to show them how central the right to vote was," Craig relates. "He was very conscious how the issue was to be presented. The SNCC people wanted ideological purity. They had people reading Fanon, Marx, Lenin on imperialism. They wanted to use the Freedom Schools for young Mississippi blacks with this kind of literature. The mothers of Stanford, Yale, and Harvard students, the *Times* reporters, would see Marxism being taught instead of the American tradition and Al was very sensitive about this. He felt there had to be control over the leaflets also. They believed the biggest threat was to have leaders telling them what to do in the Freedom Schools and what to put in the leaflets."

Among SNCC workers, the feeling that Lowenstein had a CIA connection was derived in part from his position on the Freedom Schools and the leaflets. "The left would make that charge when Al said the Freedom Schools should not have Lenin's 'Essay on Imperialism,'" Craig insists. "But Al was not censoring. He felt it was strategically unsound. It would drive Al crazy and he would take it personally."

Lowenstein and SNCC also clashed over the black church and Aaron Henry. "SNCC workers had a deep antipathy to the black clergy for accommodating themselves to segregation," Craig argues. "Al saw the black clergy as key; that they had risked their necks for years. Who spoke for the Mississippi blacks? That was the central issue. SNCC thought Aaron Henry was just another politician and a party formed to elect him would make no difference. Participatory democracy from Port Huron became an operative and romantic idea when put into operation in Mississippi. It was thought by Bob Moses to be a special and pure form of democracy which couldn't be corrupted."

In March of 1964, Lowenstein wrote in his diary: "NAA-LG Shadow Nears: NCNW Promises to Help—MW Emerging as a Key." And soon after, he wrote further: "'Infiltration' Possibility Weighed, CC Cause for Concern; Decision to Use LG Could Lead 'A' to a 'Public Dissociation.' New 'Board of Control' May Be Pressed as Summer Requisite. 'New Light' Seen On Resistance of SNCC to 'Outside' Assistance."

Lowenstein went up to Yale for a civil rights symposium where he pressed his opposition to Communists in the movement. Marian Wright (Edelman), a black lawyer from Mississippi, took issue with his position. "Gus Tyler of the NAACP Legal Defense Fund was apopleptic about the Lawyers Guild," she relates, "but I told Al, 'You can't control everything all of the time.' At a symposium at Yale, Al became livid with me for not endorsing his position of ridding the civil rights movement of Communists. He assumed I had come up to New Haven to support his position and when I didn't, he became furious. But the SNCC people were livid too. They were both unable to compromise. I believed a 'weeding out' process was unjustifiable since the vast majority of people simply wanted to accomplish the goal of getting people the right to vote. I disagreed with him and said so, but I felt the problem was on all sides and that Al had a perfect right to press his point of view."

Convinced that SNCC was not going to yield on the issue of the Lawyers Guild, and that without SNCC the Summer Project could not succeed, Lowenstein conferred at Yale with Frank Graham, who agreed that the right to select one's own lawyer might break the deadlock. Lowenstein convinced Graham to propose the solution to Roy Wilkins, head of the NAACP, giving them an out. According to an account of Lowenstein's drive with Graham back to New York, Graham agreed to approach both Wilkins and A. Phillip Randolph to press the point. The NAACP did not have to endorse the presence of the Lawyers Guild but would allow it to function separately. Ultimately Jack Greenberg modified his position and agreed to let volunteers decide if they wanted a guild or an NAACP Legal Defense Fund lawyer. He added the proviso that the Legal Defense Fund would not defend SNCC people. But SNCC remained adamant that Greenberg not be allowed to "use the orientation of volunteers as a forum to attack the guild."

Meanwhile, Mel Wulf, ("MW" in Lowenstein's diary), the legal director of the American Civil Liberties Union who supported Lowenstein's demand for a control board to oversee the Summer Project, was working to establish the Lawyers Constitutional Defense Committee (LCDC) in Mississippi. While Wulf was "open about being anti-Communist," according to Joanne Grant Rabinowitz, he was also "friendly with many guild lawyers." This ambiguity caused difficulties in Mississippi and gave rise to conflicting interpretations of Wulf's role.

At the end of March, Lowenstein wrote in his diary, "MW 'Worried,' Also, Will Push 'Board'; SNCC For Using L.G." In early April, he added: "Yale, Oberlin to Organize a 'Board' of 'Outside Students.' M.W. Sees Reversal Soon on L.G." Not only was there no reversal, Wulf insists that he wasn't trying to get rid of the guild as others were.

Liberal Bronx Congressman Jonathan Bingham, a supporter of civil rights and friend of Lowenstein's, had visited Mississippi and was upset about the guild. He arranged for Burke Marshall and John Doar of the Justice Department to meet with Bob Moses, James Forman, and Arthur Schlesinger, Jr., who had been the official Kennedy historian at the White House. Schlesinger, an anti-Stalinist of long standing, told the SNCC organizers: "There are many of us who have spent years fighting the Communists. We worked hard during the thirties and the forties fighting forces such as the National Lawyers Guild. We find it unpardonable that you would work with them."

Lowenstein and his liberal allies were apparently counting on Mel Wulf and the Lawyers Constitional Defence Committee (LCDC) to provide an alternative to the Lawyers Guild for the Summer Project and to force the guild out, though Wulf himself claims that he was merely trying to do what was right as a lawyer, offering assistance to civil rights workers in Mississippi. The genesis of the LCDC actually dated back to 1961 when Wulf first arrived in Mississippi as legal director of the American Civil Liberties Union. A letter from a black who had been convicted of raping a white woman and who was on death row in Mississippi had landed on Wulf's desk after its author had failed to interest the NAACP in his case. When Wulf went to Mississippi to meet with his client, he found not one but three condemned blacks who had been convicted of raping white women and sentenced to death. Wulf also met Bob Moses and James Forman of SNCC who were organizing in the state. Moses, in Wulf's opinion, was not ideological, but Forman was radical and hostile to liberals, while Wulf regarded himself as a democratic socialist, ideologically in the middle between the radicals and the liberals. Critical of communism, he did not engage in "Red-baiting" and believed in civil liberties for everyone.

The three blacks Wulf represented escaped the death penalty, and no executions took place in Mississippi after that. His work had required his presence in Mississippi every couple of months for durations of several weeks, and during his visits he had become well acquainted with the Mississippi situation. In 1963, when the Freedom Vote project was under way, Wulf went to campaign headquarters in Jackson to introduce himself to Allard Lowenstein, the man everybody was talking about. Lowenstein ignored him, walking away without saying a word, and Wulf's impression of him was understandably negative.

By the time the Summer Project was launched in 1964, Wulf was well aware of the hostility which the radicals in SNCC bore such establishment liberal lawyers' organizations as his own ACLU and the NAACP Legal Defense Fund. But Wulf wanted the ACLU to be involved in Mississippi, not to preempt the guild, he insists, but as a matter of principle. "The guild lawyers definitely looked down on the ACLU people as a bunch of political laggards," he concedes. "The guild was always more radical than ACLU." While acknowledging that the liberals in ACLU, with their strong anti-Communist bias, wanted to get rid of the guild, Wulf says his motives were otherwise: if the ACLU stood for anything, he reasoned, it should be in Mississippi.

Another group, the Lawyers Committee for Civil Rights under Law, was too overtly connected to the White House to inspire confidence in the Mississippi volunteers. An outgrowth of the President's Committee for Civil Rights under Law, it had been formed after a meeting at the White House called by President Kennedy in 1963 to discuss the problems and strategies of the civil rights movement. George Crockett, the black lawyer who ultimately headed the guild project in Mississippi, attended the meeting at which he detected strong anti–Lawyers Guild sentiment. "Opposition to the guild was centered in the group called 'the Lawyers Committee for Civil Rights under Law,'" he states.

Specialized in taking selected cases in order to establish precedents in the Supreme Court, rather than in handling local trial work, and in handling specific cases involving threats to civil liberties rather than civil rights, the ACLU was not organized for such an effort as the Mississippi undertaking. The LCDC was created for that purpose, but Wulf, who did most of the legwork in setting it up, was a member of the National Lawyers Guild at the same time as he was the legal director of the ACLU. Joe Rauh and other liberal lawyers found that extremely disturbing. Rauh even wrote a letter to John Pemberton, the executive director of ACLU, asking for an explanation of the apparent contradiction, and Wulf is convinced that Rauh actually tried to have him fired. Up until then, however, Wulf had functioned as a trusted member of the liberal team.

The LCDC was organized quickly. On May 20th, 1964, the formation of the committee was announced at a press conference. Hundreds of lawyers were recruited to come down south on a rotating basis. They came from big Wall Street firms and from hustling Brooklyn practices. Al Levine from Strook, Strook and Levant came down and stayed for a year. Lawyers were thrown in jail. They lived with famiies or in hotels and experienced the phenomenon of Mississippi as Wulf wanted them to. Wulf explains:

"LCDC lawyers were in courts, they were conferring with the police and with local officials and experiencing the whole thing. We were radicalizing a whole lot of New York lawyers and showing them what was going on down south."

But there were tensions between the LCDC lawyers and civil rights workers, particularly those in SNCC. At orientation sessions at Columbia the lawyers were told that they were serving the movement but that they were not the movement. In spite of this, some of the more aggressive among them did try to influence policy. They feared the left political orientation of SNCC. "It was their historic antileft political interest," Wulf asserts. "SNCC was called a tool of the Russians. But it was a figment of their imagination. SNCC was an open, democratic organization of young blacks. . . . They stopped a lot of creative politics by stifling everything to the left of the ADA."

George Crockett of the guild project in Mississippi felt the pressure from the LCDC. Formally established in Mississippi in June of 1964, the guild project "was going all right," Crockett recollects. Then, in July, LCDC, as a coalition of liberal anti-Communist lawyers supported by the NAACP, CORE, the ACLU, and both the American Jewish Congress and the American Jewish Committee, charged in. According to Crockett, "They evidently had quite a lot of money, and in those days, if you had anything, you had more than the guild had to operate on in Mississippi." Wasting no time, they opened an office in Jackson and spent a considerable amount fixing up an accommodation for their lawyers and establishing an excellent law library.

Crockett was certain that the new committee wanted to preempt the guild, but insists that because of the guild's effectiveness, they weren't able to do so. "We had an effective operation and it was an inexpensive operation. We didn't need a lot of money, and because of that, we were in a position to do things others couldn't." The hostility intensified. Prominent liberal lawyers would not even speak to old friends who were associated with the guild. The one exception was Wulf, who tried to open channels of communication between the two groups ("playing at building bridges," he says) on the grounds that they were both fighting for the same objective: the registration of voters.

30.

The "headlines" in Lowenstein's diary-newspaper for Sunday, April 12, to Thursday, April 16, 1964, reveal not only his state of mind about what was happening in Mississippi but the ambiguity of his own role. Across the top of the page, Lowenstein wrote: "Mississippi Mire: Frenzied Recruiting + Firm Withdrawal = Schizophrenia."

In the center column, he wrote:

A SUMMARY OF THE SITUATION
In Mississippi—
At Campus 'Centers'
In National Orgs—
Amongst Ind. Groups—

In the left-hand column, he wrote: "'Wrong' Decisions and 'Wrong' Group Making Them Combine to End 'Deep' Commitment; Problem Rises of Who to Tell How Much. CAMPUS 'CENTER' LEADERS IN MIXED ROLES. Obligation to Keep Them Informed Called 'Great' But Particularly on Question of 'Infiltration' Dilemma Is Acute and Has Not Been Solved."

And in the right-hand column: "Project Still 'Right,' Desire to Help Strong, But Policy Disagreements Make Presence During The Summer Seem 'Unwise' SO SPEECH SCHEDULE WILL BE FULFILLED. Participation as Lawyer 'In Ranks' Still Possible but 'Priorities' Make It Unlikely If L.G. Stays; 'Success' of Drive for Students Is a Surprise."

Lowenstein was torn between his support for the Summer Project as a worthy exercise in the registration of black voters, and his hostility to both SNCC and the Lawyers Guild. Clearly, he also felt an obligation to inform on those he believed were infiltrating the movement. If he quit the project, he would no longer be in a position to report to the "Campus Centers," whose leaders played double roles, both helping to recruit students for the Summer Project and receiving information from Lowenstein on suspected Communist infiltration.

Faced with this dilemma, Lowenstein decided to continue his speaking engagements for the Summer Project, holding out the possibility that he might join it as a lawyer "in the ranks." He would then have access to information without identifying with what he believed to be a Communist-manipulated effort. It is known that the CIA had established centers on the campuses of many American universities. In his recruiting efforts at some of these universities, Lowenstein was working with people who had been affiliated with the CIA or had participated in CIA-sponsored projects. William Sloane Coffin at Yale, whom Lowenstein wanted to head the Summer Project, had worked for the CIA. Barney Frank at Harvard had been with the Independent Research Service delegation to Helsinki, an operation which, by Frank's own admission, he clearly understood was CIA backed. Frank jokes about the role of fellow delegate Gloria Steinem, whom he describes as running around at nightclubs set up by the CIA in Helsinki, helping to win over Africans from the Communists.

Lowenstein was vacillating between wanting to quit the project outright on the grounds that the Communist threat outweighed both the benefits of information and voter registration, and wanting to help it in some way that would demonstrate his support for voter registration and allow him to inform on the suspected Communist infiltrators. Later in April, he wrote: "'A' 'withdraws' From Project After Moses Insists on L.G. and Limits Students to 400; Summer Will Be Spent Working On the Novel. (M.W. 'Wonders' If Moses Decision 'Binds' others, Sets N.O. Confab.)." Then, in May, Lowenstein noted: "Miss. 'No' final, 'A' Tells King. But He Would Help at Convention; Offer of Tougaloo Deanship Declined."

While he struggled with Mississippi, Lowenstein was also dealing with the question of his job at North Carolina State. He had been led to believe he was not going to be reappointed. He had used up the possibilities of his assistant professorship but didn't want to leave under a cloud. The chancellor, John Tyler Caldwell, was not planning to act on Lowenstein's reappointment until June. George Gullette, Lowenstein's department chairman told him that his civil rights actions were "not the issue," calling the decision on his reappointment "tough."

Lowenstein was really looking to leave honorably. He wrote in his diary in April: "Caldwell Hints at Announcement on May 29. 'A' May 'act' Sooner: NCS Honorary 'Taps' Him in Class. Surprise Blue Key Selection 'Helpful.' Quiet Display of Support Weighed as a Public Statement. Student Press May Aid."

The student support turned the tide for Lowenstein. The Blue Key award as the outstanding teacher at NC State made it virtually impossible for the administration not to reappoint him. When the reappointment came, pressure mounted for him to stay on at least through 1964–65, but Lowenstein told Gullette that he felt he should leave what he called a "dead end," finally agreeing to defer his departure until Gullette could find an adequate replacement.

John Tyler Caldwell, who does not remember any denial of reappointment in Lowenstein's case, adds: "I remember Allard Lowenstein's decision to go somewhere else. Whether I felt like he relieved us of a problem of his going, I don't know, I might have. Because Allard wasn't doing much for the university about then, except he was an extraordinary teacher." Repeating the phrase of a friend from the political science department at Stanford, Caldwell says that Lowenstein was so good, "He was a regular Pied Piper. If he started saying anything to students, why they just followed him, just like the old Pied Piper. He was an extraordinary human being."

31.

For an obscure assistant professor at North Carolina State, Lowenstein traveled in remarkably high places. On April 21, 1964, the *Raleigh Times*, reported that "Al Lowenstein, Professor of Social Studies at N.C. State, was the dinner guest of Senator and Mrs. William Fulbright of Ark. this past weekend in Washington, D.C. President and Mrs. Lyndon B. Johnson, Secretary of Defense Robert S. McNamara and Adlai Stevenson were also guests of the Fulbrights."

Lowenstein's connections at the very top of the political hierarchy and the trust he had at the grassroots level, put him in a unique position as a mediator between the Johnson administration and the civil rights movement. It is doubtful that Lyndon Johnson, who was aware of the most minute details of the government, could have been unaware of Lowenstein's CIA affiliation. Johnson knew he needed help on civil rights from someone who could be trusted not to upset the apple cart. Around the country, public opinion was rallying behind the black activists in Mississippi who wanted to establish a base within the Democratic party. With his powerful "I have a dream" speech at the March on Washington, Martin Luther King, Jr., had become a legend. But Johnson wanted the support of the blacks and the whites in the South. This required political virtuosity, and Lowenstein, who was close to Johnson's attorney general, Robert Kennedy, had that in large supply.

Deeply involved with what was going on in Mississippi, Kennedy's people were intent on keeping out the Communists and preventing a split in the Democratic party, and Lowenstein was ready to help.

When Lowenstein, who was serving as an advisor to Martin Luther King, Jr., offered to "help" at the "convention," he was referring to help with the challenge Mississippi blacks were preparing to make at the 1964 presidential convention that summer in Atlantic City. They planned to demand that their own delegates be seated in place of the all-white delegation selected by the regular Mississippi Democratic party. Though Lyndon Johnson, who succeeded to the presidency after Kennedy's assassination, was expected to be nominated, the vice-presidential nominee and the party's platform were still up for discussion.

From the Freedom Vote for Aaron Henry had evolved a Freedom party. As early as February, 1964, SNCC organizers were registering blacks in a "freedom registration" drive separate from the ongoing regular registration process enrolling blacks in the Democratic party. Moses told the COFO convention on February 9 that the purpose was to involve all blacks in the state in the democratic process. But Moses also wanted to create a political operation that would gain recognition as the "legitimate Democratic party organization in Mississippi." As Clayborne Carson has written, "This new party, soon called the Mississippi Freedom Democratic party (MFDP), was designed as a vehicle to challenge the regular party at the national Democratic Convention, to be held in August in Atlantic City, New Jersey."

Later, Lowenstein would be given credit by Norman Thomas and leading journalists such as David Halberstam for founding the MFDP, credit he would accept. But while he played an essential role in launching the MFDP, which did evolve from the Freedom Vote, it is inaccurate to describe Lowenstein as its "founder." Lowenstein advised Moses, who was influenced by his strategic sense. To this extent, Lowenstein was a catalytic agent in the creation of the MFDP.

News of the MFDP challenge to the all-white regular Mississippi Democratic party galvanized northern liberals who responded with support. In March, Ella Baker and Bob Moses approached Joseph Rauh, who agreed to help the MFDP and was named its counsel. Rauh was dedicated to civil rights and had considerable leverage within the Democratic party and the liberal establishment. As general counsel to the United Auto Workers, he had access to one of the country's most powerful unions, whose leader, Walter Reuther, was close to President Johnson and Senator Hubert Humphrey. As vice-president of the ADA, Rauh was at the center of liberal power. If the blacks of the MFDP wanted to gain access to the Democratic party and be seated as delegates to the 1964 Democratic National Convention in Atlantic City, Rauh was the perfect person to help. Rauh was a close friend and ally of Allard Lowenstein's, and Lowenstein was in and out of Mississippi, the eyes and ears of the white liberals.

Walter Reuther disapproved of Rauh's position with the MFDP, but he reluctantly acceded to Rauh's insistence and the UAW put up some money. But Rauh would soon break with Ella Baker, who thought that pressure from Johnson and the UAW limited Rauh's freedom of action. Having come to prefer Arthur Kinoy and William Kunstler, who along with Hunter Morey and Benjamin Smith comprised the COFO Legal Advisory Committee, she asked Rauh to step aside. At the same time, the UAW, fearing Johnson's wrath and not wanting to endanger Hubert Humphrey's chances for the vice-presidency, was also pressing Rauh to resign from the MFDP position. To Johnson, the Mississippi Freedom Democratic party "was like a gnat to be crushed on the way to the convention."

Rauh strenuously opposed the Lawyers Guild and objected to Baker's reliance on them. Rauh recalls: "The Lawyers Guild tried to get me thrown out as counsel for the Mississippi Democratic party. They used Ella Baker and I suppose they used Ella Baker on Al too. . . . She came in here one day and started insulting me. . . . I had enough internal fortitude to let it roll of my back, so they didn't get control and their role wasn't very significant in the Mississippi Freedom Democratic party. The Lawyers Guild was never involved primarily for the interests of the blacks. They wanted to have confrontations, and we didn't want to see confrontations. We wanted to win something. The Lawyers Guild people were not in it in '63 and they weren't in it in Atlantic City, at least as far as my recollection. I think Al felt that they would never take a position against Russia."

The MFDP was formally constituted on April 24, 1964, in Jackson. A small crowd of some 200 people showed up, but Len Holt, a black lawyer who had been the first to appeal to the Lawyers Guild for help, wrote that the meeting was permeated by a feeling of "impertinence and irrelevance; these few dare to dream of challenging the traditional Mississippi Democrats. . . . It was ridiculous by any standard other than that of SNCC." When MFDP backers were turned away from the regular Democratic precinct and county meetings, they held their own MFDP meetings and nominated four candidates for the Democratic primary in June. Fannie Lou Hamer of SNCC, a poor black woman from a sharecropper's family who became a symbol of the Mississippi struggle, ran as a congressional candidate while Victoria Gray opposed incumbent Senator John Stennis. The effort to integrate the Democratic party in Mississippi gathered momentum as the Summer Project proceeded.

Moses says that Lowenstein's influence on the Summer Project is best measured by the numbers of students he recruited. "Lowenstein had so much influence with NSA. The presence of so many NSA chapters tells you how much he influenced the Mississippi summer," he states. By Moses' account, about 1,000 Lowenstein recruits eventually came to Mississippi that summer, many of them Lowenstein loyalists with NSA connections, among whom there were products of the best prep schools and universities in America, like Greg Craig, and sons of the powerful, like Jerry Brown, whose father was California Governor Pat Brown. And there were others of more modest circumstances, like Dennis Sweeney who had dropped out of Stanford for a year to stay on in Mississippi after the Freedom Vote.

Sweeney was not well off. His father was a military man who left his family in Portland, Oregon, for an assignment in England when

Sweeney was born in 1943. Sweeney was two when he saw his father for the last time on a brief visit, after which the only news of him came when he was killed in Korea. For a while the boy lived with his grandparents and then on a boys' ranch before his mother married Jerry Sweeney and he was adopted by his stepfather. According to Teresa Carpenter, "he did not want to take his stepfather's name. He did not much like Jerry Sweeney, a perfectionist who demanded that the hair in his household be combed and the ashtrays emptied. At eighteen, he was liberated by a scholarship to Stanford."

Sweeney understood the resentment the poor blacks felt toward the wealthy white students in Mississippi. It was not unlike his own feelings toward the affluent and often arrogant students at Stanford. Like Lowenstein, who was undersized as a child and often felt left out, Sweeney identified with the underdog. Sweeney had been abandoned by his father and was from the wrong side of the tracks. Both men needed heroes and role models. Lowenstein found his in Frank Graham, Eleanor Roosevelt, Norman Thomas, and Adlai Stevenson; Sweeney found his in Lowenstein.

In his civil rights work, Sweeney discovered camaraderie and purpose. He wanted to take risks and he volunteered to be arrested during the Freedom Vote. For the Freedom Summer, he asked to be assigned to McComb, "the most dangerous assignment in the state, the place one went only if one was prepared to die," according to Carpenter. "The whites were more vicious and more inclined to violence than elsewhere. Sweeney was, furthermore, one of the first whites to integrate the project there, a fact which SNCC knew was certain to draw violence upon the McComb Freedom House. The eight blacks and two whites who shared the frame house at 702 Wall Street knew that they might be killed on a whim."

Greg Craig recollects his first meeting with Dennis Sweeney in the summer of 1964: "During the early part of that summer, I worked on the Stanford University campus. That was when I first met Dennis Sweeney. Dennis became somewhat of a hero to me. He had dropped out of Stanford for a year to go to Mississippi with Al to work on Aaron's gubernatorial campaign, and he was back at Stanford negotiating with the authorities for his reentry for the Fall semester."

As he got to know Sweeney, Craig found him "quiet, intense, a loner." But says Craig, "That was part of the charisma to me. He seemed an incipient saint. He appeared to be a very serious person, dedicated to very serious goals, capable of devoting his entire life to a cause, smoldering and burning with an almost uncontrollable passion for social justice. He was, in fact, thoughtful, apparently gentle, seemingly kind. Everyone seemed to know Dennis; everyone respected him; actually, everyone was in awe of Dennis. Unlike Al, who combined his social crusading with a sense of humor and a love of fun, life around Dennis was heavy. He was uncomfortable to be with for any period of time. Dennis never seemed able to forget the horror of what he had seen in Mississippi. He didn't talk about it much. He just seemed to be like the first person back from Dachau, not able to talk about it, his very demeanor bearing witness to the atrocities that he had seen. Dennis did make one feel somehow unworthy for not being as dedicated and pure and socially involved as he was. In that way, Dennis was a model, an ideal, and as I say, a bit of a hero. In June 1964, one could have described Dennis as being angry, as being moody, as being introverted. It would have been inaccurate then to say he was crazy."

Waves of volunteers for the Summer Project began arriving on June 13, 1964, in Oxford, Ohio, for orientation sessions at Western College for Women. They were trained in voter registration and for teaching at the Freedom Schools, and screened by psychiatrists and civil rights workers. The object of this process, writes Clayborne Carson, was to "eliminate persons who were deemed 'dangerous to the movement.'" A COFO memorandum cautioned against anyone who was "wrapped up in himself" and thus could not "reach out and help those we are dealing with." It also recommended avoiding those who were "limited in their perspectives," such as only being willing to teach in a Freedom School. Another poor candidate was the "well-meaning idealist who wants to secure equality and brotherly love for all, and is solidly anti-politics." Finally, the memorandum warned against the "bright college student" who had "all the answers" and knew "what's being done wrong" and "how to do it right." On the contrary, COFO sought people who were "realistic," "responsible," "flexible," and "understanding." Among those who were deemed acceptable was Dennis Sweeney.

But while Sweeney remained committed to the Mississippi Summer Project, Lowenstein, disturbed by Bob Moses' determination to use the Lawyers Guild, said he was withdrawing from the project, citing "personal" reasons. He contacted the Stanford recruits, advising them of his decision and telling them not to come.

In June, Lowenstein flew to Europe, writing "Finances Well Off Despite Gifts, Setbacks." He also noted: "'A' off to Europe to Ease Sudden R.D. Crisis, Reuther Spanish Trip Opposed in Frankfurt," and "Beukes Bank Position to Keep Him In Norway." Lowenstein was adept at shifting gears, keeping his international CIA work compartmentalized and separate from his domestic activities.

But while he was abroad, fear of Communism at home and the possibility that violence had been committed in Mississippi forced him to reassess his Mississippi role again. He wrote in his diary: "Norman Thomas, Schlesinger, Elder Binghams Fear Reds Are Running Project. Ask A To Return At Once, Apparently To Encourage Withdrawals; He Suggests M.W. Be Consulted, Doubts Value of Curtailing Trip. 3 Students Reported 'Missing' As First of Influx Arrives." (In addition to Norman Thomas and Arthur Schlesinger, Jr., Lowenstein was working with Congressman Jonathan Bingham of the Bronx, whose brother was also an influential liberal and whose nephew, Stephen, a Yale undergraduate, was a volunteer for the Mississippi Summer. M.W. was the lawyer, Mel Wulf.)

The three missing students were CORE volunteer James Chaney, a twenty-one-year-old black Mississippian, Michael Schwerner, twenty-four, a white New York social worker who had been put in charge of CORE's Meridian office, and Andrew Goodman, twenty-one, a Queens College student who was in the first group of volunteers to arrive in Mississippi. They had left Meridian to investigate a case of arson at a black church and had been arrested in Philadelphia, Mississippi. Denied the right to make a telephone call, they had been released from jail by Neshoba County Deputy Sheriff Cecil Price and executed on a "lonely road outside Philadelphia" by Klansmen. SNCC workers suspected that the three were dead and Moses observed coldly, "No privileged group in history has every given up anything without some kind of blood sacrifice." On August 4, their murder was confirmed when the bodies were discovered in an earth-fill dam on a farm near Philadelphia.

Lowenstein wrote in his diary in late June before the discovery of the bodies: "3 Probable Deaths 'Dictate' July Return To Mississippi, Effort to 'Rally' Liberals; Offer Of Help To Be Wired To Moses and RFK." Lowenstein now called for a "united front" in Mississippi because of the fate of the three civil rights workers, telling his student-followers that it was acceptable to join the Summer Project. Then he wrote in his diary: "N.T., RFK, Propose 'Investigatory' Mission, But 'A' Defers Trip and Decision About Status; Rustin Won't Go; P.A. Compliance Is General." Still fearful about Communist infiltration in the civil rights movement in Mississippi, Norman Thomas and Robert Kennedy wanted Lowenstein back to keep tabs on what was going on.

The violence escalated. Dennis Sweeney was the target of a bombing in McComb. "At about four o'clock one July morning, the Freedom House was bombed," wrote Teresa Carpenter. "A blast calculated at the equivalent of 17 sticks of dynamite went off six feet from Sweeney's bed. Miraculously he suffered only a mild concussion." Lowenstein observed in his diary: "Sweeney Hurt In McComb Bombing. A Off To Jackson With 'Conditions' For Broad Support of FDP Challenge, Rustin Not Hopeful—Brief Visit Will Include a 'Tour'—Rustin Scathing About White 'Guilt.'"

Lowenstein had established the basis for his return to Mississippi. He would go make a brief information-gathering trip and relay the conditions for support of the Mississippi Freedom Democratic party challenge to the white delegation at the Democratic convention in Atlantic City. Bayard Rustin, the highly experienced organizer of the March on Washington, who was strongly anti-Communist, was dubious about the outcome. The integration of the Mississippi Democratic party and support for the Freedom Democratic party clearly had its price. Lowenstein wrote again in his diary: "Rustin, MLK to Join Jackson Meeting Thursday To Work Out MDP Plan; RFK Heads Sponsors List. N.Y. 'Terms' O.K.d in Jackson; MLK will stump for FDP. 'Moses Asks A To Stay On'."

Lowenstein was making headway on the MFDP challenge. He had Martin Luther King, Jr., aboard and Robert Kennedy as a sponsor. And Bob Moses, who insists he did not see Lowenstein that summer, was, according to Lowenstein's diary, pressing for him to remain in Mississippi. The passage of the Civil Rights Act during the weekend of July 4, 1964, with its sweeping public accommodations provisions, could have caused even further violence. When white radicals working with SNCC shouted angrily that they were going out to integrate every fucking restaurant in Greenwood," Stokely Carmichael calmed them down with a brilliant display of rhetoric and reason, reminding them that their primary objective was to register as many blacks as possible and that the violence they would probably provoke would only hamper their efforts. Nearby, Martin Luther King, Jr., still the most powerful orator and respected figure of the movement, was also holding a crowd in the palm of his hand. As his voice rose and fell in the familiar cadences, a thousand people who had packed into the tiny church responded with the traditional "Amens" and "Yes, brother." Guild lawyer Sanford Katz, the only white in the audience, was grabbed affectionately as the congregation broke into "We Shall Overcome." "If King had told them to march on Meridian or fly to the moon, they would have done it," Katz asserts. The power of the Mississippi summer was being felt in Congress and the White House; a voting rights act would be passed in 1965. There was reason to believe that the Democratic party could be the vehicle for change and that blacks had a role in it, even in Mississippi.

Greg Craig remembers joining Lowenstein in Mississippi that summer: "I finally made it down to Mississippi later that summer, meeting up with Al in Jackson. He had left the state . . . because of a falling out with the other organizers of the summer project (particularly Bob Moses). But Al told me that when Schwerner, Goodman and Chaney were killed in Philadelphia, Neshoba County, it was necessary for everyone to close ranks and present a united front. Al would refrain from criticizing the political orientation of the project, and he would return and help."

Driving north from Jackson with Frank Roosevelt and another civil rights worker, Craig remembers a stop at Batesville where the atmosphere was threatening, then crossing the state border into Tennessee. "The wave of relief that swept through the car was unbelievable." he recounts. "The top of the car came off; we took the car roof down, and with the sun beating down on our heads and the wind whipping through our hair, we bellowed freedom songs and Baptist hymns all the way to Minneapolis where the National Student Association Congress was being held."

Craig had planned to drive from Minneapolis to Atlantic City for the Democratic convention with Lowenstein. But Lowenstein, short of time, flew instead, and Craig met him there.

Dennis Sweeney was also in Atlantic City, where he was involved in the effort to introduce the Mississippi Freedom Democratic party delegates to other convention delegates. Craig recalls driving around Atlantic City with Sweeney, "in a car filled with black sharecroppers who were members of the MFDP delegation, singing songs, telling stories, going from hotel to hotel, and walking into the Michigan delegation's party and the Oregon delegation's party and the Minnesota delegation's party. It was a new world for the black Mississippians, but they seemed to take it in stride. I remember Unita Blackwell, who seemed particularly fond of Dennis, bursting into song after coming out of the Oregon caucus, 'Take me home, take me home, this ain't where I b'long.'

"Dennis was a different person in Atlantic City from what he had been in Mississippi and when I met him in June on the Stanford campus. He wore dark slacks and a sports jacket; he was well-kempt [sic] and polite and friendly, Mr. All-American Boy. When we appeared at the Oregon caucus, he introduced me to Senator Wayne Morse and Congresswoman Edith Green as if he spent all his time with members of the House and Senate. They seemed to know him."

The MFDP supported Johnson while the all-white regular Mississippi delegation, smarting from the passage of the civil rights legislation, disdained the loyalty oath which pledged delegates to support the Democratic ticket if their credentials were to be accepted. Rumors of a walk-out by the South were rampant. In the confusion of a great national convention, at which the most powerful president in history was anointing himself and choosing a running mate, the question of who represented Mississippi took on increasing significance. Fearful of disruption, Johnson ordered the FBI to bug the pro-MFDP forces at the convention, including SNCC's Atlantic City offices.

Lowenstein, who considered his resignation from North Carolina State "final," since a replacement for him had been found, was calling his novel a "top priority" at the time, but he also believed a campaign position for him was "probable." Hubert Humphrey's "lead for VP Suggests Work For Him May Be Best," Lowenstein noted. Johnson, relying on Humphrey to solve the MFDP problem for him, was dangling the vice-presidency before him as an inducement. Humphrey, in turn, was relying on Walter Reuther for help, and Reuther passed the pressure on to the UAW's lawyer, Joe Rauh. Rauh, who was representing the MFDP at the convention before the Credentials Committee, knew that his support for their challenge could cost him the UAW connection. Indeed, Reuther was reported to have said to Martin Luther King, Jr., "If you don't stop those people, you'll never get another cent from the UAW."

There appeared to be no way of reconciling the demands of the MFDP and those of the all-white regular Mississippi delegation. Lowenstein wrote cryptically: "F.D.P. Prospects Fading; Rustin Rejects Role; LBJ 'Understanding' With White Party Indicated; Evers, R.L.T. Smith Weigh Public Break with SNCC. HBS, Carter Opposed to Concessions to F.D.P." Bayard Rustin, after years as an outsider, was safely ensconced in organized labor and would not challenge Reuther. Black Mississippi Democrats such as Charles Evers, also fearful of offending Johnson, sought to disassociate themselves from SNCC, while even white Mississippi liberals like Hodding Carter were against accommodating the MFDP. But Joe Rauh and Bobby Kennedy continued to support the MFDP, as Lowenstein indicated when he wrote: "Rauh, RFK Ask 'A' Aid to MFDP at Convention; He insists on 'proper bid.'"

Lowenstein then wrote: "FDP 'Atmosphere Troubling' Despite Rauh Enthusiasm; Contact With W.H. [Reuther] via H.C. Likely if 'Assurances' On Delegation Control and C.D. Are Not Obtained. Liberals' 'Box' Growing Tighter; Rustin, MLK Seek LBJ Interview— Church Parley, EFC Exhorted to Aid 'Long Mississippi Struggle'."

Lowenstein was troubled by the increasing militancy of the MFDP and its threats to rely on civil disobedience ("C.D.") at the convention. But when he received assurances that civil disobedience would not be relied on, he continued his support and wrote: "All-out Fight Underway After Aaron Henry Pledges F.D.P. EC Will Be In Charge, Appoints 'A' 'Adviser'; C.D. Out; LBJ Warns He'll 'Grind Down' Foes— COFO 'Overhaul' Due. Rauh Undeterred; A Pleads for Wires, Heads To Convention 'Relieved' to be 'Strong for F.D.P.'" Lowenstein expected a "showdown" and noted "F.D.P. Role Complicates Campaign Post Outlook." Aaron Henry, who was with the MFDP delegation, saw to it that the MFDP executive committee ("EC") would be in charge and not SNCC, appointing Lowenstein its advisor.

As Johnson's position toughened, the MFDP delegation and the civil rights workers who had accompanied them to Atlantic City grew more defiant. SNCC organizer Mendy Samstein explains that "Johnson wanted to have a unanimous convention. There was this gadfly Mississippi group bugging this up, which gave us our leverage. There was a feeling of power, of countermanding the wishes of the president." Samstein, who considered Bob Moses the major force behind the MFDP in Atlantic City adds: "It was 'heady.' It explains the anger of the Mississippi group, which I identified with and which was articulated by Bob. The press knew his influence. He was the key man; he was calling the shots."

Word eventually came down that the president was prepared to accept two at-large delegates from the MFDP as a compromise, while the regular Mississippi all-white delegation would also be seated. The two named by Johnson were Aaron Henry and Ed King. There was also a promise to prohibit segregated delegations from being seated in 1968 at the next convention but those who favored the compromise were quickly labeled sellouts by MFDP leaders and militant SNCC workers. Among the critics were Robert Moses, Ella Baker, and James Forman, as well as Fanny Lou Hamer, whose symbolic role in the struggle had been strengthened when Joe Rauh put her on television at the start of the convention as a witness before the Credentials Committee. She had told them that black prisoners had been beaten on orders from state highway patrolmen, adding: "I was beat until I was exhausted. . . . I began to scream, and one white man got up and began to beat me on the head and tell me to hush. . . . All of this on account we want to register, to become first-class citizens. If the Freedom Democratic party is not seated now, I question America."

Rauh placed himself in the middle saying that he favored the compromise but would fight to the end for the position of his client. Lowenstein later told Barney Frank that his own position had been misunderstood. "He said he was not for the compromise as stated with the two named," Frank explains. "He said they should have counteroffered to name the two delegates." Humphrey, who was waiting on pins and needles to see if he would be named vice-president, could not take a position hostile to Johnson.

The idea for the compromise had come to Johnson as he watched Fanny Lou Hamer on television. Johnson was incensed. He was going to take care of all the injustice; he wanted that accepted as a matter of faith. When the news was relayed by Bayard Rustin to the MFDP delegation that Humphrey, Walter Reuther, and Dr. King wanted to meet with representatives of the MFDP delegation, specifically Aaron Henry and Ed King, Moses requested that Fanny Lou Hamer be included and that he be allowed to attend as well.

The meeting was held in Martin Luther King, Jr.'s, suite. Rauh, in the living room, discussed a lobbying effort to seat the entire MFDP delegation. According to Lowenstein—who told his version to Rauh—Martin Luther King, Jr., Moses, and Lowenstein were meeting at the same time in the bedroom. King and Moses both agreed, Lowenstein told Rauh, that if they couldn't do any better, they should accept the two at-large delegates.

Moses insists that this separate meeting did not take place. "I didn't meet with Lowenstein at the convention," he asserts. "He was still annoyed about the Lawyers Guild." Joe Rauh asserts, "I am saying that I have a clear recollection of Al telling me that Moses and King said that if we can't get more than the two, we'll take the two." According to Rauh, who years later went to see Moses in Boston to ask him about the meeting, "He [Moses] was unclear what Al had said. He didn't say to me 'Well, Al's a liar. I never approved it.' He simply was unclear about it."

The next day, Rauh, who was not only the MFDP lawyer, but a delegate to the convention from the District of Columbia and a member of the Credentials Committee, was astonished to find Lowenstein at a meeting in Humphrey's suite where Lowenstein was apparently trying to work out an acceptable compromise with an unyielding Democratic party.

In addition to the leaders of the Mississippi Freedom Party, and Rauh himself, who came as their lawyer, the meeting was attended by a congresswoman from Oregon, Edith Green. According to Rauh, "you couldn't get in for love nor money. There were security guards and secret service and every goddamned thing, and I walked in the room, and there sitting on the bed was Al. Now I had it in the back of my head to ask that son of a bitch how the hell he got in that room. He had no official connection with either side, but there he was, and a couple of times when people were getting hot, Al said calm words that were efforts to resolve the problem. But still today, I don't know how the hell he got in that room. The only person in that room who had identical views with me was Al."

Rauh saw the dispute as basically academic and favored seating everybody. "My position was seat all of them. Seat all of the Mississippi Freedom Democratic party and seat all of the whites too. What the fuck's the difference? There weren't going to be any votes at that convention. Johnson was going to be president and whoever he mentioned was going to be vice-president. There wasn't any question of a vote coming at the convention." Yet, Rauh was committed to the MFDP challenge, and with the help of Eleanor Holmes Norton, then a recent graduate of Yale Law School, and H. Miles Jaffe, he prepared and filed a brief for the MFDP arguing that the whites should be excluded and the entire MFDP delegation seated. Norton was also handling the lobbying effort in Atlantic City for Ella Baker, approaching delegations from other states to convince them that the MFDP should be seated.

Convinced that Rauh, whom she respected, was doing his best to win the challenge, Norton was surprised to learn that Ella Baker considered him ineffective. "It's hard to know who really the players were," asserts Norton, who opposed the compromise herself, explaining: "The reason the SNCC people were turned off on the compromise was because we had seen the face of Mississippi racism up close. We had been surrounded every day by the White Citizens' Council. I disagreed, we, everybody in SNCC, with the 'two people.' But Al, Bayard, King, and Joe were all for accepting it."

Norton says, "I knew Al well and respected him. There were many in SNCC who had animosities toward Al because when Al was involved in something, he was up-front. The whole civil rights establishment wanted the compromise but Al was more visible. SNCC resented the vigor with which Al pushed it, but they resented King, everyone." And Mendy Samstein adds: "Al and his group, Rauh, Reuther, were establishment politicians, Schlesinger was a Kennedy man, so they felt like they had accomplished something, and in their minds this was good and the others were naive and inexperienced. There was an accusatory tone on both sides. Each side thought they were the good guys. Al felt offended and hurt by the anger of the Mississippi group and how it turned on their best allies, as if they were biting the hand that fed it. He could not understand Bob's argument why the compromise was unacceptable. Bob had started the Mississippi project from the day one in 1960. Bob's articulation of the issues was key—legitimacy and the rest—enough to make people feel we could not compromise. The compromise was dangerous. Mississippi was dangerous. People got killed there. To accept less than the demands of the MFDP would lead to further killings. This would appear as if it was business as usual, with a little toning down. The Mississippi people felt the establishment group didn't know the inner desperation of the situation. Al was flighty. He was in and out. He arrived at the airport, he met with Bob for five hours. He was not there the way the other people were and subject to danger."

With the tension mounting, Rauh proffered his own compromise. Having discovered that in 1944, when Johnson himself was a delegate from Texas, there had been a dispute and two Texas delegations had been seated, splitting the vote, Rauh suggested that both delegations be seated this time as well. "So my position going into the thing was seat us and don't seat them; at the convention, I floated this."

But Johnson resisted. At a meeting of powerful southern governors, he had reportedly been told point blank by John Connolly of Texas that if the black delegation of the MFDP was seated, "we will walk out." There was a growing fear that if the white southerners all walked out, the way they had in 1948 when they supported Strom Thurmond rather than Truman, then Goldwater could be elected.

When he became convinced that his own compromises would not float, Rauh continued to fight for the seating of the full MFDP delegation, with the whites excluded, though he says he knew that they weren't going to get it.

Rauh understood that nobody wanted to buck Johnson and that Johnson was prepared to go no further; while he says that he was "flabbergasted" when he first learned of it at the Credentials Committee meeting, the president had at least given the MFDP his own compromise, by naming Henry and King as the delegates. Johnson was not going to have the South walk out. The talk of backlash was escalating, and Walter Reuther told Rauh, "Joe, you're electing Goldwater with this fight." To which Rauh says he replied, "Well, that's bullshit."

Lowenstein, however, was more optimistic as he wrote in his diary: "'Fraternal' Status Rejected by F.D.P. Minority Report Assured, Victory Prospects Good in a Floor Fight. 13 Defy W.H. [Reuther] Pressure. A to 3H: 'Not Logic But Facts' Are Involved; Credentials Delay May Produce A New Offer." Lowenstein was referring to thirteen Credentials Committee members who had said that they would not yield to Reuther and had agreed to support a minority report. The strategy was to get the minority report to the floor and pass it. 3H was Humphrey (Hubert Horatio Humphrey), and Lowenstein was growing impatient with him. Lowenstein thought he had a deal for the MFDP; he had compromised himself for it.

With the issue unresolved, Rauh and Lowenstein attended an August 26 meeting of the MFDP delegation held in an Atlantic City church. At a prior caucus, the MFDP had vocally denounced the compromise without reaching a final decision. The night before the church meeting, they had met again and rejected the compromise, indicating however their support for the Rauh proposal to seat every member of each delegation who signed the loyalty oath, dividing the delegation's vote proportionally. But on Humphrey's urging, they had agreed to reconsider and hear the arguments of speakers for Johnson's compromise before taking a vote. One of the scheduled speakers was Joe Rauh.

Bayard Rustin spoke in favor of the compromise, urging the delegates not to forget their friends in organized labor, whose help they would need in the future. SNCC organizer Mendy Samstein shouted at him: "You're a traitor, Bayard, a traitor! Sit down!" The meeting, according to James Forman, was in an "uproar" when Martin Luther King, Jr., spoke. He told them that he did not intend to tell them how to vote but that he knew Hubert Humphrey would work for a strong Civil Rights Commission and that a meeting with Lyndon Johnson would be arranged. King was received politely but without much enthusiasm. He was losing his magic with this crowd.

After King, Rauh spoke. In fact, although Rauh says he was unaware of it at the time, the choice was no longer theirs to make. It had already been decided, at the highest levels, to go with Johnson's compromise, and the outcome of both the Credentials Committee meeting and the church meeting were moot. Not knowing this, Rauh told the church gathering that he considered the compromise of two at-large delegates a victory, but added, "I am with you and I want you to know we're going to work to make the resolution work." His statement provoked a tirade from Ella Baker. "Ella Baker cut up the white lib-erals, and cut me up," Rauh remembers bitterly. "And there was start-ing to be trouble even before we ever knew what we could get. So I don't know whatever caused me to say this, but at the meeting I said 'I'm going to the Credentials Committee now and I just don't know how it's going to come out, but I sort of hope there'll be tolerance for Hubert and for the others who have done so much for the civil rights fight.' That just set her off like an animal. She attacked me. I went out the door and led the fight at the Credentials Committee with Ella Baker's attack ringing in my ears."

Lowenstein, who observed the denunciations, wrote in his diary: "Samstein, Tillow Join List To Be 'Examined.' Heckling of Rustin, 'Ex-treme Misstatements' Stir Queries. Carmichael's Talk 'Wild.'" As Stokely Carmichael and other SNCC leaders started to sound more radical, Lowenstein reacted. His "list" can be viewed as an ironic har-binger of Nixon's enemies list, on which he, Lowenstein, would one day find himself. Samstein, however, discounts a political motive in Lowenstein's "list." "My sense of it is that it was a high-intensity mo-ment as far as politics go, and unique. If you look at what was being said at the moment, you would get a false impression. This makes too much of the politics and not enough of the anger." Coming from the other side, he points out, that anger took the form of a certain pre-dictable kind of criticism leveled at Lowenstein. "A lot of people were critical of Al," Samstein relates. "They didn't like his style. He was a globe hopper. The CIA allegations come from the other side of the coin. When you're feeling hostility, you frame it in political ways to justify the hostility. Al would be in the CIA and Samstein and Tillow were Communists, neither of which was true. It was 'paranoid idea-tion'—paranoid-type thinking that any normal person can be suscep-tible to under the right circumstances. This was an unusual circum-stance; life is not normally like this—college students making pronouncements on national radio."

Just as Rauh was about to enter the Credentials Committee meet-ing to wage his battle, a call came in for him from Walter Reuther. As Rauh recalls the conversation, Reuther told him, "'The convention has made its decision and I want you to accept it. It's two delegates from your crowd. A loyalty oath for their crowd, which means they'll leave. A promise that no lily-white committee or delegation will ever be accepted again and a committee to look into all of the civil rights violations in the Democratic party.' That's a hell of a lot better than what we had been offered on Sunday. And I said to Walter, 'I cannot accept it. . . . I've given Aaron Henry my word that I would never take anything without talking to him.'" At the close of the conversation, Rauh asked for a delay so that he could consult with Henry.

If Rauh was well aware that the United Auto Workers had tremendous power—it was said that Johnson didn't move without consulting Walter Reuther—he also knew that he had given Henry his word and that it would be very important to deal correctly with him. Only later did Rauh learn that on the same day the Credentials Committee met, Reuther had met with Ed King, Henry, Hamer, and Moses in an attempt "to sell them the compromise at the same time as he had just told me what it was." (Reuther told Ed King, "You have to consider all the money we put up.") Rauh recalls wryly that even as he was telling the chairman of the Credentials Committee that he would "fight to the very end" if necessary, but would prefer to consult first with Henry, "unbeknownst to me, Aaron is saying okay to Reuther. But Moses is not. And Moses is arguing with Reuther. Reuther got very rough."

Rauh recalls that while he was frantically trying to find Lowenstein to get word to Henry and pleading with the Credentials Committee for more time, the Mondale Committee preempted him by arriving to make its unanimous report. Although Walter Mondale was apparently prepared to acquiesce to Rauh's request for a delay, a self-proclaimed spokesman for the president, who was with Mondale, vetoed the idea, saying that the convention had made its decision.

"Just Walter Reuther's words," recalls Rauh. "'The convention made the decision. There'll be no delay.' And I looked at Fritz, who's then the attorney general of Minnesota, wondering if he's gonna take this shit from this little character."

Mondale made his report. "He made it sound as if I had won a million dollars," says Rauh. "And we did win a lot, but he built it all up. By that time, the Mississippi crowd [the whites] had turned down the loyalty oath and walked out, so, he said, Joe had won this wonderful victory; the racists are out, he's got two, we've got this committee, the investigation, the promise it will never happen again, I have Johnson's word, Humphrey's word, boy, you won a great victory."

Hooted down when he asked for a recess, Rauh was granted an opportunity to speak in opposition. "And I made a hell of a good speech against the settlement even though I rather believed in it, but I had to, and then we voted. And I think we got five votes against it. We needed eleven votes in order to sign a minority report. . . .

"So that was it. Then, Moses is still arguing with Reuther when the television carries 'Flash. Compromise agreed to unanimously.' And Moses lost his cool, 'cause he assumed that I had voted for it, when I had voted against it. And he went out and started attacking everybody, and said he would never talk to a white man again, and so forth. And then Mondale got on the tube and told how great a victory we had won, and I got on the tube and said I voted 'no,' and gave the truth, which was I wanted to know what Aaron felt. Well, Aaron was not giving an interview at that time and went back to the church."

There, where the MFDP delegates and their leaders were meeting, the tide was shifting to the militants. Moses told the crowd that the COFO staff was still against the compromise but that the delegates should make their own decisions. Fanny Lou Hamer, expressing the dominant mood of the gathering, shouted, "We didn't come all this way for no two seats!" When the delegates finally voted to reject the compromise, Greg Craig recalls that "there was a great sense of elation, excitement, and joy in the air, as if everyone had finally gotten over a terribly difficult decision, which, once completed, was a huge burden off of everybody's mind." Finding the happy relief "infectious," Craig says he was surprised to find Lowenstein upset.

Lowenstein, who had not been permitted to speak, had been shaken by the meeting. The rift in the Summer Project between the nonmilitant NAACP contingent and the more radical SNCC people had widened, and in the dispute over whether Lowenstein, who was not a member of the delegation, should be allowed to speak, the radicals had prevailed. Lowenstein was barred from addressing the meeting, although Robert Moses, who was not a member of the delegation but was the director of the Summer Project, was not. Moses opposed the compromise, and Lowenstein was extremely bitter, believing he had been "victimized" by the left. He was stung by the accusations that he was a traitor and a CIA agent, feeling that the way he had used ·his position to get white liberal backing for the MFDP had been misunderstood. While Robert Kennedy, who had asked him to go back to Mississippi on an "investigatory mission," became the hero of the MFDP, Lowenstein, who had done the undercover work for him in Mississippi, took the criticism.

Paul Cowan, who had been a volunteer in the Summer Project, described the assumptions which underlay that attitude: "There was a level of consciousness on which I, like Al Lowenstein and Joseph Rauh, was convinced that Communists spread political disease, that they infected everything they touched. If SNCC had received even a dollar of Moscow gold, then the organization must be polluted—that was what I instinctively thought. (I didn't know that the civil rights movement had received quite a bit more than a dollar from the CIA during those years.)" The Rev. Russell Williams of SCLC adds: "If the CIA had been giving money to the movement secretly and also was monitoring the Communists, Dr. King would not have objected. The Communists are always there in the civil rights movement. But their real goal is not civil rights. It's to disrupt the government, the capitalist system."

Part of Lowenstein's deal was that there would be no civil disobedience at the convention. But the MFDP answer to the compromise was not only a rejection, but a sit-in. His movement was now out of control. MFDP delegates went out on the floor and took the seats of the Mississippi delegates who had walked out. Because the whites had vacated the seats, the incident was peaceful. But when the MFDP returned to occupy the seats the next night, the seats had been removed. As Johnson and Humphrey were nominated, the MFDP delegates sat on the floor, a speck on the television screen in the midst of the pandemonium. When it was over, Fanny Lou Hamer called on thousands of black people to mass at the Democratic convention in 1968.

Rauh believed that the biggest blunder made by those pushing the compromise was naming King and Henry as the delegates. Had they been allowed to choose for themselves, Rauh believes that the compromise might have carried. He did not think they understood the black Mississippians and told them, "They're sharecroppers who've barely had enough to eat, but they're having one hell of a time, and they want to be represented and neither Aaron nor Ed King represents them."

Returning the credentials, which both Henry and King had refused, to the committee's counsel, Rauh was surprised to discover eleven signatures on the minority report. Five people had signed it after it no longer made any difference, to put themselves on record as having done the right thing. "Now that's the kind of crappy politics that I'll never get over," Rauh declares angrily. "On the record, they could say to Johnson, 'I saved you by not signing in time for the fight,' and they could say they were with the civil rights people."

While Rauh states that "Al and I agreed totally that we had done all we could," militant blacks and some disenchanted white students felt otherwise. In the Atlantic City episode, they saw Lowenstein as the villain. They began to believe that Lowenstein was a CIA agent, that his plane tickets, of which he had plenty, were clandestinely paid for by the government. "The CIA was a bad word," Joanne Grant Rabinowitz explains. "It was something bad to be. It haunts Gloria Steinem; the bad reputation of the CIA, the feeling that it was even sneakier then, that they were hiding something. There was a basic distrust of the government. SNCC particularly felt that the government had betrayed it, including Burke Marshall of the Justice Department. The federal government had done some bad things in the sixties, like promise SNCC people draft deferments if they went into voter registration instead of direct action."

Paul Cowan expressed their sentiments:

In many ways, I kept thinking, Al *was* a great man. He acted out the fantasies of his repressed contemporaries—those law school

274 • THE PIED PIPER: ALLARD LOWENSTEIN

classmates of his, for instance, who talked a liberal line at cocktail parties in Great Neck or Lake Forest—and he devised practical ways for the more courageous generation that followed to express its beliefs. In doing so he not only helped change Mississippi but had a large effect on the rest of the country. But he could never understand the fact that the people he sent into action would be transformed almost beyond recognition. So far as he was concerned, persons who talked publicly about their disgust with the American government—as many Mississippi residents and civil rights workers did after the Summer Project—were dangerously disloyal. Al could not understand that the young people and the black people were making an honest attempt to find their own approach toward changing America; he was convinced that a well-planned conspiracy lay behind our increasingly angry questions, our increasingly militant behavior. He fought the mythical conspiracy in a way that made him resemble the McCarthyites he despised. The tragedy was that his frenzied attitude lost him the respect and trust of students and black people, the two groups he sought to restore to his beloved imaginary America.

David Halberstam argues that the process of disillusionment was rooted in the radicalism of the Mississippi volunteers:

Young whites went to Mississippi that summer to attack segregation, but they made it clear that they were attacking the entire structure of American life and that Mississippi was merely the most visible part. Their activity led to the formation of the Mississippi Freedom Democratic Party, which caused the one sour note as far as Johnson was concerned at the convention. They were quickly put down, but what the Freedom Democrats symbolized politically, deep and abiding dissent from the processes and an unwillingness to compromise on terms dictated by the existing structure, would live and grow. By 1968 many of the people who had helped put them down at the 1964 convention were with them, and the Democratic Party itself seemed threatened.

Robert Moses says now that he believes: "If the MFDP had been seated, the attitude toward politics would have been different. The disillusionment with traditional politics began there." As for Lowenstein, Moses says merely that when he decided not to be part of the COFO militancy, he was "really out of it in terms of dealing with movement people."

Lowenstein's supporters argue that much of his rhetoric was strategic, that he understood the need for a patriotic posture to win the support of "Middle Americans." But his often heavy-handed approach inspired hostility and disillusionment in many of his young, inexperienced recruits. It disappointed Dennis Sweeney, and Greg Craig observed that "Dennis wasn't the only person angry with Al."

Many of his Ivy League and Stanford recruits were apparently angry with Lowenstein, but according to Moses, even Sweeney did not break with him. "Sweeney and Lowenstein didn't break over Mississippi," he says. "Dennis and Al worked together on Vietnam." But Lowenstein told friends after the convention that "Dennis is mad at me."

Mendy Samstein remembers that "after the convention, Sweeney was not bitter or angry at Al." He adds that "there were thousands of people who came down to Mississippi, hundreds who identified with SNCC and dozens who were part of the Mississippi cadre, and none of them would have thought of killing Al. They became lawyers, doctors, and judges. Only Dennis heard voices in his teeth telling him to kill Al. Dennis's illness was long-term, rooted in his childhood, the seeds of which go way back and the fruits were borne much later. The seed was there; the circumstances were the wrapping."

32.

After the convention, Craig visited Sweeney in his room at a Jackson motel and asked Sweeney what the problems with Lowenstein were. Sweeney, who appeared relaxed and self-assured about his political position, half-joked: "You know Al. He wants things to go his way and becomes impatient when they don't. That's just Al."

The two walked around downtown Jackson. "Dennis seemed heroic," Craig remembers. "He gave no indication of any bitterness or hatred. Lowenstein later told Craig that he was "incredibly touched" and regarded his parting with Dennis over the issues, as "symbolic of the sixties." He wanted to write a book about it. Craig paraphrases Lowenstein: "Here was this Jewish kid from New York and Dennis was a WASP from Oregon and Stanford, who had all the promise to be a leader but was soured, while Al came from a minority that had suffered but loved America." Craig concludes: "Al was à la Disraeli, a defender of the system, while Dennis was doing what he could to destroy it. But the summer of '64, they were gentle on each other."

When the convention was over, Lowenstein attended two meetings organized by the National Council of Churches in New York. A record of the second meeting, held on September 18, was kept by Mendy Samstein, who was there as one of two SNCC representatives. Also present were Courtland Cox, program director of SNCC (Moses, Forman, and other leading SNCC figures were out of the country),

James Farmer of CORE, Jack Greenberg of the NAACP Legal Defense Fund, Joe Rauh representing the UAW, Andrew Young of SCLC, several figures from the National Council of Churches, two top staff people from the NAACP, and Allard Lowenstein.

When Rauh rose to advocate that the Lawyers Guild be driven from the civil rights movement, Lowenstein replied: "I agree with you, but we must maximize cooperation. We need some understanding on how decisions are made. Right now, decision-making is metaphysical. We need a definite structure. We need a constitution. This new structure would be responsible for handling money and making other decisions."

Lowenstein called for "a commitment by the people here to the formation of a new, central body that will be regulated and democratized and broadened in its base. Questions like the Lawyers Guild would be submitted to this body and everybody would have to accept it. The problem now is we have no appeal from decisions we disagree with."

John Morcell of the NAACP expressed the reservations of others at the meeting: "In the event of decisions injurious to our national interests, no matter how democratic they might be, we must have a way out." To which Lowenstein responded: "Unless we write off Mississippi or engage in an open clash, then we must take this action which I propose. There are now lots of committed people coming back from Mississippi—lawyers, doctors, students, and others. It would be irresponsible if we were not to develop a structure. To avoid structure means to have decisions made which are not subject to the general will—authoritarian decisions made by small groups."

In the quarrel that ensued, Lowenstein charged that many who should have been participants in movement decisions had been excluded, while Mendy Samstein accused Lowenstein of taking his position "without knowing what is really going on."

Samstein felt that Lowenstein's outburst was, in a sense, his way of "getting back" at those who had refused to follow his lead in Atlantic City, and that Lowenstein may also have been jealous because of Samstein's closeness with Moses. "I had a close relationship with Bob. Al and I had a rivalry in this sense," he explains.

"Lowenstein's behavior was a constant embroiling which kept people from their work," Joanne Grant Rabinowitz asserts, expressing a harsher view of incidents like the clash with Samstein, which many believe were designed to frustrate the aims of those he opposed politically. When the transcript of the National Council of Churches meeting was circulated, Lowenstein became established as an enemy of SNCC.

Lowenstein summarized the meeting in his diary: "SNC, NAA Clash Repeatedly at Indecisive 2nd NCC Parley; Samstein 'Pulls a

Kozonguizi.' Henry to run for Senate. Official ballot spot sought. NCC parley agrees COFO, FDP must be revamped or dropped; Miss. involvement to increase."

Kozonguizi a South West African who had assisted Lowenstein in his 1959 trip to South West Africa had ultimately denounced Lowenstein over political differences, despite Lowenstein's careful cultivation of him. Now it seemed to Lowenstein that Samstein was doing the same thing, although Samstein had come to Mississippi independently of him.

Aaron Henry stayed as head of the Mississippi NAACP and became an important figure in the Democratic party. His business interests would increase and he would become chairman of the board of a television station that wouldn't sell him advertising time on the air when he ran in the 1963 Freedom Vote. When a black candidate would run for Congress in Mississippi in 1982, Henry would observe pessimistically that he had no chance to win. But Aaron Henry himself was a winner. He pulled the NAACP in Mississippi out of COFO, ended the civil rights coalition in the state after Lyndon Johnson was elected, and brought the MFDP into the regular Democratic organization. In various elections, he would support Eastland and Stennis for the U.S. Senate.

33.

In the fall of 1964, another Freedom Vote was held in Mississippi. Aaron Henry and Ed King were again the candidates, but because of the split between SNCC and the white liberals, resources for the Mississippi Project were limited and volunteers far fewer. Lowenstein indicated what his priorities were when he wrote in his diary: "'A' To 'Sound an Alarm' To Top C.R. Leadership About Infiltration."

Meanwhile, Lyndon Johnson, looking for advice about his image, turned to Gov. Terry Sanford of North Carolina for help. Sanford, in turn, asked Lowenstein for advice. Lowenstein wrote: "Sanford says Johnson wants to change image. Asks A what he would do if he were Governor of Mississippi. Gets 4 suggestions for a start." (Three years later, Lowenstein's recommendation to Johnson would be to leave office.) In the Mississippi legal battle, Joe Rauh had been dismissed as counsel for the MFDP and replaced by Arthur Kinoy and William Kunstler. Lowenstein wrote in his diary: "M.W., Now a Mississippian, in a Struggle With L.G. Over Control of Legal Efforts." Lowenstein himself temporarily dropped from the battle to attend his mother, ill with a liver malignancy, and his father, who had been rushed to the hospital with severe chest pains. A month's rest was decreed for the patriarch of the Lowenstein family.

Melvin Wulf's own view of his role in the "struggle" with the Lawyers Guild over "control of legal efforts" was far different from Lowenstein's. After the Mississippi summer ended, the LCDC opened a "permanent" office in Jackson. Wulf says he continued to be hounded by the liberals and the labor movement because of his position with regard to the Lawyers Guild. Although Rauh categorically denies it, Wulf maintains that a meeting, held in October, 1964, was set up by Rauh for the express purpose of getting Wulf fired from the ACLU. Both Rauh and Jack Greenberg, head of the NAACP Legal Defense Fund, who Wulf maintains were present at the meeting, along with a Reuther aide and Jack Pemberton, executive director of the ACLU, assert that they have "no recollection" of the meeting. Pemberton, on the other hand, confirms that he was there although he recalls no attempt by Rauh to actually fire Wulf.

Whatever the actual circumstances, any move to purge Wulf from the ACLU came to naught. Wulf, however, never spoke to Rauh again and lost all respect for Greenberg. He was embittered. "I thought Rauh was a deceitful guy. Rauh thought I was some kind of Commie. I was not. He's just a fair weather liberal."

The greatest damage done in Mississippi, according to Wulf, was the assault on SNCC: "SNCC was the most exciting, dramatic part of the civil rights movement. I think the liberals destroyed it deliberately. I know for a fact that Rauh wanted to destroy SNCC. He said they were dangerous leftists who didn't have enough sense to keep out the Communists. And to Joe Rauh's credit, he's still fighting the same battle."

Wulf is also critical of the left in Mississippi, particularly James Forman, and laments the rise of separatism and the black power movement, the direction SNCC took after Mississippi, and the falling out with the white liberals. And he is open about his criticism of Communists. He sees nothing wrong with the kind of public criticism that Allard Lowenstein engaged in, and states: "The first duty of people in politics is to criticize their enemies. I don't oppose public criticism of Communists. You're entitled to do this. This is part of free speech. But what Rauh and his bunch were doing was to treat everyone on the left of the ADA as politically unreliable and as potential subversives. They were the same as McCarthy. They just disagreed with McCarthy's methods." Wulf saw Lowenstein as part of Rauh's bunch in this respect and, for that reason, never supported him in any of his campaigns. Summing up his own efforts to get everyone to work together in Mississippi, he concludes: "I got shit from both ends. The liberals thought I was a Communist and the radicals saw me as an establishment liberal."

Ronnie Dugger, editor of the *Texas Observer* and a friend of Lowenstein's, wrote in a review of David Harris's *Dreams Die Hard* about Lowenstein's politics and the reaction of his enemies after Mississippi: "He was committed to peaceful reform within the democratic system, and therefore when necessary he opposed more radical means of change. For instance, he concluded at one point (by which time obviously he was right) that the Student Nonviolent Coordinating Committee, SNCC, had become destructive, radical, increasingly racist and insufficiently anti-Communist, and he said all these things. Therefore he came to be contemptuously hated by some young people on his left."

After extensive investigations, the FBI found no Communist infiltration of SNCC and the civil rights movement. The liberals were using an outdated experience—the union fights of the thirties when Communist infiltration of non-Communist institutions was real—as the basis for understanding the sixties.

34.

In 1964, Robert Moses and historian Staughton Lynd, who had been director of SNCC's Freedom Schools, were the speakers at a New York dinner given by the radical newspaper, *The Guardian*. Lowenstein observed: "Moses, Lynd differ on 'Popular Front' as Guardian diners hail them both." Lynd wanted to create a broad radical movement while Moses stressed local black autonomy. Someone identified by Lowenstein as "N.B." appealed to Lowenstein to "Drop Battle, Sees 'Tide' Irresistibly For SNCC; NSA Cautious." Meanwhile, Congressman Bill Ryan had joined an alliance with Joe Rauh to oppose the white racists in Mississippi, and William Kunstler was trying to work out a solution to the split in the ranks of the civil rights movement. Various liberals, Lowenstein indicated in his diary "help to reverse ADA line." That tough anti-Communist line, which was generally attributed to Arthur Schlesinger, Jr., caused problems with the more flexible ADA members, and Lowenstein joined in the effort to pursue other options in Mississippi. He was pressed to take a staff position on a planned NAACP organizing drive in the state under the direction of Bayard Rustin.

When the Mississippi NAACP voted to leave COFO and the national NAACP voted its own Summer Project, Lowenstein proposed a "cooperative format." With militancy at "a peak," according to Lowenstein, the responses were negative, and he joined Roy Wilkins, James Wechsler, and Rauh in planning a conference to establish an "alternative funnel" for funds to replace COFO. He wrote: "Wilkins, Wechsler, Rauh warned about 'Incipient Debacle.'" The new organization, which was to be set up by the National Council of Churches, would be called "Friends of Mississippi" and would "coordinate and channel national aid," he noted, adding, "Labor help likely."

Rauh, who was critical of the new MFDP legal strategy, warned against the "dream" of a coalition of liberals and radicals. Although SNCC indicated at a "Summit" in New York that it welcomed a coalition, Lowenstein warned about a "new situation," while James Forman, now regarded as the leader of SNCC, continued his criticism of Lowenstein. "'I'm Head;' Forman Calls Shots—And Most Are Aimed at 'A,'" Lowenstein noted.

William Sloane Coffin and Professor Richard B. Sewall had arranged for Lowenstein to be writer-in-residence that spring at Stiles College at Yale University. NC State was over. "'We've Lost Him': G.G. Was In Tears When He Learned Decision Was Final," Lowenstein observed in his diary, referring to George Gullette's reaction to his departure. He also planned to head for New York to work for the American Committee on Africa with Bayard Rustin and George Houser, putting his African commitments ahead of Mississippi. To further supplement his income, Lowenstein was to work for the Ford Foundation, a consultancy having been arranged for him by a friend. To bolster his domestic political career, Lowenstein would be made chairman of the Ryan for Mayor campaign with a view toward a New York congressional race. Unperturbed about his financial situation, Lowenstein considered his prospects in New York bright. To take care of Mississippi and to be sure it was in good hands, Lowenstein turned the project over to Barney Frank. He wrote: "B.F. Agrees to 'Replace' A Who Pledges Spring Month at Yale and to 'FDM' Efforts. Restored 'Unity' Helps H.R. Bid."

Lowenstein eased himself out of the Mississippi situation, recording: "April Return to Yale a Wise Compromise."

After the Summer Project of 1964, Bob Moses' position in SNCC declined as Forman's rose. At a bitter SNCC session in Atlanta in the spring of 1965, Forman defeated Moses in a policy vote on the direction of SNCC, and Moses retreated from his leadership role. Eschewing self-aggrandizement, he began to use the name Parris, encouraging leadership to develop at the grassroots level. Eventually he would leave the United States to teach in Tanzania.

It was the feeling of being part of a family that must have appealed to Dennis Sweeney, whose own family had been torn apart when he was still a child. In late May of 1964, Lowenstein observed in his diary: "Sweeney to Quit S.U. Wants E.R.F. Internship." Then in June, he added: "Sweeney 'Extraordinary' May Spend Year at Tougaloo."

The option Sweeney settled on was a ten-dollar-a-week job as a SNCC worker in Mississippi. It was a time when the leadership of

SNCC, without the moral guidance of Bob Moses, who was severing his ties to the organization, was turning on whites. But Sweeney soldiered on, getting arrested, taking difficult assignments and arguing with the SNCC black leaders about how to spend the dwindling funds that were available to them.

Sweeney also helped filmmaker Ed Pincus raise money for a project on the Mississippi experience, the end product being a documentary called *Black Natchez*, in which Sweeney appeared briefly talking to local blacks about Vietnam. Sweeney's boyish good looks are marred only by strangely jagged teeth. They were repaired by a COFO volunteer dentist, giving Sweeney an almost perfect appearance.

In the spring of 1965, returning from Cambridge where he had been conferring with filmmaker Ed Pincus after attending the first big antiwar demonstration in Washington, Sweeney stopped off at Yale to see Lowenstein. Though he had been referred to as a "writer-in-residence," Lowenstein, in fact, had no formal title at Yale. He had been offered a student dormitory room at Ezra Stiles College, there ostensibly because he was being considered for an appointment as an instructor in the English Department. FBI sources reported, however, that no such appointment was actually under consideration.

During a conversation about Mississippi and the significance of the right to vote for blacks, Sweeney argued that blacks had to decide on their own what kind of future they wanted, while Lowenstein pressed for an integrated, multiracial society. In his book, *Dreams Die Hard*, David Harris writes that Lowenstein insisted that "the kind of racial separation and exclusion SNCC was now talking about was 'racist.'" Harris continues: "The answer infuriated Dennis. The real racism was in not letting people control their own lives, he argued. If blacks wanted time to themselves, who were white people to refuse them that right? Anything else was just another white man telling them how they had to behave."

According to Harris, Lowenstein told Sweeney that the film project was a waste of time. He invited him to join the summer 1965 International Research Service mission to Algiers for the World Youth Festival. These delegations, sent out to counter the propaganda of the Moscow-backed delegates, were not casually chosen. Expenses were paid by the CIA. In asking Sweeney, Lowenstein was in effect "tapping" him for a leadership position in which he would be able to learn the realities of the Cold War. Sweeney resembled Lowenstein as an undergraduate and the prevailing theory was that the passionate ones who cared about injustice made the best anti-Communist liberals, once they knew which way was up. But Sweeney recoiled, preferring to follow his own path.

Observers of the Mississippi situation at that time concluded that

Sweeney suffered deeply from the feeling that the community he loved so intensely was coming apart. In the midst of the disintegration, Sweeney fell in love with Mary King, an attractive southern white woman who worked for SNCC as a photographer. She, knowing of his reputation as a hero in the movement, was duly impressed. When, in 1966, King was cut from the SNCC payroll, Sweeney knew it was time to leave.

Sweeney and King were married at the home of her father, a Methodist minister, in Virginia, the only invited guests being Robert Moses and his wife Donna Richards. After the wedding, Sweeney, Moses, and Richards met at the Institute for Policy Studies in Washington at a brainstorming session to see how the civil rights movement and the antiwar movement could merge into a united radical effort. They traveled to Palo Alto, where Sweeney reenrolled at Stanford and the couple concentrated on the antiwar movement, moving in with another couple engaged in similar activities. But Mary King was also a practical person. Somewhere in this chaos was the possibility of success, and Dennis Sweeney did not appear to be the man capable of achieving it. He did not follow through on projects and needed constant support. Nine months after the wedding they both realized that their marriage was not working out and they divorced. King changed her life, became a mainstream liberal, remarried, divorced, and then married Dr. Peter Bourne, a psychiatrist from Atlanta who would become President Jimmy Carter's drug advisor. She would be appointed Carter's deputy director of ACTION.

Sweeney did not seem bothered by the breakup and, after dropping out of Stanford again, threw himself into the antiwar movement, finding community again. But his bitterness toward Lowenstein would resurface later. Lowenstein also remained affected by his relationship with Sweeney and said in an interview in Stanford in 1977:

I remember one of the most bitter experiences I had in Mississippi in personal terms came about because one of the people who went down to Mississippi as a result of my efforts at Stanford was a guy called Dennis Sweeney. . . . It's a very, very illustrative story in terms of an autobiography. It's too long to tell you now, but the basic point of it was that he, after he got there, became very radicalized. He was sent to McComb. He was in very great danger physically. He was arrested when they blew up the Freedom House, and in the course of that decided that Norman Thomas and I and other figures were . . . the enemy, much more than the white power structure. And since Dennis and I had been quite close friends, it became a very, very personal thing. . . . Dennis and I had been good friends at Stanford when I was here, among the people that I worked with trying to end a lot of the social injustices here. He had been in the forefront of that. A very talented person. He went back to Mississippi during the period when SNCC was getting into "black power" and during the period when I was becoming the sort of villain in their eyes, became very much the spearhead of their campaign against me in a lot of ways. We met under very ugly kinds of circumstances in places where he would attack me from a very personal feeling. . . . He, after becoming very much involved with SNCC, ended up being thrown out of SNCC himself because he was white and, as the thing radicalized further, it became more black. They ended up accusing him of all the things that he had accused me of except it was done after he had put all of his emotion into SNCC, and it very, very badly damaged him. . . .

He called me from Philadelphia maybe two years ago out of the blue and told me that people were trying to kill him. It was a very sad sort of end for a very talented person that hacked out the fillings of his teeth because he said the CIA were using those fillings to damage his brain. And he just simply had gone to the point where I don't know if there's ever any way he could be reclaimed from this tragedy. . . . That whole situation . . . produced genuine paranoia and very often very deeply bitter and permanently damaged people. It was not limited to ideology. There was a very interesting overlap between ideology and psychology in that whole thing. . . . That people didn't snap under [the pressure] is incredible because the stresses were just constant. . . . If you understand all of that, there isn't any way that you can ever underestimate the reasonableness of going crazy.

But when Mendy Samstein saw Dennis Sweeney for the last time in 1968 or '69, he wasn't crazy. "He was disoriented and confused with what to do with his life and disappointed that the movement hadn't produced all it could," he remembers. "He was ambivalent about going back to school. He had romantic ideas about filmmaking. There was a slow development of schizophrenia, of psychosis."

If Sweeney projected his disappointment about the movement onto Lowenstein, Lowenstein himself considered his work in Mississippi had been successful. While recruiting for the Encampment for Citizenship in 1965, he visited Stanford and was interviewed by Nancy Steffen, editor of *The Stanford Daily* and a Lowenstein ally. An article entitled "SNCC: New Directions, New Problems" appeared under her name setting forth Lowenstein's views of the Mississippi debate. She wrote: "A year and a half ago, in November of 1963, Bob Moses of SNCC, addressing the Aaron Henry for Governor Campaign victory rally, spoke in praise of Professor Allard K. Lowenstein and the contribution he had made to the civil rights struggle in Mississippi.

"'He's a man who transcends a lot of situations,' Moses said. 'He was very deeply involved in this campaign and while he wasn't sufficient to bring it off, he was certainly necessary to bring it off, and without him it would never have come off as it did.'

"Several months ago, words of praise were once again raised for Lowenstein ('who has as much claim as anyone to be called the founder of the Mississippi Freedom Democratic Party') but this time not by Moses of SNCC but by Norman Thomas—speaking in angry defense of Lowenstein against SNCC and its supporters who, in some strange migration of attitude and logic, have come to regard, not only Lowenstein, but the whole spectrum of 'Liberals' as 'sell-outs' and 'traitors.'"

She described the split between SNCC and non-SNCC liberals: "Lowenstein recognizes, and has always recognized, that the vote is only one step in a process of attaining true freedom—but also recognizes that it is a necessary step—indeed a *precondition* to other liberation. . . . SNCC, on the other hand, while accepting with full vigor the notion that the vote doesn't *guarantee* social change, has apparently rejected the concomitant belief that the vote makes social change possible."

Quoting Lowenstein, who had told her, "When I first got to Mississippi [in July of 1963], everything was finished." Steffen credited him with the idea for a mock vote drive, the idea that, she wrote, "proved to be the progenitor of both the Mississippi Summer Project and the Mississippi Freedom Democratic Party. That is what Norman Thomas and others mean when they say that Lowenstein has as good a claim as any to be called the founder of the MFDP."

Lowenstein told Steffen that he saw progress in Mississippi, and that Atlantic City had been neither a "betrayal" nor a "defeat." Indeed, he said, "Atlantic City was one of the greatest proofs of the vitality of American democracy—when the President of the United States at the height of his power was forced—forced by the aroused conscience of the nation—to move to compromise."

He concluded by asserting that the country was "not in a revolutionary situation. . . . There are pockets of injustice that can, and must, be wiped out. . . . What we're going to have to learn now is to work out our problems with a sense of mutual respect. . . . If finding common ground is betrayal of principles, then we certainly don't want to ask them (SNCC) to betray their principles."

In 1979, when a Mississippi Freedom Conference reunion was held in Jackson to reassess the Summer Project, Lowenstein was shouted down when he attempted to give a scheduled speech. "His performance in Jackson was disgraceful," Joanne Grant Rabinowitz asserts. "When he got up to speak, it was so egotistical, it was as if he had created the entire movement. People just couldn't take it. The audience just wouldn't let him speak. It degenerated into a debate on free speech but he never finished. He was up against the hard-core SNCC workers who had put their lives on the line, who weren't going to take it."

Having organized a separate meeting of his own chaired by Ed King, Lowenstein reminisced to his audience: "I remember one night that has been for me, through all the events of my life since, a major force in the shaping of what I wanted to do with my life. It was a night on Lynch Street in SNCC headquarters with Stokely [Carmichael] and others, when we were told that we would all be killed, as people circled with guns and shot into the place. And the fact that we all lived through that night together, maybe it's maudlin to say, but it makes me feel that whatever my disagreements are with Stokely and the others, they are forever in my life a band of brothers with whom I share a deep sense of gratitude, affection, and respect. That will not change, however our paths may have gone in different directions since then.

"I wish Dave Dennis (of COFO and CORE) was here, and many of the early SNCC people, but Bob Moses more than anybody, because in that period, if there had been no Bob Moses there would have been nothing. It was Bob Moses everywhere. It was Bob Moses, the towering figure whose presence gave people, in the face of such fear that they didn't know whether they could go to bed at night, the sense that if he could be calm and strong and wise, we could get through what was going on. Nobody who lived through that experience would ever feel, I think, that there's any way that we could every repay the debt we owed to those people we found there."

For all his eloquence, Lowenstein could not impress these people who felt that he had opposed them before and that he was still playing politics with them. Joe Rauh, who also came to speak, recollects what Lowenstein encountered at the conference.

"Al was attacked on the same old stuff, CIA, and Al was a little shaken. What he was worried about was whether I would get the same stuff the next day. Anyway, we had breakfast the next morning and Al suggested there would be a real attack. I said I hoped he would stay for the meeting, and he said, 'Oh, no, I've gotta go.' In typical Al fashion, he would warn me but he couldn't stay to help. But nothing ever eventuated that morning. Ed King got up and was lyrical about me. That last time King spoke on this general subject about what we had accomplished, he was very, very good about me and I have the feeling he would be the same about Al."

VI

Good-Winging It Against Lyndon Johnson

35.

It has been suggested that Lowenstein's opposition to the war in Vietnam is proof that he could not possibly have been involved with the CIA: in actuality, his opposition to the war confirms his CIA involvement as much as anything. Roger Hilsman, who was the director of intelligence at the State Department from 1961 to 1963, has commented:

> Both the Kennedy and Johnson administrations were deeply divided about the nature of the struggle in Vietnam. One group saw it as part of global Communist expansionism. Although conceding that purely Vietnamese issues were also at work, they insisted the Viet Cong was ultimately inspired by Moscow and Peking, who would profit by a Communist victory strategically, economically, and politically. It followed that such an aggression could be met only by military force.
>
> The rival view agreed the insurgency was led by bona fide Communists, with full support from Moscow and Peking. But, they argued, the insurgency was more accurately described as an anti-colonialist and essentially *nationalistic* movement, feeding on social discontent in the South, over issues such as the need for land reform and whose leaders just happened to be Communist Party members. A Communist Vietnam, they conceded, would be troublesome politically to American interests in Southeast Asia, but the economic implications were minuscule. And not only was Vietnam of little intrinsic importance strategically but, they argued, Hanoi's demonstrated determination to remain independent of Moscow and Peking was ample assurance that neither would turn Vietnam into a military base.

Since the insurgency was a nationalistic, anti-colonialistic movement, they concluded, sending foreign troops would be self-defeating. Foreign troops would recruit more peasants for the Viet Cong than they could possibly kill. As President Kennedy said, "In the final analysis, it is their war."

This was the essence of the "dovish" position that Lowenstein came to avow. He took this position on the Third World, including Vietnam, because he believed it to be realistic, not because he was in any way opposed to American interests, as detractors to his right accused him of being. He was, in actuality, in the mainstream of liberal thought. There was nothing inconsistent about Lowenstein working for the CIA because it was partly a liberal institution. It was the logical place for him. It was, in fact, his friend William Buckley, Jr., who had also worked for the CIA, who was the conservative dissenter. The problem was not so much the CIA itself as Lyndon Johnson. Since the CIA is the covert arm of presidential policy, it is the president who ultimately determines the thrust of the agency. When Lowenstein became a dissenter within the agency on Vietnam, he was inevitably forced to take on Johnson.

Lowenstein was also convinced that the war in Vietnam would undermine the domestic reforms that the liberals had implemented. He was particularly fearful that the hard-won civil rights gains would be destroyed by the war as Johnson shifted the country's priorities, thus providing ammunition to SNCC radicals, who still argued that the system would not work.

Lowenstein was not against containing Communism; he was for it. He had exhorted the National Student Association in 1950 to support Truman's commitment of American troops in the Korean war. But as antiwar sentiment rose, Lowenstein came to view the effort in Vietnam as counterproductive. Sensing the need for a "loyal" opposition to the war, as opposed to the radical one, Lowenstein was also no doubt aware, as he watched the political tide move against the Vietnam War, of the implications for his own future; he wanted a legislative career of his own. There were, in fact, many reasons why Lowenstein, one of the leading anti-Communists of his time, and a CIA operative, would become a powerful opponent of a war America was fighting to stop the Communists, a war which had been launched by a Democratic administration Lowenstein himself had served and helped to elect.

36.

Lowenstein returned to the Stanford campus during the 1964 presidential campaign to address an ADA-sponsored rally for Hubert Humphrey. In January of 1965, he attended the inauguration in Washington of President Lyndon B. Johnson and Vice-President Humphrey, then returned to New York, where he was living at his parents' apartment on West 81st Street.

Lowenstein was back in New York for specific reasons. He needed to be close to the American Committee on Africa and the Spanish committees which were based there. He also wanted to run for Congress from the New York area and had to reestablish his credentials in the liberal reform movement.

Lowenstein also helped to organize the mayoralty bid of Congressman William Ryan, a central figure in the reform movement. Ryan was trying to raise $100,000 to finance his primary campaign for the Democratic nomination, and by joining the effort, Lowenstein gained access to potential supporters for his own future congressional race. Aware of Ryan's work in civil rights and his general record as an outstanding liberal, Lowenstein supported him enthusiastically.

Lowenstein also became involved in the growing issue of "campus unrest." He was invited to a conference in New Hampshire, set up by the Ford Foundation to discuss the creation of a program on youth. John Ehle, who was employed by the foundation at that time, obtained a consultancy for Lowenstein: "I was on the staff there then, was delving into campus unrest, and Al was hired at my request to help me—and later the foundation denied he was a consultant at all. Quite a remarkable set of experiences we had, chiefly at the UC at Berkeley, revealing about him and those times."

Lowenstein's job with the Ford Foundation, which, according to his diary, included a $2,500 fee, all expenses, and freedom to decide when and where he would work (an NSA grant had been approved as well), enabled him to fly to various campuses, study the causes of the unrest, and prepare a report. He particularly focused on Berkeley where President Martin Meyerson attempted to use Lowenstein as a peacemaker. Lowenstein, who was also a friend of Meyerson's, did what he could to help save Meyerson's job, but ultimately the board of trustees forced him out when Chancellor Clark Kerr had to resign under duress. "Far Left and Far Right Meet in a Very Vicious Circle to Crush Meyerson," Lowenstein wrote. But although centrist liberal Meyerson could not be salvaged, and the right was strengthened (Ronald Reagan would use the campus upheavals to consolidate his power in California as governor), Lowenstein felt he had been successful in thwarting the radicals who had hoped for more confrontation. "'Big Daddy' Salvages 'Something' Out of Berkeley's Long Days Night," Lowenstein wrote with irony. "Big Daddy" was the name radical students were using for Lowenstein, whom they regarded as a "fink" for the establishment.

A new generation of student leaders was now openly challenging authority in more extreme ways than Lowenstein had at Chapel Hill. Their rebellion was growing beyond the confines of the liberal National Student Association, which Lowenstein had continued to monitor. It was taking dangerous and unpredictable forms.

Meanwhile, Lowenstein's arrangement with the Ford Foundation became a subject of considerable disagreement. Though he had taken off for Berkeley and other destinations with the understanding that, as a Ford Foundation consultant, he would be paid for his trips, it was only after considerable haggling, particularly over his requests for expenses, that the Foundation finally agreed to reimburse him, but not until after he had stopped working for it. That happened in March, 1965, when his father died of a heart attack while Lowenstein was addressing a meeting in Berkeley on the free speech movement. Lowenstein returned to New York and on April 1, 1965, Paul Ylvisaker, the director of the Ford Foundation project on campus unrest, wrote to Lowenstein:

> This will confirm the arrangements made with Mr. John Ehle for you to serve as a consultant to the Foundation for a maximum of five days between April 1 and 9 to explore the possibility of involving youth and student groups in community action programs. We understand you will make brief visits in institutions in North Carolina, Massachusetts, California and New York.
>
> The Foundation will provide a daily fee of $50 and reimbursement for first-class round-trip air transportation to your destinations. Enclosed you will find expense report forms and certificates of time worked, which we would appreciate your filling out, signing, and returning to us. Please send your transportation stubs and hotel bills, and receipts for expenses of $25 or more.

After his father's death, friends noticed a difference in Lowenstein. "Now there was a difference between him in 1957 and him in let us say, 1967," Curtis Gans, who would join with Lowenstein in organizing "Dump Johnson," relates. "I attribute that difference to the death of his father. Up until 1966, he was willing to take an essentially behind the scenes role in a lot of things, to be a manipulator without necessarily being the up-front person except insofar as being a recruiter through oratorical talents. After his father died, he was consciously seeking the limelight in everything he did. He worshipped his father, and his father, while critical of his zigzag career, essentially gave him support whenever he needed it. His father was his anchor and his security and he could feel as if he could afford to be behind the scenes. Once his father died, he had to thrust himself forward and find his own base. I did notice that there was a different Lowenstein, a much less selfless Lowenstein after 1966." Gans cites Lowenstein's assistance to Muhammad Ali in Chicago, with his draft problems, as an example of how his friend had changed. Before his father's death, Lowenstein would have been content to work behind the scenes; afterward he wanted the identification with Ali and the notoriety that went with it.

It is also true that Lowenstein wanted to be elected to Congress. While that goal was set before his father's death, Lowenstein's all-out effort to achieve it came later. To get elected, he had to promote himself and this upset his admirers who wanted to believe that Lowenstein was a totally selfless person.

When he returned to New York, Lowenstein, who was a beneficiary in his father's will, found himself in a bitter family fight over the estate, which he wrote in his diary was valued "at $10 million." Commenting on the attitude of some of his relatives, Lowenstein also wrote: "To Heir Is Human and Noone Is Divine."

Lowenstein's sister Dorothy DiCintio explains that the dollar figure attached to the estate is misleading. The Post and Coach, a restaurant Gabriel Lowenstein owned in the Port Authority bus terminal, "made loads of money," she relates. In exchange for the right to run it, her father paid a percentage to the city of New York. In addition to the P & C, Lowenstein also had three snack bars at the terminal, all lucrative, as well as ten other restaurants in various parts of the city. "After his death, they all went," Dorothy laments. The relatives who ran the P & C were distant ones, "the uncles' nephews-in-law" is how Dorothy describes them. The worst fight was over who would get shares in the restaurants, particularly in the P & C, the big money maker. The Staten Island ferry concession, which Gabriel's brother Lazar had run, largely for his own benefit, was eventually lost to the Riese family, archrivals in the restaurant business. Gabriel left $100,000 in the stock market and very little cash. On top of this, according to Dorothy, the will was not valid.

Gabriel left half the stock market money and the P & C stock to his wife, then eighty, sick, and without an income. The rest was divided between his two sons, Larry and Allard, with the oldest brother, Bert, taking $40,000 in lieu of stock. Dorothy got the "remainder." "The P & C was worth millions," she admits, but adds that there were taxes due on all the properties. "The P & C dropped in value when the Port Authority neighborhood changed," she relates "and the city altered the facility without compensation. Willie's two nephew's-in-law ran the P & C and made a lot of money. It supported five families, and Willie [Gabriel's brother who had started the restaurant business] lived in the Sherry Netherland." His lavish life-style and the numerous hangers-on caused much of this money to evaporate. "Lazar had stock in the ferries," adds DiCintio. "It was a tremendous money-maker." Though it had been her father's idea to get the concessions on the Staten Island ferry, Gabriel had turned them over to his brother

Lazar, who, explains DiCintio, "couldn't practice law as he did in Lithuania as attorney general. Lazar was a difficult man. He set up a little office. We said, 'Lazar never takes anything that isn't his. The problem is that he thinks everything is his.'"

When Lowenstein's stepmother died in 1967, shares in the P & C were divided among Larry, Bert, and Dorothy, while Allard took cash instead. "It was a nice piece of change," says DiCintio, "but the next year it was substantially reduced, then nothing. The money on the stock exchange was used to pay the tax bill on Gabriel's estate. The sad part is that my father never built up an organization," she concludes.

The leases of some of the restaurants were in jeopardy, and one by one they closed. When Lowenstein returned from his 1967 trip to Africa and his mother was dying in the hospital, it was then that Dorothy said to him over their mother's bed: "The ferries are being taken from us. Can't you use your influence with Lindsay and his commissioners?" But Lowenstein did nothing to try to save it.

Shortly after Gabriel Lowenstein's death, before the estate was settled, Allard Lowenstein received a series of checks totaling almost $25,000 from his father's life insurance policies. At the time, Lowenstein, who lived cheaply and was reimbursed for his travels, had moved into his stepmother's apartment and was eating at the family restaurants.

Still active in civil rights, Lowenstein traveled back to Mississippi, unsure of what "posture" he should take when the Freedom Democratic party–NAACP feud "blows its lid." Robert Parris (formerly Bob Moses) was insisting that a "temporary Negro party" was "necessary" but appeared friendly to Lowenstein. "Parris Friendly, Seems Less Bitter," he noted. Then Lowenstein accepted the chairmanship of "Citizens for Ryan," convinced that he was "not a figurehead." His campaign role, he observed, was going to "delay" his "overseas travel" and he noted that "Algeria may be out."

But if Algeria was out, the Dominican Republic was not. Lowenstein would be drawn into the intrigue of the Dominican Republic to protect American interests there.

On April 27, 1965, Johnson had ordered the marines into the Dominican Republic "to help prevent another Communist state in the hemisphere." Assurances had been made at that time by the State Department that "free elections" would be held within "six to nine months," and in April 1966 Lowenstein joined the effort to recruit volunteers to observe these elections. Observers were necessary because Socialist Juan Bosch, who had been elected president of the Dominican Republic in December, 1962, in a landslide victory, no longer trusted the Americans, who had once backed him. Convinced that the Americans had been complicitous in the coup which had sent him into exile later that year, Bosch claimed that a fair election was impossible while the marines occupied his country.

Bosch relented, however, agreeing to participate in the election when his friend Norman Thomas promised to get other Americans on the left to come as observers, to make sure the elections were free of coercion and fraud. The Commission for Free Elections in the Dominican Republic was set up in New York, and Allard Lowenstein was put in charge. "By creating ad hoc groups," Curtis Gans observed, "he put himself in control." Norman Thomas was old and almost totally blind; he relied on others for his information.

On May 1, Lowenstein met at Harvard with Reverend Jack Mendelsohn and Curtis Hessler of the *Harvard Crimson* and formulated a plan to send teams of observers to the Dominican Republic before, during, and after the elections. The Commission for Free Elections set up a headquarters in Santo Domingo with a student volunteer, while Lowenstein recruited. Lowenstein was in the Dominican Republic briefly in April of 1966. In one of the reports he helped to prepare on the situation there, he stated:

> Everyone in Santiago wants observers. They say the value of observers would be that, among other things, they would improve the image of America. This view from professional men who are disturbed at the anti-Americanism. They also want a massive education campaign in the US about the Dominican Republic—to show how ludicrous the intervention was. . . . Everyone thinks Bosch will carry Santiago, which he lost in 1962. Think he could lose only in a corrupt election. They do not accept a Balaguer victory as possible.

The oligarchy was supporting Joaquin Balaguer, a one-time puppet of the dictator Trujillo and a conservative, who predicted disaster if Bosch won. The message from Balaguer was that if Bosch was elected, he would be overthrown by force. During Lowenstein's April visit to the Dominican Republic he found Bosch convinced that he would not be allowed to win. He pointed to the atmosphere of fear and the departure of his Institute for International Labor Research (IILR) aide from the island at the request of the State Department. Norman Thomas served as chairman of the New York based IILR, which had supported Bosch. Lowenstein then met with the United States ambassador to the OAS, Ellsworth Bunker, later ambassador to Vietnam. Bunker promised U.S. support for Bosch if he won, providing Lowenstein would guarantee the support of his people if the conservative Balaguer, whom Bunker backed, was elected.

When Lowenstein returned with Norman Thomas to the Dominican Republic for the elections, he found Bosch's campaign workers fleeing from the countryside to Santo Domingo. Bosch meanwhile was in New York because he feared for his life and was desperately trying to raise funds. Following Balaguer's election, Thomas and Lowenstein had agreed that neither would make a statement before flying back to the U.S., but when pressed by reporters in New York, Thomas said he had found neither violence nor fraud. "Bosch Defeat 'Free' If Not 'Fair', N.T., A Declare. M.M. Enraged. D.R. Left Teeters On Revolt Storm Over Statement," Lowenstein wrote in his diary.

At a meeting with Norman Thomas and Mrs. Bosch, Lowenstein tried to work out a different statement to the effect that the new administration in the Dominican Republic under Balaguer would look into any alleged violations, but it failed to satisfy the Bosch supporters.

At a May 1966 forum on Vietnam at Chapel Hill, Lowenstein commented: "We went into the Dominican Republic because we said that we were protecting American lives. That was when there were about 2,500 Americans. When all but 50 had been pulled out, we sent in another 20,000 Marines. We then explained that we were there to stop the Communists from taking it over. Everybody now knows that that was not going on in the Dominican Republic a year ago. I wish we could discuss that, because we made a tragic blunder in the Dominican Republic. Fortunately, there is some hope that we can reverse course there now."

With Lowenstein's help, America did reverse course in the Dominican Republic, but at the expense of Juan Bosch.

37.

In the spring of 1965, Algernon Black, still going strong at the Ethical Culture Society, contacted Lowenstein and asked him to be the director of that summer's Encampment for Citizenship to be held on the Fieldston campus. Lowenstein, who had addressed the 1964 encampment and become aware of the possibility for recruiting a new breed of student leaders, enthusiastically accepted.

Lowenstein set out to get the top student leaders in the country for the six-week program. On a trip to Stanford, he persuaded undergraduate David Harris to participate, telling him that it was to be a gathering of "future leaders." Harris had been impressed by Lowenstein when he first met him at a "bull session" at Stanford shortly before the death of Gabriel Lowenstein. "He struck the theme his life would eventually be said to have epitomized," wrote Harris. "He argued that one person can make an immense difference and that the course of history itself could be shaped by a single decision. Especially in a democracy, every person had a terribly important contribution to make."

Lowenstein explained to recruits that there would be seminars dealing with "relevant" issues that everyone was concerned with. But it would also be a kind of retreat for the political and social activists who had been on the "cutting edge" of the fatiguing battles of the 1963–64 period, particularly in the South but also on the campuses themselves. Tuition was $600 but scholarships were available for the worthy and talented. Lowenstein said he wanted these people to get together, to "interact, to unwind, to think about where to go and what to do next." Greg Craig, who attended, adds that, in fact, there was "sex and some dope."

"The kids came from everywhere—from Berkeley's Free Speech Movement, from SNCC and CORE, from Mississippi, from Harvard, Yale, Antioch, Chapel Hill, Stanford, Berkeley, Oberlin, Minnesota, Tufts, Columbia, Tougaloo, Carolina A & T, Spellman, Howard, Miles, and CUNY," Craig recalls. "They were black, white, Jewish, Italian, and WASP. There was a black woman from New York City who was special assistant to William F. Buckley, Jr., on the *National Review*. . . . The chairman of the *Yale Daily News* was there as was the editor of the *Stanford Daily*. [For a while, he (the Yalie) and she (the Daily) were a romantic item at the Encampment.] There were two of the most aggressive members of the steering committee of the Free Speech Movement at Berkeley who led and dominated every political discussion. There were the future presidents of the student governments at Harvard, Stanford, the University of North Carolina, and the University of Minnesota.

"That summer, the encampment was held on the campus of the Fieldston School in Riverdale, New York, within subway distance of downtown New York City. Fieldston School, a private secondary school associated with the Ethical Culture Society, had a grassy and somewhat secluded campus, basic athletic facilities, a cafeteria, and large classrooms that were transformed into boys' and girls' dormitories. The school was easily accessible to the parade of luminaries that Al brought to the encampment for seminarlike sessions on the lawn. Most of the people at the encampment that year were already devoted friends of Al's but complete strangers to one another. At the first meeting of the participants, a Sunday night, Al stood up before the crowd and was greeted with applause, hollers, whoops and whistles. His words that night became the lasting slogan for that six-week experience. 'The key to happiness at the Encampment for Citizenship is . . . to hang loose!' It was good advice for many reasons. First, the organization of the encampment (under Al's direction) was rocky and unreliable at best. Second, the issues that were discussed generated much heat and passion among the participants and at least once threatened to break up the entire project. Finally, the intense interpersonal relationships that developed during the summer among those high-powered, sensitive, exploring and experimental young people were absolutely exhausting for most of the participants (to say nothing of the staff members) to deal with. Barney Frank, the unsentimental Harvard teaching fellow who spent time at the encampment and went on to become Beacon Hill's representative to the Massachusetts state legislature, described the encampment as a 'loony bin filled with people who, when they're on the outside, are ordinary, squared-away people with good, common sense. They must go crazy in here.'"

Among the guests Lowenstein was able to attract to the encampment were Paul Goodman, William Sloane Coffin, Bob Moses (Parris), Paul O'Dwyer, Congressman William Fitz Ryan, City Councilman Ted Weiss, philosophers Paul Weiss and Richard Bernstein, Richard Sewall, the master of Stiles College at Yale, where Lowenstein was "writer-in-residence," Joel Fleishman, Norman Thomas, Charles McWhorter (a former assistant to Richard Nixon), William F. Buckley, Jr., James Wechsler of the *New York Post*, the president of Antioch College, John Lindsay (then the Republican candidate for mayor of New York), Abe Beame, Carey MacWilliams of *The Nation* magazine, and radical Tom Hayden.

Greg Craig remembers that David Harris was one of a group who would go down to Greenwich Village to "dig" jazz. Harris was also part of a group whose position in the debate on the war in Vietnam and President Johnson's policies set them somewhat apart. For the most part, the division within the liberal camp was between those who felt the war was threatening America's position in the world and would undermine domestic changes, and those who believed that it was a mistake to challenge Johnson because he was pressing for social goals that the liberals had worked long to achieve. An emerging third position, that of the "New Left," which attracted David Harris and others, advocated mass opposition through demonstrations on the ground that the war in Vietnam was morally wrong. Harris wrote:

The members of the New Left, almost exclusively young, sought to galvanize a moral outrage that would give Johnson no choice but withdrawal of troops from Vietnam. The war was a crime against everything the nation was supposed to be. Inspired by SNCC, but largely an unorganized network of activists, the "radicals" didn't mind offending those to their right and thought demonstrations were far more important than currying favor with congress through the Democratic party.

Lowenstein listened carefully as Robert Parris argued that Americans needed to build an entirely new society "from the ground up" and that notions of liberal democracy were obsolete.

Toward the end of the encampment, Lowenstein took some of the students campaigning with William Ryan, an underdog in the race for mayor of New York. Lowenstein told David Harris when the summer was over that his father had encouraged him to run for public office but that he had always believed it was his strength to be outside of the system to a certain extent, effecting change not from a traditional power base but among dissenters. But he was getting older, he explained, and had to find a legitimate role for himself. As an ADA liberal in Congress, he could combine his desire to make policy and his need to dissent at the same time. In fact, Lowenstein was looking at districts in Brooklyn, Westchester, and Manhattan for possible congressional campaigns.

In August, Lowenstein went to Mississippi, where he met Greg Craig, who had gone down before him. Lowenstein wanted to heal the rift between the Mississippi Freedom Democratic party and the NAACP, headed by Aaron Henry, then anxious to consolidate his own political power. Since the MFDP needed the NAACP more than the NAACP needed it, Henry got his way and was made leader, ultimately taking the MFDP into the regular state Democratic organization. According to writer Doug Ireland, who had been in the SDS and would later help in Lowenstein's only successful race for Congress, Lowenstein was in love with Greg Craig, whom Ireland describes as "stunningly beautiful and the student body president at Harvard." Lowenstein's relationship with the young men he admired was, Ireland insists, "classically Greek." But Craig and Lowenstein evidently had a Platonic relationship. From an important family, Craig was intelligent and a good worker, someone Lowenstein could trust. Craig recalls this final swing through the South: "Al arrived in his Mustang in Clarksdale in August, after the federal registrars had arrived in Greenwood. He told me that he was driving down to Bogalusa and New Orleans to meet with people who were running the Free Southern Theater and wanted to know if I wanted to go along and help with the driving. I agreed instantly."

Before heading toward Bogalusa, Craig and Lowenstein wandered through Mississippi, stopping at Lexington to drop Aaron Henry at a state NAACP conference and to look up newspaper publisher Hazel Brannon Smith, whose presses had been destroyed and her offices firebombed the preceding fall. In Greenville they visited with Hodding Carter, Sr. and Jr., and in Jackson they spent an hour with Charles Evers. "He didn't answer the door but talked through an intercom system before letting anyone in, and he had a loaded handgun on the coffee table and a shotgun behind the door," Craig relates. They spent an evening with the Bernsteins, the feisty Jewish family which had become identified with the civil rights movement in Jackson; and everywhere they went, according to Craig, "whether it was to the Bernstein's affluent house in the suburb of Jackson or whether it was to the muddy campus of Tougaloo on the outskirts of the city, Al told his friends new stories of achievement and reason for hope."

The two then headed for Bogalusa where the Free Southern Theater had been invited to perform "In White America" in an effort, says Craig, "to help diffuse the time bomb that the town had become. There had already been a number of deaths in the town, the governor had called in the National Guard, the Deacons for Defense had armed and were organized, and the town was sitting between two armed camps, festering, smoldering, waiting to explode.

"We arrived around eight o'clock at night; it was already dark. We called the phone number and were told to wait. Two cars filled with black men came out to where we were on the outskirts of town and escorted us to the theater where the performance was to take place. We passed rows of cars filled with silent white men, and we then passed rows of military vehicles filled with soldiers in riot gear. And we looked down the side streets to see police cruisers filled with white helmeted troopers from the Louisiana state police. I knew what role the Mississippi state police played in these kinds of confrontations, and I wondered whether the Louisiana state police were comparable. By the time we got to the theater, it was absolutely black night, and since we were in the poorer section of town, there were no street lights. At the door to the 'theater' there were more black males, big and well disciplined and seemingly well organized. We were searched before we were allowed in. The room was filled with black and white people, but the atmosphere was hushed and heavy. The room was set up so that one end had been cleared away to serve as the stage area. A man went up to the front and welcomed the audience to the first performance of the Free Southern Theater ever to be given in Bogalusa, Louisiana. He asked that every white stand up and identify himself so that the Deacons could know who we were, to recognize who were friends. There were about fifteen whites present—in a crowd of approximately eighty to a hundred. Al introduced himself as a lawyer from New York City; I said that I was a civil rights worker from Clarksdale, Mississippi, who was traveling with Al. The performance went forward with no disruptions.

"After the performance was completed, at around eleven, we met briefly with the performers and agreed to meet the next day at their home base at Tulane in New Orleans. Al and I decided that we would go on to New Orleans that night. To do that, we had to have an escort to leave town. Again, cars filled with black men were positioned in front and behind us, and we drove in the caravan out of Bogalusa toward New Orleans. I remember passing a gas station on the main highway to New Orleans from Bogalusa where there were five cars filled with white men, some standing alongside their cars, who were watching as our caravan went by. I can remember thinking of the ambush that might be set for the deacons on their return from wherever they intended to drop us off. The deacons took us another two miles and then signaled us to go ahead. We stopped briefly and talked, and I warned them about getting jumped on the way back. They laughed and said not to worry, that they had no intention of going back the way we had come, and there was no way that those crackers would ever be able to jump them. There was, in fact, a white-handled handgun of some sort on the front seat of the deacons' car."

As Lowenstein and Craig drove on to New Orleans, Lowenstein spoke of the book that he wanted to write about his experiences in the South and Mississippi in particular, describing what he believed had happened to the movement and to his friend Dennis Sweeney. There would be overtones of *Brutal Mandate.* He never got to write the book.

38.

That summer, William Sloane Coffin brooded about the war in Vietnam and world politics. He and his family were living in a rented cottage on Cape Cod; while his children played at the beach, he contemplated that they might not have a future at all if the world incinerated itself. "At no time was I more tempted to becoming anti-American myself," Coffin wrote. It was 1965 and Americans were raging against a handful of frustrated students who had burned their draft cards. Yet, to television and newspaper pictures of Buddhists immolating themselves, "turning themselves into burning signposts to the tragedy and insanity of the war," the most common American reaction was "Look at the kooky monk."

Coffin came up with an idea. In the fall, the United Nations was going to consider the question of admitting China to the United Nations. He reasoned that the way to begin a total rethinking of American policy in the Far East was to support China's admission. This would lead to a broad discussion of Asia in the world body and a lessening of tensions. If Americans could live with Mao, Coffin concluded, they could learn to live with Ho Chi Minh.

Borrowing a typewriter from the real estate agent who had rented him the cottage, Coffin typed a letter containing his proposal and mailed copies to a group of prominent Democrats with whom he was friendly. One replied that the idea was treasonous, but others were favorable. The best response came from Allard Lowenstein, who telephoned. Coffin was delighted to hear him say that he "would help translate the idea into immediate action." Coffin wrote:

At the time, Lowenstein was the best student organizer in the country. His moral fervor was matched by political sophistication, and he was the finest stand-up orator I had ever heard. . . . So when Al said he would help, and we had both agreed that colleges would be the best place to start, I knew that Americans for the Reappraisal of Far Eastern Policy (ARFEP) was as good as established.

Sure enough, the following month, while I helped to set up headquarters at Yale, Al set off across the country organizing campus chapters at the rate of two a day, one in the afternoon and one at night. It was enough for him to notify a contact that he was coming, and within two hours leaflets would appear announcing a meeting—which would be packed. . . . Then, after organizing a local chapter which he would put in touch with us, he would be off for the next campus, driven by a student volunteer. Occasionally he would get exercise by wrestling a local champion. It was widely believed that Al could sleep only in moving cars.

Based on the network that Lowenstein had established, a teach-in was organized on October 20, 1965, with a nationwide telephone hookup to 25,000 listeners, who heard Professor John Fairbank of Harvard, Congressman William Ryan, Norman Cousins, Norman Thomas, and Michael Harrington. Lowenstein wrote in his diary: "Yale teach-in (ARFEP)—30 campuses hold meetings—Hook-up successful. Yale, Union Crowds Large." This was followed by teach-ins with outside speakers aiding local faculty members. Lowenstein participated actively.

During that month at Yale, Coffin and his supporters collected 2,500 signatures and used them in a full-page ad in *The New York Times* with the headline "Are We Prepared to Live in the Same World With China?" ARFEP's three major points followed: U.S. recognition of China, the admission of China to the U.N., and an end to the war in Vietnam.

A *New York Times* article explained the goals of the new organization and quoted Lowenstein: "'The question of Vietnam can only be solved in the context of China and the entire Far East,' Allard K. Lowenstein, a New York lawyer who is a member of the group's national committee, said yesterday." Lowenstein also told the *Times* reporter, "We want to encourage a wider debate on the deadest limb of the tree of our foreign policy, which is our China policy. It is wrong to let groups only concerned with Vietnam monopolize the discussion."

But the response to the organization was not overwhelming. It was rejected on various campuses either because the students did not support the entry of China into the United Nations and would not criticize Johnson's war policy (the supposedly liberal University of Chicago was one of these), or because they saw ARFEP as the creation of non-radical liberals who would not deal with the question of the war in Vietnam as a reflection of the bankruptcy of American society. Coffin observed: "Despite similar ads placed in other papers by other chapters, which went on to become more active than Yale's—especially Wisconsin, Berkeley and Harvard—and despite a good journal, *China Survey*, which appeared for many months, we never really succeeded in getting the movement off the campuses into the surrounding communities. Had Al not had other fish to fry, and had he been free to devote his talents full-time to the organization, we might have succeeded. Without him we were no match for the Committee of One Million against the Admission of Communist China to the United Nations, which numbered among its most fervent members former Vice-President Richard Nixon. In the Congress, the Committee had 321 members; we had only Congressman Ryan."

Lowenstein's goal was to join Ryan in Congress. Norman Thomas was advising him to get married and get a job or he would have no credibility. Lowenstein had a job but not the one he wanted. He wanted a public platform, not a slot in the bureaucracy. He wanted to be elected. Harris Wofford remarks: "Certainly Al was ambitious. Certainly he liked the limelight. Certainly he wanted to be a heroic figure on the political, public stage and do hard things, big things. Certainly he had significant friendships. There was no sign that he wanted a lot of money. I don't know anyone who wanted to do something about the obstacles to the common good more than Al Lowenstein."

Lowenstein was driven now to be a public figure and the war in Vietnam was slowly creating a critical mass of public opinion compatible with Lowenstein's "good-wing" views. As Curtis Gans asserts: "Al had an excellent sense of the American center. He could start majoritarian movements and knew how far he could take them rhetorically and strategically."

39.

In the Democratic primary for mayor, Abe Beame, who had the support of the regular Democratic organization and Robert Kennedy, was victorious. Liberal reformer William Ryan's vote was 113,182 or 15 percent of the total, which Lowenstein regarded as a victory of sorts.

Speaking to Ryan's supporters, he told them "It took La Guardia twice." Lowenstein recorded in his diary: "And The Crowd Goes Wild." The winner in the general election was not Beame, but liberal Republican Congressman John V. Lindsay, a product of St. Paul's School, Yale, and Yale Law School, the epitome of the elitist liberal reformer, and a representative of a world Lowenstein longed to be part of.

To New York and out of the world of John Marquand came Jenny Lyman of Boston, whose father, Ronald Lyman, was a Brahman from Beacon Hill and Harvard. In wanting to break away from her background, Jenny, in fact, resembled her mother, Olivia. Also born to privilege, she had rebelled, divorced Lyman, and "left Boston in disgrace" (Jenny's words), tallying up five husbands before her death from a heart attack in St. Maarten in the seventies. After the Lyman divorce, Olivia married Harry King, who died three weeks later from a heart attack. Married again, this time to a banker, she had been living with him for fifteen years when one winter night in 1965 he was shot dead in his own home, having answered a knock at the door. The murderer was never found. But the banker had been generous with Olivia's children, and Jenny Lyman acquired an income of her own. Her mother, a large, lively, and unsinkable woman, moved to Manhattan, taking an apartment at One Gracie Terrace.

Born in Boston, Jenny Lyman had gone to the Windsor School, a private day school. But her attitude soon showed the influence of her mother, who was regarded as "offbeat" and who "summered in Bridgehampton" (a Long Island resort considered a hotbed of radicalism and promiscuity by proper Bostonians). "I wanted to get away from what I considered to be a narrow, WASP upper-crust upbringing," she asserts. "I defected. I was in a state of rebellion against what I grew up with."

Rev. William Sloane Coffin was the speaker at her graduation. Just back from jail in Alabama, Coffin talked of commitment, of "throwing your sandals in the ring." The themes of prejudice, global poverty, and the threat of war moved her. She had chosen to go to Barnard so she could be in New York, away from Boston, and with Coffin's voice ringing in her ears, she left.

Jenny Lyman had a "strong feeling about civil rights" and was "moved by the Freedom Riders." In the spring of her senior year at Barnard, where she majored in English, she visited Selma and Montgomery, Alabama. After graduation, in the summer of 1965, she joined "Crossroads Africa," a kind of mini–Peace Corps that was privately run, and spent eight weeks in a small village in Nigeria, returning to live with her mother. She also took a job with the American Committee on Africa.

Although Jenny Lyman and Allard Lowenstein had the American

Committee on Africa in common, she insists that they did not meet until shortly after her twenty-first birthday, when Sam Beard, a friend of her sister's, invited her to a party. Beard was effusive about "this spectacular guy who changed my life and pulled me out of a slump." Jenny went to the party and four hours later, "this shy, strange-looking man arrived with all of his belongings dripping out of his bag." It was Lowenstein. "This is the most wonderful man in the world?" Jenny thought to herself. She says she did not expect to see him again.

Two months after she started working at the American Committee on Africa, Jenny was released. Feeling "low and discouraged and with a degree in English lit. that was no use, for anything," she was glad to get a call from Sam Beard. "Al is going to run for Congress," he told her. "How would you like to work on the campaign?"

It was her first effort in politics. That it was for a reform Democrat scandalized her father, a passionately right-wing Republican who had contributed heavily over the years to Nixon and Reagan. "Al was the most beguiling and convincing person I had ever met," she acknowledges, allowing that she had revised her initial impression. "The regulars were the enemy. He was always talking about the regulars. He took me to lunch at the Hyde Park on Madison Avenue, one of his father's many restaurants. It was now a family corporation run by Larry. Al would outline a whole task on the assumption that you would do it. He was kind and funny. No one ever spoke in my Republican family. I was terrified of politics. He said not to worry. He didn't care if you weren't perfect. Then he drew up a list on paper napkins, people to call to convince and other responsibilities."

Jenny was stationed in a back room of the restaurant office, a few blocks from the Hyde Park. Larry had donated the room for the campaign, and she made her calls from it while Blanche and Sonya from the restaurant business took calls. Evenings she was to be Lowenstein's driver to the reform clubs as he campaigned. The only outing resembling a date occurred when he asked her to the movies and Jenny thought it was a great honor. "Poor little me," she muses. "We ended up going with five other people, including Lucille Kohn who was then ninety-three. She lived in a walk-up apartment. Her heat had been shut off and she had her windows nailed for the winter."

According to Jenny, Lowenstein "needed grandparents" and routinely visited Lucille Kohn, his old friend from the Encampment for Citizenship, in her apartment between midnight and two in the morning. He would phone her and then run over to her apartment, which was a second floor walkup overlooking Lexington Avenue. After letting him in, Kohn would return to bed and they would talk. Greg Craig, who visited her with Lowenstein, recalls:

"He would take her by the hand and tell her about the day's events. He would ask, 'What do you think about Mr. DeSapio?' or

'Who are you going to vote for for mayor?' or 'Why isn't Mayor Lindsay better at keeping the potholes repaired?' And then a long and rambling and high-spirited conversation would ensue, Lucille with her false teeth clacking away. Al interrupted with a running commentary, every now and then jumping up and darting to the refrigerator for a glass of milk and some pound cake which Lucille kept on hand for him. Lucille wore a gold medallion around her neck with a profile of John Kennedy on it. President Kennedy was her one true political hero. 'Even more than Eleanor Roosevelt?' Al asked, one night in disbelief. 'After all,' said Lucille, 'Jack Kennedy did so much more for his people.' Al would just break up laughing."

Jenny was working. This was very different from the way he had escorted Barbara Boggs around to the reform clubs in 1960. "I knew nothing but found it exciting," she insists. There were the big names in the reform movement; Ed Koch, Bella Abzug, Ronnie Eldridge, and the endless reform battles. "In the reform movement, no one was neutral," Jenny explains. "You were loved or hated. He loved wit and had a good sense of humor regardless of reverses. He wanted to be cheery in the face of adversity."

Lowenstein would frequently drop everything to go off and visit Norman Thomas. When he introduced Greg Craig and Craig's Harvard roommate to Thomas as "the leaders of the Harvard student movement," Thomas said, "Well, I went to Princeton, you know, and we didn't know very much about movements, student or otherwise." Then, walking them down his driveway and watching as Lowenstein and his friends piled into the convertible, "he lifted his cane and pointed it to the sky, like a cavalry officer leading the charge with his saber upraised. 'Long live the Harvard revolution,' he shouted with the most memorable broad grin creasing his face."

Lowenstein told Jenny his life's story as she drove him around the district. He told her that he had loved his *real* mother's family, the Goldbergs, with whom his father had kept him in touch after his mother's death. He repeated the story of how, as a very young child, he had realized his "mother" was not his real mother. No one in his family had been allowed to tell him the truth, an odd conspiracy, he said, but he had pieced it together. Jenny says that she was deeply touched when Al told her how he had said to his stepmother: "I know you're not my real mother, but I love you very much."

Lowenstein had insinuated himself into Jenny's life by this time and she had become dedicated to him. But at one point she thought it was over. "I was to have picked him up but was rushing because I was late and banged up the car," she relates. "I drove to where I was to pick him up, but he wasn't angry. He did what he called 'biting his tongue.' Al felt it was wrong to lose his temper at people, although he would do it. He would be in a political rage, never never personal.

He tried not to be personally hurt. He believed you had to adjust your expectations of people and then you wouldn't be hurt by them. He expected a huge amount, more than they could give, but he was still accepting and enthusiastic about people's talents, however minor. I had zero self-esteem, and he thought I was bright, funny, and pretty. It was tremendously important."

Lowenstein said to her: "How could you be so late? You messed me up."

They drove the wrecked car to Granson's Restaurant, a Lowenstein establishment on Lexington Avenue and 49th Street and sat in a booth. It was about 8:30 at night.

"God, I'm so sorry about the car," Jenny apologized.

Lowenstein was unperturbed.

"Don't worry about that. What I think we really should do is get married," he said.

Taken aback, her reply was, "You're kidding." Then she added, "That's a subject we'll have to think about."

Lowenstein dropped the subject temporarily, but he would bring it up out of the blue while they were driving around. "How are you doing on the subject of marriage?" he would ask. In fact, he was winning her over. Though unimpressed at their first meeting, she soon found him personally "beguiling." To that attraction was added the glamour of his public side and the promise it offered of power and fame. To Lowenstein, it was the public side that was the reality. Running for Congress was its ultimate expression.

40.

The campaign was for the seat held by regular organization Democrat Leonard Farbstein in the 19th Congressional District of Manhattan, and the battle was among members of the New York Reform Democratic Movement for the right to oppose the incumbent in the primary. It was called a "preprimary," and members of the various reform clubs in the district voted in an area that included the Lower East Side and the hook of lower Manhattan and which ran up the West Side to West 86th Street. Its strangely drawn lines gave it a saxophonelike shape within which various shades of liberalism and left-wing ideology prevailed.

Reform Democrats would vote on March 6 for their favorite reformer among a group of candidates; Lowenstein, City Councilman Ted Weiss, R. Peter Straus of WMCA Radio, and Justin Feldman, a prominent attorney.

Lowenstein's campaign was run by Ronnie Eldridge, district

leader of the Reform Independent Democrats who had run Robert Kennedy's successful campaign for United States Senate in New York State. Lowenstein had the backing of a solid group of prominent reformers but there was also resentment against him. "Al was not liked by lots of people in the West Side reform movement." Brooke Aronson Trent, who had helped him with *Brutal Mandate*, relates. "He just arrived in the midst of all these people who had put in all the time and he wanted to be the savior."

Lowenstein accused Weiss of having the backing of the "far left," while Lowenstein was accused of "Red-baiting." ("Far Left Backing Weiss, 'Red-Baiting' Laid to A," he wrote in his diary.) Lowenstein was criticized for his actions in Mississippi, but the Communist party indicated that it was "neutral" in the race. All the reform candidates opposed the bombing of North Vietnam and supported a cease-fire and an international conference to settle the issues dividing the parties to the war. Lowenstein pointed to his liberal Democratic credentials including his association with Eleanor Roosevelt, stressing his "commitment to the liberal principles which have motivated the reform movement" and to the "dispossessed," both in the district and "all over the world." Speaking on the Lower East Side, he reminded his audience of his roots: "I have a feeling of homecoming when I come to East Broadway or Madison Street or Henry Street or Grand Street or Clinton Street. . . . These streets are where my parents spent their teenage lives. . . . My mother whose maiden name was Goldstein taught at Corlears Junior High School on Monroe and Jackson Streets."

Lowenstein reminded them that his father, Gabriel Lowenstein, had taught at the Eron School and was president of the board of Madison House. "He must have helped many of you to pass your regents for college," he told them. His father had helped the children have summer vacations at Camp Felicia and Camp Madison, which he had founded. "So you see I'm not a stranger about this section," Lowenstein concluded. "I learned more than some people who live here know."

Across the top of the handwritten speech, a note instructed him: "Read; use; it may help when they think you are one of them or you know about them."

Lowenstein gained the support of liberals who were against the war in Vietnam but who were also anti-Communist. Amherst student Stephen Cohen, who lived on West 87th Street, attended campaign kaffeeklatsches and engaged him in discussions about the war. Cohen (who concluded a letter to Lowenstein on the subject by stating that his views coincided with those of moderate critics of the administration's policies who felt that Vietnam was not worth the price the U.S. was paying, but believed that some other place "might very well be worth the price") became a staunch supporter of Lowenstein's. He joined Lowenstein later in the McCarthy campaign and worked for him in his 1968 congressional race on Long Island.

Meanwhile, Lowenstein's army of friends and supporters gathered to bolster his chances. A large testimonial dinner for him was held and Barney Frank, who happens to be a talented stand-up comic as well as a clever politician, came down from Boston to serve as the emcee. Frank Graham and Norman Thomas addressed the 400 guests, among whom were the Reverend Ed King and Aaron Henry from Mississippi. After the speeches, folk-singer Phil Ochs sang. Before he became famous, Ochs had been in the habit of reading his songs to Lowenstein before he performed them. Lowenstein believed Ochs, who later committed suicide, was "emotionally fragile."

That night Ochs sang a raunchy, satirical song about "fucking in the U.S.A." Norman Thomas, who was hard of hearing, was not sure he was getting the words, and leaned forward, shaking his huge, lantern-like head in Lowenstein's direction. Lowenstein, straight and square about language, whispered: "Ochs is so lost. He needs help."

Meanwhile, Farbstein, who sat on the Foreign Affairs Committee and had fought off several other attempts by reformers to unseat him, went about his business, consolidating his support with the regular organization and the clubhouses. He and his supporters were oblivious to the attacks of reformers who charged that he was evading the issue of the war in Vietnam.

Robert Kennedy was not oblivious to the growing antiwar movement. A former "hawk," he began speaking out about the war from his new base in the United States Senate. His suggestion that the Viet Cong should be offered "a share of power" in Vietnam, put him in the Fulbright camp of the American establishment, opposed to Johnson's intransigence and personalization of the war. Lowenstein picked up on Kennedy's initiative. *The New York Times* wrote: "Mr. Lowenstein said he was grateful to Mr. Kennedy for helping make it clear that any interim regime, pending Vietnam elections, could not simply be the current regime of Premier Nguyen Cao Ky. Mr. Lowenstein suggested . . . a coalition including the Viet Cong or some sort of international trusteeship."

The New York Times called the race "one of the best political shows in town" but declined to endorse anyone. The reformers voted on March 10 in a series of rounds. The candidate with the lowest tally was dropped from the succeeding round.

Straus led the first vote with 681, Ted Weiss and Lowenstein trailing with 598 and 575 respectively, with Justin Feldman last, well behind. In the next round, Straus clung to his lead with 736; Weiss was second again with 650 and Lowenstein followed with 637. Lowenstein believed he had been eliminated by only eleven votes. In the final run-off, Weiss defeated Straus 1009 to 966, only to lose to Farbstein in the primary. Weiss was considered very liberal. Lowenstein, who was less liberal, probably would have fared better against Farbstein, but it was his problem that he was not liberal enough for the reformers but too liberal for the regulars.

Unfortunately for Lowenstein, a highly favorable interview in *The New Yorker* did not appear until March 12, two days after the election. It made him a celebrity of sorts. "Mr. Lowenstein is a thirty-seven-year-old attorney—a rugged-looking man, easy, humorous, and earnest, who can be found in a state of repose only after sensible people have been in bed for hours. By day, he races through appointed rounds of conferences, kaffeeklatsches, and rallies. At night, he takes off his shoes, squats Indian-style on the floor of a friend's apartment, and explains, in an uncannily lucid manner, what must be done about Rhodesia or Vietnam or Mississippi or Harlem."

The author, Jacob Brackman, listed the Lowenstein credentials: "The truth of the matter is that he has spent the past twenty years dashing about the globe toiling in the service of Causes: in Spain, helping the organized opposition to Franco; in Southwest Africa, investigating conditions, smuggling out anti-apartheid tape recordings, gathering evidence of oppression to present to the United Nations, and writing *Brutal Mandate*, a widely admired book about the South African situation; in Mississippi, working for 'the movement' before that became modish; in Manhattan, campaigning for William Fitz Ryan in the early days of the Reform Democratic insurgency; in Washington, serving as legislative assistant to Senator Frank Graham, and later, as foreign-policy adviser to Senator Hubert Humphrey; at Stanford, teaching international law; at North Carolina state, teaching political science; in Los Angeles, serving as a delegate to the Democratic National Convention; in Atlantic City, counseling the Freedom Democratic Party, and, from Oregon to Massachusetts, helping to found a national group called Americans for Reappraisal of Far Eastern Policy. By the time we had finished splicing this roster of credentials together, we were beginning to suspect that Lowenstein must have doubles planted in trouble spots around the world poised for action whenever the need arose."

Lowenstein dissembled when he explained how he was able to do all of this, claiming that the wisest accident of his postcollege life was "that I've never really tried to plan ahead." "I've tried to do what seemed useful and interesting as the time came. I know that occasionally people who love me have wished they knew what I was going to do, and thought it would be better for me if I settled into being a lawyer, but when I was supposedly practicing on a full-time basis I got so deeply involved in other things that I wasn't much of a breadwinner at it. You see, the priority of your goals gets complicated if you're trying to build up a law practice and are always being tangentially pulled into struggles you believe in."

He lived on the cheap, he told Brackman, which enabled him to do what he wanted. "Now, I have a very uneducated palate—I eat hamburgers and hot dogs a great deal. . . . I don't smoke or drink, and my clothes are hardly stylish, so although I've always wished there were greater sums available for the things I care about, and although I've been improvident about saving, I've been able to earn enough by teaching and occasional writing and legal work to get by."

Lowenstein told Brackman that Norman Thomas was a model for him, and that Thomas had run for office without any thought of winning. "He's been willing to sacrifice his own power to worthwhile principles, to lost individuals. That kind of life lights up the sky, and there are dozens of state senators and United States senators who have never achieved anything like it."

When asked about marriage and getting a job, Lowenstein replied: "I came very close to getting married once. But marriage, of course, can get in the way of your doing the things you are moved to do. It depends on whether you marry a person who shares your feelings of wanting to live a life of some service. I guess that goes back to your question about security. Security is something internal. And for some people to feel right inside they must know that they have a lot of money or a job they aren't going to lose. But that's a matter of what they've learned to want. I couldn't separate my life into a career part and a private part, the way many men do. I feel curious about ways of living I haven't seen and kinds of experiences I haven't had. We live a very short time. Aren't we fools to restrict ourselves arbitrarily even more than time itself restricts us?"

Lowenstein said he was a liberal when asked where he stood politically, and then spoke at length about the successes he had achieved in Mississippi with the Freedom Vote. "The real radicals always said that the country didn't care, that the country was basically indifferent to the oppression of Negroes," he stated, "but I always felt that if we could let people know what was going on, they wouldn't stand for it. 'Well,' we said, 'all right, bring people *into* Mississippi.' And so there began this sort of series of new procedures that are finally starting to make the old procedures work, even in Mississippi—where more Negroes have been registered to vote in one year than were registered in the previous century. Rednecks who'd worn buttons reading 'Never!' are now saying that we've got to accept the change. Very soon you'll have congressmen from the South who will be more liberal than congressmen from New York. Because they'll be an accurate reflection of the needs of that area."

Did that mean, asked Brackman, that "the old liberalism still works after all?" To that Lowenstein replied that although liberalism had been basically successful, people were still unhappy. "When I was in college, I think we all felt that if we could produce a society in which we'd removed the scourges of war and dictatorship and racism and poverty, we'd have a happy society. That was the liberal creed. Yet it's a fact that now, for the vast majority of our people, we've removed many of the external forms of misery, we've attained our goals, and there's still the hollowness. Our personal lives, in many cases, have been successful without being fulfilled or happy, the way we thought they would be. We live in a society today that may be even more fundamentally unhappy than the old one. We have to figure out what's missing at the center of the person now."

Lowenstein saw an answer to this problem in the kind of life he had chosen. He said: "What life is all about is how you spend the day, and each day becomes part of this totality of involvement. So you build, as you go along, a life in which you may do many things, in different situations, with different kinds of people. But it all has a common denominator that gives it some sense, some direction—the sense that your total activity is going to make a better situation for people to live in."

Brackman's interview, like the writing later on of James Wechsler, David Halberstam, Ronnie Dugger, and Flora Lewis, contributed to the creation of the Lowenstein legend. He was portrayed as a liberal gadfly without a job and without ambition who devoted his life to causes. His political ambition, his CIA connection and his flaws are not part of the legend. Certainly he cared about the goals he professed; he was for civil rights and against apartheid and Franco. But the whole issue of "authenticity" which was so hotly debated in the sixties arose because many suspected that things were not what they appeared to be, that liberalism was an illusion masking a reality of manipulation and self-interest.

They were troubled when liberals emphasized the barrenness of middle class life over the struggles of those who were trying to lift themselves out of poverty. When Lowenstein asserted that "very often, young people in our society don't take advantage of the fluidity of our society and the freedom that they have," and warned students against getting bogged down with the concerns of security, those who knew he had money of his own and suspected he had a hidden employment felt he spoke in bad faith. His criticism of marriage could also be seen, in retrospect, as less than honest, a denial of his desire to marry Barbara Boggs (who had broken off their engagement), of his courtship of Jenny, and as a sign of his refusal to deal with his own complex sexuality.

No sooner had the votes been counted in the 19th C.D. than Lowenstein began exploring other districts in Westchester and Manhattan, writing in his diary: "Race in 12 C.D. ruled out. 'Boom' in 17th Is

Growing." He would, in fact, run for Congress every two years until his death. Looking at himself in the mirror, he observed: "'Time marches on' but 'A' looks much the same." And indeed, Lowenstein was able to shrug off his defeat. Unlike many of those close to him whose disappointment was deep, he was always able to regroup, to move on. And although his friends wondered about his future, they also found cause for hope in his refusal to stop doing whatever it was he was doing. "Then the old liberalism still works, after all?" they were able to say, even if there was some doubt creeping into their voices.

41.

By 1966, doubts about the war in Vietnam had grown even within the administration. Lowenstein reflected this growing disillusionment with the war and with Lyndon Johnson when he participated in a panel debate on the Vietnam war at the University of North Carolina at Chapel Hill on May 17, 1966. Joining him on the panel were former foreign policy official George Lodge, Duke law professor Arthur Larson, and Henry Kissinger of Harvard. Lowenstein did not favor a complete pull-out from Vietnam and was opposed to the Communists. His position was characteristic "good-wing" realism, based on intelligence indicating that America could not win the war and should therefore seek to end it by negotiations. Lowenstein outlined the long history of misplaced optimism concerning the outcome of the war which he said was, in fact, "militarily unwinnable." The only way to win a war on the mainland of Asia, he said, "is to be prepared for a nuclear war." Excluding that as a rational alternative, one "basic fact" remained, he observed. "The more we continue to pour people in, the more they pour people in—and they have more people there." Concluding his statement, Lowenstein asked his audience to "face what the military situation is. We are not going to win. We are going to have more and more people committed there. We are going to have 400,000. We are going to be doubling the bombing strikes. We are going to make ourselves more and more committed to a situation from which we cannot extricate ourselves honorably, and then all of us who feel that the initial commitment was very possibly well intentioned face a much more serious question, which is what justification is there now for what we are doing there?. . ."

Lowenstein argued that the Dominican Republic had been a "tragic blunder," adding, "The tragedy of that mistake is being repeated on an irreversible scale now in South Vietnam, where in fact we are creating a situation that we can't get out of without an endless land war in Asia—for what?"

"The solution in Vietnam," he insisted, "must be a political solution, and if that's the case, then the price we pay politically for what we're doing is one of the greatest considerations in what we should be doing." Lowenstein singled out America's failure to identify with the forces for basic social change in the world as the nation's "greatest problem" and blamed "episodes like the Dominican Republic and Vietnam" for that failure. He predicted that those forces seeking social change would, in fact, cause turbulence in the world in the next decades and argued that Americans "would be much more faithful to our heritage and to our interests were we to align ourselves with these forces everywhere possible, rather than to make ourselves roadblocks as we have too often. . . ."

While he noted that "we're all using rhetoric about how we want to get free elections and a discussion that will lead to some sort of solution," Lowenstein warned that "we're not taking the steps that would make that possible when the other side gets around to it. . . . And it's that question that ought to be primary for all Americans now. Figure out a way that we can reverse course before this leads us into a collision that's desperately useless for us and that can mean the end of the whole concept of a peaceful world looking toward a decent life for people in it."

There was an increasing awareness that unless there was a peace movement within the established political process, dissent would be monopolized by the radicals and revolutionaries. Even within the CIA, "good-wing" theory apparently held that the war in Vietnam was jeopardizing hard-won domestic gains and driving young people out of the system into radical, antiwar organizations just as it was hurting America's international status, undermining the "good wing's" work in the Third World. Lowenstein offered an answer to the threat of the New Left: a loyal opposition. He opposed what Johnson was doing; he also wanted to stop the New Left. He was poised for an important role in the new liberal politics that the war was creating, ready to reject the old Cold War hard-line he himself had espoused in the past. Change America's China policy, he argued. Stop the bombing of North Vietnam and start negotiations, he pleaded at Chapel Hill.

Lowenstein saw the problem in simple terms. Stopping Communism was right. But the war could not be won. So there should be a negotiated settlement. Johnson would not negotiate. (Nor would Ho Chi Minh, but Lowenstein's position apparently failed to take that into consideration.) Johnson should be persuaded to change his policy, and if he would not, he should be replaced.

On the campuses, there was a different approach to the problem. The war, like racism, was viewed by some students as a symptom of something deeply wrong in American society, a distorted sense of values. They recognized a cultural as well as a political problem and instinctively, sought to go to the root of it, becoming authentic radicals in the process. They rejected the values of their parents and thus of their own country and what they believed it stood for.

Lowenstein could neither reject his family's values (his father was his idol) nor what his country stood for. For him the enemy was not so much Ho Chi Minh or even Lyndon Johnson. It was the "New Left" with its "new politics of alienation" as Lowenstein referred to it. The "direct action" methods of the civil rights movement were being used improperly in the New Politics, Lowenstein believed. The old coalitions of the Democratic party were splintering and Lowenstein placed the blame on Johnson. He believed that it was Johnson's refusal to implement various progressive policies, that had unleashed new forces which would perhaps never win over a majority of Americans but could nevertheless do grave damage.

There is no precise indication of authorship of the June 17, 1966, typewritten analysis of the politics of alienation in his papers, but Lowenstein's point of view is glaring:

The third milestone to the politics of 1966 is the Vietnamese war. There perhaps would still have been a New Left in 1966 without the Vietnamese war, but the war gives it its strength, its financial support, and its ability to draw together so many disparate forces. There has been nothing in American history like the war in Vietnam. Never have so many disagreed so vehemently about so much. Rarely has a nation been so committed with so little support from its people. The ever-increasing commitment to that war has created an ever-increasing splintering of American public opinion. For the liberals and radicals who helped elect Johnson and thought it meant peace, it has meant a feeling of captivity and a will to break out of that captivity even if it means upsetting other important applecarts. And for others of all political persuasions it has meant the progressive polarization of the American political spectrum from hawk to dove with many of both being anti-government. Other factors related to Vietnam also have helped the New Left gain much of its impetus. With the exception of the Civil Rights Movement of 1960–64, and the trade union movement of the 1930's, there has never been as massive a vocal and activist concern about any issue as there has been about Vietnam in 1964–66. There have been huge mass demonstrations conducted with great decorum, smaller ones conducted with much less decorum, editorials and articles in hundreds of publications, teach-ins at almost every American campus, sit-ins at a number of them, Congressional opposition and letters of protest, even candidates committed to peace who have run and won, with no apparent effect on the direction of policy. The fact that despite the massive protest, there has been no general consensus behind an alternative course, means little to protestors who have felt, quite rightly, that full-scale active participation in any and all forms of the political process deserves at least a hearing, if not a reward in a change of policy. To compound the sin and be derogated as unpatriotic or "nervous Nellies" only serves to further alienate this large segment of the American populace not only from the government but from the very basic political processes upon which government by consent of the governed was founded.

The result has been the creation of "a new politics" of alienation, which is increasingly venting its frustration with the war and other social ills through independent action in the political process. Under any of three formulations—through one-issue peace candidates, through candidates who combine the motivations of peace candidates and insurgent radical perspective toward domestic issues, or through the device of defeating Democrats regardless of their opposition if they support the war—these practitioners of the new politics seek to change the Congressional consensus on Vietnam. But though their motivations are unquestioned, and though in some areas they may perform a creative function, the net result may well be a very worse climate for a peaceful settlement of the war and for future domestic progress toward attainable social goals.

Early that summer, Lowenstein wrote in his diary: "Gans to organize Vietnamese vote group. 'A' 'Key,' agrees to July 'survey' trip 'if needed'; China group ready." The new group, organized by Curtis Gans, was to raise funds for liberal war-critic candidates who were not one-issue and who were established within the Democratic party. Participating in a July 14, 1966, meeting were Leon Shull and Curtis Gans of the ADA, representatives from the Council for a Livable World, the Industrial Union Department of the AFL-CIO, SANE, and four members of the Inter-Universities Committee, Allard Lowenstein among them.

Minutes of the meeting reported that "the group continued its discussion of the possibilities of cooperation, coordination and coalition among moderate organizations working against the war in Vietnam." The list of candidates to be supported included "Brown, Porter, Wilson, Dow, Corman, Dyal, Leggett, Todd, Vivian, Helstowski, McCarthy (N.Y.), Ottinger, Hicks, Adams, Grider, Schmidhauser, Leppert; and if entered into re-run elections, Weiss and Dubin."

Gans was assigned to prepare and circulate detailed background materials on each of the candidates. Hope was expressed that representatives of the Union of American Hebrew Congregations, the American Friends Service Committee, the Friends Committee on National Legislation, the Southern Christian Leadership Conference, and the Packinghouse, Butcher Workmen, and Amalgamated Clothing Workers unions would join the group, and another meeting was scheduled for the end of July at SANE's New York office.

Lowenstein himself was, meanwhile, preoccupied with other matters. His diary that summer indicates that he believed that his marriage to Jenny was no longer in doubt. Referring to Jenny as "I.J.," he wrote in banner headlines: "I.J. Agrees To a Date in Early Fall, Engagement is 'Undesirable.' 'Announcement Only Unsettled Question' 'A' Says 'Small Wedding Probable' Summer in Miss. For Her and Abroad for Him. 'Something Jewish' Necessary, Rest in Flux. The 'Public Life' Decision Remains, and Discussion Is Difficult; Summer Trips Unaffected and I.J. Insists It Must Ever Be Thus."

But according to Jenny, she did not consider the marriage question settled. Anxious to spend the summer in Mississippi because she felt she had "missed out" on the civil rights campaign there and wanted to tie into it in some way, she got a job, arranged by Lowenstein, on the *Lexington Advertise* in Lexington, Mississippi. The paper was run by Hazel Brannon Smith, the white journalist who had been ostracized by the white community for supporting integration. But by 1966 the "black power" and "separatist" movements had been launched and Smith was viewed as "old hat." Jenny learned from the summer, however. She lived at Smith's house, wrote a series of articles on Head Start, and got to know some of Lowenstein's associates from 1963 and '64, including the Rev. Ed King. She experienced a small town in the Deep South for the first time, though things were far quieter than when Robert Moses, Dennis Sweeney, and Lowenstein had been there a short time before.

Because Lowenstein had been raising the question of marriage with increasing frequency, Jenny says she wrote him a letter from Lexington stressing their need to get to know each other better and telling him that she believed it would be best if getting married were postponed. But when Lowenstein came to Mississippi to visit her, he made no mention of the letter. Instead, he said:

"I've just been having supper with you mother and planning the wedding."

Lowenstein had become great friends with Olivia, Jenny's mother. During his visits, at which he regaled her with funny stories and satires of the famous political figures he knew, she would feed him grape juice and "Devil Dogs." It was evident that she was very much for the wedding. But when Lowenstein told Jenny that he and her mother had been making plans for it, Jenny, puzzled, asked whether he had gotten her letter.

"What letter?" he responded.

Lowenstein went on to say that he had never received it, or must have lost it. "You know," Jenny exclaims, "everything they say about Al Lowenstein. Manipulative and all the rest. But maybe he really did lose it. He was ebullient and decided it was going to happen and it did."

By the time Jenny got back to New York, Lowenstein and Olivia were in a "conspiracy," as Jenny describes it, to convince Jenny's father to accept the marriage, though Jenny insists she still hadn't decided. "I loved Al," she acknowledges. "He was the most extraordinary person I had ever met, and I was dumbfounded that he wanted to marry me. But I didn't know him and knew it was taking a chance."

Lowenstein's first meeting with Jenny's father evidently took place before Lyman had been informed about any wedding plans because Lowenstein wrote: "Lyman meeting brief, plans not mentioned; Boston visit urged."

Pressure from Lowenstein and her mother continued and Jenny finally agreed to the marriage. She and Lowenstein traveled to her father's farm in New Hampshire, where Lowenstein was going to "ask him for her hand." Ronald Lyman was apparently puzzled by the courtship but agreed reluctantly to accept Lowenstein as his son-in-law. Lowenstein, on the other hand, liked Lyman immensely.

Returning to the farm after driving Lowenstein to the airport, Jenny found the atmosphere as chilly as a New Hampshire autumn morning. No one talked.

Finally, after a silent breakfast, Lyman spoke: "I will give a wedding," he proclaimed, "but I can't accept it. He's a different religion, a different class, a different age group, and a different race."

When Jenny told Lowenstein what her father had said, he quipped: "You should have said, 'At least he's the same color.'"

Lowenstein and Jenny agreed that she would not get a diamond ring because of their disapproval of South African racial policies. Instead, Jenny was given an opal ring. A few years later, when the band broke, the ring was replaced by one with two diamonds in a diagonal setting, given to them by a black South African woman.

The wedding took place on November 26, 1966, at "The Vale," a historic house in Waltham, Massachusetts, which belonged to Jenny's grandfather. The stately mansion was used as a museum, but the family repossessed it for this major occasion to which many were invited. Jenny's mother submitted her list and was given invitations for them. Lowenstein had the invitations copied and sent out a batch to his own list of friends—liberal political activists opposed to the Vietnam war, supporters of civil rights, some black friends, and the like. Hundreds of extras went out but most of those on Lowenstein's special list didn't come. Present, however, were Norman Thomas, Frank Graham, Franklin Roosevelt III, and Wendell Willkie II, as Jenny's father and stepmother presided over a very proper Bostonian wedding.

Lowenstein had wanted to be married by a minister and a rabbi, but William Sloane Coffin told him he would have trouble finding a rabbi to perform an interfaith marriage, which turned out to be true. After extensive searching, Olivia came up with one who made them promise not to tell anyone what he had done. The minister was Coffin, because, as he explains, "I was his closest buddy in the cloth. I don't do weddings that are not religious. I stretched it in Al's case."

The day before the ceremony there was a luncheon at Lyman's Beacon Street house. Coffin was greeted at the door by a prim Boston matron who showed him inside, where he recognized Norman Thomas. Turning to the Boston lady, Coffin couldn't resist asking her how it felt to be at a gathering with a Socialist.

"I don't know any Socialists," she proclaimed.

"Well, that's Norman Thomas, the biggest Socialist in America," he replied. The woman gasped in horror.

There had been a debate over what Lowenstein would wear. Jenny's father had wanted a full cutaway, a proposal supported by two of Jenny's brothers. Lowenstein, however, refused to put on formal attire and was backed by a third brother, who said that if Lowenstein wanted to wear a simple suit, he would wear one as well. In the end, only Jenny's father wore a morning suit. Lowenstein wore a brown business suit and Jenny wore her older sister's wedding dress and the Lyman family veil. Then Lowenstein balked at a formal cake-cutting and refused to drink any wine. "Is this grape juice?" he asked the rabbi and then broke the glass with his foot in traditional Jewish wedding fashion. Finally, to everybody's relief, he cut the cake.

The whole wedding had been an ordeal. It had been difficult for Olivia to return, having left Lyman's house "in disgrace" and having lost custody of the children. And although Lyman had been decent, had even huddled on a sofa with Frank Graham and Norman Thomas at one point for a discussion, it had been a strain on him as it had been on his daughter and her husband.

When it was all over, the couple drove away in the Mustang Jenny had wrecked during the congressional campaign. Lowenstein had wanted a honeymoon in South Africa or Spain where he had work to do but was persuaded to have a "real" honeymoon. With money borrowed from Charles Levien, his cousin's husband, they went to the island of St. Johns in the Virgin Islands, where Hubert Humphrey was also vacationing. When some Secret Service men arrived at their hotel door to invite them aboard the vice-presidential yacht, Jenny says she was dubious, afraid that their brief escape might turn into a political affair after all.

But once on the yacht, it was "funny and bizarre," she says. Jenny was "star struck." Humphrey was an "ebullient and nice man" who talked a lot and Muriel was an "impressive" woman. While they were enjoying themselves, a terrible squall came up. Muriel and Jenny swam ashore while Humphrey and Lowenstein rowed all the way in.

Just before leaving for the Virgin Islands, Jenny had realized that she had unintentionally included her birth control prescription with the marriage papers which she had mailed to the rabbi. She quickly discovered, once back in New York, that she was pregnant. Lowenstein began teaching constitutional law at City College on a part-time basis in the political science department (the department chairman was John A. Davis, who was named head of the American Society of African Culture with which Lowenstein had ties), and they moved into an apartment on West 81st Street, a block away from his parents' old apartment. When they walked into it for the first time as a married couple, Lowenstein looked around and said: "This is an apartment that every Jewish boy in Manhattan dreams of growing up in and running away from."

Yet in his married life with Jenny, he was compelled to bring her with him to neighborhoods that were, in their way, ghettos. The ostensible reason was politics. In 1966, the Upper West Side was the focal point of antiwar activity in New York and he was still trying to run for Congress (the 12th and 17th C.D.s remained possibilities). If Jenny had her doubts about the marriage, she had her reasons. She wasn't just marrying a man; she was marrying his causes.

42.

That summer, Lowenstein had a great many things on his mind. The CIA relationship with the NSA was coming to a head. Seven months before the story was made public in *Ramparts* in the March 1967 edition, Lowenstein wrote in his diary: "The CIA has subsidized NSA for a decade and breaking the ice is tough." He added later on during the summer: "CIA money shadow a spooky factor," by way of a little joke to himself. The belief on the part of New Left students that Lowenstein was affiliated with the CIA made him a prime target for their animosity toward liberals in general. They saw his activity with regard to the Vietnam War as yet another example of an inauthentic attempt to stifle a radical movement.

The CIA link notwithstanding, Lowenstein did try to accommodate some of the radical currents without upsetting the existing liberal order. The two public figures he believed might make this possible were Robert Kennedy and Martin Luther King, Jr. There was talk that Lowenstein might work for Kennedy in some capacity. In his diary, Lowenstein wrote: "RFK staff post seems out. Johnson 'wonders' if 'any' post with RFK would 'interest' A." President Johnson was aware of Lowenstein's activities, as this entry indicates. In fact, Johnson had a reputation for being acutely aware of the most minute details of government and politics.

Already opposed to Johnson, Lowenstein noted in his diary during the summer of 1966: "A favors RFK in '68 and 'failing that' would back MLK as things stand now." Johnson's speeches were beginning to sound irrational, almost hysterical to him, and he concluded that if Kennedy did not run, the next best thing would be to have a protest candidacy by Martin Luther King, Jr., who had come out against the war in Vietnam that spring. The seeds of Dump Johnson had been planted in Lowenstein's mind long before the actual organizing and the endless letters which called on the president to reconsider his policies and to discuss them with those who were concerned about the war. Having decided to oppose Johnson, Lowenstein needed to build up the momentum and make a public show of exhausting all other remedies within the system.

Lowenstein believed that what Johnson was doing in Vietnam was not unrelated to the deteriorating situation in Africa. In July of 1966, the World Court handed down its decision on South West Africa, holding that Ethiopia and Liberia had no standing to bring a case challenging South Africa's mandate because they could not show any injury to themselves. Lowenstein observed: "Court decision means 'violence,' sanctions out, anti-S.A. groups agree; SWAPO asks A to organize. Jolt is 'devastating.'" Lowenstein had played an important role in convincing the Africans to use nonviolence, pressing them to take their grievances to the United Nations and the World Court. But the United States was backing away from sanctions against South Africa, and the World Court had closed the door to a legal settlement. The Africans America had worked so hard to win over saw the Johnson administration as an enemy, and the escalation of the war in Vietnam reinforced their opinion that America was not the friend to the newly independent countries it pretended to be. Johnson would not let the U.N. deal with the Vietnam question; he was undermining all the work of the "good wing."

Lowenstein attended meetings at the Rand Corporation to formulate a new United Nations policy. He wrote: "Lengthy Rand sessions produce plan for conference to chart new approach to U.N. with 'intellectual underpinnings.'" But ultimately, from the "good-wing" point of view, only the removal of Johnson would solve the problem.

Although Lowenstein's stepmother was close to death ("'F' IS 'FAILING FAST' MEYERS SAYS—NOTHING CAN BE DONE; WAYS SOUGHT TO 'BRIGHTEN THE END.' TRIPS MAY BE OFF," he wrote), she recovered sufficiently for him to travel to Africa and Spain for extensive CIA-related work. The assassination of South African Prime Minister Verwoerd almost threw a monkey wrench into the African trip, but he accomplished his mission there. Lowenstein was troubled by bad health while abroad and jotted down: "Sharpened pain hits chest twice, A will confer S.B. on return." S.B. was Sherman Bull, who had accompanied him to Africa in 1959 as a medical student and who was by then a practicing physician. Lowenstein did not have a heart condition as he feared but would be felled at the peak of the McCarthy campaign with a gall bladder attack.

On his return, Lowenstein discovered that the New Left politics of alienation was spreading into what had been mainstream student movements. He wondered if Robert Kennedy was vulnerable because of his personal life ("RFK and MM. Was her last call to him? Is he blackmailable?" he asked himself) and feared that without Kennedy the students would turn to direct-action tactics, which he considered revolutionary and anti-America. The basic weapon of the antiwar radicals was draft resistance, advocated by radical historian Staughton Lynd. Lowenstein opposed Lynd and this tactic but he was particularly distressed to find that it was now being advocated within the NSA.

Lowenstein did not decide to organize against American policy in Vietnam until the NSA congress at Urbana in the summer of 1966. According to Greg Craig, who had just been elected president of the Harvard student council, it was the position of the radicals that propelled him into action. Lowenstein had come to Urbana to debate Stokely Carmichael. He was convinced that the main area of concern in NSA was civil rights and not international affairs. Instead, he found the radicals pressing for resistance to the draft and sympathetic to Hanoi and the Viet Cong. Craig, who was summoned to Urbana by Lowenstein, says that "Al understood that the war was infecting the political climate and knew that we had to change policy."

Instead of debating Carmichael, who failed to appear, Lowenstein faced his substitute, recently elected president of the Stanford student body, David Harris. A friend had sent Lowenstein a clipping from the *San Francisco Chronicle* describing Harris's election. Correspondent Bill Moore had written: "A tall, blond, articulate admirer of the 'New Left,' who bills himself as a revolutionary, is the new president of the Stanford University student body. . . . Harris usually campaigned in dungarees, a rumpled sport coat and sandals. He took strong stands in favor of student strikes, abolition of fraternities, abolition of the

grading system and of required courses and student voting representation on the Stanford Board of Trustees. 'I was forged with the student revolutionary spirit,' the personable victor said."

Harris, who said he admired Mario Savio of the Free Speech
Movement and radical educator Paul Goodman, had worked for
SNCC in Mississippi in 1965 but was not considered political. His
candidacy had begun as a protest ("When we started we figured the
most we would get would be 200 votes," he had said), and after his
surprise election, he had indicated that he would not attend the NSA
congress. He had spoken to Greg Craig about forming a new student
axis and indicated that he would not be going to Urbana, saying, "I
have no truck with these political types." He changed his mind about
going, though, believing he should be there to participate in the debate over the war.

That Lowenstein, by then in his late thirties, was at Urbana gave
substance to the remark of his friend from Yale Law School, the journalist Fred Graham, who said that Lowenstein was "the oldest student
leader in America." (Graham also said Lowenstein was "someone who
knows everyone in America.") But Lowenstein had a specific reason
for working with the students as the antiwar movement accelerated.
Both he and Craig concluded there was a great danger that if the
radicals prevailed, as Craig would put it at a class-day speech at Harvard, a "whole generation would be lost to the political process." Lowenstein used this phrase and singled out the pacifist Staughton Lynd
as one of the most dangerous participants in the antiwar movement
because of his advocacy of passive resistance. To the Communist
threat was added the specter of millions of young people actively resisting the authority of their government.

Lowenstein had written in his diary, "A Agrees to Debate Carmichael at NSA." But as the issue changed and Harris came forward on
the matter of draft resistance, Lowenstein wrote: "D.H. wants to
avoid jail, but plans anti-draft push. NSA to be focus of effort to develop wide protest; 'Effectiveness' a valid query, he tells A; Shurtleff
to refuse C.O." The decision of some students to refuse a conscientious objector status and to go to jail instead of doing military service
was unacceptable to Lowenstein, not only as a strategy to end the war,
but as a protest against the government. It may also have been an
uncomfortable reminder of how he had handled his own draft status
during the Korean war.

Harris introduced a series of resolutions out of the Liberal Caucus
(which was, in fact, radical), calling the war imperialist and racist.
Lowenstein and Craig disagreed. The decision makers, in their view,
were neither racist nor imperialist but were overreacting to Soviet
expansion. "Did you say it was racist, imperialist, thereby alienating
vast numbers of Americans, or did you rationally explain why it was a

miscalculation of what our own national interests were and how best to defend democracy?" Craig asks. According to Craig, "To Al, it was a nationalist war. There were two civil wars; the one between the north and the south, and the one in the south between those hostile to Thieu and those supporting him. We were drawn in by our perception that one side was Communist. It was our overblown fear of the Communists."

According to Rick Weidman (who was then president of the student body at Colgate and would later become a Lowenstein backer after serving in Vietnam), "It looked like the whole thing was going to break up. Harris wanted a resolution supporting the NLF." NSA conservatives pressed for a resolution supporting the draft as essential, while the radicals, led by Harris, wanted one calling for civil disobedience to protest the unfairness of the Selective Service. The liberals were in the middle with their own resolution which acknowledged the unfairness of the system and criticized American foreign policy, Lowenstein's position.

Harris would later write:

> He said the war was a tragic mistake. I said it was the logical conclusion of the values holding national sway. I said the war would never be ended in an election. He said it not only could, but would. He reminded people that he was no pacifist and had served as an enlisted man in the United States Army for two years. I said I wasn't sure if I was a pacifist or not, but that I was sure no one ever stopped a war by fighting in it. He said the point was "to be effective." I said the real point was "effective for what?" When asked what he would do if he were drafted, Allard said young people ought to find any deferment they could to stay out, but if they ended up being called, then they should go. I said massive civil disobedience was the most honorable strategic option we had and that I would personally refuse either to carry a draft card or be inducted.
>
> The audience got the show it had come for. "All over the room," the *Daily Bruin* editor said years later, "there was a sense that people were listening hard," and that "minds were being made up."

Lowenstein spoke for the system and he prevailed. The resolution offered by the radicals was voted down, and the watered-down resolution backed by Lowenstein passed. Harris broke with Lowenstein and went on to become a leader in the draft resistance movement, joined by Dennis Sweeney. Lowenstein pursued his liberal approach through the system.

In July 1966, Lowenstein had met with former Subcommittee on

Disarmament staff director for Hubert Humphrey Betty Goetz Lall, under whom Lowenstein had worked in 1959 as a Humphrey staffer, to develop ideas to get peace talks started. At first when they approached Humphrey's staff to discuss their ideas, they were told that the administration's position on the war had in fact "hardened." Humphrey did meet with Lowenstein and Lall in August, however. The presentation she and Lowenstein made then, as outlined in a memorandum Lall sent to Humphrey following the meeting, proposed a nine-point program: (1) United States bombing of North Vietnam would cease; (2) A Geneva-type international conference would meet within a month in conditions of a cease-fire supervised by an adequately expanded ICC; (3) Upon acceptance of the cease-fire, no further buildup of military strength on either side could take place; (4) Conference participants would be decided according to the same formula used for the conference on Laos, and given the aim of the conference to revitalize the Geneva Agreements of 1954, all parties to that conference would be participants, plus those who came to the 1961–62 Laos conference, as well as representatives from South Vietnam recognized by one or more of the other conference participants; (5) Within nine months of the convening of the peace conference the troops of the United States, North Vietnam, and other foreign military groups would begin to leave South Vietnam; (6) Six months later, all foreign troops would be removed from Vietnam; (7) Within two years after the start of the peace conference, free elections would be held in South Vietnam; (8) The government set up after the elections in South Vietnam would decide its relationship with North Vietnam, including the question of unification; (9) Both North and South Vietnam, and a united Vietnam, should it emerge, should accept a status of neutrality and ask the other members of the conference to respect this neutrality.

As Lall informed Vice-President Humphrey in a letter dated August 21, 1966, her group, which included Lowenstein and Norman Thomas, intended to discuss the plan with Soviet officials. There were also plans to present it, if possible, to North Vietnamese officials as well. "If there are some favorable indications," she wrote, "I shall hope to take several steps to present it to the President and in the most favorable light." She stressed the importance of a precise timetable for troop withdrawal and also advised Humphrey that a Chinese source had informed her that in China it was believed that "sooner or later the American people will 'force' the government to end the war," by which the source claimed they meant "at the next Presidential election—in other words the North Vietnamese should just attempt to hold out until then."

Lall indicated that some Russians with whom she had spoken had suggested that if some steps were taken in the U.S. "to show positively we are prepared to end the war," that would give them a "handle" in approaching Hanoi. The Russians were anxious to end the war, she maintained, "though not at a price that sacrifices its interests in Vietnam," thereby damaging its international status.

In concluding, she wrote: "If there is a favorable reception to our plan by the Soviets and others and if it is important to show public support for it, assuming it is first presented to the President and he does not reject it outright, I have a plan for a large Congressional Citizen Conference at the capital in January that could muster support. . . . If our work can contribute to the end of the war it certainly would be a long step forward in assisting the world, the U.S., and Johnson administration, and you to continue the pursuit of peace."

There were contradictions in this liberal peace proposal Lowenstein was working with. There was an assumption that the North Vietnamese and the "infiltrators" could be persuaded to withdraw if American troops did. Ho Chi Minh had fought the Japanese and the French; now he was fighting the Americans. There was little indication that he would relent, and there was not much likelihood that the Soviets or the Chinese would help America out of its jam. In the end, if you believed that the U.S. had no alternative to withdrawal, it meant you were prepared to give the country to the Communists, and Johnson was not.

Lowenstein was playing along with the liberals who thought Johnson could be won over. In his own mind, he was for Robert Kennedy in 1968. But he needed to put these people through their paces with Johnson so they would arrive where he was already. Careers were on the line, though, and only those with nothing to lose could afford to take a position out in front, to challenge Johnson. Lowenstein not only had nothing to lose; he had much to gain. His own career was bogged down and he saw an opening. He also had the vision to understand that unless the liberals changed course, they were all in trouble. Yet he was unwilling to accept the direct action strategy of the New Left, even though it had been effective in forcing Johnson on civil rights. He was older, of course, and more committed to his own political career. But perhaps above all, he had put his faith in Robert Kennedy, who, he believed, could set things right if he became president—just as Martin Luther King, Jr.'s, moral courage could make America understand where it had gone wrong.

In November 1966, Lowenstein and Curtis Gans met after the election and reviewed the results. "We perceived it as wonderful," Gans smiles. "Forty-seven Democrats lost in the House. It was proof that the public was repudiating Johnson." The ADA lamented the loss of Senator Paul Douglas who was defeated by his former student

Charles Percy, but both Gans and Lowenstein thought it was healthy and began to think of opposing Johnson as the "Achilles' heel of the war issue."

On December 9, 1966, Tom Hughes, the director of intelligence and research at the State Department, to whom Lowenstein had supplied intelligence information on Spain, sent him an interoffice memorandum on official stationery reading, "MEMO FOR: Mr. Allard Lowenstein. You may find a few stalks of general applicability from this underbrush of legalisms." It was a copy of a speech Hughes had made on November 14 at Stanford Law School entitled "Relativity in Foreign Policy: The Storage and Retrieval of Conviction." Off the record and not for publication, the Hughes speech argued that there was a basis in the jurisprudence of legal positivism for supporting Johnson's policies in Vietnam. Countering antiwar arguments, he stated:

We are convinced beyond a reasonable doubt of Hanoi's command and control of the Viet Cong in the South since the onset of this struggle—a rather fundamental proposition which belatedly shows signs of registering with the worldwide jury. We see no necessary reason to interpret the 1954 Geneva accords as a deliberate fraud designed to underwrite Hanoi's ascendancy and to scuttle the South. We are old-fashioned enough to think that in this case the burden of proof lies with those who believe that adverse possession by the Viet Cong, even though contested, quiets title, or that equity should somehow credit this particular brand of criminal with clean hands as he covets his unjust enrichment. We think that the other parties to the Geneva Accords deserve something more substantial than peppercorns from Hanoi when it comes to good faith consideration, let alone specific performance, in its contracts. We see no reason why the Viet Cong's employment of terror should constitute a covenant running with the land in South Vietnam, nor any reason why Viet Cong control, if vested, should not be subject to divestment.

What is more, we believe that if and when Hanoi stops rejecting the renvoi—if and when the infiltrators from the North return whence they came—the decisive element of change militarily will have occurred. We understand full well that the contingent remainder of Viet Cong, the entailed inheritance left in the South, may continue to be troublesome. But with the Northern support ended, and Northern troops withdrawn, we think the chances are good that the process of reconciliation and revolutionary development will indeed take hold, that the residual violence in the South will in fact subside, and that, as Secretary Rusk said a week ago, "the situation can become as normal as it is in most countries of the world."

Hughes was a participant in the attempt launched by Secretary of State Rusk and Under Secretary of State and former Yale law professor Nicholas Katzenbach to enlist the law schools as supporters of the war. Rusk himself would host a reception for law professors at the State Department a few weeks after Hughes's speech. Lowenstein, who was part of this community, as well as the intelligence community, was someone they wanted in their camp.

But on December 9, 1966, a draft "State of the Union" statement by the ADA was circulated. It reflected Lowenstein's and Gans's thinking, arguing that the United States policy was "essentially conservative and fearful" and resting on two cornerstones: "1. military containment of adversaries, indiscriminately defined as communism, and 2. maintenance of a status quo in the fear that any change, major or minor, is subversive to our interests and the interests of international good order." The statement concluded: "Thus we are in Vietnam to prevent the upsetting of the Southeast Asian balance of power by a change of regime or social system in the area. Toward that end we seek a stable, pro-American Saigon-based government with the 17th parallel the borderline of Chinese containment."

The ADA paper charged that

the Vietnamese war represents the single greatest threat to world security, and as it grows in size and intensity the danger increases of a massive war in Asia and even possibly of a third world war. . . . It is important . . . to note that two of the major origins of the war involved the United States directly. The South Vietnamese refused in 1956 to honor the 1954 Geneva Accords upon the advice of the United States. The Diem government—which suspended what little local democracy that existed, which failed to carry out promised reforms, which continued the Saigon tradition of corruption, which was supported only by the landed aristocracy of Vietnam, and which created the main grievances that eventually rallied the widespread hostility necessary to start and carry out a civil war—was installed, supported and guaranteed by the United States.

More important, however, are the actions of the last three years, which have turned a minor civil war into a major test of wills that seems so hopelessly incapable of resolution. During the Johnson administration, the American presence in Vietnam radically changed in size and character. From advice and support, the U.S. personnel are now the front line combatants in the war of guns and the shock troops in the war to create an entirely new Vietnamese society. From a clash of minor units on the ground, the United States had escalated the war so that daily bombing is at a level higher than the round-the-clock raids that pummelled

Germany in World War II. From a scant commitment of 10,000 troops as advisors in 1963, the United States now has more than 385,000 troops there—more than the largest U.S. troop commitment at the height of the Korean War.

Pointing to the deterioration of the United States' position in international relations because of the war, the ADA state of the union message proposed a step-by-step solution that was basically the same as the one Betty Lall and Lowenstein had proposed to Humphrey that summer: the creation of a civilian government in South Vietnam through free elections, with the U.S. and the United Nations assisting to see that all outside interference, "whether [it] be the Viet Cong or the South Vietnamese armed forces," was prohibited; the cessation of the bombing of North Vietnam; the deescalation of the war in the south; negotiations with the National Liberation Front; an international conference for finalizing the peace; and a long-range development program for Asia.

The report stated clearly, again in line with Lowenstein's thinking, that "ADA has never believed in unilateral withdrawal, but it has equally been opposed to every escalation." The basic reason given for this position was that it was not a matter of right but of reality. "For twenty years, the Viet Cong has fought, and despite more American fighting men in Vietnam than were in Korea it has consistently gained strength in South Vietnam," the report noted. "We must recognize their existence and allow them a primary role in peace negotiations. Beyond this, we must offer them some role in the future political life of South Vietnam—either as a part of a coalition government or as a recognized political party in free elections in South Vietnam. Only such an approach offers the hope that they will see an opportunity to win in peace what they cannot win in war."

The ADA position, while it was far less militaristic than Johnson's, was nevertheless firm about a major role for the United States in Vietnam. By insisting that "an early election in which all parties are able to run and campaign would speed creation of a more representative government, hasten negotiations, and make the end of the war a possibility," its authors revealed that they too assumed that the American way of doing things would provide the solution to the war. As their statement indicates, the presence of non-Communist elements in the government would actually be guaranteed by virtue of logistics. They declared: "Despite the problems of holding elections in wartime in only a part of South Vietnam, we believe such elections should be held at the earliest possible moment and that all possible assistance should be given to the present Constituent Assembly in calling these elections." Lowenstein apparently assumed that the Viet Cong could be restrained until they saw the need to accept the elections that the

United States would supervise and which would be run by the existing government. The ADA position was very like the one Lowenstein had implemented in the Dominican Republic. Beneath the passionate rhetoric it was a holding action.

The Viet Cong, on the other hand, gave every indication that they intended to win the war. Like their allies in North Vietnam, they had a clear goal: an independent, unified Vietnam with a Marxist-Leninist government. The only question was when it would happen. The "good-wing" tactic was to involve them in a democratic process in the middle of the war. But with whole areas of the country excluded from the voting, and the United States holding a key supervisory position, the Viet Cong had little reason to believe that they might "win in peace what they could not win in war." Ho Chi Minh was not Juan Bosch, who had himself only been persuaded to join the Dominican election by his supposed allies in America. The Vietnamese revolutionaries would have been fools to ignore the lessons of their own war against the French, the Geneva accords, the American actions in Cuba, the Dominican Republic, and Vietnam itself. Meanwhile, Lyndon Johnson, determined to prevent a Communist government in the South, continued to ignore his liberal critics and to escalate. As Curtis Gans observes, "It was clear that Johnson was not persuadable. He wanted an anti-Communist government in South Vietnam." But his intractability was, in fact, alienating the rest of the world from the United States. From the "good-wing" point of view, opposing him was now an imperative.

Fully aware of this, Lowenstein did what he could to show that every effort was being made to get the students into a dialogue with the Johnson administration that would lead to a policy reversal. In actuality, he was enabling the political momentum to build within the system as he diffused the radical alternative presented by SDS and the draft resistance movement.

Late in 1966 and in January of 1967, Lowenstein took a series of world fact-finding tours. He told his wife Jenny that he was talking to "lots of people about Vietnam." In the demonstration led by theologian Reinhold Niebuhr and in the individual protest of heavyweight champion Muhammad Ali, Lowenstein perceived signs of public sentiment against the war that was mainstream in nature, not radical. He would seek to capitalize on this sentiment.

Starting in the winter of 1966, letters from student body presidents, editors of student newspapers, and other student groups began to appear in the press. David Halberstam wrote: "All the ads that are appearing in *The New York Times*—Mister President, College Editors Protest Your War; Mister President, Student Council Presidents Reject Your War; Mister President, Peace Corps Returnees Will Not Condone—are the work of Al Lowenstein."

The letters, addressed not only to Johnson but to Secretary of State Dean Rusk and Secretary of Defense Robert McNamara, emphasized that moderate, patriotic students, unlike the radicals, did not want to confront their government. Explaining the letter-writing campaign, Lowenstein observed that "the war protest was getting hooked on a very narrow radical base," making it necessary to "rally moderate, reasonable student opinion." The intention was to express the concern among students aroused by "the growing conflict between their own observations on the one hand, and statements by administration leaders about the war on the other."

A draft of one of the letters which Lowenstein helped to write reads:

As students, many of us are confronted by a personal dilemma caused by the draft and the war. This dilemma crosses religious, political and social lines. A sizable number of students feel that it is unjust for students to be deferred from military service when their contemporaries must make substantial sacrifices to serve our country. Other students feel that the whole war is unjust and therefore no draft is reasonable. Still another group avoids the draft choosing deferment. Unsure about the purpose of the war, members of this group compromise their basic willingness to serve our country. In spite of their doubts, many of these students have not wanted to express dissatisfaction by demonstrating since they have a commitment to our government. We are obliged nevertheless to acknowledge that an increasing number of students and non-students, silent or otherwise, are finding it difficult to support the draft and American foreign policy.

Lowenstein drafted a letter to President Johnson for Norman Thomas' signature, dated December 26, 1966, in which Thomas advised the president that "some of us have been groping for several months to find a basis on which negotiations toward a settlement could be undertaken." Calling such a settlement "the only hope of saving the people of Vietnam from untold further suffering, and of sparing the rest of the world the ever-increasing risk of a widening war," the chances of a decisive military victory having become "more remote now than ever," Thomas said that his group had formed with the hope of discovering "some basis on which negotiations could be conducted if all parties wished to negotiate; or failing that, to evolve a formula in support of which world opinion could be rallied." He noted that thoughts about possible procedures toward such discussions had been transmitted to representatives of both sides and offered to "go anywhere at any time to explore these matters further."

Johnson still did not respond. On December 30, 1966, a letter written by Lowenstein, Abbie Erdman, a "Seven Sisters" student leader, and Clinton DeVeaux, a black student leader from Georgia at the State University of New York at Buffalo, appeared in *The New York Times* on page one, with one hundred student body presidents' signatures, as a news item. "Unless this conflict can be eased," it asserted, "the United States will find some of her most loyal and courageous young people choosing to go to jail rather than to bear their country's arms."

The letters continued into 1967. Lowenstein traveled to England where he met in London with Rhodes scholars to enlist their support for a statement criticizing Johnson's policies and supporting citizen participation in foreign-policy decision making. Lowenstein had personal friends among the Rhodes scholars, with whom he corresponded at length, and he was able to get fifty signatures. A second effort was far less successful, though, and one Rhodes scholar wrote that "an effort of 50 seems out of the question. I think what we'll do most successfully is this—a letter from about 15 of us making the original points again, in abbreviated form. . . ."

In his own remarks, Lowenstein stressed "unconditional negotiation" and emphasized the increased number of South Vietnamese desertions. He argued that there was no point drafting people to fight a war that the South Vietnamese "don't themselves want to fight."

In January 1967, Theodore Draper published "The American Crisis—Vietnam, Cuba and the Dominican Republic" in *Commentary*. A long scholarly inquiry into American foreign policy, it captured Lowenstein's attention. He marked off three sections. One read: "The notion that we are weakening, frightening or deterring China by killing Vietnamese, as if this were a case of mistaken identity, defies all logic and experience." The second stated: "But if we were serious about the two Vietnams, the least we could do is make sure that South Vietnam has an authentically Southern leadership. Premier Ky and his immediate entourage happen to be North Vietnamese. He and those close to him fought in the French armed forces to perpetuate French colonial rule. The symbol of our independent South Vietnamese state is, therefore, a Northern air-force officer, who fought against Vietnamese independence, and is on record with a somewhat ambiguous remark in praise of Adolph Hitler." The last section concluded: "As a result of one miscalculation after another, we have gradually been drawn into making an enormous, disproportionate military and political investment in Vietnam. This investment, not the vital interests of the United States in Vietnam, has cast a spell on us. The same thing would happen if we should decide to put 40,000 troops in Mauretania or even Ruritania. Once American resources and prestige are committed on such a profligate scale, the 'commitment' develops a life of its own and, as the saying goes, good money must be thrown after bad. This,

to my mind, is nothing to be scoffed or sneered at. It is serious business for a great power to back into a cockpit so far away and so little
understood, fling thousands after thousands of men and billions after
billions of dollars into it—and then have second thoughts about the
wisdom of having gambled so much for so little. The temptation is
almost overpowering to magnify the importance of the game, to try to
retrieve one's fortunes with one more raise of the ante, to be prisoners
of an ever-changing present because looking back at the past is too
painful and peering into the future is too unpromising. Above all,
there is need for some reassurance that we possess some infallible
power to come out right on top in the end."

43.

During 1966, Senate Foreign Relations Chairman J. William Fulbright, electrified the country by grilling Robert McNamara and other
Johnson officials during the hearings he conducted on the Vietnam
War. Radio and television coverage gave an increased impact to the
Arkansas senator's disenchantment with Johnson's policies. "The hearings," Curtis Gans asserts, "made it possible for responsible people to
oppose the war." Gans himself published an ADA tabloid on the hearings, enabling him to direct ADA's publicity to an antiwar posture
without actually taking a position. In September of 1966, Fulbright's
efforts led a citizens' group formed by New York psychiatrist Martin
Shepard to organize Citizens for Kennedy-Fulbright as the first public
manifestation of what would become the "Dump Johnson" movement.
Starting with a handful of activists in California and New York, their
organization grew to over 1500 people scattered throughout thirty-
eight states. Citizens for Kennedy-Fulbright received press, radio,
and TV coverage and placed ads in *The Nation, The New Republic,
The New York Times* and the *Village Voice*. The response was encouraging. Declaring their intention to get rid of Lyndon Johnson as head
of the Democratic ticket in 1968 and replace him with Robert Kennedy (Humphrey was to be scuttled for Fulbright), the group began
publishing a newsletter on January 15, 1967. In it Shepard wrote:
"Over the next year and a half we shall try to 'democratize' the Democratic Party. We believe that a party should belong to its voters, and
not to a handful of 'back room politicians.' When the November Harris
poll can show RFK preferred over LBJ 44% to 37%, we reject the poll
of 48 out of 50 state chairmen who see LBJ as the nominee in '68. By
bringing these issues before the people, and the people into their local
party organizations, we hope to bring about this transformation."

Citizens for Kennedy-Fulbright began to expand its national coordinating committee and launched Students for Kennedy-Fulbright to

coordinate activities of interested persons on some eighty campuses throughout the country. They had their ticket and they had their issue. But they did not have Robert Kennedy's agreement to run for president. Lowenstein, however, examined their newsletter, and saved Volume 1, Number 1, in his papers. Much of what he would do would be modeled on this experiment.

A week after the publication of the Citizens for Kennedy-Fulbright newsletter, Lowenstein met in Washington with Secretary of State Rusk and twenty-five of the hundred student body presidents who had signed the letter to President Johnson and Rusk. It was through Walt Rostow, the chief liberal hawk in Johnson's White House that Lowenstein had arranged the meeting, a major coup since the administration was increasingly reluctant to talk with critics. Afterward, Lowenstein related, "I found Rostow's position so arrogant, and so completely askew from my point of view, that there wasn't much we had to say to each other." Among the students who attended were David Harris of Stanford and Rick Weidman of Colgate. Weidman, a short-haired conservative, had become friends with Lowenstein after losing a wrestling match to him at an NSA congress. Weidman, who had not made up his mind about the war, remembers that Lowenstein gave Harris a tie to wear at the meeting so he would look respectable.

When they got there, Rusk told them: "We are fighting monolithic Communism and we will escalate until they capitulate."

When Jim Graham, president of the student body of Michigan State and later counsel to the Senate Subcommittee on Intergovernmental Affairs, asked what would happen if they didn't capitulate, Rusk responded in a matter-of-fact tone: "Someone is going to get hurt."

Weidman understood Rusk to mean that nuclear war was definitely an option if the resistance to American forces did not cease, and recalls that he concluded from that that the Secretary of State was "nuts."

Rusk denies this interpretation. Participating in an oral history project at Duke University in the spring of 1980, he stated that it was his opinion that "if we couldn't get an understanding on the grassroots level as to when it would be over, we should pull out." He asserted moreover that "there was no attempt to develop 'war fever' because of the threat of nuclear war," and that his opinion then was that "if we start using these nuclear weapons, the jig is up." Summing up the problem in Vietnam, he concluded: "We tried to urge the South Vietnam government to do a great many things beyond its political and administrative capacity. We pressed for thirty to forty reforms, but they couldn't do it."

Rusk's interpretation does not square, however, with the impression of the students. Lowenstein arranged one more meeting in March, this time at the International Hotel at Kennedy Airport. It was convened by William Bundy, the assistant secretary of state for Asia, and attended by about 200 people, most of them student body presidents. The featured speaker was McGeorge Bundy, William Bundy's brother, and Johnson's national security advisor. "Al suckered them into coming," Weidman insists. "It was clear that no meaningful dialogue was possible."

Lowenstein participated with the Rev. William Sloane Coffin and numerous clergy on January 31 and February 1, 1967, in a Washington Mobilization called by Clergy and Laymen Concerned about Vietnam. Assisting were antiwar liberals such as Richard Barnet, Marcus Raskin, Sanford Gottlieb, and Curtis Gans, by then director of research and publication for the ADA. They were joined by the ADA's Leon Shull. There was a silent vigil, a walk to Capitol Hill, and visits with congressmen and senators, including Fulbright. An evening worship on January 31 was led by Father Daniel Berrigan. The following day, workshops on Vietnam were conducted and a closing session was addressed by Senators Wayne Morse and Eugene McCarthy, and Dr. Reinhold Niebuhr. It was stressed, however, that those who called "this mobilization did not feel that they had a right or a specific obligation to ask all participants to participate in a particular action program following our meeting here in Washington, DC." An "action group" was formed to consider what might be done, but, they concluded, "it should be made clear that we do not preclude the possibility that no specific action will evolve from the deliberations of the action group."

Meanwhile radical students like David Harris and Dennis Sweeney continued to promote draft resistance as the form of action they believed could force an end to the war. Sweeney, after his divorce from Mary King, first lived with Harris in his Peace and Liberation Commune in Palo Alto, then joined Harris's "Resistance" project as editor of its publication, *Resist*. An effective draft-resistance and antiwar organizer, he traveled extensively, joining the 1967 peace delegation which met with the North Vietnamese and the NLF in Bratislava, Czechoslovakia. "When the rest of us would go flying off into the clouds," Harris said, "he would bring us back down to earth." But while Harris decided to go to jail rather than be inducted (Sweeney criticized him for having a "Jesus Christ complex"), Sweeney took a deferment based on his mother's dependence on him.

On a hectic swing through Palo Alto, Lowenstein spoke briefly on the phone with Sweeney, who later wrote: "I remember a phone conversation in 1967 after a long period of absence [from Lowenstein]. I was working with the students in the anti-draft movement in California, when a call came one evening to our lodging directed to someone else. I was asked to pick up the phone since Mr. Lowenstein heard I was there, and after a brief explanation of what we were doing, I remember him saying: 'Well, you're at the center of things now. The forms we were in together have disappeared, and it is up to you and those like you to provide leadership to the new wave of recruits coming along.'"

Yet Lowenstein remained a constant critic of the New Left and continued to work to keep young people in the existing system. Rather than create new forms, he strove to make the old ones more accessible. Curtis Gans explains that Lowenstein "was far less elitist" than the other leading Democrats with whom he was associated. He and Jenny cultivated obscure students, corresponding with them, encouraging them, sometimes even lending them money. The students, in turn, saw Lowenstein not only as a political mentor but as a good personal friend. They sent endless letters from all over the country and abroad reminding Lowenstein where they had met and telling him what projects they were working on. One would be going to Africa, another organizing with SANE.

Lowenstein also took on the right. That March he debated William Rusher of *The National Review* on "The Barry Farber Show" and charged that rightist organizations received CIA funds, an allegation that Rusher deflected by demanding "proof." Rusher dragged out his dossier on Lowenstein's past associations by way of showing him to be a dangerous leftist.

The irony of the exchange with Rusher was that liberal organizations had long received financial support from the CIA to counter the Communists on the left, and Lowenstein knew it. The March issue of *Ramparts* contained the exposé of the National Student Association, and although it did not implicate Lowenstein, who was at the time of the revelations chairman of the National Supervisory Board of NSA, he was attacked by the New Left. SNCC people and SDS antiwar activists seized on Lowenstein's involvement with the NSA as proof of his CIA connection. David Harris has commented: "In 1967, as throughout his life, Lowenstein responded to such criticism from the left by labeling it the usual 'distorted and dishonest rubbish' that was always slung at him from that direction. They wanted young people to abandon the political system, and he was the strongest voice against such a move, the one liberal who could persuade students to save the system by using it to change things."

By early spring of 1967, Lowenstein was probably the only relatively young liberal still trusted by much of the alienated young. While that trust was threatened by the constant attacks of the radicals linking him with the CIA, he was also now thirty-eight, eight years over the age considered trustworthy by young people.

Theodore White described him at this point:

Wiry yet frail, balding early, his eyes compelling behind their black horn-rimmed eyeglasses, a non-smoker and non-drinker, Lowenstein was a one-man excitement wherever he moved. Even alone in a room, in private conversation, his talk quivered with the intensity of convention oratory. . . . At once a romantic and an executive, a distinct philosopohical quality set off Lowenstein from a later generation of students—from the "revolutionaries," anarchists and radicals of the college generation of the mid-sixties. Whether from Frank Graham, Norman Thomas, Eleanor Roosevelt or Adlai Stevenson—all saints in the Lowenstein mystique—Lowenstein had come to the conviction that what had to be done to change America could, and must, be done within the traditional system of American party politics. Thus, in public, for those few politicians who noticed him, Lowenstein was a desperate, irresponsible, rabble-rousing student leader; but within the student movement, he was constantly engaged in a transcontinental battle with the newer, younger "revolutionary" leaders who thought of him as an Establishment fink.

We must see Lowenstein, therefore, in 1967, as a faintly preposterous character—a self-appointed, self-anointed voice of American youth, revolving from campus to campus, from California to New England, from the Bronx to Sherman, Texas, calling for revolt, while at the same time, surfacing in Washington as a self-constituted one-man lobby, pleading with whatever Congressmen or Senators he could buttonhole for an end to war and the repudiation of Lyndon Johnson. "It was like looking for your father," recalled Lowenstein some time after, "but who was I? Nobody knew who I was. There was a credibility problem. I must have spoken to twenty Senators or Congressmen. Some thought I was a kook. Some of them listened. No one defended Lyndon Johnson or the war. I told them we had the strength. I told them there was a base in the student movement. But no major figure would take the lead—I couldn't find a trigger or a fuse."

Even people close to Lowenstein wondered at his ability to travel extensively by air and incur other expenses. "Allard had the freedom to run up $500 monthly phone bills like no other mortal," recalls Curtis Gans. "He always had access to money." This is what distinguished Lowenstein from other activists of the period, according to Gans. "If he wanted to go someplace, he never hesitated," Gans concludes. Yet Gans also acknowledges Lowenstein's ingenuity in cutting costs. "If you ever traveled with him, you knew he had this great, big, giant address book, and because of his many, many political and social involvements, he used to know about six people in every town in the country," Gans explains. "And he would wander into a town and he would call two of them. They would be so overjoyed because they had not seen or heard from him for three years that one would offer him dinner and the other would offer him a place to stay. The next year he would call two other people in that community and not call the two that he had called the last time. So they hadn't seen him in three years and were overjoyed."

Other close friends laughed at Lowenstein's alleged CIA involvement. Nancy Murphy of Dudley, North Carolina, wrote him: "You need not account to me for all those C.I.A. Funds—as long as you weren't mixed up with the Bay of Pigs, I forgive you everything. . . ." And on the Upper West Side, Steve Cohen continued to work with him organizing the Forum Committee, which conducted community discussions on Vietnam and other issues of concern to the reformers. A sought-after speaker against the war at these discussions was Lowenstein's friend Norman Thomas, still active although frail and almost blind.

That April, the writer David Halberstam met Thomas at Lowenstein's apartment at a gathering which left Halberstam with some doubts about Lowenstein's method of operating and his ability to carry off his campaign to deny Johnson the Democratic party nomination in 1968. Halberstam had been introduced to Lowenstein years before by their mutual friend, the journalist Fred Graham and had been invited by an insistent Lowenstein to come meet Norman Thomas, "the most beautiful man in America." But when Halberstam got there, Lowenstein was absent. Present were Thomas, Frank Graham, Lowenstein's wife, Jenny, and a group of students.

Halberstam described the scene: "Mrs. Lowenstein, young, quite pretty, quite confused, quite pregnant, is there as well as about twenty students, none of whom know each other. It is the mark of a Lowenstein gathering that no one knows anyone else, but everyone knows Lowenstein; they all get together to share the common goal, which is whatever Lowenstein dictates."

Thomas was arguing with some of the students who insisted that the war was racially motivated. "Mr. Thomas, frail in all but voice, argues that Vietnam was a mistake, it was too much vanity, it was a nation more proud than wise; but it was not genocide," Halberstam observed. "Eventually, as the evening is breaking up, Lowenstein arrives, rumpled as ever. He introduces everyone to the people they have just spent the evening with, and packs everyone off to a West Side reform-club meeting where he then spends half the night attacking Johnson and the war and promises that the Democratic party, the party of Eleanor Roosevelt, will not permit Johnson to run again. Johnson will be beaten. The politicians are wrong. No one is for Johnson. It is in the air. Volunteers are asked for. A few put their hands up. It all seems very vague, and somehow Lowenstein is hard for me to take seriously; I have the same reservations about him that I have about Humphrey, that he is somehow intellectually promiscuous, that he jumps around from cause to cause, that all liberal causes are equal, that he is somehow the perpetual student leader, that there is a lack of toughness and discipline in him."

44.

At the New Politics conference in Chicago, where radicals and ultraliberals of all stripes met, the idea of Martin Luther King, Jr., as a third party candidate gained ground. And even as he insisted that the party of Eleanor Roosevelt would not allow Johnson's renomination, Lowenstein was apparently thinking third party too, frustrated by the intransigence, obsolescence, and obliviousness of the Democratic party. He had written in his diary in 1966 that if Robert Kennedy were not to run, he would support Martin Luther King, Jr. Since Kennedy had not offered any signs of his own candidacy, Lowenstein was promoting King.

Curtis Gans argued, however, that there wasn't time to create a third party and that even if there were, it would fall outside the mainstream, as Henry Wallace's Progressive party had in 1948. In his view, opposition to the war had to be organized within the Democratic party.

To discuss the options, Lowenstein called a meeting at Granson's, one of the family restaurants which he used as an informal "office." Curtis Gans, his wife, Genie, Norman Thomas, the liberal columnist James Wechsler, and Andrew Young were present.

When Young made it clear that King was not going to run for president, Wechsler asserted that Johnson would have to be opposed within the Democratic party. Having obtained the others' agreement on that point, Wechsler drafted a resolution in the form of a threat to Johnson, calling on him to change his policy in Vietnam or be opposed by ADA. At the upcoming ADA convention, Rauh was to read the resolution and Lowenstein would speak for it.

When the convention opened on April 2, 1967, however, and Rauh read the resolution as planned, he was met with immediate and powerful opposition led by Gus Tyler. The theoretician and organizer for the ILGWU who had fought so tenaciously against the Lawyers Guild in Mississippi, Tyler found it inconceivable that the ADA would not support a just war against Communist aggression. Founded to press for social change in America, the ADA had also been created to fight Communism. In the view of Gus Tyler and his allies, its very purpose was threatened by the Wechsler resolution, which they regarded as treasonous. Moreover, they argued, if the ADA went on record opposing Johnson in Vietnam, it would be political suicide.

When, with Rauh's help, he was finally recognized by the chairman, Don Edwards, Lowenstein ignored the three-minute limitation imposed by ADA rules, and spoke at length from the floor, without notes. "Al made the greatest spontaneous speech I have ever heard," Rauh asserts. At the end, there was a burst of applause and the resolution carried three to one. But Gus Tyler shook his head. "This is the end of ADA," he lamented. Later, when the ADA endorsed Eugene McCarthy for president in February of 1968, Tyler walked out, taking the labor people with him and shattering the old New Deal coalition.

Gans and Lowenstein expanded the effort. They asked Rauh, who was insistent that the movement could go nowhere without a candidate, to sound out George McGovern, Frank Church, Eugene McCarthy, and Robert Kennedy. Meanwhile, there were informal meetings with organization leaders in the peace movement. Gans met with Sanford Gottlieb and Paul Gorman of SANE and Bella Abzug from the Women's Strike for Peace and argued that if the peace movement were to accomplish anything meaningful, it would have to go political. But the "political solution" to the problem of the war appealed only to Bella Abzug, who provided a network of church groups with which she had been working and names of people to help organize. All of this was, in Gans' words, "low-level exploring."

On April 15, the SDS-initiated Spring Mobilization was launched, with enormous marches in New York and San Francisco. On the day of the marches, Jenny's mother, Olivia, married Dale Parkhill, an eccentric, high-living Texan then running a well-known bar in the Hamptons. The question arose whether Lowenstein would go to the wedding or the march on Fifth Avenue, but "Al went to the march," insists Jenny. In a major speech that was the highlight of the event, Martin Luther King, Jr., came out strongly against the war. Afterward Jenny and Lowenstein mingled with the antiwar leaders at a dinner in the Riverside Church.

At about this time, Lowenstein was organizing divinity students to write and publish a letter to Robert McNamara on the draft. The new Campus Coordinating Committee which he was creating as a net to catch nonradical student support on the campuses opened an office in Union Theological Seminary with David Hawk, a student there, as chairman. Aiding Hawk, whose office boasted a Watts line and a mimeograph machine, was Harvard Divinity School student Sam Brown. Two weeks after the Spring Mobilization, the letter from 1,000 seminarians, drafted by Hawk, appeared in *The New York Times*. It called on McNamara to "ease the draft" by changing the law to permit "conscientious objection to a particular war." This would solve the "dilemma" of "those law-abiding young Americans whose conscience would not permit them to fight in Vietnam."

The question of a candidate began to plague both Lowenstein and Gans. For about a month, Rauh supposedly had been talking to possible contenders for the presidency. But Gans and Lowenstein felt that "Joe got cold feet," as Gans puts it. At the end of the month, Rauh reported that no one was willing to run and that, without a candidate, the ADA was not in a position to do anything.

Gans firmly believes that Rauh never·spoke to McCarthy, and suggests that Rauh in all likelihood made the option sound all but impossible to those whom he did approach. Gans explains: "He [Rauh] was Mr. ADA, and Shull supported the war and feared the loss of labor support. The UAW opposed the antiwar movement and Joe was doing lots of labor law. Joe supported the ADA resolution but opposed the strategy of Al, Gans, and Wechsler. Rauh proposed and supported the 'peace plank' strategy."

Rauh saw things differently. "A candidate was needed, but Al was going ahead to dump Johnson even without one. I felt the ADA would be embarrassed without a candidate and the organization would be destroyed."

In May, Lowenstein was in Berkeley listening to Martin Luther King, Jr., address a large crowd on Vietnam. Also there was David Halberstam, who wrote this description: "There are 5,000 cheering people in the audience as well as several people sitting in trees for a better look. One of them is Allard K. Lowenstein. He is just in from some California school to the south, he is passing through to give focus to the dissent on Vietnam, organizing it, channeling it."

Declining Halberstam's dinner invitation, Lowenstein explained that he had to fly off to Oregon, adding, "These kids, no one really knows how alienated they are. Trying to keep them in the system is very, very hard. They're bitter and they're angry. They really resent this society. Of course, there are a lot of things in this society that are very resentable."

Lowenstein had just come from the Stanford campus, where he had urged "de-escalation" of the Vietnam War. According to the report in the *Stanford Daily*, Lowenstein had gotten a big laugh by referring to President Johnson's conduct as a "great gale of political halitosis coming out of the White House." But Lowenstein did not have a candidate to oppose Johnson, and when he was asked about 1968, he "expressed the hope" that "a Democrat other than Lyndon Johnson" would be nominated. The next day, debating with a representative of the State Department, Lowenstein claimed that "the United States does not want to negotiate an honorable peace."

Robert Kennedy did not believe it even remotely possible in June of 1967 to oppose Johnson. At a fund-raiser for the Democratic party in New York, while a gigantic crowd of antiwar demonstrators protested outside the hotel, Kennedy waxed euphoric about Lyndon Johnson as he introduced him: "He has poured out his own strength to renew the strength of the country. . . . He has gained huge popularity, but never hesitated to spend it on what he thought important. . . . He has led us . . . to comfort the oppressed on a scale unmatched in history. . . ."

In the July issue of the ADA magazine, Curtis Gans outlined the Dump Johnson strategy. "I told them basically why Dump Johnson was the way to go," Gans explains. "I wrote that if a base were created, a candidate would follow." Although Gans was on the ADA staff, the article was published under the name of Roy Bennett, a board member, so it would carry greater weight. It read in part:

> Having largely failed in the attempt to give loyal counsel to a Democratic President, the liberal community's . . . strength to bring about a change in policies rests precisely on its ability to remain independent. . . . The most effective initial strategy must be for liberals to work within the Democratic Party . . . and organization should begin in preliminary form for a primary challenge to Johnson. Hopefully this can be accomplished by a national candidate of stature who might run in opposition to Johnson, but if not it could well be done through local candidates . . . willing to oppose him in the primary. . . .
>
> Most importantly, Liberals must begin to act now. For at stake are not only the present policies of Vietnam but the political future of the next decade. . . . If there is to be an end to the political polarization that threatens to strain the very foundations of American democracy, it is for the liberal movement to begin to pose another option.

In a strong opposition article, Gus Tyler of the ILGWU, reiterated his position that the Johnson administration was capable of providing both the guns and butter, that it was an administration to which liberals had access and that Johnson and the war should be supported. The old coalition, Tyler argued, could be held together.

Joe Rauh tried to prevent a split and ended up infuriating everyone, including his friends Al Lowenstein and Jimmy Wechsler. Wechsler became so incensed that he stopped speaking to Rauh. At the June board meeting, Lowenstein and Rauh tried unsuccessfully to resolve their differences. Despite the rift, with Gans's help, Lowenstein was elected a vice-chairman of the ADA. Among his numerous accomplishments and credentials he mentioned that he had "maintained close ties with students and youth and was partially responsible for the letters written to the President on Vietnam from a group of 100 student body presidents, 800 Peace Corps returnees, 1,000 seminarians, and 50 Rhodes scholars."

When the next issue of the ADA magazine came out with an article written by Rauh advising opponents of the war to work for a "peace plank" at the 1968 Democratic convention, which would presumably renominate Johnson, Gans and Lowenstein understood that the ADA could no longer be the base of their activities. They would have to create something themselves. Gans is still incredulous. "Al and I believed we could succeed in dumping Johnson when no one else did. Two out of three people hated Johnson."

Joseph Rauh, on the other hand, still questions whether Lowenstein could have dumped Johnson if McCarthy had not decided to run, and believes it was logical and sensible for the ADA to do nothing more until its endorsement of McCarthy in February, 1968. He acknowledges, though, that he and Lowenstein fought bitterly over the question. Rauh remembers sitting on his porch one evening in July 1967, in the overpowering summer heat of Washington, arguing with Lowenstein. Rauh, frustrated and irritable, asked him, "How the hell are you going to crystallize it all without a candidate?" Lowenstein was adamant: "In the Wisconsin primary, there is a line that says 'none of the above' and I'm gonna win with that."

Rauh remained unimpressed. He insists that he did speak to all the potential candidates as he had promised. "I tried Church, McGovern, and Bobby Kennedy. Paul Douglas was a hawk. I was surprised that McCarthy did it," he asserts. "I considered him a cynic."

The ambiguity toward McCarthy would, in time, cause a great deal of pain. Harold Ickes, who had been a volunteer in Mississippi and had researched the Wisconsin primary law with Alice Brandeis Popkin, eventually broke with Lowenstein, embittered by Lowenstein's depreciation of McCarthy as a candidate after Robert Kennedy entered the race. "He was my first 'lost friend' from politics," Jenny laments. There would be others.

45.

After the Spring Mobilization, Greg Craig, who had marched with Lowenstein, joined with Carl Ogelsby of SDS, a coauthor of the Port Huron Statement, at a press conference to announce the Vietnam Summer Project at Cambridge, Massachusetts. Organized by Gar Alperovitz and Martin Peretz at Harvard and endorsed by Martin Luther King, Jr., it was a political action project designed to promote student activity against the Vietnam War. But Lowenstein, who had been involved in organizing the large spring Harvard teach-in (Henry

Steele Commager of Amherst, Stanley Hoffman, John Fairbank, and Jerry Cohen of Harvard spoke and were piped into 160 campuses), opposed the summer project and was upset that Craig had been involved in the press conference. According to Craig, Lowenstein felt "there wasn't sufficient control over the project." Lowenstein argued that some student might decide that the plight of the nuns in Vietnam would be his project and alienate the American people by saying he would "rape a nun for peace."

Lowenstein felt that "unpatriotic" behavior was unacceptable in students. Until the Vietnam War, he insisted that they had believed in the country and would have fought in World War II. The radical movement, particularly against the draft, was anathema to him. He believed that the country was running the risk of "losing a whole generation," a phrase he used repeatedly but which Greg Craig coined. "He thought the dialogue on the war would be captured by the crazies or the left," Craig exclaims, "and a whole generation would have to choose between Staughton Lynd and Lyndon Johnson."

To mobilize students within the system to get a "none of the above" vote in Wisconsin, Lowenstein transformed the Campus Coordinating Committee into the Alternative Candidate Task Force (ACT–68). Returning from his Africa trip in the summer of 1967 (Jenny had summoned him home because his mother was dying), Lowenstein met with David Hawk, Steve Cohen, and Clinton DeVeaux, who had been considering strategies for the fall, to find out what they thought was likely to happen in the antiwar movement. After the students had spoken, Lowenstein announced, "What we have to do is get rid of Lyndon Johnson." According to Hawk, as the Campus Coordinating Committee "faded into ACT–68," it became inappropriate to run it out of the Union Theological Seminary; while CCC was nonpartisan, ACT–68 was "partisan-political."

Meanwhile, the Dump Johnson campaign was entering a critical phase in its attempt to create what Curtis Gans calls the "adult base." Lowenstein geared up for a nationwide speaking tour even though he still did not have a candidate. He advised audiences to write in the names of anyone opposed to the war in the primaries and to support local candidates who shared their views. Curtis Gans, who like Lowenstein had been traveling and organizing since April, argued that if the base were created the candidate would follow, and he and Lowenstein now joined in creating that base. Lowenstein was ubiquitous as he called for the deposing of Johnson while arguing for support of the system, a kind of Trotsky of the middle class.

A pair of eccentrics (for every Coke Lowenstein drank, Gans downed a Pepsi), dark and intense, the two arrived in New Hampshire where Lowenstein was to give a speech. Dartmouth political science professor David Hoeh told Milton Viorst that Lowenstein had to be taken to a gift shop to buy a tie "that almost matched his shirt and suit." He and Gans prepared a position paper in New Hampshire that read in part: "If a president is wrong but popular, political realities may make opposing him difficult, however right; if a president is right but unpopular, supporting him may be a duty, however difficult. But when a president is both wrong and unpopular, to refuse to oppose him is a moral abdication and a political stupidity."

On August 4 there was to be a big Democratic fund-raiser in California, organized by Jesse Unruh, the speaker of the California legislature. Robert Kennedy was scheduled to address the guests and Lowenstein, also planning a California trip, arranged to travel aboard the same plane with Kennedy. "He was traveling first class," Lowenstein related. "I was tourist. That's the story of my life." Frank Mankiewicz, Kennedy's press secretary, swapped seats with Lowenstein so the senator and the anti-Johnson organizer could talk during the flight. Lowenstein was up-front. They were organizing to defeat Lyndon Johnson and were looking for a candidate. "If you want to run we'll let you," he joked. Kennedy acknowledged that the idea was valid but indicated that he was not available himself. Lowenstein related later: "I just explained to him what the Dump Johnson movement was really all about. . . . We were not Kooks, or the New Left, or just the same old peace people. I explained that we were recruiting thousands of students and many regular Democrats. . . . I tried to convince him that his stereotype of these people was wrong and that we were committed to working inside the electoral system. . . . I told him we were going to defeat Lyndon Johnson for the party nomination in 1968. I told him that with him we could do it very much more easily, but that we were going to do it with him or without him. He took it as seriously as the idea of a priest in Bogotá deposing the Pope. I knew that his instinct was to run. But . . . I had no illusions at that time that he would ever risk it." After discussing other possible candidates, including military war critic retired U.S. Army General James Gavin ("If you get Gavin, you've got a new ball game," Kennedy said.), Lowenstein said that he was on his way to talk to the California Democratic Council people, a liberal group of independent Stevenson Democrats active in the peace movement. Kennedy grew serious. He told Lowenstein that the CDC was made up of dangerous left-wingers and that Lowenstein "had too good a future in politics to get mixed up with people like that." Lowenstein demurred, saying it was ridiculous to describe the CDC in those terms. Then he said to Kennedy, "If you really think the CDC people are so bad, why don't you say so to the reporters who meet us when the plane gets in?" Lowenstein would later confess, "I was aware that I was a flea and he was an elephant."

Kennedy was met by reporters who asked him what he thought of the peace movement in California. He responded coldly, "That's a matter for the people of California to decide for themselves." Kennedy resented the CDC because it had been formed by holdouts for Adlai Stevenson at the 1960 convention in San Francisco.

The next day, Lowenstein met with Gerald Hill of the CDC to enlist his support for the Dump Johnson movement. They agreed that they needed money and staff and that they should raise $3,000, half in California and half in New York. They immediately called Curtis Gans to ask that he be the staff of something called the "Conference of Concerned Democrats," originally launched by Zoltan Ferency, the state Democratic chairman of Michigan. "Are you willing to put your body where your mouth is?" they asked him. After fullfilling his obligations as a marine reservist in summer camp, Gans resigned from the ADA and opened the Conference of Concerned Democrats in the living room of his house on Capitol Hill.

Gans's wife, Genie, compiled lists of people who had signed petitions against the war or who had responded to the various newspaper ads. To those names were added those of political people who might be sympathetic and community leaders, and the whole list was arranged by precinct. Gans prepared for a nationwide tour, armed with a list of names for each state. But while some relatively prominent politicians, such as Donald Fraser of Minnesota, gave names to Gans, only Congressman Don Edwards of San Jose, California, openly identified with the movement. The strategy was to expand the list and divide it into three parts: The more politically savvy would be categorized as Concerned Democrats. Among them, holders of public office were particularly prized. The less disciplined peace movement people and antiwar activists were put into "Dissenting Democrats," a group originally launched by the actor Robert Vaughn, the initiator of a petition drive which had called on Johnson to change his politics. Students were deployed in the Alternative Candidates Task Force, which formally came into existence at a rally organized by Curtis Gans at the August, 1967, congress of the National Student Association in Maryland.

Jenny, expecting their first child, had gone into labor while Lowenstein was in Atlanta at an SCLC rally. Speaking with him over the phone from the hospital, she could hear Martin Luther King, Jr.'s, voice in the background. Excited and frenzied, Lowenstein grabbed a plane for New York and arrived at the hospital with an almost equally anxious Curtis Gans. Gans had arranged for Lowenstein to address the huge Dump Johnson rally at College Park. It was the first rally of this kind and thousands of people had been assembled to hear Lowenstein in the heat of the summer. While Lowenstein pressed the attending physician to tell him when the baby would be born, Gans was pressing Lowenstein. "Children are born every day," he told Lowenstein. "You must come and give the speech. Thousands are waiting."

"I felt Al could walk on water," Jenny says. "I told him to go." Lowenstein told her he would be back for the birth and took off to give the speech. When he phoned from Washington, he discovered that the baby had been born at 9:00 P.M. while he and Gans had been flying south. Lowenstein drove on to College Park with Gans, gave the speech, and drove back to New York, arriving at the hospital at 2:00 A.M. to see his son, whom they named Frank Graham Lowenstein. (They would name their second son Thomas Kennedy Lowenstein, after Norman Thomas and Robert Kennedy, and their daughter, Katherine Eleanor Lowenstein, after Katharine Hepburn and Eleanor Roosevelt.) "If it were happening now, I would say, 'The hell you'll give that speech,'" Jenny asserts. "But in those days, I thought he was infallible and everything he said and did was right. If making the speech was important, he should do it."

Lowenstein gave a rousing speech at College Park, assuring the crowd that no matter who the candidate was, they would dump Johnson. The response was affirmative. As one student said, "The feeling at that meeting was that we had gone just as far as we could go through the normal procedures. They just acted as if we didn't exist, and we weren't serious. And we didn't want to go into the resistance, at least not yet. So we were ready to try what Al wanted. It was the last stop on the way."

While Lowenstein spoke, the SDS picketed him, carrying signs that read "Don't Listen to the CIA Agent Downstairs." One SDS activist called him "Hubert Lowenstein." Liberal, conservative, radical, and moderate caucuses were held. Timothy Leary, the prophet of LSD, made an appearance, as did various SDS leaders and assorted "movement" people. "The whole congress was a happening," according to Michael Stauffer of Fredonia State. Sam Brown, who was defeated in the election for NSA president by Ed Schwartz, took over as head of ACT–68 and student coordinator of the Conference of Concerned Democrats. Steve Cohen, defeated in his bid for an NSA vice-presidency, also joined the Dump Johnson campaign. As David Hawk observes, had they been elected, neither would have been available for the McCarthy campaign.

This was the first "clean" NSA congress since the fifties, with no CIA involvement. As a vice-president of NSA, Sam Brown had spent much of the spring cutting the remaining CIA ties, traveling the country speaking against the connection. But according to David Hawk, ACT–68 never really amounted to anything. "It petered out," he explains. The CCC people who worked for it—Brown, Hawks, Sue Hester, and Clinton DeVeaux—could not make something out of nothing. Without a candidate, it was difficult to organize the moderate students who were opposed to the war.

The College Park NSA congress lasted ten days. It was marked by stormy sessions and debates, and in the general turmoil, some schools withdrew. Seventeen years had passed since Lowenstein had been elected NSA president at the Ann Arbor convention where support for the Korean War had been overwhelming. Now the organization that he had nurtured was torn apart by Vietnam and the revelations of CIA support. It would not survive these strains.

After College Park, Lowenstein stayed home for a short while with Jenny and Frankie, then took off again, this time for Vietnam to observe the elections. David Halberstam reported that while he was sitting on the patio of the Continental Hotel in Saigon with John Chancellor, comparing Chancellor's "depressing stories" about official Washington with Halberstam's "depressing stories" about unofficial and official Saigon, a clean-cut young man of about twenty approached them, asking "quite surreptitiously" if they had seen Lowenstein. When Halberstam replied that he had seen Lowenstein in New York, the young man informed him, "He's here now."

"He is there to observe the elections on his own because Lyndon Johnson picked his observers and failed to include Lowenstein," wrote Halberstam. "Al had flown over, Air Lowenstein, to judge the elections, since he intends to criticize Vietnamese policy in the year to come and he does not intend to be one-upped by people asking, were you there?" Lowenstein told him that observing a Vietnamese election was almost as futile as participating in one. "Nevertheless, he seems to be known to everyone in Saigon, particularly underground politicians," Halberstam concluded.

Lowenstein had people helping him on the trip and ample funds for airline tickets and hotels. At the Tokyo Hilton where he stayed en route to Saigon, he found a note from an aide: "Al, you have appointment with Nguyen Van Phuoc at 294 Cong Ly—Buddhist student dorm. He is one of the leaders of struggle. He cannot leave because of his own security. App't. is at 4:00 pm. Your flight to Bangkok is confirmed on Air Viet Nam for 12:00 noon tomorrow. My flight is at 1:00 pm today. Won't be able to have lunch with you. If you have a moment sometime, drop a note and tell me how things turn out. Address is 567 Lincoln Ave., Palo Alto. Thank you, Joe. P.S. I suggest you see the guy and let the others go if you have to make a choice. He is by far the most interesting. 2nd choice is Kiet from Student Union—4 Duy Ton. Don't worry about calling to break appointments. They were not extremely definite anyway (except for Phuoc). PSS. Your ticket is in room on bed. Adios."

On September 5, 1967, Lowenstein, in Saigon, typed a draft "manifesto" on Vietnam. It described the government of South Vietnam as "lacking a sound legal basis" and criticized it for failing "to establish democracy or to win the people's heart." Arguing that democracy was "necessary for political stability," Lowenstein wrote: "We solemnly denounce before national and international opinion the dishonest and oppressive practices of this Government that aimed at transforming the election into a ratification of a preselected Government."

Lowenstein presented the case of the South Vietnamese dissenters to American public opinion in the manifesto. He argued: "Finally, we must address ourselves to the people and government of the U.S. whose motivation for becoming involved in the affairs of South Vietnam has often been ascribed to a desire to assist the people of South Vietnam in the achieving of genuine self-determination, that any policy carried out in Vietnam must conform to the will of the Vietnamese people. . . ," The solution, the manifesto concluded, was for the United States to "withdraw support from the minority government" whose policies continued to "oppress the majority of our people."

Back in New York, Lowenstein spoke to the press about the elections. *The New York Times*, in an article entitled "New York Lawyer Questions Fairness of Vietnam Vote," reported that "Allard K. Lowenstein, a vice chairman of Americans for Democratic Action, said today that the charges of fraud made by some of the losing candidates . . . should not be dismissed as the complaints of poor losers." Reporting as well that Lowenstein had met with Ambassador Ellsworth Bunker, the *Times* stated that he "informed Mr. Bunker that many Americans in Vietnam, including government employees, do not share the euphoric reaction to the elections that has marked the public comments of many of the official American observers." He filed his minority report on the elections and continued to travel and speak.

While Lowenstein was in Vietnam, his new baby became critically ill. The doctors were unable to diagnose his condition at first, and though Jenny was filled with fear, she did not attempt to call her husband, knowing that it would take at least four days to reach him. When his illness was identified as pytoric stemosis, requiring dangerous surgery, she found herself alone with the baby as they wheeled him into the operating room. When the surgeon asked where her husband was and she replied, "He's in Vietnam," there was great sympathy. "Oh, you poor woman," he responded. "Oh, no," Jenny tried to explain, "you don't understand. . . ."

"I was afraid," recalls Jenny, "but Al was still walking on water. I was twenty-three and still young and naive. And Al was naive too. In so many ways, he was still a 'student.' But now he was also a national leader."

That September, Lowenstein, very involved with the Vietnamese elections, breezed into his constitutional law class at City College with a green book bag tossed over his shoulder. The aged Norman Thomas was giving his annual lecture, and the class marched over to hear him speak about Vietnam and student protest. As former student Harvey

Lippman recalls the occasion, Thomas told the students, "It would be better to wash the flag than to burn it."

Lowenstein's schedule was so full that more often than not "guest lecturers" took his class for him; Jenny would collect his exam papers when he was away. David Yeres, one of Lowenstein's students at the time, explains that Lowenstein did not have a full-time appointment and that his contract was only for one or two years. "He had a very limited load," Yeres asserts. "My impression was he was teaching this one course. He always seemed to be arriving at class from somewhere else, like an airport, and leaving for somewhere else right after class."

That fall Curtis Gans also began to travel the country. In most states, three efforts were in progress at the same time: precincts were being organized by the politically knowledgeable members of the Concerned Democrats; petitions were being carried by the antiwar activists in the Dissenting Democrats; and campuses were being organized by students. Gans arranged meetings with the three different groups wherever he traveled, and then Lowenstein would arrive to address them. In two months, Gans traveled to thirty-four states, followed by Lowenstein, whose rhetorical skills were effective in winning support. The two made a particularly concentrated effort in Minnesota, New Hampshire, and Wisconsin, where delegates would be chosen early, and in New York and California because their large blocks of delegates could swing the convention.

Lowenstein himself was very much in demand as he moved towards national prominence. On September 20, Richard Gambino, director of the Elliot Institute for Human Relations, offered him $600 to give a short course on the theme "Youth in America Today." On September 26, James Arthur Johnson, director of the graduate program of the Woodrow Wilson School of Public and International Affairs at Princeton, wrote: "I have been given the high honor of inviting you to come to the Woodrow Wilson School to address the students and faculty at the Friday luncheon on October 13th. We would like to have you speak on 'The Need for a Strong Alternative to President Johnson in the 1968 Presidential Election.'" And Gerald S. Glazer at the University Center System of the University of Wisconsin in Waukesha wrote on September 27 that, having been advised that Lowenstein was one of the connected "Concerned Democrats" opposed to the current U.S. policy in Vietnam, he was anxious to affiliate with that group "and do whatever I can to prevent Lyndon Johnson (or anyone with similar views on Vietnam) from winning the next Democratic Presidential nomination. In particular, I am interested in making the 1968 Wisconsin primary a testing-ground of antiwar sentiment. Please let me know how I can participate in your efforts here in Wisconsin."

The Dump Johnson movement in Wisconsin had the support of

Donald Peterson, a county leader from the 10th district in Eau Claire who astonished author Theodore White when he gave him his card. It read "the pizza with the THIN GOLDEN CRUST, several great flavors." Peterson was general sales manager for a dairy products concern, had served as a bombardier in World War II, and was opposed to the war because of his two sons. He told White: "I felt that my sons meant more to me than the Democratic party. Everybody's willing to let other people's sons go off to the war, but not their own. But I can't commit myself to allow them to go off to that damned war. What am I in politics for, if I can't take care of my sons?"

Peterson was one of the few office holders in the Dump Johnson movement. The most prominent figure identified with the movement was Congressman Don Edwards. Alpha Smaby, a member of the Minnesota legislature, was with them, and they also had the head of the South Dakota farmers union. "I operated on the principle that you could organize the country before you could get two liberals in New York to agree," says Gans. But reflecting on the people he had to work with in the heartland, Gans describes them as "a group of political neophytes, a ragtag bunch of insurgents."

Despite Gans's crucial role, Dump Johnson became known as a Lowenstein undertaking. A friend of Lowenstein's gave this account to David Halberstam: "The Dump Johnson movement was a typical Lowenstein operation. It was Lowenstein working outside the normal apparatus, functioning almost out of his own hip pocket, using his own personal contacts and his own charisma, not responsible to anyone above him, and influencing people to the *right* of him. That's his great strength, talking to these clean-cut young kids, getting them back into the system. He doesn't work nearly as well to the left, and he loses his patience; it's as if he doesn't think people have the right to be to the left of him. Al likes to start things, but when they get out of hand and get revolutionary, he doesn't like it. The trouble is, they're bound to in this country because someone like Lowenstein is trying to work within the system and save it, but of course he doesn't have the support of the system. The system doesn't give a damn about being saved. So he starts these movements, like the Mississippi Freedom Democratic party, but when they get stalled or bounce off the system, the kids get discouraged or become more radical, just like the Mississippi Freedom Democratic party did. And they break with Al and he gets hurt, and they become a little cynical. Now this Vietnam thing, he's perfectly typecast for it. There's no one for outlining moral questions in practical terms and exciting people to the challenge ahead like Lowenstein. But what happens if it fails? Will you have more disillusioned kids, turned off by the process thinking Lowenstein fooled them?"

But Ronnie Dugger, of the *Texas Observer* described Lowenstein as an heroic figure: "He didn't even have a candidate at that time. But he came down and he was organizing and putting it together, telling us it could be done, that we were not alone. And then I remember taking him to the airport afterward and watching him walk up the ramp, and I thought, my God, there goes one man trying to take on the entire system alone, and I felt a certain chill. It was pretty damn impressive."

46.

On the Friday preceding the September 23 ADA meeting in Washington, at a dinner party given by Robert Kennedy, Lowenstein listened as Richard Goodwin suggested that Johnson was certifiably mad and Kennedy speculated that the president would withdraw at the 1968 convention. The next night, Kennedy once again gathered his friends at Hickory Hill. Present were Lowenstein, journalist Jack Newfield, historian Arthur Schlesinger, Jr., James Loeb, who had been President Kennedy's ambassador to Peru and Guinea, and Senator Kennedy, in casual dress and hippie love beads. Lowenstein, his shoes kicked off, sat cross-legged on an armchair in his typical college bull-session position.

Kennedy was moderating a debate on whether he should challenge Lyndon Johnson for the Democratic nomination. Lowenstein and Newfield were for running while Schlesinger and Loeb were opposed. Lowenstein, emphasizing "the moral imperative of stopping the war," insisted that Johnson had to be defeated and what was needed was a strong candidate in the primaries or a "no" vote in Wisconsin. When Schlesinger supported the Rauh concept of a peace plank, Kennedy said, "You're a historian, Arthur. When was the last time millions of people rallied behind a plank?" But he indicated that he was not available as a candidate.

Things came to a head with Rauh and the ADA at the September 23 ADA meeting. Lowenstein and Gans pushed for a series of antiwar, anti-Johnson resolutions but all of them were beaten back. Rauh stuck to his position that unless there was a candidate, the ADA could not go along. "Al wanted a resolution to dump Johnson without a candidate and I said no," Rauh states. "I won that fight." When Rauh's tepid "peace plank" proposal prevailed, Lowenstein was furious. In the washroom of the Statler-Hilton, he asked Rauh at least to delete the word "irresponsible" from the resolution's reference to the antiwar people, but Rauh refused. According to Gans, "Rauh and Shull of the ADA did more to undercut us than anyone, including Johnson, who didn't take us seriously." Gans acknowledges, however, that as soon as they found a candidate, Rauh was helpful in getting the ADA to endorse him. But in September, Rauh was more than dubious about the Dump Johnson enterprise. (Lowenstein himself did not like the term "Dump Johnson" and preferred something more dignified like "Stop Johnson.") To the columnist Stuart Alsop, Rauh suggested that the Dump Johnson effort was "not important."

At Cambridge, where the Young Democrats managed to pass an antiwar resolution, though they could not defeat Lyndon Johnson's candidate, Senator Eugene McCarthy of Minnesota spoke against Johnson's policies in Vietnam. He was well received. McCarthy's unhappiness with Johnson was by then well known in Minnesota, and some people were even suggesting that McCarthy might run for president. But in advancing his cause in Minnesota, Gans had to assure people that dumping Johnson was not anti-Humphrey. Gans also held back from approaching McCarthy because he knew Lowenstein still hoped to recruit Robert Kennedy. Gans was also aware of the animosity Kennedy bore toward McCarthy for having supported Adlai Stevenson at the 1960 convention. Yet McCarthy himself believed that Robert Kennedy was the best possible candidate to oppose Johnson. Thus, with Kennedy insisting that he would not be a candidate and McCarthy supporting Kennedy, Lowenstein remained emptyhanded. Without a candidate, his movement was floundering.

On October 15, Steve Cohen wrote to Lowenstein:

I have been thinking about the explanation of current anti-Johnson strategy that you made at the last club meeting, and it seems to me that it was not clear.

You said that the selection of an anti-Johnson candidate is premature for the present and that a demonstration of grass-roots anti-Johnson sentiment will eventually bring forth a candidate. But it is not clear whether you thought this would happen before the first few primaries, or after, at the convention, and it seems to me that the timing is very important.

If there is no serious anti-Johnson candidate in the New Hampshire and/or Wisconsin primary, I think that the anti-Johnson position, or slate, will fail. An anti-Johnson position, or slate, without a candidate at its head, is too abstract, too uncertain; most people want someone to vote for.

If the anti-Johnson position fails in the first few primaries, the anti-Johnson movement will be crippled, and I doubt that a serious anti-Johnson candidate will then come forward.

Consequently, a serious candidate should come forward before the primaries. As of now, Kennedy does not fit the bill, because of his categorical disavowals of interest in the race. This will cost votes, and if his name is placed on the New Hampshire ballot, or a write-in campaign is organized, and his position has not changed, it will only help to plow the anti-Johnson movement under. But it appears that the only way to get Shepard to lay off is to provide an alternative.

If a serious candidate will come forward only on the basis of a grass-roots anti-Johnson demonstration, such a demonstration should be made before the primaries, so that his name can be placed on the ballot. Yet, what more can be done than has already been done? Johnson's standing in the polls is falling, anti-war sentiment is rising, the "Negotiations Now!" campaign appears to have been successful and a good part of the Senate is attacking Johnson.

A candidate must declare before New Hampshire, sometime during the winter. If there is a man who has already expressed a serious interest privately, he should be urged to prepare to move publicly. Such a candidate need not be the favorite of all factions of the anti-Johnson coalition in the New Hampshire and Wisconsin primaries. If he scores, it will create the wide-open convention which everyone wants.

Among the doves in the senate, it seems to me that McGovern would be best suited to this role, and outside the senate, because the Democrats do not have any major state houses, one thinks of Galbraith.

Martin Shepard and his Kennedy-Fulbright clubs were pressing Lowenstein's movement to join them, which would put pressure on Kennedy to declare his candidacy. Lowenstein addressed Shepard's group and attempted to persuade them that a candidate was not yet necessary, but Shepard felt that Lowenstein was being manipulative. Though he spoke brilliantly, Shepard believed that Lowenstein was keeping the inside information to himself. Cohen, who disagreed with Lowenstein's strategy, argued that the candidate they needed did not necessarily have to be the ultimate nominee. What they required, he maintained, was someone to force Johnson out and assure a "wide-open convention," which presumably could still nominate Robert Kennedy.

Lowenstein, through young antiwar radical Marcus Raskin, then tried McGovern, a loyal Kennedy person who, in 1960, had risked defeat in South Dakota by supporting a Catholic, John Kennedy, for president. But while he was sympathetic, McGovern was up for re-election, and he declined. Lowenstein persisted, requesting that McGovern run anyway as a favorite son, but McGovern wouldn't commit himself. He suggested McCarthy.

Wayne Morse and Vance Hartke were both willing to run but neither Lowenstein nor Gans wanted them. Morse was too much the maverick, and according to Gans, "Hartke had a reputation for not always honorable fiscal involvements." But Hartke was willing to run as a "favorite son," and Morse was prepared to give Lowenstein all of his names in Oregon as well as his personal organization, which was formidable. Lowenstein then went to Frank Church of Idaho, who was also unwilling because he too was up for reelection.

Rather than go to Eugene McCarthy, who was by then sounding more and more like a candidate, Lowenstein approached Don Edwards, General James Gavin, and John Kenneth Galbraith. Edwards declined, believing himself far too obscure, Gavin said he might run, but as a Republican; and Galbraith pointed out that he was Canadian-born, a naturalized citizen. It was time to talk to McCarthy.

Lowenstein, who did not know McCarthy, wanted his own introduction and asked the columnist Joseph Kraft, a mutual friend, to lay the groundwork for him. Kraft complied, but McCarthy, while indicating a willingness to Lowenstein, still held back. If Robert Kennedy was going to run, he would not.

Lowenstein had said, "You understand I love Bobby Kennedy more than anyone else in political life." In New York, unable to restrain himself any longer, Lowenstein charged up to Kennedy's apartment and heatedly presented his case. "Everything is falling into place," he told Kennedy. "We have local organizations in New Hampshire and Wisconsin, and the California Democratic Council is already committed to running an anti-Johnson candidate in the California primary. I've been across the country thirty times and I can tell we're going to win. . . . You have to get into it. . . . We're not the West Side Reform Democrats. We are grassroots America. Johnson is finished."

But Kennedy still could not be convinced. "He said he would not run except under unforeseen circumstances," Lowenstein later related. "So I . . . said, 'I'm an unforeseen circumstance.' He recited all that business he used to recite in that period about why so-and-so said it couldn't be done. But you could see he wanted to do it. It made me very sad, but angry too. I kept saying that if things were to be judged by traditional judgments of what was possible, then of course nothing could be done. But that was the whole point. Nothing was the way it had been before and if he didn't know that, he wasn't anywhere near as smart as I thought he was; and furthermore, if he didn't try . . . it was hard to believe he cared as much as millions of people thought he did.

"He said, 'It can't be put together.'

"Then . . . I just glared at him, and said, 'You understand, of course, that there are those of us who think the honor and direction of the country are at stake. I don't give a damn whether you think it can be put together or not. . . . We're going to do it without you, and that's too bad because you could have been president of the United States.'

"I turned and flew out. He came soaring out after me, and in that familiar gesture, he turned me around with his hand on my shoulder. We both were standing there blowing our noses in this thick sense of emotion. It was really very unexpected. . . . He just said, 'Well, I hope you understand that I can't do it, and that I know what you're doing should be done, but I just can't do it.'"

Lowenstein's impatience with Kennedy had also manifested itself on September 30 when he advised a pro-Kennedy group in Pittsburgh to "ditch Bobby," assuring them that it would be easier to mobilize anti-Johnson sentiment if "no candidate were put forward at this time." He told the *New York Times*, "Some people think we have to name a candidate now, I believe there is much time to make a decision." But on October 11, Lowenstein appeared on a late-night radio program in Philadelphia with Jack Newfield and an organizer for ACT–68. Newfield recalled that "there was a uniform tone to most of the questions we received: I don't like the war, I don't like Johnson, but you guys can't be real because you don't have a candidate." Then, toward the end of the program, Newfield observed that Lowenstein had scribbled something on a piece of paper in the form of a newspaper headline. It proclaimed: "McCarthy Wins Wisconsin Primary. Beats LBJ with 60 Percent of Vote."

On October 20, Lowenstein flew to Los Angeles where McCarthy was to give a speech on Vietnam. Having been assured by Kennedy that he wasn't running, McCarthy had gone so far as to suggest to George McGovern that he might in fact run. Indicating that he was willing to "test the waters" as he put it to Lowenstein, McCarthy had expressed a desire to have his name lumped with McGovern and Church as "the sort of people" who might run. Lowenstein had succeeded in extracting permission for this limited use of their names from McGovern and Church.

In Los Angeles, Lowenstein, Gerald Hill, McCarthy's aide Jerome Eller, and McCarthy got together for a jovial breakfast in McCarthy's suite, during which McCarthy asked practical political questions about possible labor support, fund raising and volunteers. Then he broke into a big grin and said to Lowenstein and Hill, "I guess you can cut it down to one."

Lowenstein phoned Gans and raced back to Washington to firm things up. It was agreed that McCarthy would make his announcement at the convention of Concerned Democrats in Chicago the first week in December. Until the announcement, nothing would be said about it. "I was ecstatic," Lowenstein related in describing his reaction to McCarthy's decision. "It was like music, like an organ welling up in my ears." At a press conference in Washington, pressed to name his candidate, Lowenstein replied with a smile, "Who knows? Senator McThis, Senator McThat. Someone will run."

Lowenstein's arrival in Washington coincided with that of over 100,000 people—including Dennis Sweeney, fresh from a minor drug bust following a police raid of Resistance House. The radical march on the Pentagon, later documented by Norman Mailer in *Armies of the Night*, threatened to overshadow the work of the anti-Johnson liberals who were seeking a solution through the electoral process. As Lowenstein said in a major story on him written by Frederick C. Klein for the *Wall Street Journal* and dated November 1, "There's a lot of room for innovation within the democratic system, but the general strain of liberalism in this country is passive. . . . This is dangerous because it leaves it up to the radicals to act. One doesn't accomplish much by sitting back and criticizing." He asserted his conviction that "the war protest was getting hooked on a narrow radical-pacifist base," which had led him to organize college students, seminarians, and Peace Corpsmen to write "end-the-war" letters to the president.

The article, entitled "Liberal 'Shaker' Edges to Limelight," contained laudatory comments from Norman Thomas and Frank Graham. Thomas said, "He is brilliant, able and an astute political operator," while Graham added, "Al's devotion to humane causes is exceptional. He is tireless, and one of the most unselfish people I've ever run across."

Lowenstein was now cochairman of the Conference of Concerned Democrats along with Gerald Hill and Donald Peterson. "The new organization claims to have active committees in all twenty states that conduct presidential primaries or open nominating conventions," Klein wrote. But the journalist insisted that Lowenstein himself was "a trifle uncomfortable in the limelight." Although he had been a "'shaker' in almost every liberal cause extant" and was close to the powerful leaders of the Democratic party, "yet he says he prefers to operate independently and remain in the background ('I've never found that formal titles and enduring organizational ties increase one's effectiveness') and wishes 'some better-known figure' headed the dump-Johnson movement," Klein concluded. "I feel like an understudy in a Broadway show," Lowenstein told him. "I know I can't sing and dance that well, but I have to go on just the same."

The article explained that Lowenstein was able to find time for all his activities "because he has fewer financial worries than most people. His family owns interests in 10 New York restaurants, and he is director and counsel to the company that controls four of them." Besides his teaching at City College (which Lowenstein described as his "steady job"), Lowenstein also had a radio show on WBAI and wrote articles for magazines that paid little or nothing. "Mostly, they are the kind of magazines that ask you for money at the end of the year," he told Klein. "It doesn't make much sense to accept a fee and then have to go out and raise it yourself." He estimated his income at between $12,000 and $15,000 a year, including $3,000 in dividends from the restaurant company with which, according to Klein, he "finances his travels and supports a wife, Jenny, who shares his political enthusiasms, and a two-month-old son." Explaining how he managed to do this, Lowenstein said, "We don't live expensively. . . . We don't drink, play golf, buy a lot of clothing or take expensive holidays. It's really not expensive to travel if you know someone where you are going who will lend you his car, put you up and feed you. I'm not fussy about what I eat." Repeating a statement he had made earlier, he added, "Too many young people don't take advantage of all the mobility we have today. People get locked into career ladders and cheat themselves out of doing things they consider important and useful."

While Lowenstein explained that it was the dividends from the restaurants that gave him the "opportunity to do things I couldn't do otherwise" (he also said he considered the dividends to be "unearned"), Lowenstein's sister Dorothy says that by 1967 Lowenstein's income from the restaurants was insignificant. His brother Larry confirms that by then Lowenstein's only involvement with the restaurants, except in a nominal way, was as an "eater." On the other hand his tastes while traveling abroad tended toward such luxurious establishments as the Norfolk Hotel in Nairobi and the Tokyo Hilton.

It was known that Jenny was very careful with her own trust-fund money, which, she says, didn't pay much at that time anyway. And since his part-time teaching at City College paid him far less than he had earned at NC State (only $7,000 for a full-time position), the evidence pointed toward some other source of money. The far-left Progressive Labor party (a Maoist splinter group) offered one theory in its publication *Challenge*. They accused Lowenstein of being "involved up to his ears in the CIA" and of "'subverting' the leadership of an African exile movement." They also described Lowenstein as "a loyal and experienced operative" of Senator Robert Kennedy.

Lowenstein wore this kind of criticism like a badge of honor. It was helpful to the Dump Johnson effort in that it showed the movement to be moderate and patriotic, distinguishing it from the radical New Left, with its emphasis on draft resistance.

Within the Democratic party and organized labor there was intense hostility to the antiwar movement, just as there was to SNCC. Both movements reminded influential labor leaders like Gus Tyler of past Communist party activity in America. The American Communist party had been torn in the twenties by the Comintern's insistence that it adopt a policy of support for a separate nation for

American blacks. In the thirties, on the American campuses, "Communists took a pledge not to bear arms in any international conflict and stage-managed riots against the Reserve Officers Training Corps." By 1967, Stokely Carmichael was advocating a separate black nation made up of several bordering southern states, while New Left leaders like David Harris were calling on students not to serve in the armed forces. There were deep suspicions that Communists were involved in the black power demonstrations and the antiwar movement. Stokely Carmichael, who headed SNCC in its final phase, was an avowed socialist and a revolutionary, while the pro-Chinese Progressive Labor party was taking over the SDS. But though Lowenstein had provided information on radicals in the civil rights movement and had organized to counter the strength of the New Left in the antiwar movement (his letters-to-the-president campaign grew out of his confrontation with David Harris at the 1966 NSA congress), he now became a target of FBI inquiries himself and the subject of reports to the president.

On November 13, 1967, an FBI memorandum classified as secret was sent to Mildred Stegall on the White House staff. The covering letter read: "I thought the President would be interested in the enclosed memoranda regarding the West Side Liberal Democrats and Allard Kenneth Lowenstein. I am returning the correspondence regarding this matter which was furnished to Mr. Cartha D. DeLoach of this Bureau. Upon removal of the classified enclosure this transmittal letter becomes unclassified." The signature is omitted, but it is presumably that of J. Edgar Hoover.

The memorandum, subsequently declassified, summarized the *Wall Street Journal* article of November 1, identifying Lowenstein as cochairman of the Conference of Concerned Democrats "a national group seeking to deny Lyndon Johnson the Democratic Presidential nomination in 1968."

Gerald Hill, also a cochairman, was the first subject of the FBI report. Hill, who was also chairman of the California Democratic Council, was described as "an outspoken critic against United States policy in Vietnam." Hill's political associations, clearly viewed as dubious, were traced back to his term as president of the Sausalito, California, branch of the American Youth for Democracy in January 1948, when he was fifteen years old. "The American Youth for Democracy has been cited as subversive by the Attorney General pursuant to Executive Order 10450," the report stated ominously.

The information on Lowenstein contained his educational background, incidental information about *Brutal Mandate* and his opposition to apartheid in South Africa, and the investigation of him by the FBI to see if his actions had "incurred an obligation to register under the Foreign Agents Registration Act of 1938." They had not. The memorandum indicated that Lowenstein, while president of the National Student Association, had accused the "Communist controlled International Union of Students" in 1951 of "using unscrupulous deceit, distortion of facts, and confusion in carrying on a progaganda campaign against democratic nations." Lowenstein's civil rights activities and his antiapartheid work in 1960 at the time of the Sharpeville Massacre were outlined as were his efforts in 1965 to gain recognition by the United States of the Peoples Republic of China and to obtain a cease-fire in Vietnam through the creation of the Americans for Reappraisal of Far Eastern Policy. It was also noted that he had visited Spain in 1966 to make contact with "various members of the Spanish opposition whom he knew from previous trips to Spain." The memo concluded:

"The December 30, 1966, issue of *The New York Times* reported that student leaders from 100 colleges and universities had signed an open letter to President Johnson expressing their anxiety and doubts about United States involvement in the war in Vietnam. It was noted that the students' idea to write the letter to President Johnson grew out of a debate at the annual congress of the National Student Association that summer on the campus of the University of Illinois. The proposal was advanced during the debate by Allard K. Lowenstein, a former president of the Association who is now a lawyer and active Reform Democrat in Manhattan."

Lowenstein had been an observer of radical political action. Now, his own liberal politics were under scrutiny. Even a "good-wing" CIA operative was apparently subject to the anti-Communist excesses of the FBI.

47.

Lowenstein used Dissenting Democrats to take the fight to the SDS at Cornell. The Cornell SDS chapter had put him on the defensive with the Spring Mobilization, but in November he was back, urging the students to join the Dump Johnson movement, apparently with considerable success. On November 14, Nancy Roche of Cornell wrote Lowenstein to thank him for appearing, telling him "yours was The Way" and to inform him that his speech had "won many converts for the 'Dump Johnson' cause."

If Lowenstein was undercutting the SDS to his left, he was also making converts on the right, enlisting the uncommitted and conservative students who would never have joined the radicals in their movement. At the same time, his own fame was growing. Dissenting Democrats, based on West 72nd Street in New York (it may have been grassroots America, but the Upper West Side liberal Reform Democrats were still at the heart of it), reproduced the *Wall Street Journal* article and distributed it widely.

But while Lowenstein's instinct was to build up the pressure, Eugene McCarthy's was to diffuse it. Instead of making his announcement before the Concerned Democrats in Chicago in a highly charged atmosphere of public dissent, McCarthy jumped the gun and made a subdued statement of his candidacy in the Senate Caucus Room two days before. "I intend to enter the Democratic primaries in Wisconsin, California, and Nebraska," he said. "The decision with reference to Massachusetts and New Hampshire will be made within two weeks." McCarthy never actually said he was running for president. It wasn't until he had met in New Hampshire with Professor David Hoeh and a group of supporters that it was decided to drop Massachusetts, where Johnson had considerable support on the state committee.

McCarthy later stated that the reason for his announcement in Washington was a desire to distance himself from Lowenstein's group. "I had made the announcement of my candidacy two days earlier in Washington," he related. "The reason was that I did not wish to be represented as the candidate of any special group or organization, and also because I had some reservations about the tone and the criticism of the administration by some of the Concerned Democrats. Allard Lowenstein had said, for example, 'When a president is both wrong and unpopular, to refuse to oppose him is both a moral abdication and a political stupidity.'"

On December 2, McCarthy did keep his speaking engagement with the Concerned Democrats in Chicago, at a giant rally organized by Curtis Gans, Harold Ickes, and Sam Brown. Gerald Hill was to have introduced McCarthy, but as Gans describes it, "Al did his questioning act. 'Is Hill best to introduce McCarthy?' He put on pressure to speak before McCarthy and confused who was the candidate for president."

McCarthy who arrived slightly late, found Lowenstein already at the podium before a rambunctious overflow crowd of 4,000. Both ballrooms of the Chicago Hilton were packed and another 2,000 were outside. Lowenstein had pulled out some notes and told his audience, "I'm going to give you a little pep talk."

The months of tension coming to a head in him, Lowenstein gave them what the authors of *An American Melodrama* described as "a hell-raising, bawl-and-jump speech." McCarthy was furious, "raging like a caged lion" in his suite. Finally, he said to Jerry Eller, "Let's go!" and stormed into the ballroom, where Lowenstein was still at it. According to the *American Melodrama* account, "Lowenstein was boiling up to a peak, and every time he mentioned Lyndon Johnson the crowd howled for blood. 'Get this straight,' he was bellowing, 'if a man cheats you once, shame on him. But if he cheats you twice, shame on you!'"

Gans tried desperately to get him to stop, while McCarthy fumed, kicking a Dixie cup against the wall. Gans moved his finger across his throat to signal Lowenstein to cut it, and then ran up to the front shouting, "Stop it! Someone get him to stop it, for Christ's sake!" But Lowenstein continued, waving his notes and shouting, "There's only a little bit left."

During the entire tirade, Lowenstein mentioned McCarthy only once. Gans believes that McCarthy was prepared to make a good speech but got so distracted that he delivered a bad one. Most observers agree that McCarthy left his crowd in an anticlimax, but McCarthy himself thought the address was both good and appropriate. Later, he reflected in *Year of the People*:

> I thought as I prepared it that it was rather a good speech and on rereading it after the criticism was still of the same opinion. As to the tone in which it was delivered, probably no one understood at the time, but, first, it followed the speech of Al Lowenstein, which I thought was an overstatement of the case against Lyndon Johnson and which was not in the spirit of the campaign which I intended to wage. And second, the people gathered there did not need to be inflamed or exhorted. They were pretty well turned on before arriving in Chicago and were ready to hold the election immediately. They needed, I thought, a speech of some restraint if they were to be prepared for the long and difficult campaign, which I knew lay ahead. It was not a time for storming the walls, but for beginning a long march.

"I saw him as a candidate," Lowenstein said of McCarthy, "He saw himself as a moral protester for a cause." And Jenny, who sympathized with her husband's impatience with McCarthy, concludes: "Al believed in working forty-eight hours a day around the clock, which was not McCarthy's style. And there was a big rhetorical difference. Al resorted to the grossest demogoguery, but people needed this hypodermic needle of energy. He had spent one and a half years researching all of this at his own expense, and it irked him that in the middle of everything, McCarthy would take off and go to the movies."

The Conference of Concerned Democrats did not endorse McCarthy in Chicago. On December 3, the day after McCarthy's speech, Lawrence Spivak asked Lowenstein on "Meet the Press": "You were recently described as being 'a loyal and experienced operative of Senator Robert Kennedy.' What is your answer to those who say that you and Concerned Democrats are using Senator McCarthy as a stalking horse for Senator Robert Kennedy?"

Lowenstein replied: "I think it is flattering to be called the loyal and experienced operative, whatever an operative is, and Senator Kennedy wouldn't be a bad person to be loyal and experienced on the behalf of. I think he is one of the great men around, but the fact is, I don't work for Senator Kennedy or for Senator McCarthy. I would like to see all the Democrats in the country who feel discontented with the direction of the party and the country rally behind an alternative who can win, and I think that alternative is Senator McCarthy.

"Senator Kennedy hasn't in any way put me up to this or put anyone else up to it. He is very clear; he speaks very well for himself. In fact, I like what he says, but I don't tell him what to say, and he doesn't tell me what to say."

Spivak pressed him further: "Regardless of anybody's present intentions, yours and Senator Kennedy's, do you believe that a strong showing in the primaries by Senator McCarthy could lead to the nomination of Senator Kennedy?"

Lowenstein responded: 'Yes, I think a strong showing by Senator McCarthy will produce an open convention, and I think that could lead to the nomination of a great many people, almost all of whom would represent a distinct improvement over the prospects of the Democratic party if the incumbent is renominated. Senator Kennedy, like most of us, would, I believe, profit from an open convention, but I don't think that guarantees that Senator Kennedy would emerge as a candidate at all. If Senator McCarthy does as well as he is going to do, I think what will happen is that he will become a major figure on his own with momentum rising in his behalf, and there is no telling at that point what the convention will do."

Towards the end of December, Lowenstein was hospitalized because of a gall bladder attack requiring surgery. On December 26, McCarthy cabled him at Columbia Presbyterian Medical Center: "Looking forward to seeing you at the January 6th New York City dinner meeting of the Coalition for a Democratic Alternative. You and your associates have already done great work in bringing the important issues of this moment before the Democratic Party and the country. I count on you all to continue and redouble your efforts in the months to come. I am grateful for your support in my effort."

Robert Kennedy responded to questions from the press about McCarthy's chances by saying he didn't believe that Johnson would lose the New Hampshire primary. But when the Tet offensive broke out in January 1968, the spotlight fell on New Hampshire. Suddenly, Eugene McCarthy was credible. And when Johnson spoke of Tet as an American victory, McCarthy's stature increased as he continued campaigning in a low-key, moderate manner.

Lowenstein continued to keep a backbreaking schedule after his release from the hospital. On February 8, he arrived in Minneapolis for a full day of radio tapings, press conferences, meetings with campus groups, a buffet supper with the St. Paul McCarthy Committee, a speech at Macalester College, more meetings with peace groups, and a radio appearance at night. On Friday, February 9, he left for Duluth by car at 7:30 A.M. for an 11:30 press conference followed by lunch with the Duluth Concerned Democrats and a half-hour radio program in the afternoon. At 4:00 P.M., he flew from Duluth in a private university plane to St. Cloud for a meeting with the St. Cloud Concerned Democrats. Then he flew to Morris, Minnesota, for an 8 P.M. rally at the university campus, after which he flew to Anoka where a driver met him at the airport and took him to a McCarthy supporter's house for the night.

But a rift was widening between Lowenstein and Gans. The difficulties arose as the shift from Dump Johnson to the actual McCarthy campaign took place. The entire Dump Johnson organization had been put together on a budget of less than $50,000, and Gans had been paid only an extremely small sum. Debts were accumulating, and by the time McCarthy decided to run, the organization was in rocky shape. Gans was in a difficult position because, in his words, "Al had other fish to fry," meaning that Lowenstein was seeking to be a candidate for office himself.

Gans, still peeved, recalls: "Al left me high and dry with $25,000 in debts. He wanted to be McCarthy's campaign manager but McCarthy didn't trust him in that position."

When McCarthy named Blair Clark his campaign manager, Lowenstein decided to continue supporting McCarthy independently from the McCarthy campaign. McCarthy himself created his campaign organization as a separate entity from Dump Johnson, as Gans puts it, "in no relation to anything else." But, as Gans states, they still needed the old Dump Johnson people, and "only two people knew who these people were"—Lowenstein and Gans. When Lowenstein was in the hospital, it was up to Gans to make the McCarthy campaign a reality. Gans, who would be fired five times by McCarthy only to be rehired each time, was also aware that Lowenstein "really favored Kennedy" and was not enthusiastic about McCarthy as a candidate.

At this point, McCarthy hired Gans and assumed the debts of the Conference of Concerned Democrats while Lowenstein considered running for the United States Senate from New York. He maintained that the antiwar movement needed a strong New York forum for opposition to Johnson and that his contacts with both McCarthy and Robert Kennedy made him the ideal candidate. Both Ronnie Eldridge, McCarthy's New York coordinator who had also managed Lowenstein's 1966 congressional campaign, and Gans told Lowenstein that they were willing to support him but the McCarthy campaign would have to be given priority.

For a short period, Lowenstein's apartment on West 82nd Street became the hub of his Senate effort. For the first time, Jenny took a role in his political career, promoting her husband's plans among people she knew and he didn't. Greg Craig and other friends would move in for periods of time though the apartment had only two bedrooms, and there was always someone living with them, either a McCarthy supporter or one of Lowenstein's own campaign workers. Later, when Robert Kennedy finally announced, Lowenstein believed that his candidacy could unite the opposing Kennedy and McCarthy camps. But the two groups were too hostile to each other to support a common cause and Lowenstein's dream of running for the Senate evaporated.

On February 10, Joseph Rauh engineered an ADA resolution of board members endorsing McCarthy. Then the full ADA Convention endorsed him, prompting the liberal hawks to leave the organization.

At a major address delivered on March 4 in the chapel of Phillips Exeter Academy in New Hampshire, Lowenstein exhorted his listeners to give McCarthy their full support:

> Some people sit around and say, "Well, we know that McCarthy is the only candidate now running, but we ought to wait around to see if someone else doesn't emerge." Some people are still waiting for Kennedy, or waiting for Rockefeller, or Godot, I don't know. . . . What you are saying is that in the presence of a great man doing the greatest and most important political act of independence, probably in our history, standing for all the things that you know he should stand for, with a great public record to back him up, in the face of that you don't want to work, you don't want to commit yourself. I guess no one can argue with you if that's what you feel, but you should understand that it's not political realism that leads you not to take part. It's some kind of desire to find an excuse to sit it out. . . .
>
> Stand up here and in New Hampshire and then at home, and get this extraordinarily great human being who has been carrying the burden for all of us, get him the kind of support that will make him the nominee of the Democratic party and after that the next president of the United States and the first president of the United States since Jack Kennedy to understand what America's about and how to get us on the road that we started down when he was president.

Gans took charge of the New Hampshire campaign, with a huge army of college students at his disposal. He had them canvass each house three times in person and twice by phone. Every registered voter in the state was deluged by six or more pieces of campaign literature. Lowenstein traveled throughout the state in the snow, often with Jenny and the baby. "All through New Hampshire, Al and Paul Newman campaigned twenty-four hours a day," she recalls.

On the eve of the primary, Lowenstein met with Gans and Sam Brown and urged them to tell McCarthy that "he was not a good candidate." Gans was incredulous. When the results came in on the night of March 12, McCarthy had 42.2 percent of the vote on the Democratic line and a significant number of Republican write-ins, a total of slightly under fifty percent. McCarthy won twenty of the twenty-four delegates.

Lowenstein and Jenny were in New Hampshire the night McCarthy "won" the primary and learned that Robert Kennedy, who had phoned to congratulate McCarthy, had announced that he was "reassessing" his position. After a brief, unpleasant encounter with McCarthy, who was evidently displeased with him, Lowenstein, exhausted, returned to New York with Jenny and went to bed. They were awakened by a telephone call from Bobby Kennedy. "Al, baby," Kennedy told him, "I've decided to take your advice and run for president." There was a pause. "Bobby, you S.O.B., you've really done it this time," Lowenstein told him, chuckling.

When Johnson neglected to file as a candidate in Massachusetts, assuming that the state Democratic organization would take care of business for him, McCarthy picked up seventy-two delegates by default. In Minnesota, where Gans had done considerable organizing, McCarthy supporters turned out in large numbers in the caucuses, surprising the Humphrey organization.

Lowenstein worked out a "moral calculus" as Gans calls it, to reconcile his own personal conflict. He met with Jesse Unruh to plan a joint Kennedy-McCarthy delegation from California. He assisted Kennedy with his formal announcement, delivered three days after McCarthy's New Hampshire triumph, but attempted to make it part of a general movement against Johnson and the war. He continued to speak for McCarthy in states where Kennedy was not running but, at the same time, he also spoke negatively about McCarthy in private. Lowenstein argued that McCarthy had lost contact with reality after Kennedy entered the race, refusing to recognize that Kennedy was a "winner" and that he was not himself a viable candidate. Lowenstein told his cousin Alice Levien and her husband Charles that McCarthy was "sick" and that he had "gone off the deep end." As the California primary drew near, he told them that McCarthy was "mentally and emotionally unstable," "had delusions of grandeur," and "could not be relied on."

When Lowenstein informed Kennedy of his plans to run for the

Senate in New York, Kennedy responded that, "It could be fun. We could really shake them up." But by then the McCarthy people were dubious, convinced that Lowenstein was really for Kennedy. Lowenstein was obliged to cancel his Senate project and began talking about a race for Congress, prompting Kennedy to remark, "You running for Congress is like the pope running for parish priest." Kennedy began to needle Lowenstein good-naturedly, speculating aloud about what job he could offer Lowenstein to win his support for the presidency. Working his way through cabinet positions, Kennedy stopped suddenly to observe, "I know what you're thinking. You want to be secretary of the army." Lowenstein smiled sheepishly; he had been thinking about the job.

A week after Kennedy's announcement, Lowenstein found himself on a bus with him riding back to New York following a big Democratic dinner in Buffalo where the airport was totally fogged in. They talked about the war and the campaign and then Kennedy asked him to leave McCarthy for him. Lowenstein told him, "As much as I'm for you, I'm staying with McCarthy."

Kennedy nodded and then scribbled a note which he handed to Lowenstein. It read, "For Al, who knew the lesson of Emerson and taught it to the rest of us: 'They did not yet see, and thousands of young men as hopeful now crowding to the barriers of their careers do not yet see, that if a single man plant himself on his convictions and then abide, the huge world will come round to him.' from his friend Bob Kennedy."

It was three in the morning when Lowenstein got home. According to Jenny, his eyes filled with tears when he told her what had happened and how he had explained to Kennedy that he couldn't support him. Lowenstein showed her the note and went to bed. He would carry it with him, show it to others, and use it in his speeches.

The Kennedy and McCarthy camps attacked each other and tried to make deals at the same time. Curtis Gans proposed a swap to the Kennedy forces—Indiana for Oregon in the primaries. The Kennedy people published a version of McCarthy's voting record which showed him to be more conservative than his campaign indicated. Lowenstein's position was becoming untenable. Writer Arthur Herzog, who was advising McCarthy, says that Lowenstein, whom he considered "the most overblown person of the period" was "the ultimate adversary. He was to be kept away from at any cost" because he was so "disruptive." "He was regarded as a Kennedy plant," Herzog concludes.

Jenny relates that "Al faded from the '68 presidential picture in the spring of '68 after New Hampshire and Wisconsin." In the confusion and turmoil, Lowenstein had decided to heed the advice of a new acquaintance, an obscure, middle-aged Jewish housewife from Long Beach, Long Island, Harriet Eisman.

48.

Harriet Eisman in 1967 was a politically unsophisticated person deeply upset by the war in Vietnam. She was disturbed not because her major field of interest was geopolitics but because she was the mother of three draft-age sons, all deeply involved in the antiwar movement. "They gave up everything to work on the cause," she said. "I had to do something." The most important thing she felt she could do was to stir things up locally, to galvanize people into serious action.

Long Beach, a predominantly Jewish community, surrounded by the strong Irish and Italian enclaves of Point Lookout and Atlantic Beach, was once a luxurious summer colony inhabited by movie stars and rich entrepreneurs. By decree of its developer, the stores on Main Street were all built with red tile roofs. By 1968, although many once fashionable mansions were still inhabited by middle-class families, a feeling of decay had begun to set in. The beach was still magnificent, but nursing homes had opened along it; the old hotels were in disrepair and excitement had been replaced by apathy.

In this setting, Eisman, with four other women, opened the "headquarters" of the antiwar movement in Long Beach, "The Ad Hoc Committee to Stop the War." As Eisman told it, "People would see us and say 'Are you Communists or something?' These were good people we couldn't get moving." To get some action, the five opened a headquarters for McCarthy and began "looking for someone to come out and speak to whip up the community, which we were unable to do." Word of Lowenstein's rhetorical skills reached them, and when they heard he was scheduled to debate in nearby Great Neck, all five drove over to hear him. "He was the most exciting speaker I have ever heard," reflected Eisman afterward. "We went up to him after the meeting and said we were from Long Beach, a Democratic stronghold, and we were trying to organize something there and we have been trying to find someone to whip up the community. Would you come out and speak?"

Lowenstein readily agreed but proposed that, in exchange, the five women should go to New Hampshire and canvass. "Of course, when we got there," Eisman continued, "they sent us to the boondocks." When Lowenstein and his family finally appeared there, Eisman recalled that she grabbed him and asked if he remembered them.

"Everybody was doing that. We told him that we had kept our promise, we came here, now he had to come to Long Beach."

In fact, the idea of recruiting Lowenstein to run in the 5th Congressional District was beginning to interest the group and soon became an obsession with Eisman. "I had the singularity of the insane. I had this thing that if we could get someone like him, we could stir up the whole scene." Nothing else had worked. Eisman had sent out cards asking, "Why aren't you running wild in the streets, screaming 'Help, murder, police.'" Her group had distributed handouts at graduation and been "terribly reprimanded" for it. "Your child is graduating junior high today and in a few years, he will be eligible for this horrendous unfair war," was their message. It was, as she said, "real rabble-rousing."

Determined to dump Johnson and get someone elected to Congress, the group, according to Eisman, didn't really view the seat as the important thing. Rather, they believed that "a candidate for anything could motivate the whole movement, and we talked him into it." Lowenstein told them that he had been toying with the idea, though he had no aspirations for political office, and indeed Eisman described Lowenstein as single-minded at the time. "He had this one singular thing about dumping Johnson, the war had to stop. By that time, he had been around the colleges and saw the despair. He'd been to every college in the country. He was known throughout the country by the youth as the antiwar spokesman."

The 5th Congressional District was "a nice mixture," according to Eisman, but "the problem was that it was a Republican stronghold, like the rest of Nassau County. You would have to get a large number of Republican cross-overs. And the big issue was the war. When we started, there were places we would go in the county in which they withstood him, but Al had a way, it was magic, almost. When he spoke somewhere, fifty people would call the headquarters and say, 'What can I do to help?' He turned things around, there was no question about it. He had an unusual, dynamic pull. . . . He had this special quality of pulling out people. He managed to take from Nassau and Suffolk County on Long Island, in and outside the district, the most unusual group of people from all over, people who stayed involved twelve years after, and they remained good people. They didn't get ruined by power or the system."

49.

On March 21, shortly before the Wisconsin primary, Lyndon Johnson went on television and told the world that he would not be a candidate for reelection. Lowenstein heard the news while sitting in the airport, waiting for a plane to take him to Wisconsin where he was to speak for McCarthy. All the polls showed the Minnesota senator well ahead of Johnson and Lowenstein's appearance was to be icing on the cake. It turned out to be his last speech for McCarthy.

When Jenny received a telegram from Harriet Eisman and the 5th C.D. people urging Lowenstein to run for Congress in their Long Island district, she phoned him in Wisconsin to get his reaction. "Let's talk to them," he said. "It's the answer for me to get out of the Mc-Carthy-Kennedy battle. Shouldn't I do this as an antiwar candidate?" According to Jenny, Lowenstein really wanted to go to Congress, not-withstanding his protestations to the contrary. "I was for it," she de-clares. "I liked Long Beach. I saw a house I loved, near the ocean. It was early spring. Frankie was young and it was nice weather."

On April 2, McCarthy, running against a lame-duck Johnson, whose name still appeared on the ballot, won the Wisconsin primary overwhelmingly. James Wechsler commented in his *New York Post* column, "On primary night, Eugene McCarthy publicly thanked Lowenstein, whose organization of students and other concerned cit-izens, he said, had been crucial to his lonely, successful combat."

On April 4, Martin Luther King, Jr., was assassinated in Memphis, where he had gone to support a sanitation workers' strike. Rioting broke out in the ghettos all across America as the philosophy of non-violence was overthrown in frustration and despair.

Lowenstein's decision to run had been made quickly. He returned from Wisconsin, they rented a house on President Street in Long Beach and prepared for the Dissenting Democrats convention on March 31, at which the liberal Democrats of the district assembled to listen to the candidates, including aspirants for the seat of outgoing Congressman, Herbert Tenzer. Though Lowenstein liked to think of himself as a Willkie, a private citizen drafted to run for office, he was actually being criticized as a "carpetbagger" and for running in the 5th C.D. only after failing to get the nomination in Manhattan. Lowen-stein's supporters explained that their candidate had, in fact, declined to run in the 17th C.D.

Long-time liberal activist Saul Schindler had reacted favorably to Lowenstein after hearing him speak on a TV talk show. He was "very impressed with his intelligence, articulateness and enunciation of commitment to many of the issues we stood for—an end to the Viet-nam War, disarmament, civil rights." He had reservations, however, because of the "carpetbagger" issue, and was leaning toward another candidate, Albert Vorspan, a liberal, popular in Jewish circles, who had been active in the civil rights movement. When he was satisfied that Vorspan did not intend to run, however, Schindler settled on Lowenstein who became the choice of his group and of another "peace group," one of whose leaders was Fran Boehm, an activist in Women's Strike for Peace. According to Schindler, Lowenstein gave a "very convincing speech in which he repudiated the charges that he was a 'carpetbagger,' citing his roots in the area."

Al Dorfman, a handsome, vigorous, and impassioned speaker with a strong following among people who believed in civil rights was also a contender, but his bid was effectively sidetracked. As Schindler relates, "There were some spirited speeches, some quick electioneering and then the vote—with Lowenstein the victor by a narrow margin over Dorfman. Something in the process angered Dorfman's supporters and they were about to repudiate the selection of Lowenstein, or walk out of the meeting, when inspiration struck me. I quickly realized that if Lowenstein didn't have Dorfman's activist supporters with us, we, a minority, would have a hard time getting him the Democratic nomination, much less the election. I poked Fran Boehm, who was sitting near me. 'Quick Fran,' I urged, 'nominate Al Dorfman as candidate for district attorney.'

"Fran, who has a sharp mind, and a devoted following, quickly shouted, 'I nominate Al Dorfman for district attorney.'

"There was some hubbub, with Dorfman and his supporters refusing this bone which seemed to be thrown at them. There was also a recess and during that recess, I went to speak to Dorfman. I pointed out to him that for a man with his ideals and commitment to civil rights, the D.A. position could be a very useful one from which to effectuate those ideals, since minority groups and those wishing to hold public meetings and petition were often harassed by the forces of 'law and order.' Dorfman listened attentively and seemed to buy the argument. He agreed to be the D.A. candidate, was nominated, and accepted without opposition. His supporters seemed appeased, and in fact, one of Lowenstein's strongest centers of support was in Long Beach, and from these Dorfman supporters."

Having been designated as the candidate of the liberal wing of the party in the 5th C.D., Lowenstein formally announced on April 11. James Wechsler wrote in his column in the *New York Post*: "No other individual did more than Lowenstein to set in motion the sequence of events climaxed by Mr. Johnson's formal withdrawal." Lowenstein's decision to run, he added, "represents a very real turning point. . . . This unusual citizen must now settle down for a long political siege on a limited landscape. No doubt there will be intermittent flying trips to McCarthy campaign fronts in other states, but his immediate major mission is clear and he isn't running for exercise." The primary was scheduled for June 17. Lowenstein had two months.

Volunteers began to pour into Long Beach. "Before the convention, he rented a house on President Street here," Harriet Eisman recalled. "He rented a place, and all of a sudden, his kids starting arriving to work for him. He had been doing this McCarthy thing and speaking at the colleges, and this was a small, little house, and the community was not used to this sort of thing. All of a sudden, kids started piling into this little place. . . . People coming into the campaign had to clear it with me, so he would send them over to me, right? One day, knocking at my door is this big, lanky guy. 'I was told by Al to introduce myself to you, that you would be the person to tell me where to go and what to do.' You had to know that Al already had the whole thing worked out, and he said, 'I'm Franklin Roosevelt III.' In my dreams, I never. Although he looked a little bit like Eleanor, I really . . . I said, 'It's nice to meet you, and I'm Betsy Ross.' And the funny thing is, this kid comes into the campaign and says, 'Al wants me to introduce myself to you. I'm Wendell Willkie II.'"

"The campaign for the Democratic nomination turned into a bitter fight between the two wings of the party," relates Saul Schindler, who had volunteered to do public relations work for Lowenstein at a critical moment. "It was so bitter, in fact, that neighbors and friends of long-standing became bitter enemies, or ceased talking to each other. The leaders of the local Democratic organization didn't want Lowenstein and decided to back *their* candidate. That candidate turned out to be Al Vorspan." Schindler had apparently misunderstood Vorspan's initial negative reaction. Though it was true that Vorspan didn't want to run as the candidate of the liberal Democrats Schindler represented, he did want to run as the candidate of the "regular" Democratic organization.

According to Schindler, Lowenstein was criticized as a "'carpetbagger,' 'too leftist,' and 'not strongly enough committed to Israel.'" The "regular" Democrats also claimed that his campaign was "too divisive," and that he wouldn't be able to get along with the "regular" Democrats. On one occasion, Schindler seized an opportunity to refute the latter charge by grabbing a photographer to shoot Lowenstein in a chance conversation with two leaders of the Five Towns Democratic Club who were backing Vorspan. The photograph was printed in the local papers with a caption that made it seem, in Schindler's words "that harmony now reigned among us local Democrats. After Lowenstein won the primary, they did support him, so harmony was finally achieved. Al, of course, beat his Republican opponent and thus became the Congressman from the Fifth."

50.

The Vorspan campaign continued to charge that Lowenstein was a "carpetbagger." On May 9, Woodmere attorney Joseph Ruskay, who, like Lowenstein, was a vice-president of the ADA, called on Lowenstein to withdraw from the primary race against Vorspan, who was a resident of Hewlett. Ruskay said he was "profoundly shocked" that Lowenstein, who was from Manhattan, was running, and stated that it was "beyond his comprehension" how any Democrat would wish to dissent from Vorspan, who probably had the "best progressive record" in the community. Harriet Eisman and the Dissenting Democrats countered that Vorspan had not bothered to appear before their screening committee and that Lowenstein was the best candidate to run against the Republican designee, Mason Hampton. Hampton, two years younger than Lowenstein, was, in fact, a registered Conservative. Dissenting Democrats also distributed Leroy Aarons' article on Lowenstein published on May 19 in the *Washington Post*. Aarons called Lowenstein "one of the men of his generation who has truly influenced events, however subliminally." He described him as "a Renaissance man of the liberal movement, a broad-gauged individual who has advised Eleanor Roosevelt, the Rev. Dr. Martin Luther King, Jr., Norman Thomas and Robert F. Kennedy, much of the national activist student movement and most of the civil rights leadership." Among the qualities attributed to Lowenstein by Aarons were "rare compassion and humanism," complemented by a "probing, philosophical intellect, an almost medieval sense of honor and loyalty and a consuming dedication to liberal principles." "Obsessed" by the Vietnam war and convinced of the necessity to bring down the Johnson administration, "He believed that the coup could be achieved peacefully, politically and within the Democratic Party," the article concluded.

With six to eight students living in the house at all times, there were "wall-to-wall bodies," as Jenny describes it. Frankie was passed from student volunteer to student volunteer until Dee Barber, Bert Lowenstein's ex–mother-in-law and a family friend, moved in and took charge of the baby. A veteran of the civil rights movement who had worked with Lowenstein in South Carolina, Barber described herself as from a "fallen-from-money family" and told of having taught Tallulah Bankhead to play the violin. She stayed with the Lowenstein's for a year and a half. Jenny, meanwhile, was being transformed into a professional campaigner, scheduled at Hadassah meetings and similar functions, though in order to maximize the number of appearances they both could make, she never appeared with her husband. So successful was the transformation that on a number of occasions people told her she was "better than Al."

Meanwhile, McCarthy and Kennedy headed for a showdown. Kennedy won Indiana, and when McCarthy was defeated in Nebraska many thought he was finished. He rebounded, though, taking Oregon, where he spoke with intelligence and conviction. He also still had the support of the ADA, which on May 19 reaffirmed its endorsement of him.

Within Lowenstein's campaign team, nominally McCarthy supporters, there was considerable pro-Kennedy sentiment. Harriet Eisman had originally led a letter-writing campaign urging Kennedy to run. (Each letter had gone out on different-colored stationery so Kennedy wouldn't suspect that the campaign was orchestrated.) "This was before we endorsed McCarthy," she said. "There were lots of people writing. We said he had to help us save the children, America, the whole thing. He did not agree to run until we had all committed ourselves to McCarthy." After Kennedy announced, a large group of Dissenting Democrats went over to him nevertheless, while loyalists like Harriet Eisman stuck with McCarthy, though it was evident that many of them didn't care for him as a person. Eisman's husband left Dissenting Democrats disgusted because so many had gone over to Kennedy. "That was the Democrats," Eisman sighed.

June 4 was the key winner-take-all California primary, and Lowenstein was watching it carefully as he campaigned himself. As the returns came in that night, Kennedy was holding a narrow lead. If he won, his momentum could carry him to the nomination. At the Ambassador Hotel in Los Angeles, Kennedy headquarters, the mood was jubilant as word spread that Bobby would win by four percent.

Richard Goodwin, who had started with McCarthy, then switched to Kennedy, tried to reach Lowenstein by phone at about 11 P.M. but got no answer. He was calling on Kennedy's instructions and his mission was to persuade Lowenstein to join the Kennedy camp now that California had given Kennedy an insurmountable delegate lead over McCarthy. Though Kennedy trailed Humphrey, he could overtake him if the uncommitted delegates could be won over. Kennedy recognized that Lowenstein would be invaluable in this effort and in mobilizing student support. Kennedy also wanted to wish Lowenstein good luck in his primary, to let him know that he was pulling for him and that he would give him whatever help he needed.

Just before his victory speech in the ballroom, Kennedy had Goodwin phone again to tell Lowenstein that he would talk to him personally when he had finished speaking. This time, Lowenstein was home. He took the call in his bedroom and was on hold, waiting for Kennedy to come to the phone while Jenny watched the speech on television in the living room. "My God, Bobby's been shot," she screamed, as the whole nightmare unfolded on the screen. Lowenstein tore out of the bedroom and watched the pandemonium. Then he dropped everything, took off for the airport, and flew to Los Angeles.

In L.A., Lowenstein went directly to the Good Samaritan Hospital, where he encountered Ted Kennedy by chance in the elevator. Lowenstein did not have a good relationship with Ted Kennedy. The youngest Kennedy was apparently suspicious of Lowenstein's motives. Lowenstein on the other hand, did not think Ted Kennedy had the stature or the ability of his brothers. Lowenstein also viewed Ted Kennedy as an adversary in his relationship with Bobby. But when he met Kennedy in the elevator, Lowenstein did want to reach out and console him. As he told Greg Craig later, he went over to Kennedy and said, "Senator, you are all we have left," but recognized that this was political in nature and not personal. Lowenstein also told Craig that he thought to himself, "But I don't think you're good enough."

Bobby was buried in Arlington, next to his brother. Near his grave a monument was erected on which were inscribed the moving passages of his 1966 Cape Town speech, written by Lowenstein. And politics continued. Norman Thomas, near death, exhorted Lowenstein from his hospital bed, "Win this one for me, Al." The primary that Bobby Kennedy had believed to be vitally important for Lowenstein took place, and Lowenstein did win it, 14,861 to 10,908. He had beaten the "regulars."

The McCarthy forces swept the New York State primary, but the convention rules still allowed the party to select many at-large delegates. It did not come as a surprise that Lowenstein was not named to the delegation, as the county leaders sought to hold the line on the reformers.

At the Commodore Hotel in New York, where, according to the rules, the selection of at-large delegates was to be made to reflect the primary results, the reformers grappled with the regulars. When the county leaders did everything possible to thwart Lowenstein and his group, the antagonism intensified. Aristocratic McCarthy supporter Eleanor French bawled out the regulars, proclaiming June 28, 1968, "a day which will go down in the history of Democratic state politics as a day of perfidy!" And Lowenstein shouted, "You spit in the face of the notion that this convention is democratic!"

Some regulars laughed, others booed. Manhattan leader Frank Rossetti, a Runyonesque character who had spent years in the clubhouses of Tammany and whose gravel voice echoed that of Nathan Detroit, demanded of Stanley Steingut, the leader from Brooklyn, "Are we going to allow this rabble-rousing to go on?" This prompted Lowenstein and French to walk out, shouting "Fascists!" "Nazis!" "Hacks!"

Although Kennedy was dead, his people continued to battle the McCarthy backers, among whom Lowenstein placed himself. And as the fight between the two groups escalated, Lyndon Johnson began to exercise increasing control through his handpicked candidate, Hubert Humphrey. In response to this, Lowenstein created the Coalition for an Open Convention. With it, he attempted to organize anti-Humphrey sentiment and to build bridges between the Kennedy and McCarthy people, so that the Chicago convention would not be a walkover for the old Democratic leaders, Hubert Humphrey and Lyndon Johnson. But when he called its first meeting in Chicago, Mary McCarthy, Senator McCarthy's daughter, declined to attend. "Just one thousand friends of Al Lowenstein," she shrugged.

The COC was launched in typical Lowenstein fashion. He set up a dozen students in pay phones in Chicago and had them make long-distance calls to a long list of people around the country, telling them that over a thousand "disaffected Democrats" would be at the meeting at the end of June. The calls were billed to the Humphrey campaign via credit cards that had been "borrowed" by a Lowenstein aide. Lowenstein also called for an "August primary" in Ohio when voters would be polled by an army of students in order to reveal the extent of anti-war feeling. Finally, to prevent further splintering of the peace forces, Lowenstein helped to promote the candidacy of George McGovern so that Kennedy people who could not be reconciled to McCarthy would have somewhere to go at the convention. McGovern buttons were distributed near the office of the *New York Times*, in an attempt, explained Lowenstein, to create the impression of a new "groundswell." But while he stressed to the COC that their role was not as trouble-makers "who won't accept the verdict of the people," and maintained instead that "we are the verdict of the people," he refused to walk out of the Democratic party if Humphrey should be the nominee.

When a motion was introduced at the COC meeting, calling for a pledge not to support Humphrey if he were nominated, and aimed at generating energy for a fourth party (George Wallace already led the third), Lowenstein stepped down temporarily as chairman to speak against it. His persuasive skills assured its defeat but the dilemma remained. A fourth party would split the Democratic vote and guarantee a Republican victory. But if Humphrey and the old guard kept control, there would be no vehicle for lawful and legitimate protest. Paul Cowan wrote:

The half-conscious assumption of most of the adults there is that liberals like Eugene McCarthy or Al Lowenstein can contain the new rebels more effectively than Hubert Humphrey, Richard Nixon or George Wallace. They will encourage people like Reverend Jesse Jackson and the members of the student caucus to speak—protect their civil liberties—but discourage them from acting out their ideas—exalt unity to prevent disruption. The McCarthys and the Lowensteins are the most effective champions in the country of the order that the upper–middle class Americans who support them want to maintain. . . . Al Lowenstein, whom the Establishment press is billing as the founder of the New Politics, is in fact the ideal spokesman for the new politicians. He is bright enough and brave enough to communicate with the dissident groups his contemporaries fear, and enough of a master of manipulation and persuasion to keep many of the dissenters inside the framework of conventional politics. . . . Still, Lowenstein and the new politicians who make up the majority of his coalition will be remembered as sad figures, not as heroic or evil ones. In another year, Lowenstein might have been Franklin Roosevelt or Lyndon Johnson, a genius who created a pluralistic consensus and saved the country, or the villain who destroyed democracy by insisting on unity at all costs. But not now. The splits in America are too deep for any healer. No man can play the role for which Lowenstein has cast himself. . . .

While radicals like Cowan lumped the "McCarthys" and "Lowensteins" together, McCarthy and Lowenstein were losing respect for each other. On one occasion which brought Lowenstein into contact with the Senator, Harriet Eisman recalled that "McCarthy almost spit at him." Eisman put the whole blame on McCarthy. "We built this hero out of this senator and he really was a cold fish. After Bobby's death, whenever we needed Senator McCarthy for a speech, he disappeared."

With Kennedy gone, an enormous amount of energy was directed toward the Lowenstein campaign in the 5th C.D. "All the Kennedy people came to help Al at this point," Eisman recounted. "So we had working here . . . Richard Goodwin . . . Adam Walinsky, and that whole crew of people. Al was so critical, even of those guys. It had to be just the way he wanted it. They were all working in the general election. Mason Hampton was the Republican opponent. Tenzer went out and campaigned for Al. Vorspan came out also. Al had a way of turning everybody around. . . ."

Mason Hampton was a Conservative-Republican who had never held public office before. After Lowenstein was elected, Hampton, too, became a supporter until he died during Lowenstein's tenure in office. He sent Lowenstein copies of his poems, and like so much else that went on then, Eisman found it "very strange."

Not only was Lowenstein able to win over some of the most ardent conservatives ("Buckley came out here and supported him"), he attracted a whole galaxy of stars to Long Beach. "Here in this little one-horse town, we had everyone from Paul Newman, Dick Benjamin, Paula Prentiss, you name it. . . . Al would take me to the airport and say, 'Let's meet all these exciting people,' and while it didn't mean anything to me, it was very exciting to the community. All of the towns, in Nassau and Suffolk, we had a lot of fund-raisers in the Hamptons."

Many of the campaign workers ended up in Congress themselves—Tom Downey, Doug Walgren, Barney Frank, and others. Eisman recalled that Harry Chapin came from Point Lookout where he had a little coffee house at the time. Whole busloads of supporters came from Notre Dame, which would award Lowenstein its special medal. They were put right to work, canvassing door-to-door. Eisman described the routine: "In the West End of Long Beach, they were all Irish Catholic and anti-Lowenstein, and these kids, these articulate, darling kids worked day and night, and we housed them all and fed them, and they canvassed here. . . . The main headquarters was in Rockville Centre but there was a headquarters in every town. And each town had a group of women, not quite as crazy as I am, but like me, and they also managed to pull out the intelligentsia. I had never known these people existed in Nassau County. This was a really dumb place to live, and it was amazing that he managed throughout Nassau County to pull out these top people in every area."

Harriet Eisman resigned from her part-time job with a research company and coordinated most of the campaign in Long Beach and other parts of the district. Doug Ireland, Bella Abzug's campaign strategist, was brought in, though Abzug remained convinced he would lose. Ireland, who refused to sleep on the floor and insisted on a hotel room, remembers her shouting, "Al is blowing it!."

Lowenstein became the symbol of opposition to the war within the electoral process, and his campaign took on a significance far wider than the average race for Congress. A tireless campaigner, Lowenstein would have shaken every hand in the district if he could have managed it. He was up and out at dawn, working himself and his workers until they dropped. His day did not end until the wee hours of the morning. When you worked for Lowenstein, "You were involved in his whole life," Eisman explained. "He had no sense of time. I don't mean that he was always late. He worked around the clock and people who worked for him could not do that. He saw that as a total deficit. He was uncompromising; when he wanted to do something, he did it, if he had to go to all the extremes."

Lowenstein diverted his attention from his own campaign to the national convention. There was still support for McCarthy. Joe Rauh had been raising money, appearing at a "Night of Stars" rally for McCarthy at Madison Square Garden (an event for which Gabriel Lowenstein had provided the model decades before). Stuart Mott put up $100,000. The faithful still dreamed of a miracle.

Before the convention, Lowenstein made his final appearance before the annual congress of the National Student Association. It was August, the first anniversary of the "Dump Johnson" movement, launched at College Park during the 1967 NSA congress. The 1968 congress was in Manhattan, Kansas, and Lowenstein flew west with David Halberstam. Discussing the campaign, Lowenstein told Halberstam that he had believed that Humphrey could be stopped, but now McCarthy was sluggish. McGovern was winning the support of the Kennedy people, but Humphrey was building up a large lead.

When they arrived in Kansas City at one in the morning, they were met by a group of well-scrubbed Lowensteinites, "college graduates, all part of his great apparatus, all enthusiastic. They are young and clean-cut and they regale him with all the inner gossip of NSA; it is like being with a star football player when he returns to the campus after a year's absence," wrote Halberstam.

At the congress, Lowenstein was late for everything, prompting his press secretary Mary Lou Oates to resign in frustration. Oates was overwhelmed by the "far-out" influence of the California students, according to Halberstam, who heard her lament, "It's the California kids, the California kids, they're behind it all, they're way out ahead with drugs and Speed and they're bewildering these other kids at the convention and making them freak out. There's no hope." When Lowenstein finally did turn up, he was always "bouncing off people," and Halberstam was reminded of something writer Jack Newfield had once said: "Being a friend of Lowenstein's is like being on a hold button on a phone." Among those surrounding Lowenstein, one young person was heard to say, "I hope you haven't come to tell us what we can do and how we can do it because we don't need any more of that crap," but concluded by urging him on in his congressional bid.

Later, at a workshop, Tom Hayden and other New Left activists renewed the charges that Lowenstein was a CIA agent. Halberstam wrote: "He was the last head of the NSA before its CIA subsidy, yet the attacks continue. . . . It all has a familiar ugly ring." The New Left then took credit for the McCarthy campaign, as Robert Scheer argued that without the radicals, there would have been no peace movement in the first place. There was then speculation that Lowenstein would end up endorsing Humphrey. Sitting in the audience, Lowenstein commented, "All year the radical left said don't go into the McCarthy movement. It's a plot to make the peace movement look weak. Now they want sympathy for how well they did, even if cheated because the system can't work. They want it both ways."

Lowenstein finally spoke at midnight, with the SDS opposition in the audience. He tallied up what they had all accomplished during the year. They had ended, he told them, the "inevitability of Lyndon Johnson's election and we might have done more except for June fourth. We did it without a major name, money, or the mass media. We showed that the system is not so resistant to change but that it is badly corroded. Now, however, we know more about what we're dealing with. . . . Even the most recalcitrant of leadership has become more responsible on Vietnam. Hubert Humphrey found out that he always agreed with Robert Kennedy on Vietnam."

"Then, as he is speaking, the SDS people put on what is called guerilla theater," Halberstam wrote. "Someone tagged 'Big Daddy' (the Left's nickname for Lowenstein) plays a recorder and invites a bunch of kids on to Chicago. The students arrive, do a dance, and are suddenly machine-gunned down by two men in khaki. Lowenstein stops and waits until the pageant is over. 'The kids who went to Chicago were just machine-gunned by someone from SDS,' he says. Applause. 'But on the basis of past experience, they will recover.' The intensity of feeling against Lowenstein among the New Left is really astonishing. It is very deep and very bitter; he is probably their foremost enemy. In a generation where liberalism is weak on the campus and they are so strong, Lowenstein is one of the last effective liberals competing with them, and thus a very real target."

Lowenstein continued his speech: "The McCarthy people turned around public feeling on the war, made the opposition to it respectable, and only a small minority in the country now believes it can be won. This is the last stand of decaying institutions which have not met the needs of time. So that despite the enormity of your disappointment and my disappointment there are still some positive signs. The exalting fact is that ordinary people in a complex society felt they could affect the honor and future of their country and they did and out of this will come the kind of America we want."

"Is there a chance you will support Humphrey?" someone asked from the audience.

"Extremely remote," replied Lowenstein.

"So we won't be surprised if you do."

Responding to the criticisms of the radicals, Lowenstein concluded: "The problem with radical rhetoric is that it's very good, it's the best rhetoric there is in assessing liberal failures. It's very accurate there. But then with their own programs they give little more. As much as we liberals have failed and I think our failures are obvious now, I don't see any easy alternatives. We did some things, we learned some things, and the fact that Bobby Kennedy was murdered and Gene McCarthy was disorganized doesn't show me that the system doesn't work. . . . I don't have any answers, but you don't have any programs. I can see events where I'll be as much a part of the resistance as you are. I hope it doesn't happen. But I don't think the final evidence is in that we've lost everything we started out to do and that we can't get out of the war. I think with the removal of Johnson they will understand the political crush of the war and they're opportunistic enough to get out."

The radicals debated Lowenstein on whether they should go to Chicago and demonstrate. He told them not to, that it would damage the movement. But they were determined. If the convention were rigged, as they believed, the more who became radicalized, the better, even at the risk of a backlash.

Lowenstein had so many roles at the convention that it was hard to say what it was he was trying to accomplish. He was ostensibly still a McCarthy supporter. (Harriet Eisman was at work "shaking down" Jack English, the powerful Nassau County Democratic chairman, to make Lowenstein a McCarthy delegate.) On the other hand, Lowenstein was pushing his Coalition for an Open Convention on the theory that the nomination might still be pried from Humphrey if there were a candidate other than McCarthy. He was convinced that someone else might win at the convention but that McCarthy could not. The two he had in mind were George McGovern and Ted Kennedy. The sole white on the board of Martin Luther King, Jr.'s, SCLC, Lowenstein was also working to keep blacks behind an antiwar alternative rather than with Humphrey.

Lowenstein was finally named as a McCarthy delegate, having commented to Halberstam just before his last-minute selection: "Even Humphrey is going around saying he wants me on the delegation. There's a conga line. They're all on it. They all really want to keep me off the delegation. But they also want to make sure that someone else gets the blame."

Lowenstein threw himself into the frenetic, wheeling and dealing at the convention. Described by a friend as "a political nymphomaniac," he thrived on the hectic pace and bizarre hours that exhausted many others. "The rest of the world has come round to his way of living," Halberstam quipped. But all the activity was producing nothing. While the Democrats, with Humphrey's consent, went along with a tough prowar plank that Johnson insisted on, Kennedy's boomlet died down, largely because his people believed it was a trap to get him to accept the vice-presidency. The convention became an exercise in futility. Halberstam lamented:

Now, steadily, the entire convention becomes a scenario of the party's bankruptcy. Even in the Vietnam plank debate the emptiness is obvious. Most of the men arguing for the peace plank have been silent for four years, brought to the podium now to rekindle the Kennedy flame; they are the men like Theodore Sorenson who felt in March that the issue was not worthy of Bob Kennedy making the race. It is one more sad note for the party that even here, among its dissenters, there is little in the way of fresh young leadership. One listens to Sorenson and senses that in some ways the radicals are right, the Cold War put the liberals of this country too much on the defensive, that for some the price paid in fending off the right wing, fighting with conservative forces for minor victories, proving one's basic anti-Communism, took too much out of them. In the years the Democrats have been in power—and thus in a sense the liberals—the power of the Pentagon has grown to the point where it is to a younger generation *the* issue of American life. One senses that one era is ending for the party; perhaps slowly, in the embers here, another is beginning. There is no guarantee of it.

As Humphrey was being nominated, the Chicago riot was going on outside the convention hall. The Hilton was being wrecked, Mayor Daley's police were charging into McCarthy's suite, busting heads as they went. David Hoeh, the Dartmouth professor who had pleaded with McCarthy to run, was arrested as others were gassed. Lowenstein himself was arrested for half an hour because he was carrying *The New York Times.* Jenny remembers watching as Barbara Boggs was ushered away from the demonstrations by her father, then seeing her reappear in the lobby of the hotel, where she turned to Jenny and said, "These demonstrations are childish. Why don't they stop?"

Jenny looked at her incredulously. "It's Hubert. Why doesn't he stop what he's doing?"

The two women glared at each other, then Boggs said, "Well, I will go up and tell him that." As she tried to get on the private elevator to Humphrey's suite, police blocked her way. Angrily, she told them, "I'm Barbara Boggs. My father is Congressman Hale Boggs, and I've got to go up to see Vice-President Humphrey."

"I don't care who you are, lady," the cop told her. "Nobody's going up there."

Jenny left her struggling to get through.

As the rioting continued outside, Lowenstein struggled to be heard with a motion to adjourn until the city did something about the police. John Burns, chairman of the New York State Democratic Committee, refused him access to the microphone on the floor. In the pandemonium, Lowenstein tried to reach the podium but was blocked by the Illinois delegation (under the control of Mayor Daley) and an enormous circle of plainclothes policemen. Shouting, "I'm a delegate from New York trying to make a motion," Lowenstein persisted, but he was blocked by a policeman who told him, "No, you're not. You're not going to make a motion." When Lowenstein continued to push forward, another cop grabbed him: "Listen, sonny. Be a good boy. Push off. There are federal agents here and they know what you're doing and you're going to be in trouble."

As Senator Abe Ribicoff of Connecticut took the podium to denounce Daley and the Chicago police, Daley was heard angrily muttering, "You Jew son of a bitch." Lowenstein left the floor and was immediately grabbed by a furious New York reform Democrat.

"Why isn't Teddy being put in nomination?" she demanded.

Frustrated, Lowenstein answered: "Because the bigshots don't want it."

She shot back: "The bigshots didn't want Lyndon Johnson beaten and it didn't stop you. Why don't you do something?"

Lowenstein glared. "I don't know who appointed me Jesus Christ. Isn't there anyone else here?"

In the last moments, the Wisconsin delegation placed Julian Bond's name in nomination and asked Lowenstein to second it. Lowenstein, who could barely talk anyway because he had laryngitis, was blocked from speaking by opponents.

Surrounded by television newsmen, Lowenstein told them: "This convention elected Richard Nixon president of the United States tonight. That's like electing Arthur Goldberg mayor of Cairo. I never thought it would happen."

Afterward, Lowenstein met with the McCarthy caucus for the last time and, at three in the morning, led a candlelight walk of 600 delegates. McCarthy made a brilliant final speech in the afternoon, and Humphrey accepted the nomination.

Warren Ashby, Frank Graham's biographer wrote:

And the Democratic Party was clearly in disarray. The problems had been evident before 1968, but up to that time they had been interpreted as typical Democratic brawling. The convention of 1968 destroyed any illusion that what was manifesting itself in internal conflicts was anything but an infective chaos that would end in defeat. The disarray of the Chicago convention was all the more fascinating to Graham, as he watched it on television, because one of the agents of the disarray was Al Lowenstein. Graham was, and remained throughout the 1968 campaign, an ardent supporter of his friend Hubert Humphrey; and it was not lost on him that the defection of liberals led to the defeat of Humphrey and the election of Richard Nixon.

By Halberstam's calculations, Lowenstein had given 2,367 speeches and traveled 288,021 miles in the course of the Dump Johnson campaign. The last day in Chicago, he took pity on the numerous exhausted and battered students who had worked for McCarthy and gave over his room to them so they could get some sleep. Jenny finally had enough. "I don't care if they're wounded. I don't care if they're dying," she complained. Finally, the kids gave up the room. "He kept introducing them to me," she recounted, "and I kept refusing to be introduced. Perhaps I'll never be a politician's wife."

Speculating on Lowenstein's own political aspirations, someone asked her, "What do you think he's running for?"

"Some minor deity," Jenny responded.

"Are you sure its minor?" the questioner wanted to know.

51.

After Chicago, Harriet Eisman said she was "dropping out," that "it wasn't worth it." But Lowenstein sent emissaries to tell her, "You must come back." And he himself said to her, "Don't be bitter." Then Lowenstein mended his fences.

Lowenstein asked former Governor of North Carolina Terry Sanford to get him an appointment with Humphrey. "Al was covering all his bases," Sanford explains. "I did not trust him to be loyal to Humphrey in 'sixty-eight." Sanford got him the appointment and Lowenstein did meet with Humphrey. But Sanford wrote to Humphrey, "Don't trust him and don't waste any time with him," or words to that effect; Sanford does not remember precisely. "I didn't believe he would ever support Humphrey," Sanford states. "But I hope you never find that letter."

Lowenstein and Humphrey clearly reached an accommodation, as events revealed. Five weeks before the election, the ADA convention endorsed Humphrey with the proviso that the ADA disagreed with him on the war. Humphrey had criticized Bobby Kennedy for advocating the inclusion of the Viet Cong in the government of South Vietnam. "That would be like putting the fox in charge of the chickens," Humphrey had said. But as the campaign wore on, he began to make overtures to the doves without overtly coming out against the war. The polls showed him closing the gap against Nixon.

While Joe Rauh was moving into the Humphrey camp, he was also raising money for Lowenstein's campaign for Congress, which was gaining momentum. *New York Magazine*, following the campaign, described him as "short, balding and near-sighted, with the beginning of a paunch that oozes gently over his belt. He wears wash-and-wear slacks, non-descript sports coats, flapping woolen neckties, dusty brown Hush Puppies and a harassed look." Actually, Lowenstein was not short at all. He was five eleven. But as Gina Galke, one of his close friends once said, it was impossible to agree on anything about Lowenstein. "Nobody could say how tall Al was," she explains. "A group of friends could sit around and someone would ask, 'How tall is Al?' and you would get six different answers." The same could be said of his politics.

Lowenstein's rhetoric could be moderate and reassuring. "I am neither rightist, leftist nor liberal. I'm an independent, a mainstream McCarthy Democrat," he asserted. But he could also pander to the conservative sentiment in the district by attacking "draft dodgers," suggesting that "they helped to worsen the plight of actual prisoners of war."

Harriet Eisman was instrumental in recasting Lowenstein into a local. "Al belonged to the Yale Club, and the Whale Club, you know, that whole thing that not many of us were tuned into," she explains. But gradually, as the campaign moved along, Lowenstein became more "regular" and in tune with the district. He was being transformed into a middle-class Long Islander with a wife and kids.

Long Island kids joined the campaign, which had consisted originally of Lowenstein's "acolytes." Nan Windmueller, then a sophomore at Adelphi University, volunteered and was assigned to a storefront in Rockville Centre. "Working in that storefront was an incredible experience. There was such a team spirit—so full of hope and so confident that we could all make a difference," she relates.

Many of the storefronts were managed by housewives, with a sprinkling of young idealists. But on the weekends, hundreds of college students were bused in to do door-to-door canvassing for Lowenstein. District families allowed them to sleep in their homes—after all, it was for "the cause."

"A whole new world opened for me during this period," recalls Windmueller. "I met fascinating people from all over the country and I had a sense we were making history. Our storefront was around the corner from the campaign headquarters, and I occasionally had to go there on errands. I was awed by the 'pros' there and slightly intimidated by the pace. When Al was around, everything was turned upside down (this proved to be true in every campaign); he'd disagree with policy decisions, redo the campaign literature, argue with the scheduler about which events he should attend, and of course, he'd be late for every event because he'd suddenly need an emergency haircut or milkshake. Al could not accept the professional decisions. Things ran more smoothly when he wasn't around. But he was so brilliant, so inspiring, and articulate, you'd put up with anything to work for him."

Outside of the "Five Towns," which were affluent and Jewish, and Long Beach itself, which was middle-class Jewish for the most part with a few wealthy families (notwithstanding the incipient decay which would turn the town into a disaster area), there was hostility to Lowenstein, who was viewed as an interloper. There was also an undercurrent of anti-Semitism in some areas, although it was muted. When she left the storefront, Nan Windmueller experienced this disturbing part of the campaign. Asked to go door-to-door ringing doorbells and leaving literature in the hands of the homeowner, she says she did so once or twice and decided never to do it again. "It was too traumatic, too much like a personal insult, having doors slammed in my face—or nasty comments."

Just as Humphrey needed the McCarthy vote, Lowenstein needed to hold the regular Democratic organization that was behind the national ticket. As rumors persisted that he would endorse Humphrey,

Lowenstein became increasingly identified with the Democratic party. Although support for him grew, there were signs of disillusionment among some of the students.

At an emotional staff meeting, some of the staff members rejected the notion that Johnson's bombing halt heralded a change in policy sufficient to justify the endorsement. Calvin Trillin of *The New Yorker* wrote that these staff members were convinced that the attitudes of the leaders of both political parties were such that "even if the war in Vietnam ended, a war someplace else would take its place." As one of them said later, "Al argued that the American people have shown that they won't stand for another Vietnam. But we just don't believe that's the way things work. We might as well get new signs ready and just leave the name of the next country blank."

To the liberals in Nassau County, however, regardless of their reservations about Humphrey, the enemy was still the Republican party. It ran the county with complete authority, its tentacles reaching into every community, controlling patronage and even manipulating the Democratic party itself. And while Lowenstein's campaign for Congress was in a way a referendum on the war, it was also a rebellion against the dictatorship of Joseph Margiotta, the powerful Republican county leader whose word was law. A closing of ranks within the Democratic party made sense to the Lowenstein campaign; it helped him to overcome the "carpetbagger" image by stressing his position in the Democratic community at large, and it helped him with local Democrats who distrusted their own county organization, suspecting it of collaborating with the Republicans, deliberately losing in exchange for patronage.

On Saturday, November 2, Joe Rauh accompanied Humphrey to New York, where they were met at the airport by Lowenstein and Paul O'Dwyer, the Democratic candidate for Senate. The party was to attend a big rally for Lowenstein and Humphrey in the 5th C.D. Lowenstein and the vice-president rode in an open car together, and during the rally, Lowenstein and Humphrey endorsed each other.

Most of the volunteers apparently were not affected by the endorsement, although a few said that only personal affection for Lowenstein caused them to stay with the campaign. "I think we have much less faith in America than Al does," a volunteer told Calvin Trillin. "And it's not just one or two issues that bother us—it's the whole stupid framework of thinking in this country."

When Lowenstein addressed a Saturday night gathering of hundreds of high school and college volunteers, he explained why he felt obligated to support Humphrey after the bombing halt. Only one student objected.

After the final, excruciatingly long day of campaigning, Lowenstein sat in a diner in Rockville Centre, eating a hamburger and talking to an aide to Cesar Chavez, the farm-worker organizer. The aide had come from California to help elect Lowenstein, who had supported the Chavez cause. "You know when I decided to come out for Humphrey?" Lowenstein said, biting into his hamburger. "It wasn't when Humphrey made his Vietnam speech. It was when Nixon ate those damned grapes. That was the most singularly vulgar act I think I've ever seen in public life."

On election night, the students jammed the ballroom of a hotel in Baldwin to await the results. Lowenstein ran ahead all night, and about midnight, the band struck up "Mrs. Robinson," from *The Graduate*. Lowenstein arrived and they went wild, singing chorus after chorus of "The Impossible Dream."

Lowenstein told them that "the point of view of young Americans has to be heard in Congress as it hasn't been heard before."

When all the votes had been counted, Lowenstein, the Democrat-Liberal, had defeated his Republican-Conservative opponent Mason Hampton, 99,993 to 96,427. Lowenstein told Flora Lewis: "I have a certain awe about elections. The fact of being elected is high in the hierarchy of things. I was raised to think of it as a great honor, and I had never really seen myself as doing that. By the end of the campaign, I expected to win, but I had never sat down and thought about what would happen next. It seemed to me that that was best, because if I didn't win I wouldn't be as disappointed, and if I did—well, there would be plenty of time to think it out afterward. So finding myself in the House had something of an Alice in Wonderland quality about it— something amazing, because it was unexpected and because I felt this great awe for the electoral process."

VII

On His Own

52.

Lowenstein was sworn into Congress in January of 1969. His greatest regret, he said, was that his father had not lived to see it. Lowenstein's personal success was also marred by the death that winter of Norman Thomas and the constant realization that Robert Kennedy was gone. "A man was killed on the fifth of June last year, and our experiment in democracy—in political action—was stopped," he told Erwin Knoll of *The Progressive* while sitting on the Capitol steps. "You can't prove that political action can succeed, because it hasn't. But you can't prove that political action can't succeed, because I think we were on the way to success when Robert Kennedy was assassinated."

After Eugene McCarthy voted for Russell Long and against Ted Kennedy for Senate majority Whip, Lowenstein had an angry public confrontation with him in New York. "I think Al has learned his lesson very well," McCarthy explained, speaking in Brooklyn to the Coalition for a Democratic Alternative. "He has been quite restrained on what he has to say in the House of Representatives. But House members are allowed to be very rash about what they say about the Senate. He can tell you exactly what the Whip election in the Senate meant after being in the House for five days."

"It doesn't take five days in the House," Lowenstein retorted. "You don't have to be elected to anything to have views on what the leadership should be."

Lowenstein distanced himself further from McCarthy, telling *The New York Times*, "I was deeply grateful and touched when he made the fight last year but . . . wherever I go, I find I have to defend McCarthy against rather bitter comments. New Hampshire was a turning point, but we haven't finished the turn. There are now new people to be persuaded every day. . . . I don't like to take potshots at Eugene McCarthy, but I'm afraid he's brought it on himself. I remember him historically, but I've forgotten him as a contemporary."

Shortly after taking office, Lowenstein resumed his globe hopping, traveling to Biafra on his mission to try to end the fighting there. He was still hounded by the student left, which charged that he was a "fink," "Public Enemy Number One" for stifling radical change, and a "CIA spook." Lowenstein, who was subdued in Congress, turned his rhetoric not on President Richard Nixon, with whom he expected to have a working relationship, but on the radicals. He referred to them in Agnewesque terms as "the insane five per cent," adding that "they don't want to see change come. They're out to prove the system can't be made to work. They're not allies."

At the same time, Lowenstein had nothing but praise for Nixon. Hailing his proposals on welfare and tax reform and for replacing the draft with an all-volunteer army, Lowenstein stated: "On these matters, it is encouraging to know that the new administration is off to a good start . . . these first steps of the Nixon administration deserve applause."

In March, Lowenstein was invited to a White House reception, at which the freshman congressman and the president conversed. In a letter thanking Nixon for the evening, Lowenstein wrote that "it was good to have a moment to chat with you, and I hope you will in fact let me know if I can be of any use to you along the lines we discussed." "I hope Nixon ends the war," Lowenstein insisted, "I say that as a Democrat—he can have the credit."

But *Newsday* correspondent Myron S. Waldman reported that Lowenstein's "caution . . . has disappointed some of his liberal colleagues." "He's like Nixon," one liberal congressman asserted. "He hasn't started to unveil yet. He's extremely bright, but I'm sorry that he hasn't been more of a blood-and-guts guy." Another added: "He's trying to be responsible in dissent by playing ball with the establishment. They'll never let him get away with it."

As a member of the Ninety-first Congress, Lowenstein was described as "cautiously quiet," voting almost exactly as he had promised he would during the campaign against Mason Hampton; "liberally, with a view to the national interest." He sought to lower the voting age to eighteen and said in his testimony before the Senate Subcommittee on Voting Age that he might lower the voting age to twelve, if he could. He spoke and voted against a crime bill for the District of Columbia, presenting to Congress an argument prepared by the American Civil Liberties Union on the constitutional problems with the legislation. Although he lashed out against campus violence, he voted against a proposal to cut off aid to students involved in campus disorders. Lowenstein earned a reputation for being opposed to increased military spending by speaking and voting against countless military appropriations bills, venting his spleen against Nationalist Taiwan and the military junta of Greece, recipients of increased U.S.

military aid. He denounced the military base agreement with Franco's Spain and the antiballistic missile. As his term progressed, he also tried to cut military appropriations for the war in Vietnam. But he pressed the Nixon administration to sell jets to Israel.

Some of Lowenstein's votes were particularly irksome to his "Middle American" constituency. Shortly before Apollo 11 was launched for the moon landing, Congressman Roudebush of Indiana proposed an amendment that "the flag of the United States, and no other flag, shall be implanted or otherwise placed on the surface of the moon." Lowenstein caustically belittled the amendment, arguing that the flag of the United Nations would be just as appropriate. He questioned why the Congress and not the president should make this decision, asking if Nixon was perhaps not qualified. "Has he been found embracing a Union Jack in secret or abusing the memory of Betsy Ross?" Lowenstein queried. Lowenstein then asked if the amendment would make it illegal to place other emblems on the moon in future landings. "Suppose the president feels it is in the best interests of this country to plant other items in addition to the American flag—perhaps the symbols of the great religions," Lowenstein quipped, "or a symbol of peace. Must Russians be ceded permanent rights to the use of such symbols? Would that demean the flag? Or even the pictures of someone not Lenin—George Washington perhaps. Or Pope John XXIII. Or John F. Kennedy. Dwight Eisenhower. Einstein. Ghandi. . . . Personally, however, I would hope the president would not go in for a picture gallery on the moon. But if in the end the president decided to send only the American flag onto the moon, how much better off we would all be if that decision could have been made without a prior display of the narrowest form of chauvinism. We do no credit to America this way. We do her no service."

The next day, the *Helm Independent Review*, a local paper in the 5th C.D., denounced Lowenstein in an editorial. "Residents of the Fifth C.D. will be relieved to know that despite a Herculean effort on the part of their Congressman, Allard Lowenstein, the American flag will be placed on the Moon by our Apollo 11 astronauts. . . . The disappointing aspect of Lowenstein's appearance is his consistency in objecting to a modest display of American pride in its great space achievement."

Lowenstein's style would have been more appropriate to the House of Commons than to the blandness of Congress. But he also manifested a cavalier disregard for his own political future when in early August of 1970, on the eve of his reelection campaign, he chose to join only five other congressmen in voting against a bill to prohibit the transporting of pornographic materials through the mails. He also voted against the F–14 jet fighter, which was to be manufactured on Long Island, and although he later switched his vote, Lowenstein opened himself to attacks that he wasn't concerned about the economy in his district.

Lowenstein voted for tax relief, reform of military conscription and the abolition of the House Un-American Activities Committee. He supported a national health insurance program. But his chief concern was reforming the House of Representatives itself. "If the system can't be made to work, I won't be a whore and run out in the street and say it will. I can't function unless I think it will work," he observed. Lowenstein opposed the strict limitation on speaking rights in the House and the sham of the *Congressional Record.* He fought the Closed Rule of the House, which he felt arbitrarily prohibited the offering of amendments, and led the attack of young liberals against House Speaker John McCormack, first trying to overthrow him and then forcing him to accept the most meaningful congressional reform bill in memory. By eliminating the time-honored secrecy of "committee of the whole" meetings on controversial votes, the bill forced House members into taking recorded positions. To no avail, Lowenstein took on the seniority system. But he did not challenge the leadership on a personal basis. When he was assigned to the Agricultural Committee, he did not protest although his district contained only one farm. By the end of his term, Lowenstein was attacking farm subsidies for large agro-business operations.

Lowenstein's frenetic effort to reform the House and to achieve what he called "rational change" was aimed at preventing the radicals from gaining ground in their fight against the system. "I don't know what I will do if the effort to bring change through electoral democracy fails," he confessed to Flora Lewis. "The far left thinks—really hopes—that an explosion is inevitable. . . . The only thing I am sure about is that we must not fail simply because we didn't try, and try with all the energy and brains we can muster. If we fail, would I join the revolution? Would I leave the country? After all, I would be obsolete. But I don't engage in the luxury of wondering what I would do if the effort shouldn't work. I'm committed to the notion that it will work."

Lowenstein retained his close ties with the blacks in Mississippi. At a state NAACP convention which Lowenstein addressed, Aaron Henry slapped him on the back, telling the audience, "This is the one man in Washington who has a desk in his office and a secretary for Mississippi black people. He's our congressman." Lowenstein ran a kind of shuttle between Mississippi and Washington, farming out young people to help Henry. When some students were shot at Jackson State, Lowenstein arranged for survivors to come to Washington to relate their version of the incident. In his own district, where he tried to spend several days a week, Lowenstein conducted community hearings with leading political and public figures on local and national issues and set up advisory councils on problems such as housing, jet noise, transportation, and wetland preservation.

Lowenstein's speaking ability won him respect in the House. Congressman Andy Jacobs of Indiana observed him during a debate on a military appropriations bill, rising to speak while House members chanted "Vote, vote," their custom when the hour is late and the dinner hour has passed. Jacobs recalls that "the din of noise that precedes the final passage and the exit of members began to quiet down. I had never seen that happen before under the same circumstance, regardless of the established respectability of a member who chose to speak. Al Lowenstein was sonorous and saying things in a way not often heard. . . . From that moment on, Al Lowenstein built a respect from friend and foe alike at a level rare in my experience in the Congress."

Congressmen who had expected Lowenstein to behave like a wild-eyed radical were won over. The chairman of the House Armed Services Committee, Mendel Rivers of South Carolina, with whom Lowenstein clashed on the floor of the House, came to respect him, particularly as he became aware of Lowenstein's anti-Communism. When Lowenstein spoke on the anniversary of Robert Kennedy's assassination, he surprised his detractors by his deference toward Congress and his words of appreciation for it. "This is one of those times when it is particularly gratifying to be here, to be able to say a few words that will reflect the feeling of so vast a number of people for whom the wound at heart . . . has not eased with the passage of time. . . ." With such rhetoric Lowenstein won over the old-time, crusty politicians in Congress who suspected him of being subversive and resented the attitude of the young antiwar activists with whom they identified him.

But Lowenstein did not even speak in the House on the subject of Vietnam until March 26, 1969. "Some have asked," he said, "why those of us who are opposed to the war have seemed so quiet during the opening months of the new administration. Some have been quiet because of the patience traditional among Americans toward new presidents as they assume office. Some have been quiet because in a national mood of expectancy and hope, noise might fall on ears determinedly deaf. Some have been quiet in response to President Nixon's suggestion in his inaugural address that affirmative virtue might in fact reside in a period of relative silence." Lowenstein called for the gradual withdrawal of U.S. troops if the North Vietnamese and Viet Cong were willing to negotiate in good faith.

"Mr. Chairman," he later blurted out in the middle of a debate on a supplementary appropriations bill for the Vietnam War, "I feel like Alice must have felt in Wonderland. Or maybe Rip Van Winkle. We talk as if nothing goes on outside this room. We talk as if it were five years ago. We talk nonsense in circles—vicious circles. Outside this room the country spirals into worsening crisis. We are impervious. We debate the longest war in our history, the most disputed adventure of our national experience for half an hour. Thirty minutes. Then time is up. But if we cannot discuss these matters here, where can we? What is it we are so busy doing?"

Lowenstein could still be useful in keeping young Americans in the system. But at a polarized campus like Berkeley, he could still run into trouble. In the early spring of 1969, while in San Francisco for an ADA speech, he tried to mediate the dispute between students and the Berkeley administration over a vacant lot known as "Peoples Park." When the university fenced off the lot, which students and street people had been using for gardens, to convert it to a parking lot, demonstrations broke out. There were clashes with the police, and the battle escalated when Governor Ronald Reagan mobilized the National Guard and sent helicopters over Berkeley to spray tear gas, while mass arrests took place. The park had become the rallying point for a coalition of liberals and radicals which felt increasingly threatened by Reagan. When Lowenstein tried to mediate, as he had in 1965, he was told that Reagan held all the cards and that the administration no longer had any say in the matter. As one person involved in the affair put it, "Allard's indispensability disappeared." Lowenstein now seemed "just another liberal congressman, no more and no less," the participant told David Harris. Later, when Lowenstein was back in California to visit Harris, by then in prison for draft resistance, Harris dismissed him to a fellow inmate as "just some Congressman I used to know." But Lowenstein told screenwriter Marcia Borie that he had been deeply moved by the visit. Back in Washington, he would edge toward a position on the draft that would damage him politically.

When Sam Brown and David Hawk organized 253 student leaders from Harvard, Yale, Princeton, Columbia, Cornell, Stanford, the University of Wisconsin, the University of Michigan, Berkeley, and NYU to issue a statement announcing their refusal to be inducted into the army if called, Lowenstein offered to help. On April 22, 1969, with his assistance, they met in the House Agriculture Committee Room to deliver their statement to a press conference. "Along with thousands of our fellow students, we campus leaders cannot participate in a war which we consider to be immoral and unjust," they declared. "We will not serve in the military as long as the war in Vietnam continues."

Joseph Margiotta, the Republican county leader of Nassau, promptly called on Lowenstein to resign for encouraging the students to violate the law. Lowenstein countered with a letter to the local papers in his district saying, "The President, the Congress, and the American people should have the opportunity to hear and discuss the deeply held convictions of a very large number of our young people. , , , These are our men who are prepared to pay the legal penalty for standing on their convictions, and who thus function within the framework of the Constitution."

But Harriet Eisman, who had been hired after the campaign to run his congressional-district office in Baldwin, revealed that Lowenstein went much further on the draft than his statements indicated. "He took risks to help people," she related. "Not too many people know how much draft counseling he actually did. In one of the offices in the district, there was what we called the 'room of feathers.' Kids who had to see the draft board would go up there and sit until their eyes were red and their faces were swollen. These were the asthma cases." Eisman stresses that this was done in a hostile environment. "Baldwin is made up of Nazis," she remarked. "All I can say is that the Lowenstein office there was as if we put Hitler in Israel. It was unbelievable stuff."

Lowenstein insisted on wrapping opposition to the war in the flag. To Hawk and Brown's suggestion that there be a "Moratorium against the War," with students halting all normal activity in October for a day of protests, followed in a month by two days of protests and then in two months by three days of protests, Lowenstein countered with his own plan. The moratorium, he insisted, should take place on July Fourth, with everyone carrying American flags. Lowenstein also stressed that there should be rules to ban the "more left" and "irresponsible" groups of the antiwar movement. To facilitate the demonstration, he offered the use of his congressional office to Brown and Hawk.

Unwilling to participate in "Red-baiting," as they called it, Brown and Hawk also argued that July was too soon and that people should be allowed to carry whatever signs and banners they chose. Moreover, they told Lowenstein that a demonstration organized out of a congressman's office would be suspect on the campuses. Together with Margie Schlenker, who had helped organize Lowenstein's 1968 congressional campaign, and David Mixner, Hawk and Brown pressed ahead with their plan for the October moratorium. Meanwhile, on the floor of the House, Lowenstein called the American victory at Hamburger Hill "irrelevant" as he demanded the withdrawal of American troops from Vietnam.

Still striving to hold the support of nonradical students, Lowenstein was scheduled to give the Class Day speech at Harvard on June 6, 1969. Greg Craig, recalls his appearance:

"I saw Al speak for twenty-five minutes without interruption to the Harvard graduating class, an audience which, under the best of circumstances, would have been quick to criticize and slow to respond. Al was speaking after the Harvard riot had occurred, when the university administration had called the local police force to remove demonstrating students from the administration building. The police had been quick to settle old scores and to strike with their nightsticks. The congealed blood of undergraduates on the steps of University Hall and the ruts of police vans in the grassy expanse of the Harvard Yard had traumatized the university community and led to a complete shutdown of university activities. Two months later, at the Class Day ceremonies, responding to an invitation from the graduating class, Al Lowenstein rose to speak.

"It is difficult to describe the atmosphere in the Harvard Yard as Al spoke. It was quiet. He was not interrupted by applause. The members of the class listened intently to every word. And Al's words came in a rush. Al spoke of the sixties, of the South, of Mississippi, of how the Vietnam War had poisoned our most beloved institutions and derailed the movement for racial justice and equality, of how the war had embittered an entire generation of America's most idealistic and gifted young people. Al spoke of the legacy of Dr. King and Robert Kennedy, of how they had made the system work, and only the intrusion of the bullets from the guns of madmen had aborted their efforts to improve American life. Al challenged the students to live up to the examples of King and Kennedy and to become engaged in the struggle. Al quoted from Robert Kennedy's speech in South Africa (which Al helped to write) about how history is made up of the accumulated acts of courage by individuals, and every time an individual stood up against injustice and hatred, he set forth a ripple. When Al finally came to an end, when he finally stepped back from the podium, that sea of black caps arose in a single wave and gave him a standing ovation that echoed and reechoed from the walls of Widener Library and Memorial Church. Al had sent them a message that was neither gloom nor doom nor despair but one of hope and possibility. Unbelievably, that was the very message that the graduating class seemed most ready to embrace."

But Greg Craig remembers that "Al was livid" when he learned that Craig had agreed that his picture could be used for the moratorium poster. "I was critical of Al during the moratorium period," Craig states. "He didn't handle himself well. I think he should have supported it from the beginning. Al should have moved more quickly to endorse the moratorium and should have mended his fences with David Hawk and Sam Brown."

Lowenstein's main objection was that Sam Brown was "insufficiently firm" with people on the left. He insisted that there be a strong statement against violence; until the moratorium leadership disavowed domestic violence, Lowenstein would not endorse it. But Craig was convinced that if the moratorium organized by the moderate opposition to the war did not succeed, the radical New Mobilization, which had plans for a march in Washington in November, would take charge. Since the New Mobe openly endorsed violence, Craig was critical of William Sloane Coffin for allying himself with it. For his part, Coffin believed that Lowenstein's fear that there might be a Communist presence at one of the demonstrations was obsessive. Lowenstein had told Coffin that if even one Communist were discovered sponsoring an antiwar protest, the whole thing would become unacceptable. His argument, now that he was a member of Congress, was that the Congress was moving to an increasingly antiwar position. Leading members of the House and Senate were coming close to endorsing the moratorium, he explained, but "Congress would not march" if it were known that the lone Communist was on the committee.

Lowenstein attempted to organize his own effort to undermine Brown and Hawk. He warned the antiwar congressmen that, while the two were "good kids," they would not be able to keep things under control. He attempted to organize student interns working that summer in the offices of like-minded congressmen to participate in a separate demonstration, one that would exclude "the wrong people" and be nonviolent. But when Lowenstein was unable to get anything off the ground, he changed his tactics. He moved to support the moratorium and joined with Republicans Pete McCloskey of California, Don Riegle of Michigan, and Democrat Donald Fraser of Minnesota to set up a strategy center to plan and push peace legislation. A townhouse on Northwest C Street became a hub for student interns from the offices of all four congressmen, with Marna Tucker, a Texas lawyer, in charge. Lowenstein also announced plans for a "nationwide referendum on Vietnam" which never took place.

After Senators George McGovern, Barry Goldwater and Mark Hatfield introduced a resolution in July to establish an all-volunteer army, Lowenstein backed a similar bill in the House with a bipartisan group of sixty-one congressmen. When speaking on this subject, Lowenstein would refer to his own military service to show that he was not hostile to the armed forces. Joining with sixteen representatives at a press conference, he denounced the draft and mailed out form letters to his constituents in August telling them that "nothing could be more important than reform of the present draft system." Lowenstein perceived, as did Nixon, that the draft was a major irritant among young people.

On August 15, Lowenstein took off on a trip around the world that he stressed was privately paid for. Departing from New York, he visited Madrid, London, Frankfurt, Berlin, Moscow, Prague, Bangkok, Saigon, Djakarta, Sydney, Aukland, and Honolulu. In Prague for the anniversary of the Soviet invasion, Lowenstein and his aide, Columbia Law School student Tom Engel, separated in order to talk to as many people as possible. Lowenstein was tear-gassed observing antigovernment demonstrations, while Engel was arrested, held fourteen hours, and beaten.

Back in New York, Lowenstein spoke to a reporter from *The New York Times* about his meetings with South Vietnamese politicians: "I told them that the people of the United States would be watching the newly reshuffled Government to see how concerned it was with instituting social reform, releasing political prisoners, and permitting all factions to participate in government. And I made particularly clear that we at home felt the South Vietnamese must take up more of the war burden because our commitment is no longer open-ended."

Lowenstein called a press conference on September 26 to denounce Nixon's "Vietnamization" policy, repeating his remarks on the floor of the House on September 30. "This is at last the Christmas by which American boys must be on their way home," he pressed. "If the president is unable to implement policies that will bring this about, the American people will have to break with their president on his conduct of the war. It will not be the first time that this will have happened in recent American history."

Also on September 26, Lowenstein had attended a secret caucus called by the chairman of the Democratic National Committee, Senator Fred Harris of Oklahoma. Present were twelve congressman and twelve senators, including Muskie, Kennedy, McGovern, Mondale, Bayh, and Pell. *The New York Times* reported the next day that the Democrats had decided to make Vietnam an important issue for the party and had agreed that opposition to the war might no longer be a political risk but an asset. On October 7 Lowenstein, together with nine senators and representatives called a press conference to announce support for the student-backed Vietnam moratorium scheduled for October 15.

During the moratorium, Jenny spoke at rallies in the district, facing large crowds filled with hostile picketers who supported the war. At Lowenstein's request, she visited families in the district who had lost sons in the war. "Most were hostile to Al," she relates. The "muted anti-Semitism," as she refers to it, was replaced by overt hatred. "Then, things became ugly," Jenny remembers. "We got crank calls and death threats. The night of the moratorium, Al arrived at Eisenhower Park and spoke. A group of policemen surrounded him to give him police protection, there was so much hostility. There was a bomb threat and we had to remove the children, Frankie and Tommy. A lot of crank mail had a clear-cut anti-Semitic tone to it. The Finnish girl who was staying with us said that someone phoned and called her a 'dirty Jew.' The cause was right but it was a bitter experience. I was spat on and called a Communist. They picketed our house and we had rotten eggs thrown at us. The children had to live with my sister in New York."

Sam Brown booked Lowenstein to speak on October 14 and 15 at moratorium rallies at Holy Cross, Brown, the University of Connecticut, Yale, Princeton, Villanova, Georgetown, and Fordham. Afterward, Lowenstein, McCloskey, Riegle, and Fraser, the "Vietnam Coordinating Committee" in Congress, prepared a statement that forty-five congressmen endorsed. It read: "We were pleased that the expression of concern over Vietnam by the American public on October 15 was eloquent, peaceful and dignified, and therefore in the highest tradition of exercise of the constitutional right of assembly and petition for redress of grievance. It is essential that future expressions of concern about the war be conducted in the same manner."

On November 3 it was Nixon's turn. Appearing on nationwide television, he denounced opponents of the war and dismissed them as a vocal minority. Two days later, Lowenstein joined Congressman William Ryan, as part of the forty-five man contingent of antiwar congressmen in criticizing the address. Under a special order granted to Ryan, they made their case in the House, where only Congressman George Bush spoke for the war. Rebutting the criticism of Nixon, Bush cited a Gallop Poll showing that 77 percent of the viewers who had watched the president's address backed him. Lowenstein countered that "the majority will of the country is to leave Vietnam as quickly as possible."

With the radical New Mobilization demonstration set for mid-November, Lowenstein was anxious to preserve his credibility as an opponent of the war. In a press release dated November 6, he declared that "unfortunately, the President's speech left me with no choice at all but to support the activities of the 13th, 14th and 15th which are committed to peaceful and constitutional protest against a continuation of policies which I believe to be in the disinterest of this country." He was endorsing the November demonstrations, he explained, because he was not prepared to leave "the arena, the whole center stage to the people not committed to the preservation of the Constitution and this country's basic fabric. . . . I did not stop supporting the United States army in the Second World War when the Communist Party decided to support the army. I've had great difficulty with people seeking to disrupt my meetings from the left—and I have no illusions as to what many people feel about me and I have no confusion as to what I feel about what they're doing. . . . But if we're agreed that the President's policies are wrong, it's our obligation to work to change those policies."

Following the mobilization demonstration, Lowenstein denounced the disruptive demonstrators as a "small band of ruffians." In endorsing the general thrust of the protest, he wrote in the *Congressional*

Record that "it made me proud to be among so many Americans who rejected alike the importuning of those who sought to disrupt and the name-calling of those who sought to intimidate—to be among so many Americans who decided simply to stand their ground for peace, justice, Constitution and country. . . . I have participated in no event more poignant or more memorable than the long cold trek from Arlington to the Capitol. Through the anonymity of the biting darkness moved countless thousands of our citizens, guarding their candles in unbroken sequences, past the great historic shrines of this torn land and on to its centers of political power. I cannot believe that their message will be unheard in those centers, for it has already made its mark in the farthest corners of America."

House Speaker John McCormack deftly outmaneuvered the antiwar congressmen. On November 26, he introduced a resolution which affirmed the House's "support of the President in efforts toward a just peace." Calling on North Vietnam to stop fighting and pointing to various efforts made by America to have free elections and to begin negotiations, it called on "the President to continue to pressure the Government of North Vietnam to abide by the Geneva Convention of 1947 in the treatment of Prisoners of War." *The New York Times* of December 3 reported that in the Republican cloakroom, one Republican leader had snapped to another, "Now let's see them vote against that."

Nixon endorsed the resolution as a show of support for his November 3 speech. Lowenstein told a reporter: "We have to vote for it or be damned for supporting Hanoi . . . and blocking national unity." But, on the floor of the house, Lowenstein opposed it, stating: "I oppose this resolution, so innocent at first glance, so deceptive after analysis, so dangerous in the long run; it can only create further illusion in Saigon and further disillusion in this country. For, however cleverly it confuses the options now available, and no matter how many members vote for it, nothing can long obscure this determination of the American people to get their troops out of Vietnam. We do no one a service by muddying that central fact with archaic rhetoric about equivocal resolutions."

With Lowenstein demurring, the resolution passed 333 to 55. Thereafter, throughout the rest of his term, none of his legislative efforts to reverse Nixon's policies in Vietnam succeeded. Thwarted by Speaker McCormack, he tried with Congressmen Jerome Waldie and Robert Bolling to get a vote of no confidence on February 18 on McCormack's leadership. Appearing on "Meet the Press," he expressed his belief that change could come through congressional action if the procedures were altered. "But if Congress can't function democratically and can't be effective in a time of such stress," he asserted, "people will flow out into the streets. There will be more government by decree from the president. You face all kinds of troubles."

The Democratic caucus overwhelmingly rejected Lowenstein's initiative to vote down McCormack. There was growing despair among the young antiwar organizers. When, on March 26, a bomb designed to kill people exploded by accident in a Greenwich Village townhouse, killing Weathermen Ted Gold and Diana Oughton and sending Kathy Boudin into hiding, Lowenstein remarked: "If the disaffected say the alternative to Nixon is bombs in Greenwich Village, then the country will turn right to oppression. People will say, 'I'd rather have my phone tapped than be blown up.' Only they won't tap just the phones of the extremists." Then, on April 30, 1970, Nixon invaded Cambodia. Addressing the House, Lowenstein insisted that "in this constitutional republic the will of the people cannot be ignored endlessly without eating away at the framework of the nation." He was one of twenty-four congressmen to sign a letter advising Nixon: "We strongly protest extension of U.S. involvement to Cambodia. . . . After five years of futility in Vietnam, what policy lures us to intervene in Cambodia? This decision will result in increased suffering and loss of life, and will increase tensions and divisions within our country."

Protests erupted and were met by violence. On May 4, four students at Kent State University in Ohio were shot and killed by members of the National Guard called out to quell the demonstration. When antiwar students marched on Wall Street on May 8, hard-hat construction workers, who were laying in wait for them, attacked and beat them. Nixon later invited representatives of the attackers to the White House. Following disturbances at Jackson State University in Mississippi, eleven black students were shot. May 9 brought thousands to a demonstration in Washington protesting Nixon's expansion of the war. As demonstrators gathered at the Lincoln Memorial in the early hours of the morning, Nixon, who had wandered out of the White House, encountered an undergraduate from Syracuse University and told him how highly he thought of the school's football team.

Debating a military procurement bill in the House on May 6, Lowenstein had spoken in support of amendments to cut off funds for the Cambodian operation. As the debate dragged on into the night, each of Lowenstein's amendments went down to defeat. When it was finally over, Lowenstein addressed a crowd of students who had gathered to hear him on the grass near the mall. Speaking almost like a revivalist, he told them that they now had to fight Nixon and Agnew the way they had fought Johnson. With the students was reporter Michael Green, who later described Lowenstein's voice—"emotional, angry, troubled, sad, and inspiring, finding its register on their faces, summoning expressions of determination and commitment"—and the response of the students: "Their voices raged in cheers at each call to new protest. Their throats caught in silence at each touch of love and eloquence from the voice they had come to trust." As Lowenstein neared the end, he said in a lowered voice, "God only knows what will become of this country. I don't. You don't."

Lowenstein turned to Curtis Gans for help in finding language that the Democrats could agree on in a resolution calling for the withdrawal of American troops. Gans, who was now on the Democratic National Policy Council, had vowed not to work with Lowenstein again after his disillusioning experience in the McCarthy campaign. But the antiwar people in the Democratic party wanted the Democrats in Congress, as well as the council, to go on record with their opposition to the war in Vietnam. Frank Church was leading the effort in the Senate with Lowenstein pressing in the House. Since nobody wanted to be pinned down as far as a timetable for withdrawal, Gans constructed a key phrase they could all live with: "a reasonable, brief, and specified time." Instructed by Lowenstein to "take the language to Church," Gans remembers bitterly that when he did, "Church asked, 'You have the Lowenstein language?' I said to myself I would never have anything more to do with him."

Lowenstein, Fraser, Riegle, and McCloskey introduced House Resolution 1000: "Resolved that, in the absence of a declaration of war, it is the policy of the House of Representatives that fiscal year 1971 defense expenditures in South Vietnam should be limited to only that amount required to carry out the safe and orderly withdrawal of all American combat and support troops in South Vietnam by the end of fiscal year 1971. Be it further resolved that no funds in the fiscal year 71 defense budget are to be used to finance the operation of any American combat or support troops in Cambodia or Laos."

Endorsements for the resolution in the House numbered one hundred, the most for any antiwar resolution up to that point. Thirty-five Senators endorsed it, and though the resolution was defeated, there was finally a discernible shift in Congress away from the war.

Lowenstein turned his attention to the campuses, flying around the country to endorse nonviolence and denounce the radicals. He spoke at a dozen colleges in less than a month, including Jackson State. Invited to the University of Alabama by the law-school student-body president after protests against the Cambodian invasion had led to police violence against students, Lowenstein conducted hearings before 2,000 students at the student union. At the end of the seven-and-a-half-hour session, he called on the students, who had told of beatings by the police in dormitories and fraternities, to revive their "faith in the democratic process." Governor George Wallace meanwhile praised the police for keeping order. Afterward, Lowenstein received a telegram from Sheriff Jerry Crabtree, president of the Alabama Sheriffs' Association, protesting Lowenstein's Alabama appearance and calling it a "grandstand play." Responding angrily to Lowenstein's statement that "what we need to do now is to redirect the energies of this country because the republic is in grave peril," Crabtree wrote: "I agree with you, the republic is in grave peril, because we have allowed people like you on our campuses. Today we stand on the brink of a bloody revolution in this country. . . . In short, Mr. Lowenstein, we do not need or want you meddling in the affairs of the state of Alabama."

Speaking at Stanford on May 24, Lowenstein defended the liberal position between right and left as the only valid one. "If you take as proof that you can't change the United States the fact that you can't change the president in the next several years, then of course you will watch Tuscaloosa and Jackson State and Kent State and Wall Street become the order of events. That will be the pattern, because there are some people who are not going to stay out of it," he insisted. "They're going to continue out of desperation, or fanaticism, or conviction, or all three—or out of neurosis or compassion—or anything else that motivates them to not stop when you stop. They're going to go on. And then, of course, you have the country thinking it's choosing between Abbie Hoffman and Spiro Agnew—and guess who they'll choose."

The senior class of Notre Dame selected Lowenstein for its annual Senior Class Fellow Award, previously given to John F. Kennedy, Richard Nixon, Everett Dirkson, and William Westmoreland. The citation read: "Placing principle over party, you have proven yourself a person of unusual integrity and ability. A true crusader against injustice, you appear to us an example of what a legislator and an educator in this tumultuous era should be. You have made many courageous stands throughout your life. Although many of us might disagree with much of what you have said or done at specific times, we all hail the spirit of honesty and the courage which motivated your actions. . . ."

The *South Bend Indiana Tribune* reported: "The students were jammed into the auditorium, they were sitting in all the aisles, and stairways, filling the stage behind Lowenstein and standing shoulder to shoulder in the stage wings." Before he had finished, Lowenstein was interrupted by a standing ovation. In his conclusion, he quoted Martin Luther King, Jr., and Robert Kennedy, and assured the students it was not too late to show "that we are determined not to abandon this country but to reclaim it. . . . We will unite and become a nation indivisible. We must let the president know we are in a fight to save our country and let one thing be made clear—we will prevail." At the end, Lowenstein received another standing ovation, this one lasting five minutes.

To much of the country, Lowenstein's name had become synonymous with opposition to the war. Reminiscing on this period, Harriet Eisman recalled: "I remember during the moratorium, during 1969–1970, and Al was still in Congress, there was a candlelight service at

Fordham for Kent State. Al had the country in his hands at one point. He had college interns in his office from all over the country. One school in California had every student apply for his office. The thing about Al was that he was overpowering. He came into the room and took over."

Interviewed for an August 25, 1970, *Look* magazine article entitled "The Pied Piper of the New Children's Crusade," Lowenstein told Gerald Astor that there was not much time left to change things. "Time is running out," he insisted, "but we have the resources to change. We're near the top of the mountain, the question is which side do we come down."

53.

Lowenstein's life-style in Washington and that of his family in Long Beach gave the impression of modest circumstances, even financial difficulty. With money borrowed from Ruth Hagy Brod, for whom he had worked in the fifties, Lowenstein purchased a nondescript red brick house at 163 Lindell Boulevard in Long Beach. It had white siding, obscuring the brick, a perpetually broken storm door, and five bedrooms. One of four identical dwellings in a row, it was five houses away from the beach, where dreary apartments housed mental patients, welfare cases, and senior citizens dumped by Nassau County.

As a liberal politician, Lowenstein's identification was with the less fortunate economically. But there was money in his immediate family. Lowenstein himself had his congressional salary of $45,000 as well as the honoraria he collected for his extensive campus lecture tours. In addition to this, while he was serving in Washington, Lowenstein still owned 7.39 percent of Bus Travelers Inn, a Lowenstein family restaurant corporation which in 1968 paid $340,125 in rent to the Port Authority of New York to run a lucrative food concession. One source puts the annual dividend from that business during one of Lowenstein's years in Congress at $13,000. Also, Jenny had income from her trust. As Carol Hardin Kimball, the sister of Lowenstein's friend, Adlai Hardin puts it, "Jenny had plenty of money." But Lowenstein neglected to report any of this to the House Standards Committee as required. Kate Bernstein, a student who worked for Lowenstein, told Curtis Gans that one of Lowenstein's tax forms during his congressional term had reported nearly $90,000 in income.

Nevertheless, the Lowensteins lived frugally. Lowenstein never bought clothes, and sometimes, while in Washington, he would borrow a suit to go to his office. He did not keep an apartment in Washington but stayed with friends. In Long Beach, when Lowenstein returned to hold his Congressional Forums, he would give a dinner at his house for the guest speakers and invited constituents. In preparation for these affairs, which were always buffets, Jenny would open cans of string beans, which she served with cheap tuna casseroles and french fried onion rings. She was also careful to keep the refrigerator stacked with Devil Dogs and Welch's grape juice, which were Lowenstein staples, as were the milkshakes he would drink on stage at the forums, as he sat looking unsophisticated and disheveled.

Lowenstein's image was that of the family man. Neighbors came around to look after their Welsh Corgy and cats and to help them out. "People wanted to give to the Lowensteins—to do things for them," a close friend who saw him often relates. "This meant they could hang around and rub shoulders with Al and the people surrounding him. It was like a barter system. I could, for example, trade my services as a baby sitter for almost free access to the Lowenstein house. I felt they'd begun to expect that people would give and give."

This friend, who would come around often to look after Frankie and Tommy and help Jenny in the kitchen, relates that Lowenstein "was rarely home and I always felt that he was more of a visitor when he was at home than a member of the family." He and Jenny had little privacy together. There was always somebody living with them. Even between campaigns, the house was like a dormitory. "Jenny was always kept company by those young boarders, but I sensed a deep loneliness," the friend observes. "Al would come in and tickle Tommy under the chin and leave. I never felt he knew his children as people. They were part of the perfect picture he wanted—but he wasn't in the picture. Jenny told me he wanted many children and dogs—like RFK—but he shouldered none of the day-to-day responsibilities involved in raising a family. . . . He did the best he could in his relationship with Jenny and the kids. I always felt he didn't know how to really give of himself—it all seemed very superficial to me as an observer."

"It was after Al's election that I got to know him and the family," the friend relates. "I discovered that their home on Lindell Boulevard was always open and if you hung around long enough you could meet all kinds of people, including Susan Tanenbaum (one of the 'boiler room girls' for Bobby Kennedy who was at Chappaquiddick), Frank Mankiewicz, congressmen from all over the country, Bill Buckley, etc.

"The more I hung around the Lowenstein's house, the more I noticed that there was an extraordinary number of incredibly good-looking young men involved with the 'crusade.' They had a 'look' about them; preppy (or Ivy League), thick necks, broad chests, etc. Definitely country club material. Some were so perfect they could have been models. I'd never seen people who looked like that before.

Often two or three would be living in the Lowenstein house. (Jenny and Al were rarely alone.)

"Every now and then Al—this nonviolent man—would wrestle with one of these hunks. I wondered about this, but not too much.

"Then Jenny went to the hospital to have Katie. I was asked to sleep over at the house and take care of Frankie and Tommy. That evening, Al and one of those men were discussing the campaign in the living room. I heard them go up to Al and Jenny's bedroom and they didn't come down till morning.

"I was very innocent and didn't want to believe what I suspected. I felt violated for Jenny and sickened that Al might have been unfaithful with *anyone* on the night his wife was in a hospital bed after having produced his third child. I was angry and confused.

"I had befriended a Californian named Doug Chandler. . . , He was a forest fighter in his home state and a motorcycle rider. He also was a campaign worker.

"The morning after Katie was born, I called Doug at the home he was staying at in Massapequa. I whispered about what had gone on the night before. Helmi, the Finnish mother's helper, giggled knowingly at me. I wondered how much she knew and for how long.

"Doug agreed to meet me later so we could talk. He was understanding and told me that he had been working in Indonesia when he somehow met Al and they became friends. They shared a room, and Doug said he awoke in the middle of the night to find Al on top of him. Doug said he rejected the advance. My suspicions were confirmed.

"This knowledge became a terrible burden for me. I felt I had to protect Al's reputation. I also felt Jenny and the children should never find out. The only other person I told was Larry DuBois, campaigner and writer. I kept my terrible secret for years and yet probably needing to talk it out—work it out. I was eating dinner when the newscaster on TV reported Al had been shot. My stomach contracted as I thought the shooter must have been a former lover of Al's—I had almost no doubt about that.

"I couldn't keep my silence anymore. In fact, I found I didn't have to. Several months before the murder, my brother began working for Congressman William Rachford in his Washington office. Jason called me soon after he started on the job and said in an amazed tone, '. . . Al was gay!' What a relief not to have to keep my secret anymore—and I discussed it freely after the news of the shooting."

Lowenstein came from a traditional, conservative Jewish family in which sexual matters were not discussed openly. His close friend from high school, Sandy Friedman, thought Lowenstein was sexually repressed and believed that he struggled with this problem all of his life.

"I hope the gay issue and Al will not be sensationalized," says the

Rev. William Sloane Coffin. "There were lots of guys from that period who had wives and kids but who turned out to be gay. It wasn't socially acceptable so they hid it." But it was more than socially unacceptable. Homosexuals were barred from working for the CIA and could not get security clearance.

Lowenstein projected himself as a person who was not interested in sex. "Al was asexual," insists Brooke Aronson Trent, who had helped him with *Brutal Mandate*. "The energy was being in Madrid on such and such a date and Mississippi on another. When did he have time for sex?" Lowenstein continued to project this image after his election to Congress, where being gay was a certain ticket to political oblivion. "I could never think of Al as any kind of great lover," his aide Harriet Eisman shrugged. "It just didn't fit any description of him." And Sandy Friedman adds that "Allard was inhibited, in some ways crippled sexually. I don't know how he figured out how to have a baby." Friedman concludes that Lowenstein did have homoerotic tendencies. "He had these impulses but didn't know how to act on them," he asserts. "He needed someone to educate him. But Al was the charismatic figure. He didn't know what to do. To call him bisexual implies a demonstration of sexuality, but he was too inhibited. I know he loved Jenny. His ideal that he was drawn to was what he wasn't, the all-American boy. He grew up in a time of different dos and don'ts. He didn't have the freedom."

Lowenstein told friends like Friedman that his view of public service was the same as Eleanor Roosevelt's; that you didn't have a personal life if you were in public life; that you "sacrificed this." Yet it was his public life that led him to have contact with the beautiful young men he recruited for his crusades. "There was a lot of self-blindness and self-deception in Al in his motives," Friedman acknowledges. "He overlooked it. That brilliant brain wasn't turned on himself. But he couldn't have functioned if it had."

Friedman speculates that the "failure of the marriage was that he wasn't physically present eighty percent of the time. He loved those children but they were an adjunct of the political life. That's what destroyed the marriage and broke Jenny. Al's situation was never that he loved a man and loved his wife. It was not powerful to him. It didn't haunt him. He knew he had an impulse or inclination but he didn't spend much time wrestling with it. But it did give him sympathy and understanding in championing gay issues. I think he was very courageous about that. But he disbelieved his own attractiveness. He thought he was ugly. If there was some man he thought he could have a relationship with, he was incapable of it. A really deep, personal satisfying relationship was not in Allard's stars. Maybe it was because of his psychic makeup or because of his choice about the way he saw public life or causes."

Lowenstein was vain about his body and wore tight T-shirts with the sleeves carefully folded up to reveal his powerful biceps. But in his physical relationships with other men, Lowenstein was said to have stressed that all he wanted was to hold and be held. Mike Bollman, a Harvard student when he first met Lowenstein and later a campaign worker in Lowenstein's congressional race, described his relationship with Lowenstein to journalist Larry Bush:

"I would talk to him about my feelings as a gay man, and he would think about it, try it on, and ask himself, 'Do I feel like that?'

"I'm very clear about that: he needed the physical intimacy. He was struggling to understand intimacy. To him the most important issue was not sexuality, but intimacy. In his personal experience, stalling at the merely sexual was something he wanted to avoid, and he always challenged it to move beyond that.

"There is a different understanding of that as well. It's 'I can't face the issue, so let's deal with what I can face.'

"He found it a problem of wanting to be close to a young man, and having that misunderstood as a sexual pass. At some point, I know that it washes over, moving to [sexual] climax just happens. For him, there didn't seem to be that need. There was no rushing anything. . . . He would say he was very concerned about misleading people, that they would naturally expect him to go all the way. Holding was always the consummation of the intimacy which grew from talking, but I did not feel that talking was a device to get to holding."

According to Bush, "Bollman's own experience with Lowenstein led him to conclude that Lowenstein was perhaps not gay, certainly not in the 'closeted' sense that people mean when they discuss public officials who are leading private gay lives. Lowenstein's search for meaning and self-expression in his intimate relations with men went beyond the categories of gay and straight." As Bollman explained to him, "It was a natural part of the same thing, one was verbal and one more physical than that. The quality was intimacy, but without the confusion about what's okay, okay in terms of sexuality. It was always careful, caring, comfortable. Holding another man was to him part of the progression that starts with a handshake, a full-body handshake with that much greater intimacy."

Bollman concludes: "Al's politics were the politics of personal commitment, and that made it impossible for him not to reflect his personal life—and he was struggling to make this connection. They are making a great mistake if they don't tell about his personal struggle to make this connection and failings to integrate his political life with his personal life. That place where I believe this integration became the most difficult for him was in the gay rights area. The question of one's own sexual feelings are imputed."

In 1974, Lowenstein would attend a party at the penthouse of Robert Livingston in honor of Dr. Howard Brown and Bruce Voeller.

Brown, a prominent health official in the Lindsay administration and Voeller, a leading biologist at Rockefeller University, had both "come out" and acknowledged their gayness openly. Voeller, who had been married and had children, won a landmark civil liberties case that gave him visitation rights with his children over his wife's objections. Lowenstein and Voeller had a common friend in Sherman Bull. Lowenstein had traveled to South West Africa with Bull, who had later been Voeller's neighbor in Connecticut.

Lowenstein told Voeller that he wanted to talk to him alone but not at the offices of the National Gay Task Force, which Voeller headed at the time. At a luncheonette below the office, Lowenstein asked Voeller about his experiences and about the impact which his coming out had had on his wife and children. "From the outset, he said he was in the process of 'coming out' and discovering things about himself," Voeller insists. "He said he was attracted affectionally to men." Lowenstein talked with Voeller about the lack of role models for someone with his feelings. He wanted to know if people could continue to have a heterosexual relationship and a family, knowing that one of them felt the way he did. "He wanted reassurance that he would still have their love," Voeller says. "I couldn't give him that. It was painful. As I look back, I realize that some people have had close relationships of the type Al was talking about without them being sexual relationships. It hadn't occurred to me that it might or might not be sexual."

They met again several times after that and talked in general about the problem. Voeller suggested that Lowenstein talk to Howard Brown, who had been appointed health commissioner of New York, but that meeting was never arranged. Voeller was appreciative of Lowenstein's support for the National Gay Rights Bill. He stresses that there are many people far more famous than Lowenstein who lead lives as closet gays and that "in the 'grapevine' it was regarded as common knowledge that Al was a closet gay. And that 'grapevine' is pretty reliable."

When Lowenstein went to Hyde Park with his research aide Noemie Emery in 1978 to make some tapes for an oral history of Eleanor Roosevelt, he expressed his conviction that Mrs. Roosevelt had consummated a homosexual relationship with her friend the journalist Lorena Hickock. Referring to the correspondence between the two women, Lowenstein told Emery that Mrs. Roosevelt revealed her "extraordinary courage" in the affair.

In his personal life, as in his political life, Lowenstein was not able to reveal his relationships fully. He could be a tense individual, living in a frenzied state. Curtis Gans observes that "part of his frenetic activity was his escape from himself." At times, his judgment may have been clouded by inner tensions. Friends speculated that his mistakes were a reflection of an innate self-destructiveness. Alice Brandeis

Popkin, who knew him for most of his life, believed that Lowenstein had what she insists was a "death wish" and that "unconsciously, he sought to lose." Barbara Boggs Sigmund, to whom he was engaged, expresses the belief that Lowenstein had a "messiah complex" and that he was in some way responsible for his own defeat. "He discovered his vocation, to be in Congress," she asserts, "but if he had really wanted it, it could have happened. But the need to triumph over crisis in his own life overcame his search for vocation. . . . His constant running was . . . a character problem of putting himself in a position where he couldn't succeed at what he wanted to do."

Writer Doug Ireland believed Lowenstein was "running" from himself because of sexual repression and the denial of his homosexual nature. Some Lowenstein critics hint that a sense of guilt contributed to his undoing, but while it is difficult to explain those decisions most harmful to his career without some reference to his low self-esteem and his sometimes self-defeating behavior, these explanations are too simple.

Douglas Hunt insists that Lowenstein "did not seek martyrdom." Doug Walgren, a Lowenstein co–campaign chairman in the seventies, later elected to Congress himself, maintains that Lowenstein wanted to win and believed in each instance that his chances were realistic. Harriet Eisman insists that "Al always felt he could win. One thing that I felt sure about his personality was that he believed that he could turn a situation around." And William Buckley, Jr., asserts, "He wanted to be the leading liberal in Congress, with a solid foot in the academy. He wanted to be the role model for young Americans." Buckley maintains that "it was strangely important" to Lowenstein to be in Congress, and admits that he never really understood why it mattered so much to him. According to Buckley, Lowenstein once tried to explain, telling him that in Congress he could, in relatively short order, mobilize a sufficient block "to do the right thing as he understood the right thing, which he could not do from outside Congress."

Whatever part he may have played in his own defeats, Lowenstein clearly also became a victim of the system he devoted his life to saving. He believed that the American people could be educated, that if they knew the facts they would arrive at moderate solutions through nonviolence. But the "Middle American" people for whom he had tried to save the system by opposing the revolution, denounced him for being an instigator of that revolution. They ignored or misinterpreted what he was trying to teach them and rejected him.

54.

Emory Bundy, who had been put in charge of the Merrick headquarters during the 1968 campaign, was persuaded by Lowenstein to leave Oberlin, where he had been teaching, to serve as Lowenstein's chief of staff in Washington. "When Al came to Congress, he sort of regarded himself as a congressman from Mississippi," Bundy relates. "We were under orders that if any poor soul from Mississippi wanted help, we had to give it. . . . Much of the country was part of our constituency, but Mississippi was very special."

Lowenstein also put Jenny's emotionally troubled brother, Charlie, on his staff, which he loaded with numerous people. "He [Lowenstein] was the most difficult person I ever met," Bundy insists. "He misused people. The only way was his way." Bundy says he, like other staff members, was treated as a "flunkie." Lowenstein "made you do meaningless errands," he relates. "He was in that sense inconsiderate and eccentric." Harriet Eisman, who acknowledges that Lowenstein's demands alienated some of his workers, noted that "that was how he was and you accepted it or you didn't, and there were people who were tired of that sort of thing because they felt they were being used. I never felt I was being used. I felt he was an extraordinary person and I adored to do these things."

Lowenstein needed three staffs—day, night and weekend. He began his day at 9:00 A.M. when he arrived on the floor of the House, and his staff labored into the night. If he had scheduled Lowenstein to make a statement for the *Congressional Record*, Bundy knew he would have to remain until midnight, the printer's deadline for revisions. Lowenstein insisted on revising up until the last minute and once made a legislative aide hold the presses until 1:30 A.M.. Bundy often stayed on after midnight, so that, with Lowenstein finally gone, he could get routine letters out. Nothing was supposed to leave the office without Lowenstein's approval, however, and occasionally, to bypass the endless Lowenstein revisions, Bundy would forge Lowenstein's signature. Discovered, he would be berated by a furious Lowenstein.

Resentful of the way Lowenstein "abused" his staff, Bundy explained in 1969 that he wanted to leave. Lowenstein, in turn, told Bundy that he wanted to replace him, though that did not prevent him touting Bundy as someone who should be elected to the Senate from Washington in a speech he made just as Bundy was preparing to leave. But Bundy left feeling "bruised" by the experience. He felt he had "had enough of him," yet he remained under Lowenstein's spell. "I always felt he was the greatest human being I ever had a first-person encounter with," he acknowledges. "He just was not real. He was completely unlike anyone else, so distinctive in so many ways, whether it was his eccentricities or his soaring intellect and deep concerns."

Lowenstein became known in Congress for his ability to win over other representatives, including Republicans, to his point of view. "Al had more personal friends than anybody in history," Bundy asserts. "Al had more friends in Seattle than I did." Lowenstein's efforts to become part of the "club" in Congress took some bizarre twists. With Mendel Rivers, he cochaired a luncheon for Zbigniew Stypulkowski. The last "ambassador" of Free Poland before the United States recognized the Communist regime, Stypulkowski also served as an advisor to the State Department on Eastern European affairs. During the first months of his term, Lowenstein was taken aside by Rivers, an old-fashioned Southern conservative, and told: "Lowenstein, my boy, you and I may not see eye to eye on lots of things. But I like you and when you run for reelection, I will come and campaign for you, or against you, whichever you want."

While Lowenstein's national reputation and his standing in the House of Representatives was growing, the situation in his home district was becoming increasingly tenuous. He lacked patience for some of the bread and butter issues of Long Island politics. When Nan Windmueller, who became a student intern for him, researched the problems of sewage treatment, he showed little interest and he was abroad when a crucial vote was taken on key environmental legislation. But these were not serious omissions. He countered them by opposing jet noise and the landing of the Concorde. In fact, he was deprived of his political strength by external forces when his district was altered, forcing him into an election campaign that was virtually impossible for him to win.

Governor Nelson Rockefeller had been under pressure from blacks to redraw New York's congressional districts in order to consolidate the growing voting power of the black community in Brooklyn. At the time, the only safe minority seat in New York was in Harlem, and Rockefeller was seeking to create another one in Brooklyn for Shirley Chisolm, a black Democratic supporter of his.

When an officer of the International Ladies Garment Workers Union, who was also a member of the New York State Liberal party run by Rockefeller's close friend Alex Rose, brought suit against the State of New York in the United States Supreme Court, in January 1969, charging that the state's congressional district plan violated the Court's recently established one-man/one-vote rule, the Court agreed. The decision, handed down on April 7, stated that New York's congressional districts were unconstitutional and that reapportionment would have to take place prior to the 1970 election.

At the time, New York State was in the firm grip of the Republican party; the governor was a Republican and the State Assembly and Senate were both held by Republican majorities. *The New York Times* reported on January 14 that a high Republican state official with expertise in district apportionment asserted that "we can draw beautiful lines that can be as compact as a good cigar and still achieve a switch of six to eight seats for our side." The first Democrat on their hit list was Lowenstein.

The January 20, 1970, plan submitted to the legislature was so blatantly partisan that some Republicans defected. It was saved only when a sick Republican state senator was carried from the hospital to break the tie. The new 5th Congressional District spelled doom for Lowenstein. Taken from him were the "Five Towns." Lawrence, Cedarhurst, Woodmere, Hewlett, and Inwood, with their upwardly mobile liberal Democratic Jewish constituencies, had provided him with his 3,500-vote majority over Mason Hampton. In their place, he was given Massapequa, one of the toughest, most conservative ethnic blue-collar Catholic Republican towns on Long Island. There were Jewish voters in Massapequa too, but they were apt to be supporters of the Jewish Defense League. Sizing up Massapequa quickly, Lowenstein dubbed it "Matzoh-Pizza."

"Massapequa was the worst," Harriet Eisman lamented. "Places like the liberal areas in Rockville Centre and Lido Beach, everyone in Lido Beach voted for Al, there were a couple of thousand residents, and they took it out of the district. It was put in the 4th C.D. . . . It was carved out very cleverly, and I kept saying to Al, 'Look, they knew what they were doing. E.D. by E.D., they did it.'"

Itching to run against Lowenstein was State Senator Norman Lent, son of popular Republican Nassau County Judge Norman Lent, Sr., and a creature of the Joseph Margiotta machine. Lent had troubles of his own. A Protestant from East Rockaway who had served five terms in the Senate and was considered "popular," he had angered many constituents when, as chairman of the Senate Health Committee, he had allowed Nelson Rockefeller's liberal abortion bill to come up for a vote. The Right to Life movement had, in fact, been founded in the 5th C.D. at the Curiae of Ars Church in Merrick by Theresa Siller and Eleanor McCormick to protest the legislation. The new Right to Life party was committed to running candidates against all those public officials responsible for the repeal of New York's restrictive antiabortion statute. With a bill introduced by Senator Robert Packwood of Oregon to legalize abortion in all fifty states pending, the Right to Life party considered it imperative to make a strong showing in a congressional race to "send a message" to Congress that a proabortion position would lead to defeat. While Lowenstein was not favored by the Right to Lifers, their candidate for Congress in the 5th C.D. described him as "fifty-fifty," someone they could talk to. Norman Lent was their major target. They hounded Lent, following him wherever he spoke, holding up photographs of dead fetuses and the usual Right to Life paraphernalia.

Lent was also divorced and remarried, while Lowenstein's image was of a sound family man. Jenny was pregnant with Katie, their third child. In a district with a growing backlash against "permissiveness," Lent did not seem to Margiotta to be the best candidate, and he initially backed Lynbrook Mayor Francis Becker, maintaining that a Lent candidacy would cost valuable patronage in Albany. But when Becker backed down to avoid intraparty battling, Margiotta had to settle for Lent. He also called on Lowenstein to resign because he didn't represent the views of the district on the war in Vietnam.

On February 16, 1970, Lowenstein announced at a press conference that he would resign if Rockefeller would call a special election. Responding to Margiotta's charges that he didn't represent the district, Lowenstein said he would pay half the cost of the election if Margiotta and the Nassau County Republican party would pay the rest. Lowenstein gave three reasons for the special election. He said it would "assure that the people of the 5th Congressional District will have a spokesman in Congress during the next ten critical months who will represent them properly on the great problems besetting the nation." It would serve as a test of President Nixon's handling of the war in a district in which Nixon "obtained a higher percentage of the popular vote in 1968 than he did in the nation at large." And finally, he insisted, it would "reinvigorate in some small way the electoral process itself."

Newsday wrote: "Representative Allard Lowenstein's response to the Republican demands that he resign is a beautiful demonstration of political judo. He very neatly used the force of the GOP attack to send Nassau GOP Chairman Joseph Margiotta to the mat with his foot lodged firmly in his mouth."

It was known in Lowenstein circles that Lowenstein had other motives for offering to resign if a special election were held. It would give him the opportunity to run against Lent in his old 5th C.D. before the redistricting went into effect. But the Republicans did not bite. Rockefeller explained that he did not "play political games," pointing out that the New York State Constitution prohibited conditional resignations.

At this juncture, Lowenstein faced a critical choice in his career. Harriet Eisman advised him not to run for reelection in the new district, as did Emory Bundy, who told him he would lose. But the liberal New Democratic Coalition pressured him to make the fight. "By 1970, by this time, I was so pissed with the NDC because they were unrealistic," Eisman recounted. "Al was fed up with some of them, even though we were all friends. They saw themselves as purists, but they were not. If you said something like this (that running in the new district was inappropriate), they labeled you a turncoat. I think Al always had a terrible fighting nature and while I don't think they talked him into it, it reinforced what he was about to do against everybody else's recommendation. We knew that you couldn't win in that district after the redistricting if you were liberal and Jewish. There was a lot of anti-Semitism."

Other Lowenstein supporters in Nassau County and elsewhere were urging him to run for the United States Senate seat that Robert Kennedy had held until his death and which had been filled by a Rockefeller appointee, Republican Charles Goodell. Students were clamoring for him to make his Senate candidacy the "New Hampshire" of 1970 and Democrats were appealing to him to "impart new life into a leaden atmosphere—both as a campaigner and as the ultimate occupant of the late Robert Kennedy's seat."

Already seeking the Democratic nomination were Congressman Richard "Max" McCarthy of Buffalo, Congressman Richard Ottinger of Westchester, New York City Councilman Paul O'Dwyer, and former Kennedy speech-writer Ted Sorenson. Challenging Goodell to the right was James Buckley, brother of William Buckley, Jr., who was running as a Conservative. "In the scrambled Democratic Senate primary," wrote James Wechsler, "Lowenstein's legion of adherents and own qualities of spirit would give him a special advantage; he would have been a favorite over Goodell in the finals. The alternative was a grim uphill Congressional contest in a district redesigned for his discomfort."

On a drive back from Washington with Lowenstein, Max McCarthy indicated that both he and Ottinger would get out of the Senate race if Lowenstein was intent on running. According to Gerry Twombley, a student at Hofstra and a local coordinator for Ottinger in Nassau County, Lowenstein "felt that if he did make the race, O'Dwyer would withdraw and he would be one on one against Sorenson."

Support for Lowenstein grew, but he agonized over his plans until the last minute. At the Nassau County Democratic Convention in April at the old Garden City Hotel, his supporters waited anxiously for the 5th C.D. to come up for consideration. Elaine Horowitz, a Lowenstein worker, was convinced Lowenstein would go for the Senate and had let it be known that, should that be the case, she was seriously seeking the nomination. Jenny commented, "I have no idea what Al is doing."

A group including Nassau County Executive Eugene Nickerson and Gerry Twombley went with Lowenstein into the men's room. "Al was in front of the urinal," Twombley relates, "still talking, tossing the Senate race idea back and forth. As Al turned and flushed, he slapped

his hands and said, 'That's it. I'm running for Congress.' Jenny ran
after him shouting, 'What are you going to do?' Someone said, 'He's
running for reelection,' and Jenny didn't look happy. She might have
felt he should go for the Senate and use his ability on a bigger scale
and that the new district was rough. I think even Al regretted the
decision to run for reelection."

James Wechsler insisted that it was not "political masochism" that
led to Lowenstein's decision but his instinctive rejection of the "notion
of backing away from the challenge embodied in the gerrymander."
Lowenstein, he wrote, had the "capacity for transforming a local clash
into a national plebiscite. His opponent—Senator Norman E. Lent—
is a faithful follower of the Nixon-Agnew establishment on Vietnam
and a cautious political trimmer on many other matters." Lowenstein
saw the election, Wechsler concluded, as a "clear test of the 'silent
majority' legend—rendered peculiarly dramatic by the gerrymander."
In accepting the nomination, Lowenstein asked the Democrats "to
have the determination not to allow this election to be meaningless,"
adding, "I would like to see if we can't in this district carry the fight
against Nixon and what he stands for and all the Agnews that are
springing up."

There were other factors in Lowenstein's decision. Goodell was a
critic of the war in Vietnam, as was his friend Democrat Richard Ottinger, who was ultimately the Democratic nominee. James Buckley,
the Conservative, was the brother of Lowenstein's friend William F.
Buckley, Jr. Too, Lowenstein must have been loath to further his career by virtue of Robert Kennedy's assassination and he may have felt
incapable of taking his place.

Norman Lent charged that Lowenstein was "sowing the seeds of
his own martyrdom" by the way he campaigned, but the evidence
clearly indicates that Lowenstein was doing everything he could to
win. He kicked off the campaign in an upbeat mood. At a cocktail
party at the Salisbury Restaurant, where 300 friends paid $25 a head
to hear him, he shouted to the cheering crowd: "I will say in Massapequa the same thing I will say in Woodmere. I will say in churches
and synagogues the same thing I say in American Legion and VFW
halls."

Local journalist Hy Wallis listened to the speech and wrote:

Never in our fifteen years of actively being involved in some form
of government, politics, civics, writing, have we ever seen or
heard so much dedication to a man and a cause as we have seen
amongst the believers in Congressman Allard Lowenstein. . . .
They believe, as we believe. For we have followed our Congressman down the path from the day he set foot in our district to make
his challenge for the Democratic Party nomination for Congressman in the 5th C.D.

We watched him in Chicago during the '68 Democratic convention. We observed him during his campaign against Mason Hampton and saw him overcome great odds and go on to victory. We spoke to him on a night when powerful forces within the Democratic Party political machine were tearing at him urging him to throw his hat into the ring and run for the U.S. Senate.

We voiced our opinion that we felt that Al Lowenstein could best serve his country and his personal beliefs by staying in our district and running for re-election. We like to feel that our little pitch to him that night, helped him to make his final decision to run again.

55.

Lowenstein's strength was with youth. "Al had a whole entourage of admirers . . . who worked night and day, who gave up their jobs and livelihood," Harriet Eisman states. "He was known among students, there was a certain amount of glamour to Al. All his weird dress and whatever. The young people adored Al. You could come in early in the morning, he was sitting on a chair picking his toes; they would sit around discussing the affairs of state. He had a sense . . . he loved to sing, he loved old songs. He had a whole thing with jazz music . . . there was this thing about Al."

When leaders of the graduating class of Oceanside High School selected their congressman to be the Commencement Day speaker, the principal agreed to accept the choice of the majority if the senior class approved it, which they did by a vote of 386 to 204. But the school board determined that the decision involved a "controversial figure" and forced the principal to deny the choice. The students were then directed by the principal to submit a list of speakers from which he would make the final decision.

"Those of us who speak for the mainstream of American public opinion," Lowenstein declared, "—whatever our party affiliation and whatever our point of view on specific issues—will, of course, continue to speak out, despite efforts and destruction and censorship from the Left and the Right." Lowenstein, who had insisted on the removal of the writings of Lenin from the freedom schools in Mississippi, expressed his disappointment at the lesson the Oceanside students were being taught; that the "establishment tells them to work within the system, to vote, and when they do, the establishment turns its back on them."

Lowenstein spoke in June to over half the Oceanside seniors at a "supplementary graduation program" held at the Laurel Movie Theater in Long Beach. Entering to a standing ovation, he was cheered by the crowd of 700 students, their families, and friends. Echoing FDR, he told them, "This generation has a rendezvous with destiny. We are the majority of Americans not to be silenced." Quoting from Keats, he concluded, "Come my friends, 'tis not too late to seek a newer world."

In Congress, member after member, from both parties, rose at the end of the session to condemn the censorship of Lowenstein and to praise him. Each spoke for a minute, and their expanded remarks were published in the *Congressional Record* of June 18.

"I think all of us in the House," Congressman Adams remarked, "liberals, conservatives, Republicans, and Democrats, of whatever persuasion we may be—would find it to be a terrible thing if certain people in our districts were given the power to say that their elected representative was someone who could not be heard on local public school property after the school had invited him to come."

Congressman Pete McCloskey, a tough former marine who had become a close friend of Lowenstein's, portrayed Lowenstein as the savior of the system who was being unjustly denounced as its destroyer: "Perhaps more than any one of the 537 elected national leaders that serve here—in the White House and in the Congress—Al Lowenstein has been responsible for keeping the faith of millions of young people alive during these last several years of national debate and probing self-scrutiny. . . . He has counseled nonviolence and obedience to the law in places and circumstances where to do so involved far more than his credibility—indeed his personal safety."

Congressman Waldie noted with irony: "If there was ever a man in this country who has done more than any other to put out the fires of student violence and student unrest and to channel their energies into constructive channels and into the system, it is Al Lowenstein. . . . If Al Lowenstein is 'controversial' it is because the extremists who counsel violence and destruction find his opposition to their views to be too effective."

"He has gone the length and breadth of this land," Rep. Benjamin Rosenthal declared, "to preach nonviolence, to preach within the system, and to tell young people that this system can be made to work."

Congressman Martha Griffiths of Michigan summed up: "What a great final lesson in democracy for graduating seniors. Now, they know how the real world is run. I do hope the speaker chosen does not read the bill of rights. That is really controversial. What an insult to the entire Congress and to the district which elected Mr. Lowenstein. There have been few young men ever to enter this body who have arrived better equipped to be a member of this body and who have worked as diligently through established channels for relevant changes."

On Thursday, June 25, 1970, the *Helm Independence Review* of Lynbrook, Malverne, and East Rockaway, "The Family Newspaper," took exception to the House of Representatives of the United States in an editorial. Denouncing Lowenstein for participating in the "counter graduation," it chided:

Now, we think Congressman Lowenstein's inflated ego ought to be tempered by the fact that the right to hear the word of God in our schools was turned down some time ago by the Courts at the request of a small minority who felt offended by hearing words with which they disagreed. . . . Yet, we think there is a larger issue here in which Mr. Lowenstein is the main offender by virtue of his official position. In our judgment, by failing to recognize and honor the decision of the Oceanside School Board, he did, with malice, undermine the authority and responsibility of that body. The fact that he was piqued by the Board's prior refusal to permit him to use the High School for one of his political forums, is no excuse for his conduct.

It was not Lowenstein who was denied freedom of speech, the editorial concluded. In fact, the school board had been trying to exercise its freedom of speech with its decision to "turn down a request by the students for a particular speaker at graduation time." The editorial was reprinted as "a public service" by one William W. Seiffert of Oceanside and distributed throughout the 5th Congressional District.

Over the Fourth of July weekend, Lowenstein was shoved and heckled in his district by self-proclaimed "patriots." And when Jenny, visibly pregnant, tried to take their eldest son, Frankie, to a firemen's Independence Day celebration, she was barred. In early September, Lowenstein was assaulted by an angry mob of twenty picketers as he arrived to speak at the Massapequa chapter of the American Cancer Society. They blocked his car shouting "Commie" and "traitor," and brandishing signs which adivsed him to "Go Back to Hanoi."

In an article characterizing the race as a struggle between Lowenstein and the "silent majority," the *Wall Street Journal* described Lent as a "sort of mini–Spiro Agnew—a firm supporter of the Nixon Vietnam policy, a hard-slugging advocate of get-tough measures on campus violence, crime and a host of social problems."

Over the Labor Day weekend, Lowenstein traveled to Valley Forge to speak at an antiwar rally, where he was preceded at the platform by film star Jane Fonda, speaking for the Black Panthers in Chicago and the Indians occupying Alcatraz. Afterward, many of Lowenstein's constituents, hostile to Fonda because of her radical politics and her reputation for playing provocative roles, criticized him for appearing with her. And after the election, a Lent campaign aide snapped to

Gerry Twombley, "You just do not run around with Jane Fonda and expect to get elected in the 5th Congressional District."

Lowenstein dispatched students to help the campaigns of other antiwar candidates, such as Peter Eikenberry, who ran a primary against pro-Nixon Democratic Congressman John Rooney in Brooklyn. His recruits aided both Republicans and Democrats including Ogden Reid and Bella Abzug in New York, Nick Lamont of Philadelphia, Joseph Duffy in Connecticut, Father Robert Drinan in Massachusetts and Gary Hart (not the Gary Hart from Colorado) and Pete McCloskey in California. In September, he appealed to Chapel Hill, Yale, Stanford, and Notre Dame for volunteers for his own campaign, sending fliers that read, "Congressman Al Lowenstein needs you. Hundreds of students will ring doorbells and discuss the issues of the campaign. With a little help from his friends, Lowenstein can stay in Congress. Contact your campus representative."

Students responded and the house became a dormitory again, the floor strewn with sleeping bags. About 1,000 volunteers, including high school students, fanned out through the district. Lowenstein also had his celebrities. Actor Robert Vaughn, who stayed at the house, campaigned, as did stars George Segal and Ben Gazarra and New York Yankee pitcher Jim Bouton. Folksinger Harry Chapin, still unknown, churned out Lowenstein literature from his coffee house in Point Lookout. But it was not the same as it had been two years earlier. "In 1968, Al had really good volunteer help," Lowenstein loyalist Rick Weidman relates. "There was Clinton DeVeaux, president of SUNY, Buffalo, student body, David Chanin, the student body president at Trinity, Steven Cohen, now Joe Papp's main assistant. He had Margie Schlenker full-time, one of the four coordinators of the moratorium. She got all the McCarthy kids. But in 1970 the same quality people were not running the storefronts, except in Massapequa. In 1968, people thought they could end the war. In 1970, there was pessimism, less effort."

Lowenstein also continued to be assaulted by the radical left. Addressing 500 students at the State University of New York at Stony Brook, Lowenstein was confronted by an angry, hostile crowd that reacted violently when he said, "America is not in any sense a Fascist country." Lowenstein was pelted with water bombs by "screaming, cursing, yippie-oriented SDSers trying to disrupt his talk," wrote journalist Karl Grossman in the *Long Island Press*. The majority of the students cheered as he stood his ground. "Those who want to change this country's direction are not going to be bullied," he shouted. "If good people committed to change worked within the democratic system, there'd by change." Lowenstein then attacked the radicals for "engaging in the luxury of the rhetoric of violence on the grounds that nothing else works and wanting to be excused from the penalties of

violence." When some of the students shouted, "The only way is revolution," he retorted, "We have to get ourselves talking to people instead of spitting at them. This is no police state when we consider the
freedom people have to throw water bombs at a U.S. congressman
and be seated in their seats after they've done it."

The basic tactic of the Lent campaign was to identify Lowenstein
with the New Left radicals who were so hostile to him. Lowenstein
had never been part of the "New Left," although the press invariably
lumped him in with it. He had tried to organize something called the
"Democratic Left," enlisting people like liberal critic Irving Howe to
counter Tom Hayden and the SDS. But Lent was able to put Lowenstein on the defensive with his literature and statements. A "hard-
nosed, Bob Haldeman type" as Gerry Twombley describes him, Lent
knew Lowenstein had a high identification factor and acknowledged
that his only chance was to portray Lowenstein as negatively as possible. When Lowenstein staffer Arnie Miller worried aloud that "we
have to somehow overcome the notion that Al is a wild-eyed leader of
the New Left who's responsible for violence," Lowenstein added, "I'm
saddled with this whole business of kids going crazy."

Lent's fund-raising mailings set the tone. "As you know," an early
one stated, "Senator Lent will be running against Representative Allard Lowenstein, the darling of the New Left and probably the single
most polarizing force in Congress." Lent denounced Lowenstein for
being "the chief apologist in Congress for the Black Panthers." Lowenstein "blames the police for student riots and burnings rather than
the guilty students," he insisted. Lowenstein was "voting for the pornography peddlars" when he opposed the pornography bill on First
Amendment grounds. Because Lowenstein supported withdrawal of
American troops from Vietnam, Lent said he "echoes the line from
Hanoi." One piece of Lent literature showed five screaming hippie
students beating up the police. The inflammatory copy read: "Lowenstein opposed every measure to curb campus violence during his
two years in Congress. Lowenstein commends draft evaders. He participated in the November moratorium led by Communists, which
received commendation from Hanoi." Lowenstein voted "to deny
funds for Congressional investigation of the Black Panthers and other
violent revolutionary groups," the voters were told. Lowenstein was
"a liability to Israel," Lent alleged because he had first voted against
building the F–14, which was to be made by the Grumman Corporation on Long Island and which was being considered for sale to Israel.

Lent also falsely charged that Lowenstein "even voted against a
bill which would have provided military sales to permit the sale of jets
to Israel." The bill Lent was referring to was the Foreign Sales Act of
1970, which, in fact, had nothing to do with the sale of jets to Israel.
Lowenstein had actually led the fight in Congress to adopt Section

501 of the Military Authorization Bill of 1971, authorizing the president to sell jets to Israel on credit as made necessary by increased American military aid to any other Middle Eastern country. Lent accused Lowenstein of opposing funds for a Hadassah hospital in Israel; the appropriation was buried in a military spending bill Lowenstein opposed. Lent avoided talking about Vietnam except to reiterate that "Mr. Lowenstein echoes Hanoi completely in his call for unilateral withdrawal." Lowenstein was, he concluded, "the Pied Piper of youth" and "the chief architect of the Black Panthers" who "commends draft evaders."

Inflamed by Lent's demagoguery, Ray Gimmler, a New York City Fire Department captain who lived in the district, organized a "Silent Majority for Lent" which mailed 10,000 letters to policemen, firemen, veterans, and members of fraternal organizations, asking them to help defeat "our New Left Congressman." "There was all that shit-lying literature," Jenny remarks bitterly. "They did it to Frank Graham. He was philosophical but Al was not. Al told me, 'I'm going to fight them all the way. If they get away with this here, they'll get away with it everywhere.' And he started talking about 'sinister forces' and 'the dark forces' and about 'how the consequences of defying them are growing.'"

Lowenstein continued to vote against the defense budget. When $2 billion were appropriated to maintain U.S. bases in Spain, he lamented, "I can't get a nickel from the government to help the Long Island Railroad but they see fit to give away $2 billion for the privilege of maintaining bases in Spain." When the vote came up in the House in 1970 on the defense budget, it contained an extra billion dollars for the Nationalist Chinese to buy an air force, which, the Pentagon argued, was essential for their security. "What happens," Lowenstein retorted, "when Taiwan bombs the mainland with that air force? Who's going to protect the island of Formosa from retaliation? It's certainly not going to be Madame Chiang on her broomstick. It's going to be our kids going back to the Asian continent to fight another war."

Rev. Paul G. Driscoll of Our Lady Queen of Martyrs Church believed that the hostility to Lowenstein did not spring entirely from his liberal positions. "The fact is that there is a deep hatred of Mr. Lowenstein within the Catholic community . . .," he lamented. "The intensity of that hatred has to be experienced to be believed. . . . Now why is Mr. Lowenstein so hated? Is it because he is a 'radical liberal?' Or is it because he is Jewish? Both sides are involved, but I am afraid the anti-Semitic reason is more significant than many of us would like to believe."

Lent charged that it was Lowenstein who started the name-calling "by calling me 'chicken hawk,' 'gerrymander Lent,' 'mini-Agnew,' and the 'Mendel Rivers of the 1990s' . . . I didn't even know who Mendel Rivers was, but I found out he was a Southern congressman who's a racist and a drunk."

Bishop Walter P. Kellenberg of the powerful Catholic Diocese of Rockville Centre sent out a pastoral letter reminding Long Island Catholics that abortion was a violation of religious doctrine. The letter, which was read at all masses, suggested that "Catholics do all that you can in November to restore respect for life . . . and to encourage our legislators in the federal government to reject attempts to pass a national abortion law." Lent came out against the Packwood liberal abortion legislation. Incensed, he stated that he hoped the church "will not go any further than it has in getting involved in partisan politics."

When Lent, Right to Life candidate Vincent Carey, and Lowenstein appeared at debates, Lowenstein, who was prochoice, would tell the audience that anyone who didn't want to vote for him because he was too liberal, should support Carey. Carey meanwhile continued to speak favorably of Lowenstein and to denounce Lent, who had challenged Carey's petitions: "Although I wouldn't vote for either of them, if I weren't in the race . . . I must say Lowenstein is a warmer, more honest individual. You can deal with him and he listens. You can't deal with Lent. I'd much rather have Lowenstein reelected than to see Lent rewarded with a congressional seat." When Lent heard this, he insisted that Carey had been placed in the race by Lowenstein "in cahoots with a man of the cloth."

The campaign, according to Greg Craig, threw almost everything into Massapequa, where Lowenstein had 60,000 new Republican voters in his district. "Al said if he got forty percent of Massapequa and Massapequa Park, he would win," Craig asserts. "Long Beach would come out in heavy numbers. He got it, but the Democrats didn't vote for Al in sufficient numbers. They voted for James Buckley and were drawn away."

But Lowenstein pointed with pride to the "Buckley-Lowenstein" bumper stickers that could be seen in the district. It was evidence to him that he could win over the right. The reason for the erosion of the Democratic support, the NDC believed—with some justification— was that the regular Nassau County Democratic organization which was close to Margiotta and which distrusted the independent Lowenstein, was doing what it could to undermine him. Lowenstein did not compromise on the issues in the campaign. (When he sent in Thomas Clancy, a Jesuit priest, to campaign for him in Massapequa, he told Clancy "not to cut corners with the truth.") But he also had some geniunely conservative positions; he favored the death penalty, for instance. One voter said, "I feel both men are so close on everything, it's a tossup. I will probably vote for Lent." Another observed that she was "amazed at the contrast in their styles. Lent was cool, calm, and collected. Lowenstein was too emotional and talked too fast."

Driving Lowenstein's grey Le Mans convertible, chauffeuring the candidate to neighborhood speaking engagements, Gerry Twombley found that Lowenstein would often become furious over a Lent radio spot or some piece of Lent literature, then blow his speech because he was so upset. In Twombley's opinion, Lowenstein "overreacted" to Lent's accusations and allowed himself to become flustered. "The biggest criticism about Al during the campaign and after," Twombley relates, "was that he had spent too much time explaining each and every accusation. . . . He would often, in front of overflowing audiences at debates and forums, burst out in a heated lashing of his opponent. Lent told me later this was playing into his hands. . . . Besides giving him recognition, Lowenstein's emotional speeches gave Lent the opportunity to shift the emphasis of the campaign from issues to personalities."

Lowenstein was preoccupied by his effort to look like a "Middle American." "Al was fanatical about having haircuts," Twombley relates. "He got one at least once every ten days. He was fanatical also about shaving and not having a beard, or any hair on his face." Lowenstein also took to wearing an American flag on his lapel as he tirelessly shook hands throughout the district. "He was too defensive about not being an extremist," Twombley argues. "He should have concentrated on why he should be elected. We didn't feel that he had to explain his positions to his staff. He didn't have to tell us why he was not an apologist for the violent left. It was Lent's campaign literature that did it to him. Lent's first piece drove Al crazy. There was a photo showing a dejected-looking Lowenstein as though he was already beaten. Al was incensed. He was observing retarded children at the time the picture was taken. And Lent knew it was all phony."

Lent's tactics were denounced in the press. Lent, in turn, charged that Lowenstein was denying accusations that Lent had not made, in order to make him look like a mud-slinger. Lent then went to the Fair Campaign Practices Committee on the grounds that the attacks from Lowenstein were designed "in order that he would appear the victim of an ugly campaign rather than its creator." Lent also charged that a growing list of "Republicans and Independents for Lowenstein was inaccurate" and contained "names of dead persons and registered Democrats." Lent did not, however, request binding arbitration, thus avoiding an opinion on the charges and leaving the committee with the power only to analyze the campaign.

Lowenstein then went to the Fair Campaign Practices Committee himself, submitting various pieces of Lent literature. Appearing at a news conference on October 27 in New York with House Democratic leader Carl Albert of Oklahoma, Lowenstein challenged Lent to consent to binding arbitration and said, referring to his opponent's campaign, "This may not be the most dishonest campaign but it is the most cynical." Albert added that "the campaign against Al Lowenstein is using the big lie technique. . . . If successful this will really polarize America and divide its citizens."

Lent shot back: "Al Lowenstein is the toughest political gut fighter in the United States. He destroyed a president of the United States. For him to say that I'm picking on him is the height of absurdity. I'm just a country lawyer."

Just before the last weekend of the campaign, Lent consented to arbitration. Meeting over the weekend, the committee concluded on Sunday that there was too much literature and too little time to make a decision on either of the candidates' charges. The campaign ended, with the signs of both candidates being torn down in what Gerry Twombley describes as a "demolition contest."

Lowenstein's campaign got a lift from the birth of his daughter, Katherine Eleanor (traditional values), and from a string of newspaper endorsements from district newspapers as well as *Newsday* and *The New York Times*. "More in sorrow than in anger," wrote the *Long Island Graphic*, "we must comment on the conduct of Senator Norman Lent's campaign for Congress. Never before have we known him to stoop to smearing an opponent instead of campaigning on the issues, which he has done this time with a vengeance." In their endorsement, *The New York Times* stated that "in Representative Allard K. Lowenstein, Congress has a brilliant and imaginative member with unusual capacity for future service. We sincerely hope his district chooses him over state Senator Norman Lent, a moderate Republican with a respectable record in Albany, whose campaign against Mr. Lowenstein has nevertheless been marred by grossly unfair tactics." *Newsday*, the most influential Long Island paper, wrote that "no vote cast . . . will be more important than the one given to Allard Lowenstein. . . . In a real sense, the residents of the Fifth Congressional District are being asked to vote on a national candidate. Lowenstein's efforts to end that dreary and endless war in Vietnam are a matter of public record. As is his tireless work on behalf of the civil rights movement." Describing an incident at Hofstra University, where radical lawyer William Kunstler "had fanned the embers of student outrage," the endorsement pointed to Lowenstein's reasoned appeal to the students to "work within the system," adding, "It was the start of a crusade. In campus after campus Lowenstein kept the flames from becoming a conflagration." Lowenstein was, *Newsday* asserted, "a builder of bridges between generations, between ideologies, between classes. During his two years in Congress, he has been more than a lawmaker; he has been a peacemaker."

But the *New York Daily News*, read by many in the district, denounced Lowenstein in its endorsement of Lent. "Lowenstein's main interest as a Congressman," it declared, "as it was before his election, lies in shoving the Democratic Party into the brackish political backwaters of radicalism. He is one of the original Vietnam bugout boys, a fervent apologist for militants, a big spender on budget questions and one of the more profuse bleeding hearts when it comes to the 'rights' of criminals. Fifth District voters would serve their own interests and do the nation a huge favor, by electing Norman Lent."

Lowenstein's buddy from the Old Left, Jimmy Wechsler, made a valiant effort to educate the voters in Lowenstein's district. "Anyone remotely familiar with Lowenstein's history knows that he has long been a major target of New Left epithets and abuse precisely because he rejected the politics of 'confrontation' and terrorism," Wechsler pleaded. "At crucial moments Lowenstein has courageously risked the status he long ago acquired among the new political generation by refusing to compromise on the issue of nonviolence." Wechsler sensed that the dream in which he believed and which he shared with his younger friend was fading as the right gained momentum. "At moments one had a feeling of sadness about the contest," he wrote. But Wechsler still hoped that Lowenstein's "fighting spirit" combined with his "implausible" energy would turn it around. Calling the election a "plebiscite of sanity and decency," he concluded, "But he has already transformed a 'lost cause' into an inspirational battle."

At the end, Lowenstein was openly rejected by people he had appealed to. Campaigning in Massapequa, Jim Bouton would stick out his hand and say, "Hello, I'm Jim Bouton, I'd sure like to shake your hand," and people would say, "Sure." But, after a few seconds talking baseball, when Bouton would say, "I'd like you to meet Congressman Lowenstein," they would refuse to shake Lowenstein's hand. "I couldn't believe it," Bouton said over and over, "They wouldn't shake his hand."

Lowenstein had hoped to get Republican votes and counter Lent's attacks through the support of his friend the former Congressman Donald Rumsfeld, whom Nixon had named head of the Office of Economic Opportunity. Rumsfeld had made a helpful statement earlier in the campaign, calling Lowenstein "one hell of a good man," "a responsible voice speaking out about issues that trouble him," "a man who has always advocated working within the political system and I certainly have never heard him advocate the use of violence." The *Long Island Press* had blunted Lent's attack by quoting Rumsfeld and criticizing Lent's literature which portrayed Lowenstein as a violent revolutionary.

Lowenstein had gone out on a limb for Rumsfeld in Congress, assuring blacks that he was the right man to head OEO. When Nixon began to dismember the poverty program, Lowenstein came under attack, but he stuck by Rumsfeld, praising him in the House. Then, when Lowenstein turned to him for help, Rumsfeld publicly praised Lowenstein and promised an endorsement but later, ceding to pressure from the White House and local Republicans, wrote a letter, retracting any endorsement of Lowenstein. Lent made public the letter from Rumsfeld, who had not warned Lowenstein that it was coming. "Rumsfeld stabbed Al in the back at the end of the campaign," Gerry Twombley insists. "He endorsed Lent right before the election, and Al never quite forgave him."

Black voters did not come across for Lowenstein, either. Although Aaron Henry, Charles Evers, and Fanny Lou Hamer supported him and Andrew Young campaigned for him in Freeport where there was a large black population, blacks in the district remained apathetic, either not bothering to register or not coming out to vote.

"In retrospect," Gerry Twombley asserts, "I believe Al failed at his attempt to educate the voters. People just did not want to hear a lecture on the workings of Congress. They wanted to hear what their congressman had done for them."

The campaign workers were exhausted. They were drained not only by the long hours but by the sense of swimming upstream against the strong current of reaction that had gripped the country. Rick Weidman, who hadn't slept for several days, was "all burned out at the end." Alone with Lowenstein on the Sunday night before the election, Weidman told him that he would lose. "Al was angry, but I told him he would be five thousand votes short."

On a rainy election day, Lowenstein drove through the district to thank his volunteers in the storefronts. In the middle of a crowd of students, Lowenstein embraced his workers, running his hands through their hair, kissing them, and being kissed. It was, wrote *Newsday*, "a scene reminiscent of the best moments of Robert Kennedy's race for the Presidency."

On election night, over 100 volunteers who had been working in Massapequa gathered after pulling out the last voter. They milled around waiting for the returns at the Brooklyn Avenue shopping mall where a trailer dispensed refreshments. Among them was Greg Craig, who had taken time off from Yale Law School to work on the campaign. It came like a blow to the solar plexus when they heard Lowenstein was losing. Tears came to their eyes, and quietly they got into their cars and drove to Lowenstein's headquarters in Rockville Centre, where the "victory party" was to have been held.

Lowenstein was defeated by 10,000 votes out of 178,000 cast. At Carl Hoppl's restaurant, he made a quick concession speech to the crowd of young students, telling them that "if everyone in this room could have voted, we would have won . . . which means the future belongs to us." The band struck up the Notre Dame marching song (Lowenstein knew all the college fight songs by heart and loved to have them played), and he continued: "They could only beat us by distorting our views. The district would not have rejected us had they not been confused. We must look at this defeat as a warning. The loss of one congressman is not important. We know we must work hard now to reveal the issues so when the stakes are really high, as they will be in 1972 in the election of the president, we will elect a candidate on his merits." Lowenstein then sat forlornly, Jenny at his side. Behind them were the drums of the band that was to have played the rousing songs of victory. It was too much. They could not wait to get out.

By the time Greg Craig and the workers arrived, Lowenstein was already leaving. Craig was displeased with him. "Al was walking out after giving the concession speech. He gave it before his volunteers, his dearest friends, got there. Over a dozen old-time loyalists were there. It was a quick concession. He should have waited. We were all in this with him."

The final figures, after a recanvass by the Nassau County Board of Elections, were 76,127 votes for Lowenstein on the Democratic line and 8,645 on the Liberal line, for a total of 84,772. Lent, as a Republican-Conservative had 93,841, a margin of 9,069 votes. James Wechsler wrote:

> If the district had been constituted as it was in 1968, Lowenstein would have won by more than 5,000 votes—or twice as many as his margin when he staged what was regarded as an upset on Long Island. . . . Finally, and perhaps most astonishingly, Lowenstein defeated Lent and ran even with James Buckley in many sectors even while Buckley was running well against both his opponents in the Senate race. Lowenstein ran nearly 10 percent ahead of gubernatorial nominee Arthur Goldberg.

And *The New Yorker* noted that Lowenstein's "vote on the Democratic line exceeded by about five thousand that of his opponent Norman Lent . . . on the Republican line. Mr. Lent's margin of victory came from his votes on the Conservative line, where he was helped by the extremely strong showing of that party's successful candidate for the United States Senate, James Buckley."

Lowenstein interpreted his defeat as a victory of sorts. "The fact that I lost worries me less than the possibility that the results in my district will be misread," he told *The New Yorker*. "One of the most satisfying aspects of the campaign for me was that I had the opportunity to go down to Washington in the middle of it and vote against the crime bill and the military appropriations bill. A lot of people came up to me on the floor and said, 'For God's sake, don't vote against these bills, Al! You'll never survive.' I think the figures show something quite different, which is that you *can* stand against the war and against the Administration's way of dealing with the so-called social issues and you *can* survive in the face of that."

Lowenstein believed his defeat had been caused not by his positions but by the distortions of the campaign, as did *The New Yorker*. Recalling that Lowenstein had been called "an echo of Hanoi," "an inflamer of youth," and "the chief apologist for the Black Panthers," it observed that these were "odd accusations since Mr. Lowenstein is a convinced anti-Communist, the leading advocate of student participation in electoral politics, and a critic of the Panthers' infatuation with violence, and since these stands have resulted in much ill feeling toward him on the extreme left."

Lowenstein himself observed:

> There was an ominous warning in this campaign, and that is that the ugliness can get so intense that it confuses great numbers of voters. The possibility exists that the same thing might happen that happened in the nineteen-fifties, when people were swept away by distortions. The fact that this approach was used here in the suburbs of New York City this year was a surprise to me. In the case of the Fifth District, I think it's important to stress that while it hurt us in areas where we weren't able to get the facts to the people, it wouldn't have worked without the gerrymander. It didn't work in the country at large, and I don't think it will work in 1972. You just can't gerrymander the whole country. . . . The lame ducks like me will quack and the lame quacks will duck. In political terms, I'm going to work, beginning right away, to see to it that the ugliness that was unleashed all over the country is turned out of office in 1972. We have taken the measure of these people, and they can be defeated.

Lowenstein took off for Vietnam. As he was leaving the House, the doorman told him he could still use the House gymnasium. "I guess I have nothing to worry about," he quipped. His final efforts in the House were to oppose military aid to the junta in Greece and to fight the seniority system. On his last day in office, Lowenstein held a press conference on his findings from Vietnam.

Lowenstein was given a final tribute by his fellow congressmen. "Many House members seemed astonished that he could perform as he had and still be defeated," *Newsday* reporter Edward Hershey observed: "It was as if his loss had hammered home to some of them what the Gentleman from New York had been saying about their system for two years. And more than 90 of them showed up at a reception in Lowenstein's honor after the election."

Octogenarian Emanual Celler, the "dean" of the House and a representative from Brooklyn for decades, astonished his colleagues not only by appearing but by requesting to speak. "Allard Lowenstein has provided the yeast for Congress," Celler said. "Without yeast there can be no ferment. Without ferment there is no progress. Our nation has remained so great because we have always been able to progress. Without progress there is stagnation and our institutions wither and die. It is because of men like Allard Lowenstein that we progress."

House Speaker John McCormack, against whom Lowenstein had fought to reform the congressional system, came as well. "I can't remember any new member who contributed so much to the Congress in his first two years," he admitted.

Statements of praise for Lowenstein were inserted in the *Congressional Record*. On December 17, a special order of sixty minutes was held on the floor of the House to honor Lowenstein. Representative Jonathan Bingham of the Bronx, one of Lowenstein's allies in the civil rights movement, was the most extravagant in summing up the sentiments of the House: "Mr. Speaker, I suspect that no freshman member of the House since Henry Clay—and not excluding Abraham Lincoln or John F. Kennedy—has made more of an impression on this body than has Allard Lowenstein."

There was, as always, a campaign deficit to pay off. A fund-raiser was organized by Harriet Eisman and Mrs. Myron Harkavy at the Atlantic Beach Hotel, with actor George Segal as master of ceremonies and Senator-elect John Tunney as chief speaker. Just before the dinner, Lowenstein and Jenny had flown to Boston for her brother Charlie's funeral. Described in the papers as "a young auto accident victim," he had in reality been a suicide.

Lowenstein prepared his speech for the dinner. "Knowing what to say or how to say it has never been a problem for Lowenstein," wrote Ed Hershey, "which has led to a certain puzzlement among his associates. It runs against the grain of their liberal iconoclasm to accept even Al Lowenstein as Christ."

At the dinner, a sixteen-year-year old high school girl from Massapequa named Randee Flug, who had rung door bells for Lowenstein, spoke on behalf of the high school volunteers. "Politicians, writers, and parents, they all try to understand why students work in or out of the system, but they don't really understand," she said. "It's not the disappointment, the knowledge that what we are trying to accomplish fails, that convinces us to work outside the system. But rather it's disillusionment." And that occurs, she explained, when after investing their hopes, their energies, and their confidence in a candidate, it becomes evident that "what he said and what he meant were opposite things."

Lowenstein was different, she said, because in him "we saw a man who above all else honestly cared about other people." Disgusted after the invasion of Cambodia and Kent State, at the age of sixteen she had decided that it was impossible to fight the system. "It was later on in June that over the radio I heard Al Lowenstein speaking," she went on. "He talked about fighting and not simply failing because we haven't tried hard enough. I'd heard plenty of politicians saying that, but this was different. He not only said it, and meant it, but he was doing it. He was fighting and against all the odds set up against him in the election. Well, I still look at our system as a giant, inhuman machine but he's given me a new hope, and watching Al fight has given me a new spirit to fight."

When it was finally Lowenstein's turn, he repeated in defiance his new battle cry. "They can gerrymander a district," he shouted, "but they can't gerrymander a country!"

56

Lowenstein opened a community office in Oceanside on Long Island's South Shore. Harriet Eisman, whom he paid to run it, assembled a staff of volunteers from the old Dissenting Democrats. While the volunteers finished up projects begun by Lowenstein's congressional district office, Eisman booked him to speak at universities. "He was speaking around the country," she explained. "He never made less than fifty thousand that I know. And in those days, fifty was a little better than it is now." Lowenstein was also appointed to the faculty of the Yale School of Urban Studies and made a Visiting Fellow at the John F. Kennedy School of Government at Harvard.

Appearing on "Meet the Press" early in 1971, Lowenstein said, "In my view, the general feeling in this country for basic social change is greater than at any time since the bottom of the Depression." In May, with the help of Joseph Rauh and James Wechsler, he was elected chairman of Americans for Democratic Action. Dolores Mitchell of Boston, who was to have been elected chairman, pulled out when Lowenstein's candidacy was announced, though she remained angry with Rauh. "But you know," Rauh observes, "you couldn't beat Al at a liberal meeting." According to Rauh, Lowenstein, as national chairman, "got more kids interested in it than at any other time in ADA's history. At one dinner, he asked one side of the room to stand up and they were all kids. He got young people involved. It was too bad he had to defeat the first woman to be head of a political organization."

Lowenstein was not an administrator or a fund-raiser for ADA, but a "spokesman." Disorganized, he would frequently have the office cancel an appearance if he decided he would prefer to be somewhere else. Lowenstein was engaged in a massive campaign to register all the eighteen- to twenty-one-year-olds eligible to vote upon the ratification of the Twenty-third Amendment, expected that summer. He believed this effort would alter the American political landscape and drive Richard Nixon from the White House. He was, in fact, planning a rerun of "Dump Johnson"; this time, it was "Dump Nixon."

The first news of Lowenstein's plan appeared in an article by influential political writer David Broder in the March 25, 1971, issue of the *Washington Post*. "Going After the 23 Million New Voters," the headline read. "Lowenstein Plans Rerun of 'Dumping the President.'" There was a photograph of Lowenstein looking dead serious. "We may end up with an election in which Barry Goldwater looks like a popular hero compared to what Richard Nixon can get at the polls," Lowenstein stated, "and I don't think one should assume that, facing that prospect, Nixon would necessarily be a candidate." Expressing his concern about the prevailing "cynicism about whether elections mean anything," he said he found the mood, particularly on campuses, to be one of "disillusionment and resentment" with the Nixon administration but of "little enthusiasm for any of the visible candidates" against the president. Lowenstein indicated that the "vacuum and frustration" and the growing alienation could lead to a new round of marches and demonstrations which, in his view, would only serve to help Nixon "by dividing public opinion, not on the wisdom of his own policies, but on the tactics of his most extreme critics."

If the young people's distrust of politics could be overcome, a liberal election victory would become a real possibility, he argued. "For the first time since the depths of the Depression, we are in a position to assemble a majority coalition for basic changes not only in foreign policy, but in distribution of income and resources at home," he repeated. The opinion polls showed vast support for an early end to the war, he maintained, adding that with the exception of Senator Henry Jackson of Washington, all the major Democratic candidates for president supported what he termed "the views of the Kennedy-McCarthy heresy of 1968." Within the Republican party, Lowenstein insisted opposition to Nixon was "far more numerous and prestigious than the Democrats who were willing to be involved in the anti-Johnson movement at the same point four years ago." The key was to register the 23 million young voters. "If only 5 million of them vote," Lowenstein stressed, "Nixon will get half of them. But the more we can register over that number, the bigger the coalition for change."

Lowenstein announced a Patriot's Day Rally in Providence, Rhode Island, on the 196th anniversary of Paul Revere's ride. Scheduled for

April 18, the rally was to launch his bipartisan drive to "Dump Nixon," with leading Republicans and Democrats joining him on the platform. If Lowenstein's plan sounded farfetched, Broder wrote, "it should be remembered that they laughed at Lowenstein four years ago when he first sketched his plans for the 'Dump Johnson' drive. Since he lost his Long Island House seat to a Republican gerrymander last November, Lowenstein has been . . . touring the country on his usual frantic schedule, organizing for the spring offensive."

Allied with Lowenstein in "Dump Nixon" were Republican Congressmen Pete McCloskey, who opposed Nixon for the Republican nomination, and Donald Riegle, who later became a Democrat, and former Senator Charles Goodell. Leading Democrats seeking the nomination to oppose Nixon included Senators Ed Muskie of Maine, George McGovern of South Dakota, and Birch Bayh of Indiana, and Mayor John Lindsay of New York. This time, though, Lowenstein was not behind any particular candidate. In fact, he indicated that he was thinking of running for president himself. The only Democratic candidate he said he would not support was Jackson, and he dismissed the idea of a fourth party which, he said, "makes utterly no sense . . . when we're at the point where we're clearly inheriting the Democratic party."

Political pundits criticized the strategy, claiming that no matter how many eighteen- to twenty-one-year-olds Lowenstein registered, at least half of them would vote the way their parents did and would support Nixon. And Curtis Gans, who had organized "Dump Johnson" with Lowenstein, looked at the effort critically for other reasons. "Lowenstein decided to take unilateral credit for Dump Johnson," he insists. "Others got expunged from the record. It became one glorious man fighting the evils of Lyndon Johnson. Dump Nixon was a crude attempt to play on his Dump Johnson notoriety. Dump Nixon was a fraud. It was a way to get publicity for himself. His personal ambition was more obvious." Further, as Barney Frank indicates, "'dumping' assumes you were there at the construction. He didn't have the leverage against Nixon."

During 1971, Lowenstein addressed the New York Law Associates on Wall Street and explained his plan for a "Registration Summer" to organize young people to vote. He told them that if you could register a reasonable number of the 23 million new young voters, you could get them to vote in the primaries against Nixon and control the election. You could use the war, he explained, to get them involved on both sides. He also announced that McCloskey was going to challenge Nixon and that he, Lowenstein, wanted a bipartisan effort. He was on the Democratic side, he explained, with McCloskey and Riegle on the Republican.

In the audience was Nick Littlefield, a young law associate with the firm of Hughes, Hubbard & Reed. A graduate of Milton Academy, Harvard, Penn Law School, and the London School of Economics, Littlefield was a liberal Republican from Rhode Island who had served as campaign manager for Republican John Chaffee in his successful campaign for the state's governorship. The senior partner of Littlefield's firm was Orville Schell, a leading "dove" who knew Lowenstein and was helping to organize the upper crust of the legal profession against Nixon's policies in Southeast Asia.

After Cambodia and Kent State, Littlefield had become involved in the New York Lawyers Committee to End the War, Schell's organization. It raised over $200,000 for antiwar candidates, including Lowenstein, who received the most money from the committee in 1970. Littlefield came out to Long Island five or six times to canvass for Lowenstein but did not meet him. He did meet Jenny, and toured the district with Lowenstein's volunteers.

Littlefield was overwhelmed by Lowenstein's speech to the law associates. "I was so thrilled and dazzled by this man," he recounts. "He combined all his intelligence and articulateness about ending the war plus humor. It was intellect and humor combined."

A mutual friend arranged for Littlefield and Lowenstein to meet. "I met Al at Granson's restaurant," Littlefield relates. "He described the voter registration drive. I was dazzled by his commitment and ability to translate it into action." Littlefield was, in turn, attractive to Lowenstein because of the role he had played as Chaffee's campaign manager in Rhode Island, and Lowenstein asked him to run the registration program. Lowenstein was working with two leading Democrats who helped raise funds for Hubert Humphrey, Abe Feinberg and Morris Rosenberg, who put up $50,000 each. "They were both affected by their children who wanted to stop the war," Littlefield states. "The plan was to have rallies and conferences across the country. We would galvanize kids in each state to run their own registration drive. We would provide the seed money and the seed organization."

Littlefield approached Orville Schell for organizational help and was granted a half-time leave of absence permitting him to work for the firm from 9:00 until 12:00 at half pay. From noon to 5:00, he worked on voter registration. Meanwhile, Lowenstein traveled the country, visiting campuses and compiling a list of 200 students who wanted to participate. Littlefield then interviewed them and reduced the list to 75 paid interns for the training program in New York. This was the first time that Lowenstein ever paid his recruits, although some refused the money, a subsistence wage, and insisted on working for nothing. They were housed, fed, and transported by participating local communities. Among them were some of the best students from the best schools and universities in the country as well as top athletes and recognized leaders.

As the Registration Summer Project interns spread out across the country to twenty-one states, they set up local committees to mobilize the millions of first-time voters to register and participate in the convention-delegate selection process in both parties. Each regional committee carried a different name to give the drive an aura of spontaneity: "Register for Peace" in Los Angeles and Iowa, "Citizens for Alternatives Now" on Long Island, "Countdown 72" in Texas and Kansas, "Youth in Politics" in Florida, "Bi-Partisan Caucus to Stop the War" in Minnesota, "Register for a New America" in New Jersey. But everywhere the message was the same: "Beat Nixon, stop the war, insist on truth in government and turn the country around through the electoral process."

During the first phase of the project there was a series of mass bipartisan registration rallies around the country, starting with the one in Rhode Island. In July and August, the interns worked with local committees to organize youth political leadership conferences which stressed political instruction with seminars on legal and technical obstacles to registration, press relations, and organizing of special interest groups. The drive continued in the fall with more registration rallies.

Lowenstein and McCloskey spoke and helped organize in almost every state. Their list of speakers included Senators Bayh, Cranston, McGovern, Muskie, Harris, and Chiles, Representatives Riegle, Conyers, Abzug, Culver, and Chisolm, Governors Docking and Askew, Mayors Lindsay, White, and Flaherty, and prominent antiwar figures Charles Goodell, John Kerry, Daniel Ellsberg, George Wiley, Frank Mankiewicz, Jack Conway, and Eugene McCarthy.

Out of this movement, Lowenstein intended to create a "Youth Caucus" which would ally itself with the already formed Women's and Black Caucuses to influence delegate selection. The final event, from which the Youth Caucus was to spring was the Emergency Conference for New Voters in Chicago, spearheaded by the Association of Student Governments and organized by Lowenstein himself. The goal was the defeat of Richard Nixon and "the selection of national leadership prepared to change the direction of the country."

Political commentator Nicholas Von Hoffman predicted that Lowenstein would have no impact on the Republican party. McCloskey, he asserted, would never be a Republican Eugene McCarthy, given the nature of those who voted in Republican primaries. "They fail to understand that the party that would nominate Nixon will renominate him." Nixon would not pull out as Johnson had, he insisted, not even under pressure from Ronald Reagan, the most dangerous Republican candidate. "That's not going to happen either—Nixon isn't smart enough to know when he's beaten. If he were, he wouldn't be president today."

But Von Hoffman saw Lowenstein as a key factor in the coming presidential election because of his nationwide effort to register the youth vote. "If he succeeds," Von Hoffman wrote, "he will be much more important to this election than any of the candidates whose names have been mentioned here. If he can do it, and that means registering not all, but upwards of twelve million in this vote pool, he will scatter Humphrey, Jackson, the whole New Deal–Great Frontier–Fair Society groups; he will imperil Muskie and push the party in the direction of a McGovern."

In one issue, *Look* magazine featured statements by both Riegle and Lowenstein in support of the movement to depose Nixon. Riegle was backing McCloskey. Lowenstein, who had no specific candidate, argued that Johnson's policies had been rejected by the voters but that the gains made in the primaries were "destroyed" by the assassinations of Robert Kennedy and Martin Luther King, Jr., and the "president who was elected continued the rejected policies of his predecessor." Concluded Lowenstein, "Just as President Johnson broke his 1964 pledge to end the war, President Nixon has abandoned his 1968 promise to end the war. Of course, more than the war is involved, for the faith of Americans in their form of government is imperiled when Presidents are unable or unwilling to keep their word on matters of primary concern to the people."

Nick Littlefield was particularly useful to Lowenstein in kicking off the effort because of his connections in Rhode Island as a friend of the governor. At the first registration rally on April 18, which Littlefield had arranged to be held on the front steps of the statehouse in Providence, Bayh, Muskie, McCloskey, Abzug, and Lowenstein exhorted a crowd of 6,000 to vote Nixon out of the White House. There was an all-day conference on the issues and considerable press coverage, and according to Littlefield, "It was a big success."

Lowenstein then flew to Indianapolis to join former New York Republican Senator Charles Goodell on May 22 for the next event. But Republican Governor Edgar Whitcomb insisted that a $50,000 bond be posted and that the committee assume unlimited liability for any damage done at the rally on state property. Meanwhile, the state police began broadcasting warnings that any hitchhiker headed for Indianapolis before the rally would be detained until they had received FBI clearance. Local papers suggested that the rally was Communist-inspired. As a result, although the bond requirement was dropped after Mayor Richard Lugar agreed that the rally could be held in a city park, only some 2,000 people turned up, and although Lowenstein stirred the crowd with raking criticism of Nixon, Nicholas Von Hoffman called it a "flop." He wrote, "But what's so interesting is the authorities' fear and pre-emptive repression. The fear shows that he may be getting somewhere and the repression can ignite a counterforce that surely will."

Lowenstein was under scrutiny by the White House. "Because of Lowenstein's success in 1968 with the McCarthy forces," wrote White House operative John Caulfied in a memo, "an alert should go up if he surfaces with McCloskey." And on September 9, 1971, in an "eyes only" memo to Counsel to the President John Dean, Charles Colson, Nixon's hatchet man, placed Lowenstein number seven on the White House's infamous "enemies list," checking his name in blue as one "to whom I would give top priority." Lowenstein had kept his own list in Mississippi with the names of "those to be examined." Now he was on Nixon's list.

In Minneapolis, where Lowenstein shared the podium with Eugene McCarthy, 27,000 filled the hockey stadium at the Metropolitan Sports Center, and Littlefield called it "the most powerful event" he had ever experienced. McCarthy called for reform in the Republican and Democratic parties but added that "there is no magic in the two-party system." Lowenstein seemed pained by McCarthy's suggestion of a fourth-party movement. "We're here," Lowenstein shouted, thumping the rostrum, "because we're going to work for a country where the eighteen-year-olds won't have to choose between exile, jail, or going off to die in an unjust war. We are not Democrats using Republicans. We are not Republicans using Democrats. We are Americans using the electoral process to end the war and reclaim this country." At the end of the long afternoon, the thousands stood in darkness and softly joined John Denver in singing "America the Beautiful." Of the 27,000 present, 22,000 signed pledge cards to register.

On June 13, Lowenstein was on Long Island for an afternoon rally on the asphalt in front of the Mineola courthouse. Lowenstein mixed with the crowd of uncomfortable, sweating people who were signing registration pledge cards. "We are the heart of the land," Lowenstein told them. Afterward, he told Nicholas Von Hoffman, who was following him around the way David Halberstam had followed him in 1968, "The other day somebody said, 'We've tried everything and nothing works.' I told him, 'Don't feel sorry for yourselves. You act like you've thrown yourselves on spears. You haven't done much but march a few times and knock on a few doors.'" Commented Von Hoffman, "That's Allard K. He has a certain toughness."

The California rally failed to materialize. Instead, "Register for Peace," organized by Lowenstein, sent volunteers to the public beaches to register voters. McCloskey waded out into the ocean up to his knees to direct a registrar as he signed up two girls who had been swimming.

Arriving late for the Youth in Politics Conference in Florida, Lowenstein explained to the crowd still assembled shortly before midnight that plane connections had been difficult in his cross-country trip back from the funeral of Soledad brother George Jackson in California. Jackson, a close friend of radical black activist Angela Davis, was killed attempting a daring escape from prison after someone had smuggled a gun to him. Lowenstein's friend Stephen Bingham was accused of smuggling the gun to Jackson and fled.

The ratification of the Twenty-third Amendment in July gave the movement momentum as the students returned to the campuses that fall. With the chances of dumping Nixon in the Republican primaries fading (McCloskey would get only two delegates), Lowenstein gave an impassioned speech at the University of Pittsburgh calling on youth to exercise its power in the next Democratic convention to see that the country had "a real alternative" to the president. Folksinger Peter Yarrow, who was traveling with Lowenstein, sang and announced that "this whole rally is futile, meaningless, unless you pick up your body and register. We've marched long enough. Now we're going to vote." Flora Lewis wrote, "The last time I saw that kind of crowd in a park across from a Hilton hotel was in Chicago, 1968. Everything was different this time—peaceful, polite, interested more than impassioned."

On September 17, a rally at Rutgers University in New Brunswick, New Jersey, attracted thousands, and then, by midfall, "it wound down" according to Nick Littlefield. "The final event was to be a National Youth Vote Convention at Loyola University in Chicago in December, with two to three thousand delegates from each state sponsored by 180 student body presidents. This is what ultimately created the 'Youth Caucus' at the 1972 Democratic convention. I was a physical and mental wreck from carrying the organizational details from New York. Al was traveling. The interns weren't paid on time. I worked twenty hours a day and had to resume full-time work at my law firm in November. I was broke. It took a tremendous personal toll. You don't see your friends, you go broke, you don't exercise, all kinds of people are mad at you, but it is worth it. It was the most rewarding thing I had done, but I wanted some peace."

The final Chicago conference at Loyola ended in crisis, as Greg Craig relates: "Three times as many people came as expected, and they registered 7,000 people. It was heavily covered by the press and the presidential candidates. And it became like the sixties NSA congresses or civil rights meetings, with the young blacks who became militant. This happened in Chicago. There was anger by the young blacks that insufficient attention was being paid to black people. A series of demands were formulated by the Black Caucus, who took over the stage. They discounted democratic procedures to impose their agenda, just the way it happened in a series of NSA congresses.

They stated their position. 'Unless the conference elected a black chairman and met their demands, the meeting would not go forward.'

"Al faced them down. It was very scary and tense and a difficult moment for Al. His belief in procedures was in conflict with his sensitivity to the needs of blacks. There was a head-to-head confrontation and violence was threatened to Al."

This would be Lowenstein's last real showdown with the militants and radicals. On the national level, Democratic contenders were becoming irritated with Lowenstein because the only candidate he openly praised was Pete McCloskey, a Republican. Lowenstein countered by saying that he had endorsed no Democrat because as national chairman of ADA and as leader of the national voter-registration drive, he should show no preference. "It seems clear that the Presidential campaign will not yield him a national podium or focus for his views," Mary Breasted of *The New York Times* wrote on Sunday, March 17, 1972. "His natural constituency—the young—is not enthusiastic about any of the candidates." In 1971, ADA had voted to impeach Nixon. Reelected national chairman of ADA in April of 1972, Lowenstein continued to speak against Nixon's Vietnam policy. But he was not a part of George McGovern's campaign, though it was based on opposition to the war and was substantially aided by Lowenstein's efforts to register the youth vote, and Lowenstein faded from the presidential picture.

57.

Lowenstein came to accept Harriet Eisman's assessment of the Nassau County Democratic party as an appendage of the Margiotta Republican machine and blamed the party for his defeat. Because of this, he allowed the New Democratic Coalition in Nassau County to push him into a contest for Democratic county leader against Marvin D. Christenfeld in the fall of 1971, though at the time Lowenstein was still traveling around the country registering voters. The contest was surprisingly close, considering his lack of organization outside of Long Beach, but Lowenstein lost, and it was, as his aide Greg Stone put it, a "good example of Al doing something ludicrous."

The Republicans redistricted again. This time, they carved out a new 5th C.D. that was even more Republican than the one in which Lowenstein had lost to Lent. Long Beach, where Lowenstein lived, was carefully included, however, making a Lowenstein bid in the district for the seat held by incumbent John Wydler a Herculean task. Lowenstein's predilection was for a rematch with Lent, but Lent was now safely ensconced in the new 4th C.D.

Ignoring the advice of Harriet Eisman, who told him to sit 1972 out, Lowenstein began to consider the suggestion of his friend Anne Feldman, whom he had known at Yale Law School before she went to work in his congressional office. In 1972, Feldman, then active in the Brooklyn reform movement, was urging Lowenstein to challenge Congressman John Rooney, an old-guard regular-organization politician whose tenure as the Representative in the 14th C.D. in Brooklyn had been marked by controversy. Lowenstein also pondered a race against the aged Emanuel Celler in Brooklyn, but decided against it because of his personal esteem for Celler. Celler's district was middle class, Jewish, and liberal, and Eisman advised him that if he were to run, it would be more suitable than Rooney's. "What's the point of running unless I make a difference?" Lowenstein asked. But Eisman adds, "I think he changed that position later on, but that was his feeling up until the time he ran in Brooklyn."

In March of 1972, after giving a speech in Washington State, Lowenstein returned home on the same day to be visited by an emissary from the reform faction in John Rooney's district who invited him to meet with Brooklyn reform club leaders to discuss his candidacy. That same evening, he received a standing ovation from his Nassau County supporters at a dinner given by the Five Towns Democratic Club. "We belong to him and he belongs to us," said the club president, Mrs. Barbara Kaplan.

Following the dinner in Nassau County, Lowenstein drove to Manhattan for a meeting with a group organizing to protest the importation of Rhodesian chrome. He raced to Brooklyn for his meeting with the reformers and shot up to New Hampshire to observe the first presidential primary of 1972. Reporter Mary Breasted of *The New York Times* described Lowenstein as a "perennial gadfly . . . identified with left-wing causes" who "often jokes about those on the left who have accused him of working for the Central Intelligence Agency." She noted that those who had worked with him saw him as a "charismatic demagogue" who could fall into "deeply philosophical moods." Noting that Lowenstein was, at the time, "out of Congress now for nearly two years and the veteran of two political defeats," Breasted suggested that "Mr. Lowenstein must pick his next race carefully if he is not to brand himself as a loser. . . . Apparently, the next order of business is to decide whether he can best practice the art of the possible in Nassau or Brooklyn." Lowenstein told Breasted that he was having trouble deciding where he should run, adding, "The thing I'm least able to make decisions about is what I should do with myself. I can be very clear about what policies should be followed."

Beyond the requirement of residence in New York state, Lowenstein was not obliged to be a resident in the district in which he chose to run. Disregarding Gerry Twombley's warning that the carpetbagger issue would hurt him in Brooklyn, Lowenstein decided to take on Rooney. Moving into a black community in the Fort Greene section of Brooklyn, where he and his family were the only white people on the block, Lowenstein kept his Long Beach house and listed that address as his legal residence on his Brooklyn designating petitions.

A drive through the 14th C.D. was, according to Lowenstein strategist Lanny J. Davis, like a "drive through a series of European city-states." "Ethnic and cultural identities remain strong," a Ralph Nader report noted. "From the Hasidic Jewish community of Crown Heights to the Italian enclave of Carroll Gardens, posh Cobble Hill and predominantly black Ft. Greene, the fourteenth—embracing much of the Brooklyn waterfront and the northwest corner of the borough—offers a challenge to a politician's memory for national holidays, taste for ethnic foods and linguistic abilities." The pro-Rooney white ethnics were conservative, fearful of the growing black and Puerto Rican population, while the pro-Lowenstein well-educated white professionals of Brooklyn Heights were liberal and opposed to the war. The blacks and Puerto Ricans hostile to the regular Democratic clubhouse machine which excluded them from a share of power, were also generally for Lowenstein.

Rooney, who was born in the district, was a hero to the shrinking white ethnic population. An admirer of Rooney's in Washington observed, "There are no zigzags in the pipeline between John J. Rooney and the pope." At sixty-nine, Rooney was almost a caricature of the old-time ward politician. A product of Catholic parochial schools, St. Francis College, and Fordham Law School, he spoke with a classic Brooklyn accent. But this belied the immense power he wielded in Washington as the ranking member of the House Committee on Appropriations and Chairman of the Subcommittee on Appropriations for State, Justice, Commerce, the Judiciary, and Related Agencies. He controlled the expenditure of over $4 billion, including the budgets of the FBI and the State Department. And he maintained a close friendship with FBI Director J. Edgar Hoover, who made his files available to Rooney, including damaging information on his opponents.

As an assistant district attorney under William O'Dwyer, Rooney made his reputation by getting convictions against some of the most notorious criminals of the forties, "including Lepke and all those Murder, Inc., guys," he asserted. Selected to run in a special election to fill the seat of Congressman Thomas H. Cullen, who died in office, Rooney was elected on D-Day, June 6, 1944, and continued to be reelected for fifteen terms, staying on intimate terms with all the borough's county leaders. When former bail bondsman Meade Esposito finally consolidated his power and emerged as county leader in the sixties, Rooney became his confidant and had his support. Also in the Rooney camp was legendary district leader James Mangano, the last man to hold the position of sheriff of Brooklyn and a politician whose ability to deliver the ethnic vote in Brooklyn was regarded as awesome.

The vast amount of patronage Rooney controlled through his subcommittee and the $4 billion he supervised in budgetary funds were essential to the Esposito organization. In the struggle to save jobs at the Brooklyn Navy Yard, Rooney's seniority was also considered crucial to the party. And Rooney was close to the shipping companies and the Longshoremen's Union. The president of powerful Local 1814, Anthony Scotto, was a Rooney supporter. Scotto had married the daughter of "Tough Tony" Anastasia, who had run the waterfront for years and as he moved into his father-in law's shoes, Scotto was being hailed by assorted liberals as a "new breed" of union leader. When Lowenstein presented her with a paper he had prepared on his plans for cleaning up the waterfront, Harriet Eisman confronted him. "How could you come out with something like this?" she demanded. Puzzled and offended by her attitude, Lowenstein was insistent. "Unless I can stand up for my principles," he replied, "I'm not gonna work." Seeing that he was determined to issue the paper, Eisman warned him, "They're gonna mop you up with that, this is their big industry, this is where the drug traffic comes from."

Esposito and the union leaders were aware that Rooney's seat was no longer safe. In 1968, millionaire businessman Fred Richmond had mounted a "reform" campaign that cost a quarter of a million dollars and which had almost succeeded. A bitter Richmond had been convinced that Peter Eikenberry, a young attorney who had finished a distant third, had known he couldn't win but had stayed in the race to make sure Richmond lost. Eikenberry denied the charge.

In 1970, Eikenberry had opposed Rooney in the primary as the antiwar candidate. The race had received considerable publicity as a confrontation between the student-led antiwar activism which had been channeled into the electoral process and the old guard of the Democratic party, which still supported the war in Vietnam. Following the American invasion of Cambodia and the shootings at Kent State and Jackson State, hundreds of student volunteers had poured into the district at Lowenstein's direction to aid the Eikenberry campaign.

Lashing back, Rooney had told the voters that the student volunteers represented "a movement which is alien to all in which you and I believe." But he had also retreated from his staunch support for the war and Nixon's policies and, a month before the primary, had introduced a House resolution requiring congressional approval for any subsequent American military involvement in Cambodia. Of the 23,000 votes cast, Rooney received 50 percent to Eikenberry's 44, winning by 1,600 votes. Eikenberry supporters called it a squeaker but Rooney people claimed a solid margin. Two years later, reformers were convinced they could win with Lowenstein.

Lowenstein opened his campaign headquarters at 383 Pearl Street, set up more than a dozen community storefronts and enlisted an army of student volunteers. Congressman Herman Badillo and his wife Irma came to campaign for him as did light-heavyweight boxer and writer Jose Torres. Aaron Henry, satirical singer Tom Lehrer, Coretta Scott King, Dustin Hoffman, and Pete McCloskey also came.

At the Boerum Hill home of Rik and Nancy Pierce, smartly dressed supporters gathered to sit on the parquet floor and listened intently to songs by Tom Lehrer and a Lowenstein speech. To the members of the community, gentrified largely by upper-middle-class WASPs, he spoke of Rooney's "coming out of a different time in America," adding that "you have to have been in Congress to know how bad he is." To blacks who packed a church in Fort Greene he spoke of racial injustice. And when he finished, they rose and gave him the clenched fist salute. Meanwhile, his campaign churned out literature aimed at the white ethnics, endorsing tuition tax credits for parochial schools and the death penalty. Lowenstein also appeared regularly at ethnic events and on behalf of Polish, Irish, Italian, and Jewish causes.

Having signed on Anne Feldman and Arnie Miller for the campaign, Lowenstein turned to Nick Littlefield, who had returned to his Wall Street firm after the registration drive, to be the "administrative head" of the campaign. Littlefield accepted because he "was rested and rejuvenated," he says, "and this was a cause with a role." But Littlefield was also making plans of his own. He intended to give up private practice and join the U.S. attorney's office. Again, Orville Schell agreed to grant Littlefield half-time leave, but Schell advised him to get a fixed starting date in August for his job with the U.S. attorney. "Otherwise, you will be working for Lowenstein forever," Schell added.

Meade Esposito pressured black Councilman Sam Wright to run in the primary to make it a three-man race and to cut into Lowenstein's minority support. When Wright, on the advice of Mayor John Lindsay, refused, Esposito tried to enlist Lydia Rivera, a Puerto Rican, but she too refused. All other white reform candidates pulled out, throwing their support to Lowenstein. Only Irving Gross, a maverick with a long history of running meaningless races, remained in the June primary with Lowenstein and Rooney. Gross would pull enough votes to make the difference and save it for Rooney.

Esposito also cut a deal with Fred Richmond, who kicked in $3,000 to Rooney and served as his campaign chairman. In exchange for serving as the official head of the Rooney campaign, Richmond was given a seat on the City Council. Although Esposito publicly insisted that

Richmond would not have the support of the organization for Congress after Rooney retired, rumors persisted that Richmond would eventually succeed Rooney in the 14th.

Rooney referred to Lowenstein out of the side of his mouth, as "Mr. Low Esteem," and dismissed him as "a 'boid' who flies from Manhattan to run in Long Island and then, when the voters reject him there, flies to Brooklyn to run against me." When former Attorney General Ramsey Clark called Rooney one of the greatest "blights" in history on the Justice Department, Rooney shrugged: "One of those liberal 'boids' flyin' around again."

Rooney was a vocal critic of the elitism of the State Department. One of his favorite activities was castigating it and cutting its budget for programs that in any way involved contacts with Communist countries. Lowenstein felt that Rooney had a sinister side and he was convinced that Rooney was using his position in Congress to get campaign funds illegally. Demanding a federal grand jury investigation of campaign contributions made to Rooney by shipping companies, Lowenstein charged: "In the last two years, John Rooney has funneled some fifty-eight million dollars of taxpayers' money through his Congressional subcommittee to three shipping companies that have been involved in financing his political campaigns. Unless there is an investigation, one must assume there is a reason why the appropriate agencies cannot investigate."

Muckraking columnist Jack Anderson supported the charges, writing that Rooney "has been a jolly benefactor . . . of the shipping interests. Rarely has he held back a dime from the maritime subsidy program which keeps the shipping companies afloat. In election years, the shippers pay him back, in kind, with financial assistance. For instance, his Washington campaign treasurer this year is Nicholas Pasco, a lobbyist for the Moore-McCormick lines, which received $1.4 million in federal subsidies last year. It has become an election-year ritual for the shipping companies to pass the hat for Rooney." Anderson revealed that several shipping companies had, in the past, been convicted of making illegal contributions to him from "their corporate tills" but explained that the fines levied against them "were nothing compared to the whopping subsidies that the two companies squeezed out of the taxpayers." Seatrain Ship Building, Anderson noted, which received federal assistance with Rooney's support, was making billboards for the current campaign.

Cigar-chomping head of the AFL-CIO, super-hawk George Meany, who resented Lowenstein's opposition to the Vietnam War and his role in deposing Lyndon Johnson, fired off a telegram endorsing Rooney, which was read to a packed meeting of labor leaders at the International Longshoremen's Union Hall on Court Street. Tony

Scotto told them, "We must not just give lip service because it's going to be a rough and tough campaign."

Rooney lit into Lowenstein for his leadership of the ADA, describing it as a "subversive" organization. The Rooney campaign labeled Lowenstein a "leftist" whose supporters wanted "Communism" and a supporter of "SDS flag-burners," while Rooney called him a "radical and subversive." In the Hasidic neighborhoods, Lowenstein was portrayed in Rooney literature as "anti-Israel" because of his votes in Congress against the military budget. Rooney was described as a "staunch friend of Israel" while he had, in fact, opposed the sale of jets to Israel.

By religious Jews, Lowenstein was denounced for having married a "shiksa," and out campaigning, Jenny was once again spat at, this time by bearded Hasidim who banged on the car. *Brooklyn Heights Press* columnist Bob Side ran a series of columns revealing the nature of the anti-Lowenstein campaign waged by the Hasidim who were working for Rooney. One piece of literature written in Yiddish and distributed by the "Williamsburger for Rooney" praised Rooney for what he had done for Williamsburg and attacked Lowenstein. It read in translation:

His opponent, Al Lowenstein, is an assimilated Jew from Long Island who first moved to Brooklyn two months ago. It is interesting that he has settled in Fort Greene amongst his friends. This goyish neighborhood is 100 percent gentile. For those who know Lowenstein this is not a surprise for he has always danced at goyishe weddings. Whenever there has been a non-Jewish cause, he has been there. When there has been a Jewish cause, like parochial schools or Jewish relief, he did not even put a finger into the cold water. He now has the chutzpah to come to Williamsburg, put on a yarmulka and describe himself as interested in Jewish problems. He not long ago declared that he would fire the Jewish principal at P.S. 19. He is chairman of the committee to get rid of yeshivas. He gives aid and comfort to our enemies.

Called a "Communist" by Rooney-connected Hasidim, Lowenstein was also attacked by the Catholic community because he was Jewish. Michael O'Donovan, Lowenstein's twenty-one-year-old student coordinator, the son of a Catholic father and Jewish mother, and a Catholic by choice, told Bob Side that when he dropped Lowenstein literature at a convent, a nun, speaking "with loathing in her voice and distaste on her face," asked: "He's Jewish, isn't he?" Shaking hands with eighth graders at St. Charles Borromeo rectory, at a graduation rehearsal, Lowenstein was told by a student, "I wouldn't vote for a Jew." One Rooney flier exhorted voters in Catholic neighborhoods to "vote the Christian ticket," while others called Lowenstein anti-Catholic. When Rooney raised the parochial school issue at the only debate in which he took part, Lowenstein pointed to his own position in favor of tuition tax credits. Rooney went further, backing a constitutional amendment allowing for direct financial assistance for parochial schools. When Lowenstein said he opposed the amendment, he was hooted down.

Lowenstein denounced Rooney's literature as "scurrilous," and countered Rooney's charges by stressing the incumbent's absenteeism from the district and his support for the war in Vietnam. He continued to press for a complete withdrawal of American troops and a negotiated settlement and argued that the war had caused terrible economic damage to the district. As he campaigned, the tide began to shift in his favor. Bolstered by the strong McGovern organization in the 14th C.D., comprised of people like Peter Eikenberry who were also supporters, Lowenstein benefited from their meticulous effort to send as many delegates as possible to the Democratic National Convention in Miami. He found himself with volunteers at his disposal who worked more efficiently to get out the vote for him than the regular organization did in Rooney's behalf. A reform challenge to district leader James Mangano and bids by popular reformers Carol Bellamy and Mike Pesce for the State Senate and Assembly also added to the momentum and cut into the strength of Esposito's Democratic party. With polls showing him gaining strongly, Lowenstein announced to the press that he was confident of victory and stressed that his liberal point of view was going to prevail on the national level. Rooney, he said, was Nixon's favorite congressman, and both of them, he predicted, would be defeated.

The Gay Alliance of Brooklyn abandoned its policy of not backing candidates and announced its support for Lowenstein and McGovern, while Mike May, president of the notoriously antigay Uniformed Firefighters Association endorsed Rooney. The *Home Reporter* and *Sunset News* proclaimed in bold type: "GAYS BACK LOWENSTEIN; FIREMEN PUSH ROONEY."

Rooney, who had retired to bed with pneumonia and was unable to continue campaigning, was aided by a Supreme Court decision barring up to half a million new young voters in New York State because of registration technicalities. *The New York Times* indicated that the decision could have a "crucial impact" on the Lowenstein-Rooney race. A further irony was that while Lowenstein was traveling all over the country registering young voters, the registration drive in New York City was described by the press as lagging behind other regions; the Board of Elections called the effort there "very poor."

Esposito went into action to neutralize the impact of the McGovern campaign on the Lowenstein-Rooney primary. He flew to

California for a meeting with McGovern and returned to Brooklyn to announce his endorsement of him. The endorsement, described by Peter Eikenberry as a move by the regular Democratic machine to "stave off defeat of their local candidates with a cynical death-bed conversion to George McGovern," nevertheless confused voters in the district sufficiently to diffuse the influence of the presidential campaign on the congressional primary. When Esposito's organization staged an event for Robert Kennedy's daughter, Kathleen Kennedy, who was campaigning for McGovern, Lowenstein, who had been directing her tour of the fourteenth C.D., was turned away. Lowenstein was permitted to introduce McGovern several days later when he came to the district to campaign, but only after a great deal of haggling with McGovern's New York organization.

Once McGovern had Esposito's endorsement, which he thought would help him carry New York state, although he had some kind words for Lowenstein, he indicated to the press that he was "neutral" between Lowenstein and Rooney. This infuriated Lowenstein staffers, who were also supporting McGovern, although they acknowledged that the move made political sense. The McGovern delegates did run ahead of Lowenstein in the ethnic neighborhoods. That the antiwar candidate for president chose to remain neutral in a race between "the man who had founded the Dump Johnson movement and organized the campuses against the war and one of the most militant hawks in Congress," was ironic, as Lanny Davis wrote, but Lowenstein had himself been neutral in the presidential race during his voter registration campaign. Had he been an early supporter of McGovern instead of toying with the idea of running for president himself and trying to influence the Republican nomination, he would have denied Esposito this ploy and probably gained some crucial additional votes. Instead, Lowenstein had given John Lindsay a platform to launch his campaign. Lindsay aided Lowenstein, but his own neighborhood organization, originally established by Lindsay to counter the power of the regular Democratic clubhouses, had gone over to Rooney. Lindsay explained that he no longer had any control over it and that the organization had made its own deal with Esposito.

There was a moment of comic relief in Brooklyn when Kathleen Kennedy, a junior at Radcliffe, spoke for McGovern at Brooklyn Tech High School, with Lowenstein in attendance. William Buckley, Jr., described the incident:

> Then one of the students asks Kathleen, "Is it true that McGovern supported Henry Wallace in 1948?" To which question Kathleen gave the startling answer: "Yes, it's true." It's also true that Henry Wallace "was a Communist and I guess Senator McGovern was a Communist then too, but he isn't any more."

I wasn't there, but I can imagine the ashen expression on Al Lowenstein's face, and the mike-clutching that must have gone on. Al explained to the students that Senator McGovern had never been a Communist. . . . And Al concluded, "Anybody who says that [McGovern was a Communist] is speaking out of ignorance. They are trying to confuse you."

This would be the last of Lowenstein's campaigns to be covered widely in the press and treated as national news. The *Los Angeles Times* ran a front-page story on the primary in the 14th C.D. James Wechsler followed the campaign closely, turning out a series of columns on Lowenstein's cause, the viciousness of the Rooney campaign, and the American political crisis that the primary reflected. From national publications to small weeklies, Lowenstein was the topic of endless reporting and commentary. And as the June 20 primary drew near, the regular organization began to fear that Lowenstein was going to win. They took action.

Esposito sent in all of his troops, pulling workers out of Congressman Emanuel Celler's race against insurgent Elizabeth Holtzman. This and apathy were later offered as the reasons for the defeat, by fewer than 600 votes, of the eighty-year-old chairman of the House Judiciary Committee by the young, unknown woman attorney.

Just before the election, the Diocesan Federation of Home School Associations, the Catholic school association, mailed a letter to all priests in the district endorsing Rooney and calling on them to endorse him from the pulpit. Bob Side, in his columns, described their compliance. Rooney sent his own final mailings to Catholics emphasizing abortion and aid to parochial schools. Lowenstein desperately tried to answer all the attacks with mailings of his own and personal appearances. On Sunday, he stood in front of Catholic churches at mass time trying to undo the damage caused by the attacks. "In the final days," wrote Lanny Davis, "while storefronts in black and Puerto Rican neighborhoods were begging for more manpower to help out on election day, extra volunteers were allocated to Greenpoint and Hasidic Williamsburg to try to counter the last-minute smears by Rooney and the party regulars."

It was Davis's thesis that Lowenstein should have concentrated on the black–Puerto Rican–upper-middle-class WASP–and Jewish liberal reformist coalition, leaving the ethnics for Rooney. In his opinion, all of Lowenstein's campaigning in the ethnic neighborhoods only stirred up the organization's efforts and anti-Lowenstein sentiment.

But by primary day on June 20 even the regulars believed that Lowenstein was going to win by a landslide. Manipulation of the voting and irregularities were expected but because of Lowenstein's strength, it was considered impossible for the results to be overturned by the organization using such tactics. While they controlled the Board of Elections and their people were the chief polling place officials, Lowenstein had trained two to three hundred "poll watchers" to watch out for irregularities. Moreover, Attorney General Louis Lefkowitz had deputized a group of lawyers as deputy attorneys general to see to it that there were as few cases of fraud and manipulation as possible. One of them, Harvey Lippman, a young Harvard Law School graduate who had been a student of Lowenstein's at City College, was assigned to the polls as Cadman Plaza, a large apartment complex inhabited primarily by Lowenstein supporters. As the voting began, Lippman watched with bewilderment the blatant manipulation of the election process.

People in the pro-Rooney areas were efficiently processed, hustled in and out of the polls. But at Cadman Plaza, and at other liberal strongholds, voters had to wait in line for up to four hours to enter the booth. Through Lippman's efforts and the efforts of other deputies, the polling place at Cadman Plaza, scheduled to shut at 10:00 P.M., remained open until 2:15 A.M. and Lowenstein campaign workers were instructed to convince people to remain and cast their ballots because the election now seemed to be close. But throughout the day, hundreds left in disgust, refusing to vote in what had become an endurance contest. Many of the residents of Cadman Plaza were elderly and simply could not wait. On the other hand, Jack Anderson reported in his column that James Rooney, a nephew of the congressman, and his wife were recorded as having voted twice. "There has been a foul-up somewhere," florist James Rooney speculated.

According to Lippman, James Mangano arranged for the Board of Elections to change voting locations for the "benefit of the voters," but notices of the change, as required by law, were never received by voters affected by the changes. Also, election inspectors were told not to turn up in strong Lowenstein areas. Instead of mandatory Democratic and Republican inspectors, there were only Republicans in some polling places. It was common knowledge that the regular Republicans were working for Rooney.

In Lowenstein strongholds, the Board of Elections violated the law requiring two voting machines in districts with more than 750–800 registered voters. In black and Puerto Rican neighborhoods, not only was there an acute shortage of voting machines, but affidavits collected by Lowenstein indicated that various polls opened several hours late. Large numbers of black and Puerto Rican voters were turned away because their "buff cards"—registration identification cards—were mysteriously missing although they had voted at those places numerous times before. But in the white ethnic pro-Rooney districts, there was an abundance of voting machines and no one had to wait. Many voters carried with them into the voting booth what appeared to be an "official" Board of Elections card reminding them to vote which listed only the organization candidates. The cards had reached them through a bulk mailing by the Pioneer Democratic Club in Rooney's home district.

Lippman rushed to try to get a court order permitting pro-Lowenstein people to vote who had been told that they were not listed or whose buff cards were missing. As officials were preparing to close, a group of Hasidim turned up at the Board of Elections to receive blank court orders enabling them to vote. They claimed that their buff cards were missing. State Supreme Court Justice Joseph R. Corso signed the orders for these people, whose eligibility had been in question, without bothering to take testimony. (In 1974, Justice Corso was investigated by the Brooklyn District Attorney's office and D.A. Eugene Gold referred the case to the State Committee on Judicial Conduct. The Temporary State Commission on Judicial Conduct, which succeeded the committee, found in 1976 that Corso had signed the blank orders improperly, having failed to take testimony. He was reprimanded for his "carelessness and injudiciousness," and his conduct was deemed "improper.")

The results of the primary showed Rooney the winner in the 14th C.D., polling 13,868 to Lowenstein's 12,833. Irving Gross polled 1,817. A recount would reduce Rooney's margin to 801 votes out of the almost 30,000 cast. As expected, McGovern swept New York and seemed assured of the Democratic nomination for president.

Lowenstein refused to concede defeat. He announced to his exhausted wife who had asked him to pick a vacation spot, "We're not going on vacation. We're going to court." Lowenstein appealed to the hard core of his volunteers to stay with him. He asked them to work within the system rather than "scream on the sidelines." Telling them, "We won this primary," he explained that it was just as important to prove you could have a fair election in Brooklyn as it was in Mississippi.

On the Sunday following the election, Lowenstein called a meeting of those who had witnessed or experienced voting irregularities on primary day. Three hundred people from the various neighborhoods turned up in spite of the bad weather to exchange horror stories. "I personally know more than one-hundred people who were qualified to vote and were turned away," observed one black who attended. A Pole added: "In all of my 40 years of politics, I ain't never seen vote stealin' like this . . . and I seen my share in the old days."

Jack Newfield, James Wechsler, and William F. Buckley, Jr., all cried "foul." "It happens," wrote Buckley, "that Mr. Lowenstein backs enthusiastically almost every mistaken political idea that ever issued out of the social imagination of man, but that isn't the point, any more so than when us good guys sat around in 1964 worrying how many votes would be stolen from Barry Goldwater by the Democratic poll tenders. Fair elections, like precautions against accidental wars, are in everybody's interest. It is lucky for our international reputation that we didn't invite any South Vietnamese professors over to monitor the Lowenstein election." Buckley concluded, "The evidence suggests that Lowenstein would have won by something like a landslide."

Lowenstein himself observed bitterly, "If it happened in another country, we would probably send in the army to fight for free elections."

Through Harvey Lippman, Lowenstein was able to retain the services of the firm for which Lippman worked, Kornish, Lieb. Besides Lippman, Lowenstein's legal team included former Robert Kennedy aide Adam Walinsky, former head of the federal legal service program Terry Lenzner, and David Ellhorn. With Lowenstein as the plaintiff, his lawyers brought an action in the New York State Supreme Court in Brooklyn to set aside the primary results. Blacks and Puerto Ricans who had been unable to vote brought suit in Brooklyn Federal Court alleging violations of the Voting Rights Act and the Civil Rights Act. Lowenstein also went before the Fair Campaign Practices Arbitration Tribunal of the American Arbitration Association. To counter Lowenstein's offensive, Rooney also appealed to that tribunal to rule on charges that smear tactics had been used in the Brooklyn Democratic contest. Rooney's attorney was the legendary Brooklyn election law expert Harold Fisher. Meanwhile, Lowenstein established the "Committee for Fair Elections" at his office on Pearl Street, to raise money to pay for the legal battle; Congressman Pete McCloskey assisted the fund-raising campaign.

The federal case established the necessity of applying the Voting Rights Act—which Lowenstein had helped to pass so that voting abuses in the South could be ended—to Brooklyn. But on September 1, Justice Charles Rubin, after considering countless affidavits and sworn testimony of witnesses and after initially reserving decision, denied Lowenstein's contention that irregularities in the primary voting were too numerous to allow determination of a victor. Rubin rejected all but 1,509 of the 3,673 irregularities charged by Lowenstein and accepted Harold Fisher's argument that Rooney had been equally affected by any irregularities that occurred. Lowenstein called the decision "frivolous and unresponsive" and said he would go to the Appellate Division. Bob Side reported that President Nixon, fearful that Rooney might find himself without a line to run on if a new election were called and Lowenstein won, directed Kieran O'Doherty, a founder of the New York Conservative party and its vice-chairman, as well as a Nixon federal appointee, to advise the local Conservatives to nominate Rooney.

Lowenstein received the nomination of the Liberal party, as the party's Brooklyn chairman, Jacob Loft, praised him as "an outstanding national liberal leader." Lowenstein was also elected to the Democratic National Committee and selected as one of the at-large McGovern delegates to the Democratic National Convention. Lowenstein pointed to his impeccable liberal Democratic credentials and called on Esposito to end his support for Rooney, who had Richard Nixon's support and who had been nominated by the Conservative party. Offering Esposito an accommodation, Lowenstein acknowleged that he was bucking the organization by running against a Democratic incumbent, but insisted that Rooney was now closer to the Republicans than he was to the Democratic party, which he, Lowenstein, fully represented. To the public pressure exerted on him to back Lowenstein, Esposito responded by explaining that he had started with Rooney and would have to finish with him. Referring to Lowenstein, he said, "He's a hell of a nice guy, but I can't stand back and play ping pong." In fact, Esposito was incensed that he had been kept off the New York delegation to the convention and that Lowenstein had been put on it. It was widely known that Esposito had told Rooney that this was his last election with organization support and that he would have to retire. Meanwhile, Lowenstein announced that whatever happened in the election, afterward, there was going to be "all-out war" against Esposito.

On September 8, the Appellate Division, in a unanimous decision, overruled the lower court and overturned the election. In a four-paragraph opinion, Presiding Justice Samuel Rabin and Associate Justices James Hopkins, Fred Munder, Irwin Shapiro, and Marcus Christ, stated that the court found no evidence "of fraud per se." But quoting from *DeSapio v. Koch*, they noted that "we think this was one of those rare elections 'conducted so badly . . . that even though illegality of specific votes cannot be attributed to the misconduct, still it must be found that the resultant mischief held such potential for changing the result that every dictate of fairness and protection of the voters' franchise demands a new election.'" Citing specific instances of conduct by Rooney supporters that required calling the new election, the court concluded, "A fair election is the cornerstone of democracy and we find that this election did not meet the requisite standards." The date set for the new election was September 19.

Rooney was in bed in his Washington home, still recuperating from pneumonia when he was informed of the decision. He and his lawyer, Harold Fisher, agreed that an appeal should be filed with the Court of Appeals, the highest tribunal in the state. Calling the opinion "shocking," Fisher said that he would argue on appeal "that this is a departure from the normal rules that have been laid down by the Court of Appeals." He expressed confidence that he would win and observed, "In no primary that I know of have these types of irregularities been sufficient to warrant a new primary." Lowenstein was not home when Jenny received the phone call with the news of the decision. He was out campaigning.

On September 13, just six days before the second primary had been ordered by the Appellate Division, the Court of Appeals ruled four to three in Lowenstein's favor and affirmed the order calling for the new primary. No majority opinion was issued by the four judges who voted to affirm. Exuberant, Lowenstein expressed his "boundless gratitude" to his lawyers and quipped, "Democracy is alive and well, four to three."

"The issues are clear," Lowenstein said. "The problem is there is so little time. . . . If we get the votes out, we'll win." He kept up a backbreaking schedule of campaigning while Rooney vanished from sight, and Esposito took the most prominent role in the drive to stop Lowenstein.

The other major reform primary challenges had ended in June. The workers who had helped Bellamy and Pesce to succeed in their challenges had drifted away. Mangano had survived the challenge to him, and was back at the helm in his district, supporting Rooney. The McGovern campaign, which had provided much of the momentum to the insurgent races in Brooklyn, had run out of steam after a debilitating battle at the credentials committee. McGovern had managed to salvage the nomination, but at enormous cost and without the Humphrey people, the labor unions, and Scoop Jackson, whose supporters refused to come over. George Wallace, too infirm to wage the independent candidacy McGovern had hoped would split the right-wing vote, gave every indication that he was for Nixon. And when McGovern's choice for vice-president, Thomas Eagleton, was dropped from the ticket after it was revealed that he had received shock treatment for depression, McGovern's standing in the polls sank desperately low.

In Miami at the Democratic National Convention, Lowenstein had been virtually invisible. His sister describes it as a "low point" for her brother, who realized that without a victory in the primary against Rooney, he could no longer command the attention of people who had previously treated him with enormous respect. Instead, he was ignored by prominent Democrats, and leaders who had once sought his advice and support did not even speak when they encountered him on an elevator.

Lowenstein made two speeches in Miami. In one, he called on the American navy to send the Sixth Fleet into the Mediterranean to help defend Israel. An extremely hawkish effort aimed at religious Jewish voters in the district in which he was campaigning, it surprised even some pro-Israel delegates. Lowenstein also joined Gloria Steinem in nominating Texas legislator Frances "Sissy" Farenthold for vice-president. A *cause célèbre* with the women's caucus, Farenthold had been narrowly defeated for governor in Texas, where Lowenstein had actively supported her. Her candidacy in Miami was put forward by feminists frustrated by what they perceived as McGovern's abandonment of their cause. The vice-presidency provoked a heated and prolonged debate in the New York caucus, which delayed McGovern's acceptance speech for hours, forcing him to deliver it long after most television viewers had gone to bed.

The revelation of Thomas Eagleton's shock treatments and his replacement on the ticket by former Peace Corps director Sargent Shriver took away Lowenstein's headlines. And talk of a mysterious Watergate break-in at Democratic national headquarters by men with CIA connections working for the Committee to ReElect the President (CREEP) superseded the antiwar movement as the leading topic of conversation.

Though a "hard core" of about twenty-five loyalists had stayed on in September, many had left after Lowenstein's suit was dismissed in the lower court, believing that all was lost. With the McGovern campaign in disarray, the momentum of June dissipated. It looked indeed like four more years.

Among Lowenstein's opposition, however, fervor had not diminished and both the Hasidim and the right-wing Catholics mounted an even greater effort against Lowenstein than before. At a meeting, Michael O'Donovan, one of the loyal campaign workers who had remained, told Lowenstein, "Al, first you brought the blacks and Puerto Ricans together in this campaign; now for the first time since Christ died, you've brought the Catholics and the Jews together. They both don't like you."

With the country sinking further into the Nixon-Agnew backlash, Lowenstein stood virtually alone in his fight against the forces of reaction in Brooklyn. The Conservative party, the labor union hawks, organized crime, the Esposito organization, and Nixon Republicans all moved together against him.

The New York Times endorsed Lowenstein, saying the voters owed him their thanks for his "determined effort" to gather the evidence of election fraud. "It is not so much a question of who will represent the 14th Congressional District," they proclaimed, "—though we think Mr. Lowenstein is greatly to be preferred to his opponent. The real contribution the former Congressman has made is to the integrity of the election process." The *Harvard Law Review* would agree, devoting a scholarly piece to the law Lowenstein made in the election.

But on September 19, Rooney was declared the winner with 15,486 votes to Lowenstein's 13,071 and Irving Gross's 485. Lowenstein had led congressional candidates in the state in money spent on a congressional campaign. His final figure was $220,715 against

$73,622 by Rooney, as reported by Common Cause. Rooney insisted he spent only $16,017. Lowenstein had put up $12,500 of his own money; Franklin Delano Roosevelt III had contributed $6,000, and former Secretary of the Treasury C. Douglas Dillon, $1,000. Lowenstein stressed that almost $40,000 had gone for legal fees.

On September 28, too late for it to make any difference, the Fair Campaign Practices Arbitration Tribunal called on Rooney to "publicly condemn" tactics used in his behalf during the primary campaigns against Lowenstein. Rooney had not appeared at the hearing and had sent no one from his office. In its findings, the tribunal cited as unfair a leaflet on Israel which distorted Lowenstein's record, distributed by Youth for Rooney; distortions of Lowenstein's record in Congress; a letter distributed by the Veterans of Foreign Wars also distorting Lowenstein's record and positions; an advertisement in the *Polish Week* of the American Polish Committee misrepresenting Lowenstein's record and positions; and an advertisement in *Der Yid* along with a pamphlet issued by Williamsburg Jews for Rooney which not only distorted Lowenstein's positions and activities, but which constituted an "appeal to prejudice based on race, creed or national origin" in violation of the code of campaign conduct.

Harriet Eisman felt that there had been less support for Lowenstein in Brooklyn than on Long Island, though she acknowledged "the times were different too." Analyzing the defeat later, Eisman contrasted Lowenstein's reception in Brooklyn to the feelings he inspired on Long Island: "There wasn't the same 'You are my mentor, my leader, my this. . . .' They really didn't have the same emotional reaction to Al that was felt out here. Also, there was no one really selling him that way either up there, you know, the handful of us that were tremendous salespeople for him. We set the stage and we had the people that were able to get him to make it."

But Harriet Eisman never doubted that "they stole the second election." Although Lowenstein continued to insist that there had been a pattern of irregularities which prevented many people from voting, he decided nevertheless against seeking a third election and conceded defeat. At the Board of Elections, David N. Dinkins said he had no idea just how many people had been turned away from the polls and, unable or unwilling to get court orders, had failed to vote. "I think no one will ever know who won," Lowenstein concluded. Vowing to keep his office at 383 Pearl Street open to continue community work, he told dejected volunteers that they should "go out of here mad." Although he was on the Liberal line and suggested that victory was still possible, Lowenstein indicated, through his issues director, Greg Stone, that most of his efforts would go to electing other antiwar candidates. "We're making an effort of some size," Stone explained. "We're short of money."

Meade Esposito did not respond kindly to Lowenstein's attacks on him. Calling the most important factor in Rooney's victory "the personal attacks and vilification leveled against our leadership by Allard Lowenstein," Esposito asserted that "every local Brooklyn Democrat was personally affronted by the ruthless campaign of a desperate nonresident candidate who placed his personal motives above the interests of our party and our community."

Lowenstein shot back, "Wild horses could not move me from Brooklyn." In the general election, Rooney received 44,629 to Lowenstein's 23,820 as a Liberal. McGovern was crushed by Nixon, who was reelected president. Rooney was returned to Congress and Meade Esposito was still the county leader. Harold Fisher was not surprised. He had seen the reformers come and go. He'd seen them fight the mob and the corrupt judges. There had been Seabury and LaGuardia, Finletter, Eugene McCarthy, the NDC, McGovern and Al Lowenstein. They had all come and gone, but the organization endured. You either learned to live with it or you got out.

Lowenstein jockeyed to keep Meade Esposito off the Democratic National Committee, participating in a series of basement meetings at the Washington Hilton, where negotiations were taking place to fill twenty-five vacant seats. He talked of running for borough president of Brooklyn, or possibly even mayor of New York. Interviewed by a law school student, Lowenstein insisted that "the things that have gone wrong with the system can be changed more effectively if you elect people committed to change them." He maintained that he had "no regret" about his career in politics.

But Harriet Eisman observed, "Once he lost in Brooklyn, he was very dismayed." She noticed a change in Lowenstein's attitude. He no longer laughed at her ominous descriptions of organized crime, but accepted what she was saying. "He really believed in this country," she stressed. "And . . . there was nothing funny about it. I used to tell him that when the other Kennedy, John, was still president that there was a conspiracy. He always felt I had this horrible conspiratorial mind. It wasn't until years later he said, 'You know, you were right.'"

Under Nixon, fear of CIA and FBI intrusion into the lives of private citizens, which Lowenstein now shared, increased dramatically as evidence of domestic spying came to light. The infamous Huston plan to give U.S. intelligence agencies broad powers to monitor the activities of Americans was uncovered. Sinister facts about Watergate surfaced. E. Howard Hunt, who worked for the Republicans, was revealed to be a former CIA agent. James McCord, head of security for CREEP, had also been in the CIA; and the Cubans who broke into Democratic headquarters had worked for the CIA as well.

A watershed year for liberalism in many other ways, 1972 was also the year that Frank Graham, the first of Lowenstein's great liberal mentors, died, the last of Lowenstein's heroes to go.

On February 7, 1973, a Valentine Dinner Dance in Lowenstein's honor at the Tavern on the Green was attended by top luminaries from the Democratic party, the entertainment world and the media. The list of sponsors and dinner committee participants was a virtual *Who's Who* of the civil rights movement, the peace movement, organized labor, and liberal politics. Honorary Cochairpersons were Mrs. Hale Boggs, Governor Rafael Hernandez Colon of Puerto Rico, Mrs. Coretta King, Senator George McGovern, Representative Thomas Foley, Robert Strauss, the chairman of the Democratic National Committee, and Leonard Woodcock, the head of the United Auto Workers.

His old friend from Raleigh, North Carolina, attorney Wade Smith spoke, as did Senator Alan Cranston, Fannie Lou Hamer, Lucile Kohn, and Pete McCloskey. Peter Yarrow sang and Peter Duchin's orchestra played. The masters of ceremony were Barney Frank and television journalist Geraldo Rivera. They raised money for Lowenstein to pay off his campaign debt and praised him for his work. They joked about his campaigns and predicted that there would be others. But the event was tinged with sadness. The liberals were tired and they tended to look back, not forward. Lowenstein's friends wondered what he should do now that he had lost again. Some couldn't take another defeat. His friend Jim Bouton wrote:

> When the hell are you going to invite me to a victory party? I'm fed up with standing around at cocktail parties feeling like I have to express condolences. I'm sick and tired of standing at affairs where people are saying, "It's too bad he lost because Al's such a great guy," or "It's really a shame because our country really needs people like Al."
>
> Shit on all that. (Not on you, Al.)
>
> I want to go someplace where people are happy. I want to hear people saying things like, "Boy that Lowenstein machine is really brutal," and "What's Al going to do now with all that power?"
>
> At that kind of a party I could laugh and drink without guilt. I could pinch women on the fanny and say I was only celebrating. I could go in and ask big Al to fix it so I wouldn't have to pay taxes or something, or go in and ask for a political handout of some kind.
>
> If I wanted to feel like a loser I could go back to baseball.

Lowenstein attempted to put on a brave face. "There always will be moments when people of principle find themselves swimming upstream," he wrote in *ADA World* in June, 1973, as his second term as

ADA chairman expired. "There always will be sensitivities that unscrupulous, ambitious people can seek to manipulate to their own advantage. But whatever else November 1972 was, it was not a repudiation of the Roosevelt-Kennedy tradition."

Even so, he acknowledged, "One sad fact underscored by the voting is how many Americans are losing faith in the electoral process." Lowenstein exhorted his fellow liberals to offer "honest and intelligent leadership that can articulate and inspire," warning, "This will not be easy, in the face of the wealth and power to distort now concentrated in the White House, and in the wake of bullets that destroyed those best equipped to lead the effort." He called on the liberals to work for their goals "even if they seemed impossible," adding "But we should know they are not impossible—and that knowledge should increase our determination to work to achieve them." He concluded by quoting Robert Kennedy: "In any event, that is the only way we can live."

58.

Lowenstein's credo that one person could make a difference suffered from neglect during the seventies as the "Me generation" took over and liberal ideology vanished. His own faith, severely tested by the dirty campaigns and Watergate, was further shaken during 1973 by the revelation that he had been placed on a White House "enemies list."

At a series of dinner parties in his Fort Greene brownstone he discussed his future plans with such friends as Arthur Schlesinger, Jr., actor and folksinger Theodore Bikel and columnist James Wechsler. He kept his community office and continued to work on district problems as if he were a congressman, but he began to be preoccupied with other things. At one of the dinners, Lowenstein indicated to his guests that he was looking into the murder of Robert Kennedy. During a trip to England, he spoke at Oxford to a gathering of some seventy-five Americans, including Wendell Willkie II, and devoted an hour to the Kennedy assassinations, particularly Robert's. To Willkie's surprise, Lowenstein also called for a government of "national reconciliation" because the problems facing the United States were "so intractable now that they are not susceptible to partisan or ideological resolution."

In July of 1973, *The New York Times* reported Lowenstein's call for a "deeper examination of a whole range of events, from elections to assassinations, which may not have happened in the way generally accepted." Jenny insists that Lowenstein felt "cheated" by Robert Kennedy's death, and thought Nixon's victory and the country's move to the right were not entirely natural. They had been achieved by the gun, he reasoned, and his own fate, he believed, was tied to these events.

Lowenstein's attorney Harvey Lippman describes him as a "laughing stock" in New York politics, recalling that "Al practically had to sneak into Democratic dinners." Lowenstein also developed a painful back condition which forced him to hobble around. "It was shocking to see him hampered this way," Lippman shudders. Lowenstein also dyed his hair for a brief period, trying to disguise the signs of age he so resented. He worried about how he was perceived. "Al had a fear of losing because of his image as a loser," Lippman concludes.

Also in 1973, Dennis Sweeney phoned Lowenstein and asked to spend the night at his place in Brooklyn. Lowenstein, who had not heard from Sweeney in ages, agreed. "Dennis was very odd," Jenny recounts. "He sat all through dinner, very uncommunicative and reserved. And he looked strange. His teeth were pulled out. Dennis was on the brink in 1973. He didn't say much." Lowenstein stayed up late talking with Sweeney. Afterward, he told Jenny, "It's so incredibly sad. There's nothing left of what there used to be." Sweeney left in the morning.

In February of 1974, it was reported on the front page of *The New York Times* that J. Edgar Hoover, while he was director of the FBI, had helped Congressman John Rooney by supplying him with information about both Allard Lowenstein and Peter Eikenberry. Both the FBI and Rooney denied the allegations, but Lowenstein and Eikenberry were clearly targets. A "well-placed source" in the FBI said the agency "did everything we could to help Rooney get elected." According to the source, agents in the field were ordered to gather and forward to Washington whatever "background" information they could find on Lowenstein. "They didn't find anything derogatory," the source said, "but it seems he was identified with liberal and radical causes. We gave Rooney everything we knew." Lowenstein, who was in Israel when the news broke, said that he hoped "the full story of this kind of activity will come out."

Dennis Sweeney had actually preceded Lowenstein as the target of an FBI investigation, prompted by Sweeney's radical politics and suspected involvement in a fire at a Stanford ROTC building. Told that he would not be bothered as long as he stayed out of trouble, Sweeney dropped out of politics. Then, as his mental state deteriorated, he began to show signs of paranoia, becoming convinced that Lowenstein and the CIA were controlling his mind. Unable to extricate himself from Lowenstein's orbit long after he had broken with him over the civil rights movement, Sweeney went insane, imagining that back when the COFO dentist had repaired his teeth, the CIA had taken the opportunity to implant a "sensor" in his mouth. Having

harbored suspicions that Lowenstein had close CIA contacts, Sweeney now fantasized that Lowenstein and others were transmitting
messages to him through the sensor. With a pair of pliers, he pulled
out the denture bridge the COFO dentist had fitted him with, leaving
the ugly filed-down stubs of his front teeth exposed. Ironically, it was
then not Sweeney but Lowenstein who was subjected to surveillance
by the FBI as he sought to win election through the system Sweeney
had by then renounced.

Believing himself victimized by Nixon, Hoover, and Rooney, Lowenstein now experienced bitter disappointment at the hands of the
people he counted on as his supporters. Lowenstein began to organize
in 1974 to run for the United States Senate seat held by powerful
liberal Republican Jacob Javits. Besides seeking the Democratic nomination by entering the Democratic primary, he also planned to challenge Javits for the Liberal designation that party boss Alex Rose normally bestowed on his pet Republican.

At the Democratic convention in Niagara Falls, Lowenstein received 40 percent of the vote, well above the 25 percent required to
get on the primary ballot. While he was pushing for the Senate, he
was also working on the side to organize a campaign in the 14th C.D.
against Fred Richmond, the regular organization's choice to replace
the cancer-stricken John Rooney.

By her own account, Harriet Eisman and previous Lowenstein loyalists put enormous effort into "trying to talk him out of running for
the Senate." Yet Eisman arranged with Ogden Reid, to use the
wealthy gubernatorial candidate's posh suites for the Lowenstein effort and went ahead with the production of campaign materials. "He
had used up a lot of his own money and had taken out loans to pay off
debts," Eisman explains. "We had a million fund-raisers to recoup his
losses. There was a limit to how many times you can pass the hat to
the same people." But, she adds, "Al was a fighter and he wasn't going
to stop."

Lowenstein was confident he could win a primary against Ramsey
Clark, Lyndon Johnson's attorney general. His aide Greg Stone also
thought Lowenstein could defeat Javits. But Lowenstein was told by
liberal Democrats at the convention that it was unrealistic to believe
anyone could unseat Javits in a six-week campaign, that Javits actually
enjoyed the favor of liberal Jewish Democrats who didn't really want
to see him beaten. At the same time, participants at Niagara Falls
were engaging in a bizarre debate over how many Jews should be
allowed on the state Democratic ticket. Howard Samuels, who was
seeking the nomination for governor, insisted that he should be the
only Jew to run. Robert Abrams, the borough president of the Bronx,
contested this and was nominated for attorney general, while Irish
Catholic Hugh Carey became the favorite for governor. Lowenstein

wasn't able to raise the money and dropped out of the Senate race, and his dreams for the 14th C.D. in Brooklyn were swept away in the avalanche of Fred Richmond's millions.

Lowenstein was deeply hurt by what had happened in the Senate race and felt he had been abandoned by his friends. It was the first time that Harriet Eisman had told him his goals were unrealistic and that he shouldn't run. Deflated and discouraged, Lowenstein was agonizing over his future, afraid that he might be totally shut out of politics, when he was approached by Stanley Harwood to run against the incumbent congressman, John Wydler, in the redrawn 5th C.D.

Harwood was the new Nassau County Democratic county leader (Marvin Christenfeld having been deposed and indicted), and having persuaded one declared challenger to withdraw, he approached Lowenstein because he believed that with him at the head of the county ticket, the party would be given a boost. Harwood envisioned money and volunteers, though he was well aware that Wydler was deeply entrenched and had the full power of Joseph Margiotta behind him. At the same time, liberal, antiwar activists in Nassau County were pressuring Lowenstein to return to Long Island.

Greg Stone advised Lowenstein not to run, pointing out that further changes in the 5th C.D., meant that it was more conservative than when Lowenstein lost to Lent. It was, he said, the toughest district for a liberal Democrat to run in on Long Island. But Karl Grossman, who was covering the political scene for the *Long Island Press*, believes that Lowenstein's decision to run against Wydler was valid. "Wydler was probably the worst congressman on Long Island," he asserts. "He was an arch right-winger and a complete Nixonite, a real neanderthal. It was appropriate for Lowenstein to run against him."

Seeing a chance to unite the feuding factions of the Democratic party in Nassau County, Lowenstein accepted and moved his family back into their house in Long Beach. That spring, to celebrate his return, he held a Passover seder to which Nick Littlefield was invited. Since Lowenstein was the only Jew present, it was jokingly called a "gentile seder."

Lowenstein gambled that Nixon would still be in office and that the public's anger would rub off on Wydler, who was completely identified with the disgraced president. Insisting that he opposed Nixon's impeachment, Lowenstein seemed to be less concerned with what Nixon had or had not done than he was with the effect that the public outrage would have on the elections. But when Nixon resigned and Gerald Ford became president, much of the impact of the Watergate debacle was lost. In fact, Wendell Willkie II, a Republican insider, reports that Donald Rumsfeld approached Lowenstein and asked him to serve "in some capacity" as an "in-house liberal" in the Ford administration, "as a sort of Leonard Garment." Garment, a partner in the law firm Nixon had joined in New York, had served Nixon in the White House as his resident liberal.

Lowenstein's other gamble was that the vote on the right in the 5th C.D. would be split, the Conservative party having indicated it would run its own candidate. But Wydler managed to secure the Conservative designation despite strenuous objections within the party, and despite Conservative James Leonard's charge that the designation had been made in the absence of a quorum and thus was a fraud. Though a law suit was brought before Justice Beatrice Bernstein, who declared Wydler's Conservative nomination invalid, Leonard died of a heart attack and the case was lost on appeal. Lowenstein told Harvey Lippman that he suspected foul play in Leonard's death although he had no direct proof.

Lowenstein tore Wydler apart in the debates, but although the Republicans feared he was gaining, Lowenstein was defeated by a substantial margin, 91,677 to 77,356. Even so, with 46 percent of the vote, Lowenstein had made a stronger race against Wydler than any of the previous challengers.

It was demoralizing for Lowenstein to see his former volunteers getting elected while he could not win. Speaking on the phone with young Tom Downey, a former McCarthy campaign worker who had run for Congress in neighboring Suffolk County, Lowenstein asked, "Tom, did you get elected?" Downey replied that he had and asked about Lowenstein's race. "I came in second," replied Lowenstein sadly. "Al was brokenhearted when he wasn't elected," Harriet Eisman relates. "He feared not being in the public eye. But I told him to wait."

59.

Lowenstein's attempt to get to the bottom of the Robert Kennedy assassination led to increased suspicions on his part that facts were being suppressed. Invited to a meeting in 1973 by actor Robert Vaughn, star of the popular TV series "The Man From U.N.C.L.E.," Lowenstein had accepted with reservations. He went to prove his open-mindedness and to persuade Vaughn, who was his friend, "to avoid further involvement in such foolishness." He began to have doubts of his own, however, when Vaughn produced the autopsy report showing that Kennedy had been hit from behind "by bullets fired at point-blank range—that is, from a distance of several inches," as he explained later. Lowenstein thought he remembered that Sirhan Sirhan had been facing Kennedy when he shot him from a distance of several feet.

When the police report confirmed the autopsy, Lowenstein went through grand-jury and trial records for evidence placing Sirhan's gun behind, and inches from, Kennedy's head. He found none. Criminal ballistic expert William Harper had executed an affidavit stating that the bullet removed from Kennedy's head could not be matched with Sirhan's gun. Lowenstein was also confused by the fact that Sirhan's gun could fire only eight bullets but that at least ten bullets had been fired. Through the efforts of Washington attorney Bernard Fensterwald, an FBI report was obtained in 1976 under the Freedom of Information Act indicating that twelve bullets were in fact fired. Two bullets had been recovered from Kennedy's body; a third had gone through his chest, while a fourth had passed through his left shoulder pad. Five bullets had been recovered after surgery from wounded bystanders, while three more bullets had been extracted by police from ceiling tiles; bullet holes were also found in door frames. "Nobody could add seven to three and get eight," Lowenstein remarked.

Lowenstein concluded that a "propaganda campaign" was being waged to peddle "the precise reverse of the facts." District Attorney of Los Angeles County Joe Busch said on the "Tomorrow" show every eyewitness with whom he had spoken had confirmed that Sirhan had fired the gun up close to Kennedy's ear. When Lowenstein asked him to name such a witness, Busch replied, "Would you like Mr. Uecker, the man that grabbed his arm?" But Karl Uecker's testimony had refuted the official position. When Lowenstein traced him down in Germany, Uecker was explicit: "I told the authorities that Sirhan never got close enough for a point-blank shot, never," he said, irritated that he had been misquoted. "It was decided long ago that it was to stop with Sirhan, and that is what will happen," Uecker added. According to Lowenstein, Uecker was certain that Sirhan had fired only two shots before being pushed down onto a steam table. Lowenstein also conferred with Paul Schrade, a former administrative assistant to Walter Reuther and the west coast labor coordinator for Robert Kennedy. Schrade had received a gunshot wound in the head when Kennedy was killed and had serious doubts about the official version of the incident. Schrade joined with Lowenstein in investigating further. Convinced that the Los Angeles police were not telling him the truth, Lowenstein became outraged when they asked him to draw up a list of written questions to which they agreed to give only oral answers.

Lowenstein and Schrade held press conferences on December 15 and 19 of 1974, going public for the first time with their speculations after the Los Angeles police categorically refused to reopen the case. "We offer no answers today, only questions," they said in their statement. "Nor have we any prejudices or preconceptions about what may ultimately be found to be the whole truth about the assassination of Robert Kennedy. . . . In short, facts must be determined free of any dogged precommitment to any theory."

The *Los Angeles Times*, "the only widely read paper in the city where the murder occurred," as Lowenstein described it, refused to give coverage to the press conferences. In its editorial, it totally dismissed Lowenstein's efforts, ascribing his suspicions to "an unwillingness to conclude that mundane facts can explain such fearful dramas" and calling Lowenstein's arguments "wispy" and "long since discounted by authorities."

James Wechsler defended Lowenstein's involvement in the Sirhan case, arguing that he and Schrade "have surely made a compelling case for either a congressional investigation or an independent commission of inquiry." After two key eyewitnesses and four of the wounded bystanders demanded that the case be reopened and a special committee of the American Academy of Forensic Sciences, headed by it former president Dr. Robert Joling, announced "basic problems" with the ballistic evidence, the Los Angeles Superior Court in the summer of 1975, ordered the partial reexamination of that aspect of the case. Sirhan Sirhan's gun was fired as part of the new investigation.

Not all of his friends responded as favorably as Wechsler to Lowenstein's thesis that evidence of more than one assassin in the Sirhan case might have been suppressed. Some perceived in his preoccupation with Robert Kennedy's assassination a disenchantment with the system that contradicted the buoyant optimism they had come to expect of him. They preferred the Lowenstein who expressed his faith in an American system threatened only by the Communists. But the radical left had all but vanished in America, leaving the liberals, who had fought them, exhausted. The right was monolithic and uncontrolled and Lowenstein suspected that it had achieved power through sinister means.

"What happened in Robert Kennedy's death became an obsession that was a non-productive use of his enormous talents," Carol Hardin Kimball argues, while Wendell Willkie II insists that Lowenstein's speech at Oxford on the assasinations was a "mistake." And William F. Buckley, Jr., concludes that "he conceived the notion that democracy was imperiled if an intelligent question survived as to whether there might have been a cover-up of who killed this man, that it was the cover-up that was the enemy rather than the mere identification of this man rather than the other, as having been the executioner."

Lowenstein implied that, even before he went public, the Kennedys were aware of his activities related to the Sirhan case and his concerns about it but did not themselves want to become involved in assassination controversies. According to Greg Stone, however, the Kennedys froze Lowenstein out and Ted Kennedy, with whom Lowenstein's relations were already strained, became particularly remote. According to Stone, the Kennedy family took an especially dim view of Lowenstein's activities with regard to the assassinations and kept him at a considerable distance. This was not true of Kennedy allies such as Frank Mankiewicz, Arthur Schlesinger, Jr., and Richard Goodwin. Mankiewicz had done considerable research on the murders of both Kennedys and had arranged for two of David Susskind's television shows to be devoted to President Kennedy's assassination, though he failed to uncover any new evidence.

Lowenstein endorsed Representative Henry Gonzales's resolution to create a special committee to re-examine all the major assassinations. In 1976, in an essay entitled "Who Killed Robert Kennedy?" published in a collection of pieces under the title *Government by Gunplay* (an introduction was provided by ex-CIA agent Philip Agee), Lowenstein provided what editor Sidney Blumenthal calls his "most cogent statement on the RFK murder, stating his belief in the possibility of conspiracy." Lowenstein wrote:

I was once typical of many people who refused to face questions that threatened some cherished assumptions about America. We had closed our minds and didn't even know that we had done it. Then came the discovery that things had happened in our country that few of us believed could happen. The "enemies list" was my personal trip-wire. I was confused about the implications of offical tampering with my affairs but one thing was certain: tales of tapped wires and planted provocateurs could no longer be dismissed simply as signs of hysteria. If the White House, the CIA, the FBI, the Internal Revenue Service and other prime instruments of an impartial government could be used against civil rights groups, churches, members of Congress and anyone else who incurred official displeasure, clearly someone, somewhere might have organized some of the events that changed America. . . .

I do not know if there was a conspiracy to murder President Kennedy, Senator Kennedy, Martin Luther King, Jr., or Governor Wallace; I do know that it is *possible* that there was a conspiracy to murder one or more of them. If there were such conspiracies, I do not know if there were connections between them; I do know it is *possible* there were connections of some kind between some of them.

I do not know if we can ever find out the full story, if indeed there is a "full story" not yet found out. I *do* know we had better free ourselves of preconceptions so we can do our best to find out. Those of us who have preached that the electoral process is the way to decide policies and leadership ought to feel a special obligation to help this effort.

The inclusion of the Wallace shooting might have confused some of the less sophisticated students of assassination theory, but it was widely known that McGovern was counting on an independent Wallace candidacy to split the right-wing vote in the 1972 election. The near-fatal attempt on Wallace's life that left him paralyzed effectively eliminated that possibility. Though Lowenstein had, on occasion, become involved in sensational cases—the bizarre murder of Green Beret Doctor Jeffrey McDonald's wife and children is one example—it is difficult to dismiss his involvement in assassination theory, as William Buckley, Jr., tries to do, as one of his "tangents." Instead, it was a recognition by him that assassination had become a subterranean issue in American politics that could be exploited by the irresponsible, and his "good-wing" instincts led him to preempt them by involving himself at the peril of damaging his own reputation.

In 1975, Thomas Kranz, the district attorney's special counsel in the Robert Kennedy assassination investigation, wrote a report which was withheld. In an article for the *Saturday Review*, published in 1977, Lowenstein lamented the constant revisions of the report and speculated that "the Kranz report may have met the same fate as the door frames and ceiling tiles" which had been taken as evidence by the Los Angeles Police Department and never produced. After his article appeared, the Kranz Report was released in 1977. It criticized the way the official investigation had been conducted but supported its findings in general. Lowenstein, Schrade, and Dr. Joling testified soon after the report's release before the Los Angeles Board of Supervisors, providing a point-by-point rebuttal, but no further action on the case was ever taken.

60.

The winter of 1974–75 was a bleak one for Lowenstein and Jenny. He was no longer head of ADA. Out of office and without an effective base, he suffered increasingly from a sense of deflation. Long Beach was in an advanced state of decay and money began to get tight. Jenny was restless and spoke about going back to school and having a career of her own.

Lowenstein's principal frustration, as he indicated to William Buckley, Jr., was that it was almost impossible for him to get coverage for anything he said or wrote. Buckley, who put Lowenstein on "Firing Line" frequently, paying him for his appearances, encouraged him to write, believing that Lowenstein "wrote with great, great skill." But Buckley adds that Lowenstein "had to labor very strenuously to write. If he had been able to write with great facility, he might have used that particular pulpit rather than the congressional pulpit." Lowenstein himself put it more succinctly when he said to Jenny, "Writing is like shitting grapefruits."

Lowenstein began to have premonitions of his death during 1974. He called up his brother Larry and Greg Stone, and woke up a family friend, Gina Galke, who had been helping him with his manuscripts, to tell them what should be done when he died. He would begin: "When I die, this is what I want to happen." The most important thing was that he wanted William Buckley, Jr., to be a pallbearer at the funeral.

The preoccupation with death had some specific causes. During that period his physician brother, Bert, would come to the house, often at night, to treat Lowenstein's excruciatingly painful back condition or some other illness. Still targeted by haters, Lowenstein continued to get threatening phone calls and his house was fired on. In a particularly low moment, Lowenstein remarked, "Life is a shit sandwich and every day you have to take a bite."

In 1975, Lowenstein received a phone call from Dennis Sweeney, then living in Philadelphia. According to Jenny, Sweeney was incoherent and threatening. He believed people were trying to kill him. "Call off your dogs," Sweeney told Lowenstein, according to one account of the conversation. Jenny remembers that Lowenstein met Sweeney at a railway station in Pennsylvania where they spoke. At least one letter came after that blaming Lowenstein for Sweeney's family problems.

Lowenstein's ability to rebound depended to a great extent on the vast network of friends and admirers he had developed through his various crusades. If that network showed signs of waning in New York, it was as strong as ever in California, where, as Harvey Lippman puts it, Lowenstein was "revered." His powerful allies there included Senators Cranston and Tunney and Congressman Pete McCloskey, and he remained a favorite on the campuses of the state's colleges and universities. Jerry Brown, the young, newly elected governor of California was an admirer of Lowenstein's. Brown had been in Mississippi briefly and had participated in a minor way in the McCarthy campaign. Politically ambitious, he was impressed by Lowenstein's acumen and skill. Lowenstein, in turn, thought Jerry Brown had the greatest potential for growth since Bobby Kennedy, whom, he suggested, Brown resembled.

Brown approached Lowenstein and asked him to run his student intern program that summer in Sacramento and to work in a general capacity as an ombudsman and informal counselor. Taking Harvey Lippman with him as his deputy, Lowenstein flew to California while Jenny drove out with a friend and the children. According to Harvey Lippman, California marked a "reversal" of Lowenstein's fortunes. Lowenstein's confidence returned. He announced that he would not settle for less than a house with a pool for no more than $500 per month—his due, he insisted, because of who he was. That Lowenstein should suddenly "pull rank" was, in Lippman's view, "sweet," considering what he had put up with in Long Beach. In the end, Brown turned over his own Los Angeles house in Laurel Canyon to the family, while Lowenstein worked in Sacramento and visited on weekends. On one such visit, he told Jenny, "I'll chuck politics and just write movie scripts." "He wanted to write or direct," Jenny remembers. "And he felt free, riding a convertible all day, drinking orange juice, face to the sun." But he also said to her that he envisioned himself dying soon; he could be shot, he said, or it might be a heart attack. His frame of reference was different from hers, he explained, because he was approaching fifty while she was still young.

Lowenstein finally completed his screenplay about the civil rights movement, *Angus*. Marcia Borie helped him distribute it, working with him at the same time on other writing projects. Lowenstein also wanted to write a novel, a book on assassinations, and a reflection on American politics.

Lowenstein recruited University of Santa Clara law student Tom Flynn to help him supervise the forty interns under his direction. Meanwhile, he also advised Tom Bradley, the black mayor of Los Angeles. Senators Cranston and Tunney asked Lowenstein to stay and to run for Congress as a Democrat in Los Angeles. Lowenstein was offered a "safe" seat in West Los Angeles by Assemblyman Howard Burman and Henry Waxman of the "Waxman-Burman" machine, as it was known. The district was very liberal and Jewish with new people constantly moving in. Because everyone was a transient, there was no such thing as a "carpetbagger." "He could have run there and won," Harvey Lippman maintains. But Lowenstein decided against running in California.

Curtis Gans insists that Lowenstein made the decision because he still wanted to run for the Senate eventually, and with Tunney and Cranston in office, he would be blocked since they were his friends and he would never challenge them. "If Al had said, 'Let's stay in California,'" Jenny laments, "we might have saved everything. He was away from the ties and pressures of Long Island and he had real friends, in the sense that they were not political. . . . Plus he really loved California like a kid."

At the end of the summer, they returned to Long Beach. During that fall and winter, Lowenstein lectured extensively on campuses in California, including Santa Clara, Berkeley, and Stanford, and got closer to Jerry Brown. Lowenstein was on the move again, upbeat, traveling, speaking. He felt a Democratic breeze and he tried to whip it up into a gale.

In the winter of 1976, Jimmy Carter got the jump on the other candidates, winning the New Hampshire primary. Lowenstein, who was not a fan of Carter's, talked to Brown about his experiences in the McCarthy campaign, whetting his appetite for the presidency. When Carter came in fourth in Massachusetts, Brown decided to run. Lowenstein believed that had Brown gotten into the race earlier, he could have succeeded.

On March 16, Lowenstein phoned Tom Flynn to tell him that Brown was running. Lowenstein was named "political director" of the campaign, which would have its first big test in Maryland. Polls there showed Brown a distant underdog, lagging behind Carter, Wallace, Jackson, and Udall with only 7 percent of the vote. He had no organization and few backers. Lowenstein, using his influence among his many friends in Montgomery County, a wealthy suburb of Washington, helped the Brown organization raise half a million dollars, enough for Brown to blitz the state. On May 18, Brown reaped the benefits, winning with a decisive 49 percent to Carter's 37. He won every county but one, and in Montgomery, where Lowenstein had been his chief organizer, Brown beat Carter by more than two to one.

Brown then sent Lowenstein into Oregon and, on Lowenstein's instructions, Harvey Lippman into Rhode Island. Lowenstein also dispatched Flynn to Rhode Island, giving him the phone numbers of two antiwar Brown supporters. In Oregon, however, Brown was late in filing and the Oregon secretary of state refused to list him. Brown was forced to either withdraw or stage a write-in candidacy, which he decided to do.

"The effort was about the most electrifying undertaking in the entire 1976 campaign," journalist Jules Witcover wrote, "reminiscent as it was of the 'kiddie korps' that had labored so tirelessly and brilliantly for McCarthy in New Hampshire in 1968. And Lowenstein, a leading force in that earlier effort, was in the thick of things in Oregon, speaking on campuses and rallying to Brown's side many of the Democrats who gave McCarthy his primary victory over Robert Kennedy."

Frank Church won the Oregon primary, but Brown finished a strong third, just behind Carter. In Rhode Island, with Lowenstein's lieutenants in the field, delegates committed to Brown took 31 percent of the vote, leading Carter and Church. Because of Lowenstein's last-minute wizardry, Brown had become a serious contender for the presidency after serving only one year as governor. But Brown faded, and Lowenstein ultimately became frustrated with his unstructured style. Carter was nominated and the Democratic party turned to the right.

That summer, Lowenstein was smuggled into the Republican convention with William Buckley, Jr.'s credentials (two old CIA hands pulling a fast one). From the middle of a crowd on the floor, a voice shouted, "Betty Ford kissed me! Betty Ford kissed me!" To everyone's amazement, it was Al Lowenstein, beaming, having been kissed by the president's wife.

61.

In 1976, Lowenstein was felled by a painful attack of kidney stones. It was almost as if his body succumbed upon returning to Long Island and the dismal drabness of Long Beach. Influenced by the women's movement, Jenny began studying for her master's in social work at Adelphi, where Lowenstein took a teaching assignment to help pay the tuition.

Lowenstein advised a friend who was contemplating a race against Norman Lent in the neighboring 4th Congressional District that he shouldn't do it because the odds were insurmountable. He also promised Jenny that he would not run against John Wydler again. She, in turn, warned him that if he did, she was leaving, yet Lowenstein reneged on his promise and committed himself to another race against Wydler.

"Their marriage was in trouble," Harriet Eisman said. "Jenny was in a rage when he ran against Wydler the second time after he promised not to. He did run and this was the precipitating factor. At one point Jenny said to me, 'There must be something better in life for me than this.' She was torn."

Jenny refused to campaign. "During the last Wydler campaign, the relationship was untenable," she explains. "I was tired and angry because he ran again. Al was . . . mad at me because I wouldn't do what I had always done. And I was mad at him. We didn't have a personal life. . . . I feel guilty for what I did. I just walked out. He was very stubborn too. He wouldn't beg me to stay. It hurt him. He cared about me but didn't understand how to be a private person. I didn't try to help him. I just walked out the door. I think a mature person could have said, 'Let's try this or that,' but we didn't sit down and work it out."

The irony of their marriage was that Jenny was often far more politically astute than her husband. While he had assumed that Arthur Goldberg would be a strong candidate for governor, Jenny had known from the beginning that he would be a disaster and would hurt the ticket in 1970, when Lowenstein was, in fact, defeated for reelection. She had advised him to run for the Senate that year, not Congress. Had he listened to her, he might well have succeeded, but it was his weakness that he would take advice from no one.

Jenny had also advised him to stay in California and not to run again against Wydler. Knowing that he had an opportunity to run for a safe seat in Los Angeles, where he had every chance of being elected, Jenny wanted him to do it not only because she wanted a better life (although she complained to friends that she felt stuck in Long Beach and longed to live in a beautiful home), but because she understood that this was how he could win. He chose to ignore her advice, remaining a perpetual candidate and allowing his marriage to fail. There was in his behavior a suggestion of the old-fashioned patriarchal attitude of his father, a hint that although he dreamed of assimilation, he was somehow compelled to act out his traditional role. In this respect, Jenny grew while he did not. He remained apart, looking at the world "from outside," as he put it, through a "knot hole." Always the outsider, he couldn't be intimate and, in some ways, he remained the son of an immigrant.

Lowenstein was embittered by the attitude Jenny's family took about money. Although Jenny had an account managed by her brother-in-law Larry Huntington at the Fiduciary Bank, of which Huntington was president, Lowenstein told Harvey Lippman that her family never gave him the money he wanted for his political campaigns, and that he resented it. "Because he was doing good things," says Lippman paraphrasing Lowenstein, "he felt people should support him in those causes." And Carol Hardin Kimball adds, "Jenny would never spend capital. It was a problem in the marriage."

Jenny absented herself from the Wydler campaign that summer and went up to her sister's house in Maine. Then she enrolled at Boston University to finish her MSW. She took the children with her and moved into a large and beautiful farmhouse in Wayland which she rented from Devie Hamlin, a Boston socialite whom she had known as a teenager. Jenny's three sisters were all living in Belmont, another rich Boston suburb, having "returned from different points," as she puts it. Now she was returning as well. "I said to myself, 'What had my life been all about if I was coming back to what I wanted to leave,'" Jenny confesses. "I felt ashamed of leaving Al, but I couldn't stay in Long Beach."

Also back in Boston was Nick Littlefield. Lowenstein's close personal friend, his campaign manager in the Rooney effort, and the director of his youth voter-registration drive, Littlefield had stayed in Brooklyn long enough to collect affidavits and to see Rooney's first primary victory overthrown in 1972. After working for the U.S. attorney's office in New York for three years, he was named a teaching fellow at Harvard Law School in 1976 and a lecturer in law. "Nick was in Boston, in Cambridge," Jenny relates, "teaching full-time at Harvard Law School in the clinical program, working with Gary Bellow, who met Al at Yale. They were all connected."

Harriet Eisman believed Nick and Jenny were attracted to each other because of their common background. "Jenny knew Nick from the campaign," Eisman recalled. "All the young men had a crush on Jenny. Jenny had a marvelous sense of humor, she was warm, she was a kid herself, they could identify with her . . . and beyond that, I really don't know what happened. But Al was away a lot. . . . While he was doing all this campaigning, he was still continuing with his international involvements, and they were heavy duty stuff. Jenny was miserable in Long Beach. She is a good person. She felt guilty and heartsick that she was leaving. She knew she was leaving with Nick but I didn't. I said to her, 'I'm not sitting in judgment over this. Al is heartsick, so am I, but there is no one in the whole district who would not appreciate why you're doing this.'"

According to Harvey Lippman, "Al refused to admit to himself what was going on. Al got vicious about Jenny and his marital affairs. Al was so mad at Jenny, he was going to fight her for custody. But they ended with a joint custody agreement."

A shattered Lowenstein told Alice Brandeis Popkin in Washington, "My marriage is falling apart. I can't believe this is happening to me. My wife is having an affair with my best friend." In a rage at Little-field, he snapped to Harriet Eisman, "I'll never believe who she's hooked up with." But Jenny insists, "I didn't know I would marry Nick. I saw him after the 1977 separation."

On August 3, 1977, Jenny was present at a reception hosted by Andrew Young when Lowenstein was sworn in as an ambassador to the United Nations. Afterward, Jenny phoned her friend from Long Beach, Lowenstein campaign worker Nan Windmueller, who recalls the conversation: "She told me from her Massachusetts home that when Al joined the U.N. staff, where there was a reception for him, Jenny came and everyone close to them knew this would be their last appearance together as husband and wife. He called her up to the stage and gave her a present. (My parents, who were there, felt it was a contrived event meant to impress the crowd. They felt Jenny was being used and they felt sorry for her.) Jenny told me that the gift was a plaque—like one given for years of dedicated service. He probably meant well, but again, intimacy was foreign to him.

"Jenny said she'd been to a woman therapist and had wanted Al to come too, or to go to one of his own, in a desperate attempt to save the marriage. Al wouldn't go. Her fear was of repeating the pattern of her mother's life—marriage after marriage. I lectured her and said, 'Jenny, you are *not* your mother!'"

After they formalized the terms of their separation, Jenny left for good in their Toyota station wagon, while Lowenstein drove off in the other direction in his blue Volkswagen convertible. His campaign colors had always been blue; that didn't change.

After serving as general counsel to a special Massachusetts commission investigating kickback schemes in government construction contracts, Littlefield joined the prestigious Boston law firm of Foley, Hoag & Eliot while teaching part-time at Harvard. Jenny became a social worker in the black ghetto of Roxbury. After the divorce, Jenny and Littlefield were married in September of 1979. They lived in the house Jenny had rented in Wayland. "Al was in a rage and rightly so," she confirms. "Before he died, we hadn't gotten close, but we could talk." According to Littlefield, "He was really pissed when he came up for the kids and he saw this place."

After Lowenstein's death, although some of his friends resented her marriage to Littlefield, the Lowenstein family treated Jenny more or less as though she were Lowenstein's widow, taking her back into the family and validating her remarriage as if it had happened after her ex-husband's death. They felt honored to have her, and she was happy to accept the aura with which it endowed her; she also wanted her children to have the benefit of being Lowenstein's heirs.

The David Levine cartoon drawings of Lowenstein "Dumping Johnson," illustrations for David Halberstam's article in *Harper's*, hang in a bedroom in Jenny's house. Harriet Eisman commented that Jenny and Nick were living in a "strange kind of *ménage à trois* with a dead man."

Three years after his death, at a memorial service for Lowenstein in Arlington, where he was buried, it was Jenny who stepped forward first to lay a flower on his grave. Only then did the others follow her lead.

62.

After Jenny left in the summer of 1976, Greg Stone and Tom Flynn moved in to work on the Wydler campaign, both believing that Lowenstein would win. Joining the entourage was Lowenstein's new campaign manager, Paul Tully, a professional who had been a top organizer for Morris Udall's unsuccessful presidential bid.

Lowenstein put together what James Wechsler described in a column as a "rare coalition" of conservatives and liberals. He was endorsed by William Buckley, Jr., black civil-rights leader and Georgia Congressman Andrew Young, former Nixon aides Leonard Garment and Rita Hauser, conservative theoritician Ernest Vanderhag, hawkish pro-Israel Democratic Senator Henry Jackson, Governor Jerry Brown, the Patrolmen's Benevolent Association, and the Americans for Democratic Action.

Wydler countered with an endorsement from Conservative Senator James Buckley, William Buckley, Jr.'s, brother. With the polls showing Lowenstein surging, Wydler then launched a smear campaign similar to Norman Lent's in 1970. His literature charged that Lowenstein had voted against crime bills in Congress, where his had been the worst attendance record. The literature also accused Lowenstein of meeting with draft dodgers and fomenting riots. Although Lowenstein challenged him to bring the campaign literature before the Fair Campaign Practices Committee, Wydler refused.

The final result gave Wydler 56 percent of the vote with 110,366 and Lowenstein 87,868. But Lowenstein had outspent Wydler $93,568 to $90,568. He had still been able to raise money and to bring in some student volunteers; the bus from Notre Dame had come again. But now the cheering had finally stopped. Greg Stone concluded that Jenny had been right; Lowenstein could never win in this district. When Harriet Eisman advised him to look for "a solid job," Lowenstein replied, "The only job I wanted I couldn't get." The young student volunteers gathered up their sleeping bags in the lonely house on Lindell Boulevard and disappeared.

Jimmy Carter was elected president over Gerald Ford, with Eugene McCarthy running an inconsequential race as an independent. Mary King, Dennis Sweeney's ex-wife, now married to Atlanta psychiatrist Peter Bourne, surfaced, bedecked in jewelry, as a top Carter advisor headed for a big job with VISTA, the domestic volunteer agency. Although Lowenstein had not supported Carter, a number of his young people were on the transition committee. They were "ADA people, NDC types," as Harriet Eisman describes them, including Lowenstein's protégé from the civil rights movement, Barney Frank, who had been elected to Congress, and Lowenstein's congressional aide Arnie Miller, who had joined the White House staff. But Lowenstein's most influential friend in the Carter camp was Andrew Young.

Lowenstein complained to Harriet Eisman that she "had abandoned him," she related. "So I told him I would shake down Carter and get him something in the administration." Early in 1977, Eisman went down to Washington for an early morning appointment with Andrew Young and said to him, "There has to be something for Al. I can't believe that with all Al has done, that everyone is so self-motivated not to help him."

Asked by Young what it was that Lowenstein wanted, Eisman replied, "I don't know. He knows Third World leaders. . . . Maybe head of the U.N.?" To her surprise, Young said, "I want that for myself." According to Eisman, "Al felt he could work with Andy Young in some capacity, so Andy recommended him. Andy was really the one who got Al the position." Lowenstein had, in fact, wanted to be ambassador to South Africa, but this proved unattainable.

Lowenstein's first appointment in the Carter administration was as

United States representative to the United Nations Human Rights Commission in Geneva, a position held by Eleanor Roosevelt in the Truman administration. He was also named U.S. representative on the Trusteeship Council, the position held by Mason Sears when Lowenstein, cooperating with the CIA, had smuggled Hans Beukes out of South Africa so he could testify before the Fourth Committee of the General Assembly on South West Africa in 1959. Lowenstein himself had testified before the U.N. at that time on South African abuses of its mandate over South West Africa. As his aides, Lowenstein recruited Tom Flynn and Rhodes scholar Brent McNight, both from Jerry Brown's internship program, then flew to Geneva where he assigned Flynn to comb through all of Eleanor Roosevelt's speeches at the commission.

On the Trusteeship Council, Lowenstein was faced with a delicate matter: the CIA bugging of the office of the Micronesian representative at the United Nations. The Micronesian islands, taken from Japan by the United States after the war, were run as American outposts with the requirement that every year, the American government report to the United Nations on their status. Because the Micronesians were agitating for independence, the CIA had begun bugging the office of their representative and chiefs when they came to the U.N.

When the Micronesians discovered the surveillance, they protested. Lowenstein and Flynn were briefed by a "National Security officer," as Flynn describes him. Because various Micronesian splinter groups, who appeared before the Trusteeship Council to complain, were prepared to use the issue to America's disadvantage, Lowenstein insisted on a meeting with the Micronesians. On Lowenstein's advice, the United States admitted what had happened but declined to ask the United Nations to undertake a formal investigation, as only the United State had standing to do. This put Lowenstein in the incongruous position of having sought to condemn South Africa in the Trusteeship Council for mistreating Namibia, while denying the Micronesians the right to do the same to the United States for its abuse.

As Carter's spokesman for the president's human rights policy, Lowenstein put the Soviet Union on the defensive at the start of the Human Rights Commission session by taking up the cause of Soviet Jewry and the cases of dissidents Orlov, Shcharansky, and Ginsberg. When Lowenstein demanded to know why Soviet human rights activist Yuri Orlov had been arrested, he did so, insists Flynn, without State Department permission. Lowenstein's controversial deputy Brady Tyson, who had worked as a missionary in Brazil in 1967 and was, according to Frank Carlucci, "expelled for political activities" (Carlucci explains that Tyson was "helping left-wing groups"), also caused controversy. When Tyson delivered a speech attacking a number of countries on human rights, it was "unauthorized," delivered without clearance from Lowenstein. Just as in 1959, there was an appearance of spontaneity.

And, as it had in 1959, the "good-wing" policy appeared to be working. Just as Donald Grant of the *St. Louis Post-Dispatch* had picked up on the Hans Beukes story, the press picked up on Lowenstein's attacks on the Soviet Union for its human rights violations. In May of 1977, Lowenstein testified before the House Subcommittee on International Organizations of the Committee on International Relations, stressing how important he believed his assignment in Geneva had been in promoting Carter's human rights policy. Crediting Carter's permanent representative to the United Nations, Andrew Young, with having exercised considerable influence in changing the international atmosphere for America, he argued for giving human rights a high priority in American foreign policy.

At Young's request, Carter named Lowenstein United Nations ambassador for special political affairs, making him, along with Young's deputy Don McHenry, one of the five ambassadors in the U.S. delegation. Apart from his salary of $52,000, Lowenstein had an office at the U.N. mission, a paid aide, Tom Flynn, and five student volunteers. Lowenstein moved into an apartment on East 44th Street and Second Avenue, close to the U.N., and after being sworn in that summer, went to work.

According to Flynn, Lowenstein "didn't spend that much time in the office." Flynn also relates that Lowenstein was routinely briefed by the CIA people in New York. He received whatever documents he wanted and had access to top intelligence and policy-making people, including Secretary of State Cyrus Vance and White House National Security Adviser Zbigniew Brzezinski, with whom Lowenstein shared a deep suspicion of the Soviet Union. Every two weeks, Lowenstein went to Washington for consultations at the State Department and the White House; President Carter, in turn, consulted with him when he was in New York. According to Tom Flynn, Lowenstein dealt with the CIA and the State Department as though they were interchangeable, and Flynn observes that, in fact, they were often the same people. He states as well that there are "lots of CIA people working at the United Nations."

Lowenstein's office was responsible for a variety of mundane matters, including parking tickets, rent problems, and personal matters of the some 8,000 people employed by the missions of the member countries of the U.N. The failure of the Congo to pay its rent and the expulsion of the Vietnamese ambassador who was caught spying fell within his jurisdiction. But these matters he palmed off on his staff, to the chagrin of Tom Flynn. Most of the time, Lowenstein was out of the country.

With Carter in the White House, the CIA's "good-wing" approach
to Third World revolution was at its zenith. The hard line in Vietnam
had been a failure. As new revolutionary situations sprang up closer
to home, an alternative method of dealing with them became essential. Implicit in the implementation of the "good-wing" approach is the
understanding that governments established in the Third World countries should be controllable, not reactionary. With Andrew Young's
help, Lowenstein found himself in a position to put his point of view
into practice.

As a spokesman on human rights for the Carter administration,
Lowenstein took numerous trips abroad sponsored by the USIA
(called the International Communications Agency during the Carter
years and at another time, the United States Information Service, or
USIS). Lowenstein's job was to emphasize American support for human rights and to meet with opposition groups in the countries to
which he traveled. According to Flynn, there were four such major
trips: to Eastern Europe, to Western Europe and South Africa, to
black African countries, and to Central and South America. Lowenstein always managed side trips to Spain. In 1977, on his major trip
through Central and South America, he visited Nicaragua, where the
Somoza regime was under increasing pressure from opposition groups
covering the whole spectrum, right to left. The threat of Communist
revolution loomed large in Nicaragua, and the more Somoza resisted
change, the greater that threat became.

One of Lowenstein's contacts in Managua was Edgar Chamorro, a
leader of the Democratic Conservative party who also served as an
ambassador to the United Nations with the Nicaraguan delegation. An
opponent of Somoza, he had been placed in the delegation by the
dictator, who was head of the Liberal party, in an attempt to show that
political diversity was permitted in Nicaragua. Chamorro was from a
very old aristocratic Nicaraguan family which had held power before
Somoza; his party wanted a return to electoral democracy, and while
in Nicaragua, Lowenstein spent time not only with him, but with his
brother Eduardo, who had served in the Nicaraguan Congress.

The Chamorros assert that Lowenstein was instrumental in putting
the Sandinistas in power in Nicaragua. Based in Miami, where Edgar
is one of the seven-member national directorate of the Fuerza De-
mocrática Nicaragüenese (known popularly as "*contras*"), the Chamorros submit that the Carter administration backed the Sandinistas, believing them to be the only viable alternative to the Communists; they
maintain that the CIA destabilized Somoza so they could take power.
They argue that it was not bad intentions but lack of knowledge of the
true nature of the Sandinistas which led them to do so. A word they
both use to describe Carter administration policy is "misguided."

"They felt they could work with the Marxists and buy the revolution," Eduardo asserts. In his view, Lowenstein was "the leading force" behind the policy to put the Sandinistas into power which was adopted because of the "fear that unless these non-Communist leftists were put in, the Communists would take over after Somoza."

Eduardo Chamorro states that Lowenstein was from what he calls "the extreme left" of the CIA. "I still believe," he asserts, "that the CIA has different colors, shades of political opinion depending on where they are working. In the back of their minds, they believe that the Caribbean and the underdeveloped part of Latin America couldn't afford to be democratic." Eduardo Chamorro concludes that this "extreme left" of the CIA, which included Lowenstein, supported in the Caribbean and Latin America those Marxists it believed to be controllable.

Eduardo Chamorro's conclusion is that "the CIA was finally outwitted by Castro." He explains that when the Sandinistas were put into power, the Communists "overtook" the moderates and "seized control." In his opinion, Lowenstein's wing of the CIA was "academic and naive," but Lowenstein's performance was impressive. "He was like the messiah," Eduardo Chamorro relates, "telling us there was going to be a change. After he arrived, things started to change, to be more decisive in the diplomatic, political, and military areas. After Lowenstein's presence, the United States military relationship with Nicaragua weakened. Support for Somoza weakened dramatically after Lowenstein's appearance." And a friend of Chamorro's, who works primarily within Nicaragua in opposing the Sandinistas and who does not want to be named, adds, "After Lowenstein's arrival, everything happened." Asserts Eduardo Chamorro, "Everyone knew Somoza had to go. The real secret war was the one against Somoza, not against the Sandinistas."

Edgar Chamorro recalls visiting Lowenstein's office at the U.N. and spotting a copy of *The Sandino Affair* on his desk. They talked about the broad coalition which was being assembled to get rid of Somoza and the high level of activity of the United States in this period. "Lowenstein was very much in favor of the Sandinistas," the former ambassador reflects. "Lowenstein was very active in destabilizing Nicaragua. They wanted to get rid of Somoza by any means."

The Chamorro analysis is partially confirmed by Sidney Lens, senior editor of *The Progressive*, who has written:

> Sometimes Washington's tactics are crowned with quick success—as they were in Salvador Allende's Chile ten years ago. Sometimes they meet with repeated failure, as in the twenty-five year campaign against Fidel Castro's Cuba. And sometimes the outcome remains in doubt—as it does with respect to the Sandinistas of Nicaragua.

For years, the brutal Somoza dynasty enjoyed Washington's whole-hearted support as it amassed all but incalculable wealth at the expense of the Nicaraguan people. In the late 1970's when it became clear that the Somoza days were numbered, the Carter administration (in conjunction with Catholic prelates and Nicaragua's official Moscow-oriented Communist Party) tried to ease the last Somoza out of power while leaving the system relatively intact.

Lens argues that the Sandinistas would not make a deal with the United States and took power themselves. He writes further that "Washington, probing to see whether the new regime in Managua was for sale, offered a $75 million loan. But the Sandinistas refused to accede to U.S. conditions. They would not turn their backs on the revolution in nearby El Salvador, for example, nor would they reject Cuban offers of assistance. Once it became clear that Nicaragua would no longer be a submissive satellite of the United States, Washington began turning the screws."

Sandinista officials become incensed at the suggestion that the United States helped put them in power. They prefer the Lens version of what took place; the Americans did want Somoza out, but the Sandinistas took power without their help. But could they have come to power unless the United States let them? And could the United States have done this without Lowenstein, who, in 1979 after he had left the U.N., celebrated their victory with enthusiasm?

Lowenstein's aide Ken McComiskey confirms that Lowenstein was "elated" when the Sandinistas took the presidential palace in 1979. But as Eduardo Chamorro observed, "Lowenstein was an extraordinary person, but there was an enormous cultural gap. He saw an analogy between civil rights in the United States and Nicaragua. As in the case of Zimbabwe, he believed the analogy of the the United States system was applicable. But the courts were not the same in these places." But on another level, Lowenstein was a professional in the intelligence business, working in the interests of the West. There is an impossible contradiction in this. The very interests he was serving resisted the kinds of changes he wanted to take place because ultimately those changes would lead to the loss of what the interests wanted to preserve.

While he supported those left-wing movements in the Third World which he believed were capable of preempting the Communists, Lowenstein was openly critical of Third World hostility to Israel. He was emphatic in his criticism of the U.N. resolution which defined Zionism with racism. He said this was a "spiral" he had tried to reverse while at the Human Rights Commission, but admitted the goal was "noble but hopeless." The continued attacks from Third World countries against Israel, a country which enjoyed Lowenstein's strong support and whose ambassador, Chaim Herzog, was a good friend of his, forced him to redefine his attitude to the U.N., bringing his outlook closer to the neoconservatism of Moynihan and Henry Jackson. Disillusioned, he still refused to dismiss the U.N. entirely. "To abandon the U.N. would be dangerous and self-defeating," he wrote. "To abandon the effort to improve the U.N. makes no sense at all."

In November of 1977, Ed Koch, the Democratic congressman from the 18th Congressional District in Manhattan (known as the "Silk Stocking" district because it encompassed the wealthier neighborhoods of New York's Upper East Side) was elected mayor. The night Koch was elected, Lowenstein spoke by phone to some of the mayor-elect's staff, expressing his interest in the seat and exploring whether Koch would be willing to support him. Koch, he was told, would not get involved in the fight over his seat. Soon afterward, Lowenstein told friends that Ed Koch was endorsing him for Congress, and though Koch denied it, Lowenstein announced his candidacy and stuck to his story.

A special election for Koch's seat was called for February 1978. The Democratic nominee was to be chosen at a Congressional District convention. Delegates to the convention were to be selected at miniconventions attended by representatives from all the Democratic clubs and held in each of the C.D.'s Assembly Districts.

On January 5, 1978, ten days before the Silk Stocking caucuses, Lowenstein met with Harvey Lippman, his attorney. Lippman produced the separation agreement with Jenny, which Lowenstein signed, and then handed him the Federal Election Commission "initial filing" for the campaign in which Lippman agreed to serve as treasurer. Lowenstein told Lippman that in signing the separation agreement, he was ending an old life, and on signing the filing, he was beginning a new one.

Lowenstein approached his old friend, former tennis star and one-time administrative assistant to Senator Russell Long, Ham Richardson, to be his campaign chairman. Richardson, who had moved his successful investment and oil exploration business to a Park Avenue penthouse, looked at Lowenstein with sympathy and frustration when Lowenstein told him that he was taking a leave of absence from the U.N. to seek Koch's seat.

"Al, you're a jerk," he told him.

"I guess I am," Lowenstein replied, "but I can't help it. I'll probably continue to be the same."

Richardson agreed to serve as his campaign manager, believing the Silk Stocking district was Lowenstein's natural constituency. But when he saw Lowenstein campaigning on the street dressed in a hideous lemon-lime ski jacket, Richardson took him aside. "Al, you can't look like a jerk your whole life," he told him. Richardson then took him shopping for some decent clothes, picking out a suit, with which Lowenstein was delighted. "Al wouldn't let himself be merchandized the way Koch did with Garth's help," Richardson explains. "He insisted that clothes were not important. It was the issues that counted. In the early days, the people around Al were clones of himself. He had no one around who had the authority to tell him what to do and not to do. He was a great congressman but not a great office seeker."

Admirers like Congressmen Andy Jacobs and Doug Walgren came up from Washington to help. Congressman Pete McCloskey sent out a letter to the county committee members in the district describing Lowenstein as a "rare kind of public figure" who was needed back in Congress. "There have been few individuals in recent years who have had the capacity to touch the conscience of people and translate idealism into solid effort for good causes," McCloskey stated. "A few Americans—Bob and Jack Kennedy, Hubert Humphrey, Martin Luther King, Jr., Earl Warren—have had this invaluable quality, and so does Al." And political media strategist David Garth wrote, "I have known Al Lowenstein for almost 20 years. He is hardheaded, persistent and tireless. He is loved because he cares so much, and respected because he is so honorable and so effective. He was clearly one of the best Congressmen this region ever had, in part because his concerns include people everywhere, and consequently people everywhere listen to him as a friend."

Richardson held receptions at his penthouse to raise money and to introduce Lowenstein to the 600 delegates who would select the nominee. But Lowenstein's support lagged. At the packed convention held at the Washington Irving High School, Bella Abzug and millionaire City Councilman Carter Burden battled for the lead with Lowenstein behind them. Burden, a figure of the sixties himself, had been the male half of New York's "golden couple" along with his wife, Amanda, daughter of CBS's William Paley. When Lowenstein threw his support to Burden, infuriating his old ally Abzug, Burden appeared to have won the nomination. But Abzug took the battle to court where two delegates of Burden's were declared ineligible, their votes null and void. Awarded the nomination, Abzug went down in defeat to the Republican candidate, millionaire William Green, heir to the Ex-Lax fortune (and a friend of Lowenstein's from Horace Mann). Most observers believed that Lowenstein would have won the election, and Lowenstein himself, convinced of it, kept his sights on the September primary for the seat.

Back at the United Nations, Lowenstein remained a popular figure in the diplomatic community. He also continued a heavy schedule of lecturing around the country on the campuses. Speaking in late February at a symposium at Duke Law School on "protecting the right to dissent," he lauded the Carter administration's global concern "about repression and injustice." His own role, he stressed, was to involve the United States mission at the U.N. in this concern. Singling out Andrew Young for praise, Lowenstein proclaimed him "the central figure in the world on these questions," and went on to say that "for the first time since Eleanor Roosevelt represented the United States at the United Nations, an American is the central figure in the nerve center of our effort to promote human rights—that is, to reduce suffering—in the world. . . . Periodic disagreements about specific views or statements is a small price to pay for the great benefits that flow from having such a man as our chief representative at the United Nations."

But while Lowenstein continued to praise Young in his speeches, in private he was becoming increasingly critical of him over their differences with regard to policy in southern Africa. He considered Young to be too sympathetic in Zimbabwe-Rhodesia to Robert Mugabe, whom Lowenstein regarded as a dangerous Marxist-Leninist, too apt to use violence. Lowenstein believed Young was pushing the Carter administration too far to the left in the policy for southern Africa, including South Africa and Namibia. As Lowenstein became increasingly convinced that Young was trying to restrict the role Lowenstein would play in southern African (where Lowenstein regarded himself as an expert), and that Young wanted, in fact, to make southern Africa his own exclusive province, he began to distrust Young. Lowenstein himself had retreated from his militant opposition to South Africa. "He grew disillusioned with Andy Young," Harvey Lippman concludes. Increasingly sympathetic to the South African whites, Lowenstein befriended members of its Nationlist government, including South African Ambassador Donald Bell Sole and top foreign-policy aide Sean Cleary. Lowenstein was also close to the Israelis and disapproved of what he regarded as Carter's tilt toward the Arabs in the Middle East. "He would have resigned even if he didn't run for Congress," states Greg Stone, who coedited a book on Lowenstein. "It was clear he couldn't be effective and wouldn't be an errand boy. He felt his credibility was being used for stupid, ineffective policies and the perpetuation of a process with which he was dismally familiar." And William Buckley, Jr., adds that Lowenstein "retreated from the vanities of liberalism," concluding, "He changed his position on the United Nations. He no longer thought of it as an instrument with a divine warrant. He had less faith in the purity of democratic politics and the courage of the academy, and less faith in his compatriots' devotion to free speech. He was moving to an idealistic realism." Others, such as conservative Republican Wendell Willkie II and left-wing writer Doug Ireland, thought Lowenstein was moving rightward toward neoconservatism. He was also still trying to get elected to Congress.

Lowenstein notified Andrew Young early in 1978 that he would be leaving his U.N. post. He made plans in late April to run in the September primary in the 18th C.D., and on June 16 had Tom Flynn type out his letter of resignation. On July 14, in an article in the *New York Post*, Lowenstein explained his resignation, stressing his differences with the Carter administration over America's policy in the Middle East. "Israel was promised F–16's in return for a withdrawal in Sinai," he explained. "Whoever reattached these previously promised planes to a 'package' that includes planes for Saudi Arabia ignored history and flunked psychology. Breaking promises to people seared by broken promises is no way to build confidence in new promises."

But Lowenstein also wanted to detach himself from the administration because he wanted to succeed on his own in elective politics. "We worked for reform politics so everyone could participate, only to discover that nobody wants to any more," he wrote. "So now we must deal with the problem connected to so many others—the problem of how to revive and excite energies." He saw his own candidacy as the best vehicle for accomplishing that goal.

Liberal ideology had always been a basic ingredient in the excitement Lowenstein generated in his campaigns and crusades. But in 1978, not only had liberal ideology all but disappeared, Lowenstein himself, as the result of his neoconservative positions, could no longer posture as the leading liberal. Among what remained of the liberal community in New York, Lowenstein was an outcast. He supported the death penalty and he supported tuition tax credits for private schools, causing him to fail the litmus test of the Liberal party. Lowenstein had told Buckley that he was "shocked by the factual illiteracy of American students" and argued that competition in the education system was necessary to correct what he regarded as a dangerous trend. Albert Shanker and the American Federation of Teachers regarded this position as anathema. But as Buckley also pointed out, if this cost Lowenstein support among liberals, he did not attempt to hide his position from Catholics and conservatives, who favored support of parochial schools.

On a hectic day that spring, Lowenstein, who had not yet formally announced his candidacy, was met by Harvey Lippman at the airport, where they ran into Congressman Bill Green, whom they offered a lift back to the city. Jammed into the tiny seat of the Volkswagen convertible, the tall congressman, his hair windblown and his clothes disheveled as they drove him to a synagogue where he was to speak, asked Lowenstein whether he had decided to run. Lowenstein replied that he really hadn't given it any thought. After dropping Green at the synagogue, however, Lowenstein and Lippman tore over to the West Side, where Lowenstein had a meeting scheduled with his financial committee to discuss his candidacy.

By the time Lowenstein announced in June, his major opponent in the September primary, Carter Burden, had already organized an expensive campaign and had secured the Liberal party nomination. Rick Weidman, a longtime Lowenstein supporter who had come down from Vermont to take over the campaign, contends that "Burden made a deal with the Liberal party" and that generous contributions by Burden to the party determined its decision. Greg Stone points to the purchase by Burden of tickets for Liberal party dinners as the reason for his ability to get the Liberal line, which Lowenstein had never before been denied in his congressional races. But members of the Liberal party executive committee insist that it was Lowenstein's position on issues regarded as particularly crucial at a time when the party had shrunk in size and influence that led them to turn to Burden.

Lowenstein attempted to take the Liberal nomination from Burden by collecting signatures to enter a Liberal primary under the state's Wilson-Pakula law permitting such a challenge. There were about 3,000 registered Liberals in the district and Lowenstein collected some 400 signatures, but they were challenged by Burden. Because Lowenstein's lawyer was held up in a trial, and Weidman was unable to find anyone else to stand in for him, no lawyer was present while the signatures were invalidated. And because there was neither time nor money for an appeal, Lowenstein's Liberal effort was thrown out. "He fell short," Weidman laments. "We knew they were good signatures. We had phoned and got identification and he should have been over by thirty-five. Al was screaming about what a shitty thing this is, but I said we didn't have the resources to fight it." Weidman, who had tried to convince Lowenstein not to run, argued that, in any event, he should concentrate totally on the Democratic primary and forget about the Liberals.

But Lowenstein's inability to get the Liberal line damaged his candidacy. Burden effectively argued that without it, no Democrat could defeat Green. Since Burden had the Liberal nomination, if Lowenstein were to win the Democratic primary, the two of them would split the vote and guarantee Green's victory. The logic of this argument dictated against voting for Lowenstein if a voter wanted a Democratic congressman.

Burden also received the endorsement of the New Democratic Coalition, the last remnant of the old McCarthy supporters in New York, an irony that was not lost on Lowenstein. Moreover, Burden had millions for television advertising while Lowenstein was running, by comparison, a low-budget campaign. A fund-raising committee was set up with Assemblyman Tony Olivieri as chairman. Howard Samuels gave a fund-raising party at his home in Bridgehampton, and Rick Weidman organized events on Fire Island; an organization was hammered out with $100,000. But Lowenstein was plagued by staffing problems. His campaign chairman, Chris McGrath, supposedly politically well connected in the district, was unable to deliver the clubs; except for the Chelsea Democratic Club, they all backed Burden. "If he had put his weight into it, Al would have won," Greg Stone insists. "It was partly deliberate and partly incompetence," Weidman insists. "McGrath did nothing."

Lowenstein had a contingent of gay activists working in the campaign for him. He also phoned people out of his past. Bronia Kupsick, the old friend of his father's, whose daughter had attended the Ethical Culture School with Lowenstein, was among them. "He sounded desperate," Kupsick declares. She went out distributing literature for him in restaurants.

Six weeks before the primary, a city-wide newspaper strike blacked out coverage of the campaign. Without enough money to compete with Burden for television and radio advertising, Lowenstein had counted on the press to cover him and carry his positions. On August 15, William Buckley, Jr., endorsed him in his column, but because of the strike, it didn't appear in any daily paper in the 18th C.D. Called "A Liberal Indulgence," the column was published in *Newsday*, which might have helped Lowenstein had he been running on Long Island. Buckley described the liberal "Eastern Establishment" as "hoary and bureaucratic" but touted Lowenstein as the man who could revive "its idealistic vision," suggesting he could do this by filtering it "through conservative forms." Buckley wrote, "There is, in Lowenstein, a hectic idealism which it is impossible to fail to be moved by. There will be quite a few liberal Democrats in the next Congress. So why not one whose integrity and warmth will at least repristinate a movement grown cynical, bureaucratic and ineffective. . . . Allard Lowenstein belongs in Congress as demonstrably as Rudolph Nureyev belongs on the stage."

Such conservative support was confusing to liberals and it was not enough to offset the liberal support he lost. In the five-way September primary, out of some 40,000 votes cast, Lowenstein lost by about 1,200, or 4 percent. Burden, who spent $600,000 to win the primary, lost the election to Green after spending over a million. "The Burden campaign was well run," Weidman admits. "But Al would have beaten Green, who was weakened by his divorce and was down throughout the campaign against Burden. At the end, Al was O.K. Losing didn't hurt him as much as it did me."

To liberal radio commentator Barry Grey, Lowenstein was a "loser." William Buckley, Jr., countered this description of his friend with a column on America's obsession with backing winners and defended Lowenstein. But Lowenstein, as a liberal, was a loser. His running was no longer a transcendental act of faith but a mechanical response. His once total faith in the system had been replaced by a deep skepticism bordering on the cynical. Lowenstein asked, "Is independence and character more important in a politician than ideology? Has the rot of the political process proceeded far enough so that even what is right is done for the wrong reasons and the only redemption is independent, unpredictable persons in the system?"

63.

After quitting his U.N. job, Lowenstein was made "of counsel" to the international law firm of Delson & Gordon, which, besides its office at 230 Park Avenue, had branches in Djakarta, Indonesia, and Washington. The senior partner, Max Delson, an old liberal with an honorary LLD from Chungang University in Seoul, Korea, was close to Lowenstein and wanted to see him back in Congress. The second-ranking partner was Robert Delson, who had served as general counsel of the American Committee on Africa. He wanted Lowenstein to bring in clients. The firm represented numerous foreign governments and it was believed that Lowenstein would be useful because of his contacts.

It was from this base that Lowenstein made his last South African trip for which he was paid $7,000 by a group of South Africans backed by Anglo-American and Harry Oppenheimer. On this trip Lowenstein worked as a mediator between the white Nationalist government of South Africa and the black nationalist groups fighting for majority rule in Zimbabwe, independence for Namibia, and an end to apartheid in South Africa itself. "He was starting to get paid appropriately," says attorney Alice Brandeis Popkin, a close friend and political ally of Lowenstein.

Lowenstein needed to make money. He kept his own expenses to a minimum, but his child support payments were substantial, and his unusual visitation rights were predicated on his making them. The South Africans were willing to pay him a good fee because he was a valuable asset to them. He had close ties to Frank Carlucci at the CIA and he knew all the key players among the black Africans. At this stage, Lowenstein was traveling as a professional, not as a romantic and idealistic volunteer. Though previously, even when he had worked for the CIA, Lowenstein had done so for a cause, now he had to make a living, and international troubleshooting was something he did well.

In the case of the African trip, however, Lowenstein regarded the fee as his own and the South Africans as his client. "When Delson & Gordon pressed him to meet with foreign governments, he would disappear," Harvey Lippman relates. "When they wanted him to get a favor done by Teddy Kennedy, Al told them that he was involved in personal negotiations with South Africa and that he needed Kennedy's assistance. 'I only have so many chits,' Al explained, 'and this has to take precedence.'"

Lowenstein left Delson & Gordon and, after a hiatus, joined the firm of Layton & Sherman at 50 Rockefeller Plaza. A small, international firm headed by a Yale Law School classmate of Lowenstein's, Robert Layton, who was active in international committees of the prestigious Association of the Bar of the City of New York, Layton & Sherman also had offices in London and Tokyo. Although small, the firm had clients that generated a lucrative practice. Lowenstein told Harvey Lippman that he found the firm to be "less venal" than the one he had left.

With a loan advanced to him by the firm, Lowenstein purchased a condominium in Cyprus, Florida, for his vacations and future retirement. Lowenstein relocated to a new apartment on East 24th Street, and when he finally managed to get the tenant out of his house in Long Beach, he sold it. Lowenstein also placed his papers with the Kennedy Library at Harvard, which stored them at a repository in Waltham, Massachusetts. It was 1979 and Al Lowenstein was fifty. No one found it harder to believe than he did. "Life after fifty is all downhill," he told his high school friend Sandy Friedman.

Lowenstein brooded about death. He knew he had made political enemies who hated him and believed he might be shot. Edith Steinberg, a Lowenstein campaign worker on Long Island, told Lowenstein's cousin Larry Hill, "Al thought he was going to die violently. . . . He expected to die at a very early age." Lowenstein had detailed ideas about his funeral. "He wanted to have a minister and a rabbi, and he wanted someone from the black community," Steinberg related. "He was very strong in wanting specific hymns sung. He wanted a black choir from a Baptist church in Long Beach. He wanted *Amazing Grace* sung. He wanted members of Congress. . . . He was disappointed that Bobby Kennedy died first because Al said he would have given a great eulogy. . . . He wanted to be buried in an Alexander's suit—in a Farkas suit. He didn't care if it was wrinkled. He was not joking. He didn't want crying, he wanted it to be in a huge place. We used to ask him whether Madison Square Garden would be big enough."

Periodically, when he was with Harvey Lippman, he would pull out of his overstuffed briefcase a piece of paper on which he had written his funeral plans, and would ask Lippman if he had them. "I've got them," Lippman always replied gently. The service was outlined in detail. Burial was to be in Arlington cemetery near John and Robert Kennedy.

He could often be found at the Puffing Billy, the last Lowenstein restaurant, which Larry Lowenstein would close after his brother's death. "He'd have people at the Puffing Billy I wouldn't be seen crossing the street with," Harvey Lippman remarks. "But he knew that they could be useful to him in some way in the future."

On one such occasion, he commented to Lippman that he needed some new suits. "Why do you need new suits?" Lippman asked. "Oh, I just thought I could use a couple of new ones." It was the tip-off to Lippman, who knew the suits would be cheap and ill-fitting, that Lowenstein would be campaigning again.

When Ted Kennedy announced that he would challenge Jimmy Carter for the Democratic presidential nomination, Lowenstein told Tom Flynn, "I'm not a particular fan of Ted Kennedy." Dissatisfied and disillusioned with Jimmy Carter for his tilt toward the Arabs, he had told Senator Alan Cranston one night at dinner, "You should run for president." But Lowenstein came out for Kennedy, telling Tom Flynn he thought Kennedy would "knock off Carter," and began working on his behalf independently. He asked Noemie Emery, who had written a biography of George Washington and was writing one on Alexander Hamilton, to provide him with a history of the sexual indiscretions of the Founding Fathers for use in the Kennedy campaign. But Senator Kennedy, Bobby's widow, Ethel, and Kennedy's brother-in-law Steve Smith, who was managing the campaign, were still icy to Lowenstein because of the questions he had raised concerning Robert Kennedy's assassination in his 1974 joint press conference with Paul Schrade. For three months, Lowenstein was given no role. But as Kennedy's fortunes sagged, there was a thaw. Reflecting on her final contacts with Lowenstein, Harriet Eisman recounted, "The campaign was in disarray. He sounded tired. . . . He felt the Kennedy campaign wasn't going anywhere. . . . He was deeply disturbed about the country the last time I spoke with him." And Greg Stone relates that while Lowenstein "was billed as an optimist," he believed that "we were heading toward our own destruction." Stone insists that Lowenstein saw the end of the world as almost inevitable but still thought people should try to prevent the worst from happening.

Lowenstein had his own reason for supporting Kennedy and getting back on good terms with the family. He was planning another run for Bill Green's seat in Congress and expected to face a primary for the Democratic nomination, probably against former Ralph Nader associate Mark Green. Steve Smith had clout in the district; Lowenstein would need him if he were to have any chance of winning. Beyond this, the ritual of opposing the incumbent president provided Lowenstein with a *raison d'etre*, a ticket out of oblivion. He traded on his reputation as a giant-slayer. Moreover, if he ran well, he would remain an asset to his firm. The Kennedys, in turn, realized that they needed his strategic genius. As his role in the campaign increased, Lowenstein had the satisfaction of shedding his image as an outcast; the Kennedys needed him.

Jerry Brown had also announced for the presidency, and Lowenstein had close ties to his camp. Harvey Lippman and Tom Flynn were both working for Brown, who also wanted Lowenstein's help. Though he told Brown that he was backing Kennedy, Lowenstein nevertheless advised Brown to organize Wisconsin. If Kennedy faltered, Brown would be in a position to pick up the pieces, Lowenstein explained.

Lowenstein was building a new base for himself in the gay community, the old student-activist constituency having vanished. Gays responded to Lowenstein's advice to work in the system and develop a "clean machine" to obtain political clout. But they began to resent what they preceived as timidity on Jerry Brown's part in supporting their cause. They had threatened to block an endorsement of Brown in his reelection bid for governor by California's liberal CDC, which had provided the springboard for McCarthy's campaign in 1968. Summoned to San Diego by Brown, Lowenstein had addressed the powerful gay caucus and convinced them not to block the endorsement.

Kennedy used Lowenstein as an unofficial liaison to the gay community. Before the March 11 primary, Lowenstein flew to Florida to campaign in Dade County, where there was an important gay vote. Kennedy lost the Florida primary, but his margin of victory among the gays in the state was considerable, attesting to Lowenstein's effectiveness.

The night of Kennedy's defeat in Florida, Lowenstein turned up at the home of the state campaign coordinator, Mike Abrams, in Coral Gables. Reporter Randy Schultz of the *West Palm Beach Post*, met Lowenstein there for the first time, after which he declared that what interested him about Lowenstein was that his life had been "devoted to crusading, and crusading seemed," he said, "to have become anachronistic." Lowenstein disagreed and said, "I think people care just as much as they did in the sixties. Now it's a tougher world and we just have to keep reminding people that even if things are harder for them, there are still other people who won't even get a chance if we don't help." Lowenstein then launched a prolonged attack on Jimmy Carter, his voice rising as he continued to speak to another while Schultz left to file his story. "I remember thinking," Schultz related, "that he was one activist who had never stopped charging."

Lowenstein's efforts for Kennedy were not confined to the gay community. He made the rounds of the New York Democratic clubs as Kennedy's spokesman, while Harvey Lippman did the same for Brown. Late one night, as Lippman was preparing to speak for Brown at a club, the president announced that the meeting would be delayed because the speaker for Kennedy was running late. "I knew it must be Al," Lippman laughs.

Tom Flynn says Lowenstein tried unsuccessfully to persuade the Kennedy people not to try to throw Brown off the ballot in New York. As they walked down Madison Avenue after dinner at the Puffing Billy, Lowenstein told Flynn that he was proud of him for fighting to keep Brown on the New York ballot. Flynn was Lowenstein's last "student volunteer" protégé and their relations had been strained by Lowenstein's anger at Flynn for remaining at the U.N. after Lowenstein's resignation. The dinner had been a reconciliation of sorts, with Lowenstein acknowledging that he should have told Flynn sooner about his decision to run for Congress. They parted and Flynn caught a plane for Boston to work at Brown headquarters there.

Lowenstein's friends threw a party for him at Studio 54 the first week of March to celebrate the retirement of his campaign debt. A photograph taken at the affair shows model Cheryl Tiegs sitting on the lap of a grinning Lowenstein. Tiegs wrote on the picture, "Al, the way you put your arms around me . . ." A few days later, Lowenstein attended a strategy session with Steve Smith and other members of the Kennedy staff at the office of political consultant David Sawyer to plan the final media push in New York.

On Saturday, March 8, Lowenstein represented Kennedy at a rally at the Boston opera house after George Bush's son had spoken on behalf of his father. Afterward, Lowenstein and his children tried to attend a rally for John Anderson at a church in Wellesley but couldn't get in because of the crowd. He had a bad cold, and on Sunday morning, before he addressed a rally for all the candidates at a synagogue, he tried to soothe his throat with a Sucret, offered by his son Tommy. The only Democrat at the event, Lowenstein could barely speak. It was the last time his children saw him.

64.

Meanwhile, Dennis Sweeney was living alone in New London, Connecticut, his life apparently at a dead end. While working in the draft resistance movement with David Harris, Sweeney had traveled to Bratislava, Czechoslovakia, where, as a representative of the radical American "movement," he had met with a delegation of the South Vietnamese NLF and their North Vietnamese supporters. Later, however, Sweeney broke with Harris, who had elected to go to jail as a draft resister. He turned on Harris for his relationship with the folksinger Joan Baez and for not taking a draft deferment. Harris, deciding to go to jail when resistance organizers were needed out on the streets,had a "Jesus" complex, Sweeney said. "You're not supposed to let them take you," Sweeney told him. "You're supposed to stay out, however you can."

By this time, Sweeney had moved beyond nonviolence. He proposed "sabotage" to associates in the draft resistance movement and led a night raid on the Stanford naval ROTC boathouse, setting fire to it with gasoline and a burning cigarette in a book of matches. Sweeney fled the scene and avoided detection. The case was never solved by the authorities but it prompted the FBI's prolonged investigation of Sweeney. The arson threw suspicion on all the peace groups at Stanford, most of whom denounced the act. Sweeney acknowledged that the sabotage had been a "severe miscalculation." According to David Harris, Sweeney would bring it up as an example of "a very serious mistake" that had jeopardized his whole political cause.

Harris further observes: "The guilt that 'mistake' incited would also provide fertile ground for the incubation of Dennis's madness. The guilt grew as time passed and when he eventually began to believe he was being 'monitored' by what were at first only vaguely discernible nefarious forces, he was sure that his 'mistake' was the reason why."

With several others from the resistance movement, including a fellow member of the commune in which he was then living who had joined with him in the arson attack, Sweeney formed a rock group called "The Fool." The group's political purpose was to launch a "mobile education project" to mobilize "the masses," and they intended to travel in their 1941 Diamond Reo van to the 1968 convention, where they would participate in the planned demonstration. When Harris, who still had authority over the resistance movement in California, overruled him, Sweeney moved out of the commune and led his "caravan" of rock musicians and antiwar protesters on a tour of California's farm country. "Most of the two dozen or so people involved would look upon Dennis Sweeney, 'The Fool's' rhythm guitarist, as the man in charge," Harris wrote.

The mobile education project was a failure. The acid rock converted no one and the response to his political lecture on the war was hostile. At one stop, his speech was interrupted by shouts of "Commie" and "traitor." Angered, Sweeney snapped to the man who had helped him burn down the ROTC building, "This is just like goddamn Mississippi."

Disillusioned with political crusading, Sweeney tried to turn The Fool into a professional rock group to perform in clubs. But his guitar playing and singing were amateurish. When the group fell apart, he and Connie Field, who had been living with him and helping him to edit a documentary on The Fool, traveled east to Boston. In Cambridge, he sought out filmmaker Ed Pincus, whom he had met in Natchez in 1965.

Pincus had made a film of the civil rights movement in Mississippi which contained footage of Dennis Sweeney trying to raise the issue of the Vietnam War with the local blacks. In it, Sweeney is forceful, intelligent, and charismatic. The only thing wrong is the teeth; they are distorted and irregular. The COFO dentist would correct this, making Sweeney's appearance almost flawless.

Sweeney was impressed by Pincus's work and went around the country raising money for the film. When Pincus found that he had excess footage after his own work had been completed, Sweeney asked to fashion it into a film of his own about a black man named Panola. Pincus let him, but when Leni Wildflower and Paul Potter of SDS showed it after extensive editing, the film was a failure. Radicals denounced it as "condescending" and "racist." Sweeney and Field, who had returned to the west with him, traveling by motorcycle, broke up, and Sweeney went back home to Portland, Oregon. At Portland State, Sweeney tried to resume his education, but the "voices" disrupted his concentration in 1973. Convinced that the electrode had been planted in his mouth by the COFO dentist, he pulled his teeth out. Frightened, his mother took him to the Oregon State Mental Hospital for a ten-day observation, but because he never told the doctors about the "voices" and the "transmitters," he was released. When the voices persisted, Sweeney came to believe that the mechanism was somewhere in his body and that the CIA had placed it there.

Some, like Lowenstein, suggested that Sweeney had been driven insane by his experiences in Mississippi, while Mendy Samstein, who had also worked with SNCC in Mississippi and later became a therapist, believes that the seeds of Sweeney's madness had been planted long before his political engagement. Teresa Carpenter wrote, "Or, perhaps, as Field suggests, the sickness was like a virus that lay in his brain until isolation and desperation gave it the culture in which to grow." It has also been established that Sweeney dropped acid (LSD), a drug known to produce chronic paranoid-schizophrenia (as Sweeney's condition was ultimately diagnosed) in disturbed people.

In 1973, the year he visited Lowenstein in Brooklyn, Sweeney wrote to Paul Potter and Leni Wildflower for advice:

We were never really close friends, I realize, but I need some trustworthy advice so that I can begin to plan my life again instead of being perpetually on the run. . . . I don't know any more poetic way of saying it, but I am at the lowest ebb of my life now because of psychological warfare that is being made on me, since about two years ago. I don't believe I am alone in that respect, but since I am alone and have been prior to leaving California in '72 my perspective has become entirely subjective. The specific way in which this psych war had been effected has been a revelation. I am simultaneously attuned to be programmed electronically, apparently, causing obliteration of an already weak ego, social objectification and ostracization, and a freeze on my ability to reintegrate myself intellectually for not being able to work out my own thoughts from the impulses running through my skull. I have done everything I can think to do to locate it and remove it. My efforts have all been failures and usually self-destructive.

No doubt in the sixties I was party to some behavior that was politically irresponsible. If that incurred a social debt then I am willing to pay for it in reasonable terms with some sense of limits such as definition of what constitutes rehabilitative service and duration of same, as opposed to bureaucratic sadism and infinite guilt which is what I see confronting me.

More likely, I think, is that my whole life since early childhood is tangled into a kind of self-aborted preparation for social democratic leadership, where the lines of responsibility for thought and action are very muddy. Unwilling to live my life on the terms that have been revealed recently, that is as a component in a vast communication system, I think I am simply being pressured to leave the country. . . .

I take it that I cannot undo myself from this system within the system. If that is not an absolute rule then I am open to suggestions as to how to go about it, for I really don't feel up to starting over at age thirty in another culture. If that is the reality of the situation, though, I would like to know where you think I might travel to find the medical help I want. . . .

I know we're all up against it now, and I wish I were not so divided from humanity that I can't pitch in. I hope you are both in considerably better shape than me, and if I can work this out we will see each other again. Excuse me for being overly familiar with this letter, but there are some situations in which everyone seems almost equi-distant and a reach might be excusable. I hope I hear from you and that your lives go well through the next three years.

In 1973, Dennis Sweeney turned up in Cambridge, Massachusetts, and dropped in on Ed and Jane Pincus and their family. Pincus was working on an experimental film about his own life called *Diaries* which involved the filming of daily events in detail. Produced as a sophisticated version of home movies, it dwells on a generation of young, well-educated Americans who were radicalized in the sixties but who, because of the disappointments of their movement and the election of Nixon, turned inward, pushing introspection to the limits of its possibility, where the only revolution was the one they could make with their own lives. Vincent Canby of *The New York Times*, in reviewing the film, wrote:

> It is no accident that the film's most riveting moments have nothing to do with self-analysis but with the chance appearance of Dennis Sweeney, the young civil rights activist Ed worked with in the 1960's. Mr. Sweeney comes to see Ed and Jane in Boston to discuss his problem: he's receiving messages through his teeth.
>
> Ed and Jane try to talk rationally to Dennis. They suggest that he seek what's euphemistically called "help." Later they learn that Dennis is blaming them for those messages and is threatening them and their children.

After seeing a Boston psychologist who declared him harmless, not unlike many others who were walking around, Sweeney got a job in a mattress factory in Lynn, Massachusetts, and then moved to Philadelphia where he lived in the home of a minister with the United Church of Christ and worked as a free-lance carpenter. It was from Philadelphia that he phoned Lowenstein in 1975, meeting him at the railway station and refusing his offer of help. Sweeney was convinced, as he indicated to Lowenstein, that Lowenstein was controlling his mind.

Sweeney then moved to Cambridge and for a while worked as a short-order cook. He constantly harassed Pincus, turning his life into a nightmare. After a summer in Vermont, Pincus decided to move his family there permanently and commute to his job in Boston. "By 1976, Dennis Sweeney had become a problem in my life," he explained.

Sweeney had grown "ugly," charging that, with Angela Davis and Allard Lowenstein, Pincus was part of the "International Jewish hate conspiracy" that was controlling his mind and which had been "on the run since Watergate." He threatened Pincus as well as his wife and children, causing Jane Pincus to become enraged with Sweeney for refusing to take responsibility for what was happening in his life. They saw him as the remains of a failed revolution who was unable, if not unwilling, to take hold of his mind and reverse the downward course of his behavior.

Because Sweeney kept phoning Pincus to repeat his denunciations and threats, Pincus finally went to the police. They told him, however, that until Sweeney actually did something, they were powerless to act against him. When Sweeney continued to phone him at his MIT office, Pincus agreed to meet him and have it out. Sweeney had no weapon. Instead, he attacked Pincus with his fists and the filmmaker fell to the ground in the limp, protective passive resistance posture he had learned in the civil rights movement. The blows fell harmlessly on him and Sweeney left, having spent his rage and believing Pincus had been frightened off. His voice would not bother him further. Jane Pincus, fearing that harm might be done to Allard Lowenstein, whom Sweeney was denouncing, contacted a relative of Lowenstein's. It is not known if Lowenstein was ever warned, but he was aware of Sweeney's condition and hostility toward him.

Sweeney wandered down from Massachusetts. He studied carpentry in Norwich, Connecticut, and then moved to Fall River. He lived alone, in total abstinence, having lost his sexual powers in the early seventies. After Fall River, he settled in at a boarding house in the seaport town of Mystic, Connecticut, and then, in 1979, he moved to a renovated barn in New London. None of his old friends had any news of him and rumors persisted that he had committed suicide. Sweeney was then thirty-seven years old, and his landlords, Herman Hamilton and his wife, thought him a pathetic figure; he would occasionally shout to himself in his quarters for no apparent reason. He made beautiful furniture and devoted hours to varnishing it. When he wasn't working, he read books on psychology and corresponded with a Stanford professor on the brain's physiology. He also kept a journal and dwelled on the control of his mind by Allard Lowenstein.

Sweeney heard Lowenstein's voice, Bob Dylan's, and others. He could make the voices tell him what to do. The voices told him to marry a Jew and join the "Allard Lowenstein–Angela Davis" conspiracy. He blamed Lowenstein for the murder of Mayor George Mascone of San Francisco, the crash of the DC–10 in Chicago that killed 200 people, and the crash of the private jet that killed New York Yankee catcher Thurmond Munson. When his stepfather died of a heart attack while playing golf in Portland, Oregon, it pushed Sweeney totally over the brink. He flew home for the funeral and returned determined to stop Lowenstein from causing any more deaths. His plan was to confront his tormentor and get assurances from him that he would stop persecuting him, his family, and others.

Sweeney planned to get assurances from Lowenstein that he would stop the harmful control and then drive in his pickup to Portland where he would move in with his mother. If Lowenstein did not agree to stop, Sweeney knew he would have to kill him. But as Sweeney's court-appointed lawyer, Jesse Zaslov, relates, it was not just Ed Pincus and Al Lowenstein. Sweeney had a whole list of people he had to get straight. "There are a lot of lucky people who don't know how close they came," he concludes.

Early in March, Sweeney walked into Raub's Sporting Goods Store in New London and filled out a pistol permit application. He also ordered a Llana Especiala, a .38 caliber pistol which held seven rounds of ammunition. After a routine police check that uncovered no criminal record, the permit was granted, and Sweeney paid for the gun and enough bullets to kill a whole group of people. He called

Lowenstein's law office and left a message that he wanted an appointment to see him. Lowenstein was still in Florida with the Kennedy
campaign and would be returning soon. Sweeney was given an appointment for 4:00 P.M. on Friday, March 14, and he went ahead with
preparations to return to Oregon after the visit. At noon on the 14th,
he got in his pickup and drove to New York.

Sweeney arrived precisely at 4:00 at Layton & Sherman. When
the receptionist notified Lowenstein of Sweeney's arrival, he came out
to greet him and escorted him into his office. No one but Sweeney
knows what happened then. By his own account, he demanded that
Lowenstein promise "not to cause any harm to anyone near or dear"
to him. Lowenstein spoke with Sweeney for between ten and twenty
minutes, advising him that he needed help and offering to get it for
him. Sweeney got up, shook hands with Lowenstein, and pulled the
gun from his jacket, firing all seven shots into him. Then he walked
into the outer office, put down his gun and sat down. Sweeney lit up
a cigarette and waited for the police to take him away.

Lowenstein lay in agony on the floor, bleeding profusely from his
wounds. They rushed him to St. Clare's Hospital on West 51st Street
for emergency surgery as he struggled for his life. While he lay for
hours on the operating table receiving blood transfusions, the crowd
of people waiting outside grew. Jenny, who was in Wayland, had to
break the news to the children. "Daddy's been shot," she told them.
But Frankie put his face in his hands. "Don't tell me that!" he shouted
and threw down his coat.

Jenny flew to New York with the children. As they sat waiting, a
deranged, unknown young man went around comforting people. Algernon Black was there, shaking his head in disbelief. So many people
were shot dead in New York in 1980 that the Soho News called it "the
year of the gun." William Sloane Coffin got in a cab and rode down to
the hospital, thinking that it was the worst thing he could imagine.
Then he said to himself that Lowenstein had lived his life and made
his mark on history. This was the way it was bound to happen, he
concluded. While they all waited, Peter Yarrow gently strummed his
guitar and sang "Sweet Survivor." They were told at 11:00 P.M. that
Lowenstein was dead.

At the police station, the family and Harvey Lippman listened to
what had happened while Dennis Sweeney sat in a room nearby.
Among those whose death Sweeney blamed Lowenstein for was Robert Kennedy; there would be no crueler irony. Jenny was shocked to
learn that Ed King, the white minister from Jackson, was at the police
station with Sweeney. "He knew Dennis as well as Al," she states. "He
spent the whole evening after going to the hospital, holding Dennis's
hand. I couldn't imagine Ed King doing this. Ed called later and
wanted to see me and explain why Dennis did it. Ed got radicalized,

paranoid, and bitter. He was a victim of what the civil rights movement could do to people. Sweeney was crazy, but there was more of a connection between him and Al than the other people who killed leaders. They had a split on civil rights. He idolized Al and went to Mississippi because of Al, but focuses on Al as someone who misled him after Sweeney was radicalized and was one of the last whites in the movement. . . . I hate him, I really do."

Curtis Gans, who himself had brooded on Lowenstein after the McCarthy campaign, had this to say about Lowenstein and the people he recruited:

> He was a brilliant recruiter who tried to bring people to a sense of personal loyalty. The way he did this was by appealing to idealism. But he accepted no responsiblity to his recruits except as they were useful to him in a particular period. After that, they had to go their separate ways. There is a parallel to Huey Long. People were brought into the process and stayed; but he used and abused people in his personal dealings in ways that were not fundamentally honorable.

Sweeney told his lawyer, Jesse Zaslov, that he wanted it reported that during the civil rights movement, Lowenstein had approached him one night in a motel and made a homosexual proposition, but that Sweeney had rebuffed him. "This was determined as not having anything to do with the murder," Zaslov explains, not recalling the nature of the advance Sweeney said Lowenstein made. John Riek, the assistant district attorney in charge of the case, examined this possible motive and dismissed it. When Jenny came down to Lowenstein's apartment, Harvey Lippman raised it with her. "She got very hurt and started to cry," he recalls.

Zaslov relates that on all subjects but the question of the forces that had control over him, Dennis Sweeney was totally rational and had a very high IQ. Declared incompetent to stand trial by reason of insanity, Sweeney was confined to the Mid-Hudson Psychiatric Center in New Hampton, New York. According to Zaslov, Sweeney, who will not see anyone, sits quietly reading the Bible. He still hears Lowenstein's voice.

65.

On March 15, speaking in New York before the New York State United Federation of Teachers Annual Convention, Senator Ted Kennedy replaced the remarks he had planned to make on education and inflation with a tribute to Lowenstein. His words were the first to express the way Lowenstein's friends and supporters wished him to be remembered. Kennedy told the teachers:

> If no man is an island, then Allard Lowenstein was a continent, a universe, a vast expanse of compassion, conviction, and courage. These qualities drew out the best in all who knew him, but especially in the young, who heard his call and joined his ceaseless quest against injustice and indifference.
>
> He was the irresistible force that made immovable objects move. Almost single-handedly, twelve years ago, he set out to stop the relentless escalation in Vietnam. When others thought nothing could be done to change an incumbent administration and its war policy, and that no one could make a difference, he insisted that we had to try, that it had to be done—and so he did it.
>
> With his boundless energy, with his papers, his clothes, his books, and seemingly his whole life jammed into briefcases, envelopes, and satchels—all of it carried with him everywhere—he was a portable and powerful lobby for progressive principles. All by himself, he was more effective than an organization of thousands. He was a one-man demonstration for civil rights; even when he walked alone, he was a multitude marching for peace. He had a gentle passion for the truth.
>
> As much as anyone I know, he proved that one person truly can make a difference. . . .
>
> To me, he was a loyal friend who spoke with uncommon frankness.
>
> To America, he was a loyal citizen who spoke the uncommon truth. . . .
>
> Allard Lowenstein's life leaves us with the philosopher's question: "If not me, who; if not now, when?"

On Tuesday, March 18, 1980, at 1:00 P.M., the memorial service for Allard Lowenstein took place at Central Synagogue in New York. Richard Murphy, Lowenstein's old friend from Chapel Hill and the NSA, went instead to Mount Sinai hospital to be with Ruth Hagy Brod, the early supporter of the NSA who had backed Lowenstein throughout his career. Dying of cancer, she was in her bed listening to the funeral service on the radio. Radio commentator Barry Farber, once the editor of the *Tar Heel* at Chapel Hill and a former NSA official, was also at her bedside, conducting an interview. "I wish that Al could have been alive to see the outpouring at his funeral," said Brod, who died herself two months later.

Thousands lined the street outside the synagogue—campaign workers, politicians, ambassadors, friends, and the curious. The old

Lowenstein crowd talked about their new lives and jobs while they exchanged "Allardisms," the anecdotes they would always remember about the man who had now brought them together for one last time. Some wept.

Ken Lowenstein, Al's nephew, stood watch by the side entrance screening the incoming mourners, excluding all but family, close friends, and high dignitaries. The temple, which had a capacity of 2,500, was filled, while a crowd that included Bella Abzug, Gloria Steinem, members of the White House staff, and other prominent politicians had to stand in the street along with thousands of others, listening to the service over the loudspeakers.

Jacqueline Kennedy Onassis arrived followed by Governor Hugh Carey, Mayor Ed Koch, Senator Moynihan, Coretta Scott King, important congressmen, Franklin D. Roosevelt III, and the Kennedy children. Flanked by Secret Service guards, Ted Kennedy headed for the private room where the family waited, to express his condolences.

Harvey Lippman had spent three days at Larry Lowenstein's apartment planning the program. Jerry Brown phoned and said he was wrapped up with a busy schedule running for president. Lippman insists that Brown's concern was that he would be upstaged by Ted Kennedy, who was also running for president. Brown wanted to know if he was being scheduled to speak before or after Kennedy. Uncertain whether he would get to speak at all, Brown told the family he had a "bad cold" and stayed away, sending his sister Cathy in his place.

Rev. William Sloane Coffin was curiously excluded from the program. There was no minister, except for Andrew Young, and he spoke as a politician. There was no black Baptist choir. The audience, which represented Lowenstein's remarkable range of experiences, listened as Indiana Congressman Andy Jacobs linked Lowenstein with the other great modern martyrs. "Lincoln, Ghandi, Evers, Kennedy, King, Kennedy again, and now Al," he lamented. "We are tempted to the conclusion that the most dangerous thing on this earth to do is to advocate love and kindliness." Jacobs described Lowenstein as the "gentle tornado . . . who helped save our country's soul. . . ."

Andrew Young said Lowenstein was a "foundation stone" of the political movements of the sixties who was able to bring people together by giving them a "sense of ideals" as well as a "sense of continuing struggle." Lowenstein's contribution during this period and his endless quest for justice, Young proclaimed, "exemplified . . . what the prophets of the Old Testament might have done had they been allowed to live amongst circumstances such as ours."

Ted Kennedy continued on the same theme. Speaking in the familiar Kennedy cadences, he said:

There are Black people in Mississippi who can vote because he was there in the civil rights summer of 1964.

There are American sons, living out normal lives, who did not die in Vietnam, because he was there in New Hampshire in 1968 in the winter of our national discontent.

There are political prisoners in the Soviet Union whose cause was heard before the world because he was there, in the United Nations, to demand that their cases be stated and debated.

He was everywhere.

He was the man who lived for others. I always thought that somehow he was too good for this world. And in the end the world he reached out to broke him because he was the last friend of a man scorned by everyone else.

Kennedy brought bittersweet smiles to faces in the saddened crowd when he remarked, "Who but Al Lowenstein could claim among his best friends both William F. Buckley and Robert Kennedy? Bill Buckley had the good sense to endorse him for Congress. And Al had the good sense not to endorse Bill for mayor in 1965. Al would do almost anything for Bill."

Buckley, in his deep and aristocratic voice, spoke solemnly:

Possibly as a dissenter, my own experience with him was unique, in that we conservatives did not generally endorse his political prescriptions. So that we were, presumptively, opponents of Al Lowenstein, in those straitened chambers in which we spend, and misspend, so much of our lives.

It was his genius that so many of those he touched—generally arriving a half hour late—discovered intuitively the underlying communion. He was, in our time, the original activist, such was his impatience with the sluggishness of justice; so that his rhythms were more often than not disharmonious with those that govern the practical, banausic councils of this world.

His habits were appropriately disarrayed. He was late to breakfast, to his appointments; late in announcing his sequential availability for public service. He was punctual only in registering (though often under age) for service in any army that conceived itself bound to righteousness.

How did he live such a life, so hectic with public concern, while preoccupying himself so fully with individual human beings: whose torments, never mind their singularity, he adopted as his own, with the passion that some give only to the universal? Eleanor Roosevelt, James Burnham once mused, looked on all the world as her personal slum project. Although he was at home with collectivist formulations one had the impression of Allard Lowenstein that he might be late in aborting a Third World War—because of his absorption with the problems of one sophomore. Oh, they followed him everywhere; because we experienced in him the essence of an entirely personal dedication. Of all the partisans I have known from the furthest steppes of the spectrum, his was the most undistracted concern, not for humanity—though he was conversant with big-think idiom—but with human beings.

Those of us who dealt with him (often in those narrow passages constrained by time clocks and fire laws and deadlines) think back ruefully on the happy blend of purpose and carelessness with which he arranged his own career and his own schedule. A poet might be tempted to say, "If only the Lord had granted us that Allard Lowenstein should have also arrived late at his own assassination."

But all his life he was felled by mysteries, dominant among them those most readily understood by more worldly men—namely, that his rhythms were not of this world. His days, foreshortened, lived out the secular dissonances. "Behold, Thou has made my days as if it were a span long: and mine age is even as nothing in respect of Thee; and verily every man living is altogether vanity."

The psalmist spoke of Al, on Friday last—"I became dumb, and opened not my mouth; for it was thy doing." To those not yet dumb, the psalmist also spoke, saying, "The Lord is close to the brokenhearted and those who are crushed in spirit. He saves."

Who was the wit who said that Nature abhors a vacuum? Let Nature then fill this vacuum. That is the challenge which, bereft, the friends of Allard Lowenstein hurl up to Nature, and to Nature's God, prayerful, demandingly, because today, Lord, our loneliness is great.

Rabbi Alexander Schindler found no divine explanation. "The senselessness of it all," he pondered, "the tragic waste. A living thing cut down while still in the fullness of its flowering. A violent end of a life devoted to the dreams of nonviolence."

As the oak coffin was wheeled out of the synagogue, people reached out to touch it. After the service, the family and close friends gathered at Larry Lowenstein's apartment. Emory Bundy, who had not planned to go to the funeral but who went because he had received a personal invitiation, arrived and walked into a room where Lowenstein's children were watching television. Bundy had never met the younger ones, Tom and Katie. He was astonished to discover that they knew all the stories about South West Africa. Jerry Brown phoned and spoke to Jenny. Brown asked her how many times Lowenstein had been shot and how long he had lived afterward. Jenny thanked him for calling and hung up.

President Carter honored Lowenstein's request for his final resting place. Lowenstein's body was flown to Arlington National Cemetery, where on March 19, 1980, he was buried with full military honors close to the graves of John and Robert Kennedy. A loser in all of his campaigns but one, he was a winner in death.

As if fate had wanted to grant Lowenstein one final wish, Ted Kennedy swept the New York primary against Carter two weeks later. Not a few people gave Lowenstein considerable credit for Kennedy's win. But Kennedy lost the nomination to Carter, who lost the election to Reagan, the most conservative American president since Coolidge. Lowenstein had feared the election of Ronald Reagan. He felt the far left would welcome it as a final affirmation that the system could not work. Jimmy Wallace, Lowenstein's first friend at Chapel Hill, believes that if he had lived, Lowenstein would have been able to pull it out for Kennedy at the convention and that it all would have been different. Such is faith. Liberal dreams.

66.

On April 22, 1980, William F. Buckley, Jr., taped a retrospective of Lowenstein's appearances on "Firing Line" which was aired on PBS on May 11. There is Lowenstein again, expounding on everything from Yeshivas to the hostages in Iran; Eugene McCarthy, Nixon, Watergate, Robert Kennedy's assassination, human rights, South Africa, and the latest presidential contenders. Witty and articulate, Lowenstein matches Buckley phrase for phrase, riposte for riposte. Here are the two masters of political language, going at it to each other's delight.

On May 12, a controversial article on Dennis Sweeney by Teresa Carpenter appeared in the *Village Voice*. Six days later, it was reprinted in a shorter version in the *Washington Post*. Entitled "From Heroism to Madness," it suggested that Lowenstein "never dealt quite honestly in personal matters." Although Carpenter did not interview Sweeney, she related his disclosure that Lowenstein had made what Sweeney interpreted to be a homosexual advance toward him, which he rebuffed. Wrote Carpenter, "After the shooting, in fact, there were rumors that Lowenstein and Sweeney had fallen out as the result of a lover's quarrel. Everyone simply assumed that Lowenstein had approached Sweeney. (Now, from his cell at Rikers Island, Sweeney denies that they ever had a relationship. Once while he and Lowenstein were traveling through Mississippi together, they checked into a motel. According to Sweeney, Lowenstein made a pass and Sweeney rebuffed it. Sweeney is not angry with Lowenstein, he claims. Nor does he feel any shame. It's just that Lowenstein wasn't always above board.)"

After the Pulitzer Prize was taken away from another writer following revelations that the work contained false statements, Carpenter was awarded the coveted recognition of journalistic achievement. But Lowenstein's friends and family responded indignantly to what they maintained were misleading innuendoes. On Larry Lowenstein's initiative, the National News Council, an independent body set up to monitor claims of unfair reporting, examined the case and found fault with the article because Carpenter, the council explained, had implied that she interviewed Sweeney when she had not. But Carpenter's Pulitzer was not taken away as Lowenstein's brother had wished.

A debate also broke out between James Wechsler and gay activist Bruce Voeller, to whom Lowenstein had spoken about his personal problems. Wechsler insisted that Lowenstein's sympathy for gays and his support for gay rights was being misinterpreted, while Voeller argued that Lowenstein's real nature was bisexual or gay. The liberals could support gay rights, he argued, but could not accept that one of their leading spokesmen was gay himself. Voeller later acknowledged that he might have misinterpreted what Lowenstein had told him but basically stuck to his conclusion about Lowenstein's sexual preference.

Rumors flew that an article by gay journalist Larry Bush was going to appear in the *Soho News* detailing Lowenstein's gay relationships. But after a shake-up at the paper, the story was killed, with Bush publishing his article on July 14 in the *New York Native*, a gay newspaper. While Bush did not conclude that Lowenstein was gay in the commonly accepted use of the term, he revealed sufficient evidence to support Carpenter and Voeller. Bush concluded:

> Lowenstein's life poses many questions, and the debate after his death poses some specific questions that should no longer be avoided. As he struggled with his sexual identity, so also must those who chronicle his life give due respect for the many unanswered questions about sexual identity in general. As he made connections between his personal life and his public commitments, so must others acknowledge that public record exists as an important part of his life. Rather than sweep such questions aside, we would be better served by thoughtful consideration of what these issues mean as public figures reclaim their private lives, and moralistic crusaders seek to make private lives public for all citizens—not just those who have taken public roles that foist upon them an adherence to publicly proclaimed morality.

On August 17, *The New York Times Magazine* published "The Life and Death of Allard Lowenstein" by David Harris, who had given up political activism for a career as a writer. Harris related later that a former press secretary to Bobby Kennedy who had been close to Lowenstein, had phoned to ask if he planned to write anything about Lowenstein with "sexual connotations." He had told Harris that any such allegations would be a "cheap shot" and "vindictive," because Lowenstein wasn't around to defend himself. When Harris spoke to him about the pressure being exerted with regard to his story, another former Lowenstein protégé responded, "Amazing. That's exactly the kind of shit I used to do for Allard twelve years ago. It's the protégé's first duty. Allard always had to be defended from 'spurious attacks' by people with 'questionable motives.' Now that's you. Lowenstein speaks from the grave." Harris's article appeared with no reference to any pass Lowenstein may have made at Sweeney in a motel room in 1964.

Harris did start work on his book, called *Dreams Die Hard*, a critical memoir of his relationship with both Sweeney and Lowenstein. Published in 1982, it produced considerable resentment in the Lowenstein group and literary agent Esther Newberg, claiming that she couldn't understand how anyone could write something critical about Lowenstein, launched an effort to promote a book on him by James Wechsler and Lowenstein's nephew, Douglas. The Wechsler-Lowenstein book did not get written, though. Instead, Douglas Lowenstein joined with Gregory Stone to produce a collection of writings about and by Lowenstein, with a forward by Arthur Schlesinger, Jr., and an introduction by Wechsler. Highly favorable to Lowenstein, it omits any reference to the writings of Teresa Carpenter and David Harris. Newberg, a one-time Bobby Kennedy "boiler-room" girl who had been at the party with Ted Kennedy at Chappaquiddick, surfaced as Teresa Carpenter's agent.

Lowenstein's resurrection then got into high gear. The Allard Lowenstein Congressional Symposium, sponsored by the Allard K. Lowenstein Fund, of which Larry Lowenstein was president, was held in the Cannon House Office Building in Washington in March 1982. The idea was to hold the symposium annually on Capitol Hill and to invite leading political figures to discuss issues Lowenstein would have been concerned with.

Actor Mike Farrell of the popular "M*A*S*H" series launched a film project on behalf of the Allard K. Lowenstein Foundation for Political Media, calling it *Citizen*. The film, which features old clips of Lowenstein and taped interviews with over thirty of his friends, family members, and political associates, including William Buckley, Jr., Ted Kennedy, Andrew Young, and others, purports to be a "documentary about Allard K. Lowenstein . . . and the future of citizen-activists in the United States." The theme is that one person can make a difference.

A series of fund-raisers was held for the project, one at Peter Yarrow's Manhattan duplex, another on the lawn of Howard Samuels' luxurious summer home in Bridgehampton, where Ted Kennedy spoke. But in Long Beach, proposals that the Long Beach high school and Lindell Boulevard, where he lived, be renamed for Lowenstein failed because of local opposition. Only after Harriet Eisman lobbied extensively with the board of directors of the Long Beach Public Library was it renamed the "Allard K. Lowenstein Public Library." Eisman died before the official dedication, which took place on Sunday, April 25, 1982, at noon, on a clear, bright spring day.

On Friday, November 18, 1983, at three in the afternoon, Lowenstein's friends and family, including a "delegation of U.S. Congressmen and Senators," gathered again, this time near the United Nations to dedicate "Allard K. Lowenstein Square" on the northwest corner of Forty-fifth Street and First Avenue. Eight hundred of Lowenstein's friends and associates were invited. They and others also received a request from "Friends of Allard Lowenstein" for a contribution to support additional activities. It was as though Al Lowenstein were still running for something.

Reference Sources

The citations for sources from which material in the text is derived are arranged by Section and Chapter, with the beginning of a quotation or sentence in italics. A section of notes with background material to the text follows.

CODE: I = Interview
          L = letter
         LD = Lowenstein Diaries
          C = Conversation
        LP = Lowenstein Papers (Allard K. Lowenstein Papers, Southern Historical Collection, Wilson Library, University of North Carolina, Chapel Hill)

Section I Chapter 1.

"Boy Baby Lowenstein." I with Lowenstein's half sister, Dorothy DiCintio 1982–83. *"She was a very bright woman."* I with Dorothy DiCintio and Larry Lowenstein, Jan. 27, 1981 (conducted by Eugene E. Pfaff, Jr., Greensboro Public Library Oral History Program, Greensboro, NC). *"Mother, I know you're not . . ."* Ibid. *He loved these people . . .* I with Alice Levien, October 16, 1981. *In later life . . .* This was Lowenstein's explanation of the revelation. I with Lowenstein's ex-wife, Jenny Lowenstein Littlefield, May 1–3, 1981.

Chapter 2.

"The story was . . ." I with Dorothy DiCintio and Larry Lowenstein. *"Night of Stars"* I with Abraham Wechsler, 1981. *"I use the word 'restaurant' . . ."* I with Dorothy DiCintio and Larry Lowenstein. *"I'm going to take a year . . ."* Ibid. *a "cold" person* I with family friend Bronia Kupsick, 1981. *"If anything was worth doing . . ."* I with Dorothy DiCintio. *very close to her stepson . . .* I with Alice Levien. *like an adult* I with Rita Kupsick Katz, 1981. *the "professor"* I with Dorothy DiCintio and Larry Lowenstein. *"almost a genius in the field"* I with Abraham Wechsler. *William F. Buckley, Jr., observes . . .* I with William F. Buckley, Jr., June 10, 1981.

Chapter 3.
  most liberal school in New York I with Bronia Kupsick. *"penetration, revelation, turning potentialities into potencies,"* Ethical Culture Schools booklet. *"to train reformers"* Horace Friess, *Felix Adler and Ethical Culture* (New York: Columbia University Press, 1981), p. 122. *"organized democracy"* Ibid., p. 138. *"Judaism ever claimed to be . . ."* Ibid., p. 37. *"A class school, whether for the rich or the poor . . ."* Ethical Culture Schools booklet.

Chapter 4.
  "younger than all the other children in the class" I with Bronia Kupsick. *"We thought Allard . . ."* I with Rita Kupsick Katz. *"trying to save the world"* I with Bronia Kupsick. *"He was head and shoulders above . . ."* I with Judge Richard Wallach, Oct. 28, 1981. *He loved the color green . . .* I with Alice Levien. *Bronia Kupsick deliberately chose . . .* I with Bronia Kupsick. *Lowenstein wrote on Socialism . . .* Related by family friend and labor lawyer Sidney Cohen, to whom Lowenstein showed the essay. *Bob Wechsler, his classmate at Ethical . . .* I with Robert Wechsler, 1981. *When Franco won . . .* I with Dorothy DiCintio. *"The Game of Politics"* L from Samuel Heyman to the author, 1980. *"to be on a much more . . ."* I with Richard Wallach, Oct. 28, 1981. *"Go on. What happened?"* I with Bronia Kupsick. *"Runyonesque"* I with Sanford Friedman, Nov. 18, 1981. *"Machiavellian"* Ibid. *His cousin Alice . . .* I with Alice Levien. *"This is the kind of paper . . ."* I with Sanford Friedman.

Chapter 5.
  Lawrence Rossbach from Horace Mann . . . I with Lawrence Rossbach 1981–82.

Section II Chapter 6.
  "the grand affairs . . ." Jimmy Wallace, March 16, 1980 tape made by Douglas Hunt and Jimmy Wallace. *After frequent visits . . .* I with Douglas Hunt, March 18, 1981. *"We just start with the dorms . . ."* Douglas Hunt, Hunt and Wallace tape. *"had aspirations to be president"* I with Jimmy Wallace, March 21, 1981. *Rev. Charles Jones remembers . . .* I with Rev. Charles Jones, 1981 (conducted by Eugene Pfaff, Jr., Greensboro Public Library Oral History Program, Greensboro, NC). *"How long will we wait . . ."* Jimmy Wallace, Hunt and Wallace tape. *"shut up and back off"* Ibid. *"If it come to a question . . ."* Ibid. *"Before any of the students . . ."* Ibid. *"There was a quality . . ."* Douglas Hunt, Hunt and Wallace tape. *"You shouldn't be out . . ."* I with Frieda Altschul, 1980–81. *"this pilgrimage toward the Kingdom of God"* I with Jimmy Wallace. *the Communists "infiltrated" . . .* I with Douglas Hunt. *"mystical" quality . . .* I with Douglas Hunt. *"compelled, driven"* I with Jimmy Wallace.

Chapter 7.
  "back when it was not chic . . ." Jimmy Wallace, Hunt and Wallace tape. *"voted all the way . . ."* I with Rev. Charles Jones. *"The issue," recalls Wallace . . .* L from Jimmy Wallace to the author. *"Dr. Graham was going to vote . . ."* I with Rev. Charles Jones. *"went over and saw Senator Richard Russell . . ."* Ibid. *not to "tamper with . . ."* Ibid. *"I was surprised . . ."* Ibid. *"so important that . . ."* Ibid. *"And if my colleague . . ."* Warren Ashby, *Frank Porter Graham, a Southern Liberal,* (Winston-Salem: John F. Blair, 1980). *Graham was in anguish . . .* Ibid. *"a resurgent tide . . ."* *The New York Times,* quoted in Ashby. *striking down segregation . . .* *Sweatt v. Painter,* 339 U.S. 629 (1950); *McLaurin v Oklahoma State Regents* 339 U.S. 637(1950); *Henderson v. United States* 339 U.S. 816

(1950). *"had the nerve to die . . ."* I with Jimmy Wallace. *"I remember the morning . . ."* I with Richard Murphy, April 28, 1981.

Section III Chapter 8.

After the first . . . C with Henry Landau (who served as president of the American Federation of Youth) April 21, 1982. (Landau warned that the same thing would happen in the American Youth Congress.) *American student movement . . .* "the old American Student Union was gone . . ." Douglas Hunt, Hunt and Wallace tape. *"at the behest . . ."* Douglas Hunt, Hunt and Wallace tape. *"more important . . ."* Ibid. *"And then we sent . . ."* Ibid. *"anybody who made . . ."* Jimmy Wallace, Hunt and Wallace tape. *"the natural choice"* I with Jimmy Wallace.

Chapter 9.

Thus he argues . . . Cord Meyer, *Facing Reality* (New York: Harper and Row, 1980). *"All the way across . . ."* Jimmy Wallace, Hunt and Wallace tape. *"take it over"* I with Jimmy Wallace. *"group of veterans . . ."* I with Richard Murphy. *"Where else . . ."* I with Alice Brandeis Popkin, April 28, 1981.

Chapter 10.

"educate young people . . ." Article II, Constitution of the Encampment for Citizenship, from Algernon Black, *The Young Citizens* (New York: Ungar, 1962). *"farm laborer"* Application of Allard K. Lowenstein for 1948 Encampment for Citizenship, provided by Algernon Black and the Ethical Culture Society. *Cohn told him . . .* C with Sidney Cohn, 1981–82.

Chapter 11.

"heavily challenged" I with Richard Murphy. *"might have direct . . ."* FBI Report, National Student Association Congress, Aug. 23–31, 1950, File No. 100–16318, p. 9. *Finally, Allard Lowenstein . . .* I with Richard Murphy. *"He was incensed . . ."* I with William Dentzer, June 25, 1982. *"of those national . . ."* I with Richard Murphy. *"by invitation . . ."* I with William Dentzer. *"to establish COSEC . . ."* Ibid. *"CIA sponsored."* I with Barbara Boggs Sigmund, June 21, 1981. *"a clarion call . . ."* I with William Dentzer. *"Al was his own . . ."* Ibid. *"The Communists controlled . . ." Journal American*, Jan. 2, 1951. *"all opposition . . ."* I with William Dentzer. *"My God . . ."* I with Jenny Lowenstein Littlefield, May 1–2, 1981. *"This position . . ."* I with William Dentzer. *"was the conference . . ."* Ibid. *"on an ad hoc . . ."* Ibid. *"The CIA provided . . ."* Ibid. *The presence of homosexual . . .* Another interpretation of Ingram's death is that it resulted from autoerotic asphyxiation. *"I told them . . ."* I with William Dentzer. *"Oh, someone . . ."* Ibid. *"he would be . . ."* I with Richard Murphy. *"was very much opposed . . ."* Ibid. *"He regarded Henry Wallace . . ."* Ibid. *"when Richard Murphy . . ."* I with Jimmy Wallace. *"He quit . . ."* Ibid. *"His association . . ."* Ibid. *"duties in the government. . ."* I with Richard Murphy. *"So I made . . ."* Ibid. *"I am certain . . ."* I with William Dentzer. *Such writers . . .* See David Halberstam, "The Man Who Ran against Lyndon Johnson." *Harper's*, December 1968; Milton Viorst, *Fire in the Streets: America in the '60s* (New York: Simon and Schuster, 1979). *"When his poor eyesight . . ."* Edward Hershey, "Allard Lowenstein—Out But Not Down," *Newsday*, Saturday, Dec. 26, 1970, p. 4W. *"marksman."* Allard K. Lowenstein's June 24, 1955, rifle training program report (LP). *On December 15, 1950 . . .* Allard K. Lowenstein, Extract of Registrant Classifications Record, Selective Service System, prepared July 15, 1982. *The result of . . .* Ibid. *2A-S* Ibid. *"Registrant deferred . . ."* Ibid. *On February 21 . . .* Ibid. *On March 6 . . .* Ibid. *the army writing.* Order # 30 10 29 46, to Allard K.

Lowenstein from Chairman, Local Board 10, Selective Service System (LP). *Lowenstein was ordered* . . . Selective Service System, Order to Report for Induction, to Allard K. Lowenstein, April 25, 1952 (LP). *On May 2* . . . Extract. *a 2-S* . . . Ibid. *"drafted"* I with William Dentzer. *"Al wanted* . . *."* Talk by Ellison Capers Wynn, Lowenstein symposium, March 1982. *"occupation vital* . . *."* Quoted in Sol Stern, "A Short Account of International Student Politics and the Cold War with Particular Reference to the NSA, CIA, Etc.," *Ramparts*, March 1967, p. 35. *"NSA is largely responsible* . . *."* Ibid. *"out to students"* Address by Allard K. Lowenstein, National President, NSA 1951 (LP). *Rev. Charles Jones relates:* I with Rev. Charles Jones.

Chapter 12.
"would raise millions" I with Richard Murphy. *"You must be* . . *."* Ibid. *"little Catholic* . . *."* Ibid. *"The value of NSA* . . *."* Viorst. *"The people of Al's* . . *."* I with Richard Murphy. *"The NSA was ignored* . . *."* I with Paul Sigmund, June 21, 1981. *"there was no way* . . *."* I with Barbara Boggs Sigmund.

Chapter 13.
"awesome . . *, as if they* . . *."* Calvin Trillin, "The Kids against the Grown-Ups," *The New Yorker*, Nov. 16, 1968. *"the student leader of today* . . *."* L from Paul Hoffman to author, May 19, 1980. *"He would not take* . . *."* I with Rev. Charles Jones. *"Can we have* . . *."* Ibid. *"How did you meet* . . *."* Ibid. *"I was driving* . . *."* Ibid *"Have you got* . . *."* Talk by Ellison Capers Wynn. *"No, but* . . *."* Talk by Ellison Capers Wynn. I found an invitation to the wedding among Lowenstein's papers. Lowenstein's name was not on it. Whether he used it to gain entry or picked it up as a souvenir remains a question. *"Rita"* I with Larry Lowenstein. *"This is Eleanor* . . *."* Talk by Ellison Capers Wynn. *"I can always* . . *."* L from Lowenstein to his parents, from Germany, dated May 17, 1956, (LP). *"sour"* L from Lowenstein to his parents, June 25, 1956 (LP). *"the day before* . . *."* Ibid. *"general factotum* . . *."* Ibid. *"who had enormous* . . *."* James Forman, *The Making of Black Revolutionaries* (New York: Macmillan, 1972). *"There are some faces* . . *."* Ibid. *"The 1956 NSA* . . *."* Ibid. *"We are the privileged* . . *."* Lowenstein, 1956 NSA address, text supplied by Harvey Lippman, Lowenstein's attorney (LP); see also *Lowenstein: Acts of Courage and Belief*, ed. G. Stone and D. Lowenstein (San Diego: Harcourt Brace Jovanovich, 1983). *"I detest* . . *." "If you are* . . *."* LP. *"Old Boy* . . *."* I with Paul Sigmund. *"acolytes"* I with Barbara Boggs Sigmund. *"To denounce* . . *."* I with Jimmy Wallace. *"He wove a complex web* . . *."* I with Curtis Gans, Aug. 13–14, 1981. *"Allard could not* . . *."* I with Curtis Gans. *"nightly seances"* Ibid. *"fawning protégé"* Ibid. *"later became* . . *."* I with Emory Bundy, 1983. After leaving the CIA, Kiley changed careers, becoming head of the MTA in New York. *"unkind"* Ibid. *"He could have* . . *."* Ibid. *"the CIA thing* . . *."* Ibid. *"witty"* Ibid. *"outsider"* Ibid. *"They did what was* . . *."* Ibid. *"You may be aware* . . *."* Humphrey letter to Editor, Student Newspaper, dated May 7, 1959 (LP). *"Al, as requested* . . *."* Memo from Cyril to Lowenstein, May 14, 1959 (LP). *"might like to have"* Lowenstein memo to Gloria Steinem and Leonard Bebchick, May 20, 1959 (LP). *Independent Research Service* . . . See Stern, "A Short Account . . *.,"* *Ramparts*, March 1967. *"to cause trouble* . . *."* Telephone I with Eugene Theroux, 1983. *"I'm sure this* . . *."* I with Emory Bundy. *"One guy was* . . *."* Ibid. *"Al dared* . . *."* Ibid. *"much the master* . . *."* Ibid. *"It was intimidating* . . *."* Ibid. *"It was almost* . . *."* Ibid. *"Today it would* . . *."* I with Eugene Theroux. *"one of the past* . . *."* David Harris, *Dreams Die Hard: Three Men's Journey Through the Sixties* (New York: St. Martin's/Marek, 1982), p. 159. *On a piece of paper* . . . Lowenstein memo on NSA/CIA connection (LP). *the "firm"* . . . *"fellas"* . . . *"boys"* . . . *"witty"* Stern; see also Harris.

"We both came . . ." I with Richard Murphy. *"who were well known . . ."* Ibid. *"I don't want . . ."* Ibid. *"direct pressure"* Harris, p. 160. *"financial support"* Ibid., p. 161. *"used its influence . . ."* Ibid., p. 161. *"I was the one . . ."* Ibid., p. 161. *"was not involved . . ."* Ibid., p. 168. *"neither sought nor . . ."* Ibid., p. 168. *"suspicious offer"* Ibid., p. 168. *"It might have been . . ."* Ibid., p. 168. *"Curiously enough . . ."* Ibid., p. 169. *"beyond us . . ."* I with Curtis Gans. *"The CIA issue . . ."* I with Emory Bundy. *"What about . . ."* I with Jenny Lowenstein Littlefield. *"He was profoundly . . ."* Ibid. *"they should be aware . . ."* Victor Marchetti and John Marks, *The CIA and the Cult of Intelligence* (New York: Dell, 1975), p. 67. *"entrap unsuspecting . . ."* Ibid., p. 67. *"no federal . . ."* Ibid., p. 69. *"historically compassionate . . ."* Richard G. Stearns, "We Were Wrong," *Mademoiselle*, August 1967. *"If the agency . . ."* Marchetti and Marks, p. 69. *"The National Student Association was . . ."* W. Dennis Shaul, "We Were Right," *Mademoiselle*, August 1967. *"While I was with . . ."* L from Allard Lowenstein to Nathan Straus, September 29, 1959 (LP). *"They're turning inward . . ."* David Halberstam, "The Man Who Ran Against Lyndon Johnson."

Section IV, Part One. Chapter 14.
"I have seen . . ." L from Hubert Humphrey to Lowenstein, Feb. 27, 1958 (LP). *"What Al had . . ."* L from Walter C. Clemens to the author, July 23, 1980. *"Al might have had . . ."* Telephone C with George Cohen, 1983. *"excited and enthusiastic . . ."* I with Adlai Hardin, June 16, 1983. *"I can't say why . . ."* Ibid. *"foreign policy adviser . . ."* I with Emory Bundy. *"spellbinding"* I with Adlai Hardin. *"You say your people . . ."* Quoted in Allard Lowenstein, *Brutal Mandate* (New York: Macmillan, 1962), p. 3. *"the smartest person . . ."* I with Emory Bundy. *"Nothing I had heard . . ."* Lowenstein, *Brutal Mandate*, p. 4. *"got more closely . . ."* I with Emory Bundy. *"Al never was . . ."* David Halberstam, "The Man Who Ran Against Lyndon Johnson." *"Boys, don't open this up . . ."* I with Hamilton Richardson, Feb. 17, 1982. *In 1960 a press agency . . .* See Don Schechter, Michael Ansara, and David Kolodney, "The CIA as an Equal Opportunity Employer," *Dirty Work 2: the CIA in Africa*, ed. Ellen Ray, William Schaap, Karl Van Meter, Lois Wolf (Secaucus: Lyle Stuart, 1980); Africa Research Group, 1970; also published in *Ramparts* during 1970. *He had become a superstar . . .* See Schechter, Ansara, and Kolodney. *"This is just . . ."* L from George Houser to Lowenstein, Feb. 19, 1959 (LP). *"I am enclosing . . ."* L from George Houser to Lowenstein, March 9, 1959 (LP). *"internationalism of democracy . . ."* *The New York Times*, April 16, 1959, p.8. *"growing Soviet challenge . . ."* *The New York Times*, May 10, 1959, p.2. *"to mitigate . . ."* *The New York Times*, May 10, 1959, p.2.

Chapter 15.
"Franco's Charlie McCarthy" Memo from "Bill" to Humphrey, March 6, 1959 (LP). *"Since the Foreign . . ."* Memo from Lefever to Humphrey, March 10, 1959 (LP). *"Al—This matter . . ."* Note from Lefever to Lowenstein (LP). *"By this time . . ."* Allard Lowenstein, "Spain without Franco," *Saturday Review*, Feb. 7, 1976. *"You will be assigned . . ."* Memo from Humphrey to Lowenstein, March 26, 1959 (LP). *"Dear Philip . . ."* L from Lowenstein to Philip Willkie, April 23, 1959 (LP). *"the Communist conspiracy . . ."* McDowell Memorandum and Summary of 1959 Annual Informational Dinner Conference against Communist Aggression, Temple University, Urban Archives. *"But we would never . . ."* Lowenstein, *Brutal Mandate*, p. 7. *"in the ranks . . ."* I with Theo-Ben Gurirab, May 5, 1983. *"The Kerinas . . ."* Lowenstein, *Brutal Mandate*, p. 10. *police informer . . .* Report on the Political Activities of Mburumba Kerina, Dec. 1966, marked Confidential (LP). *"like a puppet"* I with Theo-Ben Gurirab. *"during the course . . ."* I

with Emory Bundy. *"deep philosophical . . ."* Lowenstein quoted by Bundy, I
with Emory Bundy. *"A nonracial movement . . ."* I with Emory Bundy. *"You are
quite . . ."* Lowenstein, *Brutal Mandate*, p. 32. *He went alone* . . . Ibid., p. 41.
"There may be moments . . ." Ibid., p. 45. *"Al wanted to look . . ."* I with Emory
Bundy. *"He had a wonderful . . ."* Ibid. *"Al didn't know . . ."* Ibid. *Sources report
that* . . . July 13, 1982. One of these sources served with US Army Intelligence.
The others, also with backgrounds in intelligence work, are close to the CIA.
Sherman Bull insists that Lowenstein had no contacts he didn't know about and
denies any CIA connection with the trip to South West Africa, as does Emory
Bundy. But as Lowenstein points out in *Brutal Mandate* (p. 41), he attended the
Congress of the National Union of South African Students in Johannesburg while
Bull and Bundy "were lining up a car and other provisions." This gave him ample
opportunity to confer with the CIA without Bull and Bundy knowing about it. *"to
undermine SWAPO's . . ."* I with Theo-Ben Gurirab. *"freedom fighter"* I with Ken
McCominsky, April 13, 1983. *"You'll get a hell . . ."* Lowenstein, *Brutal Mandate*,
p. 61. *"parading my need . . ."* L from Hans Beukes to the author, Feb. 15, 1983.
"foreign secretary . . ." Ibid. *"Desolate drive . . ."* Lowenstein, *Brutal Mandate*,
p. 70. *"It is Chief Kutako . . ."* Ibid., p. 117. *"In 1959, I . . ."* I with Emory
Bundy. *"There are no other . . ."* Lowenstein, *Brutal Mandate*, p. 143. 'Al must
have . . .' I with Emory Bundy. *"opposition figure . . ."* Memo from American
embassy in Madrid to State Department, Aug. 17, 1962. *"in which capacity . . ."*
Ibid. *"a Republican . . ."* L from Hans Beukes to the author, Feb. 15, 1983.
"United States policy . . ." St. Louis Post-Dispatch, Oct. 19, 1959. *"defend its
stewardship . . ."* Lowenstein, *Brutal Mandate*, p. 153. *"Finally, American support . . ."* St. Louis Post-Dispatch, Oct. 29, 1959. *"discredited" people* Lowenstein, *Brutal Mandate*, p. 150. *"The African, Asian . . ."* L from Hans Beukes to
the author, Feb. 15, 1983. *"I had personal . . ."* Ibid. *"a several weeks . . ."* Ibid.
"All at once . . ." Lowenstein, *Brutal Mandate*, p. 154. *"continue as . . ."* Ibid.,
p. 164. *"but rose . . ."* St. Louis Post-Dispatch, Oct. 27, 1959. *"At a critical moment . . ."* St. Louis Post-Dispatch, Nov. 3, 1959. *"It was nice . . ."* Lowenstein,
Brutal Mandate, p. 177. *"U.S. Scores . . ."* St. Louis Post-Dispatch, Nov. 3, 1959.
"general educational . . ." Memo Re Student Appeal for South Africa to George
Houser from Ann Morrissett, Oct. 22, 1959 (LP). *"The concept of world law . . ."*
Lowenstein, *Brutal Mandate*, p. 179. *"We are hoping . . ."* L from Catherine
Raymond to Lowenstein, Aug. 4, 1960 (LP). *"The police stabbed . . ."* L from
Donald Harrington for American Committee on Africa, Dec. 1959 (LP).

Chapter 16.
"Dear Al . . ." L from Hubert Humphrey to Lowenstein, Jan. 30, 1960 (LP).
"had practiced . . ." Memo from American embassy in Madrid to State Department, Aug. 17, 1962. *An FBI report* . . . File No. 105–103168. *"totally uneducated"* Conversation with Dorothy DiCintio, 1983. *"Lazar never . . ."* Ibid. *"I
found your . . ."* L from James A. Skardon to Lowenstein, Nov. 20, 1958 (LP).
"hoped to mobilize . . ." I with Emory Bundy. *"meeting two young . . ."* Roosevelt, "My Day," *Daily Magazine*, Nov. 27, 1959. *"Brutal Mandate arose . . ."* I
with Emory Bundy. *"very anxious to direct . . ."* FBI File No. 105–103168, Vol.
No. 2. *"object to any . . ."* Ibid. *"Allard Lowenstein was . . ."* Ibid. *The F.B.I.
took note* . . . Ibid. *"wasn't necessary" to run* . . . L from Ethel Grossman to
Lowenstein, Nov. 27, 1959 (LP). *"it wasn't necessary for you to go . . ."* Ibid.
"got screwed . . ." I with Robert Wechsler. *"I very much . . ."* Quoted on Ryan-
Ohrenstein stationery (LP). *"You stupid jerk . . ."* I with Robert Wechsler.
"McCarthy's nominating . . ." L from Frank Graham to Lowenstein, Aug. 2, 1960
(LP). *"I've just written . . ."* L from Lucille Kohn to Lowenstein, Nov. 16, 1960
(LP).

Chapter 17.
"The great fact . . ." LP. *"peripheral"* I with Curtis Gans. *"That's initially
. . ."* Ibid. *"The 'incident' . . ."* LP. *"Most important . . ."* Lowenstein, *Brutal
Mandate*, p. 19. *"On 19th December . . ."* Statement by Susan Mariaki Monanoe
(LP). *"spasmodic . . ."* I with George Houser, April 13, 1983. *"Invite you . . ."*
LP. *"definitely . . ." "roundabout route"* FBI File No. 105–103168, Vol. No. 2. *"a
New York lawyer . . ."* Ibid. *"be treated . . ."* Morrissett Memo (LP). *"With feel-
ings . . ."* L from Ben Wechsler to Donald Harrington, March 1, 1960 (LP).
"Oram put pressure . . ." I with George Houser. *"without any charge . . ."* L
from Marion J. Friedman to Lowenstein, June 21, 1960 (LP). *"Americans to join
. . ."* Action for South Africa, A Call to Action (LP). *"before we take . . ."* (LP). *"a
gross income . . ."* L from Gilbert Jonas to Vus C. Make, Dec. 30, 1960 (LP).
Harold Oram and Gilbert Jonas . . . See Robert Scheer and Warren Hinckle,
"The Viet-Nam Lobby," *Ramparts*, July 1965; *The Vietnam Reader*, ed. Marcus
Raskin and Bernard Fall (New York: Vintage, 1965), pp. 66–81. *"I am very
pleased . . ."* L from Ernest Wentzel to Ethel Grossman, June 28, 1961 (LP).
"condemning outright . . ." L from Adrian Leftwhich to Ethel Grossman, July 20,
1961 (LP).

Chapter 18.
"You should marry . . ." L from Ethel Grossman to Lowenstein, Nov. 27,
1959 (LP). *"his articulate idealism . . ."* I with Barbara Boggs Sigmund. *"We had
a few . . ."* L from Barbara Boggs to Lowenstein, Dec. 3, 1960 (LP). *"gone out
with . . ."* L from Barbara Boggs to Lowenstein, Dec. 5, 1960 (LP). *"if the liberal
Democrats . . ."* I with Barbara Boggs Sigmund. *"So far as . . ."* L from Peter
Ritner to Lowenstein, Feb. 16, 1961 (LP). *"I have no memory . . ."* Gregory B.
Craig, "Random Reminiscences," 1980 (unpublished). Section IV, Part Two.

Chapter 19.
"a regular Pied Piper . . ." Telephone I with John Tyler Caldwell, July 6,
1983. *"At the time . . ."* Telephone I with Kris Kleinbauer, 1983. *"heady preassassination . . ."* I with Barbara Boggs Sigmund. *"physical and manor-born . . ."*
Ibid. *"Messiah complex . . ."* Ibid.

Chapter 20.
"the question is . . ." Notes of I with Nelson Mandela, May 30, 1961 (LP). *On
May 31, 1962 . . .* LD, Vol. 1962–66 (LP). *Jacob Kahangua . . .* Ibid. *From Dar,
Nujoma . . .* See I with Sam Nujoma, "Namibia: SWAPO Fights for Freedom,"
ed. Liberation Support Movement (Oakland: LSM Information Center, 1978).
Nujoma states (p. 24): "We decided that unless we started fighting, we would
never be free. In 1962 our first cadres began military training in several friendly
countries and we began preparing for armed struggle." *This happened just . . .*
See Dubula, "The Two Pillars of our Struggle," *The African Communist*, No. 87,
Fourth Quarter 1981, p. 35; M. K. Mtungwa, "The Road of Struggle That Leads
to Freedom," also in *The African Communist*, No. 87, Fourth Quarter 1981, p.
76. The 1962 Program of the South African Communist Party stated: "The Communist Party considers that the slogan of 'non-violence' is harmful to the cause of
the democratic national revolution in the new phase of the struggle. . . ." *"free-
wheeling"* C with Lawrence de Bivort, 1982. *"left Stanford . . ."* I with Barbara
Boggs Sigmund. *according to sources . . .* These are the same sources referred
to in Chapter 15. *"there are so many . . ."* Telephone C with Victor Marchetti,
1983. *"status midway . . ."* Minutes of the 1968 "Bissell Meeting" at the Council
on Foreign Relations as reprinted by the Africa Research Group; in Marchetti and
Marks, Appendix. *"We have five . . ."* Telephone C with Victor Marchetti, 1983.

"Stick with . . ." Ibid. *When one of them takes* See Larry Bush, "The New Legacy of Lowenstein," *New York Native,* July 13–26, 1981, p. 13. *The CIA divides . . .* Minutes of the 1968 "Bissell Meeting," Marchetti and Marks, Appendix. *He clipped and analyzed . . .* I found considerable evidence of this in the LP. *"operational types"* Minutes of the 1968 "Bissell Meeting," Marchetti and Marks, Appendix. *"(1) political . . ."* Ibid. *"Sekou Toure . . ."* LP. *"at Lincoln . . ."* Lincoln University, a predominantly black university in Pennsylvania where numberous Africans recruited by the CIA were sent. *"In the early . . ."* Quoted in Ralph McGehee, *Deadly Deceits—My 25 Years in the CIA* (New York: Sheridan Square, 1983), p. 60. *"Where is Carlucci . . ." "Who the hell . . ."* Ronald Brownstein and Nina Easton, *Reagan's Ruling Class* (New York: Pantheon, 1983), p. 439. *"There is the possibility . . ."* I with Harris Wofford, May 18, 1983. *"I think you need to . . ." "It's an interesting . . ."* Ibid. *"too liberal . . ."* I with Rev. William Sloane Coffin, April 27, 1982. *"meliorist"* I with William F. Buckley, Jr., June 10, 1981. *"Freedom is indivisible . . ."* Mandela rally literature (LP). *"I have known . . ."* Eleanor Roosevelt, Foreword to *Brutal Mandate. "There is Mrs. Franklin D. Roosevelt . . ."* Lowenstein, *Brutal Mandate,* author's note.

Chapter 21.
"Roughly, the movie . . ." Raleigh Times (LP). *"The time has come . . ."* Statement of Committee for a Democratic Spain, FBI File No. 105–103168, Vol. No. 1. *"pro-Communist,"* Ibid. *"as you know . . ."* L from Carlos Zayas to Lowenstein, Dec. 10, 1961 (LP). *"This silence . . ."* Curtis Gate memo, July 5, 1962 (LP). *"ways and means"* Cable from American embassy in Madrid to State Department, Aug. 17, 1962 (per Robert H. McBride, minister-counselor). *"both from interested . . ."* Ibid. *"secret meetings" "assignment" "touch him" "fellow workers"* Ibid. *"an energetic . . ."* Ibid. *"Dr. Al. Lowenstein"* (LP). *"My second reason . . ."* L from Victor Reuther to Lowenstein, Aug. 23, 1962 (LP). *"our Spanish Committee"* L from Edward F. Gray to Victor Reuther, Sept. 10, 1962 (LP). *"Victor spent . . ."* Braden, "I'm Glad the CIA is 'Immoral,'" *Saturday Evening Post,* 1967; quoted in Marchetti and Marks, p. 67. *And David Halberstam . . .* David Halberstam, *The Best and the Brightest,* (New York: Random House, 1969), p. 154. *"setting up . . ."* L from Amadeo Cuito to Lowenstein, Sept. 10, 1962 (LP). *"this fall . . ."* Ibid. *"Confirm agreement . . ."* Quoted in L from Cuito to Lowenstein, Sept. 10, 1962 (LP). *"They have been invited . . ."* L from Cuito to Lowenstein, Sept. 19, 1962 (LP). *"They will . . ."* Ibid. *"I have seen . . ."* Ibid. *"covert arm . . ."* McGehee, p. xi. *"which I look . . ."* L from Walter Reuther to Lowenstein, Sept. 26, 1962 (LP). *"If so . . ."* L from Edward Gray to Lowenstein, Oct. 10, 1962 (LP). Gray mentions Jay Lovestone as one who might be objecting. Lovestone was a former Communist who broke with the party and became fiercely anti-Communist. *"sources" close to . . .* FBI File No. 105–103168, Vol. No. 2. *"very short . . ."* Jacobson and Gray announcement, Oct. 19, 1962 (LP). *"News is devastating . . ."* LD, Vol. 1962–66 (LP). *"Effort to Link . . ."* Ibid. *"wrong drift"* Ibid. *"Tom Hughes Asks . . ."* Ibid. *"It could have . . ."* Telephone C with Tom Hughes, 1983. *"the whole network . . ."* Marchetti and Marks, p. 14. *"as keys"* LD. *his reported income . . .* Lowenstein's 1964 federal income tax return, (LP). *"friend and advisor"* Cable from American embassy in Madrid to State Department, Dec. 4, 1963 (per Livingston D. Watrous, counselor of embassy for political affairs). *"His inability . . ."* Ibid. *"sabotaged"* LD, Vol. 1962–66 (LP). *"save the money . . ."* Cable from American embassy in Madrid to State Department, Nov. 23, 1966 (per Ambassador Duke). *"wide awake"* Ibid. *"liberalizing"* Ibid. *"the expected results . . ."* FBI File No. 105–103168, Vol. No. 1. *"In view of . . ."* Ibid. *"Al was as . . ."* I with Jimmy Wallace. *"contemporary Spanish student . . ."* L from Richard G. Stearns, international affairs vice-president, NSA, to Lewis Car-

liner, Dec. 14, 1966 (LP). *"a non-Communist . . ."* Frederick E. Berger, NSA, memo included in L from Richard G. Stearns to Lewis Carliner, Dec. 14, 1966 (LP). *"They want the cooperation . . ."* L from Nancy Macdonald to Lowenstein, Feb. 15, 1967 (LP). *"like-minded groups"* Minutes of meeting of Feb. 21, 1967 (LP). *"would not like . . ."* Ibid. *"committee of six"* L from Nancy Macdonald to Lowenstein, March 1, 1967 (LP). *According to sources . . .* These are the same sources referred to in Chapters 15 and 20. *when he neglected . . .* Acknowledgment of his non-payment was sent to him by both organizations (LP). *"unbelievably ill-conceived . . ."* L from Ambassador Frank Carlucci to Lowenstein, March 14, 1975 (LP). *"But if Carlucci . . ."* Brownstein and Easton, p. 439. *"had a relationship . . ."* I with Frank Carlucci, July 19, 1983. *"at a time . . ."* Brownstein and Easton. *"Whoever sold me . . ."* Ibid. *"was watching . . ."* Ibid. *"subvert the . . ."* Ibid. *"contacts with . . ."* I with Frank Carlucci. *"a very pro-American . . ."* Ibid. *"He was . . ."* Ibid. *"It's entirely possible . . ."* Ibid. *"had no association . . ."* Ibid. *"enormous importance"* L from James Loeb to Lowenstein, Feb. 11, 1976 (LP). *"with the minimum . . ."* Draft L, the American Committee for Iberian Freedom (Spain and Portugal), Feb. 1976 (LP). *"If we had helped . . ."* Lowenstein, "Spain without Franco," *Saturday Review*, Feb. 7, 1976.

Chapter 22.
"There were certain . . ." Telephone I with William Craig, June 30, 1983. *"an extraordinary teacher . . ."* Telephone I with John Tyler Caldwell, July 6, 1983. *"accept a temporary . . ."* Lowenstein personnel file, North Carolina State. Telephone C with Mary Strickland, Office of Provost Nash Winstead. The file indicates Lowenstein told the administration he had been asked to fill "an important post with the Peace Corps in Puerto Rico on a temporary basis." *"I never knew . . ."* I with Harris Wofford, May 18, 1983. *"he was interested . . ."* Telephone I with William Craig. *"nothing to do . . ."* *"didn't take . . ."* Ibid. *"fascinating"* I with Harris Wofford. *"never heard . . ."* Ibid. *"tied"* Ibid. *"the FBI and Civil . . ."* Harris Wofford, *Of Kennedy & Kings, Making Sense of the Sixties*, (New York: Farrar, Straus & Giroux, 1980). *"very embarrassed"* *"fallen through"* Lowenstein personnel file, North Carolina State. *"as a replacement . . ."* C with Douglas Hunt, 1983. *"as a link . . ."* I with Brooke Aronson Trent, Aug 11, 1983. *contributions to AMSAC . . .* Schechter, Ansara, and Kolodney, in Ray et al., p. 54. *"to study the effects . . ."* Ibid., p. 55. *"revolutionary round table . . ."* Ibid., p. 53. *"In the absence . . ."* Lowenstein and Marcum, "Force: Its Thrust and Prognosis," Southern Africa in Transition, Fourth International Conference, the American Society of African Culture, April 11–13, 1963, Howard University. In *Southern Africa in Transition*, ed. John A. Davis and James K. Baker (New York: Praeger, 1966). *"Communist, black racists . . ."* Lowenstein, *Brutal Mandate*, quoted in Lowenstein and Marcum. *"white tool"* *"waited four years"* *"expose him"* LD, Vol. 1962–66 (LP). *"imminent"* Ibid. *"neutrality"* Ibid. *"quiet approach,"* *"Demarche"* Ibid.

Chapter 23.
"Banda was always . . ." Telephone I with Kris Kleinbauer, 1983. *"started a ferment . . ."* Ibid. *"radical"* Ibid. *"We had a romance . . ."* Ibid. *"When things came . . ."* Ibid. *"festive"* Ibid. *"getting involved in . . ."* Wofford, p. 282. *Wofford explains . . .* I with Harris Wofford. *Q is put by wire . . .* LD, Vol. 1962–66 (LP). *K in L.A.. . .* Ibid. *K Drives . . .* Ibid. *"People thought . . ."* I with Kleinbauer. *"I wasn't too . . ."* Ibid. *"a lot of terms . . ."* C with Victor Marchetti. *"My daily entries . . ."* Stephen Bingham, L No. 17, Aug. 5, 1966, Freetown (LP). *"best African . . ."* I with Emory Bundy. *to "cause trouble . . ."* Telephone I with Eugene Theroux, 1983.

Chapter 24.
"We believe . . ." LP. *"the symbol of . . ."* Memo to Board of Trustees, National Conference of Christians and Jews, from Donald. S. Harrington and A. Philip Randolph, Co-Chairmen, American Committee on Africa, Feb. 7, 1966 (LP). *"the dubious reputation . . ."* Draft of memo to National Conference of Christians and Jews, undated (LP). *"If the United Nations . . ."* Lowenstein, in *The Record*, March 6, 1966. *"It is high . . ."* Ibid. *"providing an opportunity . . ."* Memo on Senator Robert Kennedy's visit to South Africa (compiled by members of the NUSAS Committee in Europe) (LP). *"Some believe . . ."* Quoted in Wofford. *"muddle"* LD, Vol. 1962–66 (LP). *"towards July . . ."* L from George Houser to Oliver Tambo in Morogoro, Tanzania, June 13, 1966 (LP). *Eduardo Mondlane . . .* L from George Houser to Eduardo Mondlane in Dar es Salaam, June 13, 1966. *"carry on . . ."* L from A. Philip Randolph to Lowenstein, July 22, 1966 (LP). *"fact-finding trip"* I with Jenny Lowenstein Littlefield. *"fact-finding adventures"* Ibid. *"He must have . . ."* Ibid. *"there was never . . ."* Ibid. *"Allard Lowenstein popped . . ."* Forman, p. 485. *"Forman and Howard . . ."* L from Kris Kleinbauer to Lowenstein, Aug. 10, 1966 (LP). *"Court decision . . ."* LD, Vol. 1962–66 (LP). *"amazed at . . ."* L from Donald S. Harrington for American Committee on Africa, March 1967. *"You may find . . ."* Memo from Tom Hughes to Lowenstein, Dec. 9, 1966 (LP). *"wiped out . . ."* I with Hal Minus, March 1981. *"I have to get . . ."* Lowenstein quoted by Minus, I with Hal Minus. *"bring change . . ."* Lowenstein quoted by Minus, I with Hal Minus. *"background information"* I with Hal Minus. *"We were going . . ."* Ibid. *"horrendously expensive"* Ibid. *"I've been here . . ."* L from Jenny to Lowenstein, July 3, 1977 (LP). *"During a secret . . ."* Note from Muffie Huntington to Lowenstein, July 3, 1967 (LP). *"Hope I'll catch,"* Note from Tim Hogen to Lowenstein, July 3, 1967 (LP). *"good personal . . ."* I with Hal Minus. *"improve Mozambique . . ."* Ibid. *"freedom fighters"* Ibid. *"Next time . . ."* Lowenstein quoted by Minus, I with Hal Minus. *"I felt . . ."* I with Hal Minus. *"It was great . . ."* L from Emory Bundy to Lowenstein, July 23, 1967 (LP). *"that the hysteria . . ."* Postcard signed John, postmarked Boston, April 1967 (LP).

Chapter 25.
"The trip to . . ." I with Emory Bundy. *"Al went . . ."* I with Greg Craig, Aug. 11, 1982. *"If you can get . . ."* Lowenstein quoted by Greg Craig, I with Greg Craig. *"firm commitment"* I with Greg Craig. *"In trying . . ."* Lowenstein quoted by Greg Craig, I with Greg Craig. *"It is vital . . ."* Ibid. *"morally bound"* I with Greg Craig. *"As such . . ."* Ibid. *"Stay in . . ."* Lowenstein quoted by Greg Craig, I with Greg Craig. *"Al was . . ."* I with Greg Craig. *"to Ted Kennedy"* Ibid.

Chapter 26.
"particular encouragement" "South Africa: Policy Alternatives for the United States," Report of a Wingspread Conference convened by the Johnson Foundation, April 1975, Racine, Wisconsin, p. 15. Lowenstein is identified in the report as "a participant experienced in national politics," the only participant to fit that description. George Houser of the American Committee on Africa was present, as was leading academic Africanist Gwendolen Carter. Besides them were various consultants, State Department, foundation, and corporate officials, and church representatives. The only nonwhite was Donald F. McHenry of the Carnegie Endowment for International Peace, later Andrew Young's deputy and then replacement at the United Nations in the Carter administration. *Lowenstein himself . . .* I with William F. Buckley, Jr. (Lowenstein confided this hope to Buckley). *"political activities . . ."* I with Frank Carlucci. *"Tyson was . . ."* Ibid. *"get as much . . ."* I with Tom Flynn, 1982. *"lots of CIA . . ."* Ibid. *"untenable"* Cleary

quoted by Lowenstein aide Ken McComiskey, I with Ken McComiskey, April 13, 1983. *"Lowenstein was concerned . . ."* Announcer quoted by Ken McComiskey, I with Ken McComiskey. *"How can we . . ."* I with Ken McComiskey. See Harris, p. 308. *"tangible change . . ."* I with Ken McComiskey. *"afraid . . ."* Lowenstein quoted by McComiskey, I with Ken McComiskey. *"He was too . . ."* I with Ken McComiskey. *"Al was tough . . ."* Ibid. *"He didn't trust . . ."* I with William F. Buckley, Jr. *"I had to indicate . . ."* I with Ken McComiskey. *"confused . . ."* L from Ken McComiskey to Lowenstein (LP). *"hands were tied . . ."* Ibid. *"credible" "potent"* Ibid. *"I pretty . . ."* Ibid. *"the administration . . ." "In all . . ."* Ibid. *Urangesellschaft . . . Plunder of Namibian Uranium,* Major Findings of the Hearings on Namibian Uranium Held by the United Nations Council for Namibia in July, 1980 (New York: United Nations, 1982). *widespread intimidation . . .* See *Namibia, The Facts,* (London: International Defense & Aid Fund for Southern Africa, 1980), p. 63. *"The contrast between . . ."* Quoted in *South Africa Digest,* Feb. 23, 1979. *"self-righteous" "more realistic"* I with Jimmy Wallace. *"Why must we . . ."* Sir Mark Turner, quoted in Alun Roberts, *The Rossing File* (London: Namibia Support Committee [CANUC], 1980), p. 40. *"something to work . . ."* I with Emory Bundy. *"wasn't a big . . ."* I with Ken McComiskey. *"Young said . . ."* Ibid. *"got distressed . . ."* I with Wendell Willkie II, May 2, 1983. *"Al thought . . ."* I with Ken McComiskey. *And he told James Symington . . .* L from James Symington to Larry Lowenstein, Dec. 23, 1980. *"frustration"* I with Wendell Willkie II. *"positive sign"* I with Ken McComiskey. *"Andy Young automatically . . ."* Ibid. *"He would dismiss . . ."* Ibid. *"were in basic . . ."* L from Arthur Schlesinger, Jr., to Larry Lowenstein, April 18, 1980. *"I had met . . ."* L from David (Lord) Harlech to Arthur Schlesinger, Jr., March 21, 1980. *"break the diplomatic . . ." Lowenstein: Acts of Courage and Belief,* ed. G. Stone and D. Lowenstein (San Diego: Harcourt Brace Jovanovich, 1983), p. 287. *"when Lowenstein . . ."* I with Greg Stone, June 5, 1981. *"different shop . . ."* Ibid. *"It was extremely . . ."* Stone and Lowenstein, p. 289. *"Ambassador Young has . . ."* Lowenstein Congressional testimony on Rhodesia, quoted in Stone and Lowenstein, p. 289. *"The contributions . . ."* Ibid., p. 290–91d. *"I would urge . . ."* Ibid., p.302. *"a promising . . ." "a middle course . . ." "racist"* Quoted in Stone and Lowenstein, p. 303, 304. *"in light of . . ."* Ibid., p.304. *"heavy pressure"* Stone and Lowenstein p. 310. *"Feisty British . . ."* Jack Anderson column, *Washington Post,* Jan. 20, 1980. *"confident he went . . ."* I with Wendell Willkie II. *"He called me . . ."* I with Theo-Ben Gurirab. *"I have finally . . ."* L from Ernest Wentzel to Hank Slack, June 12, 1979 (LP). *"He proposed . . ."* Ibid. *"It is very . . ."* Ibid. *"personal service" company* Telephone C with secretary to H. R. Slack, 1983. *"Mr. Lowenstein must . . ."* Telephone C with librarian, South African consulate, New York, Aug. 9, 1983. *"I don't know . . ."* Telephone I with Ernest Wentzel, Aug. 9, 1983. *"What an extraordinary . . ."* Ibid. *"I really don't think . . ."* Ibid. *"would report . . ."* I with Frank Carlucci. *"The State Department . . ."* Ibid. *"In fact . . ."* Ibid. *"worked out"* Ibid. *"It was all . . ."* Ibid. *"But I don't know . . ."* Ibid. *Oppenheimer's DeBeers.* See Brownstein and Easton, p. 444. *Harry Oppenheimer who* See generally Joseph Lelyveld, "Oppenheimer of South Africa," *New York Times Magazine,* May 8, 1983. *"I thought that Allard . . ."* I with Ernest Wentzel. *"In January and February . . ."* Memo from Mark Childress to Larry Lowenstein. *"a lot of opposition . . ."* Moose quoted by Adams, telephone C with Sam Adams, 1982. (Moose never returned calls.) *"State was scared . . ."* Ibid. *"worried about . . ."* Ibid. *"a loose end . . ."* Ibid. *"surprised that . . ."* Ibid. *"a real possiblity . . ."* I with Wendell Willkie II. *"people in ruling circles . . ."* Lowenstein quoted by Willkie, I with Wendell Willkie II. *"is quixotic . . ."* Lelyveld quoted by Willkie, I with Wendell Willkie II. *"noble spirit . . ."* Ibid. *"Al Lowenstein visited . . ."* Quoted in Harris, p. 313. *"brotherly identification . . ."* Lowenstein address to Pretoria Press Club (also Lowenstein report in Oggenblad), reported in *South Africa Digest*, Feb. 23, 1979. *"It is our duty . . ."* Ibid. *"The role of . . ."* Study Group on United States/South African Relations, 12 July 1979, Jan Smuts House, Johannesburg. *"Dad, you've done . . ."* I with Frank Lowenstein, May 1–3, 1981.

Section V. Chapter 27.
"identified with . . ." Viorst, p. 387. *"probably fill . . ." "tainted"* Andrew Kopkind, "New Radicals in Dixie," *The New Republic*, April 10, 1965, p. 14. *"SNCC was so . . ."* I with Joanne Grant Rabinowitz, Aug. 16, 1983. *"hard, cold . . ."* Quoted in Howell Raines, *My Soul Is Rested* (New York: Viking Penguin, 1983), p. 227. *"We met with Bobby . . ."* Ibid., p. 228 *"wrong" "I saw John Kennedy . . ."* Ibid., pp. 228–229.

Chapter 28.
"'No' to State , . ." LD, Vol. 1962–66 (LP). *"Caldwell perturbed . . ."* Ibid. *"statehouse politicians . . ."* C with Terry Sanford, 1981. *"On the final . . ."* Ashby, pp. 312–313. *"It involved . . ."* I with Rev. Russell K. Williams, 1983. *"He was in . . ."* Ibid. *"Early departure . . ."* LD, Vol. 1962–66 (LP). *"Responsible for . . ."* Clayborne Carson, *In Struggle; SNCC and the Black Awakening of the 1960's* (Cambridge: Harvard University Press, 1981), p. 86. *"like a college . . ."* I with Greg Craig. *"July 4—. . ."* LD, Vol. 1962–66 (LP). *"Miss 'No Gains' . . ."* Ibid. *"Only somewhat . . ." "like South Africa . . ."* Carson, p. 97. *"Jackson involvement . . ."* LD, Vol. 1962–66 (LP). *"Biracial . . ."* Ibid. *"a study . . ."* Lawrence Maddry, "Lowenstein Is Storm Center As Professor and As Author," *Raleigh Times* (LP). *"Al came . . ."* Quoted in Frederick Klein, "Liberal 'Shaker' Edges to Limelight," *Wall Street Journal*, Nov. 1, 1967. *"Lowenstein was summoned . . ."* Teresa Carpenter, "From Heroism to Madness—The Odyssey of the Man Who Shot Al Lowenstein," *Village Voice*, May 12, 1980, p. 24. *"It would take us . . ."* Forman, p. 357. *"Allard Lowenstein should . . ."* Ibid., p. 358. *"When I first got . . ."* Nancy Steffen, "SNCC: New Directions, New Problems," *Stanford Daily*, 1965 (LP). *"Moses' participation . . ."* Carson, p. 97. *"King also explained . . ."* See Harris, p. 31. *"somebody was looking . . ."* Telephone I with Robert Moses, April 15, 1982. *"Bob was awesome . . ."* I with Mendy Samstein, Oct. 14, 1983. *"Moses had . . ."* Lowenstein quoted in Harris, p. 33. *"What we had . . ."* Lowenstein quoted in Steffen. *"Ministers ran . . ."* Telephone I with Robert Moses. *"extension of . . ."* Ibid. *It gave them . . .* See Harris, p. 34; Carson, p. 97. *"I remembered . . ."* Lowenstein quoted in Viorst, pp. 390–391. *"but it didn't . . ."* Lowenstein quoted by Steffen. *"Then Bob Moses . . ."* Steffen. *"I was aware . . ."* I with Joe Rauh, Aug. 13, 1981. *"He never got . . ."* Charles Evers quoted in Klein. *"The various civil . . ."* I with Rev. Russell K. Williams. *"betrayed"* I with Rev. William Sloane Coffin. *"Yale group . . ."* LD, Vol. 1962–66 (LP). *"gentle and friendly"* C with Lawrence de Bivort. *"Ella Baker . . ."* Telephone I with Robert Moses. *"It didn't bother . . ."* I with Mendy Samstein. *"students wanted . . ."* Telephone I with Robert Moses. *"wanted self-asserted . . ."* C with Lawrence de Bivort. *"In Mississippi, I'm . . ."* Lowenstein speech, "Mississippi: A Foreign Country in Our Midst?" in Stone and Lowenstein, pp. 22–25; also in *Stanford Daily*, Oct. 3, 1983. *"A.K., 2 Yalies . . ."* LD, Vol. 1962–66 (LP). *"We are under . . ."* L from Lowenstein to his parents, Oct. 29, 1963 (LP). *"What is going . . ."* *Stanford Daily*, Oct. 27, 1963; Harris, p. 41. *"That's what he . . ."* Telephone I with John Tyler Caldwell, July 6, 1983. *"Yes, it is . . ."* Halberstam, "The Man Who Ran against Lyndon Johnson," p. 52. *"No, this is . . ."* Telephone I with John Tyler Caldwell. *"U.S. Marshals . . ."* LD, Vol. 1962–66. LP. *"bring about such . . ." "annealing process . . ."* Carson, p. 98. *"Decision still . . ."* LD, Vol. 1962–66 (LP). *"If we're trying . . ."* Carson, p. 99. *"So it isn't . . ." "I always*

thought" Ibid., p. 99. *"plea"* *"Agree Miss* . . ." LD, Vol. 1962–66 (LP). *"Summer must* . . ." Ibid. *"A.K. for JFK* . . ." Ibid. *"serious penetration . . ."* Life, Nov. 29, 1963, pp. 86–87; Carson, p. 106. *"SNCC staff . . ."* LD, Vol. 1962–66 (LP). *"The Freedom Vote gave* . . ." Telephone I with Robert Moses. *"float in . . ."* C with Lawrence de Bivort. *"Lowenstein was traveling . . ."* Forman, p. 379. *"135 page* . . ." LD, Vol. 1962–66 (LP). *"Project to be* . . ." Ibid. *"N.C. State . . ."* Ibid. *"Moses says A* . . ." Ibid. *"I turned up . . ."* Craig. *"if anything happened . . ."* Craig.

Chapter 29.
"SNCC had become . . ." James Howard Lane, "Direct Action and Desegregation: Towards a Theory of the Rationalization of Protest," Ph.D. Diss., Harvard University, 1965, p. 377; Carson, p. 103. *"shifted from . . ."* Carson, p. 103. *"The liberals were* . . ." I with Sanford Katz, 1982. *"He felt politics . . ."* Lawrence Michael Hill, "Allard K. Lowenstein: A Man Who Made a Difference," Honors Thesis, Dept. of Political Science, Harpur College, State University of New York at Binghampton, p. 40. *"stop taking . . ."* Carson, p. 105. *"insufficiently anti-Communist"* Dugger, "Book about Al Lowenstein Unjustified, Unjustifiable" (review of Harris, *Dreams Die Hard*), Dallas Morning News, 1982. *"Stalinist"* See Harris, p. 53. *"During the SNCC . . ."* I with Sanford Friedman. *"the first year* . . ." I with Curtis Gans. *"It attracted . . ."* I with Sanford Katz. *"Through the efforts . . ."* Ibid. *"Our general feeling . . ."* I with Jack Greenberg, Sept. 15, 1983. *"large-scale legal . . ."* Arthur Kinoy, *Rights on Trial* (Cambridge: Harvard University Press, 1983), p. 236. *"chimpanzees," "ought to be . . ."* Southern Justice, ed. Leon Friedman (New York: Pantheon, 1965), p. 189. *"but three . . ."* I with George Crockett, April 22, 1982. *"In the argument . . ."* Kinoy, p. 240. *"In the early . . ."* Telephone I with Robert Moses. *"The project . . ."* Ibid. *"chairperson . . ."* Ibid. *"This was out . . ."* Ibid. *"wanted a cleaner . . ."* I with Rev. William Sloane Coffin. *"There were deep . . ."* I with Greg Craig. *"the central ideological . . ."* Ibid. *"Al wanted . . ."* Ibid. *"The left would . . ."* Ibid. *"SNCC workers . . ."* Ibid. *"NAA-LG Shadow . . ." "'Infiltration' . . ."* LD, Vol. 1962–66 (LP). *"Gus Tyler . . ."* C with Marian Wright Edelman, March 1982. *According to* . . ., Harris, p. 54. *He added* . . . See Forman, p. 381. *"use the orientation . . ."* Carson, p. 107. *"open about being . . ."* I with Joanne Grant Rabinowitz. *"MW 'Worried' . . ."* LD, Vol. 1962–66 (LP). *"Yale, Oberlin . . ."* Ibid. *"There are many . . ."* Forman, p. 382. *"The Guild lawyers . . ."* I with Mel Wulf, May 5, 1982. *"Opposition to . . ."* I with George Crockett. *"LCDC lawyers . . ."* I with Mel Wulf. *"It was their . . ."* Ibid. *"was going . . ."* I with George Crockett. *"They evidently . . ."* Ibid. *"We had . . ."* Ibid. *"playing at . . ."* I with Mel Wulf.

Chapter 30.
"Mississippi Mire . . ." LD Vol. 1962–66 (LP). *"A' 'withdraws' . . ."* Ibid. *"not the issue," "tough"* Ibid. *"Caldwell Hints . . ."* Ibid. *"dead end . . ."* Ibid. *"I remember Allard . . ."* Telephone I with John Tyler Caldwell.

Chapter 31.
"Al Lowenstein, Professor . . ." Raleigh Times, April 21, 1964. See also FBI File No. 105–103168, Vol. No 2. *"legitimate Democratic . . ."* Carson, p. 108. *"This new party . . ."* Ibid., p. 108. *"was like a gnat . . ."* Halberstam, *The Best and the Brightest*, p. 429. *"The Lawyers Guild tried . . ."* I with Joe Rauh, Aug. 13, 1981. *"impertinence and . . ."* Carson, p. 109. *"Lowenstein had . . ."* Telephone I with Robert Moses. *"he did not want . . ."* Carpenter, p. 24. *"the most dangerous . . ."* Ibid., p. 24. *"During the early . . ."* Craig. *"eliminate persons . . ." "wrapped up . . ." "limited . . ."* etc. Carson, pp. 111–12. *"personal"* Harris, p. 58. *"Finances Well Off . . ."* LD, Vol. 1962–66 (LP). *"Norman Thomas Schles-*

inger . . ." Ibid. *"lonely road . . ."* Raines, p. 275. *"No privileged . . ."* Carson, p. 114. *"3 Probable Deaths . . ."* LD, Vol. 1962–66 (LP). *"N.T., RFK . . ."* Ibid. *"At about . . ."* Carpenter, p. 24. *"Sweeney hurt . . ."* LD, Vol. 1962–66 (LP). *"Rustin, MLK . . ."* Ibid. *"If King . . ."* I with Sanford Katz. *"I finally . . ."* Craig. *"in a car . . ."* Ibid. *Johnson ordered . . .* See Carson, p. 124 and citations. *"final" "top priority" "probable" "lead for VP . . ."* LD, Vol. 1962–66 (LP). *"F.D.P. Prospects . . ."* Ibid. *"Rauh, RFK . . ."* Ibid. *"FDP Atmosphere . . ."* Ibid. *"All-out Fight . . ."* Ibid. *"Johnson wanted . . ."* I with Mendy Samstein. *"I was beat . . ."* Harris, p. 71; Carson, p. 125. *"He said he was not . . ."* I with Barney Frank, Oct. 3, 1983. *"I didn't meet . . ."* Telephone I with Robert Moses. *"I am saying . . ."* I with Joe Rauh. *"you couldn't get . . ."* Ibid. *"My position . . ."* Ibid. *"It's hard to know . . ."* Telephone I with Eleanor Holmes Norton, 1983. *"Al and his . . ."* I with Mendy Samstein. *"Joe, you're . . ."* I with Joe Rauh. *"Well, that's . . ."* Ibid. *"'Fraternal' . . ."* LD, Vol. 1962–66 (LP). *"You're a traitor . . ."* Forman, p. 392. *"I am with you . . ."* Forman, p. 393. *"Ella Baker cut up . . ."* I with Joe Rauh. *"Samstein, Tillow . . ."* LD, Vol. 1962–66 (LP). *"My sense . . ."* I with Mendy Samstein. *"'The convention has . . .'"* I with Joe Rauh. *"to sell them . . ."* Ibid. *"fight to . . ." "unbeknownst . . ."* Ibid. *"Just Walter . . ."* Ibid. *"He made it sound . . ."* Ibid. *"And I made . . ."* Ibid. *Moses told . . .* Carson, p. 126. *"We didn't come . . ."* Forman, p. 395. *"there was a great . . ."* I with Greg Craig. *"There was a level . . ."* Paul Cowan, "What Makes Al Lowenstein Run?" *Ramparts,* Sept. 7, 1968, p. 50. *"If the CIA . . ."* I with Russell K. Williams. *"They're sharecroppers . . ."* I with Joe Rauh. *"Now that's . . ."* Ibid. *"Al and I . . ."* Ibid. *"The CIA was . . ."* I with Joanne Grant Rabinowitz. *"In many ways . . ."* Cowan, p. 48. *"Young whites . . ."* Halberstam, *The Best and the Brightest,* pp. 427–28. *"If the MFDP . . ."* Telephone I with Robert Moses. *"Dennis wasn't . . ."* I with Greg Craig. *"Sweeney and Lowenstein . . ."* Telephone I with Robert Moses. *"after the convention . . ."* I with Mendy Samstein.

Chapter 32.
"You know Al . . ." I with Greg Craig. *"Dennis seemed . . ."* Ibid. *"I agree . . ."* Forman, pp. 401–402. *"In the event . . ."* Ibid., p. 402. *"Unless we . . ."* Ibid., p. 402. *"without knowing . . ."* Ibid., p. 404. *"getting back" "I had a . . ."* I with Mendy Samstein. *"Lowenstein's behavior . . ."* I with Joanne Grant Rabinowitz. *"SNC, NAA . . ."* LD, Vol. 1962–66 (LP).

Chapter 33.
"'A' to 'Sound' . . ." LD, Vol. 1962–66 (LP). *"Sanford says . . ."* Ibid. *"M.W., Now . . ."* Ibid. *"I thought Rauh . . ."* I with Mel Wulf. *"SNCC was . . ."* Ibid. *"The first duty . . ."* Ibid. *"I got shit . . ."* Ibid. *"He was committed . . ."* Dugger.

Chapter 34.
"Moses, Lynd . . ." LD, Vol. 1962–66 (LP). *"Drop Battle . . ."* Ibid. *"help to reverse . . ."* Ibid. *"cooperative format" "a peak" "alternative"* Ibid. *"Wilkins, Wechsler . . ."* Ibid. *"coordinate and channel . . ."* Ibid. *"dream"* Ibid. *"Summit" "new situations" "I'm Head . . ."* Ibid. *"We've lost . . ."* Ibid. *"B.F. Agrees . . ."* Ibid. *"April return . . ."* Ibid. *"Sweeney to Quit . . ." "Sweeney Extraordinary . . ."* Ibid. *"the kind of racial . . ."* Harris, p. 105. *"I remember one . . ."* Ibid., p. 310. *"He was disoriented . . ."* I with Mendy Samstein. *"A year and a half . . ."* Steffen, "SNCC: New Directions, New Problems," Quoted in Harris, pp. 102–103; LP. *"His performance . . ."* I with Joanne Grant Rabinowitz. *"I remember one . . ."* Stone and Lowenstein, p. 301. *"Al was attacked . . ."* I with Joe Rauh.

Section VI. Chapter 35.
"*Both the Kennedy* . . ." *The New York Times*, Aug. 21, 1983, p. E5.

Chapter 36.
"*I was on* . . ." L from John Ehle to the author, March 9, 1983. "*Far Left* . . ."
LD, Vol. 1962–66 (LP). "'*Big Daddy*' . . ." Ibid. "*This will confirm* . . ." L from
Paul Ylvisaker to Lowenstein, April 1, 1965 (LP). "*Now there was* . . ." I with
Curtis Gans. "*at $10 million* . . ." LD, Vol. 1962–66 (LP). "*made loads* . . ." C
with Dorothy DiCintio. "*The P & C* . . ." Ibid. "*Lazar had stock* . . ." Ibid. "*It
was a nice* . . ." Ibid. "*posture*" "*blows its lid*" "*temporary Negro* . . ." "*Parris
. . .*" LD, Vol. 1962–66 (LP). "*not a figurehead*" "*delay* . . ." "*Algeria*" Ibid. "*to
help prevent* . . ." Harris, p. 132. "*six to nine* . . ." Harris, p. 132. "*By creating
. . .*" I with Curtis Gans. "*Everyone in Santiago* . . ." Lowenstein report (AL on
the Matum Incident) on the Dominican elections, p. 45 (LP). *Lowenstein then
met* See Harris, p. 138; see also Ruth Shereff, "Crisis over the Dominican Republic: Liberals in Wonderland," *Commonweal*, 86:198–9, May 5, 1967; Ruth Shereff, "The Committee for Free Elections in the Dominican Republic," *Liberation*,
Nov. 1966. "*Bosch Defeat* . . ." LD, Vol. 1962–66 (LP). "*We went into* . . ." Lowenstein address, May 17, 1966, in Stone and Lowenstein, p. 48.

Chapter 37.
"*He struck* . . ." Harris, p. 97. "*interact, to unwind* . . ." "*sex and* . . ." Craig.
"*The Kids* . . ." Ibid. "*The members of* . . ." Harris, p. 112. "*stunningly* . . ." I
with Doug Ireland, 1981. "*Al arrived* . . ." Craig.

Chapter 38.
"*At no time* . . ." Rev. William Sloane Coffin, *Once to Every Man* (New York:
Atheneum, 1977), p. 212. "*turning themselves* . . ." "*Look at* . . ." Ibid., p.212.
"*would help* . . ." Ibid., p.214. "*At the time* . . ." Ibid., p.214. "*Yale teach-in* . . ."
LD, Vol.1962–66 (LP). "*The question of* . . ." Quoted in Harris, p. 122–23. "*Despite similar* . . ." Coffin, p. 215. "*Certainly Al* . . ." I with Harris Wofford. "*Al
had* . . ." I with Curtis Gans.

Chapter 39.
"*It took* . . ." LD, Vol. 1962–66 (LP). "*I wanted to get* . . ." I with Jenny
Lowenstein Littlefield. "*this spectacular* . . ." Ibid. "*this shy* . . ." "*This is* . . ."
Ibid. "*low and* . . ." "*Al is* . . ." Ibid. "*Al was* . . ." Ibid. "*Poor little* . . ." Ibid.
"*He would* . . ." Craig. "*I knew* . . ." I with Jenny Lowenstein Littlefield. "*the
leaders of* . . ." "*Well, I* . . ." "*he lifted* . . ." Craig. "*I was to* . . ." I with Jenny
Lowenstein Littlefield. "*How could you* . . ." Ibid. "*God, I'm so* . . ." "*Don't
worry* . . ." "*You're kidding*" Ibid. "*How are you* . . ." "*beguiling*" Ibid.

Chapter 40.
"*Al was not* . . ." I with Brooke Aronson Trent. "*Far left* . . ." "*Red-Baiting
. . .*" LD, Vol. 1962–66, LP. "*commitment to* . . ." "*dispossessed*" Harris, p. 127.
"*I have a feeling* . . ." "*He must have* . . ." "*so you see*" Lowenstein speech, cam-
paign 1966 (LP). "*Read; use*" Written on Lowenstein speech, campaign 1966 (LP).
"*might very well* . . ." L from Stephen Cohen to Lowenstein, Feb. 13, 1966.
"*emotionally fragile*" I with Jenny Lowenstein Littlefield. "*Ochs is so* . . ." Ibid.
"*Mr. Lowenstein said* . . ." *The New York Times*, quoted in Harris, p. 127. "*Mr.
Lowenstein is a* . . ." Jacob Brackman, "Candidate" (The Talk of the Town), *The
New Yorker*, March 12, 1966, pp. 41–44. "*Race in 12th C.D.*. . ." "*Time marches
. . .*" LD, Vol. 1962–66 (LP).

Chapter 41.

"*militarily unwinnable*" Lowenstein address "Vietnam—In or Out" May 17, 1966; in Stone and Lowenstein, p.47–49. "*new politics of . . .*" June 17, 1966, remarks in untitled paper on the politics of alienation, (LP). "*Gans to organize . . .*" LD, Vol. 1962–66 (LP). "*the group continued . . .*" Report on July 14 Informal Meeting on Working Coalition, July 20, 1966 (LP). "*I J. Agrees . . .*" LD, Vol. 1962–66 (LP). "*missed out*" I with Jenny Lowenstein Littlefield. "*I've just been . . .*" Ibid. "*What letter?*" Ibid. "*You know,*" Ibid. "*conspiracy*" "*I loved Al*" Ibid. "*Lyman meeting . . .*" LD, Vol. 1962–66 (LP). "*ask him for . . .*" I with Jenny Lowenstein Littlefield. "*I will give . . .*" Ibid. "*You should have . . .*" Ibid. "*I was his closest . . .*" I with Rev. William Sloane Coffin. "*I don't know . . .*" "*Well, that's . . .*" Ibid. "*Is this grape . . .*" I with Jenny Lowenstein Littlefield. "*Funny and . . .*" "*star struck*" "*ebullient . . .*" "*impressive*" Ibid. "*This is an . . .*" Ibid.

Chapter 42.

"*The CIA . . .*" "*CIA money . . .*" LD, Vol. 1962–66 (LP). "*RFK staff . . .*" Ibid. "*A favors RFK . . .*" Ibid. "*Court decision . . .*" Ibid. "*Lengthy Rand . . .*" Ibid. "*F IS . . .*" Ibid. "*Sharpened pain . . .*" Ibid. "*RFK and MM . . .*" Ibid. "*Al understood . . .*" I with Greg Craig. "*A tall, blond . . .*" Bill Moore, "Stanford Picks a Revolutionary," *San Francisco Chronicle* (LP). "*I have no . . .*" I with Greg Craig. "*the oldest . . .*" "*someone who . . .*" Halberstam, "The Man Who Ran against Lyndon Johnson." "*a whole generation . . .*" I with Greg Craig. "*A Agrees . . .*" LD, Vol. 1962–66 (LP). "*D.H. . . .*" Ibid. "*Did you say . . .*" I with Greg Craig. "*To Al . . .*" Ibid. "*It looked like . . .*" I with Rick Weidman, May 16, 1981. "*He said the war . . .*" Harris, pp.153–54. "*hardened*" Memo to the "Council" from Betty Goetz Lall, July 21, 1966 (LP). *nine-point program . . .* Memo with letter from Betty Goetz Lall to Hubert Humphrey, Aug. 21, 1966 (LP). "*If there are some . . .*" L from Betty Goetz Lall to Hubert Humphrey, Aug. 21, 1966 (LP). "*We perceived it . . .*" I with Curtis Gans. "*MEMO FOR:*" Memo from Tom Hughes to Lowenstein, Dec. 9, 1966, with Hughes speech of Nov. 14, 1966, at Stanford, "Relativity in Foreign Policy: The Storage and Retrieval of Conviction" (LP). "*essentially conservative . . .*" ADA draft "State of the Union," Dec. 9, 1966 (LP). "*It was clear . . .*" I with Curtis Gans. "*lots of people . . .*" I with Jenny Lowenstein Littlefield. "*All the ads . . .*" Halberstam, "The Man Who Ran against Lyndon Johnson." "*the war protest . . .*" Harris, p.154. "*the growing conflict . . .*" Harris, p.154. "*As students . . .*" Draft student letter on Vietnam war (LP). "*some of us . . .*" L from Norman Thomas to Lyndon Johnson (drafted by Lowenstein), Dec. 26, 1966 (LP). "*Unless this conflict . . .*" *The New York Times*, Dec. 30, 1966. "*an effort . . .*" L from Rhodes scholar to Lowenstein (LP). "*unconditional negotiations*" "*don't themselves . . .*" Lowenstein handwritten speech outline (LP). "*The notion . . .*" Theodore Draper, "The American Crisis—Vietnam, Cuba and the Dominican Republic," *Commentary*, January 1967, pp.27–48.

Chapter 43.

"*The hearings . . .*" I with Curtis Gans. "*Over the next . . .*" Coordinator's Report, Citizens for Kennedy-Fulbright, Vol. 1, No. 1, Jan. 15, 1967. "*I found Rostow's . . .*" Viorst, p.403. "*We are fighting . . .*" I with Rick Weidman. "*Someone is . . .*" Ibid. "*if we couldn't . . .*" Dean Rusk, Duke University oral history project, Spring 1980. "*Al suckered . . .*" I with Rick Weidman. "*this mobilization . . .*" Action Group, Clergy and Laymen Concerned about Vietnam, in Washington Mobilization (Jan. 31–Feb. 1, 1967) Schedule and Materials (LP). "*When the rest . . .*" Carpenter, p. 25. "*Jesus Christ complex . . .*" Ibid., p. 26. "*I remember . . .*" Document given by Sweeney to his lawyer, printed in National News Council Complaint No. 24–81, Larry Lowenstein and James A. Wechsler against the

Village Voice and Teresa Carpenter (Filed May 4 and May 6, 1981), p. 18. *"was far less . . ."* I with Curtis Gans. *"proof"* L to Barry Farber from Benice Diamond, March 24, 1967 (LP); see also L from Benice Diamond to Lowenstein, March 24, 1967 (LP). *"Wiry yet frail . . ."* White, *The Making of the President, 1968* (New York: Atheneum, 1969), pp.81–82. *"Allard had . . ."* I with Curtis Gans. *"If he wanted . . ." "If you ever . . ." "And he would . . ."* Ibid. *"You need not . . ."* L from Nancy Murphy to Lowenstein, March 2, 1967 (LP). *"the most beautiful . . ."* Halberstam, "The Man Who Ran against Lyndon Johnson." *"Mrs. Lowenstein . . ."* Ibid.

Chapter 44.
"Al made . . ." I with Joe Rauh. *"This is the end . . ."* Ibid. *"low-level . . ."* I with Curtis Gans. *"Al went . . ."* I with Jenny Lowenstein Littlefield. *"ease the draft—" "conscientious . . ." "dilemma"* of *"those law-abiding . . ."* Quoted in Harris, p.181. *"Joe got cold . . ."* I with Curtis Gans. *"He (Rauh) . . ."* Ibid. *"A candidate . . ."* I with Joe Rauh. *"There are . . ."* Halberstam, "The Man Who Ran against Lyndon Johnson." *"These kids . . ."* Ibid. *"great gale . . ."* Harris, p. 183. *"expressed the hope" "the United States"* Harris, p. 183. *"He has poured . . ."* Harris, p. 183. *"I told them . . ."* I with Curtis Gans. *"Having largely . . ."* Bennett, "The Issue: Vietnam; The Target: Johnson," *ADA World Magazine*, 21 July 1967, p. 3M; see in same issue, Tyler, "The Coalition Must Remain." *"maintained close ties . . ."* Harris, p. 187. *"Al and I . . ."* I with Curtis Gans. *"How the hell . . ."* I with Joe Rauh. *"In the Wisconsin . . ."* Ibid. *"I tried . . ."* Ibid. *"He was my . . ."* I with Jenny Lowenstein Littlefield.

Chapter 45.
"there wasn't sufficient . . ." I with Greg Craig. *"rape a nun . . ."* Ibid. *"He thought . . ."* Ibid. *"What we have . . ."* Telephone C with David Hawk, 1983. *"faded into . . ." "partisan-political"* Ibid. *"If a president is . . ."* Viorst, p. 408. *"He was traveling . . ."* Lewis Chester, Godfrey Hodgson, Bruce Page, *An American Melodrama—The Presidential Campaign of 1968* (New York: Dell, 1969), p. 69; see also Jack Newfield, *Robert Kennedy: A Memoir* (New York: Dutton, 1969), p. 184. *"If you want . . ."* Chester, Hodgson, Page, p.70. *"had too good . . ."* Ibid., p. 70. *"I just explained . . ."* Jack Newfield, *Robert Kennedy: A Memoir* (New York: Dutton, 1969), p. 184; see also Jules Witcover, *85 Days: The Last Campaign of Robert F. Kennedy* (New York: Putnam's, 1969). *"If you really . . ."* Chester, Hodgson, Page, p. 20. *"I was aware . . ."* Harris, p. 193. *"That's a matter . . ."* Chester, Hodgson, Page, p. 70. *"Are you willing . . ."* I with Curtis Gans; Chester, Hodgson, Page, p. 70. *"Children are born . . ."* I with Curtis Gans. *"I felt Al . . ."* I with Jenny Lowenstein Littlefield. *"If it were . . ."* Ibid. *"The feeling . . ."* Halberstam, "The Man Who Ran against Lyndon Johnson." *"He is there . . ."* Ibid. *"Al, you have . . ."* Note to Lowenstein from Vietnam trip aide (LP). *"lacking a sound . . ."* Lowenstein Vietnam "manifesto," Sept. 5, 1967 (LP). *"Allard K. Lowenstein, a vice chairman . . ."* Quoted in Harris, p. 200. *"He's in . . ." "Oh, you . . ." "Oh, no . . ."* I with Jenny Lowenstein Littlefield. *"I was afraid . . ."* Ibid. *"It would be . . ."* I with Harvey Lippman, April 14, 1982. *"He had a very . . ."* Telephone C with David Yeres, 1983–84. *"I have been given . . ."* L from James Arthur Johnson to Lowenstein, Sept. 26, 1967 (LP). *"and do whatever . . ."* L from Gerald S. Glazer to Lowenstein, Sept. 27, 1967 (LP). *"I felt . . ."* White, p. 86. *"I operated . . ." "a group of . . ."* I with Curtis Gans. *"The Dump Johnson . . ."* Halberstam, "The Man Who Ran against Lyndon Johnson." *"He didn't even . . ."* Ibid.

Chapter 46.
"the moral imperative" Newfield, p. 185. *"You're a historian . . ."* Chester, Hodgson, Page, p. 73; see also Newfield, p. 185–86; Arthur Schlesinger, Jr., *Robert Kennedy and His Times* (Boston: Houghton Mifflin, 1978), p. 825. *"Al wanted . . ."* I with Joe Rauh. *"Rauh and Shull . . ."* I with Curtis Gans. *"not important . . ."* Ibid. *"I have been thinking . . ."* L from Steve Cohen to Lowenstein, Oct. 15, 1967. *"Hartke had . . ."* I with Curtis Gans. *"You understand I love . . ."* White, p. 84. *"Everything is falling . . ."* Harris, p. 210; Newfield, p. 187; see also Plimpton, ed., I by Jean Stein, *American Journey: The Times of Robert Kennedy* (New York: Harcourt, Brace, Jovanovich, 1970), pp. 223–24; Witcover. *"He said he . . ."* Harris, pp. 210–11; see also Plimpton, pp. 223–24; Schlesinger, p. 841; Witcover. *"ditch Bobby" "no candidate . . ." "some people . . ."* Harris, p. 207. *"There was a uniform . . ."* Harris, p. 207; see also Newfield. *"I guess you . . ."* Chester, Hodgson, Page, p. 75. *"I was ecstatic"* White, p. 84. *"Who knows?"* Harris, p. 216. *"There's a lot of room . . ."* Klein. *"eater"* I with Larry Lowenstein. *"involved up to . . ." "'subverting' . . ." "a loyal . . ."* Klein. *"Communists took . . ."* Gus Tyler, a book review of *The Heydey of American Communism*, by Harvey Klehr, *New York Times Book Review*, Jan. 29, 1984, p. 10. *"I thought the President . . ."* FBI L to Mildred Stegall, The White House, with Memo, FBI File No. 105–103168, Vol. No. 2. *"a national group . . ."* FBI Memo 11/10/67, FBI File No. 105–103168, Vol. No. 2. *"an outspoken . . ." "The American Youth . . ."* Ibid. *"incurred an obligation . . ."* Ibid. *"Communist controlled . . ." "using unscrupulous . . ."* *Journal American*, Jan. 2, 1951, quoted in FBI Memo 11/10/67, FBI File No. 105–103168, Vol. No. 2. *"various members . . ." "The December 30 . . ."* FBI Memo 11/10/67, FBI File No. 105–103168, Vol. No. 2.

Chapter 47.
"yours was . . ." "won many . . ." L from Nancy Roche to Lowenstein, Nov. 14, 1967 (LP). *"I intend to enter . . ."* Viorst, p. 411. *"I had made . . ."* Eugene McCarthy, *Year of the People* (New York: Doubleday, 1968), p. 58. *"Al did . . ."* I with Curtis Gans. *"I'm going to give . . ."* Chester, Hodgson, Page, p. 85. *"a hellraising . . ."* Ibid., p. 84. *"raging like a caged . . ." "let's go"* Ibid., p. 86. *"Lowenstein was boiling . . ."* Ibid., p. 86. *"Stop it!" "There's only . . ."* Ibid., p. 86. *"I thought as . . ."* McCarthy, p. 59. *"I saw him as . . ."* Harris, p. 222. *"Al believed . . ."* I with Jenny Lowenstein Littlefield. *"You were recently . . ."* "Meet the Press," Dec. 3, 1967, in Stone and Lowenstein, p. 50. *"Looking forward . . ."* Telegram from Eugene McCarthy to Lowenstein, Dec. 26, 1967 (LP). *On February 8 . . .* "Minnesota Itinerary for A. Lowenstein" (LP). *"Al had other . . ."* I with Curtis Gans. *"Al left me . . ."* Ibid. *"in no relation . . ."* Ibid. *'only two . . ." "really favored . . ."* Ibid. *"Some people sit . . ."* "Allard Lowenstein: 'Choice Between Disaster and Faster Disaster.'"* *The Exonian*, March 6, 1968. *"All through . . ."* I with Jenny Lowenstein Littlefield. *"he was not . . ."* Interview with Curtis Gans. *"Al, baby . . ." "Bobby, you S.O.B. . . ."* I with Jenny Lowenstein Littlefield. *"moral calculus"* with Curtis Gans. *"sick" "gone off . . ." "mentally . . ." "had delusions . . ." "could not . . ."* I with Alice and Charles Levien, Oct. 16, 1981. *"It could be . . ."* Halberstam, "The Man Who Ran against Lyndon Johnson." *"You running . . ."* Ibid.; Knoll, "Congressman on the Run," *The Progressive*, Aug. 1969, p. 19. *"I know what . . ."* Halberstam, "The Man Who Ran against Lyndon Johnson"; Hershey, "Allard Lowenstein: Out But Not Down," *Newsday*, Dec. 26, 1970. *"As much as . . ."* I with Jenny Lowenstein Littlefield. *"For Al, who . . ."* Viorst, p. 418; Halberstam, "The Man Who Ran against Lyndon Johnson." *"the most overblown . . ." "the ultimate . . ." "disruptive" "He was*

regarded . . ." C with Arthur Herzog, 1981. *"Al faded . . ."* I with Jenny Lowenstein Littlefield.

Chapter 48.
"They gave up . . ." I with Harriet Eisman, April 23, 1981. *"People would see . . ."* Ibid. *"looking for . . ." "He was the . . ." "We went up . . ."* Ibid. *'Of course . . ."* Ibid. *"I had . . ."* Ibid. *"a candidate . . ."* Ibid. *"He had . . ."* Ibid. *"a nice mixture" "the problem . . ."* Ibid.

Chapter 49.
"Let's talk . . ." "I was for it . . ." I with Jenny Lowenstein Littlefield. *"On primary night . . ."* James Wechsler, *New York Post*, quoted in Harris, p. 237. *"very impressed . . ."* L from Saul Schindler to author, July 12, 1980. *"No other . . ."* James Wechsler, *New York Post*, April 12, 1968. *"Before the convention . . ."* I with Harriet Eisman. *"The campaign . . ."* L from Saul Schindler to the author, July 12, 1980.

Chapter 50.
"profoundly shocked . . ." Nassau Herald, May 9, 1968. *"one of the men . . ."* Leroy Aarons, "A Man Who Cried 'Dump LBJ,'" *Washington Post*, May 19, 1968. *"wall-to-wall . . ."* I with Jenny Lowenstein Littlefield. *"This was before . . ."* I with Harriet Eisman. *"That was . . ."* Ibid. *"My God . . ."* I with Jenny Lowenstein Littlefield. *"Senator, you are . . ."* I with Greg Craig. *"Win this . . ."* Harris, p. 248. *"a day which . . ."* Chester, Hodgson, Page, p. 458. *"You spit . . ."* Ibid., p. 458. *"Are we going . . ."* Ibid., p. 458. *"Fascists!" "Nazis" "Hacks!"* Ibid., p. 458. *"Just one thousand . . ."* Halberstam, "The Man Who Ran against Lyndon Johnson." *"who won't accept . . ." "we are . . ."* Harris, p. 249. *"The half-conscious . . ."* Cowan, quoted in Halberstam, "The Man Who Ran against Lyndon Johnson." *"McCarthy almost . . ." "We built . . ."* I with Harriet Eisman. *"All the Kennedy . . ."* Ibid. *"Buckley came out . . ."* Ibid. *"Here in this . . ."* Ibid. *"In the West . . ."* Ibid. *"Al is blowing it!"* I with Doug Ireland. *"You were involved . . ." "He had no . . ."* I with Harriet Eisman. *"college graduates . . ."* Halberstam, "The Man Who Ran against Lyndon Johnson." *"It's the California . . ."* Ibid. *"He was the last . . ."* Ibid. *"All year . . ."* Ibid. *"inevitability . . ." "Then, as he . . ."* Ibid. *"The McCarthy people . . ."* Ibid. *"Is there . . ." "Extremely . . ." "So we . . ." "The problem . . ."* Ibid. *"Even Humphrey . . ."* Ibid. *"Now, steadily . . ."* Ibid. *"These demonstrations . . ."* I with Jenny Lowenstein Littlefield. *"It's Hubert . . ."* Ibid. *"Well, I will . . ." "I'm Barbara . . ." "I don't care . . ."* Ibid. *"I'm a delegate . . ." "No, you're not . . ." "Listen, sonny . . ."* Halberstam, "The Man Who Ran against Lyndon Johnson." *"Why isn't Teddy . . ." "Because the big shots . . ." "The big shots didn't . . ." "I don't know . . ."* Ibid. *"This convention . . ."* Ibid. *"And the Democratic . . ."* Ashby, p. 327. *"I don't care . . ." "He kept . . ."* Halberstam, "The Man Who Ran against Lyndon Johnson." *"What do you . . ." "Some minor . . ." "Are you . . ."* Ibid.

Chapter 51.
"dropping out" "it wasn't . . ." "You must . . ." "Don't be . . ." I with Harriet Eisman. *"Al was . . ."* C with Terry Sanford, March 1981. *"Don't trust . . ." "I didn't . . ." "But I hope . . ."* Ibid. *"short, balding . . ."* Leonard Schechter, "The Teenie Power of Al Lowenstein," *New York Magazine*, Aug. 12, 1968. *"Nobody could . . ."* I with Gina Galkie, Oct. 16, 1981. *"I am neither rightist . . ."* Harris, p. 239. *"draft dodgers . . ." "they helped . . ."* Lowenstein, handwritten memo for speech, undated (LP). *"Al belonged . . ."* I with Harriet Eisman. *"Working in that . . ." "A whole world . . ."* L from Nan Windmueller to the author, Sept.

1981. *"It was too . . ,"* L from Nan Windmueller to the author, Sept. 1981. *"even if . . ."* Calvin Trillin, "The Kids Against the Grown Ups," *The New Yorker*, Nov. 16, 1968. *"Al argued , . ."* Ibid. *"I think we . . ."* *"And it's not . . ."* Ibid. *"You know when . . ,"* *"It wasn't . ,."* Edward Hershey. *"that the point . . ."* Trillin. *"I have a certain , , ,"* Flora Lewis, "New Member," *The New Yorker*, Jan. 10, 1970.

Section VII Chapter 52.
"A man was killed . . ," Knoll, p. 17. *"I think Al , . ,"* Ibid., p. 17. *"It doesn't take . . ,"* Ibid., p. 17. *"I was deeply . . ,"* Quoted in Harris, p. 262; see also Susan Brownmuller, "Gene McCarthy Is Waiting for a Sign," *New York Times Magazine*, July 20, 1969. *"fink"* *"Public Enemy Number One"* *"CIA spook"* Knoll, p. 18. *"the insane five , , ,"* *"They don't want . . ."* Ibid., p. 18. *"On these matters, it is . . ."* Press release, Feb. 4, 1969 (LP). *"it was good to have , , ."* L from Lowenstein to Richard Nixon, March 13, 1969 (LP). *"I hope Nixon , , ."* Knoll, p. 17. *"Caution . . . has disappointed . . ."* Myron S. Waldman, *Newsday*, quoted in Knoll, p. 19. *"He's like Nixon , , ."* Ibid., p. 19. *"He's trying to be . . ,"* Ibid., p. 19. *"cautiously quiet"* *"liberally, with . . ."* *Current Biography 1971*, p. 237. *"Has he been found . . ."* *Congressional Record*, June 10, 1969, pp. 15303–304. *"Residents of the Fifth . . ."* *Helm Independent Review*, June 11, 1969. *"If the system . . ."* Astor, Gerald, "The Pied Piper of the New Children's Crusade," *Look*, August 25, 1970, p. 37. *"I don't know what , , ,"* Lewis. *"This is the one . . ,"* Astor, p. 37. *"the din of noise . . ,"* Hill, p. 9. *"This is one of those . . ."* *Congressional Record*, June 5, 1969, p. 14979. *"Some have asked . . ."* *Congressional Record*, March 26, 1969, p. 7781. *"Mr. Chairman . . ."* Quoted in Knoll, p. 19; *Congressional Record*, May 21, 1969, p. 13253. *"Allard's indispensability . . ."* *"just another . . ."* Harris, p. 267. *"just some Congressman . . ,"* Harris, p. 281. *"Along with thousands . . ,"* *The New York Times*, April 23, 1969, p. 26. *"The President, the Congress . . ."* L from Lowenstein to Long Island newspapers, May 9, 1969 (LP); *Newsday*, May 9, 1969. *"He took risks . . ,"* I with Harriet Eisman. *"Baldwin is made up . . ,"* Ibid. *"more left"* *"irresponsible"* Harris, p. 268. *"irrelevant"* *Congressional Record*, May 21, 1969, p. 13253. *"I saw Al speak . . ."* Craig. *"Al was livid"* I with Greg Craig. *"I was critical , , ,"* Ibid. *"insufficiently firm"* Ibid. *"Congress would not march"* I with Rev. William Sloane Coffin. *"good kids"* *"the wrong people"* Harris, p. 271. *"nothing could be . . ."* Form letter from Lowenstein to his constituents Aug. 20, 1969 (LP). *"I told them that , , ,"* *The New York Times*, Aug. 31, 1969, p. 2. *"This is at last . ,, ,"* *Congressional Record*, Sept. 30, 1969, p. 27723. *"Most were hostile , , ,"* I with Jenny Lowenstein Littlefield. *"We were pleased . . ."* Joint Statement on Vietnam Developments Oct. 31, 1969(LP). *"the majority will . . ."* *Congressional Record*, Nov. 5, 1969, pp. 33167–77. *"unfortunately, the President's , , ,"* Press release, Nov. 6, 1969 (LP). *"the arena, the whole center . . ,"* Ibid. *"small band of ruffians"* Marc Feigen, *The March to Washington—Allard K. Lowenstein in the United States House of Representatives 1968–70*, Senior Thesis, Dept. of History, University of Pennsylvania, April 15, 1983, p. 78. *"it made me proud . . ."* *Congressional Record*, Nov. 18, 1969, p. 34755. *"Now let's see , , ,"* *The New York Times*, Dec. 3, 1969, pp. 1, 20. *"We have to vote , , ,"* Ibid., pp. 1, 20. *"I oppose this resolution . . ."* *Congressional Record*, Dec. 2, 1969, p. 36502. *"But if Congress can't function . . ."* "Meet the Press," NBC News, Lawrence E. Spivak, producer, Vol. 14, No. 7, Feb. 15, 1970 (LP). *"If the disaffected say , , ."* Astor, p. 37. *"in this constitutional republic . . ."* *Congressional Record*, April 29, 1970, pp. 13418, 13527. *"We strongly protest . . ,"* L dated April 29, 1970 (LP). *they now had to fight Nixon . . .* See Feigen, p. 99. *"emotional, angry, troubled , , ,"* Michael Green, May 6, 1970, quoted in Feigen, p. 100. *"Their voices raged , , ,"* Ibid., p. 100. *"God only knows . . ,"*

Ibid., p. 100. *"a reasonable, brief and specified . . ."* I with Curtis Gans. *"take the language . . ."* Ibid. *"Church asked, 'You have . . .'"* Ibid. *Lowenstein, Fraser . . .* Feigen, p. 100. *"Resolved that, in the absence . . ."* House Resolution 1000, quoted in Feigen, p. 100; *Digest of Public General Bills—1970* (Washington, 1971); LP. *"faith in the democratic process"* Feigen, p. 103. *"grandstand play" "What we need to do . . ." "I agree with you . . ."* Telegram to Lowenstein from Sheriff Jerry Crabtree, president of the Alabama Sheriffs' Association, in a speech by Lowenstein, "Up for Grabs," Stanford University, May 24, 1970, in Stone and Lowenstein, p. 166. *"If you take as proof . . ."* Ibid., p. 173. *"Placing principle over party . . ."* Congressional Record, June 9, 1970, p. 19077; read into the Record by Congressman John Brademas of Indiana. *"The students were jammed . . ."* South Bend Indiana Tribune, in the Congressional Record, June 9, 1970, p. 19077. *"that we are determined . . ."* Ibid., p. 19077; quoted in Feigen, p. 108. *"I remember during the moratorium . . ."* I with Harriet Eisman. *"Time is running out . . ."* Astor, p. 38.

Chapter 53.
Lowenstein still owned 7.39 percent . . . Feigen, p. 65. *One source puts . . .* Ibid., p. 65. *"Jenny had plenty . . ."* I with Carol Hardin Kimball, Aug. 11, 1983. *"People wanted to give. . ."* Written communication to the author, Sept. 1981. *"was rarely home . . ."* Ibid. *"Jenny was always . . ."* Ibid. *"It was after Al's election . . ."* Ibid. *"I hope the gay issue . . ."* I with Rev. William Sloane Coffin. *"Al was asexual . . ."* I with Brooke Aronson Trent. *"The energy was . . ."* Ibid. *"I could never . . ."* I with Harriet Eisman. *"Allard was inhibited . . ."* I with Sanford Friedman. *"He had these . . ." "He needed someone . . ."* Ibid. *"There was a lot of . . ."* Ibid. *"failure of the marriage . . ."* Ibid. *"I would talk to him . . ."* Larry Bush, p. 13. *"Bollman's own experience . . ."* Ibid., p. 13. *"It was a natural . . ."* Ibid., p. 13. *"Al's politics were . . ."* Ibid., p. 13. *"From the outset . . ."* I with Bruce Voeller, July 29, 1981. *"He said he was . . ."* Ibid. *"He wanted reassurance that . . ."* Ibid. *"I couldn't give him that . . ."* Ibid. *"in the 'grapevine' . . ."* Ibid. *"extraordinary courage . . ."* C with Noemie Emery, March 1982. *"part of his frenetic . . ."* I with Curtis Gans. *"death wish" "unconsciously, he sought . . ."* I with Alice Brandeis Popkin. *"messiah complex"* I with 'Barbara Boggs Sigmund. *"He discovered his vocation . . ."* Ibid. *"running"* I with Doug Ireland. *"did not seek martyrdom"* I with Douglas Hunt. *"Al always felt . . ."* I with Harriet Eisman. *"He wanted to be . . ."* I with William F. Buckley, Jr. *"it was strangely important" "to do the right thing . . ."* Ibid.

Chapter 54.
"When Al came . . ." I with Emory Bundy. *"He was the most difficult . . ."* Ibid. *"flunkie" "made you do . . ." "He was in . . ."* Ibid. *"that was how he was . . ."* I with Harriet Eisman. *"abused" "bruised" "had enough . . ."* I with Emory Bundy. *"I always felt . . ." "He just was . . ."* Ibid. *"Al had more personal . . ."* Ibid. *"Lowenstein, my boy, you and I . . ."* Ibid. *"we can draw . . ."* The New York Times, Jan. 14, 1969, p. 23. *"Massapequa was the worst . . ."* I with Harriet Eisman. *"assure that the people . . ."* The New York Times, Feb. 16, 1970. *"Representative Allard Lowenstein's . . ."* "Viewpoints," Newsday, Feb. 17, 1970. *"play political games"* The New York Times, Feb. 17, 1970, p. 31. *"By 1970, by this time . . ."* I with Harriet Eisman. *"impart new life into a leaden . . ."* James Wechsler, "A Bigger Battle." New York Post, April 15, 1970. *"In the scrambled Democratic . . ."* Ibid. *"felt that if he did . . ."* I with Gerry Twombley, July 23, 1981. *"I have no idea . . ."* Ibid. *"Al was in front . . ."* Ibid. *"political masochism" "notion of backing . . ." "capacity for transforming . . ."* Wechsler, "A Bigger Battle." *"clear test . . ."* Ibid. *"I would like to see . . ."* The New York Times, April 14, 1970, p.

28. *"sowing the seeds . . ."* Long Island Press, Oct. 13, 1970, p. 3. *"I will say in Massapequa . . ."* Long Island Graphic and Roosevelt Press, July 30, 1970. *"Never in our fifteen years . . ."* Hy Wallis, "Hy Spots Freeport," Long Island Graphic and Roosevelt Press, July 30, 1970.

Chapter 55.
"Al had a whole . . ." I with Harriet Eisman. *"Those of us who speak . . ."* Press release, May 31, 1970 (LP). *"establishment tells them . . ."* Ibid. *Entering to a standing ovation . . .* Feigen, p. 106. *"This generation has . . ." "Come my friends . . ."* Feigen, pp.106–107; Press release May 31, 1970 (LP). *"I think all of us . . ."* etc. Congressional Record, June 18, 1970. *"commie" "traitor" "Go Back to Hanoi"* Evans and Novak, "The Allard Lowenstein Test," Washington Post, Sept. 9, 1970. *"sort of mini–Spiro Agnew . . ."* Norman C. Miller, "Rep. Lowenstein vs. the Silent Majority," Wall Street Journal, Sept. 22, 1970, p. 1. *"You just do not . . ."* "Lent Takes the Fifth," by Gerry Twombley, 1970 (unpublished). *"Congressman Al Lowenstein needs . . ."* Feigen, p. 123. *"In 1968, Al had . . ."* I with Rick Weidman. *"America is not in any sense . . ."* Long Island Press, Oct. 16, 1970. *"screaming, cursing, yippie-oriented . . ."* Ibid. *"Those who want . . ."* Ibid. *"If good people . . ." "engaging in . . ."* Ibid. *"The only way . . ." "We have to get . . ."* Ibid. *"we have to somehow overcome . . ."* Miller. *"I'm saddled with this . . ."* Miller. *"Senator Lent will be running"* Wechsler, "Test Case for Agnewism," New York Post, Sept. 18, 1970. *"the chief apologist . . ." "he blames the police . . ." "voting for the pornography peddlars" "echoes the line . . ."* in Miller. *"a liability to Israel"* in Twombley. *"even voted against . . ."* Ibid. *"Mr. Lowenstein echoes Hanoi . . ."* Lent–Lowenstein Oceanside debate, in Twombley. *"the Pied Piper of Youth" "the chief architect of the Black Panthers" "commends draft evaders"* Ibid. *"There was all that . . ."* I with Jenny Lowenstein Littlefield. *"I can't get a nickel . . ."* Twombley. *"What happens . . ."* Ibid. *"The fact is that . . ."* L from Rev. Paul G. Driscoll to Newsday, Nov. 18, 1970. *"by calling me 'chicken hawk' . . ."* Twombley, Long Island Press, Monday, Oct. 12, 1970. *"Catholics do all that you can . . ."* Newsday, Oct. 28, 1970, p. 11. *"will not go any further . . ."* Newsday, Oct. 28, 1970, p. 11. *"Although I wouldn't vote . . ."* Twombley. *"in cahoots . . ."* Ibid. *"Al said if he got . . ."* I with Greg Craig. *"not to cut corners . . ."* L from Thomas H. Clancy, S. J., to the author, May 22, 1980. *"I feel both men . . ." "amazed at the contrast"* Twombley. *"The biggest criticism . . ."* Ibid. *"Al was fanatical about having . . ."* I with Gerry Twombley. *"He was too defensive . . ."* Ibid. *"in order that he would appear . . ."* Newsday, Oct. 28, 1970. *"Republicans and Independents . . ." "names of dead . . ."* Twombley. *"This may not be the most . . ."* Newsday, Oct. 28, 1970. *"Al Lowenstein is the toughest . . ."* Ibid. *"More in sorrow than . . ."* Long Island Graphic, Oct. 18, 1970. *"in Representative Allard K. Lowenstein . . ."* The New York Times, Oct. 23, 1970. *"no vote cast . . ."* Newsday, Oct. 20, 1980. *"Lowenstein's main interest . . ."* Daily News, Oct. 26, 1970. *"Anyone remotely familiar . . ."* Wechsler, "Test Case for Agnewism." *"Hello, I'm Jim Bouton . . ."* Hershey. *"one hell of a good man" "a responsible voice . . ." "a man who has always . . ."* Long Island Press, Oct. 14, 1970. *"Rumsfeld stabbed Al . . ."* I with Gerry Twombley; see also Feigen, p. 126. *"In retrospect,"* Twombley. *"all burned out . . ."* I with Rick Weidman. *"Al was angry . . ."* Ibid. *"a scene reminiscent . . ."* Newsday, Nov. 4, 1970; Feigen, p. 127. *"if everyone in this room . . ." "They could only . . ."* Newsday, Nov. 4, 1970. *"Al was walking out . . ."* I with Greg Craig. *"If the district had been constituted . . ."* James Wechsler, "Anatomy of an Election," New York Post, Nov. 4, 1970, p. 47. *"vote on the Democratic line exceeded . . ."* Hendrik Hertzberg, "Lame Duck" (The Talk of the Town), The New Yorker, Nov. 21, 1970. *"The fact that I lost . . ."* Ibid. *"an echo of Hanoi . . ." "odd accusations . . ."* Ibid. *"There*

was an ominous warning . . ." Ibid. *"I guess I have nothing . . ."* The New York *Times,* Jan. 2, 1971, p. 15. *"Many House members seemed . . ."* Hershey. *"Allard Lowenstein has provided . . ."* Ibid. *"I can't remember any . . ."* Ibid. *"Mr. Speaker, I suspect that . . ."* Congressional Record, Dec. 17, 1970, p. 44720. *"Knowing what to say . . ."* Hershey. *"Politicians, writers and parents . . ."* Ibid. *"They can gerrymander . . ."* Ibid.

Chapter 56.
"He was speaking . . ." I with Harriet Eisman. *"In my view . . ."* "Meet the Press," in Stone and Lowenstein, p. 185. *"But you know . . ."* I with Joe Rauh. *"got more kids . . ."* Ibid. *"We may end up . . ."* Washington Post, March 25, 1971. *"makes utterly no sense . . ."* Ibid. *"Lowenstein decided to take . . ."* I with Curtis Gans. *"'dumping' assumes you were . . ."* I with Barney Frank. *"I was so thrilled . . ."* I with Nick Littlefield, May 1–2, 1981. *"I met Al at . . ."* Ibid. *"They were both affected . . ."* Ibid. *"Beat Nixon, stop the war . . ."* Registration Summer memo, Dec. 1971. *"the selection of national leadership . . ."* Ibid. *"They fail to understand . . ."* Nicholas Von Hoffman, "Darker Horses," Harper's, Sept. 1971. *"That's not going to . . ."* Ibid. *"If he succeeds,"* Ibid. *"president who was elected . . ."* Look, June 1, 1971. *"Just as President Johnson . . ."* Ibid. *"It was a big . . ."* I with Nick Littlefield. *"But what's so interesting . . ."* Nicholas Von Hoffman, "Registering Their Dissent," Washington Post, July 2, 1971. *"Because of Lowenstein's success . . ."* Stone and Lowenstein, p. 188. *"to whom I would give . . ."* Memo from Charles Colson to John Dean, Sept. 9, 1971, in Stone and Lowenstein, pp. 180–81. *"the most powerful . . ."* I with Nick Littlefield. *"there is no magic . . ."* Minneapolis Tribune, May 24, 1971. *"We're here . . ."* Ibid. *"We are not Democrats using Republicans . . ."* James Wechsler, "Where The Action Is," New York Post, June 2, 1971. *"The other day somebody said . . ."* Von Hoffman, "Registering Their Dissent.' *"That's Allard K. . . ."* Von Hoffman, "Registering Their Dissent." *"a real alternative"* Detroit News, Sept. 10, 1971. *"this whole rally . . ."* The Evening Bulletin (Philadelphia), Sept. 17, 1971. *"The last time I saw . . ."* Flora Lewis, "Seeking the Magic Coalition," Evening Bulletin (Philadelphia), Sept. 17, 1971. *"The final event . . ."* I with Nick Littlefield. *"Three times as many . . ."* I with Greg Craig. *"It seems clear . . ."* Mary Breasted, "Lowenstein Ponders Challenge to Brooklyn's Rooney or Nassau's Wydler." The New York Times, March 19, 1972, p. 10.

Chapter 57.
"good example of Al . . ." I with Greg Stone, June 5, 1981. *"What's the point . . ."* I with Harriet Eisman. *"I think he changed . . ."* Ibid. *"We belong . . ."* The New York Times, March 19, 1972, p. 10. *"perennial gadfly . . ."* *"often jokes . . ."* Ibid., p. 10. *"charismatic demagogue," "deeply philosophical moods"* Ibid., p. 10. *"out of Congress" "Mr. Lowenstein must . . ." "The thing I'm least . . ."* Ibid., p. 10. *" drive through a series . . ."* Lanny Davis, "Why Lowenstein Lost; Ethnics, Crooks and Carpetbaggers," Washington Monthly, September 1972, pp. 32–38. *"Ethnic and cultural identities . . ."* *"From the Hasidic Jewish . . ."* Arn Bortz, "John J. Rooney, Democratic Representative from New York," Ralph Nader Congress Project, Citizens Look at Congress, Grossman Publishers, August 1972. *"There are no zigzags . . ."* Bortz. *"including Lepke and all those Murder, Inc., guys"* Judith Michaelson, "Lowenstein Versus Rooney," New York Post (magazine), June 5, 1972, p. 12. *"How could you come . . ."* I with Harriet Eisman. *"Unless I can stand . . ."* Ibid. *"They're gonna mop you up . . ."* Ibid. *"a movement which is alien . . ."* Bortz. *"coming out of a different . . ."* The Phoenix (Brooklyn), June 15, 1972, p. 10. *"was rested and rejuvenated" "and this was a cause . . ."* I with Nick Littlefield. *"Otherwise, you will be working . . ."* Ibid.

"Mr. Low Esteem" Michaelson, "Lowenstein versus Rooney." *"a 'boid' who flies from . . ."* Davis, p. 33. *"blights,"* *"One of those liberal 'boids' . . ."* Davis, p. 33. *"In the last two years . . ."* Daily News, June 8, 1972. *"has been a jolly benefactor . . ."* Jack Anderson, "Rooney's Roster," New York Post, June 12, 1972. *"subversive"* James Wechsler, "No Place for Neutrality," New York Post, June 8, 1972, p. 43. *"leftist"* *"Communism"* Michaelson, "Lowenstein Versus Rooney." *"SDS flag-burners"* Wechsler, "No Place for Neutrality." *"radical and subversive"* Davis, p. 35. *"His opponent, Al Lowenstein . . ."* Bob Side, "The Untold Story of the Lowenstein Campaign; Lowenstein and the 14th C.D. Religious Groups" (Five Minutes From Wall Street), *Brooklyn Heights Press*, Sept. 7, 1972. *"Communist"* Ibid. *"with loathing in her voice . . ."* Ibid. *"vote the Christian . . ."* Jewish Week, June 29, 1972. *"scurrilous"* The New York Times, Sept. 17, 1972. *"Gays Back Lowenstein . . ."* Home Reporter and Sunset News, June 16, 1972. *"the man who had founded . . ."* Davis, p. 38. *Then one of the students . . .* William F. Buckley, Jr., "Kathleen Kennedy at Bat," (On the right), New York Post, June 17, 1972, p. 26. *"Anybody who says . . ."* Daily News, June 8, 1972; quoted in Buckley, "Kathleen Kennedy at Bat." *"In the final days . . ."* Davis, p. 36. *"There has been a foul-up . . ."* Jack Anderson, "Lowenstein's Quest," New York Post, Aug. 31, 1972. *"carelessness and injudiciousness"* *"improper"* The New York Times, July 1, 1976. *"We're not going on vacation . . ."* Judith Michaelson, "Lowenstein Kept Running," New York Post, Sept. 13, 1972. *"scream on the sidelines"* *"We won this primary"* Michaelson, "Lowenstein Kept Running." *"I personally know more . . ."* Davis, p. 36. *"In all of my 40 years . . ."* Davis, p. 36. *"It happens that Mr. Lowenstein . . ."* William F. Buckley, Jr., "Al Lowenstein Deserves a Fair Count, Too," Newsday, July 20, 1972. *"If it happened . . ."* Daily News, June 23, 1972, p. 45. *"an outstanding national . . ."* The New York Times, April 14, 1972. *"He's a hell of a . . ."* New York Post, Sept. 15, 1972. *"all-out war"* Ibid. *"of fraud per se"* *"we think this was one"* In Re Lowenstein v. Larkin, Appellate Division 2nd, Sept. 5, 1972. *"A fair election is the cornerstone . . ."* Ibid. *"shocking"* *"that this is a departure . . ."* New York Post, Sept. 8, 1972. *"boundless gratitude"* *"Democracy is alive . . ."* Michaelson, "Lowenstein Kept Running." *"The issues are clear . . ."* New York Post, Sept. 17, 1972. *"Al, first you brought . . ."* Side. *"determined effort"* *"It is not so much . . ."* The New York Times, Sept. 9, 1972. *"appeal to prejudice based . . ."* In the Matter of the Arbitration between Congressman John J. Rooney and Allard K. Lowenstein, Fair Campaign Practices Arbitration Tribunal, American Arbitration Association, Oct. 28, 1972. *"the times were different . . ."* I with Harriet Eisman. *"There wasn't the same . . ."* Ibid. *"they stole the second . . ."* Ibid. *"I think no one . . ."* The New York Times, Sept. 22, 1972. *"go out of here mad"* Daily News, Sept. 20, 1972. *"We're making an effort . . ."* The New York Times, Oct. 28, 1972. *"the personal attacks . . ."* *"every local Democrat . . ."* The New York Times, Sept. 21, 1972. *"Wild horses . . ."* The New York Times, Sept. 24, 1972. *"the things that have gone wrong . . ."* I with Walter P. Loughlin, January, 1973, in Stone and Lowenstein, p. 212. *"no regret"* I with Walter P. Loughlin, in Stone and Lowenstein, p. 213. *"Once he lost . . ."* I with Harriet Eisman. *"He really believed . . ."* Ibid. *"When the hell . . ."* L to Lowenstein from Jim Bouton (LP). *"There always will be moments . . ."* Allard Lowenstein, "The Watersheds of Watergate," ADA World, June 1973. *"One sad fact . . ."* Lowenstein, "The Watershed of Watergate."

Chapter 58.

"national reconciliation," *"so intractable . . ."* I with Wendell Willkie II. *"deeper examination . . ."* Quoted in Stone and Lowenstein, p. 219. *"cheated"* I with Jenny Lowenstein Littlefield. *"laughing stock"* *"Al practically had . . ."* I

Reference Sources • 527

with Harvey Lippman. *"It was shocking . . ."* Ibid. *"Al had a fear . . ."* Ibid.
"Dennis was very odd . . ." I with Jenny Lowenstein Littlefield. *"It's so incredibly
sad . . ."* Ibid. *"well-placed source" "did everything we could . . ."* The New York
Times, Feb. 25, 1974. *"the full story . . ."* Ibid. *"trying to talk . . ."* I with Harriet
Eisman. *"He had used up . . ."* Ibid. *"Wydler was probably the worst . . ."* C
with Karl Grossman, 1971. *"in some capacity" "in-house liberal" "as a sort of . . ."*
I with Wendell Willkie II. *"Tom, did you get . . ."* I with Harriet Eisman. *"I came
in second"* Ibid. *"Al was brokenhearted . . ."* Ibid.

Chapter 59.
   "to avoid further involvement . . ." Allard Lowenstein, "Suppressed Evidence of More Than One Assassin," *Saturday Review*, Feb. 19, 1977. *"by bullets
fired . . ."* Ibid. *"Nobody could add seven . . ."* Ibid. *"propaganda campaign" "the
precise reverse . . ."* Ibid. *"Would you like Mr. Uecker . . ."* Ibid. *"I told the
authorities . . ." "It was decided . . ."* Ibid. *"We offer no answers . . ." "Nor have
we any . . ."* Quoted in Stone and Lowenstein, p. 220. *"The only widely read
. . ."* Lowenstein, "Who Killed Robert Kennedy?" in *Government by Gunplay;
Assassination Conspiracy Theories from Dallas to Today*, ed. S. Blumenthal and
H. Yazijian (New York: Signet Books, 1976), p. 33. *"an unwillingness to conclude
. . ." "wispy" "long since discounted . . ."* Quoted in Lowenstein, "Who Killed
Robert Kennedy?" p. 33. *"have surely made . . ."* James Wechsler, "A Lonely
Inquest," *New York Post*, Jan. 9, 1975. *"What happened in Robert Kennedy's
death . . ."* I with Carol Hardin Kimball. *"mistake"* I with Wendell Willkie II. *"he
conceived the notion . . ."* I with William F. Buckley, Jr. *"most cogent statement
. . ."* L from Sidney Blumenthal to author, May 19, 1980. *"I was once typical . . ."*
Lowenstein, "Who Killed Robert Kennedy?" pp. 29–36. *"tangents"* I with Wil-
liam F. Buckley, Jr. *"the Kranz report . . ."* Lowenstein, "Suppressed Evidence."

Chapter 60.
   "wrote with great, great skill" I with William F. Buckley, Jr. *"had to labor
. . ."* Ibid. *"Writing is like shitting . . ."* I with Jenny Lowenstein Littlefield.
"When I die . . ." I with Gina Galke, Oct. 16, 1981. *"Life is a shit . . ."* Ibid. *"Call
off your dogs"* Harris, p. 302. *"revered"* I with Harvey Lippman. *"reversal"* Ibid.
"sweet" Ibid. *"I'll chuck politics . . ."* I with Jenny Lowenstein Littlefield. *"He
wanted to write . . ." "And he felt . . ."* Ibid. *"He could have run . . ."* I with
Harvey Lippman. *"If Al had said . . ."* I with Jenny Lowenstein Littlefield. *"The
effort was about . . ."* Jules Witcover, *Marathon—The Pursuit of the Presidency,
1972–1976* (New York: Viking, 1977), pp. 340–41.

Chapter 61.
   "Their marriage was in trouble . . ." I with Harriet Eisman. *"During the last
Wydler campaign . . ."* I with Jenny Lowenstein Littlefield. *"from outside" "knot
hole"* LP. *"Because he was doing . . ."* I with Harvey Lippman. *"Jenny would
never . . ."* I with Carol Hardin Kimball. *"returned from different . . ."* I with
Jenny Lowenstein Littlefield. *"I said to myself . . ."* Ibid. *"I felt ashamed . . ."*
Ibid. *"Nick was in Boston . . ."* Ibid. *"Jenny knew Nick . . ." "All the young men
. . ."* I with Harriet Eisman. *"Al refused to admit . . ."* I with Harvey Lippman.
"My marriage . . ." I with Alice Brandeis Popkin. *"I'll never believe . . ."* I with
Harriet Eisman. *"I didn't know . . ."* I with Jenny Lowenstein Littlefield. *"She
told me . . ."* L from Nan Windmueller to the author, Sept. 1981. *"Al was in a
rage . . ." "Before he died . . ."* I with Jenny Lowenstein Littlefield. *"He was
really pissed . . ."* I with Nick Littlefield. *"strange kind of . . ."* I with Harriet
Eisman.

Chapter 62.
" *rare coalition*" James Wechsler, "A Rare Coalition," *New York Post*, Oct. 22, 1976. "*a solid job*" "*the only job* . . ." I with Harriet Eisman. "*ADA people, NDC types*" Ibid. "*had already abandoned him*" "*So I told him* . . ." Ibid. "*There has to be* . . ." Ibid. "*I don't know* . . ." "*I want that* . . ." Ibid. "*Al felt he could work* . . ." Ibid. "*expelled for political activities*" "*helping left-wing groups*" I with Frank Carlucci. "*didn't spend much time* . . ." I with Tom Flynn. "*lots of CIA* . . ." Ibid. "*misguided*" Interviews with Eduardo and Edgar Chamorro, 1983. (The interview with Edgar Chamorro was conducted by Karl Grossman. Portions of the Eduardo Chamorro interview were also conducted by Karl Grossman.) "*They felt they could work* . . ." I with Eduardo Chamorro. "*the leading force*" "*fear that unless* . . ." Ibid. "*the extreme left*" "*I still believe* . . ." Ibid. "*the CIA was finally* . . ." Ibid. "*overtook*" "*seized control*" Ibid. "*academic and naive*" Ibid. "*He was like the messiah*" Ibid. "*After Lowenstein's arrival* . . ." Ibid. "*Everyone knew Somoza had to go* . . ." Ibid. "*Lowenstein was very much* . . ." "*Lowenstein was very active* . . ." Ibid. "*Sometimes Washington's tactics* . . ." Sidney Lens, "Our State, Their Revolutions" (Reflections), *The Progressive*, September, 1983, p. 14. "*Washington, probing to see* . . ." Lens, p. 14. "*elated*" I with Ken Mc-Comiskey. "*Lowenstein was an extraordinary* . . ." I with Eduardo Chamorro. "*spiral*" "*noble but hopeless*" Lowenstein, "Why I Quit," *New York Post*, July 14, 1978. "*To abandon the U.N.* . . ." "*To abandon the effort*" Lowenstein, "Why I Quit." "*Al, you're a jerk*" I with Ham Richardson. "*I guess I am*" Ibid. "*Al, you can't look* . . ." Ibid. "*Al wouldn't let* . . ." "*He insisted* . . ." Ibid. "*a rare kind of public figure* . . ." L from Congressman Pete McCloskey to County Committee Members, Jan. 13, 1978 (LP). "*I have known Al Lowenstein* . . ." L from David Garth to Jill Levine, Jan. 11, 1977. "*the central figure* . . ." Allard Lowenstein, "The United Nations and the Human Rights Issues," Law and Contemporary Problems, Duke University School of Law, Spring 1979. "*He grew disillusioned* . . ." I with Harvey Lippman. "*He would have resigned* . . ." I with Greg Stone. "*retreated from the vanities* . . ." "*He changed* . . ." I with William F. Buckley, Jr. "*Israel was promised* . . ." Lowenstein, "Why I Quit." "*We worked for reform* . . ." Lowenstein, "Why I Quit." "*shocked by the factual* . . ." I with William F. Buckley, Jr. "*Burden made a deal* . . ." I with Rick Weidman. "*He fell short* . . ." "*We knew* . . ." Ibid. "*If he had put* . . ." I with Greg Stone. "*It was partly deliberate* . . ." "*McGrath did nothing*" I with Rick Weidman. "*He sounded desperate*" I with Bronia Kupsick. "*hoary and bureaucratic*" William F. Buckley, Jr., "A Liberal Indulgence," *Newsday*, Aug. 15, 1978. "*There is, in Lowenstein* . . ." Ibid. "*The Burden campaign* . . ." "*But Al* . . ." I with Rick Weidman. "*Is independence and character* . . ." Lowenstein notes (LP).

Chapter 63.
"*He was starting to get paid* . . ." I with Alice Brandeis Popkin. "*When Delson and Gordon pressed him* . . ." I with Harvey Lippman. "*When they wanted* . . ." Ibid. "*less venal*" Ibid. "*Life after fifty* . . ." I with Sanford Friedman. "*Al thought he was going* . . ." Lawrence Michael Hill, p.3. "*He wanted to have a minister* . . ." Ibid., p. 3. "*He was very strong*" Ibid., p. 3. "*I've got them*" I with Harvey Lippman. "*He'd have people* . . ." "*But he knew* . . ." Ibid. "*Why do you need* . . ." "*Oh, I just thought* . . ." Ibid. "*I'm not a particular fan* . . ." I with Tom Flynn. "*You should run*" Comments by Senator Alan Cranston, Lowenstein Symposium, March 1982. "*knock off Carter* . . ." I with Tom Flynn. "*The campaign was in disarray* . . ." I with Harriet Eisman. "*was billed as* . . ." "*we were heading* . . ." I with Greg Stone. "*devoting to crusading* . . ." L from Randy Schultz to author, May 28, 1980. "*I think people care* . . ." Ibid. "*I remember thinking* . . ." Ibid. "*I knew it must* . . ." I with Harvey Lippman.

Chapter 64.
"You're not supposed to let them . . ." "You're supposed . . ." Harris, p. 242. *"severe miscalculation" "a very serious mistake"* Ibid., p. 227. *"The guilt that 'mistake' . . ."* Ibid., p. 227–28. *"Most of the two dozen . . ."* Ibid., p. 251. *"This is just like goddam Mississippi"* Ibid., p. 251. *"condescending"* and *"racist"* Carpenter, p. 26. *"Or, perhaps, as Field . . ."* Ibid., p. 26. *"We were never really close . . ."* Harris, p.297. *"It is no accident . . ."* The New York Times, Nov. 17, 1982, p. C31. *"By 1976 Dennis . . ."* Diaries, Ed Pincus, director. *"International Jewish hate . . ." "On the run . . ."* Ibid.; see Harris, p. 303. *"There are a lot . . ."* Telephone C with Jesse Zaslov, June 10, 1980. *"Daddy's been . . ." "Don't tell me . . ."* I with Frank Lowenstein. *"He knew Dennis as well . . ."* I with Jenny Lowenstein Littlefield. *"He was a brilliant recruiter . . ."* I with Curtis Gans. *"This was determined . . ."* Telephone C with Jesse Zaslov. *"She got very hurt . . ."* I with Harvey Lippman.

Chapter 65.
"If no man is an island . . ." Congressional Record—Senate, March 27, 1980, p. S3219. *"I wish that Al . . ."* I with Richard Murphy. *"Allardisms"* Hill, p. 2. *"Lincoln, Gandhi . . ."* Ibid., p. 4. *"foundation stone" "sense of ideals" "sense of continuing struggle" "exemplified what . . ."* Ibid., pp. 4–5. *"There are black people . . ."* Congressional Record—Senate, March 27, 1980, p. S3219. *"Possibly as a dissenter . . ."* William F. Buckley, Jr., Memorial Address, March 18, 1980, reprinted in National Review, 1980. *"The senselessness of it . . ."* Hill, p. 7.

Chapter 66.
"never dealt . . ." Carpenter, p. 25. *"After the shooting . . ."* Ibid., p. 25. *"sexual connotations" "cheap shot" "vindictive"* Harris, p. 330. *"Amazing"* Ibid., p. 330. *"delegation of U.S. Congressmen . . ."* Press release, Allard K. Lowenstein Square Dedication Ceremony, Nov. 8, 1983.

Reference Notes

Section I.
Chapter 1.
According to Lowenstein's cousin Alice Levien, the Lowensteins were angry when Allard became friendly with the Goldbergs, his real mother's family.

Chapter 2.
While Abraham Wechsler describes Gabriel Lowenstein as "almost a genius" in the restaurant business, Alice Levien nevertheless calls some of the restaurants "crummy."

Section II.
Chapter 7.
Truman's Civil Rights Commission, which angered North Carolina voters, was not the body later established by law during the Eisenhower administration. In 1950 there was no civil rights legislation enacted. And Frank Graham was not the only liberal southerner to be vilified in 1950. Senator Claude Pepper of Florida, called "Red Pepper" by his right-wing detractors in the Smather's campaign, also went down to defeat as the hysteria of the McCarthy period swept the country.

Section III.
Chapter 8.
Lowenstein joined the Young Republicans at Chapel Hill at the same time he joined ADA, a contradiction that is difficult to fathom. He would soon become a Democrat, but always insisted that ADA was bipartisan.

Chapter 13.
Lowenstein's efforts to keep all ideological factions in one student group were nullified when conservatives broke away from the United States Student Association m 1978 to form tne splinter American Student Association.

Section IV, Part One.
Chapter 14.
South West Africa was a former colony of Germany, which had ravaged it. Placed under South Africa's control as a mandated territory by the League of Nations after World War I, it proved to contain vast mineral resources worth fortunes. By the time Lowenstein visited South Africa in 1958, American, British, and South African interests in South West Africa were already considerable. The prizes included the largest source of gem diamonds on earth and vast supplies of zinc, copper, nickel, lead, silver, and cadmium. Uranium was later discovered in quantities unequaled anywhere else in the world. [See Hovey, *Namibia's Stolen*

Wealth (New York: The Africa Fund, 1982); *Plunder of Namibian Uranium* (New York: United Nations, 1982); *Namibia, The Facts* (London: International Defense and Aid Fund, 1980); Roberts, *The Rossing File* (London: Namibia Support Committee, 1980).]

In 1947 the Tsumeb mine, opened in 1906 and the oldest in South West Africa, was taken over from German interests by a consortium of American companies. The leading members were the Newmont Mining Corporation, a giant American producer of nonferrous metals, and AMAX, Inc., the largest mining company in America. Tsumeb Corporation accounted for 80 percent of South West Africa's total base-metal production and developed links through its American owners with powerful American politicians in both parties. Both former President Gerald Ford and Harold Brown, the secretary of defense under President Jimmy Carter, have served on the board of directors of AMAX.

The South African connection came through Harry Oppenheimer. DeBeers, his giant diamond company, which had been founded in the nineteenth century by Cecil Rhodes, was heavily involved in mining in South West Africa. Oppenheimer's international leviathan, the Anglo-American Corporation, owned Consolidated Gold Fields, which in turn purchased a controlling interest in Newmont. Oppenheimer also had large British interests in South West Africa. The British interests would expand greatly in the seventies, when Rio Tinto Zinc Corporation, a vast multinational mining operation with investments in Spain and with such powerful figures as Lord Carrington on its board, began heavily to exploit uranium in the vast Rossing Mine. Carrington, as British foreign minister, would play a key role in the Rhodesian crisis.

Kozonguizi had been involved in the early stages of the South West African Peoples Organization (SWAPO), a militant group pressing for an end to the South African mandate. But in 1959 he founded the South West Africa Union (SWANO), which became a rival to SWAPO. The basis for the rift could be laid to tribalism. Kozonguizi was a Herero, as were the others who joined with him in founding SWANO, while SWAPO, originally called the Ovamboland People's Organization, was founded by Ovambos Herman Toivo ja Toivo and Sam Nujoma.

While in London Kozonguizi based himself with the CIA-supported Africa Bureau, and later in the United States, participated in a symposium sponsored by the CIA-backed American Society of African Culture. He ultimately surfaced in South West Africa as a staff member of the Democratic Turnhalle Alliance, the group funded by South Africa to preempt SWAPO in the event of independence for Namibia, as the territory came to be called. At the writing of this book, the armed struggle for Namibian independence has spilled over into neighboring Angola, where the presence of Cuban troops threatens to escalate the struggle further.

Chapter 15.

Hans Beukes joined SWAPO in 1970 and was a member until 1976, when, according to Theo-Ben Gurirab, he was "expelled." Gurirab relates: "He went back to Lusaka, Zambia, where he was associated with Scandinavian technicians. He was involved in a conspiracy led by Andreas Shipanga, the leader of the conspiracy, in which this group of SWAPO members allowed themselves to be used by the South African military in collaborating with some Western powers to undermine SWAPO's armed struggle and leadership and to accept money to support the Turnhalle Conference, which in turn led to the formation of the Democratic Turnhalle Alliance, which until recently masqueraded as the interim government. This was done to pave the way for the alternative setup established by South Africa to run the country as a puppet."

The formation of the SWAPO-Democrats was announced in June 1978 in Sweden by former SWAPO Information Secretary Andreas Shipanga and his supporters. Strongly opposed to SWAPO, Shipanga's new group insists that SWAPO is against the election process in Namibia and "has no intention of operating in a peaceful way." According to the International Defense and Aid Fund for Southern Africa, a Christian group based in London and banned in South Africa, Shipanga was among the senior SWAPO members arrested in Zambia in 1976 after they persisted in challenging the leadership of Sam Nujoma, president of SWAPO and leader of its Soviet-backed armed struggle for Namibian independence. Released with eighteen followers from detention in Tanzania, where they had been moved in May of 1978, Shipanga returned to Namibia that August. It is commonly believed that Shipanga and the SWAPO-Dems will ally themselves with Kozonguizi's SWANO in the Namibian National Front, along with the white Federal party. Beukes had interceded on behalf of Shipanga and his supporters with Lowenstein in 1977, when Lowenstein was an ambassador to the United Nations. "In that capacity," Beukes explains, "he visited the Nordic countries soon after his appointment and renewed contact on passing through Oslo. We hadn't seen each other since the late sixties. My concern was with Namibians arrested in Zambia and Tanzania and kept in the local jails at the request of the SWAPO leadership. It was a panic move that I had much deplored, and I was hoping that Al would exert some pressure behind the scenes. The reason for asking for pressure to be exerted in such a manner was that would be effective and to avoid giving SWAPO's enemies ammunition for their propaganda weapons." (Letter from Beukes to the author, Feb. 15, 1983.)

This explanation by Beukes makes very little sense, particularly in light of Gurirab's statement about who was arrested and who was expelled from SWAPO. Beukes was close to the United States (in the spring of 1964, he was proposed for a Duke Law School grant) and, like Lowenstein, opposed the militant leadership of SWAPO, including Sam Nujoma. They worked together in the seventies to help Andreas Shipanga as the non-Communist alternative to Sam Nujoma and armed struggle.

Lowenstein, Bundy, and Bull testified before the United Nations in 1959, not as individuals but as spokesmen for Africans. Cables authorizing them to do so were sent by Chief Kutako, Chief Witbooi, and Sam Nujoma, president of the Ovamboland People's Organization (later SWAPO). The conservative Herero chief, Kutako, and the radical Ovambo, Nujoma, were united in their opposition to South Africa's enforcement of apartheid in South West Africa.

Chapter 17.
For a history and analysis of the long relationship of the African National Congress and the South African Communist party, see "Long Live the ANC-SACP Alliance!" *The African Communist*, No. 87, Fourth Quarter, 1981.

In "Fight U.S. Subversion of Trade Union Movement in Africa!" B. S. Nyameko directly accuses the CIA of creating the Pan-Africanist Congress to undermine the Communist-backed African National Congress. He writes: "Throughout Africa labour organizations are infiltrated by CIA agents posing as private individuals or under non-official cover, as employees in private companies or as U.S. Embassy staff in the Information Department or as Labour Attachés. This is how the U.S. Embassy Information Department and Labour Attaché men succeeded in establishing the PAC in 1959 to disrupt our ANC." [*The African Communist*, No. 87, Fourth Quarter, 1981, pp.56–57. See also Cohen, "The CIA and African Trade Unions," *Dirty Work 2: the CIA in Africa*, ed. Ray, Schaap, Van Meter, and Wolf (Secaucus: Lyle Stuart, 1980).]

Ever fearful of subversion, the government of South Africa, besides banning the ANC, took action against SWAPO in Namibia. In 1968 founding member Herman

Toivo ja Toivo was found guilty of offenses under the Terrorism Act. He, along with thirty-six other Namibians, were accused of being part of a conspiracy to overthrow the government of Namibia, undergoing guerrilla training, and participating in guerrilla warfare. Ja Toivo was not released until 1984. SWAPO itself has never been banned, but its members are periodically arrested, the organization existing in a strange semilegality while it engages in armed struggle for Namibian independence. The government of South Africa takes the position that SWAPO is Communist influenced. In SWAPO, President Sam Nujoma is referred to as "Comrade Sam Nujoma," and he refers to the African National Congress as "our Comrades-in-Arms." (See *Namibia Today*, Vol. 6, Feb. 1982.)

A. Philip Randolph had to force a black presence into the union movement's global anti-Communism. Although black African ambassadors were the honored guests at the dinner of the Council against Communist Aggression, the Brotherhood of Sleeping Car Porters had not been invited. Randolph wrote, insisting that his union be represented at the dinner.

A major force in the American Committee on Africa was the writer John Gunther. Entries in Lowenstein's diary suggest that he was in contact with Gunther about the extent of his own African activities.

Section IV, Part Two.
Chapter 19.

FBI sources stated that Lowenstein had a reputation for "stirring up" the students, and insisted that the administration was "not too pleased" with Lowenstein's performance, without giving specifics. FBI File No. 105–163168, Vol. No. 1.

Chapter 20.

The recruitment of academics by the CIA as experts in strategic parts of the world, including Africa, has been the subject of considerable study. Important work was done in this field by the Africa Research Group in 1969 and 1970, released in their publication "African Studies in America—The Extended Family—A Tribal Analysis of U.S. Africanists: Who They Are; Why to Fight Them."

According to former CIA agent John Stockwell, who authored *In Search of Enemies*, professors have entered into a wide variety of relationships with the CIA, mostly on a "contract agent" basis. Some professors do errands "just for excitement," he explains, while others "require plane tickets and a fee." (Interview with John Stockwell, June 26, 1984) The CIA has a wide variety of contracts available for any anticipated relationship and will produce an appropriate one for any occasion, saying, "We would suggest something like this."

Each agent, including contract agents and contract career agents, is known by his "crypt" or code name in the CIA. An academic agent performing various functions might keep up his expertise, Stockwell suggests, by clipping news articles and doing synopses, the way Lowenstein did. And while the FBIS performs this function for the CIA, Stockwell would not rule out a contract for this kind of work. Stockwell explains that as far as the kind of work an agent might do for the CIA and the benefits provided, "every conceivable relationship known to mankind has existed."

Ken Lawrence in "Academics: an Overview" [Covert Action Publications, Inc., 1979. See also *Dirty Work 2: the CIA in Africa*, ed. Ray, Schaap, Van Meter, and Wolf (Secaucus: Lyle Stuart, 1980), p. 80] relates the career of the late Professor James R. Hooker of Michigan State University's African Studies Center. "Probably one of the CIA's most effective agents," Hooker was recruited while at his first teaching position at Knox College in the late fifties and subsequently recruited other academics for the CIA.

Naomia Ware, who was married to Hooker, described her husband's work, which resembled very much what Lowenstein did: "It was strictly to evaluate the status of political parties and who seemed to have support and following. He was debriefed on, 'Do you think this guy—whoever it was, maybe Kenyatta, or Banda, or whoever, do you think this is a really decent sort of guy?' The job was to follow up his knowledge of those African leaders who had been bustling around in London, and make an on-the-spot evaluation of their constituencies." Hooker also told his wife he was involved with South African trade unions.

Ken Lawrence writes of Hooker in a way that makes him sound remarkably similar to Lowenstein: "Hooker was highly regarded by liberals and leftists, spoke out against the Vietnam War and brought Eugene McCarthy to MSU, and was personally close to leaders of liberation movements and heads of state in Africa and the Caribbean."

Lawrence concludes: "James Hooker was recruited to the CIA as a liberal. He abhorred the witch hunts of Senator Joseph McCarthy and the House Un-American Activities Committee. Ware says the CIA recruiter's argument went like this: 'None of us are ever going to get an intelligent approach unless we get you trained, intelligent people in there to tell us what's going on. If we rely on those yahoos, look what we're going to get.' Apparently this pitch continued to be effective among academics long after the McCarthy era."

The CIA was looking for bright people. Ralph W. McGehee, who joined the agency, scored 143 on the IQ test, the same as Lowenstein. McGehee was "gung ho" (see McGehee, *Deadly Deceits—My 25 Years in the CIA* (New York: Sheridan Square, 1983); so was Lowenstein.

Like Hooker, Lowenstein was a liberal who detested Joseph McCarthy and the HUAC. He also despised Communism and believed in democracy. He taught Constitutional Law at Stanford. He was a budding young Africanist (he was probably the only person in the country who taught "The Politics of Sub-Sahara Africa") at a time when expertise on the area was in short supply. Lowenstein was a perfect recruit. It should not be shocking that Lowenstein was recruited to the CIA; it would have been remarkable had he not been.

Harris Wofford, who claims no direct knowledge, expresses the belief that Lowenstein was telling the CIA what to do on certain issues that concerned him, not taking instructions as a regular agent who was simply an employee. (Telephone conversation with Harris Wofford, May 14, 1984) He also stresses that Lowenstein, like Chester Bowles, was too heavy on anti-Communist rhetoric but that his primary focus was on democracy. This analysis is astute and sheds light on the complex nature both of Lowenstein's politics and institutional affiliations. But as the recruitment of James R. Hooker indicates, the seductive technique of the CIA in recruiting liberals involved convincing them that they would have an impact on policy and could promote their point of view. At best, this was a symbiotic relationship.

Chapter 21.

Former CIA agent John Stockwell, who became involved in covert operations in Angola, confirms that the CIA had an active policy from 1960 to 1962 to get Portugal to give up its African colonies. But President Kennedy backed off after Portugal strenuously objected, particularly with regard to the Azores. (Interview with John Stockwell, June 26, 1984) Lowenstein's familiarity with and support for this CIA policy, which he was pushing in 1962, put him firmly in the "good-wing" camp.

Lowenstein's diaries were modeled after his high school newspaper he called *The Progressive*, and are referred to by this name by his family. They enabled him to keep track of all his different and complicated activities cryptically, while satisfying his unfulfilled desire to be the publisher and editor of his own "progressive" paper.

Chapter 23.
In Lowenstein's diary entries of mid-October 1964, "Q" clearly means "Question." There is a strong hint of a double meaning. Lowenstein is suggesting the possibility of marriage and also pondering the chances of the Banda escapade.

Notwithstanding the policy of keeping people with even remote connections with the CIA out of the Peace Corps, there is some evidence that this rule was bent. Peace Corps Desk Officer for Africa Cynthia Courtney had previously worked five years for the CIA front, the American Society of African Culture. Courtney may not have known of the CIA's role in the organization, and this may be why she escaped the prohibitive net. But at a party in 1980, a former Peace Corps recruitment officer told a former Peace Corps volunteer to Peru that "there was CIA in the Peace Corps," that the CIA placed people in various countries, and that reports the volunteers had been writing were funneled through to the CIA. The former volunteer who was told this had been expelled with all Peace Corps personnel from Peru in 1974 because of alleged CIA ties.

In fact, people and organizations with CIA connections had been involved in the formation of the Peace Corps. After Kennedy's election in 1960, the President-elect had asked Max Millikin, director of the Center for International Studies at the Massachusetts Institute of Technology to report to him on the idea of a Peace Corps. [See Wofford, *Of Kennedys and Kings, Making Sense of the Sixties* (New York: Farrar, Straus and Giroux, 1980).] Millikin had been director of the CIA's Office of National Estimates, and according to Marchetti and Marks [*The CIA and the Cult of Intelligence* (New York: Dell, 1975)], CIA money was used to set up the Center for International Studies at MIT, as part of the CIA's program to create research centers around the country at leading universities, giving them access to the campuses. Millikin was instrumental in setting up the center's African Research Department. Also active in pressing for a Peace Corps were Walter and Victor Reuther, whose United Auto Workers had been used by the CIA as a conduit.

The "Dear Family" salutation in the detailed mimeographed reports on the political, economic, and cultural aspects of the country the writer was describing reflected the sense of community that, in fact, existed among Americans working and living in the Third World. The concept of the CIA-affiliated American Africanists as a "family" is postulated in the ironic title of the African Research Group's report on them, "African Studies in America—The Extended Family—A Tribal Analysis of U.S. Africanists: Who They Are; Why to Fight Them."

The first "Dear Family" letters from Africa had been written in 1960 by Sam and Nancy Bowles, who had gone to Nigeria as teachers just prior to the creation of the Peace Corps. He was the son of Chester Bowles and she the daughter of liberal millionaire philosopher Corliss Lamont. Their letter of Oct. 5, 1960, described the governmental structure of the country in vivid detail, combining the insights of sophisticated social scientists with the eloquence of novelists. At one point, they noted, "We, and most of our Nigerian friends, feel that Nkrumah has gone a bit overboard, but we can't disagree with his position that the classical liberal democracy is at present inapplicable in most African countries." (Lowenstein Papers) They concluded with verses of contemporary African poets, commenting, "Most of the poets are highly nationalistic, and yet many of them are highly Westernized and completely reject the traditional cultures of West Africa." Carol Hardin Kimball, who was teaching in a Nigerian school and was the wife of Mobil executive Geoff Kimball, wrote from Nigeria in 1962 that her husband had "tied down several new consumer accounts" and was "working on kerosene-ped-dling schemes for the bush. Competition between the oil companies in marketing is very tough," she added, "although it's amazing how many people think that Mobil, Shell, BP, Esso, Texaco and Total are really the same company." Of the Nigerians, she wrote, "Nigerians are very friendly people who love to laugh and joke, but it is difficult to find really congenial ones with whom one would like to spend a whole evening." ("Dear Family" letter of March 1, 1962, Lowenstein Papers)

These letters came from all over the Third World. One Peace Corps letter from Brazil appeals: "I realize that a mimeographed note won't eliminate my letter responsibility to you, but perhaps it will serve temporarily until I can sit down and write you that long overdue letter." (Lowenstein Papers)

Stephen Bingham in 1966 gave a detailed account about trying to achieve change in local chiefdoms in Sierra Leone, writing: "The one thing which I think struck me more than anything else was that those whom I have always considered com-munity development theorists, those who are concerned not only about results but about processes, those who seemed to care about *how* one went about doing something, these people seemed to have accomplished the least and were having the most difficult time in their chiefdoms emotionally. Those whom we had looked down on in training, for not evincing sufficient concern for the theory, had moved into their chiefdoms and vigorously begun their work. One could pass this off as simply project orientation except that in some cases they had achieved dramatic success in affecting the process of change. This gave us much food for thought, all of which left us even more discouraged." (Lowenstein Papers)

Kennedy had compared the work of the Peace Corps to that of the Communists in Cuba. He wanted the volunteers to create change the American way, not the Communist way. Meanwhile, the volunteers and other young Americans in sim-ilar situations, poured information into Washington of a valuable type: intelli-gence on day-to-day life in Third World countries. It recorded the pulse of the countries, telling when and where violence had occurred, giving information on the power structure and attitudes toward America. For the most part, these were nice young people living an adventure, not quite understanding the part they were playing in the American hegemony of the sixties.

Following his graduation from Georgetown Law School, Eugene Theroux became associate professor of American jurisprudence at the University of Saigon in 1968. He was made a partner of Baker and McKenzie, a worldwide international law firm. Theroux has been a lecturer in international law with the Foreign Invest-ment Commission of China in Peking, chairman of the Legal Committee of the National Council for the U.S.–China Trade, and chairman and legal counsel, American Chamber of Commerce of the People's Republic of China. His brother Paul Theroux, whose nonfiction book on his experiences in the Peace Corps in Malawi was never published, was elected to the American Academy of Arts and Letters.

Chapter 24.

The presence of Stanley Levison's name on the executive board of the American Committee on Africa was a victory over anti-Communist paranoia. Levison was accused of being a Communist, but Lowenstein defended him against the charge, accepting Levison's version that he was a principled liberal.

Lowenstein was well acquainted with some who did not go on the cheap. In 1966, Peavey Heffelfinger traveled to Africa in luxury, describing his journey in long, detailed "Dear Family" letters. A wealthy grain dealer from Minneapolis who had once served as chairman of the Republican Finance Committee, Heffelfinger was accompanied by his wife, Elizabeth, and their daughter, Rosalie, a graduate of

Smith, where she had been head of the Young Republicans. Divorced by 1966, Rosalie had been married to Philip Willkie, the son of Wendell Willkie, and she and her husband had become friends with Lowenstein in the early fifties. After the 1952 political conventions in Chicago, Lowenstein went to Willkie's farm to work, establishing lasting ties with the whole family. Rosalie Willkie would become firmly convinced, as she told her son Wendell Willkie II, of Lowenstein's CIA ties.

As a grain dealer, Heffelfinger's interest in Africa was the AID-administered PL 480 program, under which surplus American grain was being sold for local African currencies, which were then given back to the buyer countries in the form of loans and grants. The Heffelfingers, who traveled first class, met with top AID officials, dined with American ambassadors, and were received by African heads of state. Peavey Heffelfinger described all of this (as well as his fishing trips and safaris) in his "Dear Family" letters, which were written in the most extravagant detail.

After meeting Haile Selassie in Addis Ababa, he wrote: "After all, we can meet an occasional Governor, and Hump and Milly even offered to introduce us to the Premier of Alberta, but we don't meet Emperors and Kings every day." In fact, wrote Heffelfinger, "the only other King we ever met was George Rukidi III, Omukama (King) of Toro with whom we had tea as you recall at Fort Portal, Uganda in 1961." On that occasion, Heffelfinger recalled that "when King George shook hands with me he said with a broad Oxford English accent, 'Call me King or call me George.'" (Peavey Heffelfinger, 1966 "Dear Family" letters, Lowenstein Papers)

Franklin D. Roosevelt III, grandson of President Roosevelt, first met Lowenstein after a lecture by him at the Yale Law School on South Africa in the fall of 1960. They found they were on "the same wavelength," as Roosevelt told the National News Council in 1981. Roosevelt traveled with Lowenstein in Mississippi in the summer of 1964, Roosevelt insisting that Lowenstein "taught me to be politically responsible." Lowenstein and Roosevelt shared a common interest in civil rights and South Africa, and Roosevelt was a major supporter of Lowenstein's in several of his races for Congress.

Chapter 25.

The Democratic Turnhalle Alliance, to which Lowenstein was sympathetic, was and is backed by the powerful Interessengemeinschaft, the Representative Committee of Namibia's German-speaking inhabitants. Through this committee, the DTA developed close ties with the conservative West German CDU-CSU (Christian Democratic Union and Christian Social Union), which opened an office in downtown Windhoek. The leader of the CSU, one of Germany's most conservative politicians, Franz Josef Straus, has commented: "I've heard nothing to indicate that the South African security forces interfere in the domestic politics of the country. On the contrary, their task is to provide law and order, to prevent the population from being terrorized." ("Namibian Politics: Day of the Chameleons," *LSM News*, Winter 1978, p. 16) There are some 20,000 ethnic Germans in Namibia in addition to the considerable West German investment.

The DTA has joined in an alliance with both Andreas Shipanga's SWAPO-Democrats, which Lowenstein aided, and SWANU, which Kozonguizi founded in 1959, to form the Namibian Multi Party Conference. It was created as a device to preempt SWAPO by appealing to whites, blacks, and coloreds of various political persuasions. SWANU is still held out as having had "strong Maoist leanings and Chinese connections" and current "credibility . . . gained through the years as a militant African nationalist organization." (*Financial Mail*, March 2, 1984) In actuality, it is in the alliance of parties backed by the United States and South Africa to prevent a SWAPO victory, giving strength to the argument that it was never authentic. While anti-SWAPO publications point out that SWANU was founded in 1959, a year before SWAPO, SWAPO's predecessor organization, the OPO, was in existence when Lowenstein's associate Kozonguizi founded SWANU.

Chapter 26.
Lowenstein admired Churchill, whose political career was launched when, as a young journalist, his daring exploits in South Africa while covering the Boer War made him a hero. But Lowenstein's great Africa adventures never received much publicity in the United States and had little impact on his own domestic political career.

Section V.
Chapter 27.
Diane Nash, a student leader from Nashville, pressed for direct action, while Charles Jones from Johnson C. Smith University in Charlotte, North Carolina, who had led sit-ins in Charlotte, argued for voter registration, as did Howard student Timothy Jenkins. Ella Baker asserted that Jenkins and Jones were "much more articulate and had more of certain kinds of contacts" than those supporting direct action.

Jenkins and Jones were deeply involved with the NSA. Jenkins, who was elected a vice-president of the student organization, was the NSA representative to SNCC and a go-between for the Kennedy administration. A protégé of Lowenstein, Jones (who bore the same name as Lowenstein's friend from his Chapel Hill days, Rev. Charles Jones, who was white) had met him in 1957 while Lowenstein was a graduate student at Chapel Hill, at a student mock assembly of the North Carolina state legislature of the type Lowenstein had participated in while he was an undergraduate at Chapel Hill. At Lowenstein's urging, Jones became active in the NSA's Virginia-Carolinas region and was elected its first (and only, in its history) black chairman. Lowenstein arranged for Jones to meet Eleanor Roosevelt when she came to speak at Chapel hill and impressed him with his sincerity. Calling Lowenstein an "inspiration" for him, Jones says that Lowenstein "had a capacity to be human that transcended racial perception. I never picked up any bullshit from him. I trusted him."

Involved with organizing the anti-Communist delegation to the 1959 Vienna Youth Festival, Lowenstein urged his fellow organizers to get in touch with Jones. Lowenstein wanted Jones, the son of a Presbyterian minister, to rebut charges in Vienna that blacks were mistreated in America. Accompanying Jones on the charter flight over was a team of journalists who wrote a series of stories for Knight Publishing Company which were published in its Charlotte, North Carolina, paper and syndicated in other publications, about Jones's appearance in Vienna. In the articles, Jones was portrayed as being "in juxtaposition" to Paul Robeson, Jr., son of the black singer who was a leading critic of the United States. After his return, he was called by an administrative assistant from the House Un-American Activities Committee and requested to testify as a "friendly witness," which he agreed to do. Jones consulted with Lowenstein to make certain the press would cover his statement to the committee accurately, which Lowenstein assured him he would do.

After participating in the sit-ins in Rock Hill, South Carolina, in early 1961, Jones became coordinator of voter education and voter registration for SNCC. Like Tim Jenkins, Jones became concerned about possible Communist influence in SNCC. When Jones entered Howard Law School, Robert Moses assumed the leadership of the SNCC's voter registration drive.

Paul Jacobs repudiated his own "Red-baiting" past and at the time of the 1967 disclosures of the NSA-CIA link confided to James Forman how the liberal-labor group planned to infiltrate SNCC with Lowenstein. Jacobs went on to become an antinuclear activist until his death from lung cancer, a disease he contracted as the result of exposure to radiation released from nuclear weapons testing.

Mississippi law provided that if a person believed he was being unlawfully prohibited from voting, he could cast a ballot that was then set aside until the courts could decide if it should be counted. But the problem was that blacks couldn't even get inside the polling places to vote "under protest." For this reason, it was decided to have blacks vote in places where they would not be threatened, such as black churches and local black businesses.

The National Lawyers Guild itself needed some prodding to get involved in civil rights. In 1963, its convention featured as its speaker a black attorney from Virginia named Len Holt, who roused them with a speech about the civil rights movement. Not a Communist, Holt was vehement about the need to do something in the South. Following his speech, the guild devoted the rest of the meeting to setting up civil rights programs.

The Port Huron Statement of the radical Students for a Democratic Society, drafted by Tom Hayden and Carl Ogelsby, espoused egalitarian participatory democracy. It was rejected by liberals as impractical and utopian.

Chapter 31.
Rauh hinted at the compromise to seat both Mississippi delegations by including an historical note in his brief for the MFDP that contained a summary of contested delegations in the past. The note indicated how in 1944 both Texas delegations had been seated, splitting the vote, implying that the same thing could be done with the Mississippi delegations in 1964. While Rauh's brief argued for the seating of the MFDP and the exclusion of the all-white regular delegation, the Summary of Contested Delegations actually contained a number of disputes at past Democratic National Conventions which were settled by seating both delegations, splitting the vote, i.e., Pennsylvania, 1836; New York, 1848; Georgia, 1852; Kentucky, 1864; Massachusetts, 1880; District of Columbia, Oklahoma Territory, Indian Territory, 1900; Puerto Rico, Canal Zone, Minnesota, 1936; Texas, 1944; Puerto Rico, 1960. The implication was clear, notwithstanding the rhetoric of the brief's argument.

Walter Tillow, who with Mendy Samstein was on Lowenstein's "list to be examined," was a white organizer from the North. Samstein describes Tillow as "a bit on the ideological side" and speculates that Lowenstein thought he was a Communist or a member of the Maoist Progressive Labor party, a splinter group from the Communist party. To Samstein, Tillow was like others who were "not Communists, but radicals." As for the Maoists, he concludes: "There were some Progressive Labor people around SNCC since 1963, but they were marginal." Samstein, who had been a professional historian, switched careers after his civil rights experience and became a psychotherapist.

Chapter 32.
The Jackson television station Aaron Henry became chairman of was sold to a Texas group, and two blacks, a popular anchorman and the station manager, were fired. In response, angry Mississippi black Democrats forced Henry out as a member of the Democratic National Committee from Mississippi. Henry remains a member of the Mississippi State Legislature to which he was elected.

Chapter 33.
A friend of Lowenstein's at Stanford wrote him after the 1964 Freedom Vote in Mississippi about Dennis Sweeny's reaction and his problems with the Mississippi

authorities: "Talked to Dennis several days after the election, just before the staff went into retreat. The trouble he had previously expected on November 3 of course never materialized, but he sounded very disappointed at the numerical results of the Mock Election. His trial, on the second charge ('Trespassing on public property') is slated for November 16, as you probably know. When I talked to him last, he said he thought part of the McComb staff (including himself) would start moving into the rural areas of Amite County to work. Don't know what his current status is, but will try to get him by phone again soon. Right now, the situation is apparently 'calm.' Would like to get him out here sometime in the next few months if possible—both for the sake of the campus and for his own— but want to hear your plans before I start making suggestions."

After the Summer Project, Jack Pemberton, the executive director of the ACLU, received a phone call from Joe Rauh. "Joe called me to set up a meeting concern- ing Mel's role," Pemberton affirms (Telephone interview with Jack Pemberton, Sept. 19, 1983). Wulf relates that Pemberton told him Rauh considered Wulf responsible for bringing in the Lawyers Guild and there should be a meeting to consider the ramifications of this. Wulf insisted on attending the meeting, to which Pemberton agreed. According to Wulf, it was held on Tuesday, October 27, 1964, at the Washington Hilton. Wulf insists that present at the meeting were Pemberton, Wulf, Jack Greenberg, Joe Rauh, and Jack Clayton, Walter Reuther's top aid at the UAW. He later added that James Wechsler also attended.

"I have no recollection of being involved in anything with Mel Wulf," Greenberg says. "I would be the first to assert publicly that Mel Wulf and I didn't get along but Mel doesn't get along with most people. But I would never get myself to fire him or even impair him. It would never occur to me." Greenberg recollected, upon examining his diary, that "there was a meeting I attended with Joe Rauh and somebody called Kleiman and somebody called Slayman; they always came together. From AFL-CIO. I can't remember what it was about. I am certain it had nothing to do with Mel Wulf."

Before I interviewed Jack Greenberg, I had telephoned Joe Rauh to ask him about the meeting with Wulf, who believes it was organized for the express purpose of firing him from the ACLU. Rauh had related: "That's the most ridiculous thing I ever heard. I would take an oath. That never happened. I was never in a meeting with Wulf. I find this incredible. I've never seen a story about Mississippi that mentioned Wulf. This is just news for me. I've never tried to get anybody fired for anything. . . . A hotel room with Jack Greenberg? I have no recollection of that."

I called back Wulf who countered: "There certainly was such a meeting. He set it up. The meeting happened. My recollection is that Jack was there. Joe's full of shit. He thought I was some kind of Commie, which I wasn't. He's just selective in his memory." Wulf asserts that Jack Greenberg also organized the meeting. "He was responsible for trying to purge me from the ACLU because they said I was responsible for bringing in the guild. Rauh tried to fire me. It was a Star Chamber proceeding. They jumped on me saying I brought the guild into Mis- sissippi, which I didn't. But I didn't try to kick them out."

Pemberton maintains that Rauh did not try to have Wulf ousted at the meeting. "Joe tried to persuade us of adopting a policy of non-cooperation, I think, with the Lawyers Guild. . . . And with Kuntsler and Kinoy, who were independently doing litigation there." But according to Pemberton, Wulf was not in favor of "excluding" the Lawyers Guild from the cooperation that existed among the var- ious lawyers' groups as Rauh wished, and that Rauh was "upset" with Wulf for this position. As executive director of the ACLU, Pemberton was "very much interested" in LCDC. "We were the sponsoring organization," he explains, "though we induced several other organizations to cosponsor with us. But I did not feel as threatened as Mel did by Joe's criticism. And I certainly didn't feel as Joe did that Mel was wrong to advocate cooperation."

In explaining Rauh's position, Pemberton states: "It stemmed back to his feeling that the Lawyers Guild had not disassociated itself as forcefully with American Communist leaders as the CIO had done in 1948, and that that was essential to preserving the independence of the civil rights movement. Joe felt that the Lawyers Guild's refusal to do that made them vulnerable to outside criticism; if not merely criticism from the outside, then to being used as a kind of front."

Pemberton supported Wulf. "I ultimately came to agree with Mel at that meeting," he asserts. "I went not as involved because I had more of an open mind on it. I was persuaded that the circumstances in Mississippi were such that we needed every ally we could get. . . . I did not feel it was a personal attack on Mel. One of the great things about Joe is, I felt, he was relatively free from any kind of personal rancor or retaliatory motives." Wulf, Pemberton insists, did a good job setting up LCDC, which was then run by other lawyers while Wulf continued on his ACLU job.

Jack Greenberg commented to me when I interviewed him: "I just spoke to Joe Rauh about an hour ago. . . . You called Joe? What did he say?"

When I told him that Rauh had "no recollection of the meeting," and repeated Wulf's allegations about Greenberg's role, Greenberg concluded: 'I have no recollection of that. We weren't the only ones who wanted to get rid of him. A lot of people did, but I think it's because he's disagreeable, not because of politics. But I certainly wouldn't have tried to get rid of someone for something like that. Joe has no recollection? I recall a meeting. Indeed, in looking at my calendar, I had lunch with Joe Rauh that day."

Chapter 34.

Lowenstein's "writer-in-residence" appointment was somewhat shrouded in mystery. It was the *Yale Daily News* that used the term, but others doubted that such a position actually existed. Rev. William Sloane Coffin, the Yale chaplain and a Fellow of Ezra Stiles College, had influenced Professor Richard B. Sewall, the Master of Ezra Stiles College and a professor of English at Yale, drawing him into the civil rights movement and bringing Lowenstein to his attention. Sewall stated that he offered Lowenstein rooms at Ezra Stiles College because he was considering him for a possible instructorship in the English department at Yale University. FBI sources doubted any such appointment was actually under consideration and were of the opinion that this was mentioned by Sewall merely to justify Lowenstein's residence in a Yale University dormitory. (FBI File No. 105–103168, Vol. No. 2)

Section VI.
Chapter 36.

On April 5, 1965, the accounting firm of Shapiro, Gubman, and Sitomer sent Lowenstein checks for $2,694.49 from Massachusetts Mutual Life, $1,026.60 from New York Life, and $1,554.20 from New York Life. On April 14 three more arrived; all from Continental Assurance Company, for $4,805.43, $2,800, and $2,000. On April 14 an additional three checks from Continental payable to him were mailed to Lowenstein: $4,805.43, $2,800 and $2,000. (Lowenstein Papers)

Juan Bosch, a democratic socialist opposed to the Communists, had introduced a new constitution while he was president of the Dominican Republic, limiting foreign acquisition of Dominican land at a time when American capital was seeking sugar plantations after Castro's revolution in Cuba had nationalized the plantations there. After Balaguer's election and Bosch's defeat in 1966, Gulf + Western Industries bought the Puerto Rican Sugar Company and moved into the Dominican Republic in a big way in 1967 with holdings in sugar plantations, hotels, and real estate. The founder and chairman of G + W, Charles G. Bluhdorn, had a personal interest in these holdings: he owned a luxurious home in the Dominican Republic.

Assisting American capital to achieve a secure base in the Dominican Republic was the AFL-CIO. In the elections that were held in the aftermath of Johnson's intervention, the American Institute for Free Labor Development (AIFLD), established by the AFL-CIO in 1962 to promote "free labor unions" and liberally supported with funds from the Agency for International Development (AID), backed Joaquin Balaguer, the former Trujillo puppet. According to Jonathan Kwinty [*Endless Enemies* (New York: Congdon and Weed, 1984), pp. 349–351], after Balanguer's election, George Meany, the president of the AFL-CIO, and Lane Kirkland, the secretary-treasurer of the AFL-CIO and later Meany's successor, joined with several other AFL-CIO leaders in establishing a "semi-private resort and tobacco plantation along a gorgeous stretch of white beach" in the Dominican Republic "not far from the biggest Gulf + Western sugar fields." Kwinty writes: "To create room for the resort, hundreds of Dominican peasant farmers had to be chased off the land. . . ."

Bosch himself had received considerable American support, some of it indirectly from the CIA. Following the assassination of the corrupt and brutal dictator Rafael Trujillo in 1961, elections were held in December, 1962, as the result of pressure by the Kennedy administration. Bosch came out of exile and, with the active support of Norman Thomas, was elected president in a landslide. Funding to Bosch was provided by the Institute of International Labor Research, which received money from the J. M. Kaplan Fund of New York, a foundation established by millionaire Jack Kaplan, a liberal Democrat who had owned sugar plantations in Cuba and Welch's Grape Juice, a product requiring ample supplies of sugar. A 1964 congressional investigation of tax-exempt foundations disclosed that the Kaplan Fund was affiliated with the CIA.

Bosch's party, the Partido Revolucionario Dominicano (PRD) was the enemy of the Partido Socialista Popular (PSP), the Communist party of the Dominican Republic. Bosch had spent part of his long exile in Cuba in the fifties and was very critical of Castro. (See Draper, "The Roots of the Dominican Crisis," *The New Leader*, May 24, 1965.) But the new constitution Bosch introduced curtailed foreign ownership of the land and broke up the large plantations. Consequently, in the summer of 1963, the Kaplan Fund denounced the Bosch government for being "infiltrated with Communists," although it was known that Bosch had "purged" the government of Communists, deporting some of them, and that the Communists had, in fact, infiltrated the conservative Unión Civica (UNC). After Trujillo's death and before Bosch's election, Communists had held government positions with the tacit approval of the conservative groups. [See *Dominican Republic, A Study in the New Imperialism*, Institute for International Labor Research (undated).]

Funding for Bosch was withdrawn in early autumn of 1963; there was a coup and a new military junta took over the country while Bosch escaped to Puerto Rico. Luis Homero Lajara Burgos charged that the Dominican Communists helped the trujillista generals and the oligarchic families to overthrow the Bosch government. Communists purged and deported by Bosch were allowed to return and were then rehired by the so-called "anti-Communist" triumvirate that the United States supported.

The Americans opposed Bosch because he opposed their control of his country's economy. The Communists opposed him because he preempted their issues. And the generals and the oligarchy opposed him because they were against democracy and reform.

A revolt of younger military officers against the triumvirate headed by Donald Reid Cabral broke out and was put down by the police on April 24, 1965. This was followed by a coup of older, reactionary military officers headed by air commander General Elias Wessin y Wessin, who replaced the triumvirate. This, in turn, was countered by a rebellion of younger officers and a popular uprising that caught the United States by surprise.

The PRD leaders proclaimed a return of constitutionality, issuing a call for civilian support for the younger military against Wessin y Wessin. When the so-called rebels were on the verge of victory, with most Americans safely evacuated on U.S. navy ships, Johnson ordered the Marines in under the pretext of protecting American lives. Johnson insisted he had received a cable from the American ambassador that "you must land troops immediately or blood will run in the streets, American blood will run in the streets." The actual message was "considerably more low key," reported Philip Gaylin of the *Wall Street Journal* on June 25, 1965. But on May 3, Johnson explained: "We don't propose to sit here on our rocking chairs with our hands folded and let the communists set up any government in the Western hemisphere." (Gaylin, "Dominican Flashback: Behind the Scenes," *Wall Street Journal*, June 25, 1965)

Senator J. William Fulbright, chairman of the Foreign Relations Committee, condemned the action as a grave mistake, linking it with Johnson's escalation in Vietnam. Johnson had ordered the bombing of North Vietnam on February 7, 1965, and the SDS had led a demonstration of 20,000 in Washington on April 17, 1965, with Robert Moses as the main speaker, but most Americans indicated support for Johnson's policies. Only a small minority dissented. Norman Thomas said Johnson had an "exaggerated fear of communism," and Theodore Draper charged, "When we betray the Juan Bosches of the world, we must in the final reckoning betray ourselves."

With all the evidence of threats and intimidation, it is difficult to conclude that the election was fair. According to David Harris, Lowenstein told a Stanford student who had been an observer that if the elections were challenged, the civil war would continue. His priority, Lowenstein indicated, was not to get a particular party elected but to install the electoral process. [*Dreams Die Hard* (New York: St. Martin's/Marek, 1982), p. 139.] But as Sam Halper, former head of the *Times* Caribbean Bureau, noted in *The New Leader* on May 11, 1965 ("The Dominical Upheaval"), the evidence strongly suggests that Washington had planned the future of the Dominican Republic with anti-Bosch groups. Bosch still did not fit into these plans in 1966.

The secretary treasurer of the IILR, who was in the Dominican Republic when the Committee for Free Elections headquarters were set up, and with whom Lowenstein had a student-volunteer contact, later admitted having performed work for the CIA. This further supports the contention that there was an organized effort by the United States to undermine Bosch.

The presence of the observers, which included Lowenstein, Thomas, and Bayard Rustin of Freedom House, had reduced the anti-Americanism, and since Bosch was allowed to return and resume his participation in politics in the opposition, his followers still had some reason to hope they might triumph in the future. Bosch would run again as the candidate of the left-wing Dominican Liberation party and would be defeated. Balaguer would himself be defeated in a free election by a candidate from Bosch's old party, the Dominican Revolutionary party. But the island republic would become an economic basket case in the eighties, with rioting over increased food prices and other hardships causing the deaths of numerous Dominicans. In June of 1984, Gulf+Western announced it was selling its Dominican sugar operations after making millions by speculating in sugar in the republic. The Securities and Exchange Commission, which investigated Gulf + Western, estimated that G + W made in the neighborhood of $64.5 million during 1974–75. In 1979, the SEC sued G + W, charging that Charles Bluhdorn had entered into a secret agreement with high Dominican officials to speculate in sugar. The SEC also accused G + W with transferring funds to a Dominican central bank to improve its dollar reserves on its financial statement.

G + W reached a settlement with the SEC in 1981 and in 1983. Bluhdorn died of a heart attack on his private plane as he was flying from the Dominican Republic to the United States. G + W operations in the Dominican Republic that year reached sales of $300 million, but peso devaluations and exchange restrictions on sugar export revenues precipitated the divestiture. G + W was also in the process of streamlining itself. As a vast conglomerate, it also owned Paramount Pictures and Simon and Schuster, the largest publisher of paperback and hardcover books. As *The New York Times* reported on June 30, 1984, "No officials of the Dominican Republic could be reached late yesterday to comment on G + W's plans."

Chapter 39.

A friend of Lowenstein who knew Jenny indicated to Lowenstein that Jenny was really attracted to him. The big news, he related, was that her mother was getting remarried and that Jenny would have to get out of her apartment on Gracie Square. He went on to explain that Jenny liked to have several men pursuing her at the same time to avoid a deep involvement. Another friend asked Lowenstein what he did to "get Jenny," because from everything he knew she was a formidable woman.

Chapter 42.

The "council" Lowenstein served on with fellow former Humphrey staffer Betty Goetz Lall and Norman Thomas undertook wide-ranging efforts to negotiate an end to the Vietnam war. They made contact with Mohammed Chebila in Algeria, sending a copy of their peace plan on Nov. 17, 1966. "If, in your judgment, there might be any utility in further discussion of these suggestions," they wrote, "we would be pleased to be represented at such discussions.

In response to the late–1966 letter from the student body presidents, President Johnson wrote thanking them for their "thoughtful letter," saying that Secretary Rusk would meet with them to discuss their concerns.

Chapter 46.

Lyndon Johnson remained convinced the antiwar movement was controlled by Communists. He ordered CIA director Richard Helms to report on Communist control of the antiwar movement, but Helms produced a CIA conclusion that there was no Communist control. Johnson told Helms to study it again, only to have Helms return with the same answer. And after extensive investigations, the FBI found no Communist infiltration of the SNCC. Meanwhile, the young radicals in the antiwar movement thought the liberals were trying to diffuse them, as the militants in the civil rights movement had suspected the liberals had acted in Mississippi.

Chapter 47.

At Martin Luther King, Jr.'s, funeral (King had been assassinated in April of 1968), Lowenstein showed Robert Kennedy's note to author David Halberstam.

Chapter 49.
Shortly after Johnson announced he would not seek reelection, Lowenstein found himself at a reception that President and Mrs. Johnson were attending. Making his way down the receiving line, Lowenstein shook hands with Johnson, who drawled, "Lady Bird, I believe you know Mr. Lowenstein." Silent, she coldly extended her hand to him.

Chapter 50.
Ted Kennedy vehemently denies that Lowenstein said to him in the elevator after the shooting of Robert Kennedy, "And you're not good enough." "It was quite the contrary," Kennedy asserts. Conversation with Ted Kennedy, summer 1981.
Mason Hampton, Lowenstein's opponent during the 1968 race for Congress in the 5th C.D., later died under anaesthesia during an operation to remove a mole.

Jenny's mother, Olivia, and Olivia's husband Dale Parkhill gave a famous party at the Potting Shed, Parkhill's restaurant in Bridgehampton. Dale Parkhill expressed his belief that Lowenstein would be the first Jewish president of the United States.

Section VII.
Chapter 52.
Marc Feigen observes that 1970 was a time of "disillusionment," with few resources available for "liberal causes." The movements that had brought Lowenstein to prominence, Feigen explains, had begun to disintegrate by the time Lowenstein had finally reached Congress. (See Feigen, *The March to Washington— Allard K. Lowenstein in the United States House of Representatives 1968–1970*, Senior Thesis, Department of History, University of Pennsylvania, April 15, 1983.) Yet Lowenstein himself was able to raise substantial amounts of campaign funds and often outspent his opponents, with the notable exception of Carter Burden in 1978.

Chapter 53.
On Lowenstein's failure to disclose outside income while in Congress, Feigen points out that the House Standards Committee required Lowenstein to list his ownership in stocks of companies that did business with the federal government or were subject to regulation by federal agencies. Additionally he was required to list income derived from involvement in any professional organization in which Lowenstein "or spouse is an officer or director or partner or serves in any advisory capacity from which income of $1,000 or more was derived in the preceding calendar year." Lowenstein served in an advisory capacity as a lawyer to the family restaurant company and had been a director. Also, as Feigen emphasizes, federal regulations probably were operative to a sufficient extent to mandate disclosure. The Port Authority, a state operation, was in interstate commerce and a restaurant in it was subject to federal jurisdiction for any number of reasons.

Chapter 54.
The *Long Island Graphic* and *Roosevelt Press* supported both Lowenstein and James Buckley in 1970, telling their readers to ignore party labels. In an Oct. 23, 1970, editorial, *The Graphic* wrote: "A surprising development in this most surprising of elections is the number of people who are supporting not only Allard Lowenstein, but are also for James Buckley, Conservative candidate for U.S. Senator. Buckley . . . would seem to be the antithesis of the Lowenstein image. But Clifton White, Buckley's campaign manager, has the following to say: 'Those people don't see Al Lowenstein as a politician. Al Lowenstein is a crusader, al-

ways fighting for the things he believes in, even if they're not exactly the things they believe in.'"

People who worked with Lowenstein, Gerry Twombley explained, tended to take on his mannerisms. Twombley had a messy desk like Lowenstein, and folksinger Harry Chapin drove fast, the way Lowenstein did. Chapin would be killed in a car crash on the Long Island Expressway.

Chapter 56.
Lowenstein's community office in Oceanside was over a shop called Al's Pottery, where supporter Andy Spadanuta had his business. Spadanuta's wife, Barbara, had been one of the organizers of Lowenstein's successful 1968 campaign. These Lowenstein loyalists continued to fight on Long Island against the Republican machine and for reform in the Democratic party.

A partial list of recruits for the Registration Summer reads like a *Who's Who* of student leaders: Kate Bernstein, molecular biologist and junior Phi Beta, *summa cum laude* graduate of Harvard; Mike Barrett, *magna cum laude* from Harvard and feature editor of *The Crimson*; Jay Jacobson, Chapel Hill wrestling team, Georgetown Law School, and Marine platoon leader in Vietnam; Art Kaminski, Phi Beta from Cornell and Yale Law School; Don Siegelman from Alabama and Oxford, who would later become Alabama's secretary of state; Greg Stone from Oberlin; Mitch Goldman from Bowdoin; Muff Singer, Phi Beta from the University of Texas; Rick Tuttle of Wesleyan and UCLA; Kurt Meade, a former Green Beret who was the highest decorated peacetime soldier in the country; Robert Thomas, a black who was president of his class at Exeter, a wrestler, and star football player.

Stephen Bingham, nephew of Congressman Jonathan Bingham and son of Judge Alfred M. Bingham, who was active in Connecticut politics, had become a lawyer after his experiences in Mississippi (he was arrested with Lowenstein in October of 1963) and the Peace Corps, joining a radical San Francisco firm that represented George Jackson. Bingham visited Jackson at San Quentin as an attorney but vanished after Jackson was killed trying to shoot his way out of prison. (Three guards and two other inmates were killed in the escape attempt.) Lowenstein, who was close to the Bingham family, was asked to represent Stephen Bingham but recommended Gary Bellow instead. After thirteen years as a fugitive, Bingham appeared in July of 1984 and pled not guilty to the charges against him. Bingham had gone to Milton Academy with Nick Littlefield (whose full name is Nicholas Bancroft Littlefield), and Bellow had met Lowenstein at Yale. "They were all connected," Jenny Lowenstein Littlefield concludes.

Chapter 57.
John Rooney was described by a Washington lobbyist as the "key connection for the underworld" for influential lobbyist Nathan Voloshen. Voloshen's exploits led to his own conviction and the conviction of his close friend and associate, the chief of staff to House Speaker John McCormick. See Robert N. Winter-Berger, *The Washington Payoff*, Secaucus, Lyle Stuart Inc., 1972.

The specter of organized crime haunted Lowenstein during the Rooney campaign. He related receiving threatening phone calls, and sometime after the election his Mazda was destroyed in a mysterious accident.

After the second primary loss to Rooney, Lowenstein agonized over whether he should continue the race on the Liberal line. At dinner with Jenny and some friends, he commented that he could not drop out because he would be letting the community down. Then Lowenstein said that if there was a good excuse for him not to run, he would seriously consider the alternative. Jenny turned to him, saying, "If you'd like, I'll remove a breast." (Letter to Lowenstein from Andrew S. Roffe, undated. Lowenstein Papers)

Chapter 58.
The Vietnam peace agreement was signed in Paris on January 27, 1973, and America finally began to disengage from Vietnam. Nixon suggested that a further intervention was possible if the Communists violated the truce, but Congress blocked him by enacting legislation prohibiting funds for any United States military operations in Indochina. Just as Nixon began to seek ways around the legislation, he was put on the defensive by the Watergate disclosures. [See Stanley Karnow, *Vietnam: A History* (New York: Viking, 1983), p. 656.] Lowenstein, who had gone to Paris to observe the negotiations, was not part of the formal process. On April 17, 1975, Cambodia fell to the Khmer Rouge, and on April 23 President Ford said the Vietnam War was "finished." The Communists took Saigon on April 30, 1975, changing its name to Ho Chi Minh City. But the war continued as the Vietnamese invaded Cambodia in 1978 and China invaded Vietnam in 1979. Lowenstein proclaimed his sympathy for the "Boat People" fleeing Vietnam and expressed his disillusionment with the Vietnamese Communists.

Chapter 60.
Teresa Carpenter relates that it was the Philadelphia railway station where Lowenstein and Sweeney met in the winter of 1975. (Carpenter, "From Heroism to Madness—The Odyssey of the Man Who Shot Al Lowenstein," *Village Voice*, May 12, 1980, p. 26.)

Chapter 61.
In 1976, Lowenstein's close friend from Congress Pete McCloskey was challenged by David Harris for McCloskey's San Francisco seat. Lowenstein backed McCloskey, the Republican, over Harris, who ran as a Democrat.
Lowenstein had several campaign managers in 1972. After Littlefield, Jay Jacobson took over.

Chapter 62.
According to Eduardo Chamorro, William Bowdler, who was political secretary at the U.S. embassy in Cuba when Castro took power, was with the negotiating team trying to expel Somoza. Chamorro believes that Sandinista Foreign Minister Miguel Escotto, a priest, was once close to the CIA, which now believes Escotto has "gone too far."

Chapter 64.
Dennis Sweeney, who believes that Lowenstein still lives, does not grant interviews. This version of what happened during his meeting with Lowenstein is a composite of what he allegedly said after the shooting and his written account to his attorney. He wrote of his final confrontation with Lowenstein: "I explained to him that I wanted to return to my home in Oregon, but that before I do [*sic*] so with any ability to function, I needed his word that insofar as he was aware of any anger or vendetta against me by himself and a few others, that [*sic*] he restrict it to myself and not cause any harm to anyone near or dear to me. He said that he couldn't give me that kind of pledge and that he thought I should see a psychiatrist. If I needed any help in doing so, he would be happy to assist. He said I had to begin by helping myself. . . . I then took the gun out of my pocket and said that in light of what I had seen, his statement was not good enough for me and I began to fire." [See David Harris, *Dreams Die Hard* (New York: St. Martin's/Marek, 1982), pp. 335–36.]

Chapter 65.
Jacqueline Kennedy Onassis admired Lowenstein, although he felt she didn't know who he was. On the same flight with her, Lowenstein approached her seat shyly and introduced himself. "I'm the person whose wife, Jenny, is the half-sister of Muffie Huntington, whose husband, Larry Huntington, you know. . . ." She interrupted him and said, "No, you're not. You're Al Lowenstein."

Chapter 66.
In actuality, Allard K. Lowenstein Square is really a corner. There is no square; what there is is the wish to honor Lowenstein with a symbolic gesture.

Index

Inter-American Association for Freedom and Democracy, 172
Internal Revenue Service, politically partisan use of, 461
International Confederation of Free Trade Unions (IFCTU), 79, 86, 115
International Development Foundation, 78
International Features Service, 78
International League for the Rights of Man, 101
International Research Service, 78
International Rescue Committee, 124
International Student Conference (ISC), 45, 49, 69. *See also* Stockholm conference
International Union of Students (IUS), 35, 36, 38, 42–5, 48–50, 61, 65, 70, 105, 186
Ireland, Doug, 296, 375, 406, 478
Israel, 73, 141, 195, 387, 417, 441, 449, 451, 475, 478, 479

Jablow, Joseph, 188
Jackson, George, 434
Jackson, Henry "Scoop," 428, 429, 432, 449, 465, 469, 476
Jackson, Jesse, 373
Jackson State University shooting, 397, 399, 438
Jacobs, Andy, 289, 477, 495
Jacobs, Paul, 232
Jacobson, Joel, 154, 158
Jaffe, Miles, 267
Javits, Jacob, 456
Jewish Defense League, 409
Jews and Jewish religion, 13, 15, 21; in American South, 19, 21–3; Hasidic, in Lowenstein congressional races, 441, 446, 450; in New York politics, 456; in South Africa, 89; in Soviet Union, 471
Johnson, James Arthur, 347
Johnson, Lyndon B., 37, 47, 49, 68, 109, 113, 184, 241, 271, 273, 277, 288, 312, 318, 323, 330, 332, 339, 340, 349, 366, 372, 374, 380, 456; and civil rights movement, 257–9, 264–7, 268–9, 271, 273, 274, 323; and Dominican Republic, *see* Dominican Republic; movement to dump, 44, 65, 67, 162, 197, 289, 318, 330, 334–6, 338–44, 347–55, 357–61, 363, 366, 368, 370, 375, 380, 397, 428–9, 431, 440, 443, 469; and Vietnam War, 49, 197, 286, 295, 300, 306, 310–12, 323, 325–8, 330, 331, 335, 338, 345, 432
Johnson Foundation, 212
Joling, Robert, 460, 462
Jonas, Gilbert, 79, 120, 122–5, 171
Jones, Charles, 21, 24, 30, 50, 54, 127

Jones, Tom, 54
Jordan, Hamilton, 211
Joseph, Helen, 206, 219, 222
Juan Carlos (king of Spain), 162, 168, 172

Kaplan, Barbara, 436
Katz, Rita Kupsick, 6, 8
Katz, Sanford, 245–7, 263
Katzenbach, Nicholas, 68, 325
Kaufmann, George, 53
Kaunda, Kenneth, 196–7, 219
Kellenberg, Walter P., 419
Kennedy, Ethel, 484
Kennedy, John F., 47, 58, 75–6, 100, 112–13, 124, 134, 140, 141, 149, 154, 159, 176, 248, 252, 268, 303, 351, 362, 399, 426, 452, 477, 483; assassination of, 160, 161, 181, 257, 461; on civil rights, 142, 144–5, 176, 223–5, 230, 238, 241, 253; and Franco Spain, 146, 152, 155; and South Africa, 144–5, 158, 181; and Vietnam War, 286
Kennedy, Katheleen, 442–3
Kennedy, Robert F., 60, 70, 85, 113, 188–9, 192, 195, 225, 257, 262, 263, 265, 272, 300, 319, 330–1, 344, 349, 355, 360, 364, 370–2, 376, 381, 392, 399, 401, 411, 432, 443, 454, 461, 463, 465, 477, 496, 500; death of, 371, 374, 385, 389, 411, 412, 454, 458–62, 483, 484, 492, 498; in JFK administration, 176, 224–5, 229; presidential race of, 318, 319, 323, 330–1, 336–40, 342, 350–3, 359–60, 361–4, 367, 370, 370–2, 376, 378, 423, 428; senatorial career, 305, 306, 411
Kennedy, Ted, 198, 201, 371, 379, 385, 394, 460, 483–6, 492–6, 497, 500; eulogy for Lowenstein, 493–4
Kennedy Library, 483
Kent, Rockwell, 12
Kent State University shooting, 397, 399, 400, 427, 430, 438
Kenya, 79, 176, 195. *See also* Kenyatta, Jomo; Mboya, Tom
Kenya Federation of Labor, 79, 86
Kenyatta, Jomo, 141
Kerina, Jane, 122, 125
Kerina, Mburumba, 76, 77, 88–9, 91, 100, 101, 107, 122, 125, 177, 178
Kerr, Clark, 185, 288
Kerry, John, 431
Khama, Seretse, 93, 94
Kiley, Robert, 60, 61
Kimball, Carol Hardin, 186, 190, 400, 460, 467
Kimball, Geoff, 186, 190
Kindelan, Alfredo, 82
Kindelan, Juan Manuel, 82–5, 153
King, Coretta Scott 439, 453, 495

Murray, John Courtney, 39
Muskie, Edmund, 394, 431, 432
Muste, A. J., 120, 233
Muzorewa, Abel, 205–6, 209, 212, 221

NAACP, 144, 224, 228–33, 238, 247, 251, 252, 254, 272, 275, 277, 279, 291, 296, 388; Legal Defense Fund, 124, 173, 228, 251, 253, 275, 278
Nader, Ralph, 169, 437, 484
Namibia/South West Africa, race and politics in, 61, 63, 73–7, 79, 87–91, 94–5, 103–5, 107, 118, 152, 182, 188, 196, 201–2, 204, 207–9, 218–21, 478, 482; liberation movements, *see* SWANU; SWAPO; trusteeship fight, 97–103, 122, 188–9, 192, 318; Western investment in, 202, 207, 217. *See also* South Africa
National Conference of Christians and Jews, 187
National Council of Churches, 275–6, 279
National Lawyers Guild, 246–9, 251–5, 261, 267, 278, 336
National Security Council, 211, 213
National Student Association (NSA), 38–52, 56–58, 60–70, 72, 75, 76, 94, 97, 103–5, 109, 128, 129, 134, 142, 144, 158, 183, 186, 197, 229, 264, 279, 288, 289, 331, 343–5, 356, 375–6, 494; and CIA, 42–50, 52, 57, 61, 63–70, 142, 165, 177, 178, 197, 333, 344, 345; and civil rights movement, 56–7, 114, 259; and FBI, 42–3, 66; founding of, 38–9; Freedom of Information suit, 70; funding of, 45–7, 50–1, 63, 65–6; political orientation of, 51–2, 56–7, 64, 70, 289, 344–5; South Africa involvement of, 94, 97, 103–5, 119; Spanish involvement of, 165–8; and Vietnam War, 319–21, 343–5, 357
National Student Lobby, 70
National Union of South African Students (NUSAS), 89–91, 104, 118, 125, 127, 188, 189, 214
NATO, 170
Naude, Beyers, 219
Nehru, Jawaharal, 123
Neto, Agostino, 179
Neustadt, Richard, 112
Newberg, Esther, 500
Newcomb, Elliot, 120
New Deal, 247, 337
New Democratic Coalition, 410, 435, 480
Newfield, Jack, 349, 353, 376, 446
"New Left," 165, 295, 311–12, 317, 319, 323, 333, 342, 343, 355, 356, 376–7, 417, 418, 422
Newman, Paul, 108, 127, 363, 374
New York politics: abortion issue in, 409,

444; Conservative Party, 447, 448, 450; death penalty issue in, 419, 479; Democratic Party, *see* Democratic Party: New York Reform Movement; election irregularities in, 444–8; fifth district (Nassau County) constituents, 409–10, 413–15; fourteenth district constituents, 437; Liberal Party, 78, 79, 408, 447, 451, 452, 479–80; Lowenstein in, 108, 195, 280, 288–91, 296, 408 (*see also* U.S. House of Representatives: Lowenstein election campaigns for; Lowenstein term in); reapportionment, 408–9, 412, 425, 427, 435; Republican Party, 370, 374, 383, 408–9; tuition tax credit issue in, 442, 444, 479
Nicaragua, Lowenstein in, 205, 473–5
Nickerson, Eugene, 411
Niebuhr, Reinhold, 327, 332
Nigeria, 190; Biafran civil war in, 198, 386
Nixon, Richard M., 81, 100, 164, 171, 173, 224, 295, 300, 302, 373, 380–81, 384, 386–7, 389, 393–7, 399, 410, 412, 415, 422, 448, 449, 450, 454, 456, 457–8, 489, 498; campaign to dump, 428–32, 434, 435; enemies list, 270, 433, 454, 457–8; and Vietnam War, 397, 432, 438; and Watergate, 457–8
Nkomo, Joshua, 196, 209, 211, 212
Nkosi, Morley, 144
Nkrumah, Kwame, 80, 123, 137, 141, 186
North Carolina, politics in, 29–33, 226–7, 239–40, 243
North Carolina, University of: Lowenstein graduate work at, 55, 58–9, 71; Lowenstein undergraduate days at, 18–29, 34, 36; student politics at, 23–5
North Carolina State at Raleigh, Lowenstein at, 85, 98, 145, 150, 157, 160, 174–76, 183, 225–7, 229, 230, 239–41, 243, 256–7, 264, 280, 307, 355
Norton, Eleanor Holmes, 267
Nu, U, 123
nuclear war, Lowenstein views on, 310, 331
Nujoma, Sam, 137, 152, 195, 196, 206, 209
Nyerere, Julius, 73, 123, 141, 192, 219, 221

Oates, Mary Lou, 67, 376
OAU (Organization of African States), 199–200
O'Brien, Frances, 168
Ochs, Phil, 306
O'Doherty, Kieran, 447
O'Donovan, Michael, 441, 450
O'Dwyer, Paul, 112, 295, 383, 411
O'Dwyer, William, 437